Lady Gregory's Diaries 1892–1902

Well, they don't like to be killed —
Sure they've but brought up to it — like
the Captain!

Sepr 21 — George Moore came a few days
ago, to work at Grania with Wats — He
likes Twisting of the Rope — & has made
some small alterations in it — He will
give £100 for the theatre, & I have
renewed my £25 guarantee — He tour.
mr. C Tillyra to the Island the received
him cordially, & refuses any guarantee.
will pay for the production of his own
play if it is accepted, but for nothing else
He came to dine yesterday evg. & I was
alone with him before dinner, & begged
him, for his own sake, to reconsider
this — I told him it would be said th
he had taken up the theatre only for
the production of his own work, & not
for the general good, & that he, who had
written so strongly against music halls
& bad English plays, ought to keep the
Literary Theatre quite independent of his
own work — But he is obstinate "will

Page from Lady Gregory's diary for 21st September 1900.

LADY GREGORY'S DIARIES
1892–1902

EDITED AND INTRODUCED
BY
JAMES PETHICA

COLIN SMYTHE
GERRARDS CROSS 1996

First published in 1996 by Colin Smythe Limited,
Gerrards Cross, Buckinghamshire SL9 8XA

British Library Cataloguing in Publication Data

A catalogue record for this book is available
from the British Library

ISBN 0-86140-306-1

Produced in Great Britain
Camera copy prepared from the author's text by David García
Printed and bound by
T. J. Press (Padstow) Ltd., Padstow, Cornwall

CONTENTS

DEDICATION

In memory of my grandparents
James Browne (1879-1970) of Knockgraffon, Co. Tipperary
Mary Bowler Browne (1893-1987) of Kanturk, Co. Cork

ACKNOWLEDGEMENTS

The help and kindness of many people smoothed and enriched the course of my work on this volume. My special thanks to Colin Smythe, for his encouragement and assistance throughout its evolution, and for making a wealth of unpublished Gregory materials available to me; to Dr. John Kelly, for urging me to undertake the project, and for his valuable advice along the way; and to Professor Warwick Gould, for his unfailing generosity with information and encouragement. I am also particularly grateful to Professor Ronald Schuchard and to Deirdre Toomey for their many suggestions and compendious help.

For helping me with information, encouragement, hospitality and the numerous other kinds of assistance which made the completion of this work possible, I am indebted to: Father Martin Coen, Dr. Nicholas Cranfield, Professor Adrien Frazier, David Hyland, Dr. Wendy Jones, Eckhart Lindemann, Jerome Mahony, Dr. Bruce Morris, Professor Maureen Murphy, Professor William M. Murphy, Professor Philip O'Leary, James Charles Roy, Professor Ann Saddlemyer, Professor Paul Sawyer, and Professor Trevor West.

Mrs. Elizabeth Speight, Coralie Persse, Thomas D. Persse, Mrs. Peggy Persse and Richard H. Persse generously assisted me with information on the Persse family, made many personal family documents available to me, and kindly allowed me to reproduce family photographs. I am also most grateful to the late Sir John Pope-Hennessy, to Michael Mallon his Private Secretary, and to Simon Birch, for their help with Birch family records, and for making photographs available to me. My thanks to Mrs. Vanessa Stone, W. Merriweather, and E. C. Merriweather for their generosity with Beauchamp family information and photographs. Mrs. Angela Waithman kindly helped me with information about the Waithman family, and treated me to a memorable evening of Galway and Gregory lore.

The staffs of the following institutions gave me much invaluable help: The Bodleian Library, Oxford; The British Library; The Colindale Newspaper Library; Special Collections at the Robert. R. Woodruff Library, Emory University; The Manuscript Division of The New York Public Library; Columbia University Library; The Plunkett Institute, and The National Library of Ireland. My thanks also to the staff of Olin Library at Cornell University, and particularly to Amy Blumenthal who alerted me to numerous useful sources and materials. A. D. Hawkyard at Harrow School, Mrs. P. Coote at Oxford University Press, Mrs. J. Pennington at Lancing College, and Mrs. C. Dalton at New College, Oxford, also kindly helped with information. The late Lola

Szladits, Curator of the Berg Collection of the New York Public Library, where I transcribed the diary and completed much supporting archival research for the volume, was a generous encourager of the project throughout my work there. Her assistants, Brian McInerney and Patrick Lawlor, inimitable in their welcome and humour, were memorable guides to the Berg Collection's riches and have my enduring thanks and regard.

My thanks to Anne de Winton and Catherine Kennedy for permission to quote unpublished material by Lady Gregory, Sir William Gregory and Robert Gregory; to the Earl of Lytton and to The British Library, for permission to publish extracts from Lady Anne Blunt's diary; to A. P. Watt Ltd., on behalf of Anne Yeats and Michael Yeats, to quote from an unpublished letter by John Butler Yeats; to the Fitzwilliam Museum, Cambridge, for permission to quote unpublished writings by Wilfrid Scawen Blunt; to the estate of J. C. Medley, for permission to quote unpublished material by George Moore; to Douglas Sealy, for permission to quote unpublished material by Douglas Hyde; to the estate of Diarmuid Russell, for permission to quote unpublished material by George Russell; to Alexander James, for permission to quote unpublished writings by Henry James; to John Murray Ltd., for permission to quote unpublished Lady Gregory correspondence in their possession; and to the Henry W. and Albert A. Berg Collection of The New York Public Library (Astor, Lenox and Tilden Foundations), for permission to quote unpublished material from their holdings.

Wolfson College, Oxford, was a welcoming and supportive academic home during a significant portion of my work on this volume. My special thanks to Professor Jon Stallworthy, Professor John Ashton, and the late Professor Richard Ellmann for their kindness and encouragement during my time there. My thanks, also, to Edward Wilson and to Professor John Jones for their help in earlier years.

I am most grateful to David García, who oversaw the production of this volume, and skillfully expedited its progress at every stage. My thanks also, to Salonge Crenshaw, for resolving a seemingly intractable software problem during the final stages of output.

To my family, for their encouragement in this work, as in all that has preceded it, many thanks.

And last and best thanks to Alison Case, for her constant support, loving companionship, and much more.

LIST OF ILLUSTRATIONS

Page from Lady Gregory's diary for 21 September 1990 *frontis*

Between pages 122 and 123

Lady Gregory, portrait by Lisa Stillman
Dudley Persse, portrait miniature
Frances Persse, *c.* 1890
Sir William Gregory, print by W. Roffe, after Sir Arthur Clay
Studio portrait of Robert Gregory, late 1880s
Chevy Chase, Slieve Echtge
Roxborough, Co. Galway, water-colour by
Lord Wemyss's sketch for *A Phantom's Pilgrimage*, 1893
Pencil drawing by Lady Gregory of Biddy Early's house
Lady Layard
Sir Henry Layard
Pen and ink sketches of Ca' Capello
Water-colour of Lynch's Castle, Galway
Opening Page of "The Stones of Galway"
Water-colour of S. Apollinare, Ravenna
Water-colour of Lydacan Castle
Water-colour of entrance to Clonfert Cathedral
Pencil sketch of Crabbet Park
Two sketches of Thoor Ballylee, 1895
Pen and ink sketches of Inisheer,

Between pages 218 and 219

Pencil sketch of New College Oxford by Robert Gregory
Sketches by John Butler Yeats of James Joyce
Front cover of 1900 issue of *Beltaine*
Pencil sketch of Lady Gregory by John Butler Yeats, 1903
Cameron Studio photograph of Robert Gregory, 1902
Scene from the first production of *Twenty Five*
Scene from the first production of *Kathleen ni Houlihan*
Signatures on Lady Gregory's fans
Pen and ink sketches of George Moore and Edward Martyn, by Robert
   Gregory

INTRODUCTION

As Lady Gregory often acknowledged, her marriage in 1880 to Sir William Gregory was a crucial, transforming event in her life. At twenty-seven, and lacking the social opportunities enjoyed by her elder sisters, most of whom had spent seasons in Dublin, she had seemed likely to remain unmarried, as Augusta Persse, facing a life of small family duties and local philanthropy in the neighbourhood of the Persse estate at Roxborough in county Galway. The marriage, which came as a surprise both to her own family and to local landowning society, gave her the considerable status of mistress at nearby Coole Park, and broadened her intellectual and social horizons dramatically. Gregory, thirty-five years her senior, had retired as Governor of Ceylon in 1877, having earlier served several terms in Parliament, and now lived much of the year in London, where he was highly regarded in artistic and social as well as political circles for his personability and cultivation. Though no longer in public office, he maintained an active role as a Trustee of the National Gallery, and counted writers and intellectuals as diverse as Browning, Henry James, Bright, Froude and Tennyson amongst his friends. For Augusta Persse, coming from "unbookish" Roxborough, where she had not been permitted to read novels until she was eighteen, and where her mother, a strict evangelical Protestant, would "refuse to buy some new dress or spend money on such things as furniture because the end of the world might soon be here and turn all to dust", the "fortunate marriage" was "a liberal education . . . indeed".[1] As George Moore, an occasional guest at the Gregorys' London townhouse in the 1880s, would recall, in their drawingroom "were to be met men of assured reputation in literature and politics, and there was always the best reading of the time" upon their tables.[2] To the end of her life she would remain grateful for the social skills and tolerant political and religious views she soon learned from Sir William, for the "position" and "good standing" his name and title conferred on her, and for the intellectual and artistic milieu to which he had introduced her.[3]

Yet if Lady Gregory's twelve years of marriage were a significant education, they were nonetheless confiningly conventional in many respects. As a wife, she was expected to fill the dutiful role expected of her sex no less assiduously than she had done at Roxborough, and this meant joining uncomplainingly in his interests, and enduring many long separations from their one child, Robert, born in 1881, to satisfy Gregory's penchant for travel.[4] At the time she evidently dealt with these expectations with wry humour—"We had spent so many months in Italy, months in Germany, a winter in India & one in

[Egypt] that I used to say that if ever I needed to take a trade I would be found fitted at least for that of courier."[5] In later life, though, she would candidly admit that their travels had often been "dull", and Gregory's tireless enthusiasm for visiting art galleries on the Continent a strain: "I wrote names of pictures that I might remember them to please W[illiam]. more than for my own pleasure".[6] The belated admission hints at a dutiful self-suppression that must often have been difficult to maintain, particularly given Gregory's age and the fact that most of the circles they moved in during the marriage comprised people a generation or more older than herself. In an early draft of her memoirs Lady Gregory would acknowledge that her expectations in marrying the courtly, cultivated Gregory had been much like Dorothea Brooke's towards the elderly scholar Casaubon in *Middlemarch*. She would take care in this draft to emphasize that, unlike Dorothea, she had suffered no subsequent "awakening" of discontent—"mine was an ever increasing affection"—but it is nonetheless clear that the actuality of the marriage proved something of a let-down.[7] For all her public care in portraying herself as a dutiful and contented wife—a care she would maintain throughout the forty years of her widowhood, dressing in black until her death—she was nevertheless unable to prevent a critical and disappointed note from entering her later writings about the period of the marriage.

The extensive diaries Lady Gregory kept during those married years are powerfully indicative of the extent of her self-suppression, for though they provide a conscientious record of the couple's travels and social engagements, there are only a handful of entries in an introspective vein, and Lady Gregory herself recognised when reviewing them in 1921 that much of their matter "would be of no interest to others".[8] Unsurprisingly, their entries make no direct mention of her most significant reaction against the restrictions and limitations of the marriage—a brief and clandestine affair with poet and explorer Wilfrid Blunt in 1882–83—but their record is with few exceptions equally reticent as to any of the private opinions and aspirations she harboured. The few creative writings she completed during the marriage, for instance, receive fitful mention at best. Her first major publication, *Arabi and his Household*, written as a letter to *The Times* in 1882 and subsequently issued as a pamphlet, is briefly noted, but more important and biographically significant works such as "An Emigrant's Notebook"—a series of vignettes about her childhood home which she prepared with a view to publication in 1883–84, but then abandoned—and a group of short stories she wrote in 1890–91, are not mentioned even in passing.[9] Though Sir William appears to have recognised and encouraged her creative abilities, praising her "power of writing well and piquantly" and urging her to do challenging and original work,[10] her silence concerning these early writings is a significant index of the extent to which she continued to subordinate her interests to his. The self-exploration implied in these unmentioned works, and in her few poems from the period that survive, was clearly not consistent with the models of wifely duty and motherly self-sacrifice her upbringing and culture promoted. In a unpublished fragment of autobiography written in later life, as a self-confident and accomplished woman, she would look back on her married years with the unmistakable tone of regret of one who recognises them as a period of wasted opportunity: "We both had energy—& love of Ireland. . . . we might between us have done some big thing".[11]

Paradoxically, then, while the "fortunate marriage" was the essential step into a world of intellect and social standing without which Lady Gregory's subsequent achievement as a writer and patron would not have been possible, it was only Sir William Gregory's death, and the demands of widowhood, that brought her to the independence necessary for a distinctive creative voice. As she elegantly acknowledged in 1928, "If I had not married I should not have learned the quick enrichment of sentences that one gets in conversation; had I not been widowed I should not have found the detachment of mind, the leisure for observation necessary to give insight into character, to express and interpret it."[12] The diaries presented here, covering the period from Sir William's death in 1892 until they peter out in early 1902, chart the course of a gradual but resolute remaking of her life. Widowed at thirty-nine, with a London social circle composed mainly of her husband's elderly friends, broadly Unionist in her political views, and with only a few minor publications to her name, she was by her fiftieth year an ardent Nationalist, friend to the major figures of the Irish literary movement, widely acknowledged as hostess of a 'workshop of genius' at Coole, and on the threshold of lasting literary prominence in her own right.

I

The course of Lady Gregory's life in the months immediately after Sir William's death gave scant suggestion of this radical remaking to come. Though a long widowhood had always been a likely prospect—Gregory had himself warned her in his letter of proposal in 1880 that "under any circumstances you will still be young when I am an old man"[13]—his sudden decline and death nonetheless came as a profound and debilitating shock. Besides facing the immediate challenges of taking practical charge at Coole and assuming sole responsibility for Robert, then ten years old, she also soon discovered that her financial prospects were considerably less robust than she must have anticipated. On the face of things, Gregory's Will left her adequately provided for, allowing her a jointure of £800 a year from the estate income, life residency at Coole (itself to be held in trust for Robert), and other personal property of value including the lease on their London house, but her first close review revealed a more sobering picture. Not only had the Coole rent-roll dropped significantly since the 1880s, but a substantial mortgage Gregory had taken out in 1867 also remained unpaid. (His bequest of £2000 to the daughter of a Captain Dawson of Wexford, presumably a former mistress, may have also come as an unpleasant surprise.[14]) With the prospect of further rent reductions highly likely, and with the Land War a recent enough memory to dispel any complacency on her part as to the long-term outlook for Irish estates, she swiftly recognized the need to retrench substantially.

On a practical level she responded resolutely to these new challenges, writing from the London house at St. George's Place, just three weeks after Sir William's death, of her intention "to sell this house & to let Coole—To live at either wd swallow up all I have, & I want to get things straight for Robert before he grows up". She also resolved to forgo most of her jointure so as to help to clear the mortgage.[15] On a personal and emotional level, though, she was clearly not ready to deal with the prospect of starting a new life on her own, and after returning to Coole in late Spring 1892 she slipped into a state of lethargy and depression. Her correspondence during the summer and early Autumn repeatedly acknowledges low spirits, and by that October, writing to Wilfrid Blunt, she candidly admitted to a sense of aimlessness: "I suppose some day I shall have courage & take up some line of life—but I can [at present] still do nothing but drift along, without much interest except Robert, & he is almost quite lost to me at school".[16] Even when solicited in November that year to become a political columnist for a proposed new journal, she remained listless and negative: "If in London, I believe I could do what they want, but I am doubtful, being so far away, and my plan of life is very undecided".[17] That month, with Robert at boarding school in England, and Coole let for winter shooting, she went to live at Roxborough, where, significantly, she slipped unresistingly back into the round of family duties she had apparently left behind for good a dozen years before. "I am wanted here just now" she wrote to Blunt in mid-November, "a brother suffering from nervous depression not letting me out of his sight—I am glad to be wanted anywhere".[18]

This retreat to her childhood home, and the listlessness it symptomized, were to end abruptly. Lady Gregory's brother William Norton Persse, who had become Master at Roxborough some months earlier, was in fact not merely "depressed" as she had euphemistically put it, but in the final stages of acute alcoholism. On New Year's Eve 1892, six weeks before his eventual death, he suddenly "got some delusion" that she was plotting to "lock him up" and have him displaced, and he peremptorily ordered her off the estate.[19] The shock of this expulsion finally galvanized her to recommence the diary, written conscientiously through almost all of her married life, that she had abandoned during Sir William's last illness. Her first entry, dated 8 January 1893, gives a largely self-pitying retrospective account of the thirteen month period she had left unrecorded, and dwells melodramatically on Sir William Gregory's last hours of life, his final meeting with Robert Gregory and her own sense of loss. The entry, though, also reflects the first beginnings of a resolve to face the "terrible difference" in her life and to come to terms with her changed circumstances. After a brief trip to London, where the welcome of friends helped restore her "self respect", she returned to Galway, staying at her mother's home, The Croft, and here her calmer continued reassessment of her situation symptomatically inspired her to a more substantial effort at writing. The result was the 4000-word essay "A Phantom's Pilgrimage: or Home Ruin", which she published anonymously as a pamphlet in late May 1893.

2

The essay, a political phantasy aimed at ensuring the defeat of Gladstone's 1893 Home Rule Bill, imagines a future in which the now-dead Gladstone returns from the grave, ten years after the passage of the Bill, to review the impact of his "best and greatest deed", the conferring of "self-government on an oppressed nation".[20] Instead of the prosperity and tolerance he expects, however, Gladstone finds only a starving peasantry, beleaguered landlords, lawlessness and contempt even for the Catholic Church. The essay is tightly focussed on its task of political persuasion, and gives no direct indication of what, if anything, might be personally at stake for the author in the debate, and to casual readers the anonymous work would have offered little to distinguish it from the work of the many Dublin and London Unionist pamphleteers of the time. Nonetheless, "A Phantom's Pilgrimage" clearly served as something of a personal as well as political manifesto for Lady Gregory. Written in response to the uncertainties facing her both as a Trustee Landlord concerned with her son's heritage, and as a woman trying to decide on an appropriate trajectory for her widowed life, it embodies a movement of significant self-questioning and marks an important stage in the emergence of her independent voice both as a woman, an Irish national, and as a writer.

On the surface, the Unionist sentiments of "A Phantom's Pilgrimage" seem unexceptionably orthodox, and very much the product of Lady Gregory's new anxieties as caretaker of Coole. As she had acknowledged in her diary that Spring, the "terrible Home Rule Bill" made "all Loyalists & all possessors of property tremble". The landlord couple briefly portrayed in the essay, for instance, have been ruined by staying on their estate out of "duty", and are in the course of burying their young child, who died when partisan local doctors refused to treat her.[21] The scenario clearly rehearses Lady Gregory's own uncertainty as to whether to sell Coole and thereby ensure some financial heritage for Robert, or to remain and try to preserve his "father's home"[22] and the cultural patrimony it represented, against unfavourable odds. Her uncertainty, though, was evidently not simply a function of political turmoil alone. The wife's despairing cry over her child's grave—"The child is not, and I, whither shall I go?"[23] — gestures squarely to a broader, generic anxiety as to what her role in life should be other than mother to Robert, to a fear of purposelessness if her child, her principal remaining focus of duty and womanly obligation, should die. The vignette reveals a tension between the apparently orthodox Unionism nominally motivating the essay and private concerns, less driven by ideology, which surfaces repeatedly elsewhere in the essay. For if "A Phantom's Pilgrimage" seems uncompromisingly anti-Nationalist in its aims—and Lady Gregory herself evidently considered it sufficiently so to have kept discreetly silent about her authorship of the pamphlet in later life, when it would have severely compromised her Nationalist credentials[24]—it nonetheless hints at the coming change in her political opinions, and shows the world-view that had predominated while Sir William was alive coming under the strain of a newly independent self-examination.

Most obviously, despite its seemingly party-line arguments, the essay manifests little in the way of narrow concern for Lady Gregory's own vested interests. Instead, "A Phantom's Pilgrimage" sympathetically considers the prospects for Irish people of all classes, whether landlords or tenants, strong farmers or merchants, factory labourers or children. Given that the essay's aim was to persuade all readers that Home Rule would be ruinous for Ireland, this panoramic attentiveness might be accounted for as mere political shrewdness, but it is noticeable that the essay dwells most closely and sympathetically on the fortunes of the country people likely to be most inimical to landlords' interests. The most emotive vignettes in the essay are consistently those bearing on the sufferings of the peasantry. Gladstone, for instance, uncovers a famine victim hastily buried beneath a pile of stones, revealing "a dead woman's face, looking upward. It was almost that of a skeleton", and he then enters a cottage only to find a "trembling emaciated man, with a child in his arms and two others clinging to him . . . in the last stages of starvation."[25] And significantly, while the poor are pointedly shown to have no options but starvation or crime—for even the workhouses are portrayed as having closed—the prospective fate of landlords in the essay is figured as at least partly a function of choice: they had the opportunity to leave before the onset of ruin, and even now have the opportunity to return, albeit poorer, to an "English home".[26]

A tension between Unionist orthodoxy and concern for the fate of the disempowered, and her discriminating sense of the real advantages of Ascendancy wealth, had already surfaced in Lady Gregory's earlier writings. In her autobiographical "An Emigrant's Notebook" of 1883–84, for instance—a work, like "A Phantom's Pilgrimage", inspired in part by a period of marked political crisis for the Ascendancy class (in this case The Land War) —she had likewise resisted the narrow self-interest, partisan anger and tone of threatened outrage that characterized most landlord writings of the period. Although she began the Notebook just a year after the generally liberal Sir William, fulminating against the Land League, had announced his intention to "remove everything of value to a safe place" and leave Coole forever empty—

"and if they blow up the residence I shall be very much obliged to them"[27]—
and just a year after Lady Gregory herself, in her first visit to Ireland since her
marriage, had found armed guards posted at Roxborough to protect her
family,[28] she had nonetheless taken a strikingly moderate and conciliating
view of the social and political upheavals that had occured. "Let us try not to
judge too harshly those who are against us" she writes in the final paragraphs
of the Notebook: "If in some places the people have been ungrateful, in
others they have suffered oppression and harshness and we must be glad that
such things will never be possible again." The work looks back nostalgically
at the untroubled times of her childhood at Roxborough, but nonetheless
pragmatically acknowledges widespead abusiveness on the parts of landlords,
accepts the need for change—"If the old relations have been changed we
must make up our minds to it"—and explicitly hopes for a new concord that
might "bind class with class".[29] So too in the pseudonymous Irish stories she
wrote in 1890–91, which explore relations between the Western peasantry
and a series of female outsider figures who are either English or "half-Irish".
The stories, which have a significant autobiographical component, show
Lady Gregory eagerly exploring differences of culture and class, and reflecting
on where her own loyalties should lie. The vacillation they embody between
an admiring concern for the peasantry and a self-interested recognition of
the dangers of losing caste inherent in seeking to identify with them more
closely, emphasizes, like "An Emigrant's Notebook", both how earnestly she
was engaged with the politics of identity even at this early stage, but also how
resistant she was to the notion of simple class or party loyalties.

In "A Phantom's Pilgrimage" these underlying uncertainties of political
conviction re-emerge most strikingly in a vignette which hints at Lady
Gregory's lingering admiration for the dead Nationalist leader Charles Stuart
Parnell. Towards the end of the essay, as he becomes increasingly anxious to
find some evidence of support for his policies, Gladstone arrives at the Dublin
Senate House, where he hopes to find former allies. Instead, he encounters
a mob of angry protesters. The main target of the their fury is the unnamed
figure of William O'Brien, whose desertion of Parnell in 1890 in the wake of
the O'Shea divorce scandal had ensured the Irish leader's fall, and they voice
their anger "with howls of 'Traitor!' 'Judas!' 'Who killed his master!'"[30] Their
"howls", however, directly echo Lady Gregory's own expressions of contempt
for O'Brien, for she had written to Wilfrid Blunt in 1891 comparing O'Brien
to the Biblical charioteer Zimri "who slew his master", and the phrase
remained a lasting favourite for her.[31] Amidst the overt Unionism of the essay,
the echo evokes a discordant and revealing hint of her own potential
unorthodoxy, for at the time of Parnell's fall, Lady Gregory had been
sufficiently contemptuous of O'Brien's desertion, and of the hypocrisy of
many of Parnell's denouncers, to have urged Sir William to stand for
Parliament as a Parnellite.[32]

If Lady Gregory's broader motivations in beginning "A Phantom's

Pilgrimage" stemmed from ingrained self-interest and class loyalty, then, her philanthropic sympathies and general sense of *noblesse oblige* seem to have challenged the ideological underpinnings of her Unionism quite directly in the process of completing it. The tensions implicit in the essay may well have accounted for her decision to keep the essay anonymous, for in withholding her name from the publication she clearly remained unwilling to commit herself publicly to anti-Nationalism, the cause of Landlords' rights, or indeed to any constituency espousing the kind of partisanship that might undercut her hopes for a solution fair to all the Irish people.

3

Besides resuming a debate about cultural and political loyalties begun in her earlier writings, "A Phantom's Pilgrimage" was also a significant act of creative self-assertion for Lady Gregory. The very fact of her determination to publish the essay, albeit anonymously, marked a radical departure from her deferential experiences as a wife, when Sir William had acted as arbiter over writings such as "Arabi and his Household", deciding both whether and when they should appear.[33] While hitherto her writings had been largely contingent on his notions of political expediency and literary merit, she now had the opportunity to write or publish as she alone saw fit. Along with the resumption of her diary, the publication of the essay marked the beginning of a self-conscious and deliberate search for creative work, which gathered pace as the year progressed. In the summer of 1893, having returned to Coole, she began the substantial task of editing an autobiography Sir William had left incomplete in manuscript at his death. By making extracts from his correspondence she was able to complete a narrative covering the last portion of his life, and arranged with John Murray for the book to be published the following year.

It would be easy to dismiss this work as merely dutiful, and a function principally of her avowed interest in keeping Sir William's name and achievement in public view for Robert's benefit. Indeed, many readers have concurred with Wilfrid Blunt in regarding it principally as a widow's "pious act".[34] The volume, however, also represented an elliptical exercise in writing a chapter of her own aubiography, for the unfinished portion of the book— that in which her own involvement would be greatest—was precisely the period of the marriage. Her work in completing the volume hence involved the significant question of how to insert herself into the text as both an explicit subject of the narrative and as its implicit shaper and agent: obliging her, in other words, to consider what forms of textual and editorial "I" she wished to present to the public. Her strategy in dealing with this challenge is revealing. After drawing initial attention to herself by extracting from a letter in which Gregory expresses his pleasure in the new marriage, her selections from the subsequent twelve years of his correspondence, together with the several pages of introductory commentary she wrote herself concerning his political views and accomplishments in later life, admit her only peripherally, almost always only as an implied presence, and then typically as the figure of the grieving widow. In effect, she makes herself largely invisible as an active presence; so deliberately, indeed, that Blunt, for one, was impelled to comment to her that "you effaced yourself throughout the book."[35]

In one sense this strategy of self-erasure merely followed the pattern typical of the marriage itself—dutiful deferral to the more important matter of her husband's interests and primacy—but it also, significantly, allowed Lady Gregory to effect an unobtrusive moulding of the narrative to suit her own needs and situation. Her commentaries, and the letter-extracts she saw fit to include, are organized around a series of interlinked themes, and repeatedly highlight such matters as Sir William's liberal political views, the good landlord-tenant relations on the Coole estate, and the profound sense of tradition and heritage informing Gregory's life. These themes, which Yeats would later absorb from Lady Gregory wholesale for use in his own figurations of Coole as a symbol of Ascendancy culture, simultaneously privilege and emphasize her position as both the implied and actual caretaker of the Coole tradition, and thereby tacitly enhanced her newly independent stature. At the same time, they also obliquely invited understanding and sympathy for her as a bereaved woman vulnerable to her tenants' demands. While seeming to erase herself from the narrative, in other words, Lady Gregory was able to shape a narrative trajectory which directly served her own new circumstances, just as the publication of the memoir itself gave her a popular success without compromising her perceived status as merely the dutiful widow.

As an exercise in determining how to represent herself in Sir William's text, Lady Gregory's work on the volume undoubtedly offered her an influential model for her future literary efforts. Throughout her career as a writer she would remain caught in a tension between the need to assert herself creatively and the ingrained imperatives of her upbringing and culture, which held up womanly self-abnegation as the ideal. The autobiography, her first book publication, represented a protected middle ground in which the exact boundaries of Sir William's and her own narrative shapings could remain conveniently blurred both to herself and others, and in which self-fulfillment and duty in completing the work were consequently not in obvious conflict. In future years she would occupy this middle ground with considerable skill, defining her creative ambitions in terms of work for Yeats, for Ireland, for the Abbey Theatre, for the Galway country people, or for her family. The autobiography, in other words, offered her a modest but significant apprenticeship both in the politics of self-representation, and in the strategic benefits of working through or in conjunction with another creative voice as she was to do with Yeats. As her deft response in Spring 1895 to a compliment on Robert's success in winning a scholarship to Harrow shows, she was even at this early stage shrewdly aware of how to call attention to her accomplishments while appearing to downplay them, and of how to simultaneously enjoy and seem to diffuse public praise of her work: "Lady Haliburton congratulated me about R. & said it was his *mother's* talent coming out—& I said no, it was like the book, I took no credit, I had only edited both".[36]

In October 1893, with her work on the memoir largely complete, and wanting "change of ideas", Lady Gregory embarked on the most remarkable creative initiative she was to undertake that year. On an impulse that suggests both how far she had progressed from the listlessness of the previous year, and how intent she was now becoming to find new stimulation and focus, she made an unaccompanied visit to the Aran Islands.[37] She began the visit with a brief stay on the main island, Inishmore, to which she had made a day trip six years before, but she then travelled by open curragh to the smallest island, Inishere, where she was "storm bound for five days, and lived in a cottage, on potatoes, amongst people speaking scarcely any English . . . completely cut away from the world."[38] The visit, to the almost undisturbed culture of this small island of Irish-speakers, was a most unusual undertaking for an Ascendancy woman at that time, and particularly for one travelling alone. Though few manuscript materials bearing on her motives in making the trip survive it seems probable that she was even at this early date inspired by literary sources. She had read Emily Lawless's sentimental Aran novel *Grania* shortly before or possibly during her visit, commenting on the book in at least two letters she wrote while on the islands, and had also recently read Jane Barlow's *Irish Idylls*, stories of peasant life in the boglands of Connaught, a volume she declared to be "one of my sermon books" in a letter of July 1893.[39] Her diary makes no contemporary mention of the journey, but it does confirm that she collected material during her stay towards an article about the islands, since a retrospective entry written at Christmas 1893 records: "I wrote out my notes on Arran [*sic*] — they ought to make a good magazine article." These notes do not appear to have been published or to survive, so the question of how directly she had recognized the specific potential literary value of Aran, with its Irish lore and customs, must remain speculative. We can be certain, however, that by as early as November 1894 she had made an explicit connection between her own experiences on the islands and the imaginative force of Yeats's folk-lore volume *The Celtic Twilight*, which she read soon after its publication in December 1893, for when meeting the American writer Bret Harte in London and hearing his complaint that California had become "too civilized" to inspire him creatively, she responded by telling him of Aran, and by sending him a copy of Yeats's book.[40] Well before their celebrated meeting in August 1896, in other words, she was already beginning to discover for herself the subject matter that would become central to her later literary life.

4

This renewal of creative activity was paralleled by a new social confidence. In London, where she spent the last two months of 1893, having been given the use of a town house by the Layards, Lady Gregory began to pick up the threads of her old social life and hosted several functions, noting with satisfaction in her diary a feeling of "independence and *power*" in "being able to give a dinner." The following Spring, when Sir Henry Layard's declining health made it unlikely that the house would again be so conveniently available, she determined "to find a little independent abode" and took out a lease on a small apartment in Queen Anne's Mansions, near St. James's Park, which was to be her London base for the remainder of the decade. The apartment re-established her presence securely in London society following her prolonged absences during 1892–93, and provided her with a forum in which her skills as a hostess and her increasing resolution to pursue a new social course quickly came to the fore. From 1894 onwards she brought a fresh energy to the business of cultivating new friends, evidently let many unpromising older allegiances wane, and began to orchestrate the mix of her guests more carefully and confidently. As she noted after hosting one small gathering in November 1894: "I don't think I will have more than 6 [guests] again that I may keep them all in hand myself!" Amidst the multitude of dinners and other social events recorded for 1894, one function, at the home of Lord Morris, would later acquire a significance unrecognised at the time, for it was here that she for the first time briefly "met Yates, looking every inch a poet".

The diaries for 1894 also reflect an increasingly systematic search for creative work. In the summer, for instance, having returned to Coole, Lady Gregory wrote "as an occupation" a short shory, "Dies Irae", published two years later in *The Sketch*, an article on the Disestablished Church, and an essay on "Our Boys in India", which latter both remained unpublished.[41] The eclectic subject matter of these writings attests to a lack of a clear creative focus, but equally suggests a robust determination to write. When *Sir William Gregory: An Autobiography* finally appeared in October 1894 after many delays, the enthusiastic reviews and praise for her editorial skill undoubtedly fueled this determination further. The distinguished historian William Hartpole Lecky presciently predicted that she would "go on writing, says it is 'like drink'", while she herself admitted to Sir Arthur Birch that the publication of the book had made her "feel 10 years younger."[42] As yet, however, a compelling subject was still wanting, and in a December letter she complained self-consciously of her lack of focus: "I wish I could set my mind to writing something, I fritter it away in letters and idle talk."[43]

Lady Gregory's London social circle at this time included many literary figures through whom she might well have sought a better-defined creative outlet had she wanted to. From editors of prominent journals such as James

Knowles of *The Nineteenth Century,* to dominant creative figures such as Henry James, through to avant-garde writers such as playwright and poet André Raffalovich and his companion, poet John Gray, both once luminaries of Oscar Wilde's circle, she had ample connections to drawn herself more actively into London literary life. And just as importantly, friends such as Emily Lawless and Violet Martin in Ireland offered her immediate examples of successful female literary enterprise. Her diaries, though, give no indication that she made any efforts to draw on these connections for encouragement or furtherment as a writer. Unsure of what her subject-matter should be, she at this point remained little more than a fringe participant at 'literary teas', retaining, as she had since an early age, a deferential regard for the literary elite—"the achievement of a writer was the one for which I had most admiration"[44]—but as yet uncertain how to channel her own latent ambitions. Recalling this period in her autobiography many years later, Lady Gregory asserted that even had she not met Yeats "I believe I should still have become a writer, because my energy was turning to that side." Rather than doing imaginative work, however, she conceded that she would most likely have become "a writer of middle articles in literary papers, or one of those 'dull people who edit books' I was once in the early days of our acquaintance rather hurt by hearing him speak of."[45] Her turn to a new editorial project in the winter of 1894–95, drawing on the correspondence of Sir William Gregory's grandfather, who had been Under-Secretary of Ireland 1813–31, might seem to confirm the supposition, but it was this work which led directly to her open conversion to Nationalism and which paved the way for the radical changes that would soon follow.

5

Initially, her rummages through "old Mr. Gregory's papers" merely represented a tidying of manuscripts she and Sir William had begun to organize some years before but "did not persist in",[46] and as such they were at the outset just another reflexive effort to find "dutiful" work. As she admitted to John Murray in November 1896 when proposing to forward her typescript for consideration, her original aim had been simply to "make a volume for our own library [at Coole]".[47] Her background researches into late-eighteenth and early nineenth-century Irish history while working on the papers, however, soon not only proved more interesting than she had anticipated, but also provided the challenge that finally forced her to openly confront the contradictions and tensions in her political views. In a March 1895 diary entry, for instance, she records that reading James Froude's *History of the English in Ireland in the Eighteenth Century* "has opened my eyes to the failings of landlords, & I may say of *all* classes in Ireland." In April, contemplating a forthcoming Land Bill which promised to increase tenant rights, she makes the following remarkable entry:

> I feel that this Land Bill is the last of "Dobson's Three Warnings" & am thankful that we land owners have been given even a little time to prepare & to work while it is day—It is necessary that as democracy gains power our power should go—& God knows many of our ancestors & forerunners have eaten or planted sour grapes & we must not repine if our teeth are set on edge—I would like to leave a good memory & not a "monument of champagne bottles"—& with all that, I hope to save the home—the house & woods at least for Robert.

The completion here of a shift anticipated in "An Emigrant's Notebook" a decade earlier, and hinted at beneath the formulaically Unionist anxieties of "A Phantom's Pilgrimage" written just two years before, is striking. The final eclipse of landlord power is not merely accepted as inevitable, but is seen in part as an appropriate consequence of past abuses of privilege. The passage shows Lady Gregory already psychologically preparing herself for the political and social changes she correctly recognised were to come, and summoning her determination to fight the rearguard action which was to occupy her for the next three decades — an attempt to preserve at least a symbolic part of the Coole dynasty, in the form of the house and its woods, even if the estate lands themselves were to be lost. The passage is not yet a profession of allegiance with Nationalist aims, for the acceptance and resignation it embodies in the face of the coming changes are far from signalling enthusiasm, but it marks a pivotal moment of self-conscious departure from the orthodoxies she had hitherto tried to uphold.

The impact of this ideological shift is registered only elliptically in Lady Gregory's diary in the months that followed, no doubt in part because the trajectory of her social life remained largely unchanged. Her promptness in inviting Nationalist M.P. Barry O'Brien to dine, after meeting him in early December 1895 and finding him "very sensible and moderate", reflects a new openness of opinion, and she increased her efforts on behalf of philanthropic groups specifically promoting Irish crafts and manufactures, such as "Irish Industries" and a local Gort "Brabazon" scheme; but her changing perspective resulted in few other discernible practical changes. Tonally, however, the diaries reflect a new contentment in her months spent at Coole. Whereas in the first year or so of her widowhood she evidently began to dread the solitude of life on the estate and its sharp contrast with the cultured social round of life in London—writing in 1893, for instance, that "my heart fails me at the idea of 6 weeks alone there before R[obert] comes"—from late 1894 onwards a progressively warmer note emerges, all the more pronounced given that her London apartment had by then made long stays at Coole a matter more of choice than of necessity. In Spring 1895, for example, we find her regretting not being "at home to look after the people", while by New Year 1896 she notes being "glad to be alone for a time—to 'possess my soul' & look life in the face". The style of the diaries, too, becomes markedly more relaxed during her periods in Ireland, with the dutiful and often factually dry daily entries in London giving way to a more spontaneous mode in which she takes obvious satisfaction in recording simple details: "A larch coming out in the woods—Farrell cutting ivy merrily". Her increasing pleasure in Galway life is reflected most clearly, though, in a letter she wrote to *The Spectator* in April 1895, "Irish Superstitions", which notes the "deeply rooted" survival of folklore beliefs in the area around Coole. Her authorial stance in the letter is still principally that of an onlooker—one whose interest is engaged, but for whom matters such as fairy rings or the drinking of water out of skulls remain essentially picturesque—but the new note of pride in the distinctive country life of "the West" is unmistakeable.[48]

The changed perspective embodied in "Irish Superstitions" may be obvious to us with the benefit of hindsight, but such manifestations of enthusiasm for her Irish home were probably viewed as little more than charming local chauvinism by her London friends. Only Wilfrid Blunt, one of her longest-standing correspondents, seems to have detected the shift in her opinions at this early point, remarking in a letter of January 1896 that he felt "sure that you are now among the Landlord nationalists".[49] In the course of 1896, her continued research towards *Mr. Gregory's Letter-Box* consolidated the change irreversibly. When the volume finally appeared, and Sir Frederic Burton "gravely" observed that he discerned "a tendency to Home Rule" in her editorial commentaries, Lady Gregory countered with a memorably defiant comment that signalled clearly that she had cast her lot firmly with the cause of Nationalism: "I defy any one to study Irish History without getting a dislike and distrust of England!"[50] To Wilfrid Blunt in her New Year's letter in January 1897 she reported her hopes for the formation of a "real Irish party" and her belief that "dislike to England is steadily increasing" amongst all classes in Ireland.[51]

6

By the time Yeats came to stay at Tillyra Castle in August 1896, as a guest of her friend and neighbour Edward Martyn, Lady Gregory was thus already well advanced on the road to Irish Nationalism. More importantly, though, she was by this point also well aware of the new literary movement in Ireland. Although no contemporary records survive to confirm exactly when she first read key volumes such as Douglas Hyde's *Love Songs of Connacht*, what evidence we have indicates that she had read widely in the works of the new generation of Irish writers by 1896. As we have seen, she was already in effect promoting *The Celtic Twilight* by late 1894, and Jane Barlow's *Irish Idylls* was already one of her "sermon books" in 1893—a strong indication of a broad taste for folk-inspired Irish writing. Her brief record of seeing Yeats in London in 1894 itself adopts a tone of easy familiarity in discriminating between his verse and prose work, and indicates that she had by then certainly read one of, if not both *The Wanderings of Oisin* (1889) and *The Countess Cathleen* (1892), the two volumes of lyrics he had published to that point: "At the Morrises I met Yates, looking every inch a poet, though I think his prose 'Celtic Twilight' is the best thing he has done". If her interest in Yeats did not itself lead her directly to other writers such as Hyde, via Yeats's reviews in mainstream journals such as *The Speaker* and *The Bookman*, her general zeal in keeping abreast of new literature, and her friendships with Irish writers such as Violet Martin and Emily Lawless would almost certainly have done so. Given this background, it is unsurprising that on hearing of Yeats's presence in the neighbourhood Lady Gregory should have promptly called at Tillyra to introduce herself and invite the entire party to lunch at Coole. While critical accounts have typically portrayed her, much in Yeats's own terms in *Autobiographies*, as at this point little more than a "clever fashionable wom[a]n"[52] who was only galvanized into creativity and Nationalism subsequent to their chance meeting, the trajectory of her life since 1893, her increasingly deliberate search for a creative outlet during these years, and most importantly, the evidence of events at Tillyra, makes clear that she was already shrewdly aware of the benefits friendship with him might confer, and that she sought the connection quite deliberately.

Lady Gregory's retrospective diary entry bearing on the meeting gives no hint of agency on her part, noting only that "E. Martyn had also poets with him, Symonds [*sic*] & Yeats—the latter full of charm & interest & the Celtic revival — I have been collecting fairy lore since his visit", but all accounts of the meeting evidence the directness of her intent to implicate herself in Yeats's creative work. George Moore, drawing on Edward Martyn's recollections, would write that "she seems to have recognised her need in Yeats at once", while Arthur Symons, Yeats's travelling companion, who was in the process of cementing his own friendship with Yeats, would later jealously charge that "as soon as her terrible eye fell upon him I knew she would keep him".[53] Most tellingly, Yeats himself would remember that he "had been but a few minutes [in] her library" during the visit to Coole for lunch when "she asked . . . if I could set her to some work for our intellectual movement"[54]—a sure testament to both her eagerness and her awareness of recent developments in Irish writing. Her diary entry likewise suggests that she began "collecting fairy lore" only reactively, in the wake of Yeats's visit. But here, too, Lady Gregory appears to have taken a more active and premeditated course than she wished to acknowledge. The first of the many notebooks she used to record her folklore gatherings, and which subsequently formed the basis of *Visions and Beliefs in the West of Ireland* and the numerous folklore articles she wrote collaboratively with Yeats, contains entries dated as early as 1 August 1896, almost certainly before Yeats's first visit to Coole, and well before he left Tillyra.[55] Many years later, when no longer so concerned to downplay her eagerness, she would acknowledge in *Visions and Beliefs* that she had indeed begun collecting before the meeting: "'The Celtic Twilight' was the first book of Mr. Yeats's that I read, and even before I met him, a little time later, I had begun looking for news of the invisible world; for his stories were of Sligo and I felt jealous for Galway."[56] Her gatherings after the meeting itself, in other words, merely continued and confirmed a trajectory of interest already in progress as a result of an enthusiasm for Yeats's own writings begun well before they met.

If the scent of careful planning thus hangs over Lady Gregory's part in the meeting—she was ready with tangible evidence of her enthusiasm for Yeats's work when he first came to lunch Coole, producing a letter Bret Harte had sent her in response to her gift of *The Celtic Twilight*[57]—it was planning well directed. Yeats, who had written in 1893 of folklore as being "the Bible, the Thirty-Nine articles and the Book of Common Prayer" of poetic inspiration, must have been immediately attentive to her enthusiasm for gathering peasant lore.[58] She would later recall that he visited her alone during his stay at Tillyra "to walk with me from Lissatumna to Ballylee in search of folk lore".[59] Conversation during their first meeting must also soon have turned to Aran, for Yeats had made his first visit to the islands—a stay of nearly a week —just days before, gathering material for his novel *The Speckled Bird*, and he was still "full of the subject" when he met Synge in Paris some weeks later.[60] While he might otherwise have been able to dismiss her enthusiasm for folklore as a passing fancy, her solo visit to Inishere would have provided solid evidence of her seriousness. Given that he had written in a letter of April 1895 that he was "always ransacking Ireland for people to set writing at Irish things"[61], we should perhaps be surprised only that her request that he "set her to some work for our intellectual movement" met with such a cautious initial response. In his manuscript autobiography Yeats would indeed later be obliged to record that "She sometimes banters me by reminding me that I could see nothing for her to do but read our books."[62]

For all Lady Gregory's eagerness, and the presumable appeal of her interest in folklore, however, the celebrated meeting at Tillyra was likely from Yeats's point of view just one of many such encounters with would-be recruits to the literary movement during the period. In 1901 he would remark in *Samhain* that "in Ireland just now one has only to discover an idea that seems of service to the country for friends and helpers to start up on every hand", and by 1896 he had likely already begun to feel the need to be circumspect with zealous newcomers.[63] While his interest was undoubtedly engaged, his first impressions seem to have been tempered by his distaste for the Georgian ambience at Coole, and quite possibly by an initial disdain for the formality and "Victorian earnestness" of Lady Gregory's personal manner—qualities he would later charge that "the superficial observer" might mistakenly regard as indicative of her character.[64] Though a promising connection was established in August 1896, then, it was not until Lady Gregory's return to London in early 1897 that it was resumed and began to develop into friendship.

7

As these diaries confirm, Lady Gregory's part in consolidating the connection was as deliberate and well planned as her initial overtures the previous summer. In the week before her first invitation to Yeats to dine at her apartment on 14 February 1897, she borrowed a typewriter from her friend Lady Layard and began preparing a transcription for him of the folklore she had collected since the previous August. For the dinner itself she evidently took considerable care to assemble an impressive range of company to meet him—inviting Nationalist M.P. Barry O'Brien, explorer-diplomat Harry Johnston, and painter Arthur Clay amongst others—as if to emphasize her diverse social connections. Her investment in the occasion is symptomatically apparent in her careful preservation of Yeats's brief reply accepting the invitation, and she would likewise preserve even his one-line responses to her subsequent invitations. This initial dinner was soon followed by a tea party— at which Yeats began to tell her of his hopes for a new theatre movement— to which she invited as her other guest Sir Alfred Lyall, himself a minor poet, whom she had primed with a gift of a volume of Yeats's poems. On this occasion, if not before, she would have been able to call attention to her kinship with Standish O'Grady, whose *History of Ireland* Yeats regarded as a seminal text which left "every Irish imaginative writer" in O'Grady's debt, and whom, Yeats now told her, he hoped to "stir up" to write a play.[65] Other dinners followed in turn, and to judge by a letter from Henry James, regretting his inability to come to dinner on 28 February "to meet your interesting Celt", she soon began to allow her enthusiasm for Yeats to overflow liberally into her invitations.[66] Her diary record of this dinner itself reflects a new and palpable excitement in her main guest: "I feel quite proud of my young countryman".

This emerging note of personal investment is notably evident in Lady Gregory's record of the dinner party she held on 21 March 1897, at which her guests were Yeats, Barry O'Brien, and Horace Plunkett, leader of the Irish co-operative movement. The small and exclusively Irish nature of this gathering immediately hints at a new intensity of focus, and the diary entry itself, with its unusually animated and detailed account of the conversation which took place, confirms a high degree of self-consciousness on her part about the importance of the evening. In bringing together three prominent Irish activists from different spheres—literary, parliamentary, and agricultural/economic—the dinner clearly offered a fresh perspective on the Nationalist cause, and, responding to the opportunity, its participants seem to have been briefly seized with a vision of unity centred on Horace Plunkett's potential as "the only possible leader" of the disorganised Irish factions. Lady Gregory's account shows her revelling in the promising consensus amongst her guests, but also enjoying her own energetic contributions to the conversation (on matters as diverse as the Parnell's influence on Irish political life, financial reparations, and land purchase), and her success in establishing herself as a determined Nationalist and practical strategist in their eyes. Her entry for the following day, recording Plunkett's enthusiastic letter of thanks "I don't know when I have spent such an interesting evening"—likewise suggests considerable satisfaction in her roles as both convenor and participant. The dinner undoubtedly cemented Lady Gregory's standing as an energetic and valuable ally in Yeats's estimation by demonstrating her aptitude as a facilitator and encourager, but with characteristic care she also chose this occasion to give him her typed "folk lore pages", thereby signalling her continued primary interest in his creative work. The record of the dinner marks a crucial turning point not only in consolidating the friendship, but also in the style of the diary itself. In sharp contrast to her earlier entries, Lady Gregory here suddenly adopts the present tense to describe events—"We come down & have coffee . . . Mr. O'Brien is much pleased . . . Mr. Plunkett wonders . . ."—a shift indicative of an unusually close involvement in her narrative. Rather than simply recording what occurred, the entry embodies an imaginative replaying of events, and marks the extent to which they were still repercussing for her. From this point on, as she began to be swept up in the whirl of social and intellectual changes offered by her friendship with Yeats, her entries are frequently marked by such immediacy, and by a steadily increasing self-consciousness about the importance of the events she was participating in.

By the time she left London in mid-April 1897, Lady Gregory had come to recognise the sharp contrast between the possibilities offered by her connection with Yeats, and the rhythms of her established social life. With Yeats promised as her long-term guest for the summer, and the idea that she should supply him with folklore gatherings for his use towards a new edition of *The Celtic Twilight* already broached, she had good reason to be confident about the long-term prospects for the friendship.[67] Her last entry before returning to Coole marks a pivotal recognition of eroding loyalty to elite London society, and an effective declaration of intent to cast her lot elsewhere:

> Lunch Morrises—Ld. M[orris]. disdainful of Horace Plunkett's schemes—"cods" or humbug he calls them—. . . & of the Irish Literary Society—"a set of schemers"—I did not like to say I have just been elected to it!—but very full of his own swell friends & of having dined at Sir H. Thompson's Octaves "where the Prince dines once a year"—Martin [Morris] on the other side much elated because he has just come from a visit to the old Duchess of Cleveland at Battle —& is going to spend Easter with the Percy Wyndhams at Clouds—

No, I think my poor literary society friends know more of "the things that are more excellent".

8

With Yeats's arrival at Coole at the end of July, for the first in a series of long summer stays that would continue until his marriage in 1917, the diaries embark on a rich record of matters of literary moment, charting the founding and fostering of the Irish Literary Theatre, the many visits of Hyde, AE, Moore, Synge and others to Coole and, throughout, the strengthening of Lady Gregory's friendship with Yeats. Their account of her gradual transition from folklore gatherer and secretary to prose collaborator and adviser, then to occasional contributor of "a sentence here and there"[68] in plays, and finally to formal co-author of *Cathleen ni Houlihan* and other plays with him, and of Yeats's correspondent increasing reliance on her both personally, financially and creatively, significantly augments the record of the development of their early friendship, and provides essential matter for the fuller account of their collaborative partnership now in preparation. Early entries, for instance, show Lady Gregory tentatively seeking to categorize the new friendship. "We searched for folk lore" she would write following Yeats's first extended stay: "I gave him over all I had collected, & took him about looking for more". This awkward combination of mutuality ("we searched"), self-praise for her generosity ("I gave him") and implied leadership ("I had collected") then gives way to a more businesslike mode—"when we came in I wd write them out, & then type them, very good training if I ever want to be private secretary!"—as if Lady Gregory suddenly recognized the need to restrain her enthusiasm given the still provisional nature of their relationship. Later entries show her initial exuberance in being able to assist Yeats evolving into a firm practicality in urging him to be more productive, into an increasingly tenacious direct role defending his interests (particularly in his confrontational relationship with George Moore), and finally to a determination to undertake substantial creative work in her own right. By late 1899, as one revealing entry shows, the early satisfactions of her patronage had given way, at this point perhaps only unconsciously, to a sense that her ministrations might be limiting her own creative scope: "I dreamed that I had been writing some article & that W.B.Y. said 'It's not your business to write—Your business is to make an atmosphere.'" By the latter sections of the diary the deep mutual regard that finally developed between the writers is obvious: a retrospective entry covering the summer and autumn of 1902 lists their work together on nearly a dozen projects in that period alone.

The record the diaries provide of the personal dynamics of the friendship is almost always revealing. Lady Gregory's accounts of Yeats's first confidences, for instance—from his "bitter feeling of degradation" at being poor, to "his tortures of hope & fear" regarding Maud Gonne—and her adoption of a maternally sympathetic tone in response—"Poor boy he has had a hard struggle"—add significantly to our knowledge of the personal imperatives and emotional paradigms at work in their relationship.[69] The diaries confirm that a certain reticence remained at the heart of the friendship even in its first flowering of mutual enthusiasm. Though Yeats was ready to confide many intimate details about his life and to seek Lady Gregory's advice widely on personal matters, he apparently kept much private, including the specifics of Maud Gonne's relationship with Lucien Millevoye, his own affair with Olivia Shakespear, and the details of his occult pursuits. Lady Gregory in turn seems to have respected this reticence, and to have made few personal confidences herself: Yeats apparently remained in ignorance of her brief affair with Wilfrid Blunt, just as he would later appear to have remained unsuspecting of her close relationship with John Quinn. For each, these early records of the friendship show, the central bond of their partnership remained Yeats's creative achievement and their joint ambitions as dramatists and folklorists, with the purely personal always kept essentially subservient to this creative focus. The final entries of the diary are marked by a confident tone of familiarity, and show that Lady Gregory was by that time readily critical of anything which she considered drew from Yeats's achievement—dismissing his psaltery experiments as "a fad", for instance, and fulminating about the demands made on his energies by "wretched mystics".[70] A final retrospective entry made in 1909, in which she admits to rewriting *Where There is Nothing* with him as *The Unicorn from the Stars* "to please him but against my will" effectively acknowledges the strains that had by then begun to emerge in their partnership.

As the only contemporary private record from this period by a major figure in the Irish literary movement, the diaries provide a corrective and frequently revealing counterweight to the narratives of these years written long afterwards, in the light of later autobiographical imperatives—by Yeats and Lady Gregory themselves as well as others. Lady Gregory's later self-aggrandizement in *Our Irish Theatre*, for instance, in which she cast her own and Yeats's roles in the Irish Literary Theatre in heroic proportions at the expense of many other notable contributors, is significantly undercut by her records made at the time. Though she was a dominant figure in arranging guarantees for the Theatre, and an energetic agent on behalf of Yeats's interests, the diary shows her only peripherally involved either creatively or in the day-to-day practicalities of its productions. While from the perspective of her later accomplishment as a dramatist and her centrality in establishing the Abbey her presence as a major figure in the earliest years of the theatre movement may have seemed ordained, at the time her role was even in her own view potentially tenuous: she unhesitatingly made a new Will in March 1899 after catching a bad cold, and would often refer to her contributions as those merely of an enthusiast.

Lady Gregory drew extensively on the diaries for use in *Seventy Years* and elsewhere, and the complete text presented here also reveals how routinely she bowdlerized their entries by removing or modifying material she judged too personal or revealing. In a characteristically cautious move, for instance, Yeats the "brilliant charming and lovable companion" of July 1897 would become merely a "most charming companion" two decades later. The more acid, forceful side of her personality, reflected in many summary, biting judgements of her contemporaries in these pages, was likewise quietly excised from her extracts. Some of these excisions simply reflected a change of heart—her early irritations at Hugh Lane's "second rate fashionable talk & vulgarity of mind"[71], for instance, soon gave way to affection and admiration— but most, such as her tellingly subjective first impression of Maud Gonne— "A shock to me— for instead of beauty I saw a death's head"[72]—were simply not consonant with the conciliating self-image she wished to present publicly. The complete text also allows correction or identification of the multitude of misdated and undated excerpts she later published. Casual misdates within the diary are numerous, but in 1897–98 Lady Gregory evidently mislaid a part-filled volume, continued her record in a new volume for some time, and then found and completed the mislaid volume. The resulting contorted chronology, corrected in this transcription, compounded her usual uncertainty over dates, and led to many notable errors which have unfortunately been followed widely in secondary works.

9

By January 1902, when her regular diary entries finally begin to peter out, Lady Gregory had completed the most significant years of her apprenticeship as a writer. The process of keeping the diary may have itself contributed significantly to the process of artistic self-discovery for her, in her early years of widowhood providing her with an unrecognized creative forum at a time when her aspirations to write were generally unfocussed, and in later years serving more self-consciously as record of her own remaking as a literary figure. Her success in finding a new creative focus indeed probably largely accounts for her abandonment of the diary, as she was becoming too busy, and was now sufficiently secure of her part in the Irish literary world, to feel the need to keep a record of the important events she was participating in. As she would observe in a 1903 entry regretting having let the diary lapse: "I can only comfort myself for not having written here . . . by thinking it is perhaps when one is doing least & so has least to tell, one has more time for writing it down." The last year or more of the diary conveys a sense of increasing pressure of business, with entries noting events in summary fashion or simply calling attention to some other, fuller record by means of notes such as "see Samhain" or "let newscuttings speak".[73] Her hasty synopses also show little of the stylistic concern apparent at earlier points in the diary . (Her record of a return visit to Aran in 1898, for instance, seems from its many deletions and revisions to have been made as a possible later source for a publication.) The last year or so of the diary also shows a further waning of interest in her old London life, with abbreviated comments such as "saw various people" finally giving way to a recognition that "somehow I have lost my interest in society for the present—All gatherings much the same, a want of ideas".[74] In recognition of the changed priorities the diary itself attests to, Lady Gregory gave up her London apartment in Spring 1901, and after 1903 became only a sporadic visitor to the city.

If the effective ending of her diary coincided closely with Lady Gregory's emergence to independent literary prominence, and her abandonment of a regular London social presence, it also appropriately enough coincided with the closure of other crucial chapters in her life. In May 1902 Robert Gregory reached the age of majority, and in the July of that year he assumed the Mastership of Coole. Though he would not graduate from Oxford until the following year, and thereafter chose to follow an artistic career in London and Paris, never displacing his mother's day-to-day supervision of the estate, the change represented an ending of Lady Gregory's legal responsibilities, and the symbolic completion of her anxious caretakership over his schooling and upbringing. "Thank God, these last ten years have passed more smoothly and happily than at their beginning I thought possible" she wrote to her near neighbour Lord Gough in June 1902. Although Robert still faced a "difficult part of his life", she observed, her own hopes were now less important than the choices he would himself have to make: "I trust in any case he may be of use to others, and may do his duty."[75]

For Lady Gregory, the various roles which had largely defined her life since 1880—as wife, mother, hostess in London and caretaker at Coole—had by 1902 thus been ended or left behind. What remained were the new opportunities and "duties"—as writer, folklorist, patron, Nationalist and literary hostess—that she had finally forged for herself.

NOTES

[1] For Roxborough and its lack of a library, see Elizabeth Coxhead *Lady Gregory: A Literary Portrait* (London: Macmillan, 1961) p. 10; for the prohibition on novels, and Frances Persse's evangelical beliefs, see Lady Gregory, *Seventy Years: Being the Autobiography of Lady Gregory* (Gerrards Cross: Colin Smythe, 1974) p. 15 (hereafter *Seventy Years*); for the "fortunate marriage" a "liberal education" see Lady Gregory, unpublished Holograph Memoirs, Berg Collection (hereafter: Berg).

[2] *Ave* (London: Heinemann, 1911) p. 275.

3 *Lady Gregory's Journals* ed. Daniel J. Murphy (Gerrards Cross: Colin Smythe, 1987) vol. 2, p. 281 and *passim*. Hereafter *Journals*.

4 See Brian Jenkins, *Sir William Gregory of Coole* (Gerrards Cross: Colin Smythe, 1986) pp. 266, 271.

5 Lady Gregory, Holograph Memoirs, Berg.

6 *Journals* vol. 1, p. 304

7 Holograph Memoirs, Berg. For a more extended reading of the parallels between Lady Gregory and Dorothea Brooke, see my "A Dialogue of Self and Service: Lady Gregory's Emergence as an Irish Writer and Partnership with W. B. Yeats" (D. Phil dissertation., Oxford University, 1987).

8 Holograph Memoirs, Berg. The unpublished diaries for the period 1882–91 are now in the Berg Collection, while a single volume covering the period 1880–82 is at Emory University (hereafter: Emory).

9 Two unpublished manuscript versions of "An Emigrant's Notebook" survive: an early draft in the Berg Collection, and a later draft at Emory. Lady Gregory wrote at least three short stories in the period 1890–91 under the pseudonym "Angus Grey": "A Philanthropist", published in *The Argosy*, June 1891, "A Gentleman", published in *The Argosy*, July 1894, and "Peeler Astore", of which an unpublished typescript survives in the Berg Collection. For readings of these, and the variety of other published and unpublished writings Lady Gregory completed during the period of her marriage, see "A Dialogue of Self and Service".

10 See Brian Jenkins "The Marriage", in *Lady Gregory: Fifty Years After* ed. Ann Saddlemyer and Colin Smythe (Gerrards Cross: Colin Smythe, 1987) pp. 70–84.

11 Holograph Memoirs, loose page inserted in vol. 9, Berg. Elsewhere in the Memoirs, she writes of the period as involving "squandered" potential and "wasted time".

12 *Journals* vol. 2, p. 327.

13 Unpublished letter from Sir William Gregory to Augusta Persse, 1 February 1880 (Emory).

14 Last Will and Testament of Sir William Gregory, dated 18 December 1891, Somerset House. Probate was granted on 1 June 1892. The daughter may, alternately, have been Gregory's child. No correspondence or record of prior financial support appears to survive.

15 Unpublished letter to Wilfrid Blunt, 31 March 1892 (Berg). Her use of the jointure to clear the mortgage is referred to elliptically in several of her diary entries, such as that of 7 April 1897: "£500 per ann put by for 6 years wd clear the place for Robert". She evidently later stressed her financial sacrifice to Yeats, who refers to it in *Autobiographies* (London: Macmillan, 1955) pp. 392, 455.

16 Unpublished letter of 29 October 1892 (Berg). Robert Gregory was at this point a boarder in England at Elstree School.

17 Unpublished letter to Wilfrid Blunt, circa 16 November 1892 (Berg). The prospective journal, "Tomorrow", to be edited by Margot Tennant and others, never got beyond the planning stage.

18 Ibid.

19 Diary entry for 8 January 1893. Subsequent entries cited in this Introduction are identified only when their source is not apparent from context.

20 *A Phantom's Pilgrimage* (London: West Ridgeway, 1893) p. 3.

21 Ibid., p. 13.

22 Ibid.

23 Ibid, p. 14.

24 Her only later written mention of the work comes in her unpublished Holograph Memoirs (Berg), in a passage in which she less than convincingly attempts to disavow the pamphlet both ideologically and creatively: "I have never been a meddler in Irish politics, except when I wrote, with sarcasm, I think a dull pamphlet against Gladstone's 2nd Home Rule Bill."

25 *A Phantom's Pilgrimage* p. 5.

26 Ibid., p. 14. The wife is explicitly figured as English by upbringing.

27 Unpublished letter from Sir William Gregory to Father Shannon, 1 May 1882 (Emory).

University.

[28] Unpublished letter to Wilfrid Blunt, 24 [July 1882] (Berg).

[29] "An Emigrant's Notebook" (Emory). For a fuller account of the genesis of this work in its variant forms, see "A Dialogue of Self and Service".

[30] *A Phantom's Pilgrimage*, p. 11.

[31] *Seventy Years* p. 248. Yeats, obviously drawing on Lady Gregory's usage, himself later borrowed the phrase to describe John Dillon's allied role in bringing about Parnell's fall. See *Autobiographies*, p. 366.

[32] "I want Sir William to stand as a Parnellite, against some of the Judases" (unpublished letter to Wilfrid Blunt, 3 December 1890 (Berg). Oddly, Lady Gregory excised this passage when including portions of the letter in *Seventy Years* (p. 244), despite her typical care to foreground material which displayed her Nationalist or proto-Nationalist credentials.

[33] For Sir William Gregory's initial veto of "Arabi" (later reversed), see Lady Gregory's letters to Wilfrid Blunt, 16 and 17 September 1882 (Berg). In general, as Brian Jenkins observes ("The Marriage" p. 83), Gregory "spurred his wife's literary endeavours" rather than "seeking to keep her in the background", but it is nonetheless clear that her deference to his wishes impacted significantly on her creative output. While Wilfrid Blunt immediately recognized her abilities, incorporated versions of several of her poems in his own volumes of verse, drew on her help in a number of his essays and other prose works and encouraged her unreservedly to write, Gregory most likely never saw most of her occasional poems, may have been the force behind her abandonment of "An Emigrant's Notebook" and doubtless either encouraged or concurred with her decision to publish her later "Irish" stories anonymously.

[34] Diary entry for 29 November 1894, quoted in Elizabeth Longford "Lady Gregory and Wilfrid Scawen Blunt", *Lady Gregory: Fifty Years After* p. 93

[35] Letter to Lady Gregory, 27 November 1894, quoted in Mary Lou Kohfeldt, *Lady Gregory: The Woman Behind the Irish Renaissance* (New York: Atheneum, 1985) p. 98.

[36] Diary entry for 3 May 1895.

[37] Unpublished letter to Wilfrid Blunt, 16 October 1893 (Berg). Her visit covered the period *c.* 1–6 October.

[38] Ibid. For her earlier day trip, see her Diary, entry for 28 June 1887 (Berg). This earlier visit obviously impressed her, since her discussion of the geological and archeological features of the islands in an 1890 conversation, reported by Grant Duff in his *Notes from a Diary 1889-1891*, vol. 1, pp. 224-25, indicates both enthusiasm for and knowledge of the subject.

[39] Grant Duff includes part of a letter Lady Gregory wrote to him from Inishmore in *Notes from a Diary 1892-1895*, vol. 1, p. 276, in which she compares her own sense of Aran life to Lawless's literary version. An unpublished letter from Sir Frederic Burton, 8 October 1893 (Berg) likewise indicates that also she wrote to him at length on the subject. For her comments on *Irish Idylls* see her unpublished letter to Lady Layard, [6 July 1893] (Berg).

[40] *Seventy Years* p. 274, and see also Typescript Diary, part 6 (Berg): "I had given him *The Celtic Twilight* because he said to me that he had lost his writing impulse in leaving the wild western states".

[41] "Dies Irae", *The Sketch* 25 March 1896, p. 376. Manuscripts of the two unpublished articles survive in the Berg Collection.

[42] Diary entries for 30 November and 24 October 1894.

[43] Unpublished letter to Wilfrid Blunt, 9 December 1894 (Berg).

[44] Holograph Memoirs (Berg).

[45] *Seventy Years*, p. 391.

[46] Ibid., p. 300.

[47] Unpublished letter to John Murray, 11 November 1896, Archives of John Murray Ltd. (Hereafter: Murray).

[48] "Irish Superstitions", *The Spectator*, April 1895, p. 533.

[49] Unpublished letter to Lady Gregory, 3 January 1896 (Berg).

[50] Lady Gregory, *Our Irish Theatre* (Gerrards Cross: Colin Smythe, 1972) p. 41.

[51] Unpublished letter to Wilfrid Blunt, 3 January 1897 (Berg).

[52] *Autobiographies* p. 455.

[53] George Moore, *Vale* (London: Heinemann, 1914) p. 176. Symons's remark, dating from 1912, is reported in *John B. Yeats, Letters to his Son W. B. Yeats and Others 1869-1922*, ed. Joseph Hone (London: Faber, 1944) p. 179. As Bruce Morris observes, however, in "Reassessing Arthur Symons's Relationship with Lady Gregory", in *Yeats: An Annual of Critical and Textual Studies Vol. 5* ed. Richard J. Finneran (Ann Arbor, Michigan: UMI Research Press, 1987), Symons's apparent hostility to Lady Gregory did not begin to manifest itself until after his 1908 mental breakdown, and contrasts sharply with the cordial relations between them prior to the breakdown.

[54] W. B. Yeats, *Memoirs* ed. Denis Donoghue (London: Macmillan, 1972) p. 102.

[55] The exact date of Yeats's arrival at Tillyra is uncertain, but was at the earliest 27 July 1896. It seems likely that he made the first of two trips he took to Aran from Tillyra soon after arriving, since getting local colour for his novel *The Speckled Bird* was a prime motive for spending time in the area. If so, this would have allowed insufficient time for Lady Gregory to call on Martyn and then host the subsequent lunch prior to early August. Her own diary entry, though admittedly retrospective and approximate, includes the presence of the "poets" at Tillyra as an event from "August".

[56] *Visions and Beliefs in the West of Ireland* (Gerrards Cross: Colin Smythe, 1970) p. 15.

[57] *Seventy Years* p. 308.

[58] W. B. Yeats, *Uncollected Prose* ed. John P. Frayne (London: Macmillan, 1970) vol. 1, p. 284.

[59] Holograph Memoirs (Berg). In this passage Lady Gregory recalls the walk as being the occasion she asked Yeats "& I counted much on his answer—what I could do that would best help Ireland." Though this recollection suggests a diplomatic delay on her part in asking the question, in contrast to the eagerness implied in Yeats's account (in which she posed it within minutes of his arrival in the library at Coole), it nonetheless confirms the intensity of her investment and premeditation in posing it. In *Seventy Years* p. 390, she would again recall the walk, but omit the matter of her concern about his answer. This later version claims that she had showed Yeats during his first visit "a folklore article I had written for the *Spectator*, but he was not much interested". While this has been generally assumed to be her 1897 article "Irish Visions", written just prior to Yeats's return to Coole that summer, it seems more likely to have been her 1895 letter "Irish Superstitions", a slight enough item to explain Yeats's lack of enthusiasm, which was most certainly engaged by 1897.

[60] *Autobiographies* p. 343.

[61] *The Collected Letters of W. B. Yeats* vol. 1, ed. John S. Kelly (Oxford: Clarendon Press, 1986) p. 463 (hereafter: *CL1*)

[62] *Memoirs* p. 102.

[63] W. B. Yeats, *Explorations* (London: Macmillan, 1962) p. 73.

[64] *Autobiographies* pp. 389, 392.

[65] Entry for 23 February 1897. See also *Autobiographies* p. 220. O'Grady was related to Lady Gregory's father's first wife.

[66] Unpublished letter, Henry James to Lady Gregory, 26 February 1897 (Berg).

[67] See unpublished letter to Wilfrid Blunt, 15 July 1897 (Berg), in which Lady Gregory mentions having gathered folklore for Yeats "for a new edition of his Celtic Twilight". There is no mention of this plan in the correspondence between Yeats and Lady Gregory after she left London, which suggests it was already agreed by that time.

[68] *Our Irish Theatre* p. 53

[69] Retrospective entry for summer 1897, dated 30 November 1897.

[70] Entries for 16 February and 11 February 1901.

[71] Retrospective entry dated 14 October, covering Spring 1894.

[72] Entry for 18 December 1898.

[73] Retrospective entry dated 4 January 1903.

74 Entries for 16 February 1901 and 1 April 1901.
75 Unpublished letter to Lord Gough, 6 June 1902 (Berg).

A NOTE ON EDITORIAL PRINCIPLES

Lady Gregory's handwriting, often difficult to decipher even at its leisurely best, and a speedy and abbreviated scrawl at its hasty worst, provided a substantial challenge in the compilation of this volume. When drawing on the diaries for use in her autobiography, Lady Gregory hired a professional typist in 1919 to make selected transcriptions. The surviving pages attest to the frequent bemusement of both the typist and Lady Gregory herself. Numerous blanks left in the transcriptions are marked only by a despairing query in Lady Gregory's own hand, and a multitude of what can only have been hopeful guesses on the typist's part went uncorrected. Most revealing of all, many of Lady Gregory's corrections, particularly of proper names, are themselves manifestly wrong. With repeated scrutiny, however, all but a small number of words and phrases in the manuscript eventually proved legible. These are enclosed in angled brackets—thus: < ? > —as are a few readings offered as probable but uncertain.

The transcription presented here aims to preserve the essential features of the manuscript, but inevitably this has involved some compromises. Lady Gregory rarely used full stops and was sparing in her use of commas, favouring instead a dash between sentences and frequently between clauses. I have retained this somewhat eccentric mode of punctuation, as regularization would have eliminated many clearly deliberate ambiguities of sequence, and the stream-like effect of immediacy in many of the entries. In the interests of readerly ease, however, I have generally supplied missing letters or words where they seemed required, such as to expand abbreviations or complete dates. Where this or other editorial material has been inserted, the interpolations are given in square brackets, thus: [ ]. In a few instances, I have silently deleted Lady Gregory's inadvertent repetitions of a word, such as at page turns. I have also silently corrected her occasional misspellings of ordinary words. Her errors in personal and proper names—such as "Yates" for "Yeats" or "Symonds" for "Symons"—are retained, however, since they signal an unfamiliarity that is itself often significant. One exception is Lady Gregory's repeated vacillation between "Mrs. Kay" and "Mrs. Kaye", which is given in its correct form throughout. Underlined text is represented in italics. Lady Gregory sometimes underlined titles of publications, sometimes enclosed them in single or double inverted commas, and often left them undifferentiated from the remainder of her text. In the interests of readerly ease, I have placed titles in double inverted commas throughout. In a few cases, I have silently supplied omitted closing brackets and closing inverted commas, and have also corrected Lady Gregory's often erratic usages of the genitive form.

The transcription regularizes line spaces around each new entry, although these are only occasionally present in the manuscript itself. At various points Lady Gregory made subsequent emendments to or comments on her original entries. These later interpolations are given in styled parentheses—thus: { } —and they are positioned within the original text as seems best to correspond with Lady Gregory's intended scheme of revision. In one instance, Lady Gregory evidently misplaced the notebook she was then compiling the diary in, commenced a new one, but later found the earlier notebook and resumed her entries in it. The resulting confused sequence of entries—which gave rise to many of the misdatings in *Seventy Years, Our Irish Theatre* and elsewhere— is silently rectified here. A small number of loose pages have likewise been restored to their correct chronological position. Small tears on one page have removed parts of some words, and the missing letters are approximated thus: +++.

In annotating Lady Gregory's entries I have aimed to provide specific identifications for people and events throughout, but rather than include introductory information readily available elsewhere I have assumed a general familiarity on the reader's part with the early years of the Irish Literary Theatre. Familiarity with major historical figures such as Darwin, Wordsworth and Goethe is also generally assumed, except insofar as a specific reference or connection needs additional explanation. Given the large cast of minor and occasional players in the diary entries, I have treated the editorial notes in a cumulative manner, placing principal biographical information only at the first point a person appears in the text and providing a full Index rather than extensive cross-referencing within the notes themselves. In a number of instances it has not been possible to make definite identifications, particularly where the context is not sufficient to give any purchase on a common name, or in the few instances (such as "Mr. Wallop, Lord Portsmouth's son", who might have been any one of seven sons), where a highly localized ambiguity arises. In these instances, I have generally refrained from weighing the likely options in a note. Lady Gregory's staff at Coole are generally identifiable as such from context, and are given minimal annotation.

In order to limit the already considerable extent of the notes, I have adopted short forms of bibliographical citation wherever possible. All references to books published by Lady Gregory are keyed to the Coole Edition of her works unless otherwise noted, with the exception of her edition of *Sir William Gregory K.C.M.G.: An Autobiography,* which has not yet been reissued. I give only title and pagination for all other works of which only one edition exists, title only where no direct citation from the text is included, and give full bibliographical information for other texts only at their first citation in the notes.

THE DIARIES

1892–1893

Jan[uary] 8 1893

More than a year since I have written & how sad that year has been — We got through Christmas pretty well, Robert amused himself & got on well with his father, & I was able to do a good deal for Holborn & Southwark[1] — but it was a week of fogs, very dark & cold — William hardly left his room — We had asked some "waifs & strays" to dine, but fog came on, & only Sir Edward Bunbury[2] appeared, & Wm. was not able to come down, & Robert soon got tired of sitting up — & we had a rather trying tête à tête evening — After that, we had one dinner party, to Mr. Merriman from the Cape[3] — It went off pleasantly enough — but Lady Robinson says that when she left she said to Sir Hercules "I shall never see Sir William again"[4] — He grew weaker, & less able to fight against the diarrhoea & the cold weather — & grew nervous & easily tired, but tried to keep up — One Sunday, we had Sir Samuel Grenier[5] & his wife & daughters to lunch — & Sir Hercules — & just before lunch Wm. came

[1] For Sir William Gregory (WHG), and the Gregorys' only child, Robert (RG), see Biographical Appendix. The diary opens with Lady Gregory (AG) recalling Christmas 1891, and WHG's terminal illness. The Gregorys were at that point residing in their London house at 3 St. George's Place, Hyde Park Corner. AG had been engaged in helping the poor of two South London parishes, St. George the Martyr, Holborn, and St. Stephen's, Southwark, since 1882. For some account of these philanthropic activities, see her autobiography, *Seventy Years*, pp. 80–95.

[2] Sir Edward Herbert Bunbury (1811–95), 9th Bart., M.P. and Parliamentary colleague of WHG 1847–52. Briefly a suitor to AG's sister Arabella (see p. 15 n. 80) in 1891.

[3] John Xavier Merriman (1841–1926), Cape Parliament M.P., friend of Kipling and Rhodes, and subsequently Prime Minister of the Cape Parliament 1908–10.

[4] Sir Hercules Robinson (1824–97), and his wife Nea, née Annesley (d.1904). Robinson was WHG's predecessor as Governor of Ceylon 1865–72, and thereafter Governor of New South Wales 1872–79, of New Zealand 1879–80, and High Commissioner for South Africa and Governor of Cape Colony 1880–89. He returned to Africa for a second term as Governor of Cape Colony 1895–97, and was raised to the peerage as Lord Rosmead in 1896.

[5] Sir John Samuel Grenier (d.1892), at this point Attorney-General of Ceylon.

back from the Athenaeum,[6] & said he had lost some lb[s] in weight in the last two months — This frightened me, & next morning I went to see Maclagan[7] —He told me he was seriously unwell, & that we shd try Bournemouth at once for he was not fit for the journey to Algiers — We did go there, & stayed a fortnight — A dull looking place, all churches & villas — but the sea blue — & Wm. at first seemed better, enjoying the complete idleness & rest from visitors — But though he gained a little in weight, he took more to invalid habits — At first we took a walk each morning — then a drive — & at the end even the drive became too great an exertion — We had the great delight of having Robert to spend the two Sundays with us — & he was very good in the house, tho' enjoying a run outside — so that his father was pleased, & said (in spite of the shaken state of his nerves) that he was the best little fellow he had ever known & not a bit in the way[8] — When Robert left after the second Sunday he went by an early train, & I heard him go in to say good bye, & his father said to him "Good bye my little man — mind you take good care of your mammy now, for I'm not able to do it any longer" — That was the last time they ever saw each other —

We returned to London — & packed up for the start to Algiers, towards the end of February — He hardly seemed fit for the journey & yet sunshine & warmth were the only chance — We had taken our tickets for the start on the morrow, said good bye to our friends, put everything away, I had even packed a little travelling basket with Brands [meat] essence & other invalid comforts — He was sleeping in the dining room, to save the walk upstairs, & I had been anxious about him, & watching his fire at night, lest he shd want anything for he wd have no one to sleep in his room — That night, I came & lay down on the study sofa — dozing at intervals, & going in now & then to put coal on, or give him some meat essence — At 5-00 he was sleeping very quietly, & I was worn out, having a bad headache, & I thought of going up to bed — but just then a puff of smoke came from his fire, & I thought if he awoke & found smoke in the room he might be uneasy — so that I had better wait till the maids came down — So I lay down again on the study sofa — In about half an hour I heard his voice, ran in, & found him sitting on the side of his bed,

[6] The Athenaeum, a club for "individuals known for their scientific and literary attainments", was founded in 1824, and quickly became one of the pre-eminent London clubs. For some account of WHG's circle of friends at the Athenaeum, see *Seventy Years* pp. 126–202, and see also p. 65 n. 6.

[7] Dr. Thomas John Maclagan (1836–1903), the Gregorys' doctor, and a leading specialist in fevers and rheumatism. Maclagan was one of various friends from whom AG obtained a letter of reference for James Joyce in 1902 prior to his departure to Paris (see Richard Ellmann, *James Joyce*). Maclagan treated Yeats around 1900, and may have contributed, amongst others, to Yeats's use of the name in his final version of *The Speckled Bird*.

[8] RG was at this point a boarder at Park Hill School, Lyndhurst, Hampshire. For WHG's discomforts with parentage, particularly during RG's infancy, see Brian Jenkins, *Sir William Gregory of Coole*, pp. 264–65, 295.

his strength gone, his mind gone, talking unintelligibly — I tore at the bell for Crouch — & with difficulty we got him back to bed, for he sank helplessly on the floor — I sent George off for Maclagan — & by the time he came he was a little better — with hot bottles & brandy — but still unconscious — And so began the fortnight's illness — It was a chill from the sudden snow fall in the night that had stopped the circulation, & left the brain unnourished — The first few days we had hope — He seemed to be returning to consciousness, spoke of still going to Algiers — always roused himself when Maclagan came in — I was much helped by Major Thackwell, his old & devoted aide de camp,[9] who took much care off my shoulders & left me free for the actual nursing — for I had only a nurse in the last few days, & then only for mechanical work — We had endless callers & enquirers — At first I saw some of them — Sir A. Birch,[10] Sir H. Robinson, Sir F. Burton,[11] Sir R. Peel the Speaker,[12] many many others deeply concerned — I had never seen so many *men* with tears in their eyes — Then came another snow fall, & the cold seemed to put its icy finger in, in spite of all we could do, & touch him — When Maclagan came in the evening he wd not meet my eye, & then told me the pulse was weaker — That evening he opened his eyes for the first time with full consciousness took my hand & said "The tie that has bound us is going to be loosed at last — I have loved you very much and I grieve very much at leaving you — I hope Robert will grow up a good man — I know you will be a good mother to him" — I said "Who knows but we may meet again?" — "Ah" he said "& who knows but we may not" — And then taking my hand in both his & laying it on his heart he said "Remember I die believing in God — not in an unjust God but a God of mercy — We are all God's children" —

Then he wandered, spoke a little of Thackwell's kindness "Oh what a kind world it is — so full of kind people!" & told me "not to be too extravagant about giving things away" — Yet he lingered for two or three days after that, very weak, begging to be left alone & not forced to take nourishment — often delirious — I wd not leave the room, lest he shd be conscious again & I should

---

[9] William Polson Thackwell, 73rd Perthshire regt., WHG's aide in Ceylon 1872–77.

[10] Sir Arthur Nonus Birch (1837–1914), Col. Sec. (1873–76), and then Lt Governor (1876–78) of Ceylon during WHG's term as Governor.

[11] Sir Frederic William Burton (1816–1900), artist, and Director of the London National Gallery 1874–94. WHG, a Trustee of the Gallery since 1867, had actively campaigned for the election of his fellow-Irishman to the post. Burton's best-known work is the much-reproduced portrait of George Eliot which now hangs in the National Portrait Gallery.

[12] Sir Arthur Wellesley Peel (1829–1913), M.P., and Speaker of the House of Commons 1884–95. Raised to the peerage as 1st Viscount Peel following his resignation as Speaker in 1895. Sir Arthur was the son of Sir Robert Peel (1788–1850), Prime Minister in the 1830s and '40s, whose initial AG inadvertently gives him here. As Chief Secretary of Ireland in 1812–18, Robert Peel had worked closely with WHG's grandfather, Mr. William Gregory (who served as Under-Secretary 1813–31), and later acted as WHG's political mentor when WHG entered public office as a young man.

miss it — For nineteen nights & days I never went to bed, & hardly left the room, eating my meals at last standing outside the door — My strength wd quite have failed, but for two nights Maclagan came at 10-00 & stayed 2 or 3 hours, to let me sleep — On the evening of the 5th[March] I begged him to stay the night — He sat till past 1-00 by the bedside & then went upstairs & I took his place — He was quite unconscious then & could not swallow — I could only wet his lips with a feather — I sat by him, he was breathing quietly, & then the breathing stopped — There was no sign or movement, but I saw at once that Death had come, & I rang & sent up for the Dr. and he said all was over — We had him laid out — & I sat there all night alone, writing to Robert & my mother & Layard[13] — He looked so peaceful after all the restlessness & delirium — lying beneath the Velasquez & opposite the Savoldo.[14]

When I had sent telegrams in the morning I went to bed & slept all day — I awoke in the evening, & a telegram of sympathy from Eliza[15] made me cry for the first time —

Oh my husband! do you know how little I have forgotten you!

Frank & Gerald[16] came over to take him home — We went first to St. George's, Hanover Square, where Robert had been christened, & had a memorial service for him there — I had said we wd have no wreaths as he did not like them, but at the last one came from the poor women & one from the Infant School at Holborn, & one from Miss Daiz — & in the church an immense one was carried in "from the Greek community in London"[17] — & all these he wd have liked to have —

Then we went on to Euston, & there I left him, with Frank & Gerald — & I

[13] Sir Austen Henry Layard (1817–94), archeologist and diplomat, and WHG's closest friend in later life. See Biographical Appendix. For AG's mother, see p. 12 n. 52.

[14] "Christ at the House of Martha and Mary" (also known as "Our Lord at the House of Lazarus") by Spanish painter Diego y Velasquez (1599–1660), hung in a downstairs room at the Gregorys' London house (AG press-cutting book, Gregory papers, Emory University—hereafter Emory), but WHG also owned two other works by Velasquez: "The Assumption of the Virgin" and "Sketch of a Duel in the Prado", both of which he bequeathed to the National Gallery, along with "The Adoration of the Shepherds" by Giovanni Girolamo Savoldo (c.1480–c.1548).

[15] Elizabeth Shawe-Taylor (1835–96), the third eldest of AG's six sisters, who had married Walter Shawe Taylor (d. 1912) of Castle Taylor, Galway, in 1864.

[16] Francis "Frank" FitzAdelm Persse (1854–1928) and Gerald Dillon Persse (1857–98), the sixth and eighth eldest of AG's nine brothers.

[17] WHG had been a forceful advocate of Greek and Slav interests during his parliamentary term in the 1860s (see his autobiography *Sir William Gregory, K.C.M.G.*, p. 226; hereafter *Autobiography*). The King of Serbia had awarded him the Grand Cross of the Order of Takovo in 1884 in recognition of his efforts for the region.

came back to my empty home — I went to Southampton for the next Sunday & had Robert to meet me there[18] —

At Gort, the people met him at the train & carried him to the Church — & went in to the service — And next morning the tenants came, & attended service again, old Gormally kneeling by the coffin all the time — Snow was falling & there were few able to come from a distance — but all the poor were there —

In London, I stayed for a time quite alone — getting through business & answering letters — & much helped by the kindness of friends, Sir A. Birch taking my affairs in hand, & Dr. Maclagan driving me out in the evenings —

Then came Easter, & I brought Robert over to the Croft[19] — only going one day to Coole — a sad visit to the empty house & the tenanted grave —

Then back to London — & some weeks there, some of them spent at 59 Portland Place[20] — trying to get rid of house, & get through Probate business[21] — It took patience but at last I sold the house & some furniture to Honble F. Eaton[22] for £600 (nett) & I sold some furniture at Phillips, very badly, & sent some to Christies for next season's sales — & sold some plate there, superfluous things we had used in London — I brought back to Coole Wm.'s writing table, he was so fond of it — & a cabinet & his statue model[23] — not much else of importance — & as Frank was furnishing Ashfield[24] I gave him some things —

Then back to Coole, a month alone, getting things into order & beginning life on a smaller scale —

[18] The home of AG's fourth eldest brother, Edward Persse (1838–1929), at Belvoir Hill, Southampton. Edward Persse served in the Indian Army 1859–86, retiring at the rank of Hon. Colonel, and lived at Southampton until his death.

[19] AG's mother's residence, a large house located on Taylor's Hill, on the west of Galway City.

[20] Home of Thomson Hankey (1805–93), Liberal M.P. for Peterborough 1853–68 and 1874–78, and a close friend of WHG since their time as Parliamentary colleagues.

[21] AG was joint executor of her husband's Will along with her brothers Frank, and Robert Algernon (d.1911). WHG's bequests to her included a jointure of £800 per annum to be paid from the revenues of the Coole estate, the leasehold to 3 St. George's Place, which she promptly sold, free life-tenancy at Coole, and many personal effects from the properties, but the bulk of the estate was left in trust for RG. The financial position of the estate was far from strong, however, as a sizeable mortgage remained. See Introduction, pp. xiii-xiv.

[22] Hon. Herbert Francis Eaton (1848–1925), later 3rd Baron Cheylesmore.

[23] A clay model of the bust of WHG as Governor of Ceylon by sculptor Sir Joseph Boehm (1834–90), 1st Bart. For a photo see Jenkins, *Sir William Gregory of Coole*, p. 246.

[24] Ashfield, near Gort, Co. Galway. Frank Persse and his wife had previously had their main residence in Loughrea.

Then Robert's holidays, a great happiness — he was well & strong & very obedient & good — & enjoyed his first rabbit shooting — I had a tutor for him, C. W. Little of New College[25] — very clever, good at cricket & football, gentle & kind, & Robert took to him at once —

One week after my husband's death poor Dudley died, suddenly — I had not seen much of him of late years but had saved his life when he was killing himself, & had grown fond of him then — He had little happiness in life, with his clouded mind & delusions — & it seemed sad that there was no one to write & sympathize with or comfort when he went![26] —

William[27] inherited the place — He had not been in Ireland for many years, & I had seen little of him in London — He decided to leave Algernon to live at Roxborough, only coming over himself for two months in the summer — But when he came he changed his mind, liked the power & authority, & decided to stay on, writing to tell Algernon this rather peremptorily & unexpectedly — This led to bad feeling, Algernon resented it & a family feud began — Alg. losing the agency —

I took Robert over in September, staying for a month at the Layards' house in Queen Anne St., a rest after hard work at Coole —

The day I returned I was sent for to Roxboro' & found Wm. as I had found Dudley before, killing himself with drink — I persuaded him to stop — & he & I & Rose[28] set out for a drive by Lisdoonvarna & Milton Malbay, staying away a week — & doing him much good — I went to Coole then for a few days to pack up the house, which I had let for the winter to Capt. & Mrs. Pering of Petersfield Court, Brecon[29] —

Then I went to Roxboro' — & for 5 weeks did my best to amuse & rouse Wm. who showed symptoms of melancholia — Then he & Rose went to London

[25] Charles William Little (b.1870), New College 1889–93, B.A. in Classics 1893.

[26] Dudley Persse (1829–92), AG's eldest brother, died unmarried on 13 March 1892. Severely wounded in the Crimean War, and absent from Roxborough, the Persse estate, during AG's childhood due to an estrangement from their father (see p. 111), Dudley had been a largely spectral figure to her prior to his inheriting the estate in late 1878. In the little more than a year between then and her marriage in 1880, AG acted as principal housekeeper at Roxborough, and credited herself with saving Dudley from drinking himself to death by persuading him to see a Dublin doctor (Holograph Memoirs, Berg Collection; hereafter Berg).

[27] AG's third brother, Major William Norton Persse (1837–93). Her second eldest brother, Richard, had died of tuberculosis in 1879.

[28] Rose, née Mesham (d.1909), Major William Norton Persse's wife.

[29] George Harmer Pering (b.1834), Captain 18th Hussars, described by AG in a letter of September 1892 (Berg) as "a Welsh gentleman in search of shooting".

— & I stayed at Roxboro' to chaperone the girls & boys — Gerald had meanwhile got the agency in Algernon's place — I am fond of Roxborough & grew fond of Arthur, & Robert came for his holidays & the time passed peaceably enough[30] — Then Wm., who had been drinking more or less ever since he left, got some delusion that I wanted to lock him up & put Arthur in his place — & telegraphed orders for me to go — And on the last night of the saddest year of my life, in bitter cold, Robert & I left my old home & took refuge at the Croft — Here I am wanted, & likely to stay for the present — But there is a terrible difference in my life —

4th [January 1893] — A *brutal* letter from Major William — insulting my husband's memory —

18th — To London with Robert, very glad to get away for a little holiday from complaints of the food & servants, visits of curates & controversialists,[31] & my own sad thoughts & sleepless nights — A very kind letter from the Layards asking me to look on their house as my London home — A tiring journey followed by a couple of days bad headache, not improved by taking Robert to the Pantomime. I saw him off [to school] on Saturday, dear little manneckin.

I only saw Paul[32] for a day or two, as he was knocked up & off to Cornwall for a rest — He brought J. F. Williams[33] to see me again — Sunday afternoon I went to the Grant Duffs at Twickenham for the night[34] — Godleys & Ld.

---

[30] The "girls and boys" at Roxborough, children of Major William and Rose, were mostly well into adult life. Sons William Arthur (1863–1925) and Dudley Jocelyn Persse (b.1873), and daughters Rose Charlotte (b.c.1861), Kathleen (b.1866) and Ione (b.c.1871) were all probably then resident. A fourth daughter, Millicent, had married in 1890 and was living in England.

[31] For AG's mother's contentious religious views, see *Seventy Years*, p. 267 and also above pp. 111–12.

[32] Henry Paul Harvey (1869–1948). Orphaned as a child, Harvey was brought up by his aunt, AG's friend Blanche Lee Childe, née de Triqueti. On Blanche's death in 1886, AG assumed something of her role, bringing Harvey to Coole for summer holidays, and—along with other sponsors, notably Henry James (see p. 20 n. 106)—otherwise assisting his progress. After graduating at Oxford, Harvey enjoyed a distinguished career as a civil servant, was knighted in 1911, and later edited *The Oxford Companion to English Literature* (1932) and *The Oxford Companion to Classical Literature* (1937). For Henry James's first impressions of Paul Harvey—"a source of much delectation to me"—when visiting the Lee Childes in 1876, see *The Letters of Henry James* ed. Leon Edel, vol. 2, p. 62.

[33] John Fischer Williams (1870–1947), a friend and contemporary of Harvey at Oxford. Matriculated at New College 1887 as a Classics Scholar from Harrow, and was a Fellow at New College 1893–99. Called to the Bar in 1894, and subsequently published widely on international law and politics. Knighted in 1923.

[34] Sir Mountstuart Elphinstone Grant Duff (1829–1906), friend and parliamentary contemporary of WHG. Under-Secretary of State for India 1868–74, and Governor of Madras 1881–86. AG was a frequent visitor at Grant Duff's Twickenham home, York House.

Monkswell there[35] — & the pleasant talk & being made welcome, helped to restore my self respect which had really been shaken! For the first few days I expected to see the Major round every corner, & Adelaide on her way to the Law Courts in every street![36]

I went to see Elstree [School], & decided on sending Robert there — I trust it will turn out well — Except Lady Clay[37] everyone speaks highly of it — I spent a day at Southwark seeing to the dinners & breakfasts & cheered by the welcome of the children & all — Financial business with Sir A. Birch satisfactory, I hope if Alg. & Frank consent, to pay off half C. Gregory's debt at once[38] —

The old Masters nice, especially the Romneys[39] — The Burne Jones collection disappointing & depressing, so many long faced women[40] — The new Van der Meer in the N[ational] G[allery] wd have pleased Wm.[41] — Amongst friends,

[35] John Arthur Godley (1847–1932), Private Secretary to Gladstone 1872–74, 1880–82, and Permanent Under-Secretary of State for India 1883–1909. Created Baron Kilbracken, 1909. Married Hon. Sarah James (d.1921) in 1871. Robert Collier, 2nd Baron Monkswell (1845–1909), barrister, was Under-Secretary of War 1892–95 and later Chairman of the London County Council.

[36] Frances Adelaide Lane (1840–1909), fourth eldest of AG's sisters, was at this point in the process of an acrimonious lawsuit and divorce case against her husband Rev. James Lane (1847–1910), whom she had married in 1870 despite strong parental opposition. AG considered the genius of her favourite nephew Hugh Lane (see p. 22 n. 120), their oldest child, to have stemmed from the "clash between opposing natures" of his "ill-mated" parents (*Hugh Lane*, p. 25).

[37] Lady Margaret Clay (d.1915), wife of Sir Arthur Temple Clay (1842–1928), barrister and painter. Arthur Clay was the brother of WHG's first wife, Elizabeth Bowdoin, née Clay, who had died in 1873.

[38] Henry Charles Gregory (1827–1918), WHG's cousin, had advanced a mortagage of £5500 on the Coole estate in 1867, and also acted as agent during WHG's absence in Ceylon in the 1870s and on until some time in the 1880s. RG's birth, as AG noted in 1884, had deprived him of "the doubtful good of succeeding to an Irish estate" (*Seventy Years*, p. 208). Algernon and Frank Persse were at this point acting jointly as agents to the Coole estate, hence AG's wish to gain their approval for the debt repayment. Frank Persse was subsequently sole agent for many years.

[39] George Romney (1734–1802), rival of Reynolds as the greatest portrait painter of his era.

[40] Sir Edward Coley Burne-Jones (1833–98), Pre-Raphaelite artist, created 1st Bart in 1894.

[41] "A young woman standing at a Virginal" by Delft painter Jan Van der Meer (1632–75), now more usually known as Jan Vermeer. This work was one of Frederic Burton's last major purchases before his retirement as Director of the National Gallery.

I dined with the Arthur Russells,[42] Gearys[43] — Morrises,[44] saw Ly. Lindsay,[45] Sir A. Lyall,[46] A. Gray[47] — Ly. Tweeddale,[48] Raffys[49] etc — In politics they said at first the Home Rule Bill wd not even get through the H[ouse]. of C[ommons]. but lately that the Gladstonians are in good spirit, as if they had something up their sleeve — Bad news of Gerald, which helped to hurry me back, & I came back to the Croft on the 2nd Feb[ruary] —

[42] Lady Arthur Russell, née Laura de Peyronnet (d.1910), widow of Arthur John Russell (1825–92). Russell, an M.P. 1857–85, was a brother of the 9th Duke of Bedford. In this and a subsequent entry, AG uses the phrase "Arthur Russells" to refer to Lady Russell's household, although Arthur Russell himself had died in April 1892. The Russells' children were young adults active in some of the same social circles as AG.

[43] William Nevill Geary (1859–1944), lawyer and diplomat, and his parents Sir Francis Geary, 4th Bart. (1811–95) and Lady Fanny Geary, née Prior (d.1901). Nevill Geary knew the Gregorys through their Galway neighbour Edward Martyn (see Biographical Appendix), his contemporary at Oxford and who shared rooms with him in Pump Court in the Temple in the 1880s. Through Martyn, Geary was also a friend of George Moore (see Biographical Appendix), at this point his tenant in King's Bench Walk. Geary married Florence Burke, a near neighbour of AG at Danesfield, Co. Galway, and younger sister of Lady Fingall (see p. 139 n. 85) in 1906. He published a novel and various legal works including *The Law of Theatres and Music Halls*.

[44] Michael Morris (1826–1901), Baron Morris and Killanin, and his wife Anna, née Hughes (d.1906). An eminent lawyer, Morris was the first Catholic to hold the office of High Sheriff in Ireland (of Galway, 1849–50) since 1692. Served as M.P. for Galway 1865–67, Attorney-General of Ireland 1866–67, and Lord Chief Justice of Ireland 1887–89. Distantly related to AG through his mother's family, the Blakes of Galway.

[45] Caroline Blanche Lindsay, née Fitzroy (1844–1912), author of several volumes of travel sketches and verse, and wife of Sir Coutts Lindsay (1824–1913), 2nd Bart., the dramatist, art-historian and founder of the Grosvenor Gallery.

[46] Sir Alfred Comyn Lyall (1835–1911), Lt Governor of N.W.Provinces, India, 1882–87, and long-time friend of WHG. Author of several anthropological works on India and Asia, a popular volume of poetry *Verses Written in India* (1882), and, in 1902, a critical work on Tennyson. For AG's recollections of his diplomatic career and poetic writings, and Yeats's dismissal of his poetry as "rhetoric" see *Seventy Years*, pp. 186–97.

[47] Albert Gray (1850–1928). Entered Ceylon Civil Service in 1871, serving under WHG. Resigned 1875, and was called to the Bar 1879. Counsel to the Chair of Committees in the House of Lords 1896–1922. Knighted 1919. Mayor of Chelsea 1924–25.

[48] Julia, Lady Tweeddale, née Stuart-Mackenzie (d.1937), widow of the 9th Marquess (d.1878). She worked closely with AG in the 1880s in relief work for St. Stephen's, Southwark, and continued to assist the parish until her death. Her colourful private life features intermittently in AG's letters of the 1890s, which report variously on her clandestine affair with Lord Connemara and narrow escape from publicity in his divorce trial, and her subsequent marriage in 1892 to Sir William Evans-Gordon "who I hear has a squint and is very third rate" (Berg).

[49] Marc-André Raffalovich (1864–1934), poet and novelist. Born in Russia, he came to London in 1884, quickly establishing himself as a society figure through the ostentatious use of family wealth. Now best remembered as the victim of Oscar Wilde's remark that he had come to London to open a *salon*, but only succeeded in opening a *saloon*. Replaced Wilde (once his close friend, but later a sworn enemy) as lover of John Gray (see p. 46 n. 134) during the period when Alfred Douglas began to monopolize Wilde's attentions. Published *Uranisme et Unisexualité*, one of the first extensive studies of male homosexuality, in 1896 in the wake of Wilde's trial. Converted to Catholicism the same year, and gradually began to renounce aesthetic circles. From 1905 until his death lived in Edinburgh in close companionship with Gray.

[February] 3rd — A telegram from Paul saying he has passed for the Home Civil [Service] a great cheer up![50] —

5th — Struggling against weakness & sickness — Food & the servants' crimes still in the ascendant —

11th — In the morning a telegram from Rose "William taken very ill — Heart very weak — Doctor fears the worst" — This was but a preparation for one in the evening "My darling died quite suddenly this morning" —

It is best so! he could not resist, & the mind was going, and he would have brought shame & trouble on us all — Yet I did not think I could have felt so sorry, & thank God, I can forgive him & have no bad feeling — Poor Rose has forgotten all the ill treatment & only remembers the husband of her youth! And that also is for the best —

June 17 — At Easter, Robert came back, tall & strong & well — We stayed a couple of days at the Croft, & then with great pleasure & relief I left Galway, where I had never been well or content — Ethel[51] who came over with R. stayed to take care of the Mrs.[52] — R. & I had a very happy 3 weeks at Coole — The Perings had left everything in good order — The weather was lovely, hardly a drop of rain — On Easter Sunday we went to the Workhouse & distributed tobacco to the old men & sweets to the children — We drove one day to Kilcornan — I hoped Christopher[52] wd have had something to say in favour of the terrible Home Rule Bill — but he is as much in fear of the Local Police & the National settlement of the Land Question as I myself — The farmers are not at all excited on the subject, rather fearing the tender mercies of their own leaders, but all Loyalists & all possessors of property tremble —

R. & I lived almost out of doors — he trained his retriever puppy, Croft, & I looked on & gained strength after the Galway influenza which had left me weak — Dear little manneckin, he was very obedient & affectionate & caressing — We read "Iliad" in the mornings — but did no lessons —

[50] Harvey was fifth out of all candidates, having taken a first in Classics at Oxford the previous summer.

[51] Ethel Frances Persse (1873–1966), eldest daughter of AG's fourth brother Edward.

[52] Frances Persse, née Barry (c.1816–96), AG's mother, "'The Mistress' as she was called by all, children as well as servants" (*Seventy Years*, p. 4).

[53] Christopher Talbot Redington (1847–99), Deputy Lieutenant and J.P. for the County of Galway, a major landowner, and AG's near neighbour at Kilcornan, Oranmore. Redington was one the first guarantors of the Irish Literary Theatre. For AG's later recollections of him see *Journals* vol.2, p. 313.

On the 22nd April we set out for London — Nora, Alg. & the children at the station, Nora very rude & even insolent, I suppose because I gave a helping hand at Roxboro'[54] — Poor thing, she has been near Death's door since then — We went to 1 Queen Anne St, which we had to ourselves, Enid Layard being still laid up with typhoid at Venice[55] — We arrived Sunday morning & went in the afternoon to the Zoo, where we saw a party of the Irish Delegates who had come over for the demonstration at the Albert Hall[56] — They were well received in London, Lady A. Russell had 2, the Grant Duffs 3, Lord Carlisle[57] 8 & so on, & all seemed pleased with their guests —

On Monday 24th Robert went off to Elstree [School], Paul taking him there — It was a great plunge from 20 boys to 120 — but he settled down quite happily — I went twice to see him, found him well & content, anxious to work, & getting on fast, & full of cricket — It is always a sad, sad thought that his father has lost the pleasure of seeing him so bright & promising —

I stayed in London till the 14th June, alone till the last fortnight & then the Layards came, very kind & affectionate — I spent a Sunday at Twickenham, did not much care for it, & Whitsuntide at Crabbet[58] where I was happy in the beauty of scenery & weather —

I brought out the little pamphlet I had written in Galway "A Phantom's Pilgrimage" — anonymously — & as far as appreciative words go, from those who know me to be the writer it has been a success[59] — Randolph Churchill,[60]

---

[54] Eleanor Persse, née Gough (1854–1935), wife of AG's brother Algernon. Sister of Hugh Gough, 3rd Viscount (for whom see p. 100 n. 177).

[55] The London home of the Layards. For Lady Enid Layard, see Biographical Appendix.

[56] The Anti-Home Rule demonstration at the Albert Hall on 23 April was attended by over 10,000 delegates, many of whom had come from Ireland. The second reading of the Home Rule Bill had passed the Commons by 43 votes on 21 April, but was soon to be defeated in the Lords. *The Times* for 22 April, reporting on the build-up to the demonstration, noted drily that Gladstone, being recognised when entering the Parliament buildings by a crowd of delegates "met with a somewhat adverse reception."

[57] George James Howard (1843–1911), 9th Earl of Carlisle.

[58] Sussex home of Wilfrid Scawen Blunt (see p. 29 n. 33).

[59] *A Phantom's Pilgrimage, or Home Ruin* (London: W. Ridgway, 1893), a pamphlet warning of dire consequences for Ireland and Irish landlords if Gladstone's Home Rule Bill should pass.

[60] Lord Randolph Churchill (1849–95), Tory M.P. 1874–95, Indian Secretary 1885–86 and Chancellor 1886. A staunch ally and friend of AG during her campaign on behalf of the Egyptian Nationalists in 1882–83, being one of the few prominent English statesmen critical of British policy, and at this point strongly sharing her distaste for Home Rule. Long-touted as likely leader of his party prior to his early decline and death from syphillis. Now best remembered as father of Winston Churchill and for his Unionist-rallying declaration at Larne in 1886, "Ulster will fight, and Ulster will be right!"

Lecky,[61] Billy Russell,[62] Sir H. Layard, Sir F. Burton particularly commend it
— and Lord Wemyss has drawn a clever cartoon "for the next edition"[63] — I
left London with regret — People were very kind to me, Layards first —
Morrises — Sir A. Birch — Lyalls etc, etc — & Paul is very dear to me — I went
to the Lyalls' windows to see the Imp[erial]. Institute opened — a pretty sight
with the Queen's escort of Australian & Canadian Volunteers & Princess Mary
sitting opposite her new fiancé & stiffly bowing[64] — I did not go to dinners,
& only to one play, Ibsen's Hedda Gabbler, dramatic & well acted[65] — On one
of my last days I had a morning visit from Ld. Wemyss, lunched with the
Duchess of St. Albans[66] — Ld. Selborne & Lady Sophie came to dinner
specially to meet me[67] — also Sir H. Thompson[68] — & in the afternoon we
gave a very successful tea party, Lady L[ayard]. inviting all the girls & I all the
young men, Albert Gray, Paul & Bonus — Nevill Geary, Jocelyn,[69] Jack

[61] Rt Hon. William Edward Hartpole Lecky (1838–1903), distinguished Trinity College
historian, and early sponsor of the Irish Literary Theatre. As M.P. for Dublin University, Lecky
was later responsible for inserting a clause in the Local Government (Ireland) Bill of 1898 which
revoked a long-standing law prohibiting dramatic performances other than in licensed theatres,
thus opening the way for the Literary Theatre to use venues such as the Antient Concert Rooms.

[62] William Howard Russell (1820–1907), correspondent for *The Times* since the 1840s.
Covered O'Connell's Repeal meetings and trial and rose to prominence reporting the Crimean
War (during which his phrase "the thin red line" entered popular usage). Subsequently covered
the Indian, American Civil and Zulu wars. Knighted 1895.

[63] Francis Wemyss (1818–1914), 10th Earl of Wemyss, M.P. 1841–83. For a reproduction
of his cartoon (now at Emory) see Illustrations.

[64] The opening of the Imperial Institute on 10 May 1893 was a full State function attended
by almost all the Royal Family. Reporting the event on 11 May, *The Times* (p. 9) noted that "a
special interest was lent to the pageant by the fact that it was the first occasion since the betrothal
of the Duke of York and Princess Victoria Mary of Teck upon which they have been seen together
by a representative British crowd."

[65] A translation by Edmund Gosse of Henrik Ibsen's play *Hedda Gabler*, performed four times
at the Opera Comique in May–June 1893.

[66] Grace, Duchess of St. Albans, née Bernal-Osborne (d.1926), second wife of the 10th Duke.

[67] Sir Roundell Palmer (1812–95), 1st Earl of Selborne, M.P. 1847–57 and 1861–72, Lord
Chancellor 1872–74 and 1880–85, and his third daughter Lady Sophia (d.1915).

[68] Sir Henry Thompson (1820–1904), most famous surgeon of the late Victorian period,
known also for his "Octave" dinners, so named for the number of persons present, courses
served, and time held. Created 1st Bart., 1899.

[69] AG's nephew Dudley Jocelyn Persse (1873–1943), second son of Major William Persse.

Gordon,[70] Alfred Cole,[71] Martin Morris[72] — besides Mr. Rodger[73] & daughter & Sir A. Birch & Una[74] — Sunday, Lecky & Sir A. Gordon[75] came to see me — I had a pastel portrait taken by Lisa Stillman[76] — paying for it with money gained by "A Philanthropist,"[77] "A Lily <??>"[78] & "Irene"[79] — I wanted to leave Robert something more durable than a photograph, & something pleasing enough for Mrs. Robert not to turn out of the room! — I left in better spirits about the Home Rule Bill, Ulster has been well stirred up, & all Unionists are making a good fight — The other side silent, & the Bill itself so clumsy it seems likely to fall to pieces — I think it right to go back to Coole, I have been so much away — but my heart rather fails me at the idea of 6 weeks alone there before R. comes — I am at Moyne[80] for 3 days, on my way —

June 25 — My home coming was indeed not a cheerful one — Elizabeth[81]

[70] George Arthur "Jack" Gordon (1871–1957), son of Sir Arthur Gordon (see below n. 75). Succeeded his father as 2nd Baron Stanmore in 1912. Chief Liberal Whip in the House of Lords 1923–44.

[71] Alfred Clayton Cole (1854–1920), partner in the city firm of W. H. Cole & Co. Subsequently a Director of the Bank of England, and its Governor 1911. Brother-in-law of Mary Cole (see below p. 26 n. 9), a second cousin of WHG.

[72] Martin Henry Morris (1867–1927), eldest son of Lord Morris, whom he succeeded in 1901. High Sheriff for Galway 1897, M.P. 1900–01, and Commissioner of National Education in Ireland 1903–22.

[73] Probably John Pickersgill Rodger (1851–1910), British Resident at Pahang 1888–96, Selangor 1896–1902 and Governor of the Gold Coast 1903–10.

[74] Una Birch (d.1949), eldest daughter of Sir Arthur Birch, and a lifelong friend of AG. Married Ladislaus Pope-Hennessy (d.1942), an officer who later rose to the rank of Major-General, in 1910. Proposed as editor of the *Journals* by RG's widow, Margaret Gough, in 1933, but bypassed in favour of Lennox Robinson. Author of a biography of Poe, and numerous other scholarly works. Created Dame of the British Empire in 1920.

[75] Sir Arthur Hamilton-Gordon (1829–1912), youngest son of the 4th Earl of Aberdeen (who was Prime Minister 1852–55). His own distinguished career included posts as Governor of Trinidad 1866–70, Mauritius 1871–74, Fiji 1875–80, New Zealand 1880–82, and Ceylon 1883–90. Raised to the peerage as 1st Baron Stanmore in August 1893.

[76] See the dust-jacket of this volume. Lisa Stillman, later Mrs. Jopling (d.1946), portrait artist, was the daughter of painter, journalist and art critic William James Stillman (1828–1901) who was known as "the American pre-Raphaelite", and his wife Marie, née Spartali (1844–1927), who modelled for Rossetti, was a pupil of Ford Madox Brown and a successful pre-Raphaelite painter herself. American-born Lisa and her sister Effie, a sculptor, both exhibited at the Royal Academy and elsewhere, but achieved only modest success with their work.

[77] A short story published under the pseudonym "Angus Grey" in *The Argosy*, June 1891, pp. 468–83.

[78] Not located. AG kept cutting books for virtually all her journal and newspaper publications (Emory), but this, along with some of her pseudonymous writings, is not included. No manuscript draft appears to have survived.

[79] A poem published under AG's name in *The Argosy*, October 1890, p. 352.

[80] Moyne Park, Co. Galway, home of Arabella Persse (1850–1924), AG's nearest sister in age, who had married Galway landowner Robert William Waithman (1828–1914), a widower with three children, in 1891.

[81] AG's maid.

seemed dull & odd — & things were not very comfortable — Sunday ev. worse — Monday very bad — On Tuesday morning she collapsed altogether — had to be helped up to bed by Mrs. MacManus — I cd hardly doubt what the reason was — but hoping against hope sent for Dr. Moran[82] — He pronounced her *drunk* — A great blow & shock, for I trusted & confided in her — & where to find a successor I know not — Fanny Shawe Taylor's engagement to Willy Trench announced[83] — He is nice tho' weak looking — & both families seem pleased — I hope this venture will turn out better than his first, by which he lost £7000 by Charles Wells! Very dry weather, farmers looking woefully at hayfields — but potatoes are doing well, & pigs dear — Rents being well paid — Frank says poor Mrs. Cahel's son robbed her, & she has had to sell her sheep at a sacrifice to pay — I am to give her 2 bonifs[84] to set her up again — Came to New Hall Ennis on Saturday, to the R. O'Brien's[85] — A pleasant change after a week's charing — jam-making etc — Wm.'s portrait[86] arrived safely, I left it in the servants' hall for the week that the people might come in & see it —

Sept[ember] 25 — Spiddal[87] — I am here for rest after the holidays, which I am thankful to say went off well — Robert very well & bright & happy, rather taking to fishing in preference to shooting — & devoted as before to Charlie Little who poor boy was depressed at having left Oxford, & anxious about a mastership which did not come — Tony & Wyndham Birch also spent the holidays with us, their poor mother slowly dying at Wimbledon, & Sir Arthur not able to leave her[88] — However the boys were happy enough — & all these six weeks I have heard of little but flies & worms & rods & cartridges — Elizabeth's relapses were a great trial & gave me much extra work — but that also has come to an end, & she is gone — I worked at intervals at Wm.'s Memoir, & have sent it to be type written[89] — Robert & Charlie left on

[82] John P. Moran, Gort doctor and surgeon.

[83] Frances Elizabeth Shawe-Taylor (1873–1950), daughter of AG's elder sister Elizabeth, married the Hon. William Cosby Trench (1869–1944), second son of the 2nd Baron Ashtown, on 7 September 1893.

[84] An Anglicized rendering of the Irish word "bainbh" meaning "piglet".

[85] Robert Vere O'Brien (1842–1913), a nephew of poet Aubrey de Vere (see p. 153 n. 140), and his wife Florence, née Arnold (d.1936), a niece of Matthew Arnold.

[86] Probably that by Sir Arthur Clay, painted in 1885. The current whereabouts of this portrait are unknown, but copies of an engraving based on the original survive in the Library of the National Portrait Gallery.

[87] Spiddal House, Spiddal, Co. Galway, home of Lord Morris.

[88] Arthur Egerton (Tony) Birch (1877–1923), and Wyndham Lindsay Birch (1874–1950), Sir Arthur Birch's two sons. After the death of his mother, Lady Zephine, Tony Birch adopted her maiden name, Watts-Russell, as his surname. He married Sylvia Grenfell, niece of Henry Riversdale Grenfell (see p. 45 n. 126) in 1912. Wyndham Birch served with distinction in the R.A.F. in WW1, earning the D.S.O., M.B.E. and Croix de Guerre.

[89] In his final years WHG began writing his autobiography, but he had completed only up to the period of his return from Ceylon by the time of his death. Writing to Wilfrid Blunt in July

Monday, Elizabeth Tuesday, the two black sheep were sold Wednesday, Croft went to Chevy[90] for the winter Thursday, the Birches left Friday — Pat Dooley had gone the previous week — & I am tired out, body & mind — & glad to be here — Fanny's marriage to Willy Trench was happily accomplished, & Eliza may now perhaps have a little thought & sympathy to spare for her family & friends! Lady Morris & Frances & Georgie Dillon[91] stayed with me for it — De Basterot's[92] visits were a gr comfort to me, at a time when things looked dark — Poor Killeen died of cancer, & Johnny Quin had a serious illness — & I cured Mrs. Diveney by a fortnight in Galway — & had school feast & Workhouse party & took Robert a little amongst the people, & tried to do my duty —

Jan[uary] 30 1894 — Late in October I went to London, 1 Queen Anne St — For some time my chief work was the editing of the Memoir — Sir H. Layard had sent me the letters to him, & it was hard & sad work reading through them & copying out a passage here & there[93] — At last it was accomplished & I sent the MS to Murray[94] — In about 10 days it came back, with a note saying the

1893 (Berg), AG observed: "I have interesting though rather perplexing work in editing some memoirs Sir William left, which will be very interesting even to outsiders if I can venture to publish enough. It was only lately I persuaded him to write these reminiscences, and they were unfortunately not finished." She had made a first move towards publication in January 1893, sending the manuscript to G. W. Russell (see p. 39 n. 87), who was strongly enthusiastic.

[90] Chevy Chase, a hunting lodge located in the Slieve Echtge hills, belonging to the Roxborough estate. See Illustrations.

[91] Georgiana Dillon (b.1867), eldest daughter of the 4th Baron Clonbrock (see p. 40 n. 92). "Frances" could have been either Georgiana's aunt Frances Dillon (d. 1911), or Lady Morris's daughter Frances (see p. 199 n. 5).

[92] Compte Florimonde de Basterot (1836–1904), near neighbour of AG at Duras on the Burren coast. Duras had been inherited by his great-grandfather Bartholomew de Basterot (b.1742) a Bernese aristocrat who had married a Galway woman, Frances French (whose uncle Oliver Martynn was an ancestor of Edward Martyn). Excepting Bartholomew's son, who settled in Ireland, subsequent generations retained Duras only as a summer home, but though de Basterot was principally resident abroad, he maintained the close connections with Galway families established by earlier generations. The Gregory family were first connected with the de Basterots when Robert Gregory of Coole, WHG's great-grandfather, bought part of the Duras estate from Bartholomew de Basterot. Friend of many French literary figures, Florimonde de Basterot published two volumes: an account in 1860 of his travels in the Americas the previous year, De Québec à Lima, and in 1869 of his travels in the Holy Land and Mediterranean over 1867–68, Le Liban, la Galilée et Rome.

[93] To complete the autobiography for the years after WHG's resignation as Governor of Ceylon, AG extracted passages from his voluminous correspondence with Layard between 1876 and 1892. See Introduction, pp. xviii-xix.

[94] John Murray (1851–1928), joint-head, with his brother Alexander Henry Hallam Murray (1854–1934), of the publishing firm founded by their great-grandfather in 1768. AG's choice of the Murrays, who published most of her non-dramatic work in the following decades, probably reflected a personal friendship established through the Layards. The firm had been Henry Layard's first publisher, and Hallam Murray had married Lady Layard's niece Alice du Cane (1861–1947) in 1885.

speeches & some other parts were slightly too long, but if I wd alter these, he wd make me an offer — I acceded, & waited for about 3 weeks for the offer — When it came it was satisfactory, that he wd publish at his own risk & expense, giving me half profits — This was an immense relief to my mind, I was anxious, for Robert's sake, to publish, that his father's name might be kept alive a little longer — but the risk & expense wd have been an anxiety to me — though "a good name is better than riches" & I would if necessary have laid the money out — I had not much further trouble, beyond shortening, & writing a kind of connecting preface to the letters —

I wrote out my notes on Arran — they ought to make a good magazine article.[95]

Poor Lady Birch was given over when I arrived in London, & soon after died, it was a sadly drawn out death & poor Sir Arthur had a terrible strain — I saw much of him till he started for Jamaica, & of the boys — It was a mild, stormy & unhealthy season — A few days before I left London old Mrs. Holmes & old Mary Keating both died[96] —

I spent a Sunday at Stanmore with the D'Arcys[97] to see Robert who I picked up at Elstree, & who stayed for the night, dear little man, a gr treat to us both, & he won good opinions & was not shy & enjoyed his outing — I drove him back on the Sunday evening, & we parted, with a few little tears —

I also spent a Sunday at Twickenham with the Grant Duffs — Spencer Walpole came for Sunday, rejoicing in his liberation from the Isle of Man & transfer to the Post Office[98] —

I was asked to Ld. Selborne's for a few days to meet Goldwin Smith[99]

---

95 AG visited Aran alone in the first week of October 1893 and was "storm bound for five days" on the smallest island, Inishere (see Introduction, p. xx). There is no evidence to suggest she completed the proposed article, nor do her "notes" on the trip appear to have survived.

96 Mrs. Holmes was a long-time neighbour of the Gregorys in St. George's Place. Mary Keatinge [sic] had been their housemaid at the London property.

97 William Knox D'Arcy (1849–1917) and his wife Elena, née Birkbeck (d.1897). AG had met D'Arcy, a "millionaire" who had made his fortune in mining and agricultural interests in Australia, in 1890, and managed to interest him in her work at Southwark, where he became a regular visitor and contributor.

98 Sir Spencer Walpole (1839–1907), Lt Governor of the Isle of Man 1882–93, and Secretary of the General Post Office 1893–99.

99 Goldwin Smith (1823–1910), prominent historian, constitutional scholar and critic. Regius Professor of Modern History at Oxford 1858–66, and thereafter taught in the U.S.A. and Canada.

but cd not go —

Friends were kind — I dined with the Arthur Russells, Lyalls, Leckys, Raffalovich, Childers,[100] Mrs. Kay[101] (where I met John Dillon looking gloomy & not at home in his clean shirt[102]) — etc — I even gave one or two little dinners myself — The first to Lady Morris & Martin, Fischer Williams & Paul — The next to Grant Duff & Clara,[103] the day of their arrival in town, Oswald Crawfurd,[104] F. Williams, Sir A. Lyall & daughter, Alfred Cole — It gives me a feel of independence & *power* being able to give a dinner, & helped by Gerald's snipe they went off well — I had also little teaparties, Emily

[100] Hugh Culling Childers (1827–96), M.P. 1860–92, War Secretary 1880–82, Chancellor of the Exchequer 1882–85, and Home Secretary 1886. A second cousin of AG's later friend, nationalist Erskine Childers (1870–1922), who was executed during the Irish Civil War. Hugh Childers had married as his second wife in 1879, Katharine Gilbert, née Elliot (d.1895). The Childerses were residents of St. George's Place, and had been the Gregorys' long-time neighbours.

[101] Mary Kay, née Drummond, daughter of Thomas Drummond (1797–1840), Under-Secretary for Ireland 1835–40 (and famous for his dictum "Property has its duties as well as its rights"), and widow of the noted economist Joseph Kay (1821–78), whose last work *Free Trade in Land* she posthumously edited and published in 1879. AG recalls the origins of the salon Mrs. Kay and her unmarried sister, Emily, had established, and its success "though their house [in Hyde Park Gardens] was not in the centre of fashion and their dinners were not very good" in *Seventy Years*, p. 98.

[102] John Dillon (1851–1927), Nationalist M.P. and staunch advocate of Parnell in the 1880s. First elected in Co. Tipperary in 1880, and M.P. for Co. Mayo 1885–1918. Dillon's direct activism in the Land War resulted in several periods of imprisonment, the most recent having been in 1891. After the O'Shea divorce scandal, he opposed Parnell, vying with Tim Healy (see below p. 237 n. 64) for leadership of the anti-Parnellites. AG's hostility to Dillon faded with her own increasing nationalism, and they would eventually campaign together for the return of the Lane pictures, but he remained for her a key figure in precipitating Parnell's fall, and she lastingly associated him (and Healy) with the biblical charioteer Zimri who "had no peace because he slew his master" (*Journals* vol. 1, p. 338).

[103] Clara Grant Duff, Grant Duff's eldest daughter.

[104] Oswald Crawfurd (1834–1909), civil servant and novelist. Crawfurd's father, John Crawfurd (d.1868), Governor of Singapore in the 1820s, had been a long-time friend of WHG, while Crawfurd himself, who served as British Consul at Oporto 1867–91, had been the Gregorys' host during their travels in Portugal in 1883. Sometime lover of Violet Hunt (see below p. 209 n. 50), Crawfurd was a resident at Queen Anne's Mansions during the period AG rented a flat there (see p. 27 n. 12), and was at this point Editor of *Chapman's Magazine*.

Lawless,[105] Henry James,[106] Grant Duffs, Sidney Colvin,[107] Mrs. Middleton[108] — & one for Southwark, Ly. Robinson, Ly. Tweeddale, Rogers,[109] D'Arcys, etc—

Poor Southwark, I could only go to a "Happy Evening" & undertake to collect for the Cocoa breakfasts with Sir H. Robinson's help —

On my last Tuesday in London I had a telegram from Miss Peel[110] offering a place in her gallery for the Debate on the Navy — I went, & heard Gladstone speak, his voice as clear, his indignation against the Opposition as fiery as ever — I could see no sign of age[111] — Balfour[112] began to chop him up afterwards but I had not time to stay — I dined that evening at Sir A. Lyall's, & everyone asked me about the debate, & what Gladstone had said about the increase of the Navy[113] — I said

[105] Emily Lawless (1845–1913), novelist and poet, daughter of 3rd Baron Cloncurry. AG first met Lawless as a girl, and, until she became a writer herself, was a strong admirer of early novels such as *Hurrish, Grania* and *With Essex in Ireland.* Yeats included the last of these works in a list of the thirty Irish books he considered most important in 1895 (*CL1* p. 441), but soon began to refer to Lawless disparagingly, and then ignored her work entirely once the emergence of new Irish writers in the late 1890s allowed him a greater choice of figures he could portray as key figures in the literary renaissance.

[106] AG first met novelist Henry James (1843–1916) while in Rome in 1880 on her European honeymoon travels. As she notes in *Seventy Years* pp. 181–82, an exchange of letters with WHG about James's novel *Roderick Hudson* had been instrumental in bringing about her marriage. Of their subsequent friendship, she would recall "I often met him in London but never got very near him except on the one matter of our protecting care of Paul Harvey" (Holograph Memoirs, Berg).

[107] Sidney Colvin (1845–1927), art historian and critic. Director of the Fitzwilliam Museum 1876–84 and Keeper of Prints and Drawings at the British Museum, 1884–1912. Colvin had been a long-time friend and advisor to WHG in his work as a Trustee of the National Gallery.

[108] Mrs John Middleton, whose husband was Slade Professor of Art at Cambridge and Director of the Fitzwilliam Museum 1889–93, and from 1893–96 Director of the Art Museum at South Kensington. Middleton, a friend of William Morris and Rossetti, was a morphia addict and died of an overdose in 1896.

[109] Probably Capt. John Thornton Rogers (d.*c.*1900), who had worked with AG both for Southwark and for Irish Industries since around 1890.

[110] Julia Beatrice Peel (1864–1949), eldest daughter of Sir Arthur Peel.

[111] William Ewart Gladstone (1809–98), the "grand old man" of the Liberal party. At this point in his final term as Prime Minister (1892–94), having previously been Chancellor 1852–55, 1859–66, 1868–74, 1880–82, and Prime Minister 1868–74, 1880–85, 1886.

[112] Arthur James Balfour (1848–1930), Chief Secretary for Ireland 1887–91, during which period he earned the nickname "Bloody Balfour" for his strong coercive measures against the Plan of Campaign. Leader of the Conservative Opposition 1892–95 and 1906–11, and Prime Minister 1902–05. Raised to the peerage in 1922.

[113] For Gladstone's principal speeches in the debate (19 December 1893), and his acrimonious exchanges with Balfour, see *Hansard's Parliamentary Debates,* 4th Series, XIX, pp. 1790–1813.

he had abused the Opposition for starting the subject, & had insisted that they
made it a Party & not a National question, & promised that if they waited for
3 months he wd tell them then as much as was good for them — No one wd
believe that he had made no definite promise or statement — but I was
justified in my analysis when his speech appeared next morning.

Adelaide's lawsuit with Jim [Lane], which had been going on more or less for
2 years was still on foot, & we were always afraid of a public report of it — It
has seemed impossible to arrange a compromise, but Ld. Rosebery's success
with the coal strikers had again raised the question of an arbitration[114] — One
morning I heard from Mamma that some question connected with it was
coming on, & she begged me to bestir myself — So, though with a bad cough,
I trotted off to the Law Courts, found the Registrar & after a long wait in an
anteroom was asked into Mr. Justice Stirling's[115] Chambers, where a question
"to omit clauses" was being argued — It was over in about 10 minutes, & I
retired, thinking I had wasted my time & done nothing — But Popham,[116] J.
Lane's solicitor came & introduced himself to me, & asked if any compromise
cd be effected — I wrote to Ade[laide], then went to Popham, then telegraphed
to her to come up, then had a hard week trying to get things settled — My
masterstroke was inviting Popham to dinner — This with a bottle of champagne
put both him & Ade[laide] into good humour — & they nearly came together
— but there were many anxieties & my trots back & forwards to Lincoln's Inn
frequent — However in the end the agreement was signed, & the letters in her
possession, from Jim's woman given up to me, & by me to Popham to be
burned[117] — A great feat — but costing me, besides anxiety & trouble, £125
towards paying her debts which were very heavy — & I could not say "depart
in peace, be warmed & filled"[118] & do nothing for her —

Poor little Robert had been with me for a week, the first of his holidays, & I
had been much taken from him, but he was very good, & I rewarded him with
a pantomime "The Pied Piper of Hamelin" —

[114] Archibald Philip Primrose (1847–1929), Lord Rosebery, Liberal statesman. Secretary for
Foreign Affairs 1892–94 and Prime Minister 1894–95. Rosebery had achieved a spectacular
success in mid-November 1893 as mediator in a dispute between trade unions and mine-owners
which had paralysed the mining industry for months. His arbitration, which ended the strike,
paved the way for his ascent to the Premiership.

[115] Hon. Sir James Stirling (1836–1916), Judge of the Chancery Division of the High Court
of Justice 1886–1900, and Lord Justice of Appeals 1900–1906.

[116] John Francis Popham, barrister of Lincoln's Inn. Subsequently Hugh Lane's lawyer for
many years.

[117] The agreement restored to Adelaide Lane £2000 made over to her husband in their 1870
marriage settlement. Lane remarried soon afterwards.

[118] *James* 2:16.

So I left London, my last evening a pleasant one, dinner at Lady Lindsay's to meet the Reays[119] — I felt I had done a good deal, & my last act was to get a post at Colnaghi's for Hugh Percy Lane[120] —

[119] Donald James Mackay (1839–1921), 11th Baron Reay. Governor of Bombay 1885–90, and Under Secretary for India 1894–95. Married in 1877 Fanny, née Hasler (d.1917), widow of Alexander Mitchell, M.P.

[120] Hugh Percy Lane (1875–1915), son of the failed marriage of Adelaide Persse and Rev. James Lane. AG chronicles his spectacular career as an art dealer, his rise to knighthood (1911) and the Directorship of the National Gallery of Ireland (1914), his death on the *Lusitania* in 1915, and the ensuing struggle over rightful possession of the collection of modern art he bequeathed to Dublin in an unsigned codicil to his will, in her biography *Hugh Lane*. This, his first post in the art world, as gallery assistant to Martin Colnaghi (1821–1908), the most prominent London art dealer of the late Victorian period, was arranged through a recommendation AG obtained from Sir J. C. Robinson (see p. 91 n. 136), Keeper of the Queen's pictures.

1894

I brought Robert over to Roxboro', Coole being let to Sir Charles Hunter[1] —
He had good holidays, Gerald & Arthur very kind, & dogs & rats & guns & a
carpenter's shop & forge at hand — To me it was not quite so pleasant, Rose
& the girls full of cuts at the family, intensified by their jealousy at Arthur's
marriage to Katy Gehle not being so smart a one as Fanny's to W. Trench[2] —
And after the good, the high minded, society I had enjoyed in London, they
seemed so empty, narrow, trivial & common — Rose's swagger so vulgar &
blatant — But I wrote my letters in Gerald's office, & read "Waverley"[3] to
Robert & taught him drawing & his holiday tasks — & so the time passed —
And then, Jan[uary] 24 I sent him off, alone, to school with a sad heart, &
came to the Croft — Ethel here, bright & pleasant — But the weather has
been bad & there is not much outing — & Sunday not very refreshing! The
morning sermon by a curate being on Mr. X. who read the "celebrated
Germans, Strauss & Renan"[4] & became an infidel, entirely by *want* of study —
And in the evening, Boland came, & there was controversial gossip — And
after prayers he hopped up from his knees & announced that there had been
gr mortality lately, no, not from influenza but from the extreme unction

---

[1] Sir Charles Hunter (1858–1924), 3rd. Bart. Described by AG in a letter of January 1894 as
"a confiding Saxon" (Berg), he nevertheless impressed her by paying his rent for the Coole
shooting in advance.

[2] Rose's son Arthur had married Katherine Ellen Gehle (d.1943) on 18 January 1894.

[3] Novel by Sir Walter Scott (1771–1832).

[4] David Friedrich Strauss (1808–74), German theologian. In his most influential work, *Leben
Jesu* (1835, English translation by George Eliot 1846), Strauss, a disciple of Hegel, asserted that
the gospel histories were myths and that their conflicting testimony should be sifted for an
accurate master-account. In later works he argued in favour of a new faith based on art and
scientific knowledge. Ernest Renan (1823–92), French philologist and historian, quit traditional
Christianity in 1845 in favour of a historically syncretic approach based on linguistic and
historical research. His choice of title for his major work, *Vie de Jesus* (1863), acknowledges
Strauss's influence.

administered ad lib by the priests on the smallest excuse, the effect of which was to make the patient die, & put death dues into their pockets![5]

I have offered to pay off C. Gregory's mortgage, & he begged the charge might be left on at reduced interest — & when we assented, proposing 4 p[er].c[ent]. he writes, rather disagreeably, saying it "is not fair" he shd get less than 4 1/2 —

Feb[ruary] 13 — I was very much frightened by a letter from Robert saying he had been in a form run — which was "awful" — They had to run 14 miles but he dropped out after 10 wheezing — & Mr. Wilson came back & put him on a heap of stones & rubbed him, & sent back another boy to look after him, & the other boy was delighted to escape the run — My own heart stopped at the thought of the danger he had been in, for he was always exhausted by running tho' so strong in other ways — I was afraid to write & complain lest he shd get into a scrape — so wrote to Dr. Maclagan — & had a very kind letter from him — He had [at] once had R. sent to him, examined & says he is quite sound — but has forbidden the very long runs —

I came back here on Shrove Tuesday, chiefly to avoid Ash Wednesday at the Croft! found the house in a good deal of disorder, the Hunter servants having only left the day before — No real damage done, only the carpets very dirty — The Hunters unpopular & stingy, & ungracious — No one liked them except the Archdeacon, to whom they sent some game — The Powers very popular, kind in word & act — Such an amount of linen they have soiled! "Glory be to God" says Tim "it was like a theayter to see them arriving!"

In spite of stormy weather I [am] enjoying the free & silent life here, have elbow room to write, & liberty of *thought* which is denied one at the Croft — In Stanley's life I read of "the loneliness of the selfish man"[6] — I must try to avoid that, & am likely to do so, for already the poor are at my door, & my hand

5 AG's mother had acquired a reputation as a virulent anti-Catholic during her tenure at Roxborough, an attitude AG disdained, as her diary shows. Though candid in *Seventy Years* about her mother's extremism, and critical of the sectarianism of her upbringing even in early writings such as "An Emigrant's Notebook", AG was nonetheless quick to discourage discussion of the subject by others, recognizing its potential harm to her own reputation. In 1912 she urged Wilfrid Blunt to cut an entry describing a meeting with Mrs. Persse in 1888, which asserted that he was the first Catholic she had received under her roof, from future editions of his volume *The Land War in Ireland*. George Moore's allegation in a 1914 article "Yeats, Lady Gregory and Synge" that AG had been an active proselytiser alongside her mother in her youth drew the threat of an injunction from her which persuaded Moore to tone down his charges considerably when reprinting the article as part of *Vale*. Boland was the Rev. Thomas Boland of Tuam.

6 *The Life and Letters of Dean Stanley* ed. Rowland Prothero (1894). Stanley (d.1881) was Dean of Westminster 1864–81.

in my pocket — Little Killeen has knitted a petticoat — a moth trap — but I have to buy it at a fancy price of £1, her brothers & sisters having been down with measles — Old Davy Boland has died, his wife & children all away in America, & the burial falls on me — Fleming's children are said to be left destitute, & Curtan, Wm.'s old Kinvara bailiff writes for help from the Workhouse hospital — I have a new cook, Mrs. Egan, very fat — I wish I could find something for her to do — Gerald came over Saturday to tell of his acceptance by Ethel Rochfort — It sounds hopeful, she is just 18 & must be nice from his account — & as A[rabe]lla says we shall be glad of a real lady as a sister in law after Rose![7] I am planting some larch & silvers in the nutwood to see if the rabbits are more merciful to them than those we plant in autumn. Feb[ruary] 24 — Charles has accepted reduction of interest to 4 p[er]. c[ent]. in lieu of being paid off — This is I daresay more prudent for us, tho' I would rather feel free — I have been getting the house arranged, correcting proof sheets of "Autobiography", & outside planting — In the nutwood I have planted a bare part with larch, spruce, silver & evergreen oak, & renewed, for the 3rd time the Insignis by the walk — I have had to mark some spruce, about 40 for cutting, for the tenants' use, as Frank says they are such good ones they deserve it — Today to make up I have planted 50 scotch, 30 spruce, 25 silver, 25 larch, in the clump near middle avenue which was hollow —

On April 14th Robert's holidays being over I left Coole with him for London — We parted with Ethel & Aubrey[8] at Athenry — arrived next morning at 1 Queen Anne St — The Layards had just returned from Venice, Sir Henry having been suddenly sent back by the doctor there, in consequence of an internal swelling, which he thought malignant — Poor Lady L. thought she wd never get him home alive — but did so, & Sir Henry Thompson took a more favourable view, but kept him to his room — I did not feel in the way, as she said she had determined on her way back to send for me, & was delighted to find my letter saying I was coming —

Robert & I spent our Sunday afternoon at the Zoo, & had tea with Paul — Next day, shopping, & as rain came on R. took me to an entertainment to see "Scott the missing man" who was put in an arm chair, & disappeared —

19th — I went to Mary Cole's wedding — She is 35, the bridegroom Herbert Studd 23 — Just 10 years older than Horace — The difference does not appear yet, she is so handsome though turning grey, & he looks old for his

---

[7] This marriage never came off, and Gerald died unmarried in March 1898. Ethel Rochfort (b.1876) married a Westmeath neighbour in August 1898.

[8] Edward Aubrey Persse (1881–1918), Ethel's brother, one of Edward Persse's eight sons.

years[9] — It was a pretty wedding, soldiers lining the aisle, & arum lilies filling the chancel — Eily & Maggie wore, like the bride, big hats without veils[10] — Alfred Cole came & sat by me & was rather upset, no wonder, his brother not 2 years in his grave — I have dined with them since then, Mary very excitedly happy, very demonstrative, but I wish she wd cease abusing poor Willy Cole, so far away in his Indian grave — and she did once love him — H. Studd has pleasant manners, looks determined, and contradicted some little order of Mary's to Annie — I would not like to put any man in that position over Robert! —

Seeing how serious Sir H. Layard's illness was, and that, though he might to some extent recover, he was not likely ever to leave England again, I determined to find a little independent abode for myself, lest I should be in the way of the invalid, or outstay my welcome, always so cordial — But I had been considering the matter for some time, and had come to the conclusion, that money permitting it would be unwise to give up London — I have at present many friends, but there of all places one must keep one's friendship "in constant repair" — I have the London knack of talking, which always reminds me of the Pool of Bethesda, one must be ready to pop in directly the water is troubled, (by an angel or other) or the subject changes & the chance is gone[11] — And I might probably lose that & become dull in society, whereas now I have the name of brightness & agreeability — I should lose sight of William's friends by staying away, & they may in 8 or 9 years time be of great use to Robert, as I see from Paul & others the difference made to a lad by a good start & influential friends — Then I had found it impossible to pass the winters alone at Coole, the long evenings when it grows dark at 5 or 6 are too trying, and I cannot eat alone, & both appetite & sleep desert me —

So I decided that it would be better for Robert as well as for myself that I should use my "two talents" and spend a part of the year in town — I hoped to find something in the way of lodgings at £100 a year, which was all I felt justified in tying myself to, but at the beginning of my search found nice

9 Mary Cole, née de Vere (1859–1930), a second cousin of Aubrey de Vere through her father, Horatio de Vere, and of WHG through her mother, Anne, née Burke (see p. 99 n. 171). Also distantly related to AG via the O'Hara family (see p. 30 n. 43). Her first husband, Major William Utting Cole, had died of cholera in India in 1892, leaving her widowed with three children, Horace, John, and Annie. Horace Cole (1881–1936) later achieved considerable notoriety as a hoaxster, his many embarrassments to officialdom including the "Dreadnought" hoax of 1910, in which Adrian Stephen, Virginia Stephen (later Woolf), Cole, and others impersonated the Emperor of Abyssinia and his entourage, and were received ceremoniously on board the flagship of the British Navy. Herbert Studd (1870–1947), Coldstream Guards, subsequently served in the S. Africa War 1899–1902 and WW1 (being awarded the Croix de Guerre and Legion of Honour), and was Chief of Staff of the Supreme War Council 1917–19.
10 Mary Cole's sisters, Lady Eleanor Shaw (d.1946) and Margaret Prescott-Decie (d.1949).
11 See *John* 5.1–7.

rooms at Queen Anne's Mansions, at £95, which suited me very well[12] — My friends helped to furnish them, Lady Layard giving me an umbrella stand, a Florentine carved chair, a set of tea things that had belonged to Sir H.'s aunt Mrs. Austin, & a milking stool — Paul gave me a Chippendale chair, just the right height for my writing table, Sir H. Layard a framed print from his portrait, Lady Tweeddale & the Duchess of St. Albans photos — Lady Lindsay three beautiful rugs & a cabinet, stained work — The other furniture, carpets etc cost me about £50, & the old drawingroom curtains from St. George's Place came in very nicely — One day, driving down Knightsbridge in an omnibus, I caught sight in a dealer's window (Arthur Smith) of the picture by Longhi,[13] A lady renouncing her wordly goods, which I had sold at Christie's for £21 & regretted ever since — I went to ask about it, & they wanted £50, & said they had an offer from Mr. Freshfield for £45 — However I wrote to A. Smith himself, & he came to see me & after some palavering let me have it for £28, & I was glad to get it, it & the curtains gave a look of home — And so I set up house, & liked the independence, & the absence of housekeeping & servant troubles — I gave a little tea party, borrowing chairs from the establishment, Ricardos, Lady Westmeath & Lady Elizabeth,[14] Miss D'Arcy, Lady O'Hagan[15] — And I gave some little dinners, in the restaurant, 3/6 a head — Poor Sir Henry whenever I saw him wd say "Well how are the three & sixpennies going on?" At my first were Lady Layard, Sir A. & Lady Clay, Sir Auckland Colvin,[16] Sir F. Burton & Mr. Wardle of Leek, the dyer & silk manufacturer[17] — Very bright & pleasant, Mr. Wardle a novelty & able to

[12] Lady Layard's diary for 18 April 1894 records: "I went with Augusta in the morning to Queen Anne's Mansions to see an apartment she is thinking of taking there. I liked the look of it. It is on the 3rd floor. Has an unfurnished sitting room, bedroom, bathroom and a tiny entrance. Rent £100 including service and electric lighting. A restaurant and public drawing room. I advised her to take it and she decided to do so" (British Library). Located in Queen Anne's Gate, one street away from the southern side of St. James's Park and close to the Parliament buildings, Queen Anne's Mansions included around a dozen MPs and many other notables amongst its residents. AG moved into the apartment at "Qmansions" or "Q. A. M.", as she subsequently refers to it, on 1 May 1894.

[13] Probably Italian painter and engraver Giuseppi Longhi (1766–1834).

[14] Emily, Lady Westmeath, née Blake (d.1906), widow of the 10th Earl (d.1883), and her third daughter Elizabeth (d.1923).

[15] Alice, Lady O'Hagan (d.1921), widow of the 1st Baron O'Hagan (d.1885), twice Lord Chancellor of Ireland.

[16] Sir Auckland Colvin (1838–1908). Rose to prominence as Controller-General in Egypt 1880–83. His articles in the Pall Mall Gazette, for which he was Egyptian correspondent, were pivotal in spurring British annexation of the country. His rigorous imperialism and antipathy to Nationalist leader Arabi Bey made him AG's sworn enemy until February 1886, when he promised to assist her in her campaign to improve the allowance given to Arabi, then in exile in Ceylon. AG marked the rapprochement with two poems in her diary in 1886 which celebrate the change in Colvin's formerly "cankered mind" (Berg). Colvin served as Lt Governor of N.W. Provinces, India, 1887–92, after which he retired.

[17] Thomas Wardle (1831–1909), subsequently knighted (1897) for his services to the silk industry.

talk to the ladies about embroidery silks & to Sir A. C[lay]. about Indian silk worms — & Enid & I teased Sir F. to say which of us he liked best[18] —

My next, for the Cecil Smiths,[19] was Ld. Carlisle, Hallam Murray & Sir A. Clay & Dorothy Stanley[20] — Also a success — The next I did not care so much for, it was for "Arvède Barine" Mme. Vincens[21] who Lee Childe[22] had asked me to be civil to, & I got it up in a hurry — I had Mr. Cross (as she had written on George Eliot I thought she might like to meet her "relict")[23] Edward Martyn,[24] Albert Ball, Sir A. Birch to talk city to Cross — I had a more successful lunch for Mme. Barine, T. P. O'Connor[25] who had never met her but had been devoting columns of the Weekly Sun to her last book "Bourgeois et Gens de Peu" & Oswald Crawfurd, who showed London to Zola[26] — I took Mme. B. to the Temple afterwards, to see it under Nevill Geary's guidance, & Olive Blake[27] came also, was much amused at meeting T. P. & I took her afterwards to a party at Mrs. Kay's where she was introduced to Grossmith & heard him recite[28] — I had another little lunch to give Mr. Bennett editor of the Times

[18] Lady Layard's diary records this dinner as taking place on 17 May 1894 (British Library).

[19] Cecil Smith (1840–1916), and his wife Teresa, née Newcomen. Smith was Lt Governor and Col. Sec. of Ceylon 1885–87, and Consul General for N. Borneo and Sarawak 1889–93.

[20] Lady Dorothy Stanley, née Tennant (d.1928). Married African explorer Henry Stanley (1841–1904) in 1890. Stanley, already famous for his expedition to find Dr Livingstone in Tanganyika, and his explorations of the Congo in the 1870s, was at this point the lion of London society following his expedition of 1886–89 to rescue Emin Pasha.

[21] Arvède Barine, pseudonym of Cecile Vincens (1840–1908), litterateur and biographer of de Musset.

[22] Edward Lee Childe (1836–1911), a nephew of Confederate General Robert E. Lee. He had remarried in 1889 following the death of his first wife, Blanche (see p. 9 n. 32), in 1886.

[23] John Walter Cross (1840–1924) had married novelist George Eliot (1819–1880) just seven months before her death in 1880. Mme Vincens's most recent book, *Portrait des Femmes*, had included a chapter on George Eliot. Cross was at this point a resident at Queen Anne's Mansions.

[24] Edward Martyn (1859–1923), see Biographical Appendix.

[25] Thomas Power O'Connor (1848–1929), nationalist politician and journalist. M. P. for Galway 1880–85 (during which time he was on the Executive of the Land League), and for Liverpool 1885–1929. Founder (and Editor 1888–90) of *The Star*, and subsequently founder and Editor of *The Sun*, *The Weekly Sun*, *T. P.'s Weekly*, *T. P.'s and Cassell's Weekly* and other papers between 1890 and 1927.

[26] Crawfurd had been a prime mover in encouraging the first visit to London by French novelist and reformer Emile Zola (1840–1902) in September 1893, arranging a dinner in Zola's honour at the Author's Club (of which he was President) and acting as escort on some of the novelist's tours of the city. The visit attracted much attention since Zola's work was still highly controversial, having been recently attacked in the House of Commons for supposed immorality.

[27] Probably a cousin of Lord Morris (see p. 11 n. 44).

[28] George Grossmith (1847–1912), actor and entertainer. Toured 1889–1906 with his one man show "Humorous and Musical Recitals." Joint-author with his brother Weedon of the classic comic novella *The Diary of a Nobody*.

of India[29] an opportunity of meeting Sir Alfred Lyall who he had never seen — Also Mrs. Kay & Ernest Hart,[30] both anxious to meet Sir A. — So with a lunch to Sarah Galbraith[31] some to Hugh Lane, & a final one to Harry MacBride[32] & Nevill Geary I think I did enough hospitality — I was forgetting that I asked the Whites to dine, friends of the Layards — Mr. W. had an immense admiration for Sir H. Robinson so I had him to meet him, & Wilfrid Blunt[33] as they were all "horsey" & MacBride to meet Sir H. — & that also was a success, & Mr. Blunt entertained the Whites & MacBride at Crabbet the next Sunday —

People were kind to me — I dined with the Duchess St. Albans, the Lyalls, the Ernest Harts, the Birchs, the Clays, the Oswald Crawfurds,[34] Mrs. Kay, the Knowles,[35] the Raffaloviches, Lord Reay's, Nevill Gearys (to meet George Moore,[36] E[dward]. M[artyn], Miss Milman & the Editor of the Newbery

[29] Thomas Jewell Bennett (1852–1925), Editor and principal owner of *The Times of India* 1892–1901.

[30] Ernest Hart (1835–98), surgeon and medical reformer, and Editor of the British Medical Journal 1886–98. His wife was a key figure in promoting and financing the Irish Industries movement.

[31] The Galbraiths were near neighbours of the Persses, owning the Cappard (or Coppard) estate close to Roxborough. There had been two marriages between the families in the eighteenth century.

[32] Robert Knox MacBride (1844–1905), aide to WHG during his term as Governor of Ceylon, and Director of Public Works in Ceylon 1885–97.

[33] Wilfrid Scawen Blunt (1840–1922), poet, explorer and anti-imperialist. Worked in close alliance with AG during the Egyptian campaign of 1882–83, during which period they were briefly lovers. After being banned from Egypt by the British authorities, Blunt took up the cause of self-determination in India in 1885–86 and, more notoriously, in Ireland in 1887 where he was arrested and jailed for two months. Though remaining a strong advocate of Home Rule, and invited to stand as a Parnellite candidate, Blunt returned to Ireland for only one brief visit following his release from prison, and AG's persistent efforts from the late 1890s onwards to draw him into the literary movement were rewarded with only a single play, *Fand*—based on Irish legendary material, but of minimal dramatic merit—which was performed once at the Abbey Theatre in 1907. Blunt and his wife Lady Anne (1837–1917), Byron's granddaughter, were the first Europeans to import pure-bred Arabian horses following their first travels in Arabia in the late 1870s. The stud they established at Crabbet was crucial to the popularizing of the breed in Britain, and to the certifying of Arabian blood lines.

[34] Crawfurd's wife, Margaret (d. 1899), daughter of Sir Clare Ford, British Envoy at Madrid, was a long-term invalid, partly as a result of syphilis she caught from her husband. Sir Harry Johnston (see p. 32 n. 53) would recall her as "unhappy, devoted to a man tant soit peu volage. Crawfurd himself was a fascinating man . . . but susceptible to the charms of young and talented women" (*The Story of My Life*).

[35] James Knowles (1831–1908) and his second wife Isabel, née Hewlett. After following his father's career as an architect, Knowles entered journalism, editing *The Contemporary Review* 1870–77. He founded *The Nineteenth Century*, the pre-eminent review of the late-Victorian period, in 1877, and remained its editor until his death. For AG's dismissive impressions of Knowles when they were first acquainted in the 1880s, see *Seventy Years*, p. 117.

[36] George Moore (1852–1933), novelist, see Biographical Appendix.

House Magazine[37]), Wilfrid Blunt (to meet Ld. Carlisle & Lady Lytton[38]), Mrs. Tennant,[39] the Childers (where Sir Barrington Seymour who sat next me began by reading his menu with his back to me & ended by inviting me to stay in the Isle of Wight!)[40] the Mitchell Henrys,[41] the Cecil Smiths, the Studds, Lord Stanmore — besides dropping in when I liked to dine at the Layards, Gearys, Ly. Osborne[42] (but I didn't care for that) or lunch at Morrises, Birches, Hoziers.[43]

Sir Henry & Lady Blake[44] took (at my instigation) a flat at the "Mansions" and were kind & friendly — One evening that I went up alone to dinner, a very rare occurrence as I generally dined either with friends or had a sandwich at the station (like <??>) they called me to their table where they were entertaining the Duchess St. A[lbans] & Lady Moyra Beauclerk & Ld. Burford[45] & made me dine with them very pleasantly — Sir Henry has brought some luminous beetles from Jamaica, & Lady B. wore them in her hair sometimes at night — Sir H. gave Robert two when he came for his exeat, and they were

---

37 Probably the daughter of Canon Milman of St. Paul's (seep. 62 n. 201). *The Newbery House Magazine* was a monthly religious journal.

38 Edith, Lady Lytton, née Villiers (1842–1936), widow of the 1st Earl Lytton (1831–91). Lytton had been Governor-General of India 1876–80 and a close friend of Wilfrid Blunt since the time Blunt had served as his Secretary at the British legation at Lisbon in the 1860s. The Lyttons' youngest son, Neville, married Blunt's daughter Judith in 1899.

39 Probably Gertrude Tennant, Lady Dorothy Stanley's mother, and a notable society hostess.

40 A slip for Sir Barrington Simeon (1850–1909), 4th Bart, M.P. for Southampton 1895–1906. Simeon, whose seat was at Newport on the Isle of White, was connected with the Childers through the marriage of his brother Stephen (1857–1937) to Childers's daughter Louisa (d.1925).

41 Mitchell Henry (1826–1910) and his wife Margaret, née Vaughan. Henry was M.P. for Galway 1871–85, and temporarily led the Irish parliamentary party during Isaac Butt's illness in 1878. Unseated in 1885 for his opposition to the Land League, subsequently re-elected in Glasgow, and thereafter opposed both Parnell and many of his own previously Nationalist positions.

42 Emma, Lady Osborne (d.1909), widow of the 14th Bart (d.1879).

43 William Wallace Hozier (1824–1906), created 1st Baron Newlands 1898. Married in 1849 Frances O'Hara of Raheen (d.1891), a niece of WHG's mother Elizabeth O'Hara Gregory (1799–1875). AG was also distantly connected with the Hozier family via the marriage of her uncle Robert Persse to Anne O'Hara, a cousin of Frances O'Hara.

44 Sir Henry Arthur Blake (1840–1918), served in the Irish Constabulary 1859–76, and as Resident Magistrate in 1876–82. For his vigour as one of five special magistrates appointed to "pacify" Ireland during the Land War, he was rewarded with the Governorship of the Bahamas 1884–87, and was thereafter Governor of Newfoundland 1887–88, Jamaica 1889–97, Hong Kong 1897–1903, and Ceylon 1903–07. Married Edith Bernal-Osborne (sister of Grace, Duchess of St. Albans) in 1874. In a letter of November 1888 (Berg), AG had dismissed Blake as "a bumptious, underbred man ... it is only through his sister-in-law ... that he has been pushed up so fast, and I should think he is quite unsuited to a Parliamentary Colony."

45 Lady Moyra Beauclerk (1876–1942), the Duchess's third daughter, and Charles Beauclerk (1870–1934), Earl of Burford, the Duchess's eldest son (who became 11th Duke of St. Albans in 1898).

the cause of great anxiety and excitement, had to be fed on sugar & given damp bark to nestle in — We had to take them to the Duchess of Bedford's (Chenies) where we went for a couple of days,[46] & back again, & after all our care Robert who I had to leave at Euston, left them on the platform! So next day I had to start off in search, & found them in the lost property office & sent them on by post, & one arrived alive.

I think my pleasantest dinners were at the Knowles, where I met Dr. Maclagan, Ld. Ashbourne,[47] the Wantages[48] amongst others — At Mrs. Tennant's I sat next Edwin Arnold, who is an old windbag — We were very much crowded at table & he began by telling me what a *really nice* little dinner he had been at a short time before — "We were only five — two of us were Duchesses!"[49] — I confessed to not having read the "Light of the World" & he said "Oh you will enjoy that, just listen to the opening stanzas" & repeated several pages! He told me of his reception in all parts of the world, how in an American village the post office clerk when he asked for his letters had cried "Are you indeed Edwin Arnold!" and produced the "Light of Asia" from his pocket — & the old story of the Buddhist priests in Ceylon having read him an address — He did not tell me as G. A. Sala had done, who was present on the occasion, that in welcoming him as the expounder of Buddhism in the West they had coupled his name with that of Madame Blavatsky, to his great indignation![50]

[46] Adeline, née Somers, Duchess of Bedford (d. 1920), wife of the 10th Duke. Chenies House, Hertfordshire, was their country seat.

[47] Edward Gibson (1837–1913), 1st Baron Ashbourne. M.P. for Dublin University 1875–85, Attorney-General for Ireland 1877–80, and Lord Chancellor of Ireland 1885–86, 1886–92 and 1895–1905.

[48] Robert James Loyd-Lindsay (1832–1901), created Lord Wantage 1885. Financial Secretary to the War Office 1877–80. Brother of Sir Coutts Lindsay (see p. 11 n. 45). Married Hon. Harriet Loyd (d. 1920) in 1858.

[49] Edwin Arnold (1832–1904), journalist for *The Daily Telegraph* 1860–1900, and latterly poet, whose principal works were *The Light of Asia* (1879) and *The Light of the World* (1891). AG had noted Arnold's habit of parading his acquaintance with the titled at a previous meeting in 1888, at which his boast was of a dinner "where we were only five—Three of us were Duchesses!" (Berg). Arnold was the leading candidate for Laureate following Tennyson's death, but was passed over in favour of Alfred Austin (1835–1913) in an appointment that was recognised as rewarding Austin's Tory views rather than his poetical gifts.

[50] Arnold's tour of Ceylon in 1886, while *The Light of Asia* was at the height of its popularity (eight British editions were published in 1885 alone), was a triumphal progress marked by addresses by Buddhist priests at Panadura, Kandy and elsewhere. The occasion recalled by Arnold's colleague on the *The Daily Telegraph*, novelist and veteran journalist George Augustus Sala (1828–95), was probably the address by local Theosophists (rather than Buddhists) at Colombo, at which Colonel Henry Steel Olcott (1832–1907), a key follower of Madame Blavatsky, was present. Helena Petrovna Blavatsky (1831–91), founder of the Theosophical Society in 1875, brought occult studies and eastern thought into the late-Victorian cultural mainstream through her books *Isis Unveiled* (1877) and *The Secret Doctrine* (1888). After being accused of fraudulent mediumship in 1884, Blavatsky broke with the Theosophical Society, established her own esoteric lodge in London in 1887, of which Yeats became a member.

He finally expounded his religious views, told me there was no real death or separation — "Lady Gregory — I myself have been married to two ladies, each of whom was a liberal education — They have both died — Am I sorry? Not a bit!"[51] On my other side was Lord ____ — who talked very modestly & intelligently & puzzled me by his knowledge of the West Indies, till I found afterwards he had been a schoolmaster out there, & had succeeded to the title on the death of his cousin, who had married a S. African Hottentot according to native rites, which marriage had been disallowed by the Courts in England — Stanley I met for the first time & was agreeably surprised[52] — I saw very little of him, but he gave me his arm downstairs, regretted not having had more talk with me, he had heard so much of me, & we parted with mutual compliments — H. H. Johnston was also there, a dear little pocket traveller, so small & gentle[53] — At a "literary tea" at Lady Lindsay's I met Coventry Patmore,[54] I thought he was of a bygone generation — At the Morrises I met Yates, looking every inch a poet, though I think his prose "Celtic Twilight" is the best thing he has done[55] — I went sometimes to see Jean Ingelow,[56] always kind & practical — I went once to the H[ouse]. of C[ommons]., Speaker's Gallery with Miss Peel, after tea, & once I took Mrs. White there, & showed her the H. of Lords as well where we saw Ld. Rosebery yawning in the face of Ld. Balfour of Burleigh[57] who was speaking (& no wonder) & we had tea with Mr. Ponsonby[58] —

I had to sell at a bazaar, Irish Industries in Lady Layard's place, didn't like it

[51] Arnold's first wife, Katharine Biddulph died in 1864. His second wife, Fanny Channing, whom he married in 1868 died in 1889. Several of his best poems, embodying his belief in the immortality of the soul, anticipate reunion with a lost love.

[52] WHG had not been impressed by Sir Henry Stanley and his towering reputation. Writing to AG in 1890 he had deplored Dorothy Tennant's marriage to the explorer: "she is so gentle & refined & he is such a brute—I suppose he will whack her—& he is very strong" (Emory).

[53] Sir Harry Hamilton Johnston (1858–1927), explorer, diplomat and writer on African history and geography. A close friend of Cecil Rhodes, and an ardent imperialist, Johnston was the principal architect of the treaties which established British control of some 400,000 square miles of African territory, including Nyasaland and large areas of the region which became Northern Rhodesia.

[54] Coventry Patmore (1823–1896), poet, whose principal works were *The Angel in the House* (1858) and *Unknown Eros* (1877).

[55] W. B. Yeats (1865–1939), hereafter WBY. See Biographical Appendix. *The Celtic Twilight* was first published in December 1893.

[56] Jean Ingelow (1820–1897), author of many volumes of poetry, and of several novels.

[57] Alexander Bruce (1849–1921), 6th Lord Balfour of Burleigh. Secretary for Scotland 1895–1903.

[58] Edward Ponsonby (1851–1920), secretary to the Speaker, Lord Peel, 1884–89. Ponsonby was Lady Layard's brother-in-law, having married her younger sister, Blanche, in 1875. Succeeded his father as Earl of Bessborough in 1906.

much tho' my coadjutor Lady St. Germans was nice[59] — I was mistaken for her by Princess Edward[60] & Lady H. Lennox[61] who wd come gushing to me till I got Mr. Ponsonby to tell them the mistake —

I went with Lady L[ayard]. to a show of amateur work at the Imperial Institute[62] — & while there the Princess of Wales & her daughter arrived — They came to talk to Lady Layard — & I was shocked to see the poor Princess so changed — Her lovely sad eyes remain, but her smile was forced & not in sympathy with them, & she was so bewigged & so plastered with paint that she looked like pictures of Queen Elizabeth — She was, as I never saw her before, dowdy — with a little old-fashioned cashmere "dolman" black skirt & toque — Poor thing, they say she has lost her interest in dress — She has certainly never been the same since the Duke of Clarence's death[63] — & Oliver Montague's death[64] & the Prince's devotion to Lady Brooke[65] have had their share — The poor young Princess looked delicate, dowdy & forlorn[66] —

As to good works — I did not quite neglect the old women's Monday meetings, had one successful one, gave them tea & had Lady Layard with her guitar & Cecil Smith with his banjo, & at other times went alone — I also had from 12 to 20 Southwark children on several Saturdays to picnic on the grass in St. James's Park, row on the lake & fish on its edge — Once I borrowed the Layards' carriage & let the teachers have a drive in the Park to their great joy — These parties cost me more than I could well afford, having my Coole poor

[59] This sale was held by Mrs. Edward Ponsonby at her house in Cavendish Square on 27–28 April. Emily St. Germans, née Labouchere (d.1933), was the wife of the 5th Earl of St. Germans (1835–1911), Ponsonby's cousin.

[60] Alexandra, Princess of Wales (d.1925), wife of Edward (1841–1910), Queen Victoria's eldest son, the future King Edward VII.

[61] Lady Henry Lennox, née Alice Ogilvie-Grant (d.1946), wife of Walter "Henry" Gordon-Lennox (1865–1922), youngest son of the 6th Duke of Richmond, and Treasurer of her Majesty's Household 1891–92.

[62] Lady Layard's diary records this visit on 5 May 1894 (British Library).

[63] Albert, Duke of Clarence (1864–1892), Princess Alexandra's eldest son.

[64] Oliver George Montagu (1844–1893), 4th son of the 7th Earl of Sandwich, sometime Commander of the Royal Horse Guards, and equerry to the Prince of Wales. He was Princess Alexandra's constant escort and companion during the Prince's dalliances with Lily Langtry (see p. 84 n. 101) and others. Died of tuberculosis in Egypt.

[65] Frances "Daisy" Brooke, née Maynard (1861–1938), had married Lord Brooke (1853–1924)—later Lord Warwick— at the age of 19, and replaced Lily Langtry, her role-model, as Prince Edward's principal mistress in the early 1890s. Her aptly titled autobiography *Discretions* gives a highly sanitized account of her subsequent career as a socialist activist and hostess. For her semi-successful efforts to blackmail the Royal Family in 1914 using Edward VII's love letters to her, see Theo Lang *The Darling Daisy Affair.*

[66] Louise Victoria Alexandra Dagmar (1867–1931), Princess Alexandra's only daughter. She had given birth to her second child on 3 April 1893.

as first charge, but they gave great pleasure — I also went & helped at "Happy Evenings" at the Board School —

I may put it down as a good work that I several times had Hugh Lane to lunch, either at a restaurant or the Mansions — His second rate fashionable talk & vulgarity of mind always irritated me — He did not like the situation at Colnaghi which I had got for him, abused C. & his temper & was always threatening to leave — however Colnaghi bundled him off at last, making his not knowing French an excuse[67] — One curious thing (which he told me in strict confidence) happened while he was there — Caroline, Colnaghi's head clerk, had painted from memory a picture he had long ago seen, by Frank Hals — Hugh persuaded him to send it to an auction, as an old picture, to see if anyone wd be taken in & to Caroline's horror when the day came he found that Colnaghi himself had bought it against several competitors, having given £100 or £120 for it — Colnaghi brought it in triumph to the gallery very proud of himself, tore off the back — & discovered the new canvas! Caroline, afraid to receive the money from the auctioneer, but more afraid to confess, nearly died — Colnaghi would quite die if this ever came out[68] —

I had an amusing lunch one Sunday at Lady O'Hagan's, only Dr. Klein[69] & Professor Dicey[70] there — Klein gave an account of a gipsy encampment in Wales he had once known, the Queen of the Gipsies was there, & her consort, who hailed from Waterford & who complained that if his wife slept indoors she got fever & if he slept outdoors he got cold — Dicey said he had been asked to stand up in argument against John Dillon at Oxford but had refused — I reproached him but he said "Well, I feel convinced he will invent facts on the spot which I shan't be able to refute, & I am unfortunately unable to do the same, for though a willing, I am not a ready liar".

I met at dinner at Mrs. Kay's old Sir Leopold McClintock[71] who I thought had

[67] According to Thomas Bodkin in *Hugh Lane and his Pictures,* Lane was "fairly proficient" in French, and it was his social affectations and his "inability to write a good hand" which led to his dismissal from Colnaghi's.

[68] AG later related that after being displayed for two days at Colnaghi's, the painting, in the style of Flemish portraitist Franz Hals (1584–1656), "vanished, and henceforth there was silence in the gallery about what I think we may still call a masterpiece" (*Hugh Lane* p. 33). John Caroline, manager of Colnaghi's gallery, remained Lane's lifelong friend.

[69] Klein, a Catholic priest, was an habitué of Grant-Duff's social circle. He had resigned from a Professorship in Dublin in 1888 through religious disagreements, and later left the Church (see p. 63).

[70] Albert Venn Dicey (1832–1922), Vinerian Professor of English Law 1882–1909.

[71] Sir Francis Leopold McClintock (1819–1907), officer in Arctic expeditions of 1848, 1850–51 and 1852, and leader of the celebrated 1857 expedition which determined the fate of Sir John Franklin's lost expedition of 1845–47. As AG would recall in *Seventy Years,* p. 292, "it was reading articles by him in the *Sunday at Home* long ago that gave me an interest I have always kept in Arctic voyages."

died in past ages, & at the same dinner a young Mr. North, whose mother I had made acquaintance with one day waiting at the Waterloo Station for Robert, & who told me that when he went to school, aged 11 he did not know how to read, but was now leading member of the junior Bar[72] — He & the rest of the company were much amused to hear this —

Almost every day I made a pilgrimage to Queen Anne St. to see, or enquire for Sir Henry, & see Enid — At first Sir H. Thompson had spoken hopefully of him & asked him to dine at one of his "Octaves" though some way off — & they made plans for Scotland, & talked of Venice, & of moves to the country — But the internal swelling was increasing all the time[73] — Sir Henry sometimes when I saw him alone said the end was coming — I never contradicted him as others did, for I believed it to be the case, & I do not think a man in clear possession of his intellect ought to be deceived on the most important subject of all — He was allowed down, & out driving at last, but after a few days he got a heart attack out driving in the Park which nearly carried him off — He lived for 2 or 3 weeks after that, but did not come downstairs again — Poor Enid watched him devotedly, though the nurse was able to do most for him — He was always kind to me, up to two days before his death sent for me, & sent his love to Robert, but unconsciousness was gradually creeping on — On July 5 I lunched with Mme. Barine & her husband & T. P. O'Connor, & hurried off to Euston to meet Robert who had been sent up for a bandage for his knee which had been put out at cricket — I took him to Queen Anne St. to enquire, & found poor Enid lying on her bed listening to the heavy unconscious breathing in the next room — He had been speechless since morning — I promised to come back, & came about 9 — & found Eliots, Du Canes etc[74] in the hall & heard he had died about an hour before — I was going away, but just then Mr. Ponsonby came down & said Enid had been asking for me, & I went up & found her quite stunned & bewildered — It reminded me so much of my own trouble two years before that I broke into passionate sobbing, & she tried to soothe me — They took her to see the body, but she came back saying "He is not there, that is not Henry" — We feared for her brain, got her to the upper room & I stayed with her all night — At five she asked what time it was & when I told her said "then morning has come" & burst out sobbing & was less rigid after that — I spent each night with her till the funeral — or rather the cremation — which she did not seem to feel specially, though I had, just as at Kinglake's cremation, a feeling of horror, &

[72] Possibly Frederic Keppel North (1860–1948), called to the bar in 1884, and later a circuit court judge.

[73] Cancer, initially manifested in Layard as a tumour in the groin.

[74] In-laws of Lady Layard. Her younger sister Constance (1844–1916) had married Col. Charles Eliot (1839–1901), youngest son of the 3rd Earl St. Germans and a groom of the Privy Chamber 1871–99. Her eldest sister Maria (1834–1902) had married Richard Du Cane (1821–1904).

spent the afternoon driving with good, kind Maclagan[75] —

The next Saturday to Monday I spent at Chenies, with her & the Duchess of Bedford, bringing Robert, who had an exeat for the Eton & Harrow match — Enid was a little better, the Duchess very kind & charming, a large hearted, large minded woman, very attractive — On Sunday she showed me all the Russell monuments in the old church, a great deal of English history to be learned there — I felt so much for her, & indeed for Lady Layard, as we three widows[76] sat together at morning service, Robert the only child amongst us! He was delighted with the trout in the stream & the perch in the pond, & the great dog "Aleuve", & it is a comfort to see him so free from self consciousness, with a nice simple manner, tho' very merry —

Dear little man, I went to see him on a Sunday & on a Saturday half holiday & we had a nice walk and chat together — I meant to send him to Harrow this autumn, but Mr. Royle begged me to leave him at Elstree till Easter, to try for a scholarship, & after consultation with Paul & Fischer Williams, & through him with Mr. Wilson at Elstree I have consented, especially as Mr. Bowen could not receive him at Harrow till Xmas — Mr. Royle says he ought never to be lower than 2nd in the school, if not first, but that he drops if not taken notice of & stirred up, & that Harrow masters will take more trouble with him if he enters as a scholar — I trust I am acting rightly — I took time & counsel before deciding —

I wrote a little, as an occupation, a short story "Dies Irae" founded on the Marcus Lynchs[77] — and an article on the Disestablished church, & on "Our boys in India"[78] none yet published — A little story "A Gentleman" was published in the July number of Argosy, without my name, I had sent it some time before[79] —

Politics subsided — In the early spring a Gen. election seemed so likely that

---

[75] Cremation was a recent innovation, having been legalized in 1888 largely due to the efforts of Sir Henry Thompson, Layard's doctor, who considered interment unsanitary and offensive. The Gregorys' friend Alexander Kinglake (see p. 65 n. 6) had been one of the first prominent public figures to be cremated, in 1891.

[76] George William Russell, 10th Duke of Bedford, had died on 23 March 1893.

[77] AG initially proposed this story, based on the marital breakup of a Galway couple she knew, to Henry James as a plot for a novel. Recording the "anecdote" in his diary for 23 January 1894, James was briefly interested enough to envisage "a rather strong short novel—80,000 to 100,000 words" though he did not pursue the project (The Notebooks of Henry James ed. F. O. Matthiessen and K. B. Murdock). "Dies Irae" was published under AG's name in The Sketch 25 March 1896, p. 376.

[78] These two articles were not published, but survive in manuscript in the Berg Collection.

[79] This story, which AG had probably written as early as Autumn 1890, appears under the pseudonym "Angus Grey" in The Argosy July 1894, pp. 72–81.

Murray would not bring out my book, but Lord Rosebery jigged through the session, passing Sir W. Harcourt's Death Duties, passing the Evicted Tenants' Bill, to be rejected by the Lords — Lord Rosebery wd better have waited till Gladstone's promises had been dispersed by time, & come in with a programme of his own[80] —

I saw more of Paul than I had done for some time, & he was very kind & good & helped me much in many ways — Poor boy, he has come out of his troubles with a kind of gentleness, rectitude & goodness very uncommon —

I returned to Coole on July 23, staying a day at Moyne on the way — A few busy days, then Robert came home, not very well, pale & thin & with a cough, & then a feverish attack — He looked so pulled down that Frank wanted me to keep him at home for 6 months feeding up before going to Harrow — But this would have been a great drawback & injury to him, & I am thankful to say he soon began to pick up, plenty of milk & fresh air working wonders, & by the time the holidays ended he was as plump & hearty as anyone could wish — Arabella came on a visit — & the Morris boys, Edmund & Charlie,[81] the house at Spiddal being in the hands of builders — Charlie a bright clever little fellow — but Edmund greedy & more — & the Birch boys who were next to arrive did not amalgamate with them —

Tony, Wyndham & Una Birch, with Mr. Watson the "holiday tutor" chosen by Sir Arthur came for the summer, with footman, housemaid & lady's maid — Mr. Watson was not very interesting or of much use, except to hold up to the boys as a warning against over smoking, his hand shaking, & his mind apparently becoming vacant from this cause — Una a straightforward girl, nice to Robert, but with an immense opinion of herself & a domineering manner — This much improved when her father came for the last fortnight & Ethel — who roused her up — The whole visit went off well poor children, I was glad to have them for these lst holidays since their mother's death — & they seemed thoroughly to enjoy the free out of door life & were very grateful — They paid for what they cost me extra, as I could not well have afforded to entertain so large a party — & I was delighted to make the house so cheerful for Robert, feeling it better for him that it shd be filled with his contemporaries than mine — I took Tony to Galway for a day, & got him leave to fish — & he got 7 salmon, & was photographed contemplating them — Afterwards

[80] Rosebery became Prime Minister following Gladstone's resignation in March 1894, accepting the position as a compromise candidate at the urging of Queen Victoria and others anxious to block Sir William Harcourt (see p. 40 n. 95). The estate duty provisions of the 1894 budget were in fact Harcourt's work, promoted reluctantly by Rosebery, who correctly recognised that they would accelerate the drift of landowners from the Liberal party.

[81] Michael Redmond Morris (1878–1902) and Charles Ambrose Morris (1880–1899), the two youngest of Lord Morris's four sons.

all the party came in & got a lot of mackerel & various salmon & Sir A. shot a seal —

I feel so glad that another summer having gone bye, we are still on good terms with our people — We had the schoolfeast (122 children) & the Workhouse party — And all the people are nice & cordial, & bring little presents for Robert as of old — Little Rourke was in the Workhouse Infirmary, & Robert went to see him there & gave him one of his own 5/- pieces, & distributed sugar sticks to him & the old men. The holidays ended, all went back, R. in good heart with Tony who was very sad — R. was top of the school in his holiday task — We had some rather painful episodes re his dog Croft, who worried geese & stole eggs & legs of mutton, & has now been presented to the postman in Galway, with a hope of return in case of reformation.

Miss Margaret Stokes[82] came for a night — It was a wet summer, but the hay crop, saved at last by sunshine is magnificent. The potatoes only middling — Prices pretty good — it may be called a good year so far —

The Mrs. came for 10 days at the end, with 3 servants, who idled, ate & smashed — She was not in good humour, & wd not drive with my one horse, so restlessly prowled about the house, & held forth on family affairs — She had begun by a desperate fight with Frank, who she threatens to cut off without even a shilling, because he is bringing up his children "idolators" — I wd not agree, & we were not much in sympathy — I don't want to live to be old! —

Now (Oct[ober] 14) I have had a fortnight of complete solitude & freedom & much enjoyed the lovely weather & the changing tints of the leaves — I have been very much out & about, looking after woods, gates and fences. I am so anxious to keep the place in good repair for Robert — The Vineries are being done up, they were beginning to go to pieces —

I have begun going through the box of old Mr. Gregory's papers, which Wm. & I once or twice began to do together but did not persist in[83] — Some of his early letters, from Harrow to his grandfather are there, dated 60 years ago! Truly we are such things as dreams are made of — I live literally "looking before and after" back over his life — forward to Robert's — God help me to be a good woman and to bring him up well — He is now all I wish him —

---

[82] Margaret MacNair Stokes (1832–1900), prominent Irish archeologist, and illustrator of Ferguson's poems. Daughter of William Stokes (1804–78), distinguished physician and President of the Royal Irish Academy 1874, and sister of Celtic scholar Whitley Stokes (1830-1909).

[83] The papers of WHG's grandfather, Mr William Gregory, from the period of his service as Under-Secretary of Ireland 1813-31. This material formed AG's next editorial project, *Mr. Gregory's Letter-Box.*

Now I am anxious to get to London, because the "Autobiography" must soon be out, & I can do more for its success on the spot — It is a great relief having done all the work connected with it, a good deal to look back on —

16th — Left Coole — Arrived London next morning — The little flat looked clean & cosy, with fires & a new Belgian housemaid — I went to Murrays & found the book ready, & to be published in a few days, & they had never forwarned me — It looks very well got up & is attractive to look through — I do trust it will be a success — I found a note from Arabella saying she was laid up at Rices[84] house at Hampstead so went there, very tired — & came back more tired still — Paul to dine with me — Too tired to sleep —

18th — Spent the morning writing notes regarding the book to friends in the Press & any I thought could aid it — Then to Murrays to consult — They are rather muddled because of the dual control, John very energetic, Hallam not caring for the business & preferring art, & it seems to me they make a good many mistakes between them, but they were very nice & cordial — I sent off a good many presentation copies, on business to F. Lawley,[85] Humphry Ward,[86] George Russell,[87] T. P. O'Connor, Labouchere[88] — Then to the Speaker, Ld. Rosebery, Dr. Maclagan, E. Martyn, Major Thackwell, Ld. Dufferin,[89] Charles Gregory, Dr. Welldon,[90] Mr. MacBride, Father Fahey,[91]

[84] Mrs. Rice was Robert Waithman's sister, Arabella's sister-in-law.

[85] Francis Charles Lawley (1825–1901), youngest son of the 1st Baron Wenlock, was elected M. P. in 1852, became Gladstone's private secretary later that year, and formed a close friendship with his parliamentary contemporary WHG. His promising political career ended in disgrace in 1854, and he left for America (see p. 52 n. 163). After covering the American Civil War for *The Times*, he returned to England in 1865, becoming a correspondent for *The Daily Telegraph*, a position he retained into the 1890s. He was also a popular essayist and sporting writer.

[86] Thomas Humphrey Ward (1845–1926), critic and journalist, now best remembered for his quintessential late-Victorian anthology *The English Poets*, and as husband of novelist Mrs. Humphrey Ward (see p. 55 n. 175).

[87] George William Erskine Russell (1853–1919), politician and writer. M.P. 1880–85 and 1892–95, and Under-Secretary of State for India 1892–94. Cousin of Lord Arthur Russell. Russell had read WHG's autobiography in manuscript in 1893 and encouraged AG to publish.

[88] Henry Labouchere (1831–1912), M.P. for Northampton 1880–1906 and founder and editor of the journal *Truth*, notorious for its swingeing political exposés.

[89] Frederick Temple Blackwood (1826–1902), 1st Earl of Dufferin, and Marquis of Dufferin and Ava. Under-Secretary of State for India 1864–66, Governor–General of Canda 1872–78, Ambassador at St. Petersburg 1879–81, at Constantinople 1881–84, Viceroy of India 1884–88, Ambassador in Italy 1888–91, and France 1891–96. A long–time friend of WHG, and the Gregorys' host during their Indian tour of 1885–86.

[90] Dr. James Edward Welldon (1854–1937), Headmaster of Harrow School 1885–98. Subsequently Bishop of Calcutta 1898–1902, and Canon of Westminster 1902–06.

[91] Rev. Dr. Jerome Fahey (1843–1919), parish priest of Gort, and a scholar of Galway history and genealogy. His 1893 volume *The History and Antiquities of the Diocese of Kilmacduagh* had dealt knowledgeably and generously with the history and achievements of the Gregory family, drawing on genealogical records subsequently destroyed in the burning of the Four Courts in 1922, and

Dr. Moran, W. Blunt, Lady Dorothy [Stanley], Ld. Clonbrock,[92] besides one to Paul — I think Wm. would approve of this list — And I gave old Waithman one, to keep him in good humour — To Hampstead again to sit with A[rabella] — Paul looked in in the evening — A better night —

19th — A little shopping, wanting some things for my room — Then to Hampstead — Then on the way back I called at F. Lawley's — He came up saying he had only two minutes for me as he had to write at once three columns on Randolph Churchill, having heard there was a telegram saying he was not expected to live — However he promised to review the "Autobiography" for the D[aily]. T[elegraph]. if sent to him before Sunday, & talked over it a good deal, & then we talked of Randolph, & he was delighted I had come as I happened to know some of his best characteristics, his success in administering the Famine Fund in Ireland, the passionate attachment of his sisters to him, & above all his great success at the India Office as Secretary of State, & also the very good impression he had made in India during his tour there, by sympathetic interest in the affairs of the natives & prudence, dignity & reticence, rather unusual not only in him but in any travelling politician — Toby M. P. best summed up his career long ago in Punch "There goes a man with a great future — behind him"[93] —

F. Lawley says that though Ld. Rosebery is so inscrutable & unconfidential to his colleagues that he has offended them all, he made himself so popular at the Foreign Office that the very dogs there wd wag their tails at the word "Rosebery", his kindness extending even to the messengers, while to young clerks & secretaries he was most generous & gracious, encouraging their interest in art or archeology & asking them to Mentmore —

20 — To Albermarle St. about F. Lawley's copy, found only Hallam [Murray] there, & no one knowing who had got copies & who had not — Truly as the Capt.[94] used to say "One bad general is better than two good ones" — But he said they were most grateful to me for doing so much, as many authors left all the trouble to them — I sent a few more presentation copies, one to Sir Wm. Harcourt, in gratitude for his kind thought of asking Robert from Park Hill for the first Sunday after his father's death[95] — Had a little clothes shopping

he had worked with WHG in researching and organizing the restoration of local sites of archeological and historical interest.

[92] Luke Gerald Dillon (1834–1917), 4th Baron Clonbrock, diplomat and Lieutenant of Co. Galway.

[93] Henry W. Lucy (1845–1924), political commentator for *Punch* under the pseudonym "Toby M.P." Randolph Churchill died a few weeks later, on 24 January 1895.

[94] Probably AG's late brother Dudley, a Captain in the 7th Fusiliers during the Crimean War.

[95] Sir William Harcourt (1827–1904), Liberal statesman. Chancellor 1886 and 1893–95, and during Gladstone's last decade in Government his right-hand-man. Harcourt's country residence was at Lyndhurst, close to Park Hill School.

& then went to see the Ricardos — I met Lecky & stopped to speak to him & he, as usual with his head carried like a giraffe's never saw me, & a man looked derisively at me, thinking apparently that I had accosted Lecky & been rejected! Froude's death in the papers[96] — F. Lawley says the Empress Frederic said to someone that the death of the Czar, which seems very near, won't be such a great loss after all, as he is nothing wonderful & his son has quite enough brains & will have the cleverest wife in Europe — Not that the Empress's own talent did her own poor husband much good as far as public life went[97] —

21 — To St. Margaret's Westminster, an immense crowd to hear Canon Farrar preach on St. James[98] — eloquent but not much in it save a few moral exhortations — Lunched Robinsons — Lady R. says they want Sir Hercules to go back to the Cape, & Cecil Rhodes writes by every mail urging him to do so[99] — On to Lady Lyall, who gives but a poor account of Sir Alfred, interspersed with complaints of his obstinacy in not giving her a new kitchen range — Then to condole with Lady Geary about Nevill's departure for Sierra Leone — I think I should go there too if I had to live in Warwick Square! — Dined Grand Hotel with Waithmans — Wrote to Buckle[100] about reviewing book — A bad night —

22 — Very tired, after a sleepless night — Went to see the Waithmans & the Birchs — & to the Stores — but so sleepy I had to come home, & very anxious, it being the eve of the publication of the book — Dined off a piece of bread & a pear & went to bed early —

23 — Awoke anxious — flew to the "Times" & was relieved to find a review in,

96 James Anthony Froude (1818–94), eminent historian and editor of Carlyle.

97 The "Empress Frederic" was Queen Victoria's eldest daughter, Victoria Adelaide (1840–1901), who had married the future German Emperor, Frederick III, in 1858. He had died in 1888, having been Emperor for little more than three months, their son becoming William II (Kaiser Wilhelm). Victoria Adelaide retained the courtesy title of Empress Frederick, with her daughter-in-law being Empress William. Alexander III (b.1845) Czar of Russia from 1881, died on 2 November 1894. His son Nikolai I, succeeded him as Emperor in 1896, but was murdered in July 1918 in the wake of the Russian Revolution along with his "clever" wife, Queen Victoria's grand-daughter Alexandra Feodorovna (b.1872), and their five children.

98 Rev. Frederic William Farrar (1831–1903), Canon 1876–83, Archdeacon 1883–95, and finally Dean of Westminster 1895–1903.

99 Cecil Rhodes (1853–1902), architect of British imperial expansion in Africa, and founder of the De Beers consortium. Successfully effected British acquisition of Bechuanaland as a Protectorate in 1884, and thereafter, with the reluctance of British Government to espouse openly imperialist aims, used his British South Africa Company as a de facto instrument of British expansion, annexing Matabeleland, Mashonaland (later called Rhodesia) and large areas that were named British South Africa. For Rhodes's motives in promoting Robinson's return to South Africa, see p. 126 n. 26.

100 George Earle Buckle (1854–1935), Editor of The Times 1884–1912.

rather a dull & un-appreciative one, but still in a good place — Then in the reading room I found F. Lawley's enthusiastic article in the Telegraph — a fairly good one in Morning Post, & one in Daily News giving plenty of quotations — And at Murrays I got the Standard's which had come out a day too soon, which made the Times angry, but is very full — & all are kind & none have discovered the mistakes in Greek & elsewhere[101] — So I felt a load roll off me, I should have taken it to heart so terribly if the book had fallen flat — Now it has had its good start & must stand or fall by its own merits — I have also nice letters from those I have sent it to, & the Murrays are most amiable, thanking me for my exertions! Farewell to Waithmans — Called on Mrs. Crawfurd — Paul in the evening —

24 — A wet stormy day — Rather pleased at the excuse to stay in & rest & arrange my little rooms — Dined Birchs — sat next Sir Ralph Thompson, Paul's chief at the War Office,[102] & made myself agreeable to him — Sir A[rthur]. asked if I did not feel 3 inches taller at the success of the book — I said no, but 10 years younger, which is true! They had a copy from the library with notice "This book being in *great demand* it is to be returned as soon as possible" — Mr. Hegan Kennard[103] & Mr. & Lady Agnes Daniel also there —

25 — The day began by the H[ouse]. maid breaking my repeater watch — Went to see Maclagan who is enthusiastic about the book — Lady Dorothy to tea, very amiable, & Maud Morris[104] — Paul dined —

26 — To Mudie's[105] — The foreman told me there was a great run on the book & he himself has not been able to take it home to read, & they had just sent for a further supply — A nice letter from Ld. Dufferin, he will send me his mother's poems in return[106] — New Gallery to see portrait collection —

---

[101] See *The Times* 23 October, p. 6; *The Daily Telegraph* 23 October, p. 6; *The Morning Post* 23 October 1894, p. 6; *The Daily News* 23 October, p. 6; *The Standard* 22 October, p. 2. Lawley's two-column review praised the Autobiography as one of the most "entertaining and instructive" volumes published in recent years. Lawley also paid AG a deft compliment by observing that WHG's second marriage had ushered in the happiest years of his life: "The perfect harmony and sympathy of taste which bound him to his second wife is attested to by the affection which breathes from the few pages of 'Conclusion' which she has added to his Autobiography and to the tender care with which she has edited its pages."

[102] Sir Ralph Wood Thompson (1830–1902), Permanent Under-Secretary for War 1878–95.

[103] Colonel Edmund Hegan Kennard (1835–1912), 8th Hussars, and A.D.C. to Lord Abercorn (then Viceroy of Ireland) 1867–68.

[104] Maud Morris (d. 1957), third daughter of Lord Morris. She later published a biography of her father, *An Irishman and his Family: Lord Morris and Killanin* (1937).

[105] The foremost London lending library of the time.

[106] Dufferin had edited *Poems and Verses by Helen Lady Dufferin,* a collection of verse, dramatic sketches and other writings by his mother, Helena (d. 1867), Richard Brinsley Sheridan's grand-daughter, which had just been published by John Murray. Dufferin's affection for his mother was renowned. In the early 1860s, he had a tower built on his estate at Clandeboye for which he

Watts's old Mrs. Percy Wyndham the best[107] — Dined Gearys to meet the Derings on their way from Sofia to Mexico[108] —

27 — Rain, a quiet day —

28 — Westminster Abbey — Lunched Ricardos, Dr. Chepmell there[109] — Lecky came to see me in the afternoon — Then to Twickenham for the night — Grant Duff asked what was thought of Rosebery's speech against the Lords[110] — I said I had not heard, but that my own feeling was akin to that awakened when the Emperor of China the other day, after long silence during which he had seen his armies shattered & his fleets sunk, had at last spoken to announce his resolve of depriving Li Hung Chang of his yellow jacket[111] — G. D. thought this a most delightful idea —

29 — Back to London —

30 — The day began with nice letters from the Prime Minister & the Chancellor of the Exchequer (Rosebery & W. Harcourt) & a present of his mother's poems from Ld. Dufferin, from the Paris Embassy — Pouring rain

commissioned works in her honour, including poems by Tennyson and Browning, and he continued to add to the collection in "Helen's Tower" long after her death.

[107] One of the best-known portraits by George Frederic Watts (1817–1904), painter and sculptor, completed around 1870, and loaned frequently for exhibits during his lifetime. The portrait itself was "old" work, but Mrs. Wyndham, née Madeline Campbell (d.1920), who had married Wilfrid Blunt's cousin Percy Wyndham (1835–1911) in 1860, was still in her social prime. She had also modelled for Watts for "The Three Graces" and "Orpheus and Eurydice" (1872).

[108] Sir Henry Nevill Dering (1839–1906), 9th Bart. Consul-General in Bulgaria 1892–94 and Envoy Extraordinary to Mexico 1894–1900. Married Rosa Underwood (d.1922) in 1863. Dering's father and Geary's father were half-brothers.

[109] Dobrée Chepmell, Maclagan's predecessor as the Gregorys' doctor. A diagnosis AG records after consulting him "about my bad headaches and frequent sickness" in 1889 confirms that he shared the Victorian medical profession's suspicion of intellectual women, and suggests why his services may have been dispensed with: "He says it is from a nerve connecting stomach & brain—& that the brain has been taking the nourishment the stomach ought to have" (Berg).

[110] Increasingly frustrated by the power of the Lords to block legislation passed by his Liberal administration in the Commons, Rosebery made a swingeing attack on the intransigence of the "irresponsible second chamber" and its unelected Tory majority in a speech at Bradford on 27 October. His progressively more hostile comments (as in a speech at Devonport on 11 December in which he attacked the "indefensible privileges" of hereditary peerage) earned him the ire of Queen Victoria and many others who shared her hostility to democracy and the challenge it was increasingly posing to the old aristocratic order.

[111] Li Hung Chang (1823–1901), a key figure in promoting industrial and military "self-strengthening" in China from the 1870s, was stripped of political office by Tsai T'ien Kuang Hsu, Emperor 1875–1908, following the catastrophic Chinese losses in the Sino-Japanese War of 1894–95, which ended Chinese suzerainty over Korea. He was subsequently rehabilitated, and helped negotiate the Boxer protocols in 1901.

all day — read & wrote & called on Mrs. Crawfurd & Albert Gray came to see me, & I dined with Lady Lindsay, only Henry James there, charming & pleasant as usual —

31st — Headache, & depressed, the reaction from excitement of last week — Paul dined —

1st Nov[ember] — Wrote duty letters — Sir G. Bowen[112] to tea — Notice in "Truth."[113]

2nd — A telegram from Miss Peel asking me to Sandy for Sunday — so accepted, & then had to trot to Durrant & Sykes & back to them again, to get my dress in time[114] —

3rd — To Sandy — a very pleasant evening, the Speaker very well & charming, the 3 girls nice & cordial. Mr. Gore from Oxford & Sir T. Wade from Cambridge, full of China on which he had just been giving a lecture[115] —

4th — To church & heard old Mr. Richardson preach on the death of the Czar![116] — Pleasant walks in the woods & talks — Such a treat to hear what is going on in the world of thought — The Speaker very full of Froude's "Erasmus" & Haussenes "1814"[117] — Then talk of poets — Sir T. Wade all for Scott, the Speaker all for Wordsworth, Mr. Gore for Browning — The evening ended by Mr. Gore reading from "The Flight of the Duchess" — not a good selection & not well read — The Speaker read "Rugby Chapel" most beautifully, interrupted by prayers, & his beautiful reading of a chapter of "Micah"[118] — The Speaker had been reading my book aloud to his daughters, & all are delighted with it — I asked who he thought best of our Irish orators

---

[112] Sir George Ferguson Bowen (1821–99), Governor successively of Queensland, New Zealand, Victoria, Mauritius and Hong Kong in the period 1859–73.

[113] *Truth* 1 November 1894, p. 988.

[114] Madame Durrant, a court dressmaker in Bond Street, had made clothes for AG since 1880. Sykes's, in Hanover Square, were dress and corset makers.

[115] Charles Gore (1853–1932), Librarian of Pusey House, Oxford, 1884–93, a key figure in the University Anglican community, and author of several influential works on faith and the ministry. Later Bishop of Worcester 1902–05, of Birmingham 1905–11 and Oxford 1911–19. Gore was a cousin of Edward Ponsonby, Peel's secretary. Sir Thomas Francis Wade (1818–95), Ambassador at Pekin 1871–83 and Professor of Chinese at Cambridge from 1888, had been a contemporary of WHG at Harrow School.

[116] See p. 41 n. 97.

[117] *Life and Letters of Erasmus*, a series of Lectures delivered by Froude at Oxford 1893–94 and published in 1894. *1814* by Henry Houssaye [*sic*], an account of Napoleon's downfall and the restoration of Louis XVIII, was published in 1888.

[118] "The Flight of the Duchess" a poem by Robert Browning, "Rugby Chapel" a poem by Matthew Arnold, and *Micah*, one of the shortest and most poetical books of the Old Testament.

— He said, for mob oratory, O'Brien[119] — Then I asked who was the best orator he had ever heard & he considered a minute or two till I suggested Bright[120] — & then said yes, facile princeps[121] —

5th — Back to London — Lunched with the Morrises, his Lordship looking much altered by his illness, with a white beard & haggard eyes — He still takes a pessimistic view of Ireland, thinks we have not touched bottom, that the new land bill will pass, & Morley appoint the new Commissioners, & property be sliced away by degrees[122] — There is a good review in the Spectator & also in the "Athenaeum" — the classical errors noted — but not unkindly[123] — Paul looked in — A rather sad evening, but it ended with an offer, to make a fresh start —

6th — To Southwark Bd. School & saw Mrs. Hills[124] — Mr. Dodge out but have written to ask if I can help in any parish work[125] — Then to School of Languages about French class — I must break through my present idle habits & work at something — Afternoon I had quite a tea party, Sir A. Colvin, Mr. Grenfell,[126] Ld. & Lady Morris, Mr. Ball — Ld. M. says Rosebery is just like his horse Lades, they both began by winning the Blue Ribbon, one the Derby the other the Premiership — & neither has distinguished himself by doing anything since[127] — Father Healy, when Ld. Plunket was talking of the validity of orders, being asked "What should I do if two of your priests come to me for ordination?" "Make them take the pledge" promptly replied Father H. — When he found Matt D'Arcy arranging his library of books bought for

[119] William O'Brien (1852–1928), journalist, and Nationalist M.P. 1883–1918. Founder and Editor of the Parnellite newspaper *United Ireland* in 1880, activist in the Land War and co-author with John Dillon of the Plan of Campaign. Opposed Parnell after the O'Shea divorce trial, but remained a central figure in Irish politics as founder of the United Irish League, and as a key figure in the land conference which ushered in the Wyndham Act in 1903.

[120] John Bright (1811–89), Liberal statesman and noted orator. M.P. 1843–89, forceful advocate of Free Trade and the repeal of the Corn Laws, and strong proponent of Irish disestablishment.

[121] i.e. "easily first".

[122] John Morley (1838–1923), distinguished politician and writer. M.P. 1883–1908, and Chief Secretary of Ireland 1886 and 1892–95. Created 1st Viscount Morley, 1908. Biographer of Burke, Cromwell, Gladstone and other political figures.

[123] *The Spectator* 3 November 1894, pp. 614–15, a complimentary, if rather turgid, review. Frank Lawley's contribution to the *Athenaeum*, 10 November 1894, p. 178, noting inaccuracies in WHG's Greek, was a letter rather than a review.

[124] Mrs. Mary Emilia Hills, Mistress of the school.

[125] Rev. William Dodge, Vicar of St. Stephen's, Southwark. The Gregorys had also assisted him in charity work in his former parish, St. Mark's, Deptford, in the early 1880s.

[126] Henry Riversdale Grenfell (1824–1902), M.P. 1862–68, and Governor of the Bank of England 1881.

[127] Rosebery's horse Lades was Derby winner in 1894. Increasingly uncomfortable with his position, Rosebery resigned in June 1895 after just fifteen months as Prime Minister. Ironically, another of his horses, Sir Visto, won the 1895 Derby.

ornament which he called his "old friends" he said "I'm glad to see you don't cut them"![128] — Mr. Grenfell, who brought an introduction from Ly. A. Russell came to say that Ld. Carlingford would like some small alterations made re Ly. Waldegrave if there is a 2nd edition, but he is pleased with the mention of her on the whole[129] — I dined Sir G. Bowen to meet his brother & Sir C. Bulwer[130] — Poor old Bowen very shaky & repeating himself —

7th — To Newman St. & joined the drawing class[131] — began at the "Clytie"[132] & was surprised to find I could get it tolerably on to the paper — Lady Robinson & the Leckys & A. Gray called to know if little Dudley whose death in the hunting field was announced in the Times was a near relation[133] — Tea at John Gray's[134] where I talked to H. D. Traill — I was rather vague as to what he had written, but noticed he rather winced when I said John Morley was the best biographer of the day, & I find he has written some![135]

[128] This "Morris" anecdote is given in Maud Wynne's biography of her father *An Irishman and his Family*, p. 95. Father Healey, parish priest of Little Bray, Dublin, and a notorious wit, was a neighbour and frequent guest of Lord Plunket, Archbishop of Dublin (see p. 74 n. 45). Matt D'Arcy, a parishioner of Father Healy, was a wealthy distiller.

[129] Samuel Chichester Parkinson-Fortescue (1823–98), 1st Baron Carlingford, Chief Secretary for Ireland 1865–66, 1868–70. Married in 1863, as her fourth husband, Frances, Countess Waldegrave (d.1879), a close friend of WHG in the 1860s and a key figure in helping him gain the Ceylon Governorship.

[130] Probably Sir Henry Ernest Gascoyne Bulwer (1836–1914), diplomat and colonial administrator. Governor of Borneo 1871, Lt Governor of Natal 1875 and Governor 1882. High Commissioner in Cyprus 1886. Retired 1892.

[131] Most likely at Heatherley's, a teaching studio AG had first enrolled at in 1889.

[132] Either the 1878 sculpture by George Watts, or the 1892 painting by Lord Leighton, both of which were based on the legend of Clytie in *Metamorphoses*.

[133] *The Times* 7 November 1894, p. 5, reported the death of Colonel Dudley Persse of Belville in an accident while hunting with the Galway Hounds. Col. Persse (1839–94) was the sixth son of Burton Persse (d.1859), brother of AG's great-grandfather William Persse (d.1802).

[134] John Gray (1866–1934), Wilde's lover in the early 1890s, and rumoured at the time to be his principal model for Dorian Gray. Friend of Arthur Symons (see p. 118 n. 47) and frequenter though not member of The Rhymer's Club, Gray established himself as a poet with *Silverpoints* (1893), a volume now prized as the quintessence of 1890s design for its binding, typography and layout by Charles Ricketts. Gray turned increasingly towards Catholicism from 1894 onwards, and published a series of four Christmas "Calendars" from 1895–98 each containing twelve devotional poems for the year. AG was evidently a close enough friend to receive a copy of each of these privately circulated works, of which only 100 copies of each were printed. Her choice privately-bound copy of the Calendars (Berg) attests to her regard for Gray's work. Ordained in 1901, Gray served as curate and, from 1905 until his death, as parish priest of St. Peter's, Edinburgh, a new church built largely through the benefaction of his close companion André Raffalovich.

[135] Henry Duff Traill (1842–1900), journalist, critic, and biographer of Coleridge, Sterne and numerous political figures. Contributor to *The Daily Telegraph* 1882–96, Editor of *The Observer* 1889–91 and Editor of *Literature* 1897–1900.

8 — To Newman St. — Tea first with Miss Childers[136] & then with Sir A. Lyall, the first time I had seen him since his illness — He said Ld. Dufferin is put out at the story about Mrs. Norton & denies it, but that Spencer Walpole says it is absolutely true[137] — He also 'hears' Vaughan is alive still, I do not believe he is[138] — Then he by way of consolation said "the responsibility is not yours, as the Memoirs were so evidently written for publication" — I having so expressly stated they were not! Altogether I felt I brought away wounds from the house of a friend — Major Gregory[139] called & lost me a visit from Paul, who has been made private sec[retary] to Knox[140] —

9 — Newman St. — Called Lefevres[141] — Gerald & Jocelyn[142] to tea, the former with his arm in a sling having had his wrist cut open by a pane of glass brought down on it by a falling brick as he sat in the club — Then Henry James, whose visit is always benedictory & then Paul, the new private secretary — Then I ran round & dined with Lord & Lady Morris — The best & most tranquil evening I have had for a long time —

10 — To Elstree — Found Robert with all the boys at a football match, & spent the afternoon watching it, balanced on a board to save one's feet from wet

[136] Probably Milly Childers, Hugh Childers's daughter.

[137] By Sir William's account (*Autobiography* pp. 85–86), Sidney Herbert (1810–67), then Secretary for War, confided a secret decision by the Cabinet in December 1845 in favour of repealing the Corn Laws to his mistress Mrs. Norton (see below p. 49 n. 152), who, in return for a substantial cheque, promptly alerted *The Times*, which published the story on 5 December 1845. The betrayal shook the Conservative Government and led Peel to resign (though, with Lord John Russell's failure to assemble a consenting Cabinet when offered the Premiership, Peel in fact remained Prime Minister).

[138] WHG had fought a duel with a certain Captain Vaughan in 1851, following chicanery on Vaughan's part with regard to a horse Gregory had entered in the 1850 Ascot Stakes. Since duelling had by then been made illegal and carried the death penalty if a killing occurred, WHG, a crack shot, informed Vaughan that he would miss with his first shot, if Vaughan missed, but shoot to kill if a second were requested. Vaughan's shot narrowly missed Gregory who then "took deliberate aim, by way of giving [Vaughan] a comfortable moment, and . . . fired in the air" (*Autobiography*, p. 152). Vaughan then declined a second shot.

[139] Major Francis Hood Gregory of Styvechall (d.1909), last of the English branch of the Gregory family (for the history of which see Vere Gregory, *The House of Gregory*).

[140] Sir Ralph Henry Knox (1836–1913), Accountant-General of the War Office, 1882–97, and Permanent Under-Secretary of State for War 1897–1901. Harvey was shortly afterwards promoted to be private secretary to Lord Lansdowne (see p. 83 n. 90), Knox's superior at the War Office.

[141] George Shaw-Lefevre (1831–1928), Liberal M.P. 1863–85, 1886–95. Supporter of the North during American Civil War and a strong advocate of Home Rule. Married Lady Constance Morton (d.1929) in 1874. Created Baron Eversley in 1906.

[142] Dudley Jocelyn Persse (1873–1943), second son of Major William Persse. Met Henry James, whom he appears to have narrowly missed on this occasion, in 1903, and quickly became the focus of the novelist's intense affection, remaining an occasional but loyal companion until James's death.

grass — R. looked well, tho' not quite so plump as when he left Coole — We had tea with Mr. Wilson who speaks very well of him — All the masters seem kindly men, & I think my little manneckin is in good hands — He was told to bring a friend to tea & I was glad he chose his rival Barnes — Heavy rain came on as I was walking to the station & I got back late & wet —

11 — To Ch[rist] Church, Victoria St., very unsatisfactory — very empty, very full of millinery, green altar cloth, green markers, green banner — & the curate, who had greenish hair preached in green bands — on the means "to catch men" — a science he has certainly himself not mastered — Lunch Lady Dorothy's, where were the Frederic Harrisons,[143] H. H. Johnston, Sir H. Bulwer & Bret Harte,[144] who is quiet & modest & was much interested in hearing of the Isles of Aran — He says California is too civilised now for romance — F. Harrison has improved in appearance, his hair grown grey & has lost much of the "epicier"[145] look — H. H. Johnston, the little pocket traveller, quite charming, with his gentle quaint sayings & look of power — His hope is to colonize Central Africa with Indians — He spoke of the want of nurses but says he wd prefer male ones, as the "Sisters" want to flirt, & if you resist flirting & getting engaged to them they write books abusing you — He sent me afterwards his "unexpurgated" blue book to read — with some remarks about erratic missionaries which the F[oreign]. O[ffice]. had made him strike out[146] — Gerald & F. O'Hara[147] to tea & Paul came to dinner —

12 — To opening of Gibbon Exhibition at British Museum[148] — Grant Duff opened it & Frederic Harrison showed us the chief treasures — Rain came on, so I stayed to study the sculpture & Elgin marbles, & came to the conclusion that while the Greek debt is in such an unsatisfactory state it is a comfort to think we held on to the latter — Home to lunch, when I entertained Rose — Dined Raffy [Raffalovich], sat next H. D. Traill, who also talked to me all the

[143] Frederic Harrison (1831–1923), ardent pacifist and close ally of AG in protesting British policy in Egypt in 1882–83. President of the London Positivist Committee 1880–1905. His wife Ethel, née Harrison, d.1916.

[144] Francis Bret Harte (1839–1902), novelist and short-story writer. Established his reputation with works set primarily in California, but spent the last decades of his life in Europe, serving as American Consul in Germany 1878–79 and Glasgow 1880–85. Harte was during this period living openly in a menage à trois, and was consequently being blackballed by much of London society.

[145] i.e. "grocer".

[146] Johnston's Blue Book (Government publication, 1894) gives an account of the military expedition which under his leadership established of Nyasaland as a British Protectorate. In his autobiography (The Story of My Life, p. 286), Johnston recalled that even the sanctioned version of the publication "made a small sensation."

[147] Probably Fanny O'Hara, a cousin of WHG.

[148] An exhibition commemorating the centenary of the death of historian Edward Gibbon.

evening pleasantly enough — but I don't care for Raffy's parties & again resolve to abjure them —

13 — To Newman St., & stayed 3 1/2 hours, getting interested in finishing "Mercury carrying off Pandora" — Then A[rabel]la's commission — Home tired — Major Gregory — Dined Lyalls — Sir Alfred better —

14 — Terrific gale & rain all day, but at 5 I went with Mrs. O. Crawfurd to the Author's Club tea party[149] — met Hamilton Aide[150] & young Ives, Bness. Malortie's son! a most ingenuous youth — Dined with the Morrises, Lady M. & Maud went to the play, so I sat with Ld. M. & had a long talk, about E. O'Flaherty etc[151] — He told me exception was taken to my putting the story about Mrs. Norton in the book, but that he defended me on the right ground, that of its having already been published in "Diana of the Crossways"[152] — Also that Vaughan's widow is alive, which I did not know — and when I came home I found a letter from F. Lawley saying all S. Carolina will be up in arms about the tarring & feathering story,[153] & all the Foreign & Colonial Office about the Queen not having been told about the Ceylon appt[154] — However, "better the wounds of a friend than the kisses of an enemy"[155] —

[149] Oswald Crawfurd was at this point Chairman of the Author's Club.

[150] Charles Hamilton Aide (1826–1906), novelist, dramatist and inveterate society figure.

[151] Edmund O'Flaherty had acted as WHG's political agent from 1847 and gradually assumed a large role in managing his gambling debts. In 1854, O'Flaherty absconded to the United States after forging WHG's signature on numerous bills. In the court case which ensued, Gregory correctly distinguished between his own and O'Flaherty's signatures, and was acquitted of both complicity and responsibility for the debts. By WHG's account, O'Flaherty died in 1887 under the assumed name of Captain Stewart, following a colourful career in New York.

[152] Caroline Norton (1808–77), a grand-daughter of the playwright Richard Brinsley Sheridan, enjoyed considerable popular success as a novelist and poet. Widely regarded as the most beautiful woman of her era, she married Hon. George Norton in 1827, only to separate from him in a famous divorce case in which Lord Melbourne was cited as co-respondent. Her acrimonious court battles with Norton to gain control of her own literary earnings paved the way for the subsequent repeal of the Married Women's Property Act. After her divorce she led a colourful career as a literary and political hostess, marrying Sir William Stirling-Maxwell in 1877. Meredith's novel *Diana of the Crossways* features an incident based on the *Times* anecdote, and drew on Mrs. Norton as the principal model for its central character.

[153] During a tour of the U. S. A. and Cuba in 1859–60, WHG witnessed the tarring and feathering of a stonemason in Columbia, South Carolina, who had expressed anti-slavery views. Though he was to be strongly pro-Confederate during the Civil War, the spectacle shocked Gregory, who included a graphic description of the event in his memoirs (*Autobiography*, p. 199).

[154] WHG was apparently promised the Ceylon Governorship by Foreign Office Minister Lord Granville (1815–91), through Lady Waldegrave's influence, some two years before the appointment was made official. By WHG's account (*Autobiography*, p. 256), Granville insisted on the promise being kept secret "as her Majesty objected to any promise of such appointments being given without her first being consulted."

[155] *Proverbs* 27.6: "Faithful are the wounds of a friend; but the kisses of an enemy are deceitful."

15 — Gibbon lecture in the afternoon — Grant Duff spoke, & then F. Harrison who I did not think a sympathetic speaker[156] — I gave a little dinner in the evening, Grant Duffs, Leckys, Bret Harte, Lady Morris & Fischer Williams — It went off tolerably, but Lady G. D.'s dullness is poison — I don't think I will have more than 6 again that I may keep them all in hand myself!

16 — Lunch old Bowen — Then to see Sir F. Burton who is laid up with a bad foot — I saw H. Murray in the morning, & he said a second edition might be wanted any moment, so I must have corrections ready, so I went off to F. Lawley for his copy, in which he says he has marked 16 mistakes! but he wants it for the next day or two to write an article for Bailey's Magazine — We made friends & I withstood him about Carolina! — Found a note from Murray on my return, saying they had had another order during the day, which increases the probability of a reprint being required — so spent the evening over corrections.

17th — Was just going out when a messenger arrived with a note from Murray saying things were going so well that all corrections must be sent straight to the printer at Beccles on Sunday night! I went as usual to see Sir F. Burton, & then the Tennants where there was a fine accumulation of bores, Ly. Lyall, Ly. Hart[157] etc — Then Mrs. Lynn Lynton[158] — Dined at the Childers, only the O'Connor Don[159] & Sir Neville Chamberlain,[160] not very lively & I had a heavy influenza cold.

18 — A Sunday of rather hard work — I spent the morning over corrections as best I could, but F. Lawley who had promised me his marked copy wrote at the last moment that he wanted it — & besides I might not like to see the marginal notes he had written in it! Albert Gray sent me Ceylon corrections

---

[156] Grant Duff's speech and Harrison's following address were published in *The Transactions of the Royal Historical Society* 3rd Series, IX pp. 25–9, 31–48. Noting the occasion in his own diary, Grant Duff, in contrast to AG, judged Harrison's paper "quite admirable" (*Notes from a Diary 1892–1895*, vol. 2, p. 133).

[157] Hester, Lady Hart, née Bredon (d.1928), wife of diplomat Sir Robert Hart (1835–1911), 1st Bart.

[158] Eliza Lynn Linton (1822–98), novelist and journalist, and at this point a resident of Queen Anne's Mansions.

[159] Rt Hon. Charles Owen O'Conor, The O'Conor Don (1838–1906). Liberal M.P. 1860–80, and a staunch advocate of Home Rule, but left the Irish parliamentary party after refusing to take a pledge of loyalty to Parnell. At this point he was serving on the Irish Financial Relations Commission, chaired by Childers, which was examining charges of over-taxation of Ireland by Britain since the Union, and of which he would become Chair following Childers's death in 1895.

[160] Gen. Sir Neville Bowles Chamberlain (1820–1902), Commander of British forces in the Indian wars of the 1850s and 60s.

& I had been given others by various people — Lunched with the Robinsons, Sir Hercules said the book had kept him up for two nights till 2-00 —

I had, ever since reading Ld. Dufferin's memoir of his mother, felt some remorse at having published the story of Mrs. Norton, which I had before looked on as so far away, & so well known that there could be no indiscretion in publishing it[161] — And I had heard that "some people" said I should not have left it in — While sitting with Sir Frederic, I spoke of it, & he thought it ought to be modified, so on leaving him I went to Sir A. Lyall, & said the new edition had been called for, & that I was not happy about the Norton story — He said he had been just on the point of, in spite of his infirmities, coming to see me, on that very subject — He & Spencer Walpole had been examining it that morning & found discrepancies, & that it did not agree with the account in the Greville Memoirs — and Henry Reeve wd be sure to attack it in the Quarterly[162] — We did not think it could be left out, having no matter ready to take its place, & Sir A. tried to alter it but found that impossible — So we decided to leave out the cheque part, & to add a note, saying that so many discrepancies had been pointed out to me that I felt sure that if my husband had himself lived to revise his memoirs he wd have by enquiring into details have been led to doubt the truth of the story —

Then home, to meet Mr. Grenfell, with pages of amendments of Ld. Carlingford's to be inserted! Then came Paul to dine, & we were till nearly midnight trying to get the corrections into order, he correcting the classical mistakes — I was really ill by this time & all my bones aching — but we got the corrections off by post —

[161] Dufferin's "memoir" of his mother, prefixed to his edition of her poems, makes clear a connection AG had evidently been unaware of: Mrs. Norton had been his aunt, being second of the three famous "Sheridan sisters" of which his mother had been the oldest. See also p. 42 n. 106.

[162] Henry Reeve (1813–95), journalist for *The Times*, and from 1855 until his death Editor of *The Edinburgh Review*. Reeve had edited a multi–volume edition of *Greville's Journals*, the controversially candid political memoirs of Charles Cavendish Greville (1794–1865), an intimate of many prominent statesmen of his day, which bear extensively on Cabinet affairs at the time of the Norton case. The Journals make no mention of Mrs. Norton and attribute the "leak" to Lord Aberdeen, but their accuracy regarding many elements in the Repeal drama is certainly questionable. Reeve had a personal interest in defending his friend Greville's versions of events since he himself features in the pertinent passages. Despite AG's retraction of the anecdote, Reeve proceeded to refer acidly to its revival as "calumnious and unfounded" in an article on Meredith's novels in the January 1895 issue of the *Edinburgh Review*. And though Dufferin wrote privately to AG on 22 November (in response to an apologetic letter on her part) urging her to "dismiss the matter at once from your mind" (Berg) it was he who appears to have prompted Reeve's comments, writing to Reeve in late December, pointing out the revival and insisting on his ability to prove it erroneous (see John Knox Laughton, *The Memoirs of Henry Reeve*).

19 — A tremendously strong letter from Lecky by first post, on the Norton story — almost *commanding* its withdrawal — This would have made me wretched had I received it at first, when I did not know if there would be a second edition, or if I had taken no steps of my own accord — Directly after breakfast I went to Murrays, luckily John was there, that invertebrate Hallam quite in the background — He at first said it wd be impossible to make the omission altogether, but when I showed him Lecky's letter he said at once "We must leave it out" — to my great relief. We tried to fill the page in with a bit from the Greville Memoirs but found it impracticable, & then we settled to alter the paging of the chapters, & I added a note, withdrawing it — It is curious that Sir H. Layard tho' objecting to so many small & trivial anecdotes never made a remark on this —

Then I had to go to F. Lawley to find out what some of the mistakes noted by him were (chiefly very trivial) — He attacked the Greville Memoirs & said they gave a false account of his "ruinous episode" which was really the most creditable one of his life — & rapidly gave details, from which I gathered he had tried to screen his friend <?Pully> Glyn[163] — but I did not clearly understand either the story or the refutation — Back to Murray with these — Then to Sir F. Burton — & back to give Miss Dexter tea — such a nuisance & she asked me so many *prying* questions about Paul & his uncle — Then Albert Gray — till past 7 & then dressed in a great hurry to dine with the Grenfells & meet Ld. Carlingford — I was so depressed by the Norton episode I dreaded him, but he was very nice, thanked me warmly for the "tribute" to Lady Waldegrave published, but produced a long note to be inserted! chiefly clearing the character of one of his predecessors, Lord Waldegrave — This to my relief I found would be possible & rather interesting[164] — He says Northbrook tells an excellent story, the inaccuracy of which I forgive as it is so good — N. says I sent him a copy of the book, saying he might like to have it as some members of his family were mentioned in it (I really said because

---

[163] Lawley's disgrace is recorded in some detail in *Greville's Journal 1852–60* (entry for 4 August 1854), with Lawley's name deleted from the account. A prominent young M.P., and Gladstone's Private Secretary, he had been prospectively appointed Governor of South Australia when rumours arose that he had amassed huge gambling debts. (Greville does not mention the more damaging rumour, current at the time, that Lawley had used his position to advantage on the stock market in an effort to pay these debts). Though defended by Gladstone in the Commons (*Hansard's Parliamentary Debates*, 3rd series, CXXXV pp. 1226*ff.*), Lawley was forced to resign in disgrace. The Journal gives no support for Lawley's claim to have been screening a friend, but Glyn was probably his close contemporary and fellow Gladstone confederate, George Glyn (1824–87), later 2nd Baron Wolverton, M.P. 1857–73, Secretary to the Treasury and Gladstone's Chief Whip 1868–73.

[164] See *Autobiography* (2nd edition) pp. 255–56. George Edward Waldegrave (1816–46), 7th Earl, was Frances Waldegrave's second husband. The first edition describes him as "one of the most debauched, drunken rowdies of the day" and recounts how he spent a year in Newgate Gaol (accompanied by his wife) for his part in a manslaughter case.

[Sir] W[illia]m had been his guest at the Durbar which he describes) & that when he looked in the Index all he could find was "Bruiser Baring, card sharper"![165]

20th — To Ld. Carlingford for some alteration in his note, & to say I must say he had given it to me — at which he hesitated saying in that case he must examine into the facts more closely! He had no objection to *my* becoming responsible for them! However, I insisted — He showed me the portraits of Lady Waldegrave & spoke much of her — "You have no idea what life with her meant" & wished so much I had known her — I asked leave to publish the story of her rebuking Lord Normanby, but he thought it better not "though tempted" as he had never heard it & thought "it might lead to questions" — He is evidently feeble, & living on her memory[166] — In the evening (having with some little difficulty got Murray to again alter the page, which makes a delay) he sends me a quantity of further alterations to make! — To the Stores, for Robert's hamper, & to Sir F. [Burton] — And called on Mrs. Murray & found poor J[ohn]. M[urray]. there, who I thought wd have hated the sight of me, but they had just written to ask me to dinner — He says he has never known an author who has given away so many copies of his book as Lord Dufferin, which indeed I believe, having seen it on most tables — Home dead tired, read "The Manxman."[167]

21 — The usual round — Tired — Paul to dinner, very kind —

22 — Lunched with Knowles — He was astonished at my withdrawing the Norton anecdote, says it was quite true & she was a bad lot & he has not heard a single person object to it! But had I heard from the Vaughans? They were likely to object to the duel story — Voting for the School Board going on, great squabbling & excitement & much bad feeling over the 4th R., Religion — Sir Frederic, & Lady A. Russell, who asked me if *O'Flaherty's* family objected to the account of his misdoings! — Dined Leckys — He serene & kind, but I can't help feeling there is something a little artificial about him — Ld. Reay

[165] For the Durbar at Calcutta in 1876, at which Lord Northbrook was host of the Prince of Wales and many other notables, see *Autobiography* pp. 352–53. Northbrook (1826–1904), born Thomas Baring, was Viceroy of India 1872–76, and succeeded his father as 2nd Baron in 1866.

[166] Marriage to the influential Lady Waldegrave in 1863 had galvanized Chichester Fortescue's political career, quickly bringing him appointment as Chief Secretary for Ireland 1865–66 and 1868–70, in which position he was responsible for both the Irish Land Act and the Disestablishment of the Church of Ireland. After he was raised to the peerage as Lord Carlingford in 1874 it seemed only a matter of time before he would return to high office, but though he accepted appointment as Lord Privy Seal in 1880 at Gladstone's urging, Lady Waldegrave's death seems to have drained him of life and, prematurely aged, he soon withdrew from public life.

[167] Novel by Hall Caine (1853–1931).

white & shadowy — Earles[168] — Miss Shaw,[169] rather blatant, probably from association with Moberley Bell[170] — I wd say with The Times, but Sir D. Wallace[171] was also there, quiet & modest as ever — Also the Netherlands Minister & his wife, & at one time the conversation on one side of the table went on in Dutch![172] I was tired & rather depressed —

23 — As usual — But I had to go, with headache & pains in the bones, to open the sale of work at Southwark, Ly. Morris having failed — Made a short speech & bought something at each stall —

24 — Tried in vain for an "opener" for the sale, but had to go again, & buy the stuffed globe fish at £1-1/-. Coughed all night —

25 — Stayed in all day — to try & cure my cold. Gerald & H. Lane to lunch — Paul came, but cd not stay to dinner, & I had not courage to go up alone.

26 — Newman St, & Sir Frederic, & correcting more proofs — & Paul came & dined —

27 — To call on Mrs. F. Harrison, & lost my way getting to Argyll Rd.[173]

28 — Finished with Newman St., the Venus de Milo, which Mr. Crompton complimented me on — A dreary call on Mrs. Mansfield[174] & then Sir F. [Burton] — & then the Morrises who I stayed & dined with, & nearly persuaded Ld. M. to write an article, or dictate it, on the "Autobiography" for

[168] Probably Charles Earle (d.1897) and his wife Maria (d.1925). Maria Earle was one of the celebrated Villiers sisters, along with her sisters Lady Loch (see p. 102 n. 185) and Lady Lytton.

[169] Flora Shaw (1852–1929), protégée of W. T. Stead (see p. 174 n. 48) on the *Pall Mall Gazette* in the 1880s, and by the early 1890s Colonial Correspondent for *The Times*, she was a crucial figure in reporting African events in a manner favourable to her idol Cecil Rhodes. A star witness in the Jameson Raid Inquiry, she managed to defuse the most incriminating evidence against Chamberlain and Rhodes by her creative testimony (see Elizabeth Longford, *Jameson's Raid*). Married Colonel (later Lord) Lugard in 1902.

[170] Charles Frederic Moberley Bell (1847–1911), nemesis of AG during 1882–83 as he provided a staunchly Imperialist version of events leading up to and during the British annexation of Egypt in his capacity as Egyptian correspondent for *The Times* (a post he held from 1865–90). At this point Assistant Editor of *The Times* (1890–1908) and, along with Flora Shaw, providing a similarly Imperialist perspective on Cecil Rhodes's services to Empire in Africa.

[171] Sir Donald Mackenzie Wallace (1841–1919), Director of the Foreign Department of *The Times* 1891–99. His 1883 volume *Egypt and the Egyptian Question* had provided a relatively impartial version of Egyptian affairs during the period of annexation.

[172] Baron von Goldstein (1831–1901), Dutch Envoy to Britain 1894–1900. Lecky's wife, Elizabeth, née van Dedem (d.1912), was Dutch.

[173] Sir Frederic Burton's residence, at 43 Argylle Rd.

[174] Emma Mansfield, née Clay (d.1908), sister of Sir Arthur Clay and widow of Horatio Mansfield (d.1887).

the 19th Century —

29 — A fog — Wrote letters — & got to Argyll Rd. Called on Mrs. Humphrey Ward who is very proud of her son having gained the Balliol — I was able to congratulate her on this more sincerely than on the *il*legitimate success of her novels — "Marcella" in its eleventh thousand![175]

30th — Tried to draw one of Stevens's casts at S. Kensington[176] but failed & must try again — Sir F. [Burton] — & then to Holborn to Mrs. Craven[177] in answer to an urgent invitation — this was to ask me to help at their bazaar! I nearly cried but consented — Dined Murrays, a very pleasant dinner — I sat between Grant Duff & Evelyn Cecil,[178] & afterwards talked to Mrs. Lecky then to Lecky, then looked at some of the family treasures, MS of Ld. Byron etc[179] — then to Mr. Lidderdell who was in great spirits, the Baring affair having that very day come to a happy end[180] — Lecky prophecies I shall go on writing, says it is "like drink" — The Murrays rather in a state about my book, the 2nd edition can't be got out till next week, & they haven't a single copy left of the first — But it was their own fault for not having more confidence & starting it sooner —

[175] Mary Humphrey Ward (1851–1920), novelist, critic and historian. Niece of Matthew Arnold, she had married Humphrey Ward in 1872. Her repeated theme, that Christianity should forgo belief in the supernatural in favour of social missionary work, necessarily earned the distaste of AG, at this period deeply concerned with the loss of faith in her culture. Even at their first meeting in 1888 AG had "felt I was doing wrong in rendering homage as it were to a woman who had made herself a half contemptuous judge of Christ and a wholly contemptuous one of Christianity" (Diary, Berg). *Marcella* (1894) may have been particularly irritating to AG, as it narrates the crushing of a young woman's ambitions to use for social good the power she has attained through marriage to an older landowner, whom she respects but does not love. Ward's son Arnold Humphrey Ward (1876–1950) was a scholar at Balliol College, Oxford, where he was Chancellor's Prizeman, Craven Scholar, Newcastle scholar and took a double first. After serving as a correspondent for *The Times* 1899–1902 he entered politics and was an M.P. 1910–19, but failed to achieve further public success after his mother's death in 1920.

[176] Alfred Stevens (1817–75), sculptor, painter and designer. The cast (see diary entry for 10 December 1894) was a model for "Truth," from one the two pairs of figures "Truth and Falsehood" and "Valour and Cowardice" which form part of Stevens's major work, the Wellington Monument in St. Paul's.

[177] Florence Dacre Craven, wife of the Vicar of St. George the Martyr, Holborn.

[178] Evelyn Cecil (1865–1941), Barrister and politician. Assistant Private Secretary to his uncle, Prime Minister Lord Salisbury (see p. 85 n. 104), 1891–92, 1895–1902. M.P. 1898–1929, and created 1st Baron Rockley in 1934.

[179] AG describes some of the Murrays' literary treasures, collected principally by John Murray the second (1778–1843), the close friend of Byron and Scott, in *Seventy Years*, p.109.

[180] Rt. Hon. William Lidderdale [*sic*] (1834–1902), Governor of the Bank of England 1889–92. Lidderdale's prompt action in November 1890 in establishing a guarantee fund when the giant Baring Brothers banking house seemed likely to collapse from a mass of bad loans to Argentina was widely credited with having prevented a general collapse in the London markets. Final elimination of the guarantors' responsibilities was not completed until 1894.

[December] 3rd [i.e. 1st] — Fog — & headache, but got to Argyll Road, & dined with the Lefevres — George a little pompous — Lady Constance introducing no one, so that I only found at the end of the evening that Wemyss Reid[181] was there, who I should have liked to talk to — I had Mundella[182] next [to] me, & after dinner Frederic Harrison came and talked to me, very much pleased with the "Autobiography" which he has been reading — G. Lefevre said "This is a shocking party to have asked you to" — but I said having dined with Lecky & Grant Duff the night before I was covered with a film of respectability that would carry me through all dangers!

2nd — Lunched Ricardos & met Sir Horace & Lady Rumbold[183] — he not quite so depressed as usual — On to Sir F. [Burton] who entertained me with an account of the Treasury objecting to pay £1 he had given to the Blenheim butler when he went to inspect the pictures[184] — Home, to see Paul who is not very well — Dined Morrises expecting them to be alone — but they had asked Ld. Ashbourne & Sir G. Fitzgerald[185] to meet me — A pleasant evening enough, but I couldn't get at Ld. M[orris]. about the article I want him to write.

3rd — Drawing at S. Kensington & Sir F. [Burton] & visits, only saw Una Birch.

4 — Paul took me to dine at Previtali's, & to "Money"[186] — very nice & kind of him — but he was not well, & the play was dull enough.

[181] Sir Thomas Wemyss Reid (1842–1905), Editor of *The Speaker* 1887–99.

[182] Rt Hon. Anthony John Mundella (1825–97), M.P. 1868–97, and expert on trade legislation.

[183] Sir Horace Rumbold (1829–1913), 8th Bart. Envoy Extraordinary to Argentina 1879–81, Sweden and Norway 1881–84, Greece 1884–88, the Netherlands 1888–96, and Ambassador at Vienna 1896–1900. Married Louisa Crampton in 1881.

[184] In 1884, Burton had been the driving force behind the acquisition of 12 pictures from Blenheim, including an outstanding Madonna by Raphael, for the National Gallery. The Trustees had to obtain special Parliamentary approval for the purchase since the £70,000 paid for the Raphael was then highest sum ever paid for a painting and massively exceeded the Gallery's annual grant of £10,000. WHG had been a lone voice arguing against the payment of such a sum, and his misgivings were proved well-grounded when the Government subsequently insisted that its special appropriation for the work be repaid from the Gallery's regular grant over seven years, hence preventing any further acquisitions during that period.

[185] Sir Gerald Fitzgerald (1833–1912). Director-General of Accounts in Egypt 1879–85, and remembered by AG as being "good-humoured" in his disagreement with the Gregorys' views on Egypt: "He, like so many others, had received some kindness from my husband when a young man in Galway town, and he did not lose his temper ... [though] he would sometimes threaten to come in return and wave the green Land League flag at the gates of Coole" (*Seventy Years*, p. 38). Served as Accountant-General of the Navy from 1885 until his retirement in 1896.

[186] A five act comedy by Edward Bulwer Lytton, first performed in 1840. This production was at the Garrick Theatre, where it ran for 107 performances.

5 — Dined Morrises — Major Ross of Bladensburg arguing for Home Rule! & protection.[187]

6 — The chief event was tea with H. H. Johnston at the end of my passage[188] — His drawings beautiful & very interesting, & he himself such a modest tidy dapper little creature to rule so much of Africa! We sat at his little tea table & he poured tea from a little tea pot, & spread a little napkin over his knees lest any crumbs should fall — and on the walls were some rather terrible pictures of vultures & men hanged from the "tree of death" — I asked how he had taken first to Africa, & he said from his childhood he was interested in it, & wrote a story when he was about 9 which turns on adventures there — When he grew up he took to art & went through an artist's training, but his health was so bad he was sent abroad, to Tunis, which awoke all his desire for Africa again — He tried to get a Consulate, but he looked so ill & fragile that no one thought him worth getting a post for. Then he persuaded his father to advance him money (like the Prodigal Son) and set out for the Congo on his own account. When he came back he published his book on it, & easily got a publisher, whereas he had never before been able to find one — And he has stuck to Africa ever since & is as strong & well as possible. He hopes to be allowed to visit India on the way back, about renewing the Sikh contingent, & wants to go by Rome and Constantinople that he may see the Pope and the Sultan! Such great mind in little body! — He came back to my rooms & sat a long time, a most interesting talk into larger worlds.

7 — Mr. Pirkis, interviewer, came to see me from "The Lady" — I had at first objected to being interviewed but gave in for the sake of an extra advt. of the book, & also the hope of getting a good word said for Southwark — But I had taken the precaution of writing my interview & sending it to him beforehand, so hope to be spared vulgarity[189] — Hugh Lane to lunch —

8 — It has been too foggy all the week to draw — & the mornings are rather frittered in letter writing — 2nd edition out today, at last — I have been every day to Sir F. [Burton] — I found him reading "The Mill on the Floss" for the first time in spite of his intimacy with George Eliot — He says at the time it appeared he was much taken up with his art, & that her novels excited him so much that they threw him off his balance & stopped his work — He told me again the history of her marriage — Lewes, a clever witty man (tho' much her inferior) living in a half bohemian set neglected his wife a good deal — Then he was enraged at finding that she had been seduced by _____ . She promised amendment & he kept her on, but finding she broke her promise,

[187] Major John Foster Ross-of-Bladensburg (1848–1926), soldier and military historian. Chief Commissioner of the Dublin Metropolitan Police 1901–14.
[188] Johnston was a fellow resident of Queen Anne's Mansions.
[189] This interview was apparently not published.

he put her away altogether — Then, being devoted to George Eliot, who was alone & not much known, she consented to live with him — She had no religious scruples, but felt in the long run very bitterly the having cut herself away from social life — She was visited by great ladies when once famous, but cd hardly ever be persuaded to go into society[190] —

Mr. Cross had by his business capacity & hard work retrieved his own affairs & those of his family, & she had put her affairs into his hands for some time, neither she [n]or ~~Cross~~ Lewes understanding money matters — After the death of Lewes, Cross gave himself up entirely to her service, & being ordered abroad, she married him, there being about 20 years between them — Sir F. speaks enthusiastically of the charm of her conversation, & the expression of her eyes when she talked —

9 — Fog — & Ld. Morris wrote backing out of his article — Sir F. told me a story which I had heard before rather differently — it was told him by Lord Lytton — When Shuvaloff came to England he was anxious to see Gladstone informally & applied to a mutual friend (un petit Juif bien sale nommé Hayward) who said it could be easily arranged — & in a few days he had a letter signed "Laura Thistlethwayte", inviting him to dinner, to meet the G[rand]. O[ld]. M[an].[191]— He soon found however that Gladstone's ignorance of

---

[190] Burton first met George Eliot during her stay in Munich in early 1858, becoming fast friends with her and George Henry Lewes (1817–78), the philosopher, critic and historian of philosophy, with whom she was living. Lewes had married Agnes Jervis in 1841, with four sons being born to the couple by 1848. In 1849, a year in which Lewes was frequently away lecturing, Agnes became pregnant by Thorton Hunt. As an advocate of free love, Lewes accepted the situation with equanimity, continuing to work with Hunt as co-editor of *The Leader* and treating the illegitimate child as his own, but when Agnes again became pregnant by Hunt in 1851, he ceased to regard her as his wife. Unable to afford a divorce (and in any case lacking suitable grounds to petition, having initially condoned the relationship) Lewes remained legally married. His open relationship with George Eliot, which began in 1854, and became widely known when she took his name in 1857, scandalized Victorian society (then at the height of its fascination with and revulsion from the idea of the "fallen woman") not least since it represented a defiant challenge to, rather than merely transgression of, convention. Lewes and Eliot were consequently much ostracized, and lived largely abroad in their years together.

[191] Count Petr Andreievich Shuvalov (1827–89), Russian Ambassador to London 1874–79. Laura Thistlethwayte (d.1894), courtesan turned evangelist, first met Gladstone in 1865, and became his closest intimate (though not his mistress) from 1869 onwards. Representing a suitably ambivalent fusion of corruption and virtue renewed, she evidently appealed acutely to his desire to 'court evil' while doing good: Gladstone had long engaged in "rescue work"—covert encounters during which he would attempt to persuade prostitutes to reform, often followed by episodes of self–flagellation, indicative of the displaced eroticism and moral self-testing the encounters involved. The dinner referred to in Burton's anecdote probably took place on 8 December 1876, an occasion when Gladstone's diaries record his meeting both Shuvalov and a Mr. Hayward at Mrs. Thistlethwayte's house (*The Gladstone Diaries* ed. H. C. Matthew, IX, p. 176, and see also VIII, pp. *ciii–cvii* and *passim*). Mrs. Thistlethwayte's singular influence on Gladstone was widely known and the subject of much gossip in elite Victorian circles. AG had reported to Wilfrid Blunt in 1888 that Mrs. Thistlethwayte "has returned to Hampstead and drinks sherry all

Russia was so complete that there was no use in talking to him, he spoke of a town as a sect! so Mrs. T. came to the rescue & embarked them in a discussion as to whether arms or legs are of greatest use to us! Dined Gearys.

10 — Finished drawing Stevens's "Truth" at S. Kensington — Sir F. spoke of his appointment to the Gallery — He was persuaded to think of it by Boxall,[192] & consented, chiefly to save it from becoming an appanage of the R[oyal]. Academy — {He disliked the idea of becoming a cockshy for the Press} — He refused however to apply, & absolutely refused to send testimonials, though Boxall at Gladstone's request begged him to do so — Gladstone had a "scruple" against appointing him because he was not an Academician! He had quite put the thought out of his mind when one day a messenger arrived from the Treasury, just as he was going out, bringing him the offer — He had hoped, & been assured by Boxall he wd have time to go on with painting — but has never been able to touch a brush — The Gallery had needed a great deal of renovating — Many of the pictures were in a filthy state — Boxall had had two or three cleaned, but was so intimidated by the outcry in the papers that he had them rubbed over again with brown varnish! Sir F. waited till the arrangement of some of the rooms was being altered, then quietly had some cleaned, & no one was the wiser — And he certainly has taken a very independent position all through —

11 — (The same continued) — The Queen is supposed to have a grudge against the N[ational]. G[allery]. because the P[rince]. Consort once offered a collection of pictures he had bought at a sale to it, & as it largely consisted of rubbish Boxall ventured [to] propose making a selection from it, which was indignantly refused & the offer withdrawn — Immediately after Sir F.'s appointment he was sent for by Ld. Beaconsfield[193] (his appointment was about the last act of Gladstone's then Govt. & when Boxall went to see him at Downing St[reet] about some final arrangement he found him just preparing to go and resign office to the Queen at Windsor, & described his face as perfectly demoniacal) — There were some drawings left by Landseer

day and won't last long" (Berg). Abraham Hayward (1801–84), barrister, journalist and influential critic, was a key figure in encouraging AG to write *Arabi and his Household*, her first publication, and was a staunch ally during her efforts on Arabi's behalf in 1883. Though critical of Hayward's overbearing manner, and alluding directly to his "dingy" manner of dress in her 1895 article "Eothen and the Athenaeum Club" (see p. 65 n. 6), AG clearly regarded him favourably. The anti-semitic slur against him she includes here in French quotes Shuvalov rather than her own views. In *Seventy Years* (pp. 129–30) she attributes the statement directly, though disguising Shuvalov's identity by referring to him as "a Russian Lady".

[192] Sir William Boxall (1800–79), artist and Director of the National Gallery 1865–74.
[193] Benjamin Disraeli (1804–81), created 1st Earl of Beaconsfield 1876. M.P. 1837–76, Chancellor of the Exchequer 1866–68 and Prime Minister 1868 and 1874–80.

for sale, & he having been a royal favourite, the Queen had expressed a desire
they should be purchased by the N. G.[194] — The subject had already been
brought up at a meeting of the Board — Ld. Hardinge[195] had just been
appointed a Trustee & had tried to insist that this purchase should be carried
out in obedience to the Royal wish — "He misunderstood his position, &
having been Chairman of the Trustees of the B[ritish]. Museum where such
such a position carries weight whereas with us it is nothing, he tried to insist
on carrying his point — I absolutely refused, first on the ground that there
is no money granted to the N. G. for the purchase either of drawings or water
colours — in fact anything on paper — These belong to the British Museum's
dept — And secondly I refused to entertain the idea because it had been
proposed by Royalty — I thought it would be a very bad precedent & lead to
many evils if we allowed ourselves to be dictated to on matters of art by Royalty,
or Majesty itself" — Lord Beaconsfield then sent for him, & though more
courteously, conveyed to him the same request, to which he made the same
answer — "When I was leaving & Ld. B. was ringing the bell, I turned back,
& with courage that I am now astonished [at], I said 'I hope Mr. Disraeli that
we quite understand each other — It is quite impossible that I should
entertain this proposal' — Dizzy, slightly taken aback, answered civilly, &
never bore me any grudge as Gladstone wd have done, but always treated me
with great consideration & liberality in all matters connected with the
Gallery."

He spoke of the treatment of artists by Royalty — Some artists employed to
decorate a kiosk at Buckingham Palace returned the money given them, it was
so little — Tom Landseer the celebrated engraver was sent for to Windsor to
instruct the Queen & Prince Consort in etching which they had taken up —
He was shown into a room — & presently a flunkey arrived with a tray on which
was an etching plate — This he was requested to prepare & having done so
it was taken away, & he was sent a message that that was all that was required
of him, & either offered money or asked what his charge was — He shook off
the dust of the Castle from his feet absolutely fuming with rage[196] — A

[194] Sir Edwin Landseer (1803–73), the most popular painter of the mid–Victorian period,
specialized in sentimental and moralistic animal scenes. As Queen Victoria's principal "court"
painter in the 1840s and early 1850s, he was a frequent guest of the royal party during their
summers in Scotland from 1842 onwards. The sale in 1874 of works left following his death
realized nearly £70,000.

[195] Charles Stuart Hardinge (1822–94), 2nd Viscount, M.P. 1851–56, and Trustee (from
1876, Chairman of the Board) of the National Gallery 1868–94.

[196] Tom Landseer (1798–1880), elder brother of Edwin, and whose reputation was largely
grounded on his frequent use of his more famous brother's paintings as subject for his
engravings. For an account of this 1842 incident, when the elder Landseer accompanied his
brother to Windsor for a rapid demonstration of their respective skills, see Campbell Lennie,
Landseer: The Victorian Paragon.

sculptor was talking to P[rince]. Albert, who asked him if he knew Threep[197] — "Oh, Threep is a very good sculptor — and *cheap!*" — with a snap of the fingers — Carl Haag, who a was a favourite gave an amusing account of his first day at Balmoral[198] — He was summoned there to paint the Prince Consort, and was deposited on the road side by the coach, with his portmanteau — At last he found someone to carry the latter, & having enquired his way proceeded on foot to the Castle — Next morning he was sent for by the Prince who said "As I shall not be able to sit till tomorrow, I would like you to paint my two new dogs" — These were accordingly sent for & he began to draw them — He was presently interrupted by a message that the Queen wished to see him, so he took off his painting garb, put on his frock coat, & was ushered to the garden where her Majesty informed him that a photographer having arrived to do some groups, she thought he might help in the arrangement of them — He proposed a couch, & H. M. thought this an excellent idea & sent for one — But it never arrived, as no one could be found whose business it was to bring couches to the garden — So at last some groups were done without it, & then the Queen asked if he wd like to go & sketch during the afternoon at Glenaquoich(?) & a pony wd be put at his disposal — Glad to escape, he set out on his pony with sketch book etc, when he heard a shout "Mr. Haag" — & looking back saw a flunkey who said the Queen wished to see him again — So he dismounted & came in, took off his riding things & again got into the frock coat, & was taken to the drawingroom where Her Majesty received him with "Why Mr. Haag I thought you were at Glenaquoich" — "I was starting but was told your Majesty wished to see me" — "Who said I wished to see Mr. Haag?" — There was consternation in the royal circle & at last it was discovered that there had been a discussion on some subject & she had said "If Mr. Haag were here he could tell us all about it" & some officious person had rushed off & sent for him[199] — Dined with Lady Morris & Maud —

12th — Dead tired after Argyll Road & Holborn bazaar. Dined Mrs. Kay —

[197] Frederick Thrupp [*sic*] (1812–95), sculptor who executed work for the House of Lords and other public buildings.

[198] Carl Haag (1820–1915), watercolourist, resident in England from 1847. An account of his career as a "royal" artist, and numerous reproductions of his Highland paintings are included in Delia Miller, *Queen Victoria's Life in the Scottish Highlands*. Victoria ended her patronage of Haag in 1865 on the grounds that his charges were too high. Haag responded by demanding (and obtaining) a copyright payment when she included engravings from four of his paintings in her 1868 book *Leaves from the Journal of Our Life in the Highlands*.

[199] This kind of experience was suffered even by favoured artists such as Landseer, whose correspondence frequently registers irritation at the demands of his royal hosts. Glen Quoich, Invergary, home of Landseer's lifelong friend and patron of artists, Cabinet Minister Edward Ellice (1781–1863), was a frequent site for painting excursions by royal favourites, and a scene from the valley forms part of the background of one of Landseer's most famous works, "The Monarch of the Glen". Glen Quoich was a full day's ride from Balmoral, however, and Haag's destination was more likely the Duchess of Bedford's encampment at Glen Feshie.

Sat between Billy Rogers[200] & Canon Milman[201] — poor H. H. Johns[t]on opposite between Miss Drummond[202] & Ly. C. Lefevre — & I had G. Lefevre all the evening — The only interesting thing he told me was that John Morley said to Ld. Rosebery "I should like to review your 'Pitt' " — "Then why don't you do it?" — "If I did you would probably never speak to me again!"[203]

13th — Mrs. Craven's brother in law at Holborn bazaar told me he had been at Toulon last year when a fête was going on to celebrate the re-capture of Toulon from the English — Mr. Wm. Saunders M. P.[204] & some other radicals there drew up a document, setting forth their regret that England had ever meddled there, & taken a place which had not belonged to her — This caused much amusement, & on the fete day they appeared with tricolour rosettes in their button holes — & were mistaken for members of the Salvation Army! —

15th — Robert came from Elstree — Corney Grain[205] —

16th — Westminster Abbey — Lunch Sir H. Robinson's — Then to see Sir Frederic, & then Sir A. Lyall, the first time I had seen him since his operation — looking worn & wasted & very much depressed, feels it a break & his life over — & suffers from lack of faith in anything —

17 — Shopping with R. — Lunched with the Duchess of Bedford & Lady Somers,[206] who took Robert out "to have a good look at him" & gave him £1 — We bought toys for Xmas tree.

[200] William Rogers (1816–96), Queen's Chaplain, Prebendary of St Paul's 1862–96, and a prominent educational reformer.

[201] Rev. William Henry Milman (1825–1908), Minor Canon of St. Paul's. Son of the eminent divine Henry Milman (d.1868), who had been Dean of St. Paul's.

[202] Emily Drummond, Mrs Kay's sister.

[203] *Pitt*, a political biography of William Pitt "the younger" (1759–1806), who became Chancellor of the Exchequer aged 23 and Prime Minister at 24, was published in 1891 as part of the Macmillan "Twelve English Statesmen" series, of which Morley was editor. The story is somewhat exaggerated, for though Morley was critical of Rosebery's style, he freely acknowledged the essay-like vigour of the work, and its clear popular success (see Robert Rhodes James, *Rosebery*).

[204] William Saunders (1823–95), founder and proprietor of the Central Press (which became the central News Agency in 1890), and its manager 1884–95. M.P. for Hull 1885–86 and for Walworth 1892–95.

[205] Corney Grain (1844–95), popular singer, story–teller and comedian.

[206] Virginia Somers (1827–1910), widow of the 3rd Earl Somers (who had died in 1883) and mother of Adeline, Duchess of Bedford. One of the celebrated seven Pattle sisters, Virginia was a noted beauty, drawing sincere tributes well into her old age.

18 — Had a busy day — Lunched Haliburtons,[207] sitting next Arthur Cecil,[208] very gouty & sorry for himself, & complaining that a remedy he tried to keep his hair on is turning it yellow — Then to see Lady Lindsay & to say good bye to Sir F. Burton — Robert meanwhile at the Birchs — Dined Beaumonts[209] — & it was a pleasant farewell to my London visit — Grant Duffs — F. Harrisons — Ld. Ashbourne — G. D. says Klein had been finally sent out of the Church of Rome by the Pope's last encyclical, on Scripture & Science[210] —

19 — Took Robert to be photographed by Mr. Cameron who gave him a photo of Lady Somers's picture[211] — Dined Morrises — home to find Richard[212] waiting for us — Then packing, & the wind howling — Set out at last & had a wretched journey, crowded train, rough crossing, late for mail train, went on to Galway to lunch at the Croft instead of waiting at Athenry — Home at 7 — after 23 hours en route!

21 — A wretched day of headache, but the boys all right — Poor Coole looks dreary — but I feel it my right place, & must try to stay on & do my best by it.

[207] Sir Arthur Lawrence Haliburton (1832–1907), War Office official 1869–95, and Permanent Under-Secretary of War 1895–97. Raised to the peerage 1898. His wife, Lady Mariana Haliburton (d.1919), had previously been married to Sir William Clay, 2nd Bart., (brother of Sir Arthur Clay and of WHG's first wife, Elizabeth) who had died in 1876.

[208] Arthur Cecil (1851–1913), youngest son of the 2nd Marquess of Salisbury, and uncle of Evelyn Cecil.

[209] Wentworth Beaumont (1829–1907), created 1st Baron Allendale 1906. M.P. 1852–92. Married Edith Pomeroy-Colley, née Hamilton (d.1927), his second wife, in 1891.

[210] *Providentissimus Deus* (18 November 1893), guidelines for Biblical research issued by Pope Leo XIII (1810–1903).

[211] Henry Herschel Cameron, son of the renowned Victorian photographer Julia Margaret Cameron (1815–79). Cameron ran a portrait studio at 70 Mortimer St., London, from c.1885–95, and at 31, George St., Hanover Square, from c.1896–1905. Photographs of RG by Henry Cameron dating prior to this 1894 session survive (see Illustrations). Henry Cameron's brother Hardinge had served as WHG's Private Secretary in Ceylon in the early 1870s, a post which apparently owed something to Gregory's friendship with Lady Somers (Julia Cameron's sister), and the family connection had continued until WHG's death. Julia Cameron's work was at this point enjoying a renewed vogue, in part through the 1893 publication of *Alfred, Lord Tennyson and his friends,* a series of her finest portraits (and including an introduction and some photographs by her son Henry), and following the first retrospective exhibition of her work (again including some photographs by Henry Cameron), mounted in 1889.

[212] Richard Persse (b.1879), fourth son of AG's brother Edward.

1895

The Croft. March 11 1895.

The Xmas holidays went off well & happily — Two of the Elstree masters, Richardson & Sanderson came for a fortnight & seemed to enjoy the shooting, which they had every day — I was glad it shd not be wasted as we cd not let it, & good workers rather than idlers shd have so pleasant a holiday, & they have been kind to Robert — In themselves they were not interesting, & Mr. Sanderson's unpunctuality & want of manners rather trying —

Gerald at Ashfield *all* the time! Arthur & Katy came for the woodcock shoot — She is bright & has a pretty manner — I hope it may turn out well — Ethel also came — Robert took very much to shooting — In the evenings chess & "Quentin Durward" & "Westward Ho!"[1] were in favour — Then, on Jan[uary] 21 they left — I found Ethel was anxious to go home for a holiday, & to see her family — so I offered myself here in her place till the end of March —

The weather has been terribly severe, a very heavy snowfall & long frost, the roads everywhere impassible for a long time — I was sorry not to be at home to look after the people — but wrote to the doctor to order blankets etc at my expense when wanted — & gave old Farrell a suit of warm clothes, & others money, & subscribed to the Gort coal fund — & I think they got on pretty well —

I have been rather sorry for myself here! The old burden of Lime Park[2] — & the perpetual talking of servants & food & what "Madell says" — & the drives

---

[1] *Quentin Durward* (1823), a novel by Sir Walter Scott. *Westward Ho!* (1855), a novel by Charles Kingsley.

[2] AG's mother repeatedly changed her Will during the 1890s to reflect her swiftly-changing displeasure with her children. Mrs. Persse eventually left Lime Park, an estate of 530 acres neighbouring Roxborough, her most substantial asset, to AG's brother Henry.

daily to Gallagher, MacNamara, Cloherty & Lipton[3] — & the dirt & disorder, all trying — And I got a sort of fever for some days which left me weak — I am better now March has come (in spite of its sad anniversaries![4]) for I can think, *next month* I will be at home, & see R. again — He writes cheerily always, & I hear nothing but good of him — There are some ecclesiastical quarrels going on — Mr. Berry[5] has lessened the size of the napkin over the "elements" — & Mr. Mack the hotel keeper refuses to come to the Sacrament till it has reached the proper size again — In his sermon yesterday he said "I suppose there is not one person in this church who does not accept every direct statement of the Scripture as absolute truth" — I wonder if I shall ever hear that said in a London congregation!

I have read through my old diaries of all these years — very sad reading — yet I am glad I kept them — I have been writing an article on "Eothen & the Athenaeum" & am not sure if it is too personal for publication[6] — I brought in the pieces of wood sent me from Ceylon, hoping to get a bookcase made for Robert — But Donohoe is too "drinky" — & made a gr compliment of doing up an old chair for me — said "he wd not do it for everybody there are so many cantankerous people about" — & Rippingham told me *he* was the only man in Galway who cd make it, but his wife said "Yes, but it 'ud take him seven years" — & the Industrial School carpenter cd not take anything so elaborate — & the Technical one has his hands full — so I was nearly in despair when Frank recommended one called Simon, & he has set to work & I hope will make a good job of it —

I am beginning to sketch "The Stones of Galway" — When I can escape from Gallagher & Macnamara! — I have been reading Froude's "English in Ireland" which has opened my eyes to the failings of landlords, & I may say of *all* classes in Ireland in the past,[7] & makes me very anxious to do my duty & to bring Robert up to do his —

March 29 — My last day at the Croft!! — I am only sorry to leave the birds, two blue tits come every day to be fed, & chaffinches & robins & sparrows — I have read Balfour's "Foundations of Belief" & was disappointed — He says well that there are many wide spaces where Science is silent — & that we should be very unwilling to give up any portion of the fair inheritance (of Faith) left to us by

---

[3] Respectively a butcher, wine merchant, ironmonger and tea seller in Galway City.

[4] "This month of dates—4th [1880] my marriage—6th [1892] my husband's death—15th [1852] my birthday" (*Journals* vol. 2, p. 400).

[5] Rev. James Fleetwood Berry, Rector of St. Nicholas's, Galway.

[6] This article, about historian Alexander Kinglake (d.1891), author of the acclaimed Eastern travel volume *Eothen,* and the circle of friends he and WHG had shared at The Athenaeum, was published in *Blackwood's Magazine,* December 1895, pp. 797–804.

[7] *The History of the English in Ireland in the Eighteenth Century* (1873–74), by James Anthony Froude.

our fathers — Yet he testifies by his own vagueness to how little of that inheritance is even now left to us[8] — I felt it wd drive readers to the Pope or General Booth[9] or anyone who holds conviction — & am rather confirmed in this view by Edward Martyn's delight with it — he holding that conviction already —

Yesterday we drove to Spiddal to see the new house, now nearly finished — Lady Morris, Martin & Eileen[10] there — Martin has begun canvassing Galway by making a speech at the Jury in favour of Galway as a packet station[11] — The Bishop has not spoken to him on the subject, but told me that he would be glad to see him in as what Galway wants is the development of industries & material help — but that he could not support him against a Home Ruler as he must "go with the times" — but will not allow him to be denounced by the priests —

Martin had all the gossip about Julia Peel's engagement to Mr. Maguire — He has been absolutely fascinated & devoted to her for two years, but she let him dangle, but would have taken any other good offer in the meantime — However none turned up, & Cecil Rhodes before he left England took her for a walk, & said she was running the chance of losing one of the best men in the Empire — He went out to Africa with £30 in his pocket & has now put by £250,000 — & manages all the S. African companies — He is small, quiet, just tolerated by Julia — Is to give up Parnellism & probably politics[12] —

The Speaker's resignation has come as a great surprise even to his own family[13] — With all his graciousness, they say he hardly speaks to his children — he was so wrapped up in his wife that he never made friends with them —

April 8 — Came back to Coole on the 1st — delighted to be at home & free again — The house in good order — Some of the larch in nutwood a good deal nibbled, but what was last planted, & that in Bull park[14] not touched —

[8] Arthur Balfour's *The Foundations of Belief: Being Notes Introductory to the Study of Theology*, published Febuary 1895, an urbane manifesto arguing for theism, in which Balfour ultimately acknowledges the bankruptcy of his efforts to reconcile rational and non-rational sources of belief.

[9] Rev. William Booth (1829–1912), founder and Commander-in-Chief of The Salvation Army.

[10] Eileen Elizabeth Morris (d. 1924), youngest of the Morris daughters, later a Carmelite nun.

[11] Morris adressed the Galway City Grand Jury (of which he was a member) on 20 March. For a report see *The Galway Express* 23 March, p. 3.

[12] Julia Peel's marriage to Rhodes confederate James Rochfort Maguire (1855–1925), Parnellite M.P. for N. Donegal 1890–92 and for West Clare 1892–95, took place on 24 April. Maguire did indeed give up politics.

[13] Peel announced his intention to resign on 9 March, and made his valedictory speech in the House of Commons on 8 April.

[14] Pairc-na-tarav ("the bull field"), one of the seven woods of Coole.

They are annointed with Dickson's "preserver" which seems good — "Mike John" is installed as keeper[15] — an addition to expense, but it is cheerful to see him about with dogs (Jap & Rover) & gun — & it was necessary to have some one to look after the woods — He has detected 4 lads from Gort cutting down & carrying off trees from Inchy, & summoned them last Saturday — but the summons server Mr. Glynn who does not want to quarrel with his neighbours did not appear to prove the service when wanted — & then there was a long case between a Diveney & a Donoughue who had quarreled the day after Patrick's Day (which seems to need no other explanation) & then the magistrates, Mr. Bagot[16] & Mr. Pery[17] went to their lunch which lasted an hour — & then A[rch]. D[eacon]. Daly[18] informed Mike the case was adjourned — & then he went to take a cup of tea with Mary — & while there a policeman called him back — & said it was coming on — however it was finally adjourned for a fortnight, no one in this country being in a hurry!

There has been a little trouble with Hanbury, who, or his mother, owed one & a half year's rent — He promised to pay a year, but then backed out, & Frank had his jennet seized — He wanted to get it back on the ground of the debt being his mother's, not his, but Frank had spared the mother's cow, & wd not give in, & it was put up for auction & he only bid 11/- for it — so Mike brought it back here, & shut it up in the stable — & then he & Mike John had to sit up at nights in the loft, lest there shd be a rescue! Today, Hanbury came again, having I hear in the meanwhile tried to "take the law of us" but failed — He says his mother is giving him up the land & that he will now get on all right, so I consented to his taking the jennet, in consideration of paying a 1/2 year's rent in May — So we parted, & to my gr joy the jennet has raised the seige!

Then came Mrs. Pat Corley with a long story of a projected lawsuit with the Quins about a right of way, & wanting a letter to the magistrate — or the lawyer — or anyone in fact — & a pair of boots to take her little girl to Court — I preached peace and arbitration, refused the loan for the boots — but promised to give a pair & also the £1 already spent on the lawyer in case of an arrangement —

I am anxious this week about Robert going up to Harrow for the scholarship exam — His masters speak so well of him I sometimes think he must get one — & then I remember his little careless ways, & the excitement he will be in about going home — & hope dies —

---

[15] "Mike John" Dooley, AG's principal groundsman at Coole for more than three decades.
[16] John Christopher Bagot (1856–1935), J.P. for Co. Galway, and a resident of Gort.
[17] The Hon. de Vere Pery, Resident Magistrate, of Kinvara.
[18] Ven. Henry Varian Daly, Dean of Gort. In 1872–74, Daly had been minister at Killinane, the church attended by AG during her Roxborough years.

J. Morley last week in his speech on the Land Bill quoted from the "Autobiography" the account of the Kinvara tenants, & spoke of Wm. as one who had never been a harsh landlord.[19] I feel that this Land Bill is the last of "Dobson's Three Warnings" & am thankful that we land owners have been given even a little time to prepare & to work while it is day — It is necessary that as democracy gains power our power should go — & God knows many of our ancestors & forerunners have eaten or planted sour grapes & we must not repine if our teeth are set on edge — I would like to leave a good memory & not a "monument of champagne bottles" — & with all that, I hope to save the *home* — the house & woods at least for Robert.

15th — All Tuesday & Wednesday I was miserably anxious about R. & his exam — not altogether lest he shd fail, but that the strain of two such long days wd be bad for him — & then if he failed there wd be nothing at all gained to make up — & if he won, it wd not be worth the sacrifice of health. Tuesday was not so bad, for I drove to Kinvara with Frank who went to inspect the castle of Dungora which E. Martyn wants to make safe[20] — & I sketched — & the drive was nice — On my return, first came Father Fahey then Mrs. Martyn[21] then the Roxboro' girls — Next day I was alone — & took down & mended the breakfast room chimney border, & was out till dark cutting ivy — & cd not read, or sleep at night — Thursday I thought if there was any good news I should have a telegram before 10 — but none came — & each time I passed the front windows I looked out in vain — At last at 11-20, just as I was going to start to meet R. I saw "Johnny from Gort" coming to the door — I had not courage to go down, but stayed on the stairs, & Marian[22] brought me 3 telegrams — looking scared — "Gregory first classical scholar — Heartiest congratulations" was Mr. Sanderson's — & there was one from Harrow & one from Mr. Richardson, & all had arrived in Gort before 10 & been delayed there — I was quite upset by the reaction & relief, & Marian rushed down & told "Johnny from Gort" who calmed me by demanding something extra for

[19] *Hansard's Parliamentary Debates*, 4th Series, XXXII, pp. 741–42 (2 April 1895). Besides the Coole and Kiltartan estates, WHG had inherited considerable acreage at Kinvara, eight miles to the west of Coole. He sold this and other outlying properties in 1857, when settling the bulk of his racing debts. Although most of the tenants on the land he sold took out long fixed leases prior to the sale, at his urging, to ensure their future security under a different landlord, the Kinvara tenants did not do so. After the sale the rapacious new owner raised rents substantially, and "killed the goose for the golden egg, [for] the town of Kinvara was all but ruined, and all the best tenants ran away" (*Autobiography*, p. 129)

[20] Dunguaire Castle, on the shores of Kinvara Bay had at one time been part of the Gregory estate. Built on the site of the royal rath of King Guaire, fabled for his generosity and lavish feasts, the restored castle is now, appropropriately enough, a banqueting centre.

[21] Annie Martyn, née Smyth (d.1898), Edward Martyn's mother.

[22] Marian McGuiness, AG's long-serving parlour-maid, who replaced the drunken Elizabeth in 1893 and was a key figure in the Gregory household until debilitated by a stroke in 1927.

bringing good news, & also that I shd forgive his son who is one of the tree-cutters in Inchy — Then to the station — where I greeted my little mannekin with the news when he stepped out safe & sound, rosy, & more solid looking than usual — pleased to hear of his success, but much taken up with "Croft" who had met him at Athenry —

Many congratulations ever since — Dr. Welldon writes that he passed "a brilliant examination" — Mr. Bowen that he was "clearly first — some of the Greek was too much for him, but his Latin excellent, the Latin verses capital" — & Mr. J. Sanderson writes that he hears the Latin verses carried the day, the last stanza especially being super excellent! And the little creature is as merry as if he had never opened a book, romping with Croft & Jap and China & making acquaintance with Rover — & today making a kite — & he is as obedient & affectionate as ever — each time I wonder if he ever *can* have such happy holidays again — Easter Sunday we went to the Workhouse after church with tobacco for the old men, oranges & sugar stick for the children — & the remains to the old women! & there was a poor little smiling mite, Thomas Corless from Kinvara, who had fallen over a stone wall & was much injured — We gave him what we could, & again this morning drove in to see him & brought him the kangaroo game & other toys — & sweets etc — & I left £1 for him to take home — I have been in a very liberal mood since R.'s return — so much the better for the people's seed potatoes!

And after all my tortures during the 2 days exam — I find it was quite thrown away, as R. enjoyed himself extremely, the morning drives to Harrow & seeing racquets played for the first time — & says "when you got interested in the work the time simply flew & the 2 1/2 hours of Latin verses seemed like 20 minutes" — He was evidently not nervous, & not the least intimidated by being marched into a small room with Dr. Welldon & 2 other masters, & asked to define such words as "plagiarism" which he did not know & "demur" which he defined as "to object to a thing, not want to do it, a sort of shirking" — He also acquitted himself well in the subjects of the Waverley novels — but could not give the reasons for the Disestablishment of the Welsh Church!

16th — Mary Rourke, for clothes to go to America — so some of those I got from the Galway sewing class came in useful, supplemented by 5/- & an order on Sheehan for £2 — Robert very much taken up making a new kite, that of yesterday having flown away — This is an improved one with pink eyes, gold spectacles & a brown paper beard — He shot a rat last night & is now trying for a pigeon — Diveney has been to Galway to see his daughter & says she is middling content with the Infirmary now, but that the first day she went in she was put to sleep in a ward as high as the top of that tree, & 4 corpses walked out before her — & she told the Dr. next day she would go straight home, & then he put a little girl with her that has the same complaint Johnny Quin of

Kiltartan had last year — & then she was satisfied to stay — Mrs. Grubb[23] called — Says a woman in George St. Gort who had married a widower was at last induced to lay the ghost of his first wife who kept troubling her by appearing by killing a cock & sprinkling her pillow with it — but it was not successful — she died.

Ap[ril] 30 — Left Coole, after a very bright open air holiday — R. low at leaving, I dead tired, & a storm getting up, which we encountered in its full force at night — I had never suffered so much on that journey or been so knocked to pieces — R. not so bad, & able to give me a helping hand, & we got some sleep & were better when we got to London — but by some mistake the rooms were not ready, & it was very wretched sitting amongst tubs & sweeping brushes until we cd get some breakfast — Then I unpacked while R. ran across the Park to see Paul & [Fischer] Williams & then we went first to the Stores & then to Cheapside in search of a cricket bat — not however to be taken to Harrow — as that is "swagger" but to be left in my charge till sent for — Then clothes etc — & then, in a scrimmage to Baker St. — without R.'s bags & missing the train we aimed at — by carelessness of the Qmansion people — Poor R. looked a little downhearted at making such a plunge into the unknown — & tho' he met 2 or 3 boys he knew they were also low & did not seem particularly glad to see him — & I was put out because they were so smart & he a little worse for the journey & general wear — I came back sad enough to my empty rooms — but found Paul waiting for me — kind & affectionate & his visit helped me — & then having dined off 2 cucumber sandwiches I very gladly turned into bed —

May 2 — Much rested — To Durrant re clothes — & Mann's for a hat — & looked in at Lady A. Russell's, & heard particulars of Clara Grant Duff's engagement — Mr. Jackson is a business man[24] — (I wish I could introduce him to Archie Grubb who called in the morning to know if I cd help him into a business house for a year to qualify him for the Union Bank) but was at Balliol, & thus in her estimation not poetic enough, he plays the piano — & has a very good head — Then to see Sir F. Burton who I found much restored — He gets to the Athenaeum every day so is off my mind — Then to see Lady Robinson, who burst into tears, & says going to the Cape will kill her & she hates it — & that what she feels so much is Sir H. not having consulted her or thought of her feelings — & that he has given up £4000 a year to go — so it is loss of income — & will kill them both — Then in came Sir H. — & asked sarcastically if she had been turning on the waterworks, & said "the best of

---

[23] A Gort neighbour. For AG's efforts to assist her son Archie, see p. 72 n. 39.

[24] Frederick "Fritz" Huth Jackson (1863–1921). For Clara Grant Duff see p. 9 n. 34 and p. 19 n. 103. The couple married in May 1895 (see p. 73) and became AG's lifelong friends. Jackson was subsequently Director of the Bank of England.

going out was — that Lady R. was so pleasant about it" — He is I think low about going & no wonder — especially after the attacks made on him by the Times & Spectator[25] — but says he was asked in a way he could not refuse — Just as he came in a message arrived from Ld. Clinton[26] saying the Queen wished him to dine & sleep at Windsor on Saturday — so I asked Lady R. to dine with me — & he showed me down — asking me to speak seriously to her about the way she was talking & the annoyance she was giving him & that if she talked like that at the Cape it wd be fatal — so there is a skeleton in that cupboard. Back just in time to receive Paul who came to dinner — He says Capt. Percy is torturing the War Office with his newly invented combined spade & pick, which he wishes to have adopted by the British Army — When Paul showed him that the spade digs into your ribs, he said it would be quite easy to remove it — leaving the invention a common garden pick!

3 — To Academy Private View — a fine day, & I enjoyed seeing so many people & hearing voices again — Of the pictures I was struck by Sargent's portrait of Coventry Patmore[27] — & liked Millais' S. Stephen & "Disciple"[28] — I met Lady Reay, the Humphrey Wards — Lady Lindsay — H. Aide & the Tennant party — lots of friends & acquaintances — Lady Haliburton congratulated me about R. & said it was his *mother's* talent coming out — & I said no, it was like the book, I took no credit I had only edited both — & Billy Russell took off his hat with a low bow & cried "Bien dit"! Then I went to lunch with Sir John Pender[29] who looked happy sitting between 2 Marchionesses, Dufferin & Tweeddale — Lady Selkirk[30] also there — & Bayard[31] & Ld. Tweeddale[32] & a

[25] *The Times* had reported on 28 March that an Opposition motion had been carried in the Cape Parliament recommending against Robinson's reappointment as Governor of South Africa on the grounds that he was too closely identified with Rhodes and the De Beers Company to be an impartial administrator. These charges were repeated in *The Spectator* on 30 March. An editorial in *The Times* on 30 April launched a new attack on Robinson, directly blaming his failure to establish border security forces in Swaziland for recent Boer incursions and the vagueness of official boundaries of British influence in the region.

[26] Lord Edward Pelham-Clinton (1836–1907), groom-in-waiting to Queen Victoria 1881–94 and Master of the Royal Household 1894–1901.

[27] Two portraits of Patmore by John Singer Sargent (1856–1925) were exhibited at the Royal Academy in 1895. Three-quarter face and profile sketch, the two works were completed (along with a third, front face) in September 1894. The profile sketch has consistently been regarded as one of Sargent's finest portraits.

[28] "St. Stephen" and "A Disciple", both completed in 1895, and amongst the last works of the pre-Raphaelite painter John Everett Millais (1829–96).

[29] Sir John Pender (1816–96), textile merchant, key figure in the development of the transatlantic telegraph system, and M.P. 1872–85, 1892–96.

[30] Cecely James, née Egerton (d.1920), widow of Dubar James (1809–85), 6th Earl of Selkirk.

[31] Thomas Francis Bayard (1828–98), U.S. Senator 1869–85 and American Ambassador to Britain 1893–97.

[32] William Montagu Hay, 10th Marquess (1826–1911), who had succeeded his brother in 1878.

lot of others — Mrs. Henry Reeve[33] & Mrs. Goodhall & 2 men I didn't know were at a little table with me — a sumptuous repast — Then back to Academy — Lord Lovelace,[34] Birchs etc etc, not a gr crowd — Home to receive Christopher Redington, who hopes he may do something for Mr. Treston[35] in spite of his discouraging letter — Rather discouraged at not having found anyone to meet Lady Robinson & puzzling who to write to — & went up to dinner — & as I finished a gentleman came over & spoke to me — Sir George O'Brien[36] — who has given up Hong Kong & the colonies — so he & his sister were promptly engaged to dine next day —

4th — A little shopping — & looked in at "Irish Industries" & was warmly congratulated by Ld. Duncannon[37] & the Dcss. St. Albans about R. — & by some lady unknown on the Auto[biography] — Then tho' tired to the Tennants, & met Sir Henry & Ly. Cunningham,[38] who were delighted to come & dine & just made up my party nicely — & home just in time to decorate my table, dress & receive them — it went off pretty well, dinner rather slow in starting — but Lady R[obinson] waked up & was very entertaining abusing the Colonies — I am afraid she won't be cured of that — tho' I gave her my lecture as she left — & told her how if she knew what it wd be to lose her husband she would never vex him by a word — but follow him on her knees & do her best for him —

May 5 — To St. Paul's — The music very fine — & the freedom of being unknown in church after Galway & Gort such a blessing! But during the sermon my thoughts were chiefly bent on what to do for Archie Grubb — & I wrote to A. Cole on my return, hoping he may help[39] — Sir Frederic in the afternoon, nice to see him about again —

Poor Mr. Maguire got a chill on his wedding day — & the next day but one Mrs. M. telegraphed for her sisters to come to Waddesdon as she felt so bored! —

[33] Christine Reeve, née Gollop, wife of journalist Henry Reeve (see above p. 51 n. 162).

[34] Ralph Gordon Milbanke (1839–1906), 2nd Earl of Lovelace. A grandson of Byron, and brother of Lady Anne Blunt.

[35] Redington was at this point serving as a Commissioner for National education. Treston was subsequently appointed schoolmaster at the Kiltartan National school, and later tutored RG privately in mathematics.

[36] Sir George Thomas O'Brien (1844–1906), Ceylon Civil service from 1867 (serving under WHG), Auditor General of Ceylon 1890–91, Col. Secretary at Hong Kong 1892–94, and Governor of Fiji 1897–1902. Assisted AG in 1890–91 in her efforts to improve conditions for Egyptian Nationalist leader Arabi Bey during his exile in Ceylon.

[37] Walter William Ponsonby (1821–1906), 7th Earl Bessborough and Lord Duncannon.

[38] Sir Henry (1832–1920) and Lady Harriet Cunningham (d.1918). Cunningham was Advocate-General at Madras 1873 and Judge of the High Court, Bengal 1877–87.

[39] AG did engineer some form of opening for Grubb, receiving thanks from his mother on 24 May 1895 (Berg).

6th — A letter from Robert — a little downhearted I think — finds Harrow "very different from Elstree as you have to find out everything for yourself from other boys & the masters hardly tell you anything" — He invites me to go down & see what is wanting for his room, & this of course I jump at —

7 — A letter from A. Cole, hopeful I think abt A. Grubb —

9 — To Harrow to see R. — I took my photo & Wm.'s — And in the morning the housemaid brought me the butterflies H. H. Johnston had promised to leave for R., & I thought forgotten — So I flew to the nearest framer & persuaded him to put them in a case at once for me to take —

I found my little man in his tiny room, looking cool & comfortable in loose grey trousers & a blue coat — He had been a little lonely at first — the only new boy in the House & rather "out of it" — feeling in the way in their games — but is beginning to settle down — We went out shopping & got a little clock & some plants & a blotter & stuff for a new curtain & the room looked much more homelike when we had arranged it & taken down some of the fans — We also proceeded to a grocer for some supplies — as if you spend 7/6 you get a book of American views! This however was rather a fraud — however we cut out the best ones & stuck them up — I went in to see Mr. Bowen, a quiet elderly gentleman — has not read the Autobiography so I have sent him a copy — I came back late & fagged with the heat — but happier about him on the whole.

10 — Some books for R. — as his library consists of "Charles O'Malley"[40] which wd not fit in very well with the grove on Sunday — Fitting clothes — & leaving cards — very tired — but went to dine with Lady Layard just arrived & I think better & stronger & with more courage —

11 — Off to Waterloo to see the Robinsons start — both more cheery, Lady R. pleased with the bouquets & bustle — Sir H. hoping to come back very soon on leave thinks "there will be some little tangle that wants undoing in a year's time" — He promised to be kind to Peyton & Alec[41] — Then home to dress & back to Waterloo & on to Twickenham for Clara Grant Duff's wedding — A lovely day — & she looked pretty & the church beautifully decorated — Then to York House to see the presents — & a scramble for refreshments not very well managed — The Duchess of Albany[42] there, looking very young & bright — The bridegroom very determined look[ing] with "eyes of dangerous

---

[40] *Charles O'Malley, the Irish Dragoon,* novel by Charles Lever (1806–72).

[41] Dudley Peyton Persse (b.1869) and Alexander Annesley Persse (1871–1941), eldest two sons of AG's brother Edward. Both settled permanently in South Africa.

[42] Princess Helen (d.1922), wife of Queen Victoria's youngest son, Prince Leopold (1853–84), Duke of Albany.

grey" — Home with the Morris girls & had tea with them —

12 — Lunched Ricardos — Chepmell & Miss Higgins[43] there as usual — She
says Ld. Rosebery's doctor undertakes to cure him if he will go away for a week,
but he won't — but now he is going to the coast of France to look for a
habitation for his daughters who are going there — Miss H. says it is high time,
as they are very badly educated, tho' Sybil is now 15[44] — & their knowledge
of French is very rudimentary — He takes gr pains about their reading,
choosing books for them — but they have the same teachers they had at 8
years old —

Evening, St Margaret's to hear Ld. Plunket speak, on Count Campello & the
Italian reformed church[45] — His voice beautiful still — but too much *wag*
motion of the head —

Nov[ember] 1 — A long interregnum — I must try to go back —

May 14 — Began French lessons with Mme. Secretan, to gain greater facility
in talking — which I find weak — my compositions & translations into French
better than I expected —

15th — Dined Sir Arthur Clay's —

16th — Dined Lady Lindsay —

17th — Dined Sir A. Haliburton's —

18th — To Maldon, Little Totham, Paul's farm house — very pretty &
peaceful — & he is better & happier for having it — We worked hard in the
garden & went to church on Sunday —

20th — Dined Beaumonts' — I remember sitting next Mr. Macmillan — And

---

43 Emily Higgins, daughter of the journalist, bon viveur and Garrick Club stalwart, Thackeray's
close friend Matthew Jacob Higgins (1810–68), who had been known universally as "Jacob
Omnium".

44 Sybil (1879–1955) and Margaret Primrose (1881–1967).

45 William Conyngham Plunket (1828–97), 4th Baron, Bishop of Meath 1876–84 and of
Dublin 1884–97, was a staunch supporter of the Italian Reformed Church, an evangelical group
headed by Count Henry di Campello and others, which had broken from Catholicism in favour
of simpler doctrines based on the New Testament, the independence of Church and State, and
the abolition of both Latin liturgy and the celibacy of the clergy. Plunket's support, directed also
to similar Reform movements in Spain and Portugal—like Italy, countries where the Catholic
Church was dominant—led to bitter charges of proselytising by Irish Catholics who suspected
him of trying to foment a new Reformation. Plunket was also the bête noire of Irish Nationalists
for his outspoken opposition to Home Rule.

after dinner the Dutch Minister talked to me all the time, in French — & I was glad to have had my lessons —

21 — H. Lane & Archie Grubb to lunch! — Ev. Mme. Blumenthal's[46] —

24 — Dined Mrs. Kay — Respectable but dullish party — Leckys etc —

25 — To Weymouth, Sat to Monday to stay with Lady Layard[47] — Poor thing, she isn't good for much as yet —

25 — Afternoon Ly. Lindsay — I think it was then I met Coventry Patmore —

26 — Weymouth again —

27 — Opening Empire of India Ex[hibition]. — Tea Mrs. Dugdale[48] — Dined Ld. Stanmore —

29 — Dined Morrises —

June 1 — to Harrow —

9 — Dined Seymours —

10 — Dined Birches — Sat next Admiral Sir E. Commerell,[49] who told Una afterwards he had had a delightful companion —

12 — "Faust"[50] — a little party for Olive Blake — N. Geary — Paul — Mrs. Martin,[51] 10-00. Dull —

13 — Mary Hozier's marriage to Lord Lamington[52] — She very late — A crowded reception — He very handsome — She looked better than usual — but will never be anything but plain —

[46] The wife of composer and musician Jacques Blumenthal (1829–1908), who was pianist to Queen Victoria.

[47] Lady Layard was visiting her brother Monty Guest at Weymouth.

[48] Mrs. Alice Dugdale (d.1902), sister of George Otto Trevelyan (see p. 108 n. 10). Her daughter Adelaide (d.1890) had been the wife of Lord Peel, the Speaker.

[49] Admiral Sir John Edmund Commerell (1829–1901), Admiral of the Fleet 1892–99.

[50] One of seven performances of Gounod's opera at Covent Garden between May and July 1895.

[51] Probably Anna Selina Martin, née Fox (d.1906), mother of novelist Violet Martin (1862–1915), AG's second cousin.

[52] Charles Napier Cochrane-Baillie (1860–1940), 2nd Baron Lamington, married May Hozier (d.1944), daughter of William Hozier (see p. 30 n. 43) on 13 June 1895. May Hozier was WHG's second cousin through her mother Frances O'Hara (see p. 30 n. 43).

15 — Maldon again — a pleasant rest —

19 — Dined Miss Hozier[53] —

20 — Tea, H. Aide —

21 — Ev. — Mrs. Bradley — rather pleasant — Canon Gore took me out on the leads to see the Abbey roof by moonlight — Dean Bradley gave a little discourse in the Jerusalem chamber[54] —

22 — Archbishop of Canterbury's garden party —

23 — Ham House[55] — Dined Morrises.

24 — Southwark Teachers' drive in Lady Layard's carriage — Dined Knowles — a very smart party — The Duke of Cambridge (who has just been forced to resign)[56] — Ld. & Ly. Brassey[57] — Lady Dorothy — Miss Higgins — Lord Warwick[58] — Ld. & Lady Ashbourne — The Duke more cheerful than we expected — but Ld. Rosebery's resignation makes him hope for a change of Govt & that he may be reinstated.

25 — Tea with Ld. & Ly. Morris at the H. of Lords, to make acquaintance with old Col. Talbot, the "Pat" of Ld. Talbot's letters[59] — & Henry Howorth sat &

53 Probably Catherine Hozier (d.1930), Mary Hozier's sister.

54 Gore (see p. 44 n. 115), was Canon of Westminster 1894–1902. Rev. George Granville Bradley (1821–1903), a close friend of Tennyson, and half-brother of the Shakespeare scholar A. C. Bradley, was Master of University College, Oxford, 1870–81, and Dean of Westminster 1881–1902. His wife was Marian, née Philpot.

55 A mansion on the south bank of the Thames near Richmond, owned by the Earls of Dysart. Completed in the 1670s, the house was a symbol for Restoration excess and prodigality. Presented to the National Trust in 1948.

56 George (1819–1904), 2nd Duke of Cambridge, the eldest son of George III's seventh son, had been Commander-in-Chief of the Army 1856–95. Throughout 1894, Rosebery's Government had been pressing for his retirement and replacement with a career soldier appointed by Parliament rather than by Royal interest. In June 1895, with the Duke continuing to refuse to resign, he was effectively dismissed by Secretary of War Henry Campbell-Bannerman (1836–1908). The resulting political furore contributed to Rosebery's resignation later that month. The Liberals were voted out of office in the July elections that followed, but the Duke of Cambridge's hopes of reinstatement were unanswered in the new Tory administration headed by Lord Salisbury.

57 Thomas Brassey (1836–1918), 1st Earl Brassey, and his second wife Sybil, née Capell (d.1934).

58 Frances Guy Greville (1853–1924), 5th Earl of Warwick. Formerly Lord Brooke (see p. 33 n. 65), he had succeeded his father in 1893.

59 Col. Wellington Patrick Chetwynd-Talbot (1817–98), eighth son of Charles Talbot (1777–1849), 2nd Earl Talbot and Lord Lieutenant of Ireland 1817–21 during Mr. William Gregory's tenure as Under-Secretary. Evidently AG had now begun to read the Under-Secretary's

talked to us[60] — Says Mrs. Gully allows Mrs. Labby to preside at her tea table, Labby having virtually made Gully Speaker[61] — & that this causes much scandal — Tea with Katie Currey[62] — such a painted wreck — one eye fixed!

26 — "Fedora" with Paul.[63]

27 — Harrow —

29 — Spent a night at Southampton to see the children & select some for Coole! I asked Richard for a companion for R[obert]. — & E[thel]. & M[arion] chose Gwin for the other — & then finding Standish wd. take to heart being left behind I invited him too[64] — Weymouth —

1st July — Lunched Canford[65] with Enid, & chose a place for Sir Henry's monument.

2 — Dined Morrises — Academy ev. party.

3 — Harrow speeches — Spoiled by the Duchess of Teck,[66] first proposing herself — then being very late & upsetting all arrangements — And my ticket had not reached me & I had difficulty in getting a place — And there was no one I knew at Mr. Bowen's lunch — However my little Robert looked very smart in his new white waistcoat — & we walked to the swimming bath —

---

correspondence (which would form the basis of her next book, *Mr. Gregory's Letter-Box*) with a view to publication. Col. Talbot was serjeant-at-arms to the House of Lords from 1858–98.

[60] Sir Henry Hoyle Howorth (1842–1923), a noted archeologist, and M.P. 1886–1900.

[61] William Court Gully M.P. had been suggested as Peel's successor as Speaker by Labouchere in the absence of another candidate acceptable to the Liberal interest. As *The Times* reported on 4 April (p. 9), Gully lacked "that intimate ready knowledge of the forms of the House and the practical questions arising out of its daily work which is indispensable to a Speaker. . . . There is no pretence that the Government believe Mr. Gully to have any other positive recommendation for the post than that he sits on their own side of the House." In the event, he proved to be highly competent, was elected to the post for a second term, and was created 1st Viscount Selby on his retirement in 1905. Married Elizabeth Walford (d.1906) in 1865. "Mrs. Labby" was Henrietta Labouchere, née Hodson.

[62] Probably Katherine Currey (b.c. 1860), eldest sister of novelist Violet Martin.

[63] An adaptation of Victorien Sardou's play by Herman Merivale at the Haymarket Theatre, starring Mrs. Patrick Campbell (see p. 294 n. 287) in the title role.

[64] Marion (1878–1955), and George Standish Persse (1877–1932), were Richard and Ethel Persse's nearest-aged siblings. "Gwin" was possibly a nickname for Edward Persse's youngest daughter, Gertrude (b.1887).

[65] Canford Manor, Dorset, principal seat of Lady Layard's brother Ivor Guest (1835–1914), 1st Baron Wimborne.

[66] Princess Mary of Cambridge (1833–97), Queen Victoria's cousin (being the second daughter of George the Third's seventh son, Adolphus), who had married Francis, Duke of Teck (d.1900) in 1866.

4th — Lunched Sir G. Bowen — & met B[isho]p. of Derry & Mrs. Alexander.[67]

5th — Dined Alfred Cole — A very pleasant dinner — Mr. Welldon — Mr. Lyttelton (Head Master of Haileybury)[68] — Vice Chancellor of Cambridge & wife[69] — Mr. & Mrs. Thackeray Ritchie[70] — Welldon very amiable & pleasant — I had met him before, one day I came to Harrow & was sitting on the cricket field he came over & sat between R. & me — & talked for a long time & seemed to have been much struck with the "Auto" — especially the story of the soldier of the Cross[71] —

6th — To Maldon for my last Sunday — The Blunts to lunch —

9th — To Ireland — It was a very hot season, & my poor little rooms were baking — & the struggle to dress & get about without maid or carriage rather trying — But it is better to keep going & not drop out until Robert starts in life — The General Election broke the season up — every one off to canvass.

1895

The summer in Ireland went off well — The Tories having swept the country at the elections, Home Rule has disappeared — & the Nat[ionalist]. leaders when heard of at all, are heard of as fighting with each other — Our own people were very nice & amiable, bringing little presents to Robert & paying their rent — tho' Mr. Hanbury has never re-appeared! — Edward Martyn has however had some trouble with his people — & his steward was fired at at our gate — & he himself is protected by police & hardly goes out[72] — The Miss Franks attempted to "boycott" me for having gone to see the prisoner who assaulted them in jail! but I wrote an amiable letter of apology — & rather a hollow truce has been patched up between us —

I had a fine house full for the holidays — Robert, very well — at first keen about cricket, then about shooting — Standish, poor little fellow, his back more deformed than any I have ever seen & is easily tired but very keen about sport — Gwin — absolutely silent — rather dull — practised a good deal —

[67] William Alexander (1824–1911), Bishop of Derry and Raphoe 1867–93, and of Armagh 1893–1911. Married Cecil Frances Humphreys (d.1895) in 1850.

[68] Edward Lyttelton (1855–1942), Headmaster of Haileybury 1890–1905, and of Eton 1905–16. Brother of politician Alfred Lyttelton (see p. 142 n. 103).

[69] Charles Smith (1844–1916), Master of Sidney Sussex College from 1890, and Vice Chancellor of Cambridge University 1895–97. Married Anne Hopkins, 1883.

[70] Richmond (1854–1912) and Anne Thackeray Ritchie (d.1912), she being the eldest daughter of Thackeray, and a popular novelist and short story-writer herself.

[71] See *Autobiography*, pp. 331–32.

[72] Martyn's tenants had asked for fair rents to be established on his estate, but he had refused. His agent was shot near the Coole gate-lodge following a hearing at the Gort Land Court. For a report see *The Galway Express*, 27 July, p. 4.

I did not care about her — she fidgetted < ?? > always looking at us silently with expressionless eyes — I felt she was like the baby who saw his nurse steal something & thought "I will tell of you when I am able to speak!" Richard, very amenable & straightforward — I liked him best — Ethel, at the end, half asleep — probably from the effect of the Croft life — Mme. Secretan I had engaged, from a sense of duty to Robert, to teach French — but she was not a success — greedy, ill-tempered & huffy — & worried me a good deal — Tony [Birch], who was idling in London after his [Army entrance] exam — I had asked — & he came & stayed for 5 weeks — very nice, gentle & affectionate — Poor boy he was very low in the exam — & much disturbed in mind — but in the end it was settled he should go & work at Hanover & try again, so he left, very sadly — but with 2 trophies of the chase — a stag's head he had shot at Chevy — & a 10lb pike he had caught in the lake & with my assistance stuffed, after the directions of a book on Taxidermy I had bought for Standish's benefit — The school feast & Workhouse feast went off well — & I feel glad that a great deal of pleasure was given to many during the holiday time —

My little Robert was still quite obedient & very affectionate — & happy all day, riding Shammy or playing cricket — & at twilight inviting me out shooting with him! The lake kept pretty full all the time — I had hired a type writer, to learn on — & found it a great comfort on wet days, all the children liking to learn —

Mr. Simon of Galway at last finished Robert's bookcase — a gr success — but it won't hold many more than his present books — I bought a new car, the old one being hopelessly jolty — I got a little knocked up myself, from housekeeping — or rather from carving for so many I did not feed myself very well — The Waithmans came for a few days — he just taking to photography & doing it very badly — De Basterot at home, & always kind — Lady Geary & Nevill at Tillyra at the end, & he often came over — The Dr. brought his pigeon trap for the boys one day — a great amusement.

On Sept 19 we all set out — Ethel, Rd. & Standish for Galway — Gwin for Millmount[73] — Robert & I for London — I, as usual, very much tired by the journey — but R. quite fresh, went off to see Paul at the War Office, & after our shopping hired a boat & rowed me about on St. James's Park — I saw him off to Harrow in the evening — & came back very tired — & Paul came to dine, but reproached me for coming over as he had meant to come for a week to Coole — The weather very hot & oppressive — & I not at all well, only fit to lie on the floor & cry — but revived by degrees.

[73] Millmount House, near Loughrea, Co. Galway, residence of AG's brother Henry.

Then Lady Layard came to town, to move from Queen Anne St. to Savile Row — & I had no further time on my hands, finding plenty to do in helping her — She dined here, & I had Sir F. Burton & Miss Lyall to meet her — & I went backwards & forwards & ended by staying there — Then, when we had labelled all the furniture & looked through the books & there was nothing else to be done, I persuaded her to come away — & we went first (Sep 29) to Winchester — & saw the Cathedral by moonlight, a lovely warm night — And next day the school & the round table & "St. Cross" & the quaint old houses — a delightful place — Then we went to Salisbury & saw that Cathedral also first by moonlight — & next day drove to Stonehenge — a weird impressive place — but the weather changed & we got wet & I caught cold.

Then on to Inwood, Merthyr & Lady Theodora Guest — where we stayed 10 days — He was in his room all the time having hurt his leg out riding — Lady T. clever & plain & self confident — & let us do what we liked — The daughter, Augusta, devoted to dogs, riding & rabbitting — plain but unaffected[74] —

We made expeditions from there to Sherborne, a curious old town with fine church — To Wells, very quiet & damp — Cathedral & moated Palace beautiful — To Glastonbury — quite lovely — The ruins of the church founded by Joseph of Arimathea very beautiful — & the whole Vale of Avalon quiet & peaceful enough to be the grave of Arthur & Guinevere — To Wimborne Minster — very fine, with a little library of chained books — & on to lunch at Canford to see Sir Henry's grave — One or 2 people came to stay — a very queer-looking Miss Gray — & a Mr. Larios, M. F. H. of the Gibraltar hounds —

9th [October] — Back to London — the weather cold, & my little rooms look snug — Poor Enid had to come up too — having had a letter saying the painters couldn't get the right colour for her drawingroom walls — She came to dine with me — & Paul — & Mr. Bond.

10th — Ly. Layard dropped in to lunch — & also N. Geary — & also Margaret[75] — who I did not know was near town — She looks fagged poor thing — but says the children enjoyed Coole immensely & that Richard tears off my autographs & keeps them — as he is sure they will be valuable some day! — I dined at the Lyalls — Sir Alfred much better, but a sudden attack of lumbago had crippled him — Mr. Clodd sat next me — talked of folk lore &

74 Inwood, Blandford, Dorset, home of Thomas Merthyr Guest (1838–1904), second oldest of Enid Layard's brothers, his wife Theodora, née Grosvenor (d.1924), and their only daughter, Augusta (b.1879).

75 Margaret Persse, née Tulloch (1849–1932), Edward Persse's wife.

superstitions[76] — The Walpoles & Bernard Hollands[77] also there —

11th — Margaret to lunch — & I took her to Private View New Gallery, portraits — Leckys — Mr. Gibbs by Huntington there[78] — & Margaret seemed amused by dresses etc — E. Layard to dinner.

13 — Sunday — Lady L., Sir F. Burton & Sidney Colvin dined with me — The latter struck with the print of Pitt I had brought over to be framed — says it is very rare — he does not think it is in the British Museum — & those of Fox & Burges[79] he also thinks very good —

14 — L. Layard & Mlle. de Perpignan[80] to lunch — We all agree as to the extraordinary indiscretion of Sir E. Malet making a speech against outsiders being put in office[81] — he who has been so extra cautious all his life — Tea Mrs. Lecky.

15 — Olive Blake wrote begging me to chaperone her & "2 male cousins" to dinner & play & I assented — though expecting to bore & be bored — But about 6 "Mr. Phipps" was announced & introduced himself as my host — & turned out to be one of the "New" set[82] — a friend of Paul & C. Little so we

[76] Edward Clodd (1840–1930), banker and folk-lorist. President of the Folk Lore Society 1895–96. Clodd may have seen "Irish Superstitions", a letter by AG published in the April 1895 issue of *The Spectator*, but her interest in folklore was evidently insufficiently developed for her to seek closer acquaintance with him at this point. When they next met, in November 1897, she promptly invited him to dinner to meet WBY.

[77] Bernard Holland (1856–1926), Private Secretary to the Duke of Devonshire 1892–94 and nephew of Sir Alfred Lyall. Married Florence Duckworth (a distant relative of Virginia Woolf) in 1895.

[78] A work by American portraitist Daniel Huntington (1816–1906).

[79] Statesman Charles James Fox (see p. 108 n. 10), and his parliamentary contemporary Sir James Burges (1752–1824), Under-Secretary for Foreign Affairs 1789–95, and an advocate for the abolition of slavery.

[80] Mlle. de Perpignan was a key figure in the household of the German Crown Prince Frederick and Princess Royal, having had charge of their children in the 1880s. Lady Layard's diary (British Library) records this lunch as taking place on 15 October.

[81] Sir Edward Malet (1837–1908), British agent and Consul General in Egypt 1879–83, during which period he earned AG's lasting antipathy for his opposition to Arabi Bey. Served as Ambassador at Berlin 1884–95, and had recently announced his intention to resign. *The Times* (14 October, p. 5) had reported Malet's speech at Berlin on 11 October in which he had deplored speculation that his replacement as Ambassador would be "an outsider of distinction" rather than a career diplomat. In an pathetic and possibly unconscious effort to justify his own mediocre abilities, Malet had argued that "a very brilliant man" would almost certainly fail in the position through lack of the "self-abnegation and reticence" in his opinion necessary for success.

[82] Edmund Bampfylde Phipps (1869–1947). Student at New College 1889–93, where he was a contemporary of Paul Harvey, Fischer Williams and Charlie Little. Tutor to the children of the Duke and Duchess of Connaught 1893–96. He later had a successful career in education, being Deputy Secretary for Elementary Education 1926–29. Knighted in 1917 following a wartime appointment as General Secretary of the Ministry of Munitions 1916–17.

IRISH

had plenty to talk about — We dined Cavalry Club — & went to "An Artist's Model"[83] which I thought dull & vulgar & so improper I was sorry for Olive — but it turned out she had been there before! Mr. Phipps is tutor to the Duke of Connaught's children — & says his lot has fallen in pleasant places — tho' Paul declares he is no better than an upper footman — I had heard a story of him, which he confirms that one day when the Royal children were having tea, at Balmoral, little P[rin]cess Ina of Battenburg[84] was very naughty — & he said "I wish I could go to lunch with the Queen & see how you behave there" — Next day at lunch, P[rin]cess Ina said "Gan-gan"! — "Well my dear" says Her Majesty — "Gan-gan — Mr. Phipps says he would like to lunch with you" — There was a dead silence — the ladys in waiting horrified — Afterwards H. M. asked what the meaning of this was — & fortunately someone had been present & was able to give the correct version — A few days afterwards H. M. invited him on an expedition — & they had tea together — a party of 6 — & he had to explain to her the difference between Rugby & Association football —

18 — At 9·00 a tap at the door — & in walked old Waithman! wanting to know about his Velasquez, just come over — Rather a shock to me to find he is actually staying in the Mansions & liable to drop in at any hour!

19th — Took him to Christies — Where Mr. Taylor said in his opinion it was *not* Velasquez but he would take Mr. Woods opinion on it.[85]

20 — Lunch Ly. Maxwell[86] — Dined with Mr. Geary at the Savoy —

21 — Mr. Geary — Mr. Williams & Miss Alderson[87] came to dine & to "Walkyrie"[88] the music fine — but 4 hours too long — Miss de Perpignan says the old Emperor[89] said to her he wd rather sit in the saddle for 4 hours in a

---

[83] A musical comedy by Owen Hall (libretto), Harry Greenbank (lyrics) and Sidney Jones (music) which ran for 392 performances at Daly's Theatre and The Lyric from May 1895.

[84] Princess Victoria Ena (1887–1969), daughter of Princess Beatrice (1857–1944), Queen Victoria's youngest daughter, and Prince Henry of Battenburg (see p. 93 n. 142 and p. 113 n. 27). Later Queen of Spain through her 1906 marriage to Alphonso XIII (d.1941).

[85] After the death of her sister Arabella in 1924, AG helped settle her estate, and arranged the sale of this painting, its authenticity still in dispute (see *Journals* vol. 1, p. 520). Henry Woods, R.A. (1846–1921), was a prominent artist and designer.

[86] Lady Lilias Maxwell, née Aberigh-Mackay, wife of Sir William Edward Maxwell (1846–97), Governor of the Gold Coast 1895–97. This meeting marks the start of AG's efforts to secure Nevill Geary's appointment as Attorney-General for the Gold Coast.

[87] Nelly Alderson, daughter of Lady Layard's second eldest sister Katherine (1837–1926), who had married Rev. Cecil Alderson (1836–1907) in 1861.

[88] Richard Wagner's "The Valkyrie" [*Die Walkure*], this being the second of six performances between October and November 1895 in a season of Wagner at Covent Garden.

[89] Frederick III (d.1888), see p. 41 n. 97.

hot sun than listen to Wagner's music for two! Mr. Taylor writes that Woods agrees in his opinion that the picture is an early Velasquez! — but won't fetch much at a sale — so old W[aithman]. is comforted.

27 — Lunch Lady Haliburton — Sir Arthur spoke very kindly of Paul (who is private sec. to Lord Lansdowne[90]) says Ld. L. likes him very much & he shows much ability — on to Twickenham, dined with the Grant Duffs —

28 — Tea A. Gray to meet his bride Mrs. Grosvenor[91] — a lady with plenty of self possession —

30 — Dine Ly. Lindsay — I am in the hands of Chamberlain American dentist & am now gagged with elastic so hardly able to eat or speak — & fearing the hot soup will melt the elastic & cause it to explode! — Lady Lauderdale[92] — Miss Higgins — Sir Hubert Miller[93] — Mrs. <?Cartwright> & "Anthony Hope" Hawkins[94] who was next me — Very pleasant — Miss Higgins had been to Curraghmore about a fortnight before Ld. Waterford's death — & says he was quite off his head then — & Lady Waterford will think it a relief — as she dreaded leaving her 2 girls in his charge[95] — The Prince of Wales has written to Ly. Cork saying they are delighted about Princess Maud's marriage & that she arranged it all herself[96] —

Mrs. & Miss Walpole[97] came to have a lesson in type writing — Still gagged by dentist — eat & speak with difficulty so keep much shut up —

2nd Nov[ember] — To Dr. Maclagan about the sort of rash, eczema that troubles me in cold weather — He says it is from want of food — that I have got into a very low state — So I must try to pay more attention to my meals —

[90] Henry Charles Petty-Fitzmaurice (1845–1927), 5th Marquess of Lansdowne. Chief Secretary for War 1895–1900 and Foreign Secretary 1900–05.

[91] Sophie Grosvenor, née Williams (d.1938), widow of the Hon. Thomas Grosvenor (1842–86), whom she had married in 1877. Grosvenor, the second son of the 1st Baron Ebury, had been Secretary at the British Legation at Pekin 1879–83. Her father, S. Wells Williams (d.1884), Secretary to the American Legation to China 1856–76, and from 1877 until his death Professor of Chinese at Yale, was the leading American Sinologist of his time.

[92] Lady Ada Lauderdale, née Simpson (d.1931), wife of the 14th Earl.

[93] Sir Charles John Hubert Miller (1858–1940), 8th Bart.

[94] Anthony Hope Hawkins (1863–1933), novelist who published under the name Anthony Hope. Best known for *The Prisoner of Zenda*. Knighted 1918.

[95] The 5th Marquess of Waterford had committed suicide on 23 October 1895. His widow, Blanche, died of cancer in 1898. The two daughters were twins, Susan and Clodagh (b.1879).

[96] Princess Maud (1869–1938), Prince Edward's youngest daughter, married Prince Christian of Denmark on 22 July 1896. Emily, Lady Cork, née Canning (d.1912), wife of the 9th Earl of Cork, was a daughter of the 1st Earl of Clanricarde (see p. 87 n. 114).

[97] Spencer Walpole's wife Marion, née Murray (d.1912), and their daughter Maud (1870–1949).

& more money for them! Which I always grudge —

3rd — Lunched Sir A. Lyall — a wet afternoon — but am interested in reading Burke — Morley's life of him (for the 2nd time) & his speeches[98] — And I have borrowed Ly. Layard's type writer & find it satisfactory as I can work in the evenings — Rather encouraged to write by Blackwood's warm reception of my "Eothen" article — Reports of Robert not quite so satisfactory, "careless", "inattentive" which frets me.

4th — Wet day — Type writing — & to Chamberlain — who put a new gag on my teeth — Tea, Sir Alfred Lyall & George Moore to meet each other — & then Nevill Geary who was to have met Sir R. Meade who was kept at the Col. Office & didn't come[99] — Then, being dressed & hungry, went to 3 Savile Row & dined with E. Layard & Ld. Duncannon — He hears Philip Currie will be in a scrape for leaving Constantinople in the middle of a crisis[100] — & anyhow he is unpopular & hasn't done well — Ly. Duncannon had been to see Ly. Waterford who greeted her with "What a record for my children! Their father blew his brains out & their mother died of cancer!" A second gushing letter from Blackwood about my "Eothen" article — & enclosing cheque for £10-10/- — which will just pay for Robert's bookcase.

5 — Day began with a letter from Robert — saying he was 4th in class & marked "Good".

6 — A wet dark day — only went across in the afternoon to Mrs. Crawfurd's — & just as I came back Ld. Morris came in — full of scandal — that it was Sir Robert Peel who stole Mrs. Langtry's jewels![101] — & that the Duchess of Hamilton is expecting her confinement, & it is thought, lst that the Duke is too long dead — & secondly that he was away in Spain in his last months —

[98] Edmund Burke (1729–97), statesman and philosopher. Morley's biography *Burke* was published in the English Men of Letters series in 1887. Morley had also published *Edmund Burke: A Historical Study* in 1867.

[99] Sir Robert Henry Meade (1835–98), Assistant Under-Secretary of State for the Colonies 1871–92, and Permanent Under-Secretary 1892–97. Meade's support would have been of considerable influence in gaining Geary the Gold Coast appointment.

[100] Sir Philip Henry Currie (1834–1906), Ambassador at Constantinople 1893–98. Graphic details of Turkish massacres of Armenians were being received in London throughout late October and November 1895, leading eventually to joint action by the European powers (see p. 105 n. 2). Currie returned to Constantinople in late November, but continued to fail to impress in his post, and was transferred to Rome in 1898, officially in consequence of poor health. He was later raised to the peerage as Baron Currie of Hawley.

[101] Lily Langtry (1852–1929), celebrated as "The Jersey Lily" for her beauty, and notorious as Prince Edward's mistress in the late 1880s and early 1890s. As her looks faded in middle age, she parlayed her fame into a successful career as an actress. Sir Robert Peel (1822–95), eldest brother of Speaker Peel, was Chief Secretary for Ireland 1861–65, and had been a close friend of WHG.

for this to be his child[102] — & that May Lamington refuses to sleep with Lord L. — & that Mrs. Langtry is living with Ld. Shrewsbury & Lady S. with a Mr. Burnaby[103] — What a world! He thinks Ld. Londonderry was very foolish to refuse the post of Privy Seal with a seat in the Cabinet — Ld. Salisbury gave him time for reflection & a second offer, but he wd only take the head of a department[104] — N. Geary took me to dine at Romanos' — & we went to see "Her Advocate"[105] — so absurd as to be amusing —

6 — Bright sunshine — but troublesome jobs — Miss Bentley to sew — & went to Chamberlain — & to have stays tried on & hair shampooed — Tired — & went up to dinner — which I couldn't eat — I don't know what I am to do about food —

7th — Very low & tired & cried from weakness — Bread & butter for breakfast & 6 oysters for lunch — Then tried to make an effort — & went & bought some knives & plates etc to try if I can't manage to dine "at home" next time Paul comes — I sympathize now with his horror of restaurants — Met Lecky in the street & stopped to give him my good wishes for the election — He is low about it — says he did not want to stand but was begged to do so — & that he would rather not get in at all than by a very small majority — And he refuses to give his religious opinions — says they are a matter for himself[106] — I went in afterwards at Lady Arthur Russell's — & Flora[107] told me of a lady at Dr. Vaughan's[108] who asked who that tall man was & was told Mr. Lecky the writer — She asked what he had written, & on hearing "The History of Rationalism" said "Then this is no place for me" — & marched off —

Sir R. Meade came to tea at last, to meet N. Geary but I doubt that it did much

[102] William Hamilton, 12th Duke, died 16 May 1895. *Burke's Peerage* records only one child born to the couple, in 1884. Lady Hamilton, née Montagu, remarried in 1897.

[103] Charles Talbot (1830–1908), 19th Earl of Shrewsbury, and his wife Anna, née Cockerell (d.1912).

[104] Robert Arthur Cecil, 3rd Marquess of Salisbury (1830–1903), Conservative statesman, had just begun his third term as Prime Minister, having previously headed the Government in 1885–86 and 1887–92. This, his final term, continued until 1902. Charles Stewart (1852–1915), 6th Marquess of Londonderry, had been Lord Lieutenant of Ireland 1886–89 during Salisbury's earlier administrations, but apparently paid dearly for this refusal, serving only as Chairman of the London School Board 1895–98 and Postmaster General 1900–02 during Salisbury's third term.

[105] A legal drama in three acts by Walter Frith, which ran for 65 performances at the Duke of York's Theatre between September and November 1895.

[106] Lecky was standing for the Dublin University parliamentary seat. Candidates' religious views were a major electoral issue due to the current debate over the possible opening of a Catholic University.

[107] Flora Russell (1869–1967), Lady Arthur Russell's eldest daughter.

[108] Dr Herbert Vaughan (1832–1903), Bishop of Salford 1872–92 and Archbishop of Westminster 1892–1903.

good — He decidedly said there was no chance of his being sent up to Coomassie as political officer, as the Governor is sure to choose a man on the spot — He was rather exhausted, Chamberlain having come back from his tour in a preternatural state of energy[109] — & keeping them all up to the mark — Evening brought a letter from Claude Phillips[110] saying the picture is not Velasquez & whoever it is by, is an inferior one — What a blessing I am out of reach of old Waithman!

A wet day again — but took N. Geary (with a very bad cold) to lunch with Lady Maxwell & talk about the Gold Coast — R. Maxwell gave me some stamps for Robert — Then to Chamberlain & finished with him, my teeth as he says being now "as straight as anybody's" — but I was horrified in the evening to hear from Lady Layard that her bill is £86! He said mine wd be "an inexpensive affair" — but anyhow I shd have had tusks in a short time — & I don't think I ought to let myself grow repulsive — Called on Mrs. Lecky — who is anxious & eager about the election — & worried by all the letters they receive — some asking questions, some for subscriptions already! Dined Ly. Layard's, she is low now from want of occupation, the house being settled — And Mr. <?Rate> has lost his interest in doing up Springfield, finding it is to be a Du Cane domicile —

9th — To Harrow. Found R. at the station gate, rather shy in his little tail coat & flat straw hat — an absurd little object enough, for he keeps his baby face — We spent most of the time watching a football match — then settled about having his photo done for the Elstree book, & bought him a tablecloth — & fruit & biscuits — & had tea at the confectioners where he was rather put out by some boy stuffing bits of cake into the hole in his hat — Mr. Richardson who had been playing in the match came & talked to us — R. seems to be getting on better in work, & likes his drawing — A gt cheer up seeing him! & it was a lovely day, & the scene in the football fields very pretty —

10 — To St. Paul's — A quiet afternoon, only E. Martyn, whose attempt to compromise with his tenants has failed — He is very low at the prospect of having to stock the land & begin farming — Read the "Vailima Letters" through[111] — rather pretty —

---

[109] Rt Hon. Joseph Chamberlain (1836–1914), who had recently been appointed Secretary of State for the Colonies, a post he retained 1895–1903. He had commenced his term with an energetic review of the Colonial Office, during which he had introduced sweeping reforms. Father of future Prime Minister Neville Chamberlain.

[110] Claude Phillips (d.1924), Barrister, art critic for *The Daily Telegraph* and Keeper of the Wallace Collection 1897–1911.

[111] *The Vailima Letters*, a selection of Robert Louis Stevenson's letters to his lifelong friend Sidney Colvin, written between 1890 and 1894 from Vailima, the home on Samoa where novelist and essayist Stevenson (1850–94) spent most of his last four years. Edited by Colvin and published in 1895.

11 — Tony [Birch] appeared in the morning, looking well, rather *distrait* — Sir A. & Una away — he stayed to lunch & we went & looked in at the Nat[ural]. Hist[ory]. Museum — Evening dined at Previliti's & to "Trilby"[112] with Paul — good acting the play well adapted — but I was in some pain — & sad — Lord Dufferin was sitting a little way behind & I went & spoke to him & hoped he had forgiven me — He said quite — & held my hand — & said it was Murray's fault — but I refused to agree to that — but he said the upshot was good — & that it was Ld. Aberdeen who had let the secret out — as he has now discovered by making researches — He has had a letter from Ld. Stanmore saying this — I asked if there wd be anything about it in Sidney Herbert's Life & he said, yes probably — I hope old Stanmore will do it graciously![113] A letter from Ld. Clanricarde[114] — who does not think the Velasquez genuine — Paul says Chamberlain sent to say the Expedition wd be wanted for Ashanti — in anticipation of the meeting of the Cabinet![115]

12 — To Southwark Board School — then to see Ly. Lindsay & Mrs. Poynter,[116] & dined Lady Layard — Eda Alderson was at Hatfield the other day,[117] & they talked of Sir Philip Currey's sensitiveness, crying at the play — & Ld. Salisbury said "He seems very sensitive about everything except the sufferings of the Armenians" — Yet he cried him up in the Guildhall speech.[118]

[112] A four-act adaptation of George du Maurier's novel by Paul M. Potter, starring and directed by H. Beerbohm Tree, which ran for 254 performances at the Haymarket Theatre 1895–96.

[113] Murray had published both WHG's autobiography and Lady Dufferin's poems, and hence might have been expected to perceive the possible offence the Mrs. Norton story might give. Despite his renewed assurances of amity, Dufferin proceeded to add an intemperate note to the fourth edition of his mother's poems, fulminating at length against WHG's "silly and injurious" repetion of "idle rumours" (*Poems and Verses by Helen Lady Dufferin* 1895 edition, pp. 59–60). Lord Stanmore's biography of Sidney Herbert, eventually published in 1906 (also by Murray), ignored the matter of *The Times* leak entirely, concentrating solely on the politics of Peel's position on the Corn Laws. George Gordon, 4th Earl of Aberdeen (1784–1860), Secretary of State for Foreign Affairs in Peel's Cabinet 1841–46, and later Prime Minister, the father of Sir Arthur Gordon, 1st Lord Stanmore.

[114] Hubert Canning (1832–1916), 2nd Earl of Clanricarde, second son of the first Earl. Both the first Earl, and his son Lord Dunkellin, who died young in 1867, had been close friends and political associates of WHG. The 2nd Earl, who succeeded his father in 1874, was a notoriously harsh landlord.

[115] Preparations were in hand for a military expedition to the Ashanti regions of the Gold Coast to end slaving raids being carried out by King Prempeh of Kumasi.

[116] Agnes Poynter, née Macdonald (d.1906), wife of Edward John Poynter (1836–1919), R.A., who was Burton's successor as Director of the National Gallery 1894–1905.

[117] Eda Alderson, Lady Layard's niece (see p. 82 n. 87). Lord Salisbury's wife, Georgiana, née Alderson (d.1899), was Eda's aunt, hence the many familial Alderson visits to the Salisburys' country residence, Hatfield House, Hertfordshire, recorded in this and subsequent entries.

[118] For a report on Salisbury's speech at the Guildhall on 9 November 1897, in which he praised Currie's "judgement and skill and tenacious labours" regarding Armenia, see *The Times* 11 November, p. 6.

13 — Tried tying a fly — but only got as far as putting the wings on — To Barr for bulbs for Paul — & Mudie's — & when I came back Lady Arthur Russell called —

14 — Ordered Xmas groceries at the stores, & missed Sir A. Lyall, Lady Layard & N. Geary — but the latter came later — Dined Leckys — Sir A. Lyall — Mr. & Ly. Victoria Plunket[119] — Count Bylandt — Goldstein — & others — Sir Alfred startled at hearing I have written a paper on the Athenaeum Club, but I told him I had been discreet & had not put in about the gentleman who takes his boots off before the fire or the one that steals the soap — He asked if I had put in the one who on being spoken to by a member he had not been introduced to, rang the bell & said "Waiter, I think this gentleman wants something — he is speaking!"

I talked to Lady Victoria afterwards, curiously like her mother, which gives her an old look, but evidently much brighter & more intelligent — Says Ld. Dufferin was delighted with "Trilby" & had gone to sup with the actors & actresses afterwards — Then Lecky talked to me, more resigned about his election — but says if he gets in it will interfere with his literary work — & he wished to write about the beginning of this century in Ireland — after the Union.[120]

15 — A note from Paul saying he wd come & dine — so went to buy provisions to try my new system of dinner in my room — pleasanter — & enough to eat — soup — cold chick[en] & beef — stewed peas — then cheese — but very troublesome & cost a good deal — & I had to sit up till midnight to wash up — Paul very kind & affectionate — but anxious I shd move to a better flat with my own servant — & I can't afford that, & carry out my intention of freeing the property for R. without touching his father's little legacy — & I don't like to stop my charities & grow selfish —

15 [i.e. 16th] — To Maclagan, who orders me strychnine — & repeats that I am in a low state — but I see no present prospect of getting out of it! — In the afternoon Mrs. Crawfurd called & Miss Higgins & Albert Gray & Mrs. Grosvenor — the latter rather impressed with her own importance — & set off talking of her distinguished friends — At a dinner party she has heard Gladstone talk the entire time on asparagus — which he planted, divided, cut, etc — till everyone was bored to death — Dined Birchs — Sir Henry Bulwer

[119] Hon. William (1864–1920) and Lady Victoria Plunket (d.1968). She was a daughter of AG's friend Lord Dufferin. William Plunket succeeded his father (see p. 74 n. 45) as 5th Baron Plunket in 1897, and was Governor of New Zealand 1904–10.

[120] Lecky never completed this project, and most of his publications following his election consisted of reprints of earlier work.

& old Lily Gordon[121] there — I had gone over at 5 & called at the Tennants, a dull visit — & what snobs they are! & I found on my return I had missed Henry James.

16 [i.e. 17th]— To Westminster Abbey — Lunched Haliburtons — & sat between Sir Redvers Buller[122] & Admiral Sir __ MacDonald[123] — & opposite Ld. Morris — R. Buller says Mahaffy is tormenting his life out to be made an English Dean[124] — Old F. Leveson Gower[125] has just been staying at Hawarden where he found the G. O. M. extraordinarily well but Mrs. Gladstone a good deal broken. When he was leaving Gladstone said "So glad to have got you here — & I hope you will repeat the visit *every* year!" Gerald & Dr. Moran appeared in the afternoon — Dined Lady Layard — Monty Guest[126] has been in the house 2 days — & she has only seen him once — & he has taken the spare room she was to have for his valet — he is a selfish creature.

18 — Fog — so had a fire & mended my stockings peaceably during the morning — Then it cleared — & I got to Lady Lindsay's tea — pleasant enough — talked to Miss Higgins, Lecky, Dorothy Stanley & Sidney Colvin — & a Mr. Gill who thinks of going to Ceylon — & Martin Morris walked home with me — Sir Lewis Morris[127] — & Burne Jones & Sir A. Lyall also there.

19 — A cheery letter from Robert, 1st in class — Lunched Ly. Layard & took her to Southwark Bd. School — made the children do a Scripture exam — that she might see they are taught the Bible — & they sang "Jesus, Lover of my Soul" and "I heard the Voice of Jesus say" — I hope she will get interested in the place — Tea with her, & when walking home met Paul who had been here —

20 — Called on Mrs. Dugdale, Rose & Mrs. Beaumont, all at home — Paul dined, says it is the German Emperor who is rather double faced about the Turkish question — He has been talking to the military attaché to the Russian

---

[121] Probably Caroline Emilia Gordon (d.1909), widow of Lord Stanmore's brother Alexander (d.1890).

[122] Sir Redvers Henry Buller (1839–1908), veteran of the Ashanti, Zulu and Egyptian campaigns, and Chief of Staff in the 1881 Boer War. Served as Under-Secretary for Ireland 1887, and returned to active duty as General Commander-in-Chief of British Forces in Natal 1899–1900 (see p. 231 n. 33).

[123] Admiral Sir Reginald John Macdonald (1820–99), who had retired in 1884 after 51 years of service in the Navy.

[124] John Pentland Mahaffy (1839–1919), Fellow in Ancient History 1864–1919, and Provost 1914–19, of Trinity College, Dublin.

[125] Edward Frederick Leveson-Gower (1819–1907), Liberal M.P. 1846–47, 1852–57, 1859–85.

[126] Montague Guest (1839–1909), third eldest of Lady Layard's brothers.

[127] Sir Lewis Morris (1833–1907), poet, knighted 1895.

Embassy—who says he really believes Russia is acting straight on this question — & does not believe there is a written treaty about a Chinese port—but that question won't come on for two years when the railroad is finished[128] — Headache in the night.

21 — A telegram from Nevill Geary saying he has been ordered to the Gold Coast — so our trouble has not been thrown away[129] — To Cecy Parnell's wedding at the Plymouth Brethren Hall in Welbeck Street, a shabby-looking place — a little table with green cloth representing an altar — some flowers on the chimney piece above it — Cecy looked nice, fresh & good humoured — & her dress white silk, fashionably made—The bridegroom Mr. Mandeville too much in the ordinary "goody man" line — with rather wild eyes — & no repose — evidently longing to give us an address on his own account[130] — First we sang a hymn — & then a "Brother" gave an extemporary prayer — "Lord, provide the wine for this marriage feast" — "Amen" from the bridegroom — etc — Then he read, with a running exposition passages from the Bible bearing on Matrimony — but was interrupted by the Registrar, a shabby looking man who had taken his seat at the green table — & who pointed at the clock — 10 to 3 — & observed that if not celebrated before 3 the marriage wd not be legal — So the bridegroom repeated a form of words something like this: "I promise that I will live with and act towards Sarah Cecilia Parnell as her true & faithful husband, according to the principles laid down in the word of God" — & she repeated the same form — & the ring was put on as a memorial of this — Then they signed their names in the register — Then another hymn — & an address on the bad marriages of the Bible — Abraham's wife was 90 — Moses married a black woman etc — with application that Christ in wedding the Church is ready to wed sinners—Then extemporary prayers were requested from the congregation — & one or two men responded — one prayer for "her Ladyship & all the Parnell family — & also the aged Mrs. Mandeville" & after another hymn all was over — It was less solemn than a church marriage, & I think its simplicity wd have been

[128] For Russia's refusal to join other Western powers in threatening action against the Sultan, see p. 105 n. 2. Diplomatic agreements between Britain and Russia were in progress on the issue of their respective competition for trade with China, at this period becoming rapidly more accessible through the construction of new railways. For diplomatic manoevres regarding the development of the Trans-Siberian railway, and events leading up to the Russian seizure of Port Arthur, see C. J. Lowe *The Reluctant Imperialists*.

[129] Geary's appointment was, however, a doubtful success, and by February 1896 he was already writing to AG in some depression as to his situation "in this cruel land" (Berg). In 1897, when a new appointment was apparently in the offing, Sir William Maxwell wrote privately to AG bluntly acknowledging her "hand in shaping [Geary's] plans" and recommending that Geary not look for a further posting in Africa as he had been "too much of a dilletante" in Accra (Berg).

[130] Sarah Cecilia Parnell (1868–1912) was a second cousin of Charles Stewart Parnell, being the only daughter of his cousin John Parnell, 2nd Lord Congleton. Her husband, Henry Ambrose Mandeville (1841–1917), was a widower with three daughters.

impressive if only the texts — the promise of fidelity, & a hymn had been given
— but the ramshackle prayers & address spoiled it — The reception crowded
so I only stayed a minute — & went to call on Miss Lefevre[131] — who was
excited over John Dillon's marriage which had taken place that morning, at
8-oo to exclude friends & the Irish Party! Miss Matthew is very bright & clever
& had been in love with Dillon for 8 years! but he wd not marry while there
were any evicted tenants! which may account for his keeping up the agitation
so long — Now, the Matthews said it cd not draggle on any longer — so he
condescended to name a day[132] — as there are now so few ev[ic]t[ion]s!
Madeline Lefevre[133] has become a member of a School Board — & is
astonished to find how much religion is taught — & she persuaded their
clergyman who had been hanging aloof to join — & he also is astonished, &
confesses he cd not do the instruction much better himself — Then called on
Miss Meade — Dined Lady Layard who hears Dufferin is to resign before his
time is up & be made Sec. of State for Foreign Affairs[134] — I hope he will be
given an ear trumpet —

22 — Gerald to lunch — Told me of Kathleen's engagement to Willy Burke
— Rather a shock being connected any more closely with that family![135] but
it is a good thing one of them shd marry — Took Ly. Layard to Southwark
"Happy Evening" & taught the children "Fly Away Pigeon" & "Earth, Air &
Water" — Dined Newton Robinson[136] — rather sorry for myself driving miles
in the rain — but found the dinner very pleasant, I was between my host & H.
O. Arnold Forster[137] — who talks incessantly — but is pleasant enough — &

[131] Probably Emily Shaw-Lefevre, youngest sister of George Shaw-Lefevre (see p. 47 n. 141).

[132] John Dillon and Elizabeth Mathew [sic] (d.1907), whom he had first met in 1886, were married by the Bishop of Galway at Brompton Oratory on 21 November 1895. AG's account is characteristically snide at Dillon's expense. Though long a familiar in her family circle, Dillon appears to have given Miss Mathew no clear indication of a serious attachment, nor to have disguised his belief that his fear of tuberculosis, a lifestyle that offered minimal opportunities for domesticity, and his modest income, made him a poor candidate for marriage. He was prompt in proposing when she eventually indicated that he should either be an acknowledged suitor or leave her social circle (see F. S. L. Lyons, *John Dillon*).

[133] Madeleine Shaw-Lefevre, Emily's sister.

[134] Dufferin in fact remained in his post as Ambassador to the French Republic until 1896, then retired from public life.

[135] Kathleen Persse, second daughter of AG's brother Major William, married William Creagh Burke of Cloonlee in June 1896. AG's existing connection with the family was via WHG's aunt Elizabeth O'Hara, who had married a Burke.

[136] Sir John Charles Robinson (1824–1913) and his wife Marian, née Newton (d.1908). Robinson was Crown Surveyor of Pictures 1882–1901. Their children adopted the surname Newton-Robinson.

[137] Hugh Oakley Arnold-Forster (1855–1909), M.P. 1892–1906, and Secretary of State for War 1903–06. A nephew of Matthew Arnold, he had been adopted along with his sister (later Florence O'Brien, see p. 16 n. 85), by W. E. Forster (see p. 130 n. 43) and his wife Jane, Arnold's sister, following his father's death.

Lewis Morris was at the other end of the table — & his ineffable expression always amuses me —

23 — Rather a bad day in the way of food — rusks for breakfast — went up to lunch & had beefsteak pie quite uneatable from toughness — & dined, at 9-00 off bread & butter & cucumber — not being able to face either the restaurant dinner or 2 eggs I had brought in. Went to a private view of Rohenhofer(?) pictures — didn't care much about them — Called on Lady Clay — & then on Ly. Haliburton — who says Paul is "too critical" — so I suppose, as he thought, Sir A. found him too outspoken on his notes for the Times which he had asked him to criticize[138] — Ly. H. says Sir A. has taken one of the War Office men to Brighton for change — as he has been completely knocked up by all the work lately & especially by a new envelope that has been issued, into which the paper used will not fit without extra folding — this has got on his brain! What a horrible idea!

24 — Westminster Abbey — One idea in the sermon, Michael Angelo walking round to criticise his pupils' drawings wrote on one that was too cramped "wider" — & Christ looking at us may sometimes touch our heart with the same word — Lunched with the Duchess of Bedford, very affectionate & kind & her new house in Hertford St. beautiful — We spoke of Enid — & of the dangers of querulousness — Tony & Una & E. Martyn in the afternoon — & dined Ly. Layard's — E. Martyn had seen a notice in the Athenaeum of my forthcoming article —

25 — Lunched Ly. Layard & on with her to Whiteley's to choose things for Xmas tree — china ornaments & vases for girls — neckties & mufflers for boys — Called on Mrs. Grosvenor but she had left her flat — & I cd not get a bus — & walked home & arrived tired & tealess — & Paul called while I was dressing — & N. Geary dined here & the dinner was bad — & we went to a very dull play "Benefit of the Doubt"[139] but then had supper at the Savoy, excellent soup & chicken which revived me & saved me from a headache that was coming on.

26 — To Mudie's — & called on Mrs. John Murray — Mrs. Crawfurd, Mrs. Maclagan & Ly. Maxwell — & had a quiet evening, reading M. Arnold's letters[140] & dining at 9 — off bread & butter & cucumber! — I got into a

[138] Haliburton's letter "The Condition of the Army", countering criticism of recent Army reorganizations, was published in The Times 3 December 1897, p. 6. Correspondence on the issue drew three further letters from him over the following week.

[139] A three-act comedy by Arthur Wing Pinero, managed by J. Comyns Carr (see p. 159 n. 173), which ran at the Comedy Theatre for 74 performances in October and December 1895.

[140] The Letters of Matthew Arnold, 1848–88, a newly published two-volume edition compiled by AG's friend G. W. E. Russell.

crowded 'bus coming from Mudie's with my arms full of books — all the passengers got out at Piccadilly Circus — & a red haired woman walked up to me (at the end of the 'bus) & said "Next time you 'ave the misfortune to knock a person's 'at off perhaps you'll 'ave the manners to apologise!!" I stared amazedly & she was gone before I had even time to laugh!

27 — Lunched Ricardos, & did some calls — one on Mrs. Gowing who wrote the Belgravia Review of Wm.'s book[141] — she is rather cracky — says Galway was too hot for her when she took to literature — & if she went out every item of her dress was remarked & had all over the Co[unty] — she complimented me very much on my part of Wm.'s book — Paul dined, & says he heard a man saying at the London Library the other day that it was the most interesting biography he had ever read in his life — P. Henry of Battenburg had been to the War Office about going to Coomassie — The Queen has been very keen about it — & telegraphed to Ld. Lansdowne in the middle of the night that Ld. Salisbury had consented & she hoped he wd not make any further objection[142] — Paul says the Duke of Devonshire is lazy & has not half so good a head as Goschen, who he is not pulling very well with[143] — Ld. Lansdowne is enormously painstaking but spends too much time on details & in laboriously writing out his reasons for all decisions — which will probably bring him more worry than if he left them alone — Ld. Morris had written to Ld. Lansdowne asking him to take Martin as Private Sec. — & he declined & took Paul! I can't help being delighted — for they were not very good when I asked them to help Paul on — "Blackwood['s Magazine]" arrived, I gave it to Paul.

28 — Daily News reviews magazines — begins "Blackwood has an extremely interesting article by Lady G." — & gives extracts[144] — 6 woodcocks from Moyne, sent them to Knowles, Sir A. Lyall & Ly. Haliburton — Wet day — Mrs.

[141] Emilia Aylmer Gowing, née Blake, (d.1905), novelist, poet and dramatist, and widow of actor and comic dramatist William Aylmer Gowing (1822–92) with whom she had jointly edited *The Play* 1881–84. Her review of WHG's autobiography appeared in *Belgravia*, September 1895, pp. 23–38.

[142] Prince Henry, who had spent the years since his marriage to Princess Beatrice in 1885 as a glorified gentleman-in-waiting, clearly saw the Ashanti expedition as the ideal opportunity to emulate his three brothers, each of whom had experienced military service. Victoria was initially opposed to Henry joining the expedition, even sending a doctor to warn him of the dangers to his health in Africa, but eventually relented due to his eagerness.

[143] Spencer Compton Cavendish (1833–1908), 8th Duke of Devonshire, was Chief Secretary for Ireland 1870–74, Secretary of State for War 1882–85 and at this point Lord President of the Council, an office he filled from 1895 to 1903. His brother, Frederick Cavendish, was one of the victims of the Phoenix Park murders in 1882. George Joachim Goschen (1831–1907), 1st Viscount, was an M.P. 1863–1900, Chancellor of the Exchequer 1887–92 and First Lord of the Admiralty 1871–74, 1895–1900.

[144] *The Daily News* 28 November 1895, p. 6, a review of AG's "Eothen and the Athenaeum Club" (see p. 65 n. 6).

Hawthorne & Mrs. Crawfurd called — & I had a note from Humphrey Ward in which he said his wife wd be at home at tea time — so went — & found rather an uninteresting lot — I told her I was amused in M. Arnold's letters at the serious way he speaks of croquet — & she laughed & said he was a wretched croquet player, but quite happy to spend hours knocking the balls about on a steep slope on which they played — On to Lady A. Russell, <?rat trapping> & the girls' manners wretched! Diana retired to a corner & wrote[145] — Flora sat by the fire reading, but occasionally looking up to contradict her mother — Dined Ly. Layard — Found a pleasing note from Paul, who likes my article —

29 — Wet — Mr. Gibbs called — & I went to open Southwark Sale at 6 — Poor people, it was pouring, & customers were scarce — & I spent £2 instead of one — however I got some things that will do children & old women at Coole so didn't grudge it so much.

30 — Wet again — read M. Arnold & Sat[urday]. Review — & went to Lady Layard, M. Morris walking across the Park with me, to take her on to Sale at Southwark — The Dcss. of Bedford's carriage so we made a smart arrival — & there were more people & it was a fine night, & she looked imposing so all went off well — I stayed & dined with her — Tired & didn't sleep.

Dec[ember] 1 — "Observer" has a notice of my article "An entertaining article by Lady Gregory containing some delightful anecdotes & one of the best & brightest chapters of reminiscence we have read for some time — Lady Gregory says of Kinglake that 'his words seemed to crystallise into epigrams as they touched the air'".[146] Westminster Abbey & lunched Sir A. Lyall — Spencer Walpole & Mrs. Lecky there, very pleasant, Sir Alfred says I always have "the very latest" — & I kept up my character — as they had not yet read M. Arnold's letters — & I had not only done so, but read, in the morning, John Morley's paper on them in the XIXth Century[147] — I had dreamed that Sir A. said "Matthew Arnold will be read when Nineveh is forgotten" — & the saying pleased him — & he hopes I will dream on — Mrs. Lecky very anxious about her husband's election — she had a telegram saying the nomination had gone off well — but the uproar so great that the speeches cd not be heard. Theodore Watts told Sir A. that Swinburne is much hurt at M. Arnold saying

---

[145] Caroline Diana Russell (b.1874), Lady Arthur Russell's youngest daughter.

[146] *The Observer* 1 December 1895, p. 7.

[147] "Matthew Arnold", *The Nineteenth Century* December 1895, pp. 1041–55, a courteous review of Russell's new edition of Arnold's letters in which Morley nonetheless makes plain his view that few collections of correspondence, Arnold's included, merit publication on literary grounds. Morley also voices the opinion that there are "probably not six Englishmen over fifty now living, whose lives need to be written", and hints at editorial injudiciousness on Russell's part in including matter which might give offense to living persons.

he takes 100 words to say what cd be said in one — & it was an ungracious thing to print as it was in allusion to Swinburne having sent him a present of "Tristram of Lyonesse"[148] — Tea Sir G. Bowen — deaf & bothered — but on literature quite bright.

2nd Dec[ember] — A kind letter from De Basterot — Then a wire from Paul asking me to go to tea & chaperone an Essex young lady, which I did, tho' at some inconvenience. Very tired & faint all the morning — & the stairs at St. James St. rather too much for me — took Tony Birch there who I met coming to see me — Then with Lady Layard to tea at Mr. du Cane's — rather pleasant, Mr. Thesiger[149] & Mr. Maryon Wilson[150] there — Home very tired — A good notice of "Eothen" in Evening Standard — "very interesting — a string of delightful anecdotes" & gives some extracts[151] — Slept badly.

3rd — Daily Telegraph says "an interesting article — but some of the Eothen sayings might as well have been left unrecorded" — this is the first unfavourable word that has been said[152] — Out to do some tiring shopping — & then to Kensington Infirmary to try & learn if there is any work our old paupers at Gort cd be taught to do — but my heart rather failed at the sight of the beautiful knitting, iron work etc — but perhaps patch work & coarse crochet or knitting wd be possible — Home to my little tea party, which only consisted of Ly. Layard, Henry James & Sir F. Burton — the latter a little X about the Athenaeum article — H. James very kind as usual, but I was sorry I did not have him alone, & enjoyed his benedictory talk — Dined Walpoles — they apologised for a small party as they had had 4 puts off at the last, but I was well enough off as I was next my host, who is extremely agreeable & a mine of knowledge — I told him of Morley saying in his M. Arnold article that there are probably not more than 6 men over 50 now living in England whose lives will be worth writing — & we tried to pick out 6 but only got to Gladstone, Ld.

[148] Russell's selection of Arnold's correspondence included an 1882 letter to Grant Duff in which Arnold noted having received a gift of "Tristram of Lyonesse" a poem of nearly 6000 lines by Algernon Charles Swinburne (1837–1909). Arnold remarks that "Swinburne's fatal habit of using one hundred words where one would suffice always offends me, and I have not yet faced his poem, but I must try it soon" (*Letters*, vol. 2, p. 232). Arnold had composed his own well-known work "Tristram and Iseult", a dramatic poem of some 600 lines, around 1850. Poet, novelist and critic Theodore Watts (1832–1914), who changed his name to Watts-Dunton in 1896, was Swinburne's closest friend, and took care of him from 1879 onwards as Swinburne's health declined.

[149] Frederick John Thesiger (1868–1933), eldest son of 2nd Baron Chelmsford. Succeeded his father in 1905 and served as Viceroy of India 1916–21. Married Frances Guest (d.1957), eldest daughter of Lady Layard's brother Lord Wimborne, in 1894.

[150] Spencer Maryon-Wilson (1859–1944), later 11th Bart.

[151] *Evening Standard* 2 December 1895, p. 2. Though strongly praising her work, the review characterizes AG's article merely as very interesting "gossip".

[152] *Daily Telegraph* 3 December 1895, p. 7.

Salisbury, Herbert Spencer & Ld. Dufferin — but he said a very good 100 pages could be written about Lord Peel — Ly. Edmond Fitzmaurice was there, in blue velvet — I wonder where poor Lord E. is![153] — I had Harold Russell[154] on my other side, but was luckily not dependent on him & Martin Morris discoursed me after dinner.

4th — Morning Post slight notice "interesting".[155] Lunched Sir G. Bowen to meet Mrs. Hemloke & Lady V. Sandars[156] & others — Mr. Campbell was there who used to give Lady Bowen money for Southwark & he professed to be "touched" by my remembering this — & offered to send some more, & I have since received £3. And Mrs. Lewis who was there said Lady Robinson had asked her "not to forget the Southwark children" — & said she had not known where to send her annual £2 — but now will send it me — Sir George says Ld. Lamington consulted him some time ago as to how to obtain a Col. Governorship & he recommended him to marry, but he fears it will be written to Queensland that May had quarrelled with him about a garden party, gone to bed instead of receiving the guests — & then bolted for home — Where she stayed a week before she cd be induced to return to him[157] — She is taking the old Governess to Queensland — "such a help to look after the dinners!"

With Martin Morris & E. Martyn to the Carlyle Centenary meeting, to hear John Morley speak — which was a great delight — hearing instead of reading for once his luminous sentences — He spoke of Wordsworth & Goethe having "a radiant sanity of vision — a serene humanity" — The lecture is very well reported in the Times so I can keep it[158] — Then A. Birrell[159] spoke, very well & brightly, with jokes & epigrams, & it was good to see J. M.'s enjoyment of it. F. Harrison proposed vote of thanks — but not very well — J. M. said he

---

[153] Lord Edmond George Fitzmaurice (1846–1935), second son of the 4th Marquess of Lansdowne, M.P. 1868–85, 1898–1905 and Under-Secretary of State for Foreign Affairs 1882–85 and 1905–08. Married Caroline FitzGerald in 1889. Their marriage had in fact been annulled in 1894.

[154] Harold John Russell (1868–1926), Barrister in the Temple, eldest son of Lady Arthur Russell. Married Lady Victoria Leveson-Gower (b.1867), daughter of the 2nd Earl Granville and niece of F. Leveson-Gower (see p. 89 n. 125) in 1896.

[155] Morning Post 4 December, p. 2.

[156] Lady Virginia Sandars (1828–1922), youngest daughter of the 2nd Marquess of Headfort, widowed in March 1893.

[157] Lamington had apparently profited by the advice, being appointed Governor of Queensland soon after his marriage to May Hozier in 1895. She was Extra Lady of the Bedchamber to H.M. Queen Mary, which perhaps explains Lamington's fear of immediate damage to his political career from her display of pique. After serving in Queensland 1895–1901, he was Governor of Bombay 1903–07.

[158] Morley's speech at the meeting honouring the centenary of the birth of Thomas Carlyle (1795–1881), is reported in detail in The Times 5 December, p. 6.

[159] Augustine Birrell (1850–1933), Chancery barrister and writer, later Chief Secretary of Ireland 1907–16 and a key ally of AG in her efforts to get the Lane pictures returned to Ireland.

hardly believed anyone now living had read all through "Frederick the Great",[160] but E. Martyn & I, we two Galwegians, said simultaneously to each other "I have done so" — John Morley comes nearer my idea of an inspired teacher than anyone I have heard, or read, of living writers — & makes one at least grope after the "radiant sanity of vision" that we want so much in poor Ireland[161] — Dined Ly. Layard.

5th — To Whiteley's for sweets for Xmas tree & Workhouse — Back at 3 — No time for lunch, as I expected Sir A. Lyall — cut a bit of bread & butter & was just beginning to eat it when Sir H. Cunningham arrived rather prosy — Then Sir A. — who was put out at finding him here, thinking him a bore, & that I had asked him — Then off to Kensington Square to call on Mrs. [Newton] Robinson — then back to meet Paul at 6 — Then dressed & to Hyde Park Gardens to dine with Mrs. Kay — pretty hard work for a *foodless* day — Mrs. Kay's party looked seedy & miscellaneous — Ross of Bladensburg etc — but I sat between Lord Lingen, who was interesting on educational matters[162] — & Mr. Barry O'Brien, a Nationalist, sub-editor of The Speaker, & very sensible & moderate in conversation[163] — He believes in Home Rule, but thinks there is no chance for it until all the present members are swept off the Board — Quite agreed with me that Dillon has done for himself as a Nationalist by marrying an Englishwoman — says he has been talking to one of the writers on the "Freeman['s Journal]" who has been travelling in Ireland, & who says the only one thing in which all parties are agreed is the failure of Morley's Govt. — He (B. O'B.) believes A. Balfour is the only man who has any understanding of Ireland — & believes he wd have swept the whole country if he had gone over & made a speech against Cromwell, who he is not an admirer of, when the Liberals proposed to erect a statue to him — We agreed on the extraordinary stupidity of even enlightened men like Morley & Bryce in Irish affairs, in having ever thought the Irish wd let such

---

[160] Carlyle's *Frederick the Great*, published in six volumes 1858–65.

[161] Morley was inevitably a sympathetic figure for AG since he shared her regard for Carlyle's "Gospel of Labour," which saw dutiful work as the best antidote to the moral and intellectual confusions of the age. His advocacy of "focalizing"—attending to a single question and resolving it in a simply expressed form, rather than attempting to elaborate a master-system which would take account of its complex relation to other issues—undoubtedly provided a congenial (and morally-based) model for her own literary career.

[162] Ralph Wheeler Lingen (1819–1905), 1st Baron Lingen, sometime Governor of Rugby and Bedford Schools, and Secretary to the Education Office 1849–69. Permanent Secretary of the Treasury 1869–85.

[163] Richard Barry O'Brien (1847–1918), barrister, writer and nationalist. Co-founder of the London branch of the Irish Literary Society, and its President 1906–11. Biographer of Wolfe Tone, Parnell and others, and a prolific writer on the Irish Land Question, he had published a biography of Thomas Henry Drummond, Mrs Kay's father, in 1890. O'Brien subsequently became Editor of *The Speaker*.

a proposal pass.[164]

6th — Lunched Ly. D. Nevill,[165] met George Moore, Mrs. Hodgson Burnett,[166] Mr. Dasart & Martin Morris — Lady D. very amiable, & all pleasant enough — Bought a "Pall Mall [Gazette]" & saw that Lecky was elected all right, so sent a telegram of congratulation to Mrs. L.[167] — Tea Mrs. Hemloke, & then to Ly. Maxwell's — Dined Ly. Layard.

7th — A letter of farewell from Nevill Geary asking if I wd go & see him off — found he wd be at the Temple at 11-30 — so went off there & saw him for a moment, going off in good spirits — Then to Christie's, & saw Mr. Woods about the Waithman picture — Mr. Woods said "Well, I must say you are a Lady with a great many friends" — He believes it is genuine but doesn't think the public sufficiently educated to give much for it — Poynter has seen it but he doesn't know what his opinion is — Then lunch & to see the mezzotints at Colnaghi's & then took 'bus to Holland Villas Rd. & went to see Jean Ingelow who I thought a good deal changed & broken & rather inconsequent in talk — She has given up writing for some months — She is always cheerful, & says she has no reason to complain of literature or of her publishers — as she has made a good deal — She is reading M. Arnold's letters & thinks them "rubbish" — but liked him and Mrs. Arnold, used to stay with them — Browning's poems she thinks "vulgar" — but likes Mrs. B.'s[168] — When I mentioned Lewis Morris she asked "Is that the shopman?" Poor thing, I

[164] A proposal to erect a statue of Oliver Cromwell in the grounds of the Palace of Westminster had precipitated one of the series of fiascos which brought the end of Rosebery's Premiership in June 1895. A Cabinet request for a vote appropriating the necessary funds provoked outrage from Irish Nationalist M.P.s, and an embarrassed withdrawal by the Government. Morley, Chief Secretary for Ireland 1892–95 and the key figure in the Liberals' Irish policy after Gladstone's resignation, appears to have let his admiration for Cromwell's forcefulness—a quality he had also admired in Parnell and others—blind him to the urgency of retaining Nationalist support if Rosebery were to remain in power. He subsequently published a biography of Cromwell in 1900. James Bryce (1838–1922), Regius Professor of Law at Oxford 1870–93, and a Liberal M.P. 1880–1907 was likewise a member of Rosebery's Cabinet as Chancellor of the Duchy of Lancaster 1892–94. Later Chief Secretary to the Lord Lieutenant of Ireland 1905–07, and raised to the peerage as 1st Viscount Bryce in 1914, he was a prolific writer on political and constitutional matters, and a forceful advocate of Gladstone's Home Rule policies. He had edited The Handbook of Home Rule (1887), essays by Morley, Gladstone, Barry O'Brien and others on the Irish Question.

[165] Lady Dorothy Nevill, née Walpole (1826–1913), youngest daughter of Horatio Walpole, 3rd Earl of Orford (d.1858), and widow of Reginald Henry Nevill (d.1878).

[166] Frances Hodgson Burnett (1849–1924), novelist, dramatist, and author of Little Lord Fauntleroy and The Secret Garden.

[167] Lecky beat his opponent for the Dublin University seat by a margin of 1757 to 1011 votes. Polling had closed early enough on 6 December for the result to be published in London evening papers.

[168] Poetess Elizabeth Barrett Browning (1806–61), author of Aurora Leigh and Sonnets from the Portuguese, married Robert Browning in 1846, and lived mainly in Italy thereafter.

hardly think I shall see her again — A quiet evening, & none too soon, for I was very tired. Editor of Sketch will pay me 4 guineas for short story sent "Dies Irae".[169]

Sunday Dec[ember] 8 1895[170]

Westminster Abbey. Lunched Maxwells — & then to see Annie Maxwell & Mary Studd[171] — & then home & got through the bundle of Sir Henry Layard's letters I had taken to sort — All to Ly. C. Schreiber,[172] & little of interest in them, except a touching one written the day after his marriage — Dinner — E. Martyn, to console him for N. Geary's departure — & Sir A. & Lady Clay, Mrs. Kay, George Moore, Mr. Barry O'Brien, & Arthur Du Cane[173] — It went off well, dinner better than usual, plenty of talk, G. Moore & Sir A. had worked in the same atelier in Paris 20 years ago, & never met since — Mr. O'Brien very interesting & G. Moore quiet & pleasant —

9th — Lunched with Ly. Layard & went with her to Southwark, to the School — Then back & dressed & went to a crowded tea party at John Gray's little rooms — no one I knew — but I was introduced to Mrs. Lilly[174] & liked her — Then back again, & found the Birch boys here, & when they went had to dress for dinner, dead tired, & off to Humphrey Wards — which ought to have been pleasant but I did not find so, I suppose from being so tired — I sat between old Horsley[175] & H. Ward, who has deteriorated, looks sullen, & sneered at every person & thing mentioned — his daughters excepted[176] —

[169] Published in *The Sketch* 25 March 1896, p. 376.

[170] This entry marks the beginning of a new exercise book. On the inside front cover AG wrote in pencil beneath the date "1896" two Biblical quotations: "He that ruleth let him do it with diligence" (*Rom* 12.8) and "But I am among you as one that serveth" (*Luke* 22.27).

[171] Annie Maxwell (d.1914) was Mary (Cole) Studd's mother. Born Anne Celestine Burke, she married firstly Francis Horatio de Vere (d.1865) and secondly Rev. Charlton Maxwell (d.1895). She was WHG's cousin, being the daughter of Anne O'Hara (d.1844), sister of WHG's mother Elizabeth.

[172] Enid Layard's mother, Lady Charlotte Schreiber, née Bertie, then Guest (1812–95), whose celebrated translation of *The Mabinogion* was a major contribution to the Victorian revival of interest in Arthurian legend and Romance studies, not least through its influence on her close friend Tennyson.

[173] Arthur George Du Cane (1866–1942), Inner Temple barrister. Third son of Richard and Maria Du Cane (see p. 35 n. 74).

[174] Probably Susannah Lilly, wife of William Samuel Lilly (1840–1919), Secretary of the Catholic Union of Great Britain 1874–1919.

[175] John Callcott Horsley (1817–1903), painter, and Treasurer of the Royal Academy 1882–97.

[176] Dorothy (1874–1964) and Janet Ward (1879–1956). Janet married George Macaulay Trevelyan, son of George Otto Trevelyan (see p. 108 n. 10) and himself a distinguished historian, in 1904.

He says Hugh Gough is looked on as a thorough donkey at Washington, & was the butt of his college when at Oxford, but had seemed to improve meanwhile — He keeps Ly. Georgiana under lock & key, & doesn't let her amuse herself as she wd like[177] — The Lionel Custs were there, she very pretty & gracious, I wished, looking at her that Paul could find a woman like that to marry[178] — Also the Du Mauriers — He told me he had been astonished at the success of "Trilby" — had written it "in corners" to amuse himself — & that he himself prefers "Peter Ibbetson" — but his new book contains quite a different heroine[179] —

10th — Shopping for home & Xmas — & called to try & see Poynter about R. W[aithman]'s picture & looked at Colnaghi's mezzotints — & called on Mrs. Walpole — Paul dined, & told me he is drifting (or it seems to me being forced) into an engagement with Miss Gilmore, the girl I had chaperoned at his rooms — He asked my advice, very hard to give as I desire his happiness, & think he wd find it in home & marriage — but he confesses he does not like her family, thinks there are more charming & refined women in the world, but has so few chances of meeting them it isn't worth while waiting — Poor boy — he is only 26 — & I believe she has thrown herself at his head, & then got her brother to speak to him. He is not in love — yet likes her & thinks she has got to like him — A bad night, & headache —

11th — Fog, without & within — Lunched Raffys, but rather vexed as they had promised to be alone — but had the usual over-dressed women & shady looking men — Then to Lady Layard with my embroidery — & she offered me the 2 bookcases she thought of selling — which will be delightful for Coole — Then to Mrs. Knowles — & then in, on chance of Paul coming, which he did — Just the same pros & cons but he has yeilded to me in not speaking to Mr. Gardner the clergyman who is to come & dine with him, so is still uncommitted — & he has written to ask Henry James to see him, for consultation — so my responsibility is divided — & I feel quieter — He asked me at the end which it wd make me happier — if he went on or broke off —

[177] Hugh Gough (1849–1919), succeeded his father as 3rd Viscount in May 1895. Entered the diplomatic service in 1873, serving as Secretary of the British Embassy at Washington 1894–96, at Berlin 1896–1901, and as Minister Resident at Dresden 1901–07. Married Lady Georgiana Pakenham (d.1943) in 1889. Besides being near neighbours in Galway, AG and the Goughs were connected through the marriage of Gough's sister Eleanor (d.1935) to AG's brother Robert Algernon. Hugh Gough's nephew Guy Gough (1887–1959) would marry Margaret Parry Gregory, RG's widow, in 1928.

[178] Lionel Henry Cust (1859–1929) and his wife Sybil (d.1934). Cust, an art historian, was Director of the National Portrait Gallery 1895–1909.

[179] George Lois Du Maurier (1834–96), novelist and dramatist. His novels *Trilby* and *Peter Ibbetson* were published in 1893 and 1891 respectively. His "new book" was the novel *The Martian* posthumously published in 1897. Married Emma Wightwick in 1863.

& honestly I could not say — or dared not say, not knowing enough of the girl —

12 — Mary Studd in the morning, & the Birchs — I think putting in for an invite for Wyndham — & giving me one to a Ceylon lunch! at which my spirit rose! & I refused — & Una then, looking rather ashamed asked me to dine, & I accepted for Sunday — Afternoon a gale rose, & terrific rain, & I did not get out — but at 6 poor Paul came — as before — still undecided but wishing to drift — which is what I wish him least to do — If it were F. Williams or anyone not so dear to me, I wd say "You are going too cheap, take another turn out of yourself" — but he wants a home so much, & I have such a habit of spoiling him & it hurts me to refuse him anything, even my consent to what I cannot quite approve of — I suppose I shall go through it all over again some day with Robert! — The gale abated & I got to dinner with Ly. Layard — Mrs. Alderson & Nelly there, & they had been to Hatfield & lunched with the Salisburys — No political news, except that G. Salisbury[180] said Sir P. Currie says the Sultan has aged extraordinarily during the crisis & looks 70 — Lady Layard spoke of Ld. Salisbury's want of confidence in those around him, & said at Con[stan]t[ino]ple he would not allow Sir H. to trust any of the secretaries — so that she had often to copy despatches — The whole Cyprus treaty is in her handwriting[181] — Nelly Alderson says Lord Cranbourne[182] & "Gwen" do all his private work — & a sort of servant secretary, attached to the house — the so called private secs nothing but the most formal work — but she declares it is to save giving them trouble!

13 — A very restless night, a debating society going on in my head over Paul's affairs — I wish he had a more impartial adviser — Then I thought perhaps he had better speak to Mr. Gardner about it — he will know if there is anything actually against the girl — or if she has been engaged before — Tried to "lay the ghost" of these debates by writing them down, & sending them to Paul, before he goes back to Totham — Rather cheered up by a beautiful bouquet of game sent by Dr. M[oran]. — 9 snipe & 2 teal! which I sent on to Lady Haliburton — & then "Mr. Spencer Walpole" was announced & had come to ask me to dine to meet Sir West Ridgeway[183] — & luckily I was free, & had just been wishing I had something to distract my thoughts in the evening — & he

[180] Gwendoline Cecil, second eldest of Lord Salisbury's daughters. She later published a biography of her father, *The Life of Robert, Marquess of Salisbury, to 1892* (4 vols., 1921–32).

[181] Under this 1878 treaty, which Layard negotiated, Turkey ceded control of Cyprus to Britain in return for a monetary payment and British protection against Syria. Salibury was at that time Secretary of State for Foreign Affairs.

[182] James Edward Gasgoyne-Cecil (1861–1945), Viscount Cranborne, Salibury's eldest son, who succeeded him as 4th Marquess in 1903. He followed his father into politics, becoming Lord Privy Seal 1903–05 and Leader of the House of Lords 1925–31.

[183] Sir Joseph West Ridgeway (1844–1930), Under–Secretary for Ireland 1887–93 and Lt Governor of the Isle of Man 1893–95.

sat & chatted pleasantly for a little — on over reading he said that Ld. Acton[184] had read 18 books on a Saturday to Monday in the country! No wonder his lecture on History had such an undigested effect! Out, to Hunt's Registry to try & get a girl for Coole, & then looking for "Federation files" to bind letters — & then chose a knife for R.'s Xmas box — a real beauty! Very pleasant dinner at the Walpoles — 3 ex-Governors of the Isle of Man, my host, West Ridgeway, & Ld. & Lady Loch,[185] also Ld. & Lady Rendel[186] — Sir A. & Ly. Lyall — the Wentworth Beaumonts & a Col. Murray — I sat next Sir Alfred — he says India is pretty peaceable except that the Amir is in a perfect fury at not being allowed to send a representative here — so all the hospitality to the Shah <??> is rather wasted — Ld. Elgin is jogging along pretty well, but will never have a name as a successful Viceroy[187] — Sir A. pleased because I asked his son over to shoot — Talked afterwards to Lady Loch, who has a nice gracious manner like Ly. Lytton — Lord Loch told me he liked his Cape Govt. immensely, there was so much important work to do, & you had immense power as High Commissioner tho' not so much as Governor — Sir West Ridgeway asked me a good deal about Ceylon & said he had enjoyed Wm's book so much, & having himself been for some years in the Under Secretary's Lodge, where Wm. was born, he felt he had a connection with him & was following Wm.'s footsteps — A very pleasant evening, & I slept well, a great mercy!

14th — Engaged a housemaid who has lived for 3 years at the Japanese Embassy! Lunched Knowles — only Hamilton Aide there, but pleasant enough — he gave me his "King Arthur" for Robert — Called on Ly. Lindsay — & tea with Mary Studd & dined Ly. Layard & went to hear the "Electrophone" with Mrs. Alderson at Pelican House, Shaftesbury Avenue! It was rather my idea of an opium den — people sitting apparently in a torpid state round with tubes to their ears. When I sat down & applied my tubes, I heard a song in the "Artist's Model" — & then clapping, but it sounded to me like the dentist's voice when one is recovering from gas — far away & harsh & without melody — Then other plays were turned on — but I soon made off — but might as well have stayed there, for I could not get to sleep till 2 — worrying myself — & so pointlessly — over Paul's affairs — At dinner they spoke of Ly. Salisbury's extravagance, it is her idea that there has always been a plentiful table at Hatfield & so there is always much too much of everything — & of course gr

---

[184] John Emerich Acton (1834–1902), 1st Baron, M.P. 1859–66, Lord-in-waiting to Queen Victoria 1892–95, and Professor of Modern History at Cambridge University 1895–1902.

[185] Henry Brougham Loch (1827–1900), and his wife, Elizabeth, née Villiers (Lady Lytton's sister). Loch was Governor of the Isle of Man 1863–82, of Victoria 1884–89, and Governor of the Cape of Good Hope and High Commissioner for S. Africa 1889–95. Raised to the Peerage as 1st Baron Loch in July 1895.

[186] Stuart Rendel (1834–1913), 1st Baron Rendel, M.P. 1880–94, and his wife Ellen, née Hubbard (d.1912).

[187] Victor Bruce (1849–1917), 9th Earl of Elgin, Viceroy of India 1894–99.

waste — curious as for a long time they had to live on a few hundreds a year.
She manages everything — house, stables & all —

15 — Westminster Abbey — but had again slept badly & was tired — Lunched
Lady Dorothy, not much of a party — Oswald Crawfurds — Sidney Colvin, Mr.
D'Arcy — & a horrid "buck parson" — the subdean of the Chapel Royal —
however I was able to ask Mr. Crawfurd for my missing sketch book — & Mr.
D'Arcy said he wd send a cheque to Dodge — S. Colvin spoke rather
sneeringly of Ld. Morris & said people were getting tired of him — & "he
doesn't take his Duchesses as his daily bread!" — Frank Lawley paid me a long
visit, delighted with my Kinglake article — a little with the wrong news as
usual, having heard a few days ago such alarming news of Ld. Salisbury's
health that he had written an obituary notice of him! Also that the one "leader
of men" in the Ministry is Ld. Lansdowne! He said he had met Cecil Rhodes
in the summer & he had said his chief relaxation is having translations of the
classics read to him — that his sight is going, & in a year he will be quite blind
— but he said "I am not going to be like your old chief, I will still keep the helm
in my own hands".[188]

Dined Birchs — they were alone, & it was rather dull, Sir A. holding forth, but
no common talk.

16th — Rain & storm — & had to go to Stores & do my shopping there as best
I could — Lunched Ly. Haliburton — then to Knowles's American friend's
picture show — Then back to Qmansions to meet Henry James who had
telegraphed to say he wd come — though I had asked him *not* to — until he
had seen Paul — But I daresay it was for the best — he was so kind — so clear
sighted — so decidedly against the marriage "too soon — too sudden — & not
inevitable enough" — & was horrified at the thought of Miss Gilmore having
herself spoken of the neighbours' gossip — "A nice girl would have pre-
tended not to know what he meant — but wd not have been there the next
Monday" — Paul was to dine with me — but at 6 it struck me to go up & ask
for a table — & they could not promise one — so I had to meet him downstairs
& ask him to take me to dinner — very ignominious — & honesty forced me
to tell him I had seen H. James — which put him out very much — but I was
too tired & too wretched to care — He came back & we argued the whole thing
over & over — I afraid to say too much & give my real opinion of that second
rate self satisfied little woman who is trying to run him down — & he in a
reckless fit born of loneliness, rather wishing to plunge into marriage, if only
to be extinguished & have nothing more expected of him — And then at the
end he told me that on his last journey down, he had twice evaded her, but

---

[188] Rhodes's physical deterioration from around 1894 was pronounced, but he did not go
blind. Lawley's "old chief" was presumably Gladstone, to whose retirement Rhodes apparently
alluded.

at the last station there was no escape & she had begged him to come & see her — & on his decidedly refusing had been "very much upset" — A dreadful woman! & if he is always to be waylaid at railway stations how can he escape — He was to go to H. James at 10 — so I bid him goodbye with a very heavy heart knowing that I could never bear to see him again with that triumphant woman at his elbow[189] —

17 — Robert in the morning — looking well — & we had a hard day — off to the City for fireworks for the tree — & to get clothes for him — & he lunched with the Birchs & I with Ly. Layard, & then for his shopping to Sloane St., & back to finish packing dead tired but cheered by a nice note from Paul — saying he has decided to give up the idea "if circumstances are not too strong for him" & thanking me very gratefully — I don't quite know for what[190] — Off to Ireland, meeting Richard & Lucy the new housemaid at the station — A wakeful night but fine crossing — but lost some luggage.

18 — To Coole — the house clean & all well — but I had to start work at once to get things unpacked.

18 — ~~Shooting~~ — Mr. Richardson arrived — He had been very kind to Robert his last Elstree term & I thought it ungrateful not to ask him again.

19 — Shooting — Arthur — Frank — Sir T. Burke[191] — J. Shawe Taylor[192] — Dr. Moran — 47 pheasants, 9 1/2 couple cock — bad, owing to mild weather.

20 — 6 1/2 couple cock — A poor day — but fine — Katy, Rosie & Miss Gehle[193] came over — All left in the evening

[189] Recalling this episode, and Henry James's help, AG would write that "four hands were needed in place of two to draw our nurseling from the slippery edge towards which he was tending, half-willing. . . . He said that in such a time of crisis Henry James was a more comfortable guide than I, and this I can well believe, for guarding against the natural jealousy of a woman when another threatened to come into the life of even an adopted child, I weighed and balanced and tried to be just, looking on every side. 'And what did Henry James say?' 'He just said it was impossible, that I must put it out of my head.' The best of advice, yet we can hardly imagine one of those beings who people his pages speaking on any matter, light or serious, in such brief and decisive words" (*Seventy Years* p. 182).

[190] "I have made up my mind to try and forget what I have been hoping for this last week— or at any rate to try and resist the temptation to allow the matter to grow. I will try to be firm and to influence circumstances; though I cannot be sure of success, especially if circumstances are strongly against me. Anyway I have made up my mind not to drift. . . . Very many thanks for what you have suffered in this affair. I make no doubt you have done me a very great service" (Emory).

[191] Sir Theobald Burke (1836–1909), soldier and veteran of the Crimean and Indian wars.

[192] John Shawe-Taylor (1866–1911), eldest son of AG's sister Elizabeth. In 1902 his call for aconference of representative landlords and tenants helped break the long stalemate over the Lnd Question and ushered in the Wyndham Land Act of 1903.

[193] Katherine Persse, née Gehle (Arthur Persse's wife), together with Arthur's sister Rose Charlotte (b.1852), and, presumably, one of Katherine's sisters.

1896

Jan[uary] 7 — A good deal of hard work over since I last wrote — Xmas — very expensive! — Workmen, servants — old women — Workhouse (tobacco, toys etc). Then the day after, Xmas tree — for the school & tenants' children — china ornaments for girls — ties & comforters for boys, sweets, crackers tea & buns for all — & Robert displayed his magic lantern with gr effect — Very tired after it.

Mr. Richardson left 30th, he had had bad weather but very fair sport — Edward Martyn letting us shoot over Tillyra being a gr help — He took a fine bundle of game away & seemed grateful — The boys have called the ferrets "Squasher & Ted" one being big & hairy — the other small & perky — Tony Birch arrived 4th — having failed in his exam — got 500 marks less than last time so the idea of the Army is given up "a good thing too" he says ingenuously "as there seems likely to be war!" There does indeed seem a likelihood of war — The President's message in America[1] — the Sultan's calm obstinacy[2] — the rash march of Jameson into the Transvaal[3] — & now the German Emperor's

---

[1] On 18 December 1895, President Cleveland had issued a hostile ultimatum to Britain regarding the two countries' long-running dispute over the borders between British Guiana and Venezuela, following Britain's refusal of an American offer of arbitration. After a week of rapidly increasing diplomatic tension, Britain backed down and agreed to negotiate a settlement.

[2] A warning note had been sent to the Turkish Sultan by six European Ambassadors urging a prompt end to Turkish massacres of Armenians and requiring immediate civil rights reforms. At this point the Sultan, perhaps encouraged by Russia's refusal to join in the threated sanctions and military intervention, was calling the Western Powers' bluff.

[3] "Jameson's Raid", engineered by Cecil Rhodes, was an armed incursion into the Transvaal from Bechuanaland by a force of over 400 British mercenaries led by Leander "Starr" Jameson (1853–1917), Rhodes's right-hand man in annexing Matabeleland in 1893. Riding quickly towards Johannesburg, Jameson's force hoped to foment a civil war and gain control of the Boer state for Britain. The plan failed miserably: Kruger's troops forced Jameson to surrender well outside Johannesburg, and anti-Boer activists within the city were rounded up and imprisoned. The raid was promptly denounced by Colonial Secretary Joseph Chamberlain and others in Government, and in a subsequent inquiry was portrayed as the product of Jameson's individual rashness. The complicity of Cecil Rhodes and many at the highest levels of Goverment (including

message of congratulation to Kruger, so insulting to England[4] — An interesting letter from H. H. Johnston in Central Africa — which seems one of the only quiet dominions at present.

Robert has shot his first woodcock his first cock pheasant & his first snipe — but yesterday was out ferreting — & as the ferrets were a long time coming out he put his gun against a tree, & went on all fours to bark at the cows like a dog — & they came behind him & knocked the gun down on a stone & it is badly dented — Such a baby! for the Vth form (he did well, was 3rd in exam & gets his remove to middle division) & I had been quite anxious about his brain the evening before, he was so intent on draught problems — tho' mastering them in a moment.

Jan[uary] 22nd — The boys left yesterday — all having gone on well during the holidays — except that the last day poor little Russ[5] was thrown from a car — & died last night — Mike John was thrown on his head, but not hurt — the boys had driven on the car to Tillyra & I followed later with Geraldine[6] to pick them up & take them on to Roxboro' and it gave me a shock thinking what might have happened if the pony had shied on the way there instead of coming back —

Tony left, not in very good humour — seemed jealous at R[ichar]d. killing more birds than he did — & was either boisterous & rowdy, or in the depths of depression, I don't think I will ask him again — Robert very happy to the last moment — went out shooting & ferreting before they started — I saw them off — then went to the Workhouse & saw the Master — who says the old men are delighted with the "Freeman's Journal" I am taking for them — I

Chamberlain himself) in planning the raid, was widely suspected, but the official enquiry produced a whitewash. To the majority of the population at this time of high Empire and rampant nationalism, Jameson's supposed impulsiveness was well-intentioned, the ride itself a heroic effort, and only its failure to be lamented. The raid was celebrated in epic tone by the Poet Laureate, Alfred Austin, in his poem "Jameson's Ride", and also provided the inspiration for Kipling's poem "If". Jameson subsequently flourished, serving as Prime Minister of Cape Colony 1904–08, and being raised to the peerage in 1911. He was buried next to his mentor, Rhodes, in Bulawayo.

4 Jameson crossed into the Transvaal on 30 December 1895 and surrended late on 2 January 1896. The following day Kaiser Wilhelm telegraphed a message of congratulations to Boer President Paul Kruger for his success in "defending the independence of the country" without having had to call on the aid of "friendly Powers". Besides implying that the Transvaal—at that time still under British suzerainty—was indeed independent, the telegram's clear suggestion that Germany would be willing to support Boer efforts to claim sovereignty caused a storm of outrage and jingoism in Britain, during which the fact that Jameson had failed, and the illegalities the action had involved, were largely ignored.

5 One of the Coole dogs.

6 Probably a maid.

spoke to him about the Brabazon scheme[7] & he is quite hopeful — says some can make nets & some straw mats — Sister Xavier has been roused by my saying the men look dull to start a bookcase — & I am to give her some books — Saw Ethel off to Roxboro' & was left quite alone — the house so silent that when I went up to dress for dinner I thought I was going to bed & turned the lamp down! But I am glad to be alone for a time — to "possess my soul" & look life in the face — & I want to plant outside — & to arrange & copy letters within — & anyhow I have spent my money & could not well get away —

Jan[uary] 31 — Have planted about 1400 trees, in nutwood & clump in "45 acres" — larch, spruce — silver — scotch — & some evergreen oaks & new lilacs in nutwood — & Frank has been over today & advised me to get 1000 birch, as a man had been over from England buying them at L. Cutra, for clog soles — anyhow they are very silvery, showing through dark foliage — I have been studying seed potatoes! & wrote to Talbot Power[8] — to ask advice — but he writes back that he is not an agriculturalist — but will send me a ton of "flourballs".

My chief visitors have been Howley, for a "note" to the sub sheriff to get him off a fine for non attendance at jury — (done I think) & Mrs. Prendergast wanting £10 to buy out her son who has enlisted but this I refused — as he seems to be a professional poacher — My chief grievance has been the Garryland shooting where they bagged 58 pheasants! our pheasants — reared at our expense! — & have offered no compensation of any sort — I am chiefly sorry that Robert shd find so soon the little grasping turn of his relatives — but Castle Taylor has always had a crooked name[9] — I went to Moyne for 2 days — A[rabella] seeming low & with troubles overhead! My letter had missed — & no carriage to meet me — & I had to walk the whole 5 miles! — but it was a fine afternoon & I enjoyed it — & I think cheered up A. — but what a life! shut up nearly all the winter with bronchitis — no money no interests or power of helping anyone outside — just skinning the rats for the W[aithmans]'s benefit.

Today the Mrs. & Eliza [Shawe-Taylor] unexpectedly to lunch — but Frank had arrived also unexpectedly & a beefsteak had been put down for him — which did very well — & he had brought over a draft Will for the Mrs. which seems fair but I suppose she will object to —

7 Reginald Brabazon (1841–1929), Earl of Meath, promoted numerous philanthropic organizations in Britain and Ireland, involving fund-raising for hospitals, education and economic self-help.

8 Sir John Talbot Power (1845–1901), 3rd Bart, Wexford landlord and J.P., and member of the Power distilling family.

9 The Garrylands woods, adjoining Coole, were part of the Shawe-Taylor estate, Castle Taylor.

Feb[ruary] 13 — Nothing new — planted 1000 birch in nut wood — & some dog wood & sallys elsewhere — Been to Workhouse with books — but it is slow work trying to start the "Brabazon scheme" — The master said I must first get leave from Local Govt. Board — & G. Morris writes back (after a fortnight) that the application must be made by Guardians — & warns me of the "local & religious jealousies" that so often bring the best intentions to nought in Ireland — I knew that well enough! & am working hard to overcome them — Robert has not written this week — which saddens me a little, as if he was beginning to think less of me — Have ordered a ton of "Wonder" seed potatoes from Muldoon's — if they turn out well I won't grudge my £5 — but if the people don't appreciate them, or they don't turn out well, I shall feel a fool for my pains — Having seen that Cecil Rhodes is going to Bulawayo (where Peyton is) I have written to Sir Hercules asking him to recommend Peyton to him — I hope he will give him the management of a gold mine at the least! Working away, still at Ld. Talbot's letters — & see my way to making them interesting enough to publish — if his family don't object — but they probably may — Arranging Wm.'s letters still in "Federation files" — & reading with gr delight, for the 2nd time G. Trevelyan's "C. J. Fox"[10] — The days go by very quickly.

13th — Frank for rent — Throws cold water on my Workhouse scheme — says I will never get anyone to go on with it when I am away — & that the Guardians will be too suspicious to give leave — as they have just found to their disgust that the Industrial School built at the Convent has to be paid for out of the rates — However the more difficulties appear, the more I see that if I don't surmount them nobody else will — so I am writing to enlist Father Fahey — Mrs. Prendergast has given up the idea of buying her son out of the army — but wants money advanced to buy a cow — & we are doing this for her. Farrell of Lissatunna wants larch for rafters so I went with Mike & marked two — tho' it goes to my heart cutting a tree.

14 — Finished Ld. Talbot's letters — Drove to Perys — Brennan is to dig Mrs. Quirk's potato field.

15 — Church — & went to see old Farrell & engaged him to cut ivy from the trees "by contract" that he can choose his own days & hours — He looked comfortable sitting by the fire with his wife — who has grown quite clean & smart — & says her daughters are very good — sending her clothes & a few shillings now & again —

[10] *The Early History of Charles James Fox*, by Sir George Otto Trevelyan (1838–1928), a history of the eminent statesman (1749–1806) and advocate of religious and political liberty, who as Foreign Secretary introduced the legislation which made Grattan's Irish Parliament possible. Trevelyan, from 1882 2nd Bart., a distinguished politician as well as historian, was M.P. 1865–97, and Chief Secretary for Ireland 1882–84.

17th — An amiable letter from Dr. Fahey promising to call tomorrow — Found another packet of Ld. Talbot's letters! A cheery letter from Robert — Walked a gr deal, & cut ivy — & fell through a paling, hurting my knees —

18 — Another letter from Father F. — not I think quite so amiable — & saying he had forgotten it was Shrove Tuesday — & can't come.

19 — A larch coming out in the woods — Farrell cutting ivy merrily.

20 — £5 from Sir H. & Lady Robinson & Mr. Dasart from the Cape for Southwark children — just as I had been puzzling how to provide for them — Father Fahey called — Quite willing I should start Brabazon scheme — but I said I must have some R[oman]. C[atholic]. support in Gort — as if it was all done by Protestants there wd be an outcry sooner or later — & as he knows of no-one at present with sufficient time & energy — it must stand over —

21 — Got thro' a lot of writing — & in the afternoon got Marty & 93 ash saplings he had dug up in the wood, & proceeded with him & Cahel to plant them along the walls — at back of Kiltartan chapel — & other wall of park — If they succeed, it will have been a good days work — towards Robert's firing in the future.

March 26 — I had meant to stay here all the spring, peacefully — but one Sunday Ethel & Katy came over to ask if I wd go to the Croft for a bit, to let Ethel stay on at Roxboro' — So, rather ruefully I packed up a bundle of my papers & copybooks, & started for Galway next day — missed the train at Athenry — had to wait 6 1/2 hours, till 9 pm! Very sorry for myself — & it was too cold to sketch, but I had a packet of Mudie's books with me — & read the "Greville Memoirs" — & I walked through the town, & bought 2 china figures of Parnell & Gladstone[11] — Arrived late & tired at the Croft — & found that Arabella had unexpectedly come there — However she was more or less of an invalid, & the Mrs. had been nervous about having her alone — & she begged not to be left tête à tête with the Mrs. — & Ethel wanted to stay on & meet a 'Major' at Roxboro', so in the end I stayed a fortnight — very unwell all the time — first with neuralgic headaches — then violent attacks of sickness, whether from the food — or the carriage or the hot rooms I know not. There were compensations — for I got a dear little pup "Rip" for Robert — & I went & interviewed Sir Thos. Moffett at the College[12] — & he not only lent me several books useful to me but told me anecdotes of Ld. Whitworth — Ld.

[11] AG describes these in "Clay People Long Famous", *Arts and Decoration* April 1930, pp. 106, 117, 133.

[12] Sir Thomas William Moffett (1830–1908), Professor of History, English Literature and Mental Science at Queen's College, Galway from 1877 and President of the College in the 1890s.

Talbot etc which will be a help if I publish[13] — The Mrs. of course, talking of
Lime Park etc — & of Alfie's affairs[14] — which are very bad — he owes £1500
at the Bank — & so will have only £1500 clear out of the £3000 she leaves him
— She seemed hard about him, made me very angry by mimicking his accent
as if it were not her fault! & talked of "poor Eliza" & "poor Arabella's" poverty
— She talked of leaving £3000 instead of £1500 to Adelaide which she could
only do by taking from the others — & I was uneasy, as she had a reckless tone,
& one didn't know what idea might come to her — However I kept my temper
with her, & she seemed to enjoy the visit — said it was her "annual treat" —

I was very anxious while there about Robert, measles having broken out at
Harrow — & he got them & was shut up in his room alone, & had a very dreary
time — & I was out of reach & did not like to indulge myself in the expense
of going over — Then I was anxious about the journey — & finally he arrived
safely, March 18 — with Richard, who I had asked at the last moment, not
liking R. to have so long a holiday alone — as looking at the lambs frisking
about I reflected that it would be very dull for one little lamb to be shut up
with 2 or 3 woolly old sheep — R. arrived without cold, or any ill effects from
the measles, only a bit thin & pulled down — & finds his gun & bat grown
heavy — but is picking up —

The Mrs. had come to see me off at the station, & looking back, it struck me
that she had a pale, languid look, & the thought flashed across me that I
should not see her again — & I went back & opened the carriage door to say
good bye — & said I wd bring Robert in to see her — which she did not seem
to notice at the time — but everyone says she spoke of it & clung to his coming
afterwards — She got a little chill or illness a day or two afterwards & stayed
in bed — her writing for a few days was very shaky so that I felt uneasy — but
on Saturday I had a very well written letter — asking me to bring the boys in
at once — I wrote to her as usual on Sunday — & on Monday morning had
a note from Henry, saying she had passed away quite suddenly on Sunday
morning[15] — She had been very well the day before (but had evidently a touch
of fever) had seen Mrs. Martin & Mr. Boland — had a long séance with Henry,
who says they settled everything about the sale of Lime Park except her
signature — & no urging would persuade her to put that, as she said it was
Saturday night, she would do it on Monday morning! She had not eaten her
dinner — but had tea & bread & butter — & got up in the morning after 8

---

[13] Charles Whitworth (1752–1825), 1st Baron, Lord Lieutenant of Ireland 1813–17 during
Mr. Gregory's tenure as Under-Secretary. Lord Talbot (see p. 76 n. 59) was Whitworth's
successor, 1817–21. AG includes numerous anecdotes about both men, and extensive extracts
from their correspondence with Gregory, in *Mr. Gregory's Letter-Box.*

[14] Alfred Louvaine Persse (b.1859), AG's youngest brother.

[15] Frances Persse died 22 March 1896. Henry "Harry" Persse (1855–1928), was AG's seventh
brother.

— begun dressing — then said "tired" & lay down — Chetham saw a change in her face & called Henry & Ethel in, just in time to see her pass away —

April 11

There was a very large funeral, rich & poor attending[16] — Torrents of rain — R[ichar]d went from here — It is strange to think of her long life being over — I can hardly say if it was a very happy one — An only daughter, an heiress, she married at 17 a man with 3 children, with a fine place & good looks — masterful & taking his own way — & not much accustomed to the discipline of life[17] — He seems to have treated her, to the end of his life, much as a spoiled child — doing as he liked in gr things — & giving her a dress or paying her compliments to pacify her — The long lawsuit over the Castleboy property kept him poor for many years[18] — & he unfortunately thought of opening a sawmill, & supplying it by cutting down great quantities of timber at Roxboro' — This much disfigured the beautiful place, annoyed us all, caused a permanent quarrel with his eldest son, & much indignation in the others[19] — My mother tried to get round him sometimes to stop it, but without effect, & she was of a light nature, "frivolous" poor Richard[20] used to say — & did not go to work in earnest — It was unfortunate, in my opinion, that she "took to religion" so violently — the religion of the extreme Irish evangelical school — resting more upon doctrine than on works — Hell was inevitable for those who, however good, gentle, benevolent or virtuous, did not adopt the Shibboleth of "free grace", "washed in the blood" etc — The way to gain credit with the Almighty was to try & convert R. Catholics — or at

[16] *The Galway Express* for 28 March reported that the funeral, which took place on 26 March, was attended by "persons of all creeds and classes of the community, a substantial proof of the high esteem in which the deceased lady was held by the people of Galway, who, by her amiable and charitable disposition had won the admiration of the rich and the affections of the poor." The records that survive in the Galway press of her charitable giving in the 1890s suggest that this was no formulaic tribute, and that Mrs. Persse had indeed largely overcome the reputation for strict sectarianism she had acquired while mistress of Roxborough.

[17] Dudley Persse (1802–78), AG's father, married Frances Barry as his second wife in 1833. His three children by his first marriage were Dudley, Katherine (Wale) and Maria, who died unmarried in 1883.

[18] AG's grandfather, Robert Persse (d.1850), conveyed the Castleboy estate to his son Robert Henry (d.1884) in a deed drawn up in 1830, following the commital into a lunatic asylum in 1828 and death the following year of his second cousin Robert Parsons Persse, the legal owner of the estate. In 1835, AG's father, Dudley Persse (d. 1879), contested the conveyance, claiming Castleboy, and he eventually won a long series of acrimonious and costly lawsuits against his own brother in 1852. A pamphlet privately printed by Robert Persse's son, Capt. Robert Persse, in 1894 (*Castleboy: A Deed of Settlement Suppressed in a Court of Justice*), shows that the affair was recontested in 1874 and again in 1881, and continued to repercuss. The pamphlet makes a strong case for the existence of an 1807 Deed which Dudley Persse had deliberately and illegally suppressed, and which would have made Robert Persse's claim undeniable.

[19] This was the principal cause of AG's brother Dudley's enlistment and absence from Roxborough during her youth (see p. 8 n. 26).

[20] AG's second brother, Richard Dudley Persse, who had died of tuberculosis in 1879.

least turn them against their own religion — to read no book that you did not previously know was written according to yr own plan of salvation — to abstain from balls & theatres — to eschew High & Broad Church doctrines equally — Doing this, you might be greedy, untruthful, uncharitable, dishonest — in moderation — that did not really matter — you wd be "washed in the blood" at last — She had taught my father this lesson so effectively, that he did not see why he shd refrain from cutting down his son's timber — spending on any passing fancy the money he ought to have provided for his children with — devoting a gr deal of time & thought to the pleasures of the table —

Venice May 2
I never finished this, & then my poor mother's death was driven into the background by another interest — Paul wrote to propose himself for a week at Easter — & came — a long promised visit — I almost feared to ask if he had quite given up the Gilmore affair — but he said he had, but was not quite sure it might not have turned out well — He was a little low, having had notice to leave Totham — & also Fischer Williams had just become engaged to a Miss Boyd[21] — & his leaving St. James St. wd break up the little semblance of a home thay had together — Well, Ethel came — she was to go home with Richard — & within 48 1/2 hours they were engaged — & head over ears in love — a very good arrangement — & I am so glad to have at last helped to make my dear Paul really happy[22] —

A week of sunshine, the woods bursting out every day into fresh decorations of blue bells & primroses & may & green leaves — & the young people treading on flowers —

Then we crossed to London — 2 days there — then farewell — & I came on to Venice — rest at last for body — if not for mind — Arrived Ap[ril] 29 at 5 a.m. — To Mrs. Eden's garden[23] —

May 1 — Rain — did not go out — Old Ct. Mocenigo who is real possessor of Cyprus[24] — & declares himself to have had a romantic attachment for Lady Dorothy Nevill! Then the Cremornes — & Cte. Belmondo — & the Princess

---

[21] Florence Keown-Boyd, whom Williams married later in 1896.

[22] On receiving the news Henry James wrote to AG: "it is all most interesting and satisfying, and as the dear boy himself says, inevitable. . . . I take the greatest pleasure in knowing that he is thus still, in a manner, under your wing. And I delight particularly in what you tell me of the young lady" (Berg). The couple married at Southampton on 8 August.

[23] Sibyl Frances Eden, née Grey (d.1945), wife of Sir William Eden (1849–1915), 7th Bart., and mother of future Prime Minister Anthony Eden. A close friend of Lady Layard, and like her, resident part of each year in Venice.

[24] Count Alvisa Mocenigo (1822–1903), head of an old Venetian family which had provided many Doges of the city. The Pallazzo Mocenigo, on the Grand Canal, was close to the Layards' Ca' Capello, and had been rented by Byron 1818–21.

of Montenegro[25] — Venetian society has been scandalized by the infatuation of the [German] Emperor for the Countess Morosini, said to be the most beautiful woman in Italy — He went to see her & stayed an hour & 23 minutes, the mob waiting outside on the traghetto & counting the time — He ended by asking her to the private lunch that was to have settled the triple alliance, to meet the King & Queen [of Italy] — & after lunch gave her his arm & marched off to show her the ship, leaving their Majesties to the care of the Empress — Yet she is said to be quite respectable —

10th May — Paul writes "Work in plenty, tho' Bulawayo is quite safe now the Nile affair is still in a state of confusion — Nobody knows exactly what is intended — Such a funny quarrel: the late Gov[e]r[nor] promised the Duke [of Cambridge] that on condition he would resign he should be allowed to hold the great Parade on the Queen's Birthday. Of this Lord L[ansdowne] had never heard, & Ld. Wolseley was calmly making his preparations & giving his address when the Duke steps in & says *he* is going to take the salute[26] — Wolseley says that he will see him blowed first! the Duke & the Queen furious — Ld. L. in a worse temper than I have ever seen him — At last to prevent them from coming to fisticuffs the Queen deputes the Prince of Wales to receive the salute!"

Paul told us at Coole that the embalming materials for P. Henry had been on the wrong ship — & when he died the telegram announcing it ran "Prince Henry died in Coromandel on navy rum". This had to be altered before transmission to the Queen[27] — Paul had been in rather a scrape about a letter sent by the Queen, a translation of one from P. Henry to her — beginning "Gracious Mamma" & asking leave to go with the expedition — It was shown to Ld. Wolseley etc — & then thinking it rather amusing he put it away instead of into the waste paper basket — After a little came notes & telegrams — asking why that valuable letter had not been returned! & first there was a fuss at its being unexpectedly demanded — & then Ld. L. when it was discovered asked sarcastically if his secretaries were making a collection of autographs —

May 19 — We have been Sat[urday] to Monday to Vescovana, Ctesse. Pisani's

[25] Princess Olga of Montenegro (1859–96), only daughter of Danilo II (1837–60).

[26] Garnet Wolseley (1833–1913), the premier military commander of the late Victorian period. A veteran of the Burmese War 1852–53, Indian Mutiny 1857–59, the Ashanti and Zulu Wars, and military commander in the Transvaal 1880, Egypt 1882, and Nile Expedition 1885. Raised to the peerage in 1882, and had replaced the Duke of Cambridge as Commander-in-Chief of H.M. Forces in 1895 (see p. 76 n. 56), evidently to the Duke's continuing chagrin. Wolseley remained as Chief of the Army 1895–1900. Lord Lansdowne was responsible for the Parade arrangements in his capacity as Secretary of State for War 1895–1900.

[27] Prince Henry died of fever on a hospital ship off Sierra Leone. In the absence of embalming materials, his body was preserved for transportation back to Britain in a rum-filled tank made of biscuit tins.

— an amusing change — a great farm on the plains — fat & fertile — tilled by white oxen — The Countess full of energy — looking after every detail on the farm — having the "bed sores" of the oxen washed before her eyes — but also full of enthusiasm for art & literature — could not sleep one night because Don Antoni[o] had been reading us the story of Ginevra from Boccaccio — A talk with her opens the windows of the mind — Yet I think *love* is lacking, she has no good word to say of the people she lives amongst.[28] We are happier at Kiltartan —

20th — Robert's birthday — 15 years old! I have looked forward rather to this birthday as an epoch, because my first *real* recollections of myself are at 15 — & because I first knew Paul at that age, & know how well we have got on ever since — & that I have not *bored* him but been always on terms of warm friendship — so I hope it may be the same with my little son.

I went with Lady Layard to Passini's studio,[29] where her portrait was being done, & looked through a portfolio of his sketches — He said — "Ah, Madame, ce n'est que mon hôpital" — & I said "Ah Monsieur, je vois que vos malades sont en train de commencer leur vie d'immortalité!"[30]

June 7 — Count Seckendorff has been here for a few days[31] — a pleasant change — He leaves today to meet the Empress at Trieste — He says the Emperor was led on by his advisers to send the congratulatory telegram to Kruger — & is now very sorry that he can't go to the Cowes Regatta, & wanted to do so all the same — But he is very "rusé"[32] & is already trying to make friends — has invited a large party of English naval engineers to Berlin, & sent one of the officials who did most to egg him on against England, to meet them at Hamburg — He is only afraid of one person in the world, that is, his mother

---

[28] Countess Evelina Millingen Pisani, daughter of Dr. Julius Millingen (one of the doctors who bled Byron to death), and widow of Count Almoro Pisani, a nobleman descended from Venetian Doges. Her three thousand acre farm near Padua, stocked with five hundred oxen for ploughing, is described in *Days Spent on a Doge's Farm* (1893) by Margaret Symonds, wife of John Addington Symonds (1840–93). Don Antonio was the parish priest at Vescovana. Two stories in Boccaccio's *Decameron* feature a Ginevra, the more famous being the ninth story from the second day (which Shakespeare used as a plot source for *Cymbeline*), in which Ginevra's fidelity is the subject of a wager between her husband and a merchant who wins the bet by describing her bedchamber after hiding in a chest. In the sixth story of the tenth day, which might have been more disturbing to AG given the circumstances of her own marriage, Ginevra is one of two young women desired by an old King, who is persuaded to resist his passion and arranges for their marriage to younger men.

[29] Louis Passini (1832–1903), Italian watercolourist, portraitist and genre painter.

[30] i.e. "Ah, Madam, it's merely my hospital . . . Ah, Sir, I see that your patients are about to begin their immortality".

[31] Count Theodor von Seckendorff (d.1910), Court Chamberlain and Secretary to the Empress Frederick from 1865 until her death, and friend of the Layards since the 1870s.

[32] i.e. "cunning".

— He can wind the Queen round his little finger, & is "aux petits soins" with her[33] — She said to Seckendorff "I am afraid the Empress does not know how to manage her difficult son, but I understand him quite well!"[34] He persuaded her to become Colonel of one of his Regts., that he might in return have an English honour of the same kind — & is especially proud of having been made an English Admiral, & when he comes to stay with his mother in the country, comes down to dinner in a naval jacket!

S[eckendorff]. laments that the Empress's daughters are so brainless & don't care to look beyond their own affairs — & are no companions to their mother — P[rin]cess. Charlotte thinks of nothing but playing with her babies & is entirely under the dominion of her nurses[35] — Sir E. Malet is not lamented at Berlin, but was harmless, never did anything — The Empress complained that he was no resource to her, & she wd never have been treated so badly if Ld. Ampthill had been there, he wd have gone to Bismarck or the Emperor & said it cd not be allowed[36] — but Malet actually *shook* before them — Seckendorff dined with the Malets pretty often, but never met any men worth meeting, or of any distinction, except an occasional passer-through — Enid says P[rin]cess Victoria[37] was a dreadful flirt — always attached herself to a little officer of the steam launch that took them on expeditions — & used to save cakes from tea for that "*dear* little fellow" — Enid said to Admiral Canevaro[38] (who had lived 5 years in England) re duelling — "You know we get on without it in England", and he answered "Oui madame, mais c'est different — vous avez le boxe!"[39]

8th — Ctesse. Pisani, Passini & Belmondos to dinner — Too much screeching — but some interesting talk as to how the C[rown] Prince of Austria had come by his death — Passini says his brother saw the dead body — & said that whereas a suicide's head is usually just pierced by a ball, his whole skull was smashed[40] — Sir C. Euan Smith afterwards — He is very indignant with Ld.

[33] i.e. "waits on her hand and foot".

[34] Kaiser Wilhelm II (b.1859), Queen Victoria's grandson, being eldest son of her eldest daughter, Victoria Adelaide (1840–1901), the Empress Frederick.

[35] Kaiser Wilhelm's sister Charlotte (1860–1919), the Empress Frederick's eldest daughter.

[36] Odo William Russell (1829–84), 1st Lord Ampthill, British Ambassador at Berlin 1871–84. Malet's appointment to Berlin had been highly controversial, with *The Times* issuing a memorably insinuating paragraph (15 September 1884, p. 9): "Sir Edward Malet's promotion, though it will occasion general suprise, is less sudden than that of his predecessor. . . . It may be assumed . . . that Lord Granville selected the new Ambassador after full reflection as to his special fitness for a post in which a man of second-rate abilities could hope for no success." By 1885 AG was already reporting in correspondence that Malet was considered "childish" at Berlin (Berg).

[37] Victoria (b.1866), the Empress Frederick's second daughter.

[38] The Italian Minister for Foreign Affairs.

[39] i.e. "Yes Madam, but that's different—You have the sport of boxing!"

[40] Crown Prince Rudolf of Austria (1858–89), eldest son of Franz Joseph I (1830–1916), had killed himself and his mistress Maria Vetsera in 1889.

Rosebery — Lady E. S. says he was taken from India & put in the diplomatic service — & then was sent to Morocco — There were French intrigues — & after a time Ld. R. wrote to suggest his coming home to consult — He did so, leaving his daughter in Morocco — For 4 months he dangled on, Ld. R. always refusing to see him, making some excuse of going to Mentmore etc — At last A. Rothschild insisted on an interview being granted — & then Ld. R. said, he had already appointed West Ridgeway as successor — No apology or reason — Ld. Salisbury professed to be indignant, but has been nearly a year in office & has done nothing.[41]

15 — I dreamed that John Morley was lecturing on some one — I know not who — & afterwards Sir A. Lyall came to me & said "was not that a fine expression in the lecture 'He had no time for trysting with sin'" — Sir C. E. Smith says he was at Windsor when he came back from Zanzibar — & the Queen said "I am afraid you have had a good deal of trouble with the Germans" — He bowed — Then "& with the Missionaries" — He bowed again — & she said "I have been talking over religious matters with my Munshi — & have come to the conclusion that difficult as I have always found it to understand the doctrine of the Trinity when explained in my own language, I shd find it impossible if explained in any other"[42] — He says she is completely in the hands of her Indian servants — Lady E. S. says there is a terrible fever at Zanzibar — in which, after death the temperature goes up to 115 [degrees] — 107 [degrees] is death.

December 14 1895 [1896]

Seven months since I have written! This must not happen again —

End of June — back to London — a very uncomfortable arrival — Paul had written so unhopefully about getting rooms — & so urgently about Ethel not being well & needing me — that I decided on evicting Monckton M.P. & returning to my own rooms — He resisted — said he had a right to a month's notice — I had to get the agreement from Coole — in his own writing, saying he took the rooms by the week — An uncomfortable business — & an

[41] Sir Charles Euan Smith (1842–1910), Minister at Tangier 1891–93. His diplomatic career did not recover from this hiatus until he was appointed Minister Resident at Bogota in 1898. Alfred de Rothschild (1842–1918), was partner in the influential Rothschild banking concern.

[42] Victoria's "munshi" (literally "clerk") was Abdul Karim, an Indian servant she had engaged in 1887. Karim, in his mid-twenties, quickly insinuated himself into Victoria's favour, parlaying his position from that of servant to that of member of the Household. By the early 1890s he had been granted a royal residence, was being seated amongst the gentry at Royal dinners, and appeared officially in the Court Circular. Besides teaching her Hindustani, his appeal seems to have been the possibility his religion offered for a Hereafter in which she could be reunited with Prince Albert. Karim was promptly repatriated on Prince Edward's accession to the throne.

uncomfortable week in lodgings before I could get in[43] —

Then Robert got whooping cough, & was shut up in the Harrow sanatorium — & I was dragged in pieces, trying to be with him as much as possible — & to look after Ethel's affairs — We got through the trousseau buying all right — & Maclagan did her health much good — She was gentle & obedient, but apathetic — it was sometimes like dragging a sack of Indian meal about the town —

Paul very happy, very much absorbed in his love & his own affairs — they were much like Lady Layard's green parrots, devoted to her till introduced to each other, & then, tho' accepting the food & sticks she brought, resenting her approach, & trying to peck her hand — It is nature — & selfishness — but I am more than ever for short engagements —

I had only 3 weeks — & not much time to think of myself — A pleasant dinner at Knowles — met Col. Yate now British agent at Meshed[44] — Also at Lecky's — where a Count von Limburg Stirum who sat next me asked leave to invite my son to dine at his club! — Also at the Lyalls — & some others — & lunch at Ly. Dorothy's — & garden party at Lambeth where I stood admiring the poor Archbishop's courtesy & good looks — standing the whole long afternoon to receive his guests that none might miss his greeting — Had J. Knowles & Flora Shaw to tea — she talked for 1 1/2 hours, without ceasing — he for the other half hour — Col. Yate escaped — I was late for dinner — all *re* Rhodes — to whom she is devoted — Lunch at Haliburtons — G. Russell.

On the whole a hurried worried time — End of July — Robert fit to travel — had Richard up to meet us — left Margaret [Persse] in my place at Qmansions — off to Ireland.

August — The 3 Beauchamp girls arrived, stayed 7 weeks — Bright, innocent — childish — Poor things they have felt the want of their mother[45] — Holidays went off fairly well — tho' rather noisy — & more romping with Rd. than I liked — Robert very keen about cricket — challenged Gort who beat us — & then return match in which they beat ~~him~~ us again.

43 Edward Philip Monckton (1840–1916), barrister, and M.P. for Northampton 1895–1900. Monckton subsequently took a flat of his own in Queen Anne's Mansions, and remained on cordial terms with AG. AG's temporary lodgings were at 15 Chester Terrace, S.W.

44 Lieut-Col. Charles Edmund Yate (1849–1940), Consul-General at Meshed in Persia, 1896–98.

45 Frances, Geraldine and Gertrude Beauchamp, daughters of Gertrude Persse (d.1876), the sister AG had been closest to, and Edmund Beauchamp (1833–1921), whom Gertrude Persse had married in 1873 as his second wife. Beauchamp, who also had a daughter by his first marriage, married for a third time soon after Gertrude's death, fathering two further daughters and two sons.

The Bourgets at Duras[46] — came here one day — & I went there one day —
She is a charming woman — he pleasant, doesn't look poetic — E. Martyn had
also poets with him, Symonds[47] & Yeats — the latter full of charm & interest
& the Celtic revival — I have been collecting fairy lore since his visit — & am
surprised to find how full of it are the minds of the people — & how strong
the belief in the invisible world around us —

In August, Eliza Shawe Taylor died at Kingstown after a long illness[48] — So
strange that she & our mother should pass away in the same year — It seems
as if a whole generation had gone — Such a breaking up of the home in which
she had been the master spirit! I saw on the day of the funeral that Walter's
brain was affected — & warned Fanny, who did not heed — & just a month
afterwards he was tended into a lunatic asylum — He had pinned his faith to
her not only in earthly but spiritual matters (something like the poor old
Master with his wife) & believed she wd get him safe to heaven — & when she
died — it was as if the Papacy had ceased to exist to a devout R[oman].
C[atholic]. — he had no landmark — & went off his head.[49]

Fanny also left rudderless — had been so dependent on her mother she seems
incapable now of choosing a servant without her — I went to her for a
fortnight — then to Castle Cor for two days such a Castle Rackrent — it has
set me looking for deficiencies here — especially as Conny says it was during
Willy's minority the house went to pieces, & I don't want Mrs. Robert to say
that of me![50] — So I have had the boat mended — the lower W.C. panelled
& papered — the baths sent to Dublin & painted — Kitchen & hall chairs
mended etc, etc.

October & November, I paid these visits & spent a week with F. S. Taylor[51] —

46 Paul Bourget (1852–1935), French novelist, critic and psychologist, and his second wife,
Minnie, née David (d.1932).

47 Arthur Symons (1865–1945), poet, essayist and critic. WBY had shared lodgings with
Symons at Fountain Court, Temple, over Winter and Spring 1895–96, this being his first
domicile independent of his parents. The move reflected WBY's intent to pursue his relationship
with Olivia Shakespear (1863-1938), but also marked a brief period of close concord with
Symons, who was at this point preparing his major critical work *The Symbolist Movement in Literature*
(1899) and exerting significant influence on WBY through his knowledge of contemporary
French literature.

48 AG's elder sister Elizabeth died on 24 August 1896.

49 Shawe-Taylor, who had been High Sheriff of Galway in 1868, recovered and survived until
1912. For his daughter Fanny (Trench), see p. 16 n. 83.

50 Castle Cor, Kanturk, Co. Cork, was the home of AG's mother's family, the Barrys. William
Norton Barry (1820–71), AG's cousin, had died while his only son William Barry (1859–1935)
was still a child, leaving the estate in the charge of his second wife Elizabeth (d.1926). Willy had
married Constance Walker (d. 1899) in 1881.

51 Probably Francis "Frank" Shawe-Taylor (1869–1920), Walter Shawe-Taylor's second son.

& wrote in "Erin" on the Convent Industries[52] — & designed blinds to be worked there for exhibition — & had old Mullins's house thatched — & made up "bottles" for hooping cough & other ailments — & generally did my duty — & some little jobs about the place —

All this time I have off & on been going through old Mr. Gregory's letterbox — At Venice I copied a good deal of what I had already written out in type writing — Lord Talbot's letters & others — These I sent to Lord Peel to ask if I might use them without indiscretion — & he says yes — Then I copied more — & then wrote 5 introductory chapters — & sent the whole to Murray — He submitted the MS to two experts & writes back that some of the letters are excellent matter — some dry & dull — they must be sifted & grouped & I must write a continuous narrative with them — in the style of the introductory chapters which are to remain as they are "so brightly written & so pleasant & readable" — They don't take into consideration that I have exhausted all my ideas & information!

So I have written to try & get hold of 1200 letters of old Gregory's to Sir R. Peel, in Mr. Parker's possession[53] — And I started off for Dublin & spent a week there, reading in the National Library, with an introduction from Sir T. Moffett to Mr. Lyster the librarian[54] — And I have filled some gaps — & laid in some knowledge — but I have also learned how much more valuable one grain of original matter will be than any amount of reproducing — so I cling to the hope of my 1200 letters.

I dined with old Henn[55] — & after many efforts extracted an anecdote of O'Connell & one or two of Ld. Plunket from him[56] — And his sister Mrs. Latouche gave me a nice recollection of O'Connell[57] — But this was all the *tradition* I gained by my visit —

[52] No issues of this publication appear to have survived, but AG's short essay was reprinted as a broadsheet, which describes *Erin* as "an Illustrated Journal of Art and Industry".

[53] Charles Stuart Parker (1829–1910) was compiling a biographical selection of Peel's papers. John Murray had published the first of Parker's three projected volumes, covering Peel's career until 1827, in 1891.

[54] Thomas William Lyster (1855–1920), Librarian of the National Library of Ireland 1895–1920. Immortalized in the ninth section of *Ulysses* as an urbane encourager of literary aspirants.

[55] Thomas Rice Henn, Q.C. (1814–1901), County Court Judge of Co. Galway 1868–98.

[56] Daniel O'Connell (1775–1847), "The Liberator", was the founder of the Catholic Association and architect of Catholic Emancipation, enacted in 1829. His Repeal Movement drew huge support in the 1840s and seemed likely to win some form of political autonomy for Ireland, but was doomed first by Coercion Acts which banned mass assembly and then by the onset of the Famine. William Conyngham Plunket (1764–1854), 1st Baron, was Attorney General for Ireland, 1822–27, and Lord Chancellor of Ireland 1830–35. The Plunket anecdote attributed to "an old member of the Irish Bar" (*Mr. Gregory's Letter-Box* p. 124), is presumably Henn's.

[57] Probably the long anecdote from "an old lady" given in *Mr. Gregory's Letter-Box* pp. 19–21.

A pleasant dinner at George Morris's[58] — He doesn't think much of Gerald Balfour — dry & wooden — Lady Betty charming & so anxious to please — He has served under 12 Chief Secs. & Arthur Balfour shines amongst them all[59] — "He was vexed if you didn't give him your own opinion — He'd say what he thought, and lean back against the chimney piece & turn up his coat tails & say 'Now tell me what *you* think' — I declare if that man had given me a kick, I'd almost have been ready to say thank you for it!" Of Morley he speaks with profound repugnance. Neither does Mr. Lyster think much of G. Balfour — A Cambridge manner" —

Home to Coole again — only 10 days now alone before R. comes —

Telegram & letter from Paul — asking if he & Ethel might come after all — said yes — They arrived, much wrapped up in each other —

22nd — Robert & Tom[60] & G[eraldine]. Beauchamp — The former looking well — Came out 4th in Vth class — Xmas very busy — Workhouse children & old men — School feast, tree & fireworks — etc, etc —

Shooting 28th & 29th Arthur, Frank Ruttledge Fair[61] — Paul, Dr. M[oran]. — Gerald failed so Robert took a gun & killed 7 pheasants — 1 woodcock — 1 rabbit — Total 81 pheasants 25 cock — A lovely day — 29th It poured — They went to Inchy [Wood] but had to give over at lunch time — Paul not well — & ungracious which made the burden of entertaining harder —

31st — Paul left — Ethel stayed — The old year has brought many changes — their marriage, my mother's death — Eliza's death —

Robert has had two broken terms — with measles & whooping cough — but on the whole has come on well — & is still gentle, obedient, straightforward.

The tenants have behaved well, paying their rents & showing civility —

---

[58] Sir George Morris (1833–1912), Lord Morris's brother. M.P. for Galway 1867–68, 1874–80. Commissioner of the Local Government Board of Ireland 1880–91, and its Vice–President 1891–98.

[59] Rt. Hon. Gerald William Balfour (1858–1945), was at this point Chief Secretary for Ireland (1895–1900), as his more politically successful brother Arthur "Bloody" Balfour had been 1887–91. Married Lady Elizabeth "Betty" Lytton (1867–1942), eldest daughter of the Lyttons (see p. 30 n. 38) in 1887, and eventually succeeded his brother as 2nd Earl of Balfour in 1930.

[60] Thomas Beverly Persse (b.1884), sixth son of AG's brother Edward.

[61] AG's niece Rose Persse, eldest daughter of her brother Major William, had married Major Robert Fair Ruttledge (1852–1912) of Mayo on 8 May 1896, whose brother Francis (1853–98) this was.

For myself, I think I have stayed too much at home & a little lost touch with London — However I have I think done good work with the Gregory letters — which have kept me from work in any other direction — I have spent too much money — that is given away too much — Ethel & Paul — Richard going to Africa[62] — A. Grubb d[itt]o — all drains upon me — but all I think money well laid out — helping them in the start —

The New Year opens with some anxiety, the revision of rents has led to 25 pc reduction where brought into Court — and one cannot blame ours if they follow the example — But with R.'s expensive education still going on — it will make a great difference to us.

[62] Richard Persse (b.1879), fourth son of AG's brother Edward, served in the South Africa war, but later settled in England.

1897

Jan[uary] 1 — To Ballylee with Ethel & Geraldine to take wine & jam to Miss Shaughnessy & bawneen, tea & money to old Diveney —

Jan[uary] 25 — Last day of the holidays, which have passed quickly & quietly & without any unpleasantness — save Paul's little aberrations from good manners — & for these he has apologised — Elizabeth Persse[1] has been elected to Higgins College — a great mercy & relief to me — Roxboro' agency shifted from Gerald to Frank — a sad business — & Arthur put the doing of it on me — but it might have been worse — had a stranger been put in —

Feb[ruary] 2 — We came over on 26th — R. went on to Harrow — We lunched with Lady Layard — & then went to buy photo printing things for R.'s Kodak — Paul

Paul came to see me — anxious to make friends.

28th — Looked for clothes — & dined with Lady Layard — Lady Selbourne[2] there, a Jewish looking woman wearing something very like a wig.

29th — To South Kensington with Enid about her tapestries she wants to sell — & Mr. Cole showed us curious Copt embroideries[3] — Back to lunch with

---

[1] Probably AG's cousin Elizabeth Margaret Persse (d.1910), daughter of AG's uncle Robert Persse (d.1884).

[2] Lady Beatrix Selborne, née Cecil (d.1950), eldest daughter of the Prime Minister, Lord Salisbury. She had married the 2nd Earl Selborne (then Sir William Waldegrave Palmer) in 1883.

[3] Alan Summerly Cole (1846–1934), son of Sir Henry Cole (1808–82), the key figure behind the development of the South Kensington Museum and Director of its Department of Science and Art 1858–73. Alan Cole acted as his father's secretary 1868–73, and remained with the Museum after his father's death, becoming Acting Assistant Director of Art in 1898. A leading figure in organizing the development of Irish arts and crafts and lacemaking, and a member of the Irish Industries Association, he published extensively on silks, lace and textiles.

Lady Gregory, pastels, by Lisa Stillman (see p.15, note 76).

Lady Gregory's parents: above left, Dudley Persse, probably *c*.1840; above right: Frances Persse, *c*.1890. Below left, Sir William Gregory, an engraving by T. Roffe in the Grillion's Club series, after the painting by Sir Arthur Clay (p.16). Below right, a portrait by Cameron Studios of Robert Gregory, *c*.1886 (p.63).

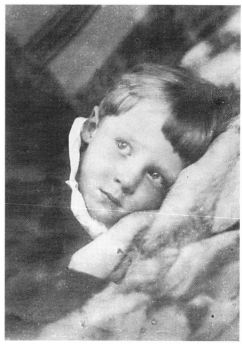

Above: Chevy Chase, the Persse family's hunting lodge in the Slieve Echtge Hills. Below: a water-colour of Roxborough, Co. Galway, the Persse family seat, c.1890. Courtesy Richard Persse.

Above: A water-colour by the Earl of Wemyss of W. E. Gladstone on a steam engine intended to illustrate Lady Gregory's anonymous pamphlet, *A Phantom's Pilgrimage* (1893). In the event, a similar line drawing was used. Below: a pencil sketch by Lady Gregory of Biddy Early's House in the Glenderee Mountains, dated June 30 1897 (p.147).

Above left, Lady Layard, second wife of Sir Henry Layard (right). Below: pen and ink sketches by Lady Gregory of Ca' Capello, the Layards' palazzo in Venice, dating from May 1896 (p.112–16).

Above "Lynches Castle", Galway, a water-colour sketch by Lady Gregory. Below: the first page of Lady Gregory's March 1895 sketchbook which she called "The Stones of Galway".

Three water-colours by Lady Gregory: above left, S. Apollinare Nuovo, Ravenna, painted 15 May 1889; above right, Lydican, 22 August 1888; below left, Clonfert, 1888, with her notes "10th or 11th century. Founded by S. Brendan 558, Burned 7 times by the Danes". Below right, pencil sketch at Wilfrid Scawen Blunt's home Crabbet Park, dated May 21 (no year given).

Above: pen and ink sketches of Thoor Ballylee, drawn on 14 August 1895. Below: Ruin of St Goban's Church, Inisheer, and the Tree of Inisheer, both drawn on Lady Gregory's visit to the island in May 1898 (pp.185–86).

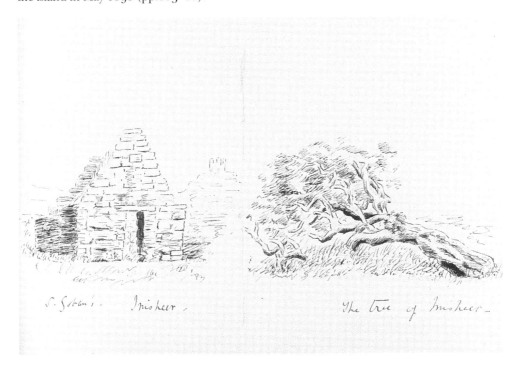

her — Lady Sophy Palmer there & Lady Waldegrave[4] came in afterwards —
I ran away, saying I must leave before any more Countesses came — but went
in to tea with Lady Lindsay, & Lady Malmesbury[5] came in — Dined Paul &
Ethel — the little house pretty, chiefly with my things — Ethel with a cold —
all the talk about the possibility of their taking a country box — Pleased to see
them happy —

30 — Dined Birchs —

31 — Service Westminster Abbey — Charity sermon in aid of the first Welsh
church built in London — Lunched Knowles — Sir J. Ferguson[6] — & a Miss
Freer, full of the Hebrides — second sight — & the iniquities of the Duke of
Argyll, Sir John Ord & Lady Gordon Cathcart[7] — Mr. Gibbs & E. Martyn in
the afternoon —

Feb[ruary] 1 — Very wet gloomy & muddy — & only got to Cheyne Row[8] —
But a nice letter from Robert saying he has got into the 6th [form] — a visit
from Lady Johnston who seems very nice & pretty & has asked me to dine[9] —
& a telegram from Enid asking me to dine which I did very pleasantly with her
& Lady Sophy [Palmer] — She has offered me a bicycle if I like to learn —
which opens up a great vista of the coast & the Burren hills! Lady Sophy says
that she was delighted with "Esther Waters" — which she read because she
heard I thought so much of it — & then she recommended it to Lady Salisbury
who she was going to Hatfield with, & who tried to buy it at the Hatfield station
but the stallkeeper said "Oh we would not take that book"[10] upon which Lady
S. picked out "A Yellow Aster",[11] "A Superfluous Woman"[12] & "The Heavenly

---

[4] Lady Mary Waldegrave, née Palmer (d.1933), wife of the 9th Earl Waldegrave. Lady Sophie
Palmer (d.1915) was her sister, both being daughters of Lady Selborne.

[5] Sylvia, Lady Malmesbury, née Stewart (d.1934), wife of the 4th Earl.

[6] Sir James Ferguson (1832–1907), 6th Bart. Kilkerran. Governor of S. Australia 1869–73,
New Zealand 1873–75, Bombay 1880–85, and M.P. 1886–1906. Under-Secretary in the Foreign
Office 1886–1901.

[7] Ada Goodrich Freer (1865–1931), sociologist and member of the Society for Psychical
Research. Author of The Outer Isles (1902), and co-editor (with John, Marquess of Bute) of The
Alleged Haunting of B[allechin] House (1899). The former volume refers to "brutalities" inflicted
on their tenants over many years by some of the major landowners on the Hebrides, including
Sir John Campbell-Orde (1827–97), 3rd Bart, George Campbell (1823–1900), 8th Duke of
Argyll, who had evicted many tenants, and the Gordon estate.

[8] 18 Cheyne Row, where Paul and Ethel Harvey were now living.

[9] Lady Winifred Johnston, née Irby (d.1933), daughter of the 5th Baron Boston. She had
married Sir Harry Johnston in October 1896.

[10] George Moore's 1894 novel was controversial for its frank treatment of working class
poverty and for its strong critique of women's subordinate place in the conventional Victorian
marriage.

[11] Novel by Kathleen Mannington Caffyn (d.1926), published under the pseudonym "Iota".

[12] Novel by Emma Frances Brooke (d.1926), who also published poetry and novels under the

Twins"[13] — & said, "then how can you with any consistency keep these".

2nd — Fog — Read thro' my folk lore[14] — which reads well — Went to see Sir F. Burton who looks changed & fragile — & Lady Clay.

3rd — Rain & fog — To Mudie's — & to borrow Enid's type writer — & began copying my fairy lore —

4th — Rain — but left a few cards & saw Mrs. Maclagan & Lady Tweeddale — Dined Sir H. H. & Lady Johnston — sat between him & "Mr. Guthrie" — who only at the end of dinner I felt must be Anstey, he was so original & pleasant[15] — Also talked to Orchardson, a rather Don Quixote looking lanky creature — very quaint & agreeable — Sir H. said he used to be very hard on him in the life school of Academy & he says he is proud of it, as it did him so much good[16] — Oswald Crawfurds — Miss Flora Shaw —

5th — Rain — Did not get out all day — but Sir A. Lyall came to see me in the morning — Says his nephew Bernard Holland wrote the financial report & Childers never saw it[17] — & when B. H. went to Devonshire House last week the Duke said "Well, you've put all the fat in the fire!" —

7th — To the Temple, to hear Welldon preach — it seemed to bring me nearer to Robert — Lunched Ricardos — dined Lady Layard —

8th — H. P. Lane to lunch — & then to see Ethel — & dined with the Birchs & went with them to Nansen at the Albert Hall[18] — very interesting — he looks so nice & bright & talks so simply — & the magic lantern slides were beautiful bringing the ice fields & the Northern lights before one — We were better off than the Royalties who had to screw their necks round to see them — The Hall

pseudonym "E. Fairfax Byrrne". A friend of Shaw and the Webbs, she served on the Fabian Executive Committee 1893–96.

[13] Novel by "Sarah Grand", pseudonym of Frances Elizabeth McFall (1854–1943), novelist and feminist. *The Heavenly Twins* (1893) was controversial for its strong critique of marriage as an institution and its frank mention of venereal disease.

[14] This was material she had collected since meeting WBY the previous summer and was now preparing to present him in typed form.

[15] Thomas Anstey Guthrie (1856–1934), novelist who published under the pseudonym F. Anstey.

[16] William Quiller Orchardson, R.A., (1835–1910), best known for portraits and subject pictures. H. H. Johnston had been a student at the Royal Academy 1876–79.

[17] Presumably a report relating to the Irish taxation question which Childers should have seen as Chair of the Irish Financial Relations Committee.

[18] Fridtjof Nansen (1861–1930), celebrated explorer of the North Pole, lectured on "Some Results of the Norwegian Arctic Expedition" under the auspices of the Royal Geographical Society. For a report of his speech, see *The Times* 9 February, p. 10.

crammed — To supper with Mauldslies[19] — he an explorer, very pleasant & cheery — home at midnight —

9th — Lady Layard came & took me out driving & then I came to meet Henry James at tea time — very anxious to know all about "our boy" — Dined Lyalls — Mme. de Novikoff[20] there & monopolised Sir A. — & there was a dull Mr. Gordon & a duller Mr. Bennett — but I enjoyed myself all the same — Sir A. much struck with the simplicity & sincerity of my people's fairy talk —

10th — Rain — so took a coupé & did visits, found Lady A. Russell at home — & met the Duke of Bedford who I had not seen since India[21] — Mrs. Humphrey Ward — who has taken a house at Kendal, to study local colour[22] — Mrs. Newton Robinson, Mrs. Williams the bride — Mary Studd — rather a trying visit — H. Studd there & the baby whimpering & a genl. upset — Dined Cheyne Row — rather bored —

12 — Called Stillmans — dined A. Gray — dullish people, none I knew except MacBride —

14 — Westminster Abbey — Eyton[23] — Dinner here — W. B. Yeats — Sir H. H. & Lady Johnston — Sophie Lyall — Alfred Cole — Barry O'Brien — Sir A. Clay — Very pleasant, at least I enjoyed it myself very much, liking them all — & they got on well — An argument at dinner as to who Conan Doyle had meant in a speech the night before by "the greatest man this century has produced."[24] B. O'Brien was for Napoleon, Sir H. for Darwin — Yeats for Goethe — A. Cole stirring them all up — but as none wd agree on the premises, I had to intervene at last —

16th — Lunch Savile Row to meet Mrs. Borwick — Re the Cretan question —

[19] Probably Alfred Maudslay (1850–1931), who had carried out extensive archeological and anthropological research in Central America. His wife Anne, née Morris, d.1926.

[20] Madame Olga Novikoff (1848–1925), Russian journalist and political writer. Initially suspected by some of being a spy, her unofficial ambassadorial work and friendship with Gladstone helped turn hostility between Russia and Britain in the later 1870s into entente. Eulogized by her friend William Stead (see p. 174 n. 48) in 1907 in his edition of her correspondence and memoirs, *The M.P. for Russia*.

[21] Herbrand Arthur Russell (1858–1940), 11th Duke of Bedford, a cousin of Lady Arthur Russell's late husband. A.D.C. to Lord Dufferin (Viceroy of India) 1884–88, and escort of the Gregorys during their tour of India in 1885. AG's friend Adeline, Duchess of Bedford, was the widow of Russell's elder brother George, the 10th Duke, whom he succeeded in March 1893.

[22] For her Lake District novel *Helbeck of Bannisdale* (1898).

[23] Rev. Robert Eyton (b.1845), Canon of Westminster since 1895.

[24] Arthur Conan Doyle (1859–1930), creator of Sherlock Holmes, had spoken at the annual dinner of the Irish Literary Society at the Café Monico, 13 February. For a report see *The Weekly Sun*, 14 February, p. 10.

We spoke of the German Emperor's domineering ways — Lady L. says he was so indignant at the Duchess of Sparta joining the Greek Church that he ordered her never to come into Germany again, that if she did, he would have her arrested at the frontier — upon which she took the first train & came — knowing he would not dare to carry out his threat — The Empress told Lady L. his maimed arm was caused by the clumsiness of the German doctors at his birth — Sir H. Thompson told her there had once been an abcess in his ear — & a bit of bone had been taken out but there is no further disease — We took Mrs. Borwick to Southwark & showed her Board School etc — Evening to "Rosemary"[25] with M[a]cBride — a pretty, sad piece, spoiled by the last superfluous act —

17th — Dined Leckys — Sat next Lord Loch — who had been to hear Cecil Rhodes examined by the Committee — & thinks he came badly out of it — his answers not straight & he had not even read the Blue books — & Lord L. is very down upon Miss Flora Shaw who seems to have precipitated the revolution[26] — Have had 2 bicycling lessons at the Queen's Club — The first simple torture, like sitting on a skate balanced on a cartwheel — I felt as if the machine was an "infernal" one — trying to compass my destruction — The 2nd, sat more comfortably — but can't yet get the balance —

18 — To Harrow — Robert with a cough & cold, but says they are on the mend — Has been doing Aristophanes with Mr. Welldon — says he is a dry teacher — does not digress like the other masters — Some of his Kodak photos have come out very well — & he is cheery enough.

19 — Bad headache, having been tired by Harrow — & a wet day but went to dine at Savile Row — & went through some of Sir Henry's MS with Miss Oswell the typist.

20th — Sir A. Lyall to lunch — then Miss Oswell from 2:30 to 10 — hard at the MS all the time — finished the Spanish & began the Turkish — It is amusing to read of Sir H.'s first interviews with the Sultan — & how he remonstrates about the Bulgarian atrocities & H[is]. M[ajesty]. pathetically

[25] A four-act play by Louis Parker and Murray Carson, which ran for 195 performances at the Criterion between May 1896 and March 1897.

[26] Rhodes appeared before the South African Committee enquiring into the Jameson Raid for six days in February. Lord Loch was a long-time personal enemy of Rhodes, having consistently attempted to maintain African policy directly under the aegis of the Crown during his term as High Commissioner for South Africa 1889–95. Rhodes had ensured that Loch would not be reappointed to this post and engineered the return of Hercules Robinson "a doddering, dropsy-inflicted, clearly compliant, aging sycophant who was almost literally in Rhodes' pocket" (Robert Rotenberg, *The Founder* p. 527). Flora Shaw had been a catalyst for Rhodes's plans in her capacity as Colonial Correspondent for *The Times*.

declares that as for himself — he would not hurt a fly![27]

21st — Sunday — To St. Saviour's, Southwark to see if it has been much spoiled by the restoration — I can't say it is improved to my mind — Met Sir H. & Ly. Cunningham — & we walked about the church afterwards — Then on to lunch with the Lyalls — a Persian there — I asked Lady L. who he is & she says "I forget his name — but he was our A.D.C. or something at some place in India, I forget where" — Yet in talking of the Indian hospitals she was quite eloquent & practical — Back to Qmansions & had a long visit from Lecky — very kind & pleasant — more lively & less mysterious I thought than in his pre-Parliament days — He said that when his "Rationalism" came out it was much talked of & sold quickly — the "Morals" which he had always preferred himself lagging behind — But of late it has been coming on, & they are now all but abreast as far as sale goes — In the same way, he divided his "History of Ireland" from that of England because it had grown so out of proportion — & though it has far more original matter in it the England has been selling very much better — He disparages his "Leaders of Public Opinion" only wants to keep the O'Connell, & to re-write that — He is anxious if he ever finds time to write on the Famine & the Tithe War, so little, comparatively, is known about them[28] — Thinks we have a financial grievance, but that 90 millions is too much to ask — Then in came Sir F. Burton — looking certainly aged, but in very good humour — delighted with my fairy lore — he does love Ireland — & so does Lecky — Then Edward Martyn — It was 7 before I was free — & rushed to Cheyne Walk where Paul had begged me to come & dine — but they had begun without me — he was not sure I was coming — Oh how much rather I would never go there as a guest —

[27] Layard had compiled a Memoir of about a million words bearing on his terms as Minister in Spain 1869–77 and as Ambassador in Turkey 1877–80. With AG's success in editing WHG's autobiography doubtless in mind, Lady Layard prepared this material for the press, but it was not published. John Murray retained a typescript of the work, but Foreign Office opposition to the release of the material, together with the certain unpopularity of Layard's anti-Russian and pro-Turkish stances at the time the Memoir might have been published, seem to have prevented its appearance. Murray did eventually publish *The Autobiography and Letters of Sir Henry Layard* edited by Sir Arthur Otway in 1903, but this work covers only the period up to Layard's appointment as Ambassador at Madrid. Layard's relationship with Sultan Abdul Hamid II of Turkey was initially amenable, with the Sultan voicing apparent distaste for the massacres of Bulgarians which had begun shortly before his accession to the throne in 1876. The Sultan soon showed increasing signs of mental instability however, sheltering abjectly in the British Embassy in May 1878 in fear of an attempt on his life and later suffering a delusion that Layard himself was an assassin. Layard's increasing perplexity as to his standing with the Sultan compounded the suspicions of many in the Foreign Office that he had been naive in his initial estimates of Abdul Hamid, thereby compounding the pressure for his removal as Ambassador.

[28] Lecky never completed this project. His major works *A History of the Rise and Influence of Rationalism in Europe* (1865), *A History of Morals from Augustus to Charlemagne* (1869), *A History of England in the Eighteenth Century* (1870–90), *A History of Ireland in the Eighteenth Century* (1892) and *Leaders of Public Opinion in Ireland* (1861, later variously expanded and revised), all remained in print during this period and for a considerable time after his death.

22 — Dined Lady Lindsay, pleasant enough — A. Grove[29] on one side — Sir A. Lyall the other — Ld. & Lady Shand,[30] Miss Higgins etc — Sir A. came & talked to me after dinner also — until Lady Lindsay came & said it was a scandal! & separated us. He likes Matthew Arnold's Tristram better than Swinburne's — it touches the heart more, tho' the latter a better workman — The Americans he says will never produce a great poem because they are so passionless — We wandered into politics — & he is very angry at my saying there is more love of country in Irish than Englishmen — his eyes flash dark & he indignantly denies it — also he warns me that we Irish must not speak ill of the Saxon for ever — "we are getting a little cross about it — We will never let you go — You are tied to us like a wife to her husband & you must make the best of it". Yes, I say, but we want our arrears of pin money — "Oh — you shall have that — indeed you shall — & all you like — only try to be content & to like us" — Then Lady Lindsay intervenes — & I go & prattle with Grove — but at the last we find a bond of sympathy in "Esther Waters" —

23 — Get on much better with my bicycle — the 4th half hour — Go a good bit alone — Lunch & drive with Mary Studd — Tea, Sir A. Lyall & Yeats — who get on very well, I can see Sir A. is taken with his simple, modest, enthusiastic way — Yeats stayed on — he is very full of play writing — doesn't like "Mariana" he has just been to see[31] — He is delighted with E. Martyn's new Celtic one[32] — "Splendid & stirring" — He, with the aid of Miss Florence Farr,[33] an actress who thinks more of a romantic than a paying play is very keen about taking or building a little theatre somewhere in the suburbs — to produce a romantic drama — His own plays, E. M.'s — one from Brydges[34]

[29] Thomas Newcomen Archibald Grove (1855–1920), Founder of *The New Review* and its Editor until 1894, and M.P. 1892–95, 1906–10.

[30] Alexander Burns Shand (1812–1904), 1st Baron Shand, and his wife Emily, née Meymott.

[31] A translation by James Graham of José Echegaray's play, starring Henry Irving (1838–1905, the most acclaimed actor of the late-Victorian era, and Hermann Vezin (see p. 303 n. 27), produced at the Court Theatre, for five matinée performances only, 22–26 March 1897.

[32] *Maeve*, published in 1899 and first produced by the Irish Literary Theatre in February 1900.

[33] Florence Farr Emery (1860–1917), George Bernard Shaw's lover in the early 1890s following the breakdown of her marriage to Edward Emery (1861–1938), whom she had married early in her career as an actress and divorced in 1894. Met WBY in 1890, and became a co-initiate of the Golden Dawn in October that year, though she subsequently broke with the Order, joining the Theosophical Society in 1902. Served as general manager during the first season of the Irish Literary Theatre in 1899, and toured widely with WBY in the first decade of the new century helping him demonstrate his theories of speaking to the psaltery. Ended her career in the theatre abruptly in 1912 to head a girls' school in Ceylon, where she died of cancer in 1917.

[34] Robert Bridges (1844–1930), one of the few poets of prominence in the generation older than WBY, elected Poet Laureate in 1913. The Bridges play WBY had in mind was almost certainly *The Return of Ulysses*, which WBY had praised as "a triumph of beauty" and "perfect after its kind" in his recent review of Bridges's work (*The Bookman* June 1897).

— & he is trying to stir up S. O'Grady[35] & Fiona McCleod[36] to write some —
He believes there will be a reaction after the realism of Ibsen, & romance will
have its turn — He has put "a great deal of himself" into his own new play —
"the shelter of the Waters"? — & rather startled me by saying about half his
characters have eagles' faces[37] — I asked him to write something in "Celtic
Twilight" to ensure my not giving this copy away[38] — & he cannot remember
one single line he has ever written — & has to copy a bit by itself! — I had given
Sir Alfred one copy of his poems & had lent Sir F. Burton the other — & had
asked him to tea — but he writes that he is so pleased with the verses — those
of a true poet — that he is afraid of breaking the spell if he comes — & that
he wd rather keep his poet ideal! — Dine Ly. Layard —

24 — Half round the course on my bicycle — Miss Oswell & MS in the evening.

25 — Too windy for bicycle — so wrote letters & this up — Lady Layard
call[ed] for me to take tea at the Temple with A[rthur]. Du Cane — She had
been to Buckingham Palace to see the Empress — who is not at all well, & is
much worried about Greece & Crete — She read her a letter from the

[35] Standish James O'Grady (1846–1928), nephew of AG's father's first wife Hon. Katherine
O'Grady (d.1829). After early years spent as a barrister and journalist on *The Dublin Daily Express*,
O'Grady turned to literature on discovering the history and literature of Gaelic Ireland. His two
volume *History of Ireland* (*The Heroic Period*, 1878 and *Cuculain and His Contemporaries* 1880) was
regarded as a seminal text in the early years of the Irish Renaissance by WBY, AE and others, as
it provided them with an indigenous racial mythology upon which they could build. In the early
1890s, O'Grady extended his vision of an heroic mythological Irish past in works such as *The Bog
of Stars*, treating Elizabethan Ireland, but from the mid-1890s his main energies were turned to
contemporary politics, and in particular the Financial Question. In 1898 O'Grady bought and
edited *The Kilkenny Moderator* in an effort to promote his conservative belief that only a
responsible and active Protestant Ascendancy could successfully lead Ireland. On its closure
following a libel suit he founded, edited and wrote most of the material for the *All Ireland Review*,
which ran from 1900 to 1907. Belatedly recognising the inevitable decline of his class, O'Grady
left Ireland in 1918, settling in England, where he died in 1928.

[36] "Fiona Macleod" was a literary alter ego created by William Sharp (1856–1905), poet,
biographer and novelist. Although Sharp published extensively under this second name, "Fiona
Macleod" was not merely a pseudonym. He sustained the fiction of the beautiful and elusive
Scottish poetess for several years by supplying bogus itineraries for her, and by conducting her
correspondence from plausible forwarding addresses using disguised handwriting—so successfully
that *Who's Who* included separate entries for the two writers. WBY only came to realize that she
was a fictive identity some time later in 1897. Sharp never completed any plays for the Irish
Literary Theatre.

[37] Yeats had been at work on *The Shadowy Waters* since 1894 or earlier. The play was first
published in 1900, and not produced until 1904.

[38] AG's copy of *The Celtic Twilight*, with the first quatrain of WBY's poem "Into the Twilight"
inscribed on a preliminary blank leaf, is now at Emory.

Duchess of Sparta saying Greece *must* have it[39] — Dined Sir A. Clay's — a
large, long dinner I didn't care much about, tho' next a *worker* Mr. Powell(?)
who made the glass for the mosaics in St. Paul's[40] —

27th — Came in for the afternoon for Miss Oswell but a lot of visitors came
— Mr. Ball & R. B. Martins[41] & Duchess of Bedford & Martin Morris — A nasty
cold —

28th — Cold bad, but engaged to Verekers to lunch so had to go — but a cruel
one — 16 — not beginning till 2-20 & lasting till 3-30. Ld. Gort pleasant
enough — but cd give me no legends of Harrow tho' his father had been
Byron's fag there[42] — Back & missed Grant Duff — who will be cross as he
called by appointment — Dinner at home — Mrs. Vere O'Brien — G. [W. E.]
Russell — Yeats — Sir H. Cunningham — G. R. extremely agreeable &
amusing — quite in the vein — anecdotes — poems — rhymes of all sorts —
He told us of Gladstone's want of humour — that he had showed him a very
funny letter from a clergyman asking for preferment, oddly worded — saying
it was an old promise of Ld. Beaconsfield — & that his wife "the only child of
an Earl now dead" wd be much disappointed if he did not get it — Gladstone's
only remark was "What a curious thing he shd expect me to keep a promise
of Beaconsfield's" — Mrs. O'Brien said Forster[43] used to say Gladstone had
a sense of humour somewhere — for that at a drawingroom he had said
"there's someone standing on my wife's train & she doesn't know it" — &

39 Civil war had broken out on Crete in June 1896 between Mahommedans aligned with
Turkey, and Christians protesting the Turkish Sultan's expansionist aims and massacres of
Armenians. When efforts to ensure constitutional protections for Greek-aligned Christians
failed, Greece sent an occupying flotilla to Crete in early February 1897. A limited war between
Greece and Turkey followed in April, in which Greece was defeated. Following pressure from
the European powers, however, Crete remained autonomous.

40 Head of the glass firm James Powell & Sons, Whitefriars, which supplied decorative glass
for many of London's major public buildings in the late Victorian period.

41 Probably Richard Biddulph Martin (1838–1916), banker and M.P., and his wife Mary, née
Crozier.

42 Standish Prendergast Vereker (1819–1900), 4th Viscount Gort. His grandfather Charles,
2nd Viscount Gort (1768–1842), had been the principal force behind the development of Gort
town, and initiated the building of Lough Cutra Castle. Charles's son John (1790–1865), 3rd
Viscount Gort, Byron's junior contemporary at Harrow, was forced to sell the estate during the
Famine, and it passed shortly afterwards to the Gough family. Thereafter, the family's Irish base
was in Co.Limerick. Lord Gort's mother Maria (d.1854) was the elder sister of Katherine
O'Grady, Dudley Persse's first wife, but though AG herself thus had no blood connection with
him, she, like all the Persse children by Dudley's second marriage, regarded the Verekers as
cousins (see *Journals* vol.1, p. 616).

43 William Edward Forster (1818–86), M.P. 1861–88, and Chief Secretary of Ireland 1880–
82. Forster had been the reluctant introducer of the 1881 Coercion Bill, but resigned following
the Kilmainham Treaty. His replacement, Lord Frederick Cavendish, was murdered in Phoenix
Park shortly after arriving in Dublin. Forster, like the Gregorys, had been a strong critic of British
military action against Egypt in 1881.

Gladstone had gone into uncontrollable fits of laughter over this!

G. R[ussell]. was at a meeting where a missionary told them that in the dialect of his district "cousin" & "enemy" are synonymous terms! — Yeats very charming, I feel quite proud of my young countryman — He gave an interesting account of the other George Russell "A.E." — who was a brilliant art student — & one day came & told his fellows he had decided to repress his artistic side — & to go into a shop as accountant — There he has been ever since — the shop keepers say they never had so good an accountant — but he is quite careless about his prospects — Sometimes he writes his delicate mystic verses — & in the evening clerks — anyone with a laden soul come to him & he tries to teach them the spiritual life — Sometimes the wild blood comes to life again — a little time ago he thought of going to America & living there as a pavement artist![44]

March 1 — Bad cold — but got to Q[ueen's].Club & got on very well with bicycle — afterwards Ly. Layard & Ly. Morris —

2nd — Bad cold — E. Layard — Began Parker's letters — reading & typing.

4th — Still in the house — Grant Duff called, his son's marriage with Miss Walpole broken off[45] —

5th — Out for the first time, still very weak — With Lady Morris to the meeting of Irish Industries at Londonderry House, having been put on the Council & accepted for the sake of Gort — Lady Londonderry[46] proposed a subscription to bring Irish workers to Earls Court & we all had to give — then a proposal was read that we shd give a lace shawl to the Queen — but that I am glad to say was rejected — Lunch Lady D. Nevill, no one interesting except Mr. Massingham(?) editor of Daily Chronicle[47] — he laments the Press getting by degrees so entirely into the hands of financiers — Drove with E. Layard — Tea Ly. Trevelyan[48] — home very tired —

6th — Lunched Ly. Layard & went to see Watts's pictures — Then to Mrs. Lawley[49] — In the morning Paul & Mr. Monckton —

44 George William Russell (1867–1935), poet, painter, mystic, and subsequently an editor and Irish agricultural organizer. WBY's friend since youth. See Biographical Appendix.

45 The engagement was with Arthur Grant–Duff (1861–1948), who was in the diplomatic service.

46 Theresa, née Talbot (d.1919), wife of the 6th Marquess (see p. 85 n. 104), and daughter of the 19th Earl of Shrewsbury (see p. 85 n. 103).

47 Henry William Massingham (1860–1924), champion of Liberal causes as Editor of *The Daily Chronicle* 1895–99, and of *The Nation* 1907–23.

48 Caroline, Lady Trevelyan, née Philips (d.1928), Sir George Trevelyan's wife.

49 Henrietta Lawley, née Zaiser, Francis Lawley's wife.

12th — Hardly yet over my cold — & have made some very bad attempts at bicycling — so shaky & nervous — Have been helping Ly. Layard with her MS — It is curious to read the Sultan's profession to Sir H. [Layard] — "He could not bear to tread on a fly" — & is horrified at the idea of Spanish bullfights — & speaks of his love for animals & birds — I don't know if he was deceiving himself as well as Sir H. at that time —

Nellie Alderson says Gerald Balfour is far & away cleverer than Arthur — that the latter has charm of manner but little real talent — & that he never did or does anything without previously consulting "Uncle Robert"[50] — "Uncle Robert" is furious at the 100 M.P.'s having ventured to send an address of sympathy to the Greeks — says he ought to be left alone to arrange the Cretan business & criticized afterwards — all very well, but it might be too late then[51]—

Yesterday 11th Ly. Layard lent me her carriage & I took Ethel for a drive & some visits — Dined Haliburtons — a large party — Sat between Sir Edward Bradford, such a gentle quiet little man to be over all the London police,[52] & a Mr. St. John, a future Ld. Bolingbroke[53] — Also there Ld. & Ly. Morris, Ld. Poltimore,[54] Ly. Duncannon, Sir F. & Ly. Jeune,[55] Ld. & Lady Harris[56] — Rider Haggard[57] — Ld. Morris in gr spirits, abusing the H. of Lords "Sure I have to be *pa-aid* to sit in it — Sure if I'd known in me young days I'd ever be in it I'd have practised making speeches in a graveyard!"

[50] Arthur Balfour's "Uncle Robert" was the Prime Minister, Lord Salisbury. Salisbury had given Balfour his start in politics, appointing him his Private Secretary while Secretary of State for Foreign Affairs 1878–80.

[51] Though strongly disposed against the Turkish Sultan, Salisbury pursued a markedly laissez-faire policy regarding Crete, and after the defeat of Greek forces in April 1897 was slow to defend Greek interests against the occupying Turkish military forces (see p. 133 n. 61). When he finally took a more active role in arranging peace talks in May 1897, however, he was highly successful in arranging a constitutional settlement which protected Greek interests on Crete.

[52] Sir Edward Ridley Bradford (1836–1914), Commissioner of Police of the Metropolis, 1890–1903.

[53] Either Rev. Maurice William St. John (1827–1914), grandson of the 3rd Viscount Bolingbroke, who had long been the heir presumptive, or more likely his eldest son, Henry (1854–1921). Henry Mildmay St John (1820–99), 5th Viscount, was the last surviving male descendant of the 4th Viscount, but married for the first time in 1893 when aged 73, producing a son, Vernon, in March 1896, who succeeded him. AG seems to have been unaware of this unexpected survival of the direct lineage.

[54] Augustus Frederick Bamfylde (1837–1908), 2nd Baron Poltimore.

[55] Sir Francis Jeune (1843–1905), Judge Advocate-General 1892–1905, and created Baron St. Helier in 1905. His wife Mary née Stewart Mackenzie (1844–1931), a great-aunt of Clementine Hozier, was a noted London hostess.

[56] George Canning Harris (1851–1932), 4th Baron Harris. Governor of Bombay 1890–95. Married Lucy (d. 1930), 2nd daughter of the 3rd Viscount St. Vincent, in 1874.

[57] Henry Rider Haggard (1856–1925), author of *King Solomon's Mines* and many other popular novels.

12th — To Queen's Club but suffered miseries of nervousness & must give up the bicycle till I am quite strong again — Dined Archibald Groves — Sat between Sir John Ardagh[58] & Mr. Lucy — Also there Sir H. & Ly. Cunningham, M. Morris — Henry Arthur Jones[59] — Mrs. Ridley[60] — Sir J. Ardagh was in Turkey during the Russian war — says Sir H. Layard was a complete dupe & did very badly! He is very anti Greek & Cretan — & above all anti Cecil Rhodes & all his works — I said to Mr. Lucy, what I had said to others — that the best support the Cretans have had yet is from Punch, with the cartoon of the "kind Turkish policeman" who is to take care of the weeping little boy[61] — He says it is a gr difficulty to know beforehand what cartoons to have — that it must be Crete next week — & they don't know yet what turn things will have taken.

13 — Mr. Richardson to lunch, is leaving Elstree & setting up a school — Type writing letters — & then to Savile Row — dined & did MS all the evening.

14 — Westminster Abbey — Lunched Duchess of Bedford — Lady Somers there still beautiful — A. Cole afternoon —

15 — My birthday! Paul looked in in the morning — & a letter from Robert in the evening — Did MS at Savile Row —

16 — Nellie Alderson here with MS & stayed to lunch — Hugh Lane to meet her — Ly. Layard's carriage, so took Ethel & Mary Studd for a drive in Battersea Park — Then tea with Ethel, then to M. Studd again — & dined Monteagles[62] — Sat next Mr. Maxse, ed of Nat. Review[63] — who was interested about Folk lore & the Celtic Movement — Ld. Monteagle on my other side — After dinner had a talk with Horace Plunkett on Irish co-operation[64] — Leckys, Miss Chamberlain — poor Lecky with a bad cold after his Irish visit.

17th — Type writing in the morning — Then Chelsea House Irish Ex[hibition].

[58] Major–General Sir John Ardagh (1840–1907), Director of Military Intelligence 1896–1901.

[59] Henry Arthur Jones (1851–1929), one of the most popular dramatists of the London commercial theatre.

[60] Alice Ridley, née Davenport (d.1945), wife of Sir Edward Ridley, Q.C. (1843–1928). Authoress of *The Story of Aline* (1896), a biography of Mrs Craven (see p. 260 n. 160).

[61] *Punch* 13 March 1897, p. 127. The cartoon, with the boy representing a Cretan, was in ironic reference to Lord Salisbury's statement in the Lords on 2 March that "it would be a rash act to withdraw the Turkish troops, who are really the only safeguard against disorder".

[62] Thomas Spring Rice (1849–1926), 2nd Baron Monteagle, and his wife Elizabeth, née Butcher (d.1908). Their daughter Mary (1880–1924) would play a prominent part in the Howth gun-running episode in 1914.

[63] Leopold James Maxse (1864–1932), Editor of *The National Review* 1893–1932.

[64] Horace Curzon Plunkett (1854–1932), Irish agricultural reformer and politician. See Biographical Appendix.

— where I watched over my blinds without success — very tired & rather
forlorn — Then Lady Morris came to my help & took me about & got some
hopes of orders — & Ld. Duncannon introduced me to some newspaper
ladies (one of the Daily Independent!) — it will make the nuns very happy if
their work is mentioned — Tired afterwards, but went to the Albert Hall
festival for S. Patrick's Day — rather disappointing, the voices lost in the gr
space, & not a very good selection —

19 [i.e. 18th] — Looking thro' letters — & then to Savile Row to do MS &
lunched — Then to Chelsea House, a very tiring afternoon & didn't do much
with my blinds — tho' they were admired — Home half dead — & off to dine
at [Vere] O'Brien's — where I sat next my nice host, with that wretched little
bumptious Arnold Foster on my other side — & afterwards had a long talk
with Horace Plunkett — He wants to make a speech in the Financial Debate,
but is not very well up in Irish grievances — & asked for hints — I told him
to go to Froude — & then offered to make some extracts from him, which he
gladly accepted — then I told him Barry O'Brien wd be the man to prime him,
& I wd ask him to dine on Sunday if he cd come — & this he jumped at[65] —
On to the Grant Duffs — as dreary as I expected — Albert Ball — Flora Shaw
— Mme. Goldstein — Japanese Minister — I made off very soon —

19 — Did some typing — Mrs. Martin & Ethel to lunch — the former said she
had desired her niece to call for her at 5-30! Luckily having Lady L.'s carriage
I cd take them both out — Took my bundles of letters to old Parker to try &
get the rest & found he had gone to Scotland again! — To Mudie's for Froude,
& then drove in the Park — Met Willy Peel when I came back, he is off today
to Salonica, on chance of a fight, to write for the Daily Telegraph[66] — Dined
Lovelaces — sat between Harold Russell & Leonard Courtenay[67] & had some
pleasant talk with the latter — After dinner first talked to Mrs. Beaumont,
then Ly. Lovelace[68] & when the men came, Henry James & Lord Lovelace sat
down one on each side — one at a time wd have been better as common

---

[65] Plunkett made his first speech in the Irish Financial Relations debate shortly afterwards on
30 March (see *Hansard's Parliamentary Debates*, 4th Series, XLVIII, pp. 157–61), and drew on AG's
assistance, presenting an historical overview of Irish grievances based on Froude's *History of the
English in Ireland in the Eighteenth Century*. As urged by WBY and O'Brien on 21 March (see diary
entry for that date), Plunkett made his speech "strong" by for the first time aligning himself with
the Nationalist majority amongst the Irish members.

[66] William Robert Peel (1866–1937), eldest son of Speaker Peel. Succeeded his father as 2nd
Viscount Peel in 1912. M.P. 1900–06, 1909–12, and Secretary of State for India 1922–24, 1928–
29. Created Viscount Clanfield 1929.

[67] Leonard Courtney [*sic*] (1832–1918), M.P. 1876–1900, Financial Secretary to the
Treasury 1882–84, and Deputy Speaker 1886–92. An habitué of Grant Duff's social circle,
frequently confused with William Leonard Courtney (1850–1928), Editor of *The Fortnightly
Review*.

[68] Lady Lovelace, née Mary Wortley (d.1941), Lord Lovelace's second wife.

ground was not quite easy to find — but we got on to the Byron letters which Lord L. is editing[69] — The Ripons[70] also there — & Freshfields[71] — a pleasant evening in those beautiful rooms — & Lady Layard's carriage to fetch me seemed quite in keeping!

20 — Worked at Froude for Mr. Plunkett — Lunched Borwicks — good natured people, not interesting — Then to see Sir F. Burton, about whom I was anxious — & with some cause — for he looks very much worn, & complains of giddiness in the head — & is anxious about himself — He is delighted with Yeats's] poetry but still sticks to not meeting him — The only poets that did not disappoint him were Rossetti & William Morris — Swinburne was vain & excitable — & not genuine — Tennyson grumpy & posing — Browning charming as a friend — but not answering to the poetic ideal — I did not stay long as there was someone waiting for him — but he stood looking rather wistfully at the hall door as I left, & I felt a sinking of heart, as if I would not often be there again — Then to enquire for Jean Ingelow — but since she had a fit a year ago she keeps to her room — Then to Mrs. Aylmer Gowing, looking very cracked with her hair hanging down — she had had it washed! She presented me with the poems she had written "in memory of her husband"[72] — Then to the Morrises, very bright & cheery — & home to a sandwich & typing Froude — & looking thro' my folk lore which I had rescued from Sir F. —

21st — Got to church, & had a quiet afternoon typing from Froude — only the Birchs — Dinner, Rt. Hon. Horace Plunkett, Mr. Barry O'Brien, W. B. Yeats — some very interesting talk — Mr. O'Brien arrived first — & said he wd be so glad to meet Mr. Plunkett — as all sections of Nationalists of late have been agreeing that he is the only possible leader to unite all parties — Yeats, just back from Dublin, corroborates this — He has been trying to reconcile conflicting committees re the '98 Centenary — but there is a great deal of squabbling[73] — He says "every man who has time on his hands & a little industry has a secret society of his own" — Then Mr. Plunkett came & we went up to dinner — a little tentative conversation first — Then Mr. Plunkett [said] his grudge against Parnellism is that Parnell so mastered & dominated his

[69] Lovelace's book *Astarte*, renewing the controversy concerning Byron's incestuous relationship with his half-sister, Augusta Leigh, and based principally on letters between Byron, Lady Byron and Augusta Leigh, was published in 1905.

[70] George Frederick Robinson (1827–1909), 1st Marquess of Ripon, Governor-General of India 1880–84, Secretary for the Colonies 1892–95. Married Henrietta Vyner (d.1907) in 1851.

[71] Douglas Freshfield (1845–1934), traveller and mountaineer. Member of the Council of the Royal Geographical Society 1878–94 and its Vice-President 1905–08. Editor of *The Alpine Journal* 1880–89. Married Augusta Ritchie (d.1911), sister of Richmond Ritchie (see p.78 n. 70).

[72] *Sita, and other Poems* (1895).

[73] For tensions between the London and Dublin branches of the '98 Centennial Association, which was organizing events to mark the centenary of the 1798 uprising, see p. 168 n. 22.

followers as to crush national life instead of developing it, as has happened when there has been a national awakening in other countries — Mr. O'B. says, it was necessary he should dominate for the campaign, & that he was a great general — I say, we see Mr. P.'s contention is true, by the helpless disorganisation parties have fallen into since his death, & ask Mr. O'B. what he would do at this moment in Ireland if he had power there — He says "I would make Mr. Horace Plunkett our leader & follow him" — Yeats agrees enthusiastically & says "we all want it" — Mr. Plunkett reddens & is evidently touched, tho' his quiet restrained manner is unchanged — Yeats asks him how far he would go — he says, to a large measure of local Government — but not separation — & not yet Home Rule they are not ready for it — We urge him to make his speech strong — Mr. O'Brien tells him how he said to a Cabinet Minister "No Irishman ever gets anything from you till he goes to you with the head of a landlord in one hand & the tail of a cow in the other" — Mr. P. is delighted, says if he could put things like that he might indeed think of being a leader —

We come down & have coffee, & I give them cigarettes & we talk finance — Mr. O'Brien's point is, that it ought to be rubbed into the Govt. that it was their own Protestant colony they destroyed in destroying trade — My point is, that the Liberals, & indeed the Govt. have confessed already the enormity of England's conduct in the past — & by way of making up, gave liberally of the landlords' money, the Church money or anything they could get at the expense of others — but as soon as it comes to their own money & the case is put before them, they say — oh now, we must have another commission, & button up their pockets — Mr. O'Brien is much pleased at my saying "It is not getting the money that is the important thing — it is getting all Ireland into line" —

None of us have a good word for Dillon — I ask B. O'B. what he thinks of him, & he says "What Parnell did — that it is a wonder the Irish people haven't found out what a consummate fool he is" — Mr. Plunkett wonders Redmond[74] hasn't made more way — O'B. thinks it is the difficulty of succeeding such a man as Parnell — I think it is the dead weight of the priests against him, they were afraid to resist Parnell until England did so — but tried by way of make up to crush Redmond with all their force — Mr. P. never met Parnell — he once had an appointment with him about the industrial scheme — but he did not keep it, & wrote afterwards to say he was going to Ireland, & wd be hard

74 John Redmond (1856–1918), Nationalist M.P., assumed leadership of the Parnell loyalists following Parnell's death. A key figure in facilitating the reunification of the Irish Parliamentary party in 1900, he was elected leader of the new coalition, a position he retained until shortly before his death. His influence declined sharply following the 1916 Easter Rising and the emergence of Sinn Fein.

to find there — Mr. P. thinks he was quite unlike an Irishman — but Yeats says it is quite Celtic to have that strong will — look at Zola & Balzac, with what tenacity they work out an idea, while an English novelist never has a true scheme — Morley told O'B. that he had once driven Parnell to a meeting where he was to make a speech — & was very anxious to know what he was going to say — but he was silent all the time — When he got near the destination, he took a little box from his pocket — unfolded its wrappings & began carefully unpacking it — Morley looked on breathlessly thinking some clue or cabalistic sign wd appear — At last a flower was revealed, which Parnell placed in his buttonhole! — Mr. P. is much disgusted with Dillon's behaviour on the financial committee, upsetting the whole coach by his silly amend-ments[75] — He is also disgusted by a deputation sent over to London who he had to introduce — Alderson etc — & who had no suggestions to make to Hicks Beach[76] — but cd only say "We hope there will be no further enquiry" — which as H[icks]. B[each]. afterwards said, they might as well have written on a post card — The party did not break up till 12 — Mr. Plunkett going first — Mr. O'Brien looked at Yeats when he had left & said "We could go fast with that man as a leader" — but is a little sad that he doesn't go in more for Home Rule — yet confesses he is wiser to stick to agricultural co-operation for the present —

His courteous restrained manner — good looks & some quality in his voice are all in his favour — & he must have some magnetic influence to have got over the suspicions of the farmers & induced them to co-operate — I gave him my Froude notes — & Mr. O'Brien his agricultural pamphlet[77] — & told him to send him in return his little Hist[ory] of Ireland[78] & I gave Yeats my folk lore pages — so I think I did my best for them all — But whether any good to Ireland will come from the meeting is another question — Yeats says "every man in Ireland & a little industry has a secret society of his own" — And when I put forward my hopes of land purchase he says, or quotes some one else, that England has always betrayed its garrison — The Protestant industrial colony — the Church — the landlords — now there are the priests, who still keep a sort of order, to betray — & then only remain the peasant proprietors — so let us put off their creation — & consequent extinction — as long as possible.

75 For Dillon's suspicions regarding the Childers Committee and the Financial Relations Bill, and the grounds of his long-lasting hostility to Plunkett, see Trevor West, *Horace Plunkett, Co-Operation and Politics* pp. 80–82.

76 Sir Michael Hicks Beach (1837–1916), 1st Earl St. Aldwyn. M.P. 1864–1906, Chief Secretary for Ireland 1874–78 and 1886–87, Chancellor of the Exchequer 1885–86 and 1895–1902.

77 Plunkett's 1894 pamphlet *The Irish Agricultural Organisation and its Aims.*

78 *Ireland* (London: T.Fisher Unwin, 1896), a brief history edited by O'Brien from an MS supplied by Unwin, and published in The Children's Study series.

22 — Mr. Plunkett writes "I don't know when I have spent such an interesting evening as I did last night — Why are there not more such evenings? . . . I am half thinking of seconding Blake's motion on the Financial Relations so as to ensure getting in early in the debate & before a minister has given the official non possumus[79] — But I must ponder on the step as it would be a capitulation to Dillon who prevented us from having a resolution which all Unionists could support."

A bicycle lesson at St. Peter's — very uphill work learning to mount! The 2 Borwick girls & Ethel to lunch — the latter in a flannel shirt of Paul's with her red cloak huddled over it! rather hard on me after all my trouble with her trousseau! Drove with her, & went to a dull tea party at Mrs. Vere O'Brien's — Home to Miss Oswell, & correcting the Layard MS for the evening —

23 — Bicycle — & when I came back a long visit from old Parker, bringing the letters at last — He is a regular Kafoozalem — & sat prattling as if neither he nor I had work to do — He told me Peel had been fond of pistol practise at Harrow — & also of shooting — He & a friend kept guns at a house some distance off — One day after they had left their guns a master met them & asked where they had got the birds they were carrying & the friend said "Oh, Peel is such a wonderful shot with a stone!" — He thinks he will have one vol ready by Xmas — the next six weeks later — but they haven't yet got leave, or asked it to publish his letters to the Queen — & now he hears she is herself writing a book, & may say, I will publish what is proper shd appear, & the rest must be left unpublished[80] — He has heard that Peel once apologised to some one he had affronted by his coldness for his "unfortunate manner" — Then Miss Alderson, & we did 2 hours of Sir H. Layard's MS — very interesting, the Sultan actually now suspects him of a design to assassinate him —

Then drove, to Ly. Morris, & to a very dull tea at the Deanery, Westminster — Dined Murrays — the house always charming, the staircase where Byron & Scott first met — the grate where Byron's MS was burned — the screen made by Byron's fencing master under his direction — the corrected MS of many authors — A speech of Peel's much corrected — "I have never done anything of that sort" said Gladstone when he saw it, forgetting a speech equally corrected in his own writing, in Murray's possession — which he

[79] Edward Blake (1833–1912), who served as Nationalist M.P. for S. Longford 1892–1907 following a distinguished parliamentary career in Canada, introduced his motion for financial reparations for Ireland in a long and powerful speech on 29 March (*Hansard's Parliamentary Debates*, 4th Series, XLVII, pp. 1577–98). John Redmond, rather than Plunkett, seconded the motion.

[80] Parker's two projected volumes completing the work were not published until 1899, but did include Peel's correspondence with Queen Victoria, by royal permission.

showed us[81] — The party less pleasant than usual — Ld. & Ly. Grimthorpe[82] — he a surly ill conditioned looking old wretch — Sir H. Cunningham, Mr. & Mrs. Thesiger — Mrs. Bishop, from a tour in China[83] — I sat next Mr. Gathorne Hardy, full of his own collection of drawings — & when we diverged to the Financial Question rude & sullen[84] — a regular Saxon — Mr. Thesiger pleasant enough —

24 — Lady Fingall[85] came to lunch, to talk Gort Industries, & I think will be a help — We are to make aprons for the stall holders at her Punchestown bazaar — Drove her home, & to Chelsea, Ethel with a headache, I went out for phenacitine for her — Then sat with Mary Studd — then to call at the Monteagles & found all the young people dancing jigs! Then home to Miss Oswell, correcting Layard MS all the evening, & very tired to bed —

25 — To Harrow — found R. very well & bright — bought football group with his photo — We met Mr. Welldon, very affable — asked us in to tea but I refused — I had read his letter in the Times in the morning appealing to the Turf to reform itself from within, as the stage has done[86] — & sympathized with him — He is not sanguine, but I believe any reform can be brought about after the abolition of duelling — Home very tired —

26 — To see E[lizabeth]. Persse at Northfleet — a charming little house with view of the river & the ships — poorly enough furnished — I promised her a carpet, & went & chose it at Tecloars on my return — Dined Ly. Layard — She has given me her type writer in lieu of the bicycle — Home dead tired, too tired to sleep.

28 — Lunched Haliburtons — Sir Vincent & Lady Barrington[87] — he

[81] Byron and Scott met for the first time at the Murrays' house at 50 Albermarle St. in April 1815. John Murray 2nd and others burnt the manuscript of Byron's unpublished memoirs there in May 1824, shortly after Byron's death, in a misguided effort to prevent speculation about his personal life.

[82] Edward Beckett (1816–1905), 1st Baron Grimthorpe, K.C., J.P. and Chancellor of York 1877–1900. Married Fanny Lonsdale (d.1901) in 1845.

[83] Mrs. Isabella Lucy Bishop, née Bird (1831–1904), celebrated for her remarkable solo travels in Korea, Japan, Tibet and elsewhere, which she documented in a series of popular volumes.

[84] Probably Alfred Gathorne-Hardy (1845–1918), M.P. 1886–95, youngest son of Gathorne Hardy, 1st Earl of Cranbrook.

[85] Elizabeth, Lady Fingall (d. 1944) wife of Arthur James Plunkett (1859–1929), 11th Earl of Fingall, and daughter of AG's near neighbour George Burke of Danesfield, Co. Galway.

[86] "The Jockey Club and Betting Rings," *The Times* 25 March, p. 11.

[87] Sir Vincent Kennet-Barrington (1844–1903), grandson of Sir Jonah Barrington (1760–1834), the Irish lawyer and M.P. whose famous *Memoirs* exposed the bribery and corruption behind the Irish Parliament's vote in favour of Union with Britain in 1800. Kennet-Barrington, a medical reformer and founder of the Red Cross Society, married Alicia Sandeman in 1878.

grandson of Sir Jonah, all for Home Rule & balloons — & Mr. Woodall — Dinner, Lady Layard, Sir H. & Ly. Johnston — George Moore — Sir H. Cunningham who was to have come had influenza — & I had not time to get another man, & found the evening dullish, neither of my ladies quite making out G. Moore[88] — who is as enthusiastic as I am about Yeats —

29 — Drove with E[nid]. L[ayard]. to Powells — to see the monument he is making for St Margaret's church, <?to> Sir H. — I found it was he who had sat next me at the Clays dinner — He showed me his mosaic, glass etc — much of it beautiful & interesting — Tea with Lady Duncannon — Home & off to Holloway, escorted by M[a]cBride to see "Shemus O'Brien" at the Parkhurst Theatre[89] — a queer little place, more like a meeting house or concert hall — chocolates hawked about between the acts — The cast fairly good — & the music very pretty —

30 — Typing, & some shopping with E. L. — & to Chelsea to see Ly. Lovelace etc — Dined Raffalovichs — the society there considerably changed — chiefly 'verts — Miss Gribbell has already the look of a Papist of 20 years standing[90] — Dullish, & glad to get home —

31 — Dead tired — Typed some of E. L.'s letters — She has given me a quantity of her copies of Sir H.'s letters to correct! just when I have so much work on my own hands — Dined Sir Barrington Simeons — Sat next Mr. Pember Q.C.[91] — curiously he was to have met me at the 2 last Wednesday dinners, that were put off by deaths — He was pleasant & agreeable — The Maxses there, & a lot I didn't know, but a pleasant evening enough —

Ap[ril] 1 — M[a]cBride came & took me to look for a bicycle at the Stores, but didn't seem to know much about them — Lunched Borwicks — Mr. Jay, of "The Jago" — looking like a nigger, but interesting, full of life & interested

[88] Lady Layard recorded in her diary that Moore was "rather paradoxical—& evidently pleased with himself" (British Library).

[89] "Shamus O'Brien" a two act Comic Opera by George Jessop (libretto) and C. Villiers Stanford (music, see p. 269 n. 197), founded on a poem by Joseph Sheridan LeFanu, had originally opened at the Opera Comique in 1896.

[90] Florence Truscott Gribbell (1843–1930), an intimate friend of André Raffalovitch's mother, entered the Raffalovitch household as governess to André in 1873, moved with him to London as his housekeeper-companion in 1884, and thereafter served prominently as hostess of his social gatherings. Worked closely with AG in her relief-work for St. Stephen's, Southwark, from the mid–1880s on.

[91] Edward Henry Pember, Q.C. (1832–1911).

in his work[92] — Mr. Richards M.P. for Finsbury[93] — amusing, tho' as Mrs. Du Cane said "trying to hold on to his h's" — He had been converted to our Financial grievances during the debate, & tho' his friends dissuaded him from going against the Govt he abstained from voting — Then helped E. L. with her shopping — & then home & worked at her letters till bed time — very tired —

April 2 — Worked at E. L.'s letters till 3, when I finished them off — Went to consult Sir A. Birch about a bicycle but without much result — To Mudie's & De Brys[94] — & back tired — Dined Cheyne Row, same as usual — E[thel]'s symptoms — & the pros & cons of houses —

3rd — Rather a wasted day, going to Lady Fingall's with pattern apron, to find she was away — lunched Savile Row & drove with E[nid]. to a dressmaker who was out — Dined Lyalls — fairly pleasant but he looked tired & Maud Walpole was there, her first appearance since the breaking of her engagement, & rather sad — Sir A. talked of Tennyson — Once, when he walked with him, Tennyson repeated one of his own poems — & Sir A. said "I suppose you wrote that some time ago?" — "I suppose you think I couldn't do it now" growled the Laureate. Watts told Sir A. that Tennyson had been one day to see him in a state of gr. depression — said he wished he had never written a line — he was only fit to be a civil engineer — Watts said "You should not give in but try to look bravely at things as your own heroes wd have done, King Arthur or Galahad or Ulysses,"[95] but for answer Tennyson pointed to his knuckles & said "Gout in the hand" in his sepulchral voice —

4th — A quiet Sunday — Westminster Abbey — & Sir F. Burton in the afternoon — he described an amusing scene when Browning was showing off his son's first pictures[96] — not very good ones — & Tennyson came to see them & walked round in his cloak & hat, looking much disgusted & giving an occasional growl while Browning cheerfully & quietly did the honours — He

[92] "The Jago" was the name given to the Shoreditch area of London, one of the poorest parts of the East End, by Arthur Morrison (1863–1945) in his 1896 realist novel *A Child of the Jago.* Arthur Osborn Jay (1858–*c.*1943), was Vicar of Holy Trinity Church, Shoreditch, and author of *A Story of Shoreditch, Life in Darkest London* and other works urging improvement of the area.

[93] Henry Richards (1851–1905), M.P. for Northampton 1884–95 and for E. Finsbury 1895–1905.

[94] A chocolatier in New Oxford Street.

[95] Watts and Tennyson were lifelong friends, with Watts at Tennyson's suggestion building a house in 1873 at Freshwater, Isle of Wight, close to the Laureate's. Watts painted some seven portraits of Tennyson, and in 1898 embarked on his monumental bronze of the poet, which now stands near the Chapter House at Lincoln Cathedral.

[96] Robert "Pen" Browning (1849–1912), exhibited from 1877 on as a painter and sculptor. Despite considerable talent, his artistic life was lastingly overshadowed and disrupted by his parents' reputations.

once met him at Lockers[97] — & Tennyson having helped himself to some cheese straws suddenly began to dash them over the table with his fork in a fit of petulance, saying "beastly things" — Carlyle had said to Lewes "It's a pity to see that man wasting his great heart in bits of verses" — "Why, what would you have him do?" said Lewes — & Carlyle gave a great guffaw — his habit when he was taken aback & said "What's before him!"

Sir A. Lyall spoke rather disparagingly of Morley the other night — says his words & speeches are so different — & that he is not gaining ground — He does not think he cares at all for Ireland — I asked what he really cares for, & Sir A. says "power" — Dined Savile Row — Elaine Guest sang nicely[98] — Talked bicycles with L. Du Cane[99] —

5th — Letters — Recd. Robert's £100 legacy[100] & went to lodge it in Nat. Penny Bank but was driven away by the die away airs & unbusinesslike ways of the young "ladies" — & took it to B[ank]. of England, to lodge for me — Shopping & tea at Mrs. Skilbecks[101] — & dined Lady L. — Miss Oswell came & helped me to clean type writer — Heard from N. Geary of his return —

6th — L. Du Cane to lunch & went with him to buy my bicycle — a Humber Wolverhampton — £24 — a large sum which I can't very well spare — but cd not put off buying having promised Robert that he shd learn in the holidays — Recd my £200 back from Ethel, & lodged it — very glad to see it again! My accounts tolerably satisfactory — £500 per ann put by for 6 years wd clear the place for Robert — but I want to do it in 5 years, when he will be of age — Had dress tried on — & went to see Ethel at Chelsea — very tired & headache in the night —

7th — N. Geary to lunch — looking very well & bright after Africa — We went on to see Lady Maxwell — Dined Mr. Horace Plunkett[102] — Fingalls, Castletowns, Alfred Lytteltons[103] — Mrs. Fitzgerald & some man — I was next Lord Castletown & had some financial talk — He says he is no Home Ruler

97 Frederic Locker (1821–95), poet and antiquary. Friend of Wilfrid Blunt, through whom AG had met him in the 1880s.

98 Elaine Guest (b. 1873), third daughter of Lady Layard's eldest brother, Lord Wimborne.

99 Louis Du Cane (1863–1937), second son of Richard and Maria Du Cane (see p. 35 n. 74).

100 From AG's mother.

101 Beatrice Skilbeck, née Knowles, daughter of James Knowles. She had married William Wray Skilbeck (1864–1919), Knowles's principal editorial assistant, in 1894. Skilbeck succeeded Knowles as Editor of The Nineteenth Century in 1908.

102 Plunkett had written in response to AG's dinner of 21 March that he would invite "a few Irishmen and women of the better sort and a few sympathetic English folk into my bachelor quarters to meet you" (Berg).

103 Alfred Lyttelton (1857–1913), M.P. 1895–1906, and Secretary of State for the Colonies 1903–05. Married Edith Balfour in 1892.

but is a Nationalist — he believes from an Imperial point of view Home Rule wd be a mistake — & also that it will never be granted — I told him there was disappointment that his H[ouse]. of L[ords]. speech was so much milder than his first[104] — & he says it is impossible to speak in the depressing influence of the H. of L. — Lord Salisbury had said to him as he came out "This was very different from yr tone in Ireland" — & he said "Yes, & I have known you speak very differently in the hustings to what you do in this house" — His object in that violent speech was to attract the attention of the people & get their confidence & bring them into line — I asked what we are to do now we are fairly in line — it is no good making a general agitation, we shd go at one point, such as tobacco growing & insist on its being granted —

He also has been collecting folk lore — & believes as firmly as Yeats in the "dim nation" — Mr. Plunkett, talking of Irish tactics in Parliament told us how one night there was a naval debate — & Redmond got up & talked for 20 minutes & took a division on every motion — at last in the Lobby Mr. P. said to him "Now do tell me, as a friend, what pleasure it gives you to keep us all out of bed — & what the Navy estimates matter to you — what are you aiming at" — "What I'm aiming at" said Redmond "is that I want to have a boat slip at Kilrush"! — & for this he was impeding the whole Imperial business.[105]

9th [i.e. 8th] — Lunched Savile Row — a crowd of the "family" I was sorry to have dropped in for — said good bye to Enid who leaves for Ireland in the evening — Shopping & saw Lady Simeon[106] — & came late to tea with Lady Johnston & Sir Harry — Then dressed for dinner, & as I was starting heard " 'anson for Sir 'Arry Johnston" called down the telephone — & when I got to the Grays I was told they were of the party! Sat between A[lbert]. G[ray]. & an uninteresting golf man but afterwards had a long talk with Sir H. H. J. on the religious ideas of his African people —

9th — Sir Auckland Colvin at 11 for a long talk — He is very sore indeed with Ld. Roberts for his attack upon his father, which he has just been answering in the N. Century[107] — He has really settled into a country place — & abjures

[104] Bernard Fitzpatrick (1849–1937), 2nd Baron Castletown, had introduced the Financial Relations Bill in the Lords on 5 March 1897, urging reparations to Ireland on the taxation question, but in a milder tone than his preliminary statements the previous Parliamentary session. He subsequently founded the Pan-Celtic Congress, an umbrella organisation for Celtic cultural nationalists, and was amongst the first subscribers to the Irish Literary Theatre. Lady Castletown, née Ursula St. Leger (d.1927), was daughter of the 4th Viscount Doneraile.

[105] Redmond had spoken repeatedly during debates over supplementary Naval estimates in March 1896, arguing along with Tim Healy for a fairer share of expenditures in Ireland.

[106] Lady Simeon, née Isabella Dutton (d.1936), Sir Barrington Simeon's wife.

[107] Frederick Sleigh Roberts (1832–1914), created 1st Baron Roberts in 1892. Served with distinction in the Indian and Afghanistan Wars. Appointed Field Marshall in 1895, and Commander of Forces in Ireland 1895–99. For his recall to active duty in 1899 to take command

society — He speaks quite indignantly of the "Cromerising" of Egypt — all the officials there speak think & write Cromerese — and he is only second in despotism to the Czar[108] — Drove Ethel & L. Du Cane to the Stillman picture ex[hibition] — met Lady Lyall in a gr state of mind because Sir A. has told her the breakfast club is to meet at their house in the morning — & has not helped her at all to prepare a menu — I advised relays of hot toast — for which they ought to be much obliged to me — Ran off to see Mrs. Kay — had 6 oysters for dinner on the way home — & went early to bed — Heard Mrs. Egan has broken a rib, & can't probably cook for some time —

10th — Trying on at Durrants — & lunched Raffalovich to meet Lady Denbigh,[109] John Gray, Mr. Dwyer — a young barrister who lives at Newman Hall, in the East End — The conversation very Papistical — Miss G[ribbel] & Raffy as full of Fathers fasts & formulas as they used to be of the stage — Lady D. a little bored, kept trying to talk to me — Great rejoicing over the conversion of Aubrey Beardsley which has just been effected by a Jesuit priest at Bournemouth — He is dying of consumption & was unhappy at the thought of leaving life so young — but now is quite peaceful & happy — tho' wishing to live a little longer to look at things in the new light cast upon them by Faith — Raffy has sent him to the Riviera at his own expense[110] —

To Chelsea to see Mary Studd & her new baby — then back at 7 to find a note from N. Geary saying we are to dine at Romanos' at 7 sharp & go to the "Geisha"[111] — so flew into my clothes & got there not very late — The Geisha a silly & vulgar performance to my mind — but as N. says "Now we know what

in South Africa, see p. 256 n. 142. In his book *Forty-One Years in India: From Subaltern to Commander-in-Chief* (1897), Roberts had been critical of the part Colvin's father had played in events during the mutiny at Agra in 1857. Colvin's counterblast was published in *The Nineteenth Century* April 1897, pp. 556–68.

[108] Evelyn Baring (1841–1917), created 1st Baron Cromer 1892, 1st Earl 1901. Commissioner of the Egyptian Public debt 1877–79, Controller-General in Egypt 1879 and British Agent and Consul-General 1883–1907. Vigorous agent of British imperialism in Egypt, and antagonist to AG in her efforts for the Egyptian Nationalists in 1882–83.

[109] Cecilia, Lady Denbigh, née Clifford (d.1919), wife of the 9th Earl of Denbigh.

[110] Aubrey Beardsley (1872–March 1898), the avant-garde artist whose brief but meteoric career was ended by tuberculosis. Beardsley met Raffalovich in 1895 shortly after being dismissed as Art Editor of *The Yellow Book* in the wake of Oscar Wilde's arrest, publisher John Lane considering him too closely associated with Wilde in the public eye because of his designs for *Salomé*. Raffalovich immediately began to provide generous support to Beardsley, then in highly straightened circumstances, paying him an allowance and financing his frequent moves in search of a suitable climate. Beardsley's last months were spent principally at Bournemouth, where he received instruction and entered the Catholic Church in early 1897, and Mentone, on the Riviera, where he died. In 1904 Raffalovich and Gray published a memorial volume of their correspondence with the artist.

[111] "The Geisha: A Story of a Teahouse" a musical drama by Owen Hall (libretto), Harry Greenbank (lyrics) and Sidney Jones (music), which enjoyed an extraorinarily successful run of 760 performances at Daly's Theatre between March 1896 and May 1898.

the taste of Royalty is" — the Prince having been there 4 times — N. G.
consulted me about a letter from a lady, a distant connection of his, who he
knows very little & has never received any civility from — who writes to ask him
for a loan of £40! She is married to a man with £10,000 per ann. — but "can't
ask him for this" — speaks of an illness she has had etc — I advise no answer
to the letter which he acknowledges wd be [the] most prudent as well as
easiest course — but he has a sort of chivalrous feel[ing] that one ought not
to refuse a woman money — but we agree in suspecting some trap — & his
name is of too much value to be put at such a woman's mercy —

11 — To the Abbey — and to lunch with the Hoziers — pompous & dull —
Mr. Barry O'Brien called in the afternoon — & I asked him to join our dinner
which he did — It went off very pleasantly Nevill Geary — Yeats — George
Moore — A. Du Cane — Miss Childers. Yeats the feature of the evening —
He brought me "The Secret Rose" which G. Moore is enthusiastic about —
and I read aloud a rather absurd review of it in the "Saturday" which he had
not seen[112] — He says George Russell's poems are not so good now — as they
are dictated by the spirits & the scansion is all wrong — He only paints now
on the whitewashed walls of his lodging — as he is sure it will be all
whitewashed over when he leaves it — & to paint anything that will last wd be
"a bond upon his soul"[113] — He signed his poems AE — but the publisher
insisted on separating the letters — a gr grievance to the writer who says that
the dipthong exactly by its sound expressed the mood of his soul[114] — We also
talked of J. F. Taylor who B. O'Brien is asking to write a pamphlet on the
Financial question[115] — Yeats says he & Mrs. Besant[116] are the two best orators
he has ever heard — that Taylor is very quarrelsome — will never join any
party — but if any party joins him he immediately secedes from it — There

[112] *The Secret Rose* had just been published, and the anonymous notice in *The Saturday Review*
10 April 1897, p. 365, was the first review of the book to appear. Moore subsequently voiced his
enthusiasm in "Mr. Yeats's New Book", *The Daily Chronicle* 24 April 1897, p. 3.
[113] For George Russell ("AE") see Biographical Appendix. For reproductions of his mystical
murals on the walls of 3 Upper Ely Place, see Henry Summerfield *That Myriad Minded Man*.
[114] "I signed the first essay I wrote 'Aeon'. The printers then as now found some difficulty in
making out my writing & on the proof it appeared as AE? . . . It was later made into 'A.E.' as my
first publisher thought A.E. looked like the initials of somebody but 'AE' did not suggest any
person living in this or any other world" (unpublished letter in editor's collection).
[115] John F. Taylor (1850–1902), barrister, journalist and orator, recalled by WBY as one of
the powerful "tragic" figures against whom he had measured himself in his youth (*Au* pp. 96–
7), and who features in the Aeolus episode of *Ulysses* for his eloquence in the cause of the Irish
language. Taylor had published a biography of Owen Roe O'Neill in 1896, but did not complete
the proposed pamphlet.
[116] Annie Besant, née Wood (1847–1933), the prominent social reformer, who had joined
the Theosophical Society under the influence of Madame Blavatsky in 1889, worked with WBY
in the Esoteric Section of the Society in 1889–90, and later led one of the rival factions when the
organization split after Madame Blavatsky's death in 1891. She was a notoriously brilliant
speaker, on occasion speaking for hours without notes.

was or is some debating club in Dublin where there was one surviving Unionist who was carefully preserved & tended, for sake of argument — & one evening when Y. went in he heard Taylor roaring at this balancing member "Sir, I tell you, I'll put your head in a bag" — He & Moore rather scoff at A. Beardsley's conversion — I was afraid to tell them Raffy had had a hand in it — Pleasant talk — it will be long before I join in such again —

{Parnell called Dillon "a black peacock" — Mrs. Gladstone had told someone that she had never known Gladstone nervous except the day Parnell was coming to Hawarden[117] —

Miss Childers had heard of the consternation in the Hawarden household when Parnell was late for dinner & did not turn up at all for breakfast — B. O'Brien hears Gladstone says that if he were now in Parliament he wd bring Home Rule out of the financial question within 2 years — }

12th — Packing — & to the City to buy cricket things — Mr. Bowen only allowing R. up in time to catch the train — & to Tecloars about changing E. Persse's carpet, which they promise to do — Lunch Morrises — Ld. M. disdainful of Horace Plunkett's schemes — "cods" or humbug he calls them — & of Taylor who he says is a third rate orator — & will never go far — & of the Irish Literary Society — "a set of schemers" — I did not like to say I have just been elected to it! — but very full of his own swell friends & of having dined at Sir H. Thompson's Octaves "where the Prince dines once a year" — Martin on the other side much elated because he has just come from a visit to the old Duchess of Cleveland at Battle — & is going to spend Easter with the Percy Wyndhams at Clouds[118] — No, I think my poor literary society friends know more of "the things that are more excellent" — A hurried packing — & met R. at Euston —

13 — Arrived at Coole after the usual tiring journey — The country saturated with water & everything looking grey & we had a wet afternoon. Even with R. I feel a little chill coming back to the grey silence & the small cares — But that will pass away in service for others — & I feel much for the people, not able to sow their crops —

14 — A good night's rest, & sunshine between the showers — Frank came

---

[117] Presumably Parnell's visit of 18–19 December 1889, at which he and Gladstone discussed what form the next Home Rule Bill should take, and specifically what degree of Irish representation should remain at Westminster if an Irish Parliament were formed. The discrepancies between Parnell's and Gladstone's accounts of this meeting were to be a particular focus of difficulty for Parnell in the course of his fall from leadership the following year.

[118] Catherine, Duchess of Cleveland (1819–1901), née Stanhope, was the widow of the 4th and last Duke (d.1891). Clouds, Wiltshire, was the Wyndhams' country home.

over — he is strong on the financial question & has written some letters to the Daily Graphic about it[119] — He says our tenants can't go into Court for about 2 years — but are sure to do so then — that means a large reduction — but if they ought to have it, better so — Pigs are selling better now the middleman has been abolished — I begin to form an idea of a pamphlet on finance — in Q[uestion] & A[nswer] form? or a conversation?[120] The weather still broken — such a month of March has never been known they say! Mrs. Lally came down to ask me to get her husband off, he is to be sent to Galway Gaol for 2 months for drunkenness & "she wouldn't mind, if she had anyone to do the spring sowing" —

1897
Nov[ember] 30 — Queen Anne Mansions — I have written no diary for a long time — I forget when the last entry was[121] — A great pity for the summer was an interesting one — After the Easter holidays Lady Layard came for three weeks — I took the old police barrack at Burren & we spent 3 weeks there — & the sea did her much good — I picked up some folk lore there & wrote an article for the Spectator "Irish Visions"[122] — Then I began ++++ting more folk lore — & ++++ for a couple of days to Chevy, & drove across the mountains to see the house of Biddy Early[123] —

One evening Sergeant Hanlon brought me in some trout — & as next day was

[119] Only one of Frank Persse's letters appears to have been published (*The Daily Graphic* 10 April 1897, p. 9). This argues succinctly for a fairer tax system, noting that taxation of commodities is regressive, and hits the generally low-income Irish disproportionately hard.

[120] AG completed this plan the following year in *A Short Catechism on the Financial Claims of Ireland*, which uses her initial idea of question-and-answer form. See below p. 168 n. 27.

[121] AG had apparently misplaced the last volume of her diary at this point, and this entry marks the beginning of a new manuscript book.

[122] Lady Layard arrived at Coole on 6 May, and she and AG stayed at Burren on the Galway coast between 10–18 May. At Burren, Lady Layard recorded, AG went in search of "stories of the fairies of which she is trying to collect a quantity for publication. They are firmly believed in by all the peasants hereabouts, & Mr. Dhooly who is our present cook spins long yarns about them & gives Augusta valuable accounts which she immediately writes down." AG also astonished Lady Layard and their jarvey by entering a rath: "On her reappearance she told me it was dark & like a beehive—by the aid of matches & a candle she had made out there were kind of cells... in many places she had had to crawl on hands & knees & was glad to get back again to light & an upright position ... The peasants believe them to be the abode of fairies & would even be afraid to venture inside them. Our gossoon said he did not know of more than 3 people who had ever ventured inside & evidently thought Augusta very adventurous" (Layard Diary, British Library). Lady Layard left Coole on 25 May after paying visits to Tillyra, Chevy Chase and Ballylee Castle. "Irish Visions" was published anonymously, *The Spectator* 10 July 1897, pp. 46–7.

[123] Biddy Early, née Connors (1798–1874), a renowned wise woman and herb healer who had lived near Feakle, across the Slieve Echtge mountains from Coole. She was widely rumoured in the Galway region to be still alive at this point. AG collected numerous stories about her powers which she later included (along with a detailed account of her journey across the mountains by pony-cart) in *Visions and Beliefs in the West of Ireland* pp. 31–50.

Friday I drove over to Tillyra to offer them to Mrs. Martyn — There I found
W. B. Yeats just arrived from Dublin, white, haggard voiceless, fresh from the
Jubilee riots which he had been in the thick of, having been led into them as
escort to Miss Gonne — However he had by main force & lock & key kept her
from reaching the mob when they came into collision with the police[124] —
Black flags had ++++ distributed & windows b++++ it was not a very dignified
proceeding — & he himself disapproved of it — not because of disrespect for
the Queen for he thinks it was right to make some protest against the unhappy
misgovernment & misfortunes of Ireland during her reign — but that he
thinks the impulse shd come from the mob people themselves, & not be
thrust on them from above — Some episodes were amusing — he heard
"Cheers for the French" & then some man cried "And boo for the Germans"
— & another said "Why do you boo the Germans, don't you know they're the
worst enemies of England now?" — "Are they so?" said the other, "Then hi for
them!" — And going into the Theosophical Society afterwards he saw a tall
Theosophist who he had last seen lying on his face on a hill side striving after
unearthly visions, sitting in triumph with a thick stick by his side with which
he had just knocked down a policeman.

I was a little in disgrace myself about the Jubilee — George Gough[125] had
ordered a bonfire to be lighted at Lough Cutra — & then had written to all
the neighbours calling on them to do ditto — I refused, saying that after the
long & marked neglect shown by the Queen to Ireland I thought it right to
preserve an attitude of respectful disapproval — W. S[hawe].Taylor wrote &
declined on the ground of turf being dear — E. Martyn wrote that he had no
turf himself, but he hoped that those of his tenants who have bogs might see
their way to lighting bonfires — George Gough was sadly grieved by my
disloyalty & wrote an impassioned letter — a sort of wail over a lost soul — In
the end the Bagots, Galbraiths & Arthur [Persse] (with English wives) lighted
fires — the people did not go near them or take any notice — Next night, St.
John's Eve, the mountains were alive with bonfires, & the people in crowds
round them —

At the end of July, a week before the holidays, Mr. Yeats came to stay with me,
bringing his friend George Russell "AE" — He had told me he had described
him in "Rosa Alchemica" — & when one Monday morning I had a sudden

[124] For Maud Gonne (1865–1953), WBY's beloved, see Biographical Appendix. For his
account of the demonstrations and rioting in Dublin on 21 June 1897 to mark Queen Victoria's
Diamond Jubilee, see *Au* pp. 367–68, and *Mem* pp. 111–13, in which he recalls preventing Maud
Gonne from leaving the National Club in Rutland Square to join the crowds. In her first letter
to WBY following the riots, Maud Gonne asserted that the death of an old woman crushed by the
crowd "would not have happened" if he had not restrained her (*Always Your Friend: The Gonne-
Yeats Letters 1893–1938*, ed. Anna MacBride White and A. Norman Jeffares, p. 73).
[125] George Gough (1852–1900), Hugh Gough's younger brother. See also p. 271 n. 207.

intimation that they would be with me by lunch time, I looked over the passage & found "with his wild red hair, fierce eyes & sensitive lips & rough clothes, Michael Robartes looked something between a peasant, a saint & a debauchee" — so I was rather apprehensive[126] — & went down to meet them feeling quite shy — but to my relief found a gentle quiet man — apparently "more in dread of me than I of him" as Mrs. Quirk said of the leprechaun[127] — but really perfectly simple, composed — & self restrained — 8 years ago he was the most promising student in the Dublin Art schools, but one day he came & said, as well as I understand, that the will is the only thing given us in this life as absolutely our own, and that we should allow no weakening of it — & that art which he cared for so much would he believed weaken his will — And so he went into Pim's shop as cashier, & had been there ever since, & Pim says he is the best cashier he has ever had — He works till 6 in the evening, has £60 a year, out of which he not only supports himself but helps others poorer than himself — edits the "Theosophist" writing it in great part — has formed a little band of mystics believing, I think, in universal brotherhood & re-incarnation — He said one evening "this life bores me — I am waiting for a higher one" — His "Homeward Songs by the Way" have gone into a second edition here, & have a great sale in America[128] — On Saturday afternoon, & Sunday, his only holidays, he goes to the Wicklow hills & wanders there, sometimes lying down & seeing visions of the old Celtic Gods — of these he has done some beautiful pastel drawings — The first afternoon I took the two poets across the lake to the cromlech & there they sat until they saw a purple clad Druid appear — Next day we went to the Burren hills, to Corcomroe — a grey day — but it pleased them, & we heard fairy lore from a young man there, the <?? ??> on the Macnamara estate — I wish I could put down the brilliant conversation of the evenings — G. R. very quiet, but the other most brilliant — pouring out his ideas in rapid succession — hair splitting — fanciful — full of wit & poetry, deep & subtle thought — His stories of his London friends wd make us laugh till we cried — Poor Lionel Johnson getting

[126] WBY arrived at Coole with AE on Monday 26 July 1897, to begin his first long stay at Coole. After a brief stay with Edward Martyn at Tillyra following the Jubilee riots in Dublin, he had gone to stay with his uncle, George Pollexfen (see p. 208 n. 45), at Rosses Point, Sligo. AG's "sudden intimation" of their arrival was presumably the receipt of WBY's letter confirming their travel plans, which would have arrived that morning. See *The Letters of W.B.Yeats,* ed. Allan Wade (London, 1954; hereafter *L*) p. 287. WBY's description of Robartes (somewhat modified in AG's memorial reconstruction), appears in "Rosa Alchemica", first published in *The Savoy* in April 1896, and subsequently included in *The Secret Rose*, published in April 1897.

[127] A phrase from a local story AG included in *Visions and Beliefs* pp. 229–30.

[128] AE studied intermittently at the Dublin Metropolitan School of Art between 1883 and 1890, and began work as a clerk at Pim's, a Dublin drapery store, in August 1890. *The Irish Theosophist*, founded in 1892, ran until late 1897 with AE as a major contributor, and was then succeeded by *The Internationalist*, of which he was Dublin editor. For AE's reasons for wanting to turn from art, see WBY's article "A Visionary", published in *The Celtic Twilight*. AE's first volume of poetry, *Homeward: Songs by the Way*, was published in June 1894 and reprinted in 1895.

very drunk & then beginning to uphold the infallibility of the Holy Catholic church — begging him & some other not to leave him, & then, fearing they would be too much elated saying "After all you are nothing but two fellows drinking with me"[129] — Whibley at a literary dinner, getting into a squabble with Heinemann & saying "All you are fit for is to put your name on the outside of books"[130] — Mrs. Emery whose husband used to drink, & to steal half crowns from the pockets of her visitors' great coats in the hall — & who says "I must be cynical to escape the discredit of my virtues" — ~~Bullen~~ {or Smithers?} the publisher who arrives at his rooms so drunk as to make a scandal in the neighbourhood[131] — John Lane the publisher, who likes to imagine he is anything else & says "I am engaged to be married to a young lady in America & she said 'I should like you to be Mr. Yeats's publisher'", & so on[132] —

Mr. Russell left in a few days having to go back to his cash office — but Mr. Yeats stayed for two months — a most brilliant charming & lovable companion — never out of humour, simple, gentle — interested in all that went on — liking to do his work in the library in the midst of the coming & going, then if I was typing in the drawing room suddenly bursting in with some great new idea — & when it was expounded laughing & saying "I treat you, as my father says, as an anvil, to beat out my ideas on" — Poor boy he has had a hard

[129] Lionel Johnson (1867–1902), poet, fellow-member with WBY of the Rhymers' Club, and cousin of Olivia Shakespear. Johnson was one of WBY's closest London friends in the early 1890s, introducing him to Walter Pater, and acting as an erudite critic of his work. WBY in his turn influenced Johnson to a brief enthusiasm for his Irish roots, reflected in his temporary but active participation in the Irish Literary Society and his collection *Ireland with other Poems* (1897). Johnson's asceticism led him to a increasingly rigid and devout Catholicism, but he was by this point already in terminal decline from the alcoholism which eventually caused his early death in 1902. For WBY's own use of this anecdote and his characterization of Johnson as one of the "tragic generation" see *Au* p. 213.

[130] Charles Whibley (1859–1930), essayist and journalist whom WBY had met through W. E. Henley (see p. 156 n. 154), and at this time working for the *Pall Mall Gazette*. William Heinemann (1863–1920), was the founder of the Heinemann publishing house.

[131] Arthur Henry Bullen (1857–1920), scholar of Elizabethan literature, and co-founder in 1891 of the publishing house Lawrence and Bullen, which published WBY's *The Celtic Twilight* (1893), *The Secret Rose* (1897), and his edition of *The Poems of William Blake* (1893). In 1904 Bullen founded the Shakespeare Head Press, which published, amongst other Yeats works, the de luxe 1908 *Collected Edition*. Leonard Smithers (1861–1907), publisher and bookseller, was notorious for dealing in erotica, and acted as publisher for more daring works by Beardsley, Wilde, Symons and others. He was at this point publisher of *The Savoy*, and putative publisher of WBY's *The Shadowy Waters* (which was eventually published by Hodder and Stoughton instead).

[132] John Lane (1854–1925), co-founder of The Bodley Head in 1887 with Elkin Mathews (1851–1921), and who retained the Bodley Head name following the dissolution of their partnership in 1894. Lane and Mathews had published *The Second Book of the Rhymers' Club* in 1894, and Lane alone was at this point contracted to publish WBY's *The Wind Among the Reeds* (published 1899) and AE's *The Earth Breath* (published September 1897).

struggle — For some time, when he was working at his "Usheen" & at the Blake book he had hardly enough to eat, & not enough for decent boots or clothes — & he says the bitter feeling of degredation haunted him for a long time — He got a job of copying at the Bodleian once, spent a week there, got £5 — & lived on currant buns all the time — & made himself ill thereby[133] — Then he worked at the British Museum — & used to go gladly to an acquaintance (Countess de Bremot?) near, for a cup of coffee, his ~~chief~~ only afternoon meal — until one day she proposed for him! one of her arguments being T. P. O'Connor married a woman of no character — & see what a help she has been politically to him! — So he made his escape & had no more coffee[134] — Now he has turned the corner & his name is up — but he works very slowly — & I think starves himself — He says not — He makes his own fire in the morning & cooks eggs & bacon — & has a chop for dinner — but luxury is far from him — And then there is his love for Miss Gonne preying on him — He fell in love with her ten years ago, & for 2 or 3 years it "broke up his life" — he did nothing but write to her & see her & think of her — Then he grew stronger — & tho' still idealising her he did not feel it in the same way — But lately, at the Jubilee riots it all came back to him — & he suffers tortures of hope & fear — But I am bound to say that his healthiness of mind & body increased while at Coole — so that he wrote afterwards "my days at Coole passed like a dream, a dream of peace."[135]

We searched for folk lore — I gave him over all I had collected, & took him about looking for more — And whoever came to the door, fishwoman or beggar or farmer, I would get on the subject, & if I found the stories worth having wd call him down that he might have them first hand — We found startling beliefs & came to the conclusion that Ireland is Pagan, not Xtian — But this will appear in the articles he is bringing out[136] — Then when we came in I wd write them out, & then type them, very good training if I ever want to be private secretary! Robert & Geraldine [Beauchamp] & Henry[137] shot & bicycled & boated & cricketed & the summer flew quickly by — Robert very

[133] WBY spent a week at the Bodleian Library in Oxford in August 1888 copying from the Caxton edition of *Aesop's Fables* for an edition by Joseph Jacobs, published in 1889 by David Nutt. His first volume of poetry, *The Wanderings of Oisin*, was published in 1889, and *The Works of William Blake*, which he edited in collaboration with Edwin Ellis, in 1893.

[134] Anne, Countess de Brémont [*sic*], neé Dunphy. Briefly a member of the Golden Dawn, which she joined in late 1888, and author of various romances, a volume on Oscar Wilde and several collections of poems. T. P. O'Connor had married Elizabeth Howard, née Paschal, the daughter of an American lawyer-journalist, in 1885. She ambitiously promoted O'Connor's career both politically and socially, but the marriage foundered around 1898, and the couple lived apart from 1905 on.

[135] For WBY's letter, see *L* p. 288.

[136] A series of six articles, commencing with "The Tribes of Danu" published in *The New Review*, November 1897, pp. 549–65. For the remainder of the series see *UP2* p. 54.

[137] Henry Wilfred Persse (1885–1918), AG's brother Edward's seventh son. He was killed in action in World War I.

well & strong — rather idle — but very keen about cricket & shooting — We
beat Gort — & then we were beaten by them —

Standish O'Grady came to stay with us — but during dinner the first
ev[ening] he had a telegram calling him away as Revising Barrister to Belfast
— he had mistaken the time by a month! He is a fine writer — but has not had
the recognition he deserves — If he were a Scotch writer writing of old Scotch
history his books wd be in every house — He is now a little over excited on the
Financial movement.

Next day, after his early start, another of my best countrymen arrived, Horace
Plunkett — He is working himself to death in his Agricultural Organization
movement — but he is doing a great work in Ireland, teaching the farmers to
get over their suspicions of each other, & to manage their own affairs — Even
if the immediate movement should fail, this will tell in the future — We had
asked the farmers to meet him, but it was a fine day after long rain, & very few
came — but he came & talked to them outside the hall door, explaining the
methods — with so much courtesy & earnestness that he won their hearts[138]
— His quiet manner, with so much enthusiasm underneath, strikes one very
much — E. Martyn came & stayed for his visit — I saw Mr. Plunkett off in the
morning & took him to the Convent, & he gave a loom to the workroom —

The result of this little national-literary stir was that Robert, near the end of
the holidays said "he would give anything to learn Irish" — We tried in vain
for a teacher — all speak but none know the grammar — so we began with
a primer & mastered the first exercises, taking them out to Mike to get the
pronunciation right[139] — But the partridge shooting interfered at the end,
R.'s first chance, which he owed to the Jubilee extra week — He was pretty
successful, getting a good many birds at Coole — & making biggest bag at
Tillyra — The Birch boys came for the last 10 days, very glad to find themselves
back again — Then the holidays came to an end, & I was left alone —

Celtic Theatre — Edward Martyn having written a new play "Maeve" with Celtic
motive, lent it to de Basterot — & I read it while with him & admired it very
much — E. Martyn & Yeats drove to Duras one drenching day, & when we had
had general conversation for a long time I divided the party by taking Yeats
into "Mr. Quin's office" — & there we had tea & talked, & the idea came to
us that if "Maeve" could be acted in Dublin, instead of London as E. M.

[138] Plunkett arrived at Coole on Friday 10 September, and left for Limerick the next day. AG
had invited him specifically to assess the prospects for forming a co-operative at Kiltartan.

[139] This was the start of AG's third (and finally successful) effort to learn Irish. A childhood
interest in the language had been ignored, while lessons she took from one of the Coole
gardeners in 1888 had ended though his suspicion that her enthusiasm was a form of mockery
(*Seventy Years* pp. 317–18).

thought of—& with Yeats['s] "Countess Kathleen" it would be a development
of the literary movement, & help to restore dignity to Ireland, so long
vulgarised on the stage as well as in romance — & we talked until we saw
Dublin as the Mecca of the Celt — This was the beginning of our movement
— A day or two after Yeats came to see me at Coole — & it began to take
practical shape — guarantors were thought desirable — & I gave the first
guarantee — Then he wrote a programme, approved by E. Martyn — & then
I wrote to Aubrey de Vere, who sent a charming answer, with his blessing[140]
— This I added to the programme, & sent it to a few others — amongst them
Lecky asking him to give £1 guarantee — He was the first to respond, most
warmly, promising £5 — With his name, I wrote to Lord Dufferin, & he also
responded amiably — & after that, except for the actual labour of typing
programmes & writing letters, all went smoothly, people of all parties
responded, & we had soon a splendid list of guarantors, & nearly all the
money (£300) required[141] —

Then E.M. & Yeats went to Dublin to work — found much encouragement
& enthusiasm — but the way was blocked by the practical difficulty of getting
a theatre — The two existing ones were engaged for the time wanted (besides
demanding absurd prices) & then they thought of a hall or concert room —
But there is an old act, passed just before the Union, inflicting a fine of £300
on anyone who gives a performance for gain in an unlicenced building —
And a claim for a special license has to be argued before the Privy Council,
& costs at least £80 in fees — I am all for having the Act repealed or a bill
brought in empowering the municipality to license halls when desirable —
but the matter rests so at present[142] —

I spent a few days at Tillyra to meet a "Celtic" party — William Sharp, an

[140] Aubrey de Vere (1814–1902), from an early age friend to many of the greatest figures of
his time, became a disciple of his father's friend Wordsworth (and later introduced Wordsworth
to Tennyson, whose work he also championed), and a close associate of Carlyle and Sir Henry
Taylor. His substantial poetic oeuvre during the second half of his life, consisting largely of
graceful but unexceptional lyric and narrative works modelled on Wordsworth, met with only
modest popular success, but in consistently choosing Irish themes, drawing on Irish legendary
materials and expressing a patriotic fidelity to his country he served as a significant precursor to
the Irish Renaissance, and was a symbolically appropriate figure to anoint the efforts of the new
generation, as AG clearly recognised. As a Catholic landlord, de Vere was an enlightened activist
on behalf of religious equality and the need for land reform in Ireland. His letter is quoted in
part in *Our Irish Theatre* p. 21. De Vere was distantly related to both Sir William and AG through
his brother's marriage to Anne Burke (see p. 26 n. 9).

[141] For the principal guarantors, almost all friends of AG, see WBY's "Important Announcement—Irish Literary Theatre" (*UP2* p. 133).

[142] With the help of Lecky and others, the law was subsequently changed by means of a clause
was inserted in the 1898 Local Government Bill authorising occasional licenses (see *Our Irish
Theatre* pp. 24–5).

absurd object, in velvet coat, curled hair, wonderful ties — a good natured creature — a sort of professional patron of poets — but making himself ridiculous by stories to the men of his love affairs & entanglements, & seeing visions (instigated by Yeats) — one apparition clasped him to an elm tree from which he had to be released — Martin Morris also there, & Dr. Moritz Bonn, an odious little German, sent to me by Horace Plunkett, studying political economy & not seeing "what relation the Celtic movement had to it"[143] — And Dr. Douglas Hyde came[144] — full of enthusiasm & Irish — I took him & Sharp to the cromlech & to Kilmacduagh — & he began talking Irish to Fahy, near Cranagh — who to my pride came out with legends of Finn & Ussian galore — I was able to help Dr. Hyde to get some MS from "one Connor", who had left there for Galway a year ago, & who I finally traced to a butcher's shop at Clare[n]bridge — but whether they are worth anything I know not[145] —

Afterwards I spent 10 days at Spiddal very pleasantly, for fine weather had come at last, a sort of Indian summer, & the Atlantic was beautiful — Lord M[orris]. very cross, very violent against literature & writers, thinking Martin is going that way[146] — I ran down to the school & had an Irish lesson when I could — & picked up some folk stories — At the end Lord M. left & E. Martyn & Yeats came — I had arranged an interview with a witch doctor for the latter of which he will doubtless give an account[147] — I tried to stir up the masters at the school to collect stories — & finally offered a prize for stories written down by the children either in English or Irish — They have since sent me eleven, not much new in them[148] —

[143] Moritz Julius Bonn (1873–1965) spent the summers of 1896–98 in Ireland studying questions of colonisation and economics under Plunkett's aegis, publishing his work in 1906 as *Die Englische Kolonisation in Irland*, which he dedicated to Plunkett. For Bonn's recollections of his friendship with Plunkett and of meeting many of the most influential Irish figures of the time, see his "A la recherche du temps perdu" in Alan Denson ed., *Printed Writings of George W. Russell (A.E.), A Bibliography* pp. 15–21.

[144] Douglas Hyde (1860–1949), folklorist, poet and key figure in promoting the revival of Gaelic. See Biographical Appendix.

[145] In a letter of 23 October 1897 to Hyde, AG mentions obtaining this manuscript from "one Conolly" (NLI). It appears not to have contained significant material since Hyde fails to mention it as a source in his publications, though he cites other material AG provided.

[146] Martin Morris had recently published an essay "The Philosophy of Poetry" in *The Nineteenth Century* (September 1897, pp. 504–13), and had collected others into a volume about to appear under the title *Transatlantic Traits* (see p. 159), but this was the only book he would publish.

[147] WBY's and AG's collaboratively written essay "Irish Witch Doctors" published in *The Fortnightly Review* for September 1900 (*UP2* pp. 219–36) includes an account of the witch doctor, and his comments on WBY's poor eyesight. AG included a variant account in *Visions and Beliefs* pp. 69–73.

[148] AG offered a shilling per story, and eventually published the material she received as "Children's Folk Tales" in *The Kilkenny Moderator* Christmas Number, December 1898, p. 25. The masters at the Spiddal National School, both Irish speakers, were P. Greaney and Daniel Deeney.

Then back to Coole, for some hard work alone — I had sent "Mr. Gregory's Letter Box" re-arranged to Murray at the beginning of the summer — but he was still not satisfied — I had obeyed his direction to group the letters — but he now found there were too many groups — & a harking back on dates, & that it wd not pay its way[149] — Then I sent it to Longmans who said shortly "It would not be a good commercial speculation" — I showed it to de Basterot, & much like Murray, he wrote delighted with my own first chapters, but stuck when he got into the letters — Then I laid it by for the holidays, at the end trying to do a little to it, but without much time or heart — After Spiddal I set really to work, re-arranged, cut, wrote in, shed a good many letters — did my best with it — just as I was coming over sent it to Smith & Elder[150] — & they like my own part very much, but don't think much of the material — doubt its paying its way — won't publish at their own risk, but will "put it in a special light" if I will publish on commission —

I went & consulted Murray & then Smith, Q.C.[151] — Both say it will be a literary success, & is extremely well done — at least all of my own that is in — but Irish history is at a discount — However I have decided to risk it, as I think it will be for Robert's advantage to publish — Already, Smith told me he had never heard of Mr. Gregory, & cd not find him in the Dict[ionary of]. Nat[ional]. Biography, but since he has read the MS he has directed the editor to put him in[152] — And then I wrote to Lord Peel to ask if I might use Sir R. Peel's letter to Mr. Gregory, giving his reasons for his change of front on Cat[holic] Emancipation, & he has given it — (it had been given to Parker for his long delayed vol) & that will be a help[153] — & Smith is now more hopeful, & doubts that I will lose money after all — I am anxious about it, having no money to throw away, but I think I am doing right — So now the proofs have begun coming in — {I didn't lose — it paid its way}.

Deeney subsequently published a collection of folktales, *Peasant Lore from Gaelic Ireland*, in 1900, which WBY reviewed with in a generally supportive tone (though critical of the idiom of Deeney's translations), *UP2* pp. 216–18.

[149] AG had initially sent her manuscript to Murray in November 1896. After rearranging the volume along the lines he suggested, she resubmitted the work in June 1897, but Murray again declined to publish (Murray archive).

[150] The publishing house founded by George Smith (d.1846) and Alexander Elder (1790–1876). In some subsequent entries, AG personifies the firm, although unlike Murray's it was no longer run by descendants of its founders.

[151] Reginald John Smith Q.C., (1857–1916), partner in Smith & Elder, and Q.C. since 1894, and at this point also Editor of *The Cornhill Magazine*. Not related to George Smith, Smith and Elder's founder.

[152] An entry for Mr. Gregory subsequently appeared in Volume 22 (Supplementary volume 2) of the Dictionary, along with an entry for WHG.

[153] See *Mr. Gregory's Letter-Box* pp. 161–63. The letter, written in 1829, was subsequently included by Parker in the second volume of his edition of Peel's papers in 1899, though with variant readings of the manuscript.

I came over to London early in November — sorry to leave the Indian summer days & the long starlight walks with the dogs, & the beauty of the leaves — but the evenings were long & it was time to move — So I came, & was sorry — dank weather, & I was tired & depressed — & didn't know who was here & thought no one wanted me & wondered why I had come — But some cordial greetings soon changed the face of things —

I lunched with the Knowles one Sunday, & Knowles asked me to write a folk lore article for the 19th Century — rather awkward as I didn't like to say I had given all my material to Yeats — so I put it off as well as I could — but Knowles followed me out saying "I'll give you no peace or ease till you write it" — A few days afterwards I heard from Yeats that his second article had been returned by Henley, who had promised to take the whole series for the New Review — as the New Review is disappearing, turning into a 3d weekly paper — & he himself retiring — A gr blow, as it would have been so easy to write the series straight off, & wd have brought in a nice sum every month — So I asked leave to send the article to Knowles — & ask[ed] him to take it instead of one from me — & after a week he wrote having only just read it — accepting — & asking for another to follow it — So all was for the best for he will very likely take the series — & this will introduce W. B. Y. to another circle — He is pleased — & has been told that there is no use in approaching the XIXth Century unless you have a title yourself or are introduced by someone with a title[154] —

He has given a lecture on The Celtic Movement at the Irish Literary Society[155] — There was some bother over it — for Graves[156] without consulting him asked Sharp to be chairman — W. B. Y. was furious at this — & declared it wd bring ridicule on the whole movement — so asked E. Martyn to take the chair, & on his assent wrote to tell Sharp he had already invited him & wd not like to disappoint him —

[154] William Ernest Henley (1849–1903), poet and journalist. Editor of *The Scots Observer* (after 1892, *The National Observer*) 1889–94 and *The New Review* 1895–97, Henley was an important early friend and promoter of WBY, giving him his first regular opportunities to place his work, and introducing him to a wide literary circle, including Oscar Wilde and Charles Whibley, at his social gatherings (see *Au* pp. 126–29). WBY's and AG's "second article", "The Prisoners of the Gods", was published in *The Nineteenth Century*, January 1898, but the remainder of the series was published elsewhere.

[155] WBY's speech, "The Celtic Movement", delivered to the London Irish Literary Society on 4 December 1897 is reported in *The Pall Mall Gazette* 7 December, p. 12, and *United Ireland* 11 December, pp. 2, 5.

[156] Alfred Percival Graves (1846–1931), poet, anthologist, and father of poet Robert Graves. Author of some of the most popular late-Victorian songs and ballads, including "Father O'Flynn". An inaugural member of the London Irish Literary Society, he served as its Secretary from 1892 until April 1900 when he resigned (claiming ill health) in consequence of WBY's position regarding Queen Victoria's visit to Ireland (see p. 258 n. 152).

E. Martyn told me this — & I am afraid I was not very polite for I said "*you* chairman" in an incredulous tone — but it was really too absurd — He grew uncomfortable then & said he wished to get out of it — if anything else cd be managed —

Meanwhile Yeats had seen Sharp who refused to withdraw! so Yeats determined to change the subject of the lecture & read his folk lore article instead — & was very unhappy over it all — So one morning I telegraphed to him for Sharp's address — then to Sharp himself — & when he came I told him that Yeats's friends were of opinion the Celtic movement wd be injured by them merging into one camp — that they shd rather be allies like the Unionists & Tories — that he had determined to change the subject & read the folk lore article — that this wd probably prevent Knowles from accepting it — & this wd be a great loss "for what is the boy to live on" — Sharp was very stiff at first — had been asked — & pressed — & had offered to resign, Graves had written back that his honour was pledged — At last, getting no "forrarder" I thought perhaps if I pressed it it wd make him turn against Yeats — so I said "Will you come & dine on Sunday to meet Yeats & the Leckys" — "Might Mrs. Sharp come too?" said he — & of course then I knew the battle was over — & only discussed details — So Alfred Nutt[157] was put in the chair, & all went well — the lecture charming, & his delivery so good & voice, & all so natural — When it was over I had a little "festa" in its honour at the Metropole — the Sharps — & W.'s father & sisters[158] & Miss Borthwick[159] — & Symons & Mrs. Emery — it went off very pleasantly — old Mr. Yeats charming — so all ended well.

Horace Plunkett is quite with the Celtic movement — asked E. M[artyn]. & Yeats to the Ag[ricultural]. Organization dinner & made Yeats speak — a

[157] Alfred Trubner Nutt (1856–1910), publisher, folklorist and Celtic scholar. Manager of the publishing house established by his father, Editor of *The Folk-Lore Journal*, organ of the Folk-Lore Society (of which he was a founder, and President in 1897), and founder of the Irish Texts Society in 1898.

[158] AG had met WBY's father, the artist John Butler Yeats (1839–1922), and his sisters Susan "Lily" Yeats and Elizabeth Corbet "Lollie" Yeats (for whom, see p. 163 n. 3) at Bedford Park for the first time a few days earlier. In subsequent entries she refers to John B. Yeats as "Mr. Yeats" to distinguish him from WBY.

[159] Mariella Norma Borthwick (1862–1934), born and raised in England, became a Nationalist after witnessing evictions in Ireland in the late 1880s. Learned Gaelic as a member of the Southwark Irish Literary Society, and joined the Gaelic League in 1895, serving on the General Committee and as an organizer, and as Secretary of the Oireachtas in 1898. Worked in publishing in Dublin until 1919, when she suddenly left Ireland, possibly on being diagnosed with the degenerative condition that eventually killed her. Lived most of her remaining years on Skye.

charming little speech "like a rose leaf falling among a lot of agricultural implements"[160] — And he has been very kind about the Theatre — & rushed to see the Attorney Genl. & to see me on his one day over here — And he has taken George Russell out of Pim's & made him an organiser of rural banks — I hope this may turn out well — Mr. Russell writes me a very cheery letter & sends me a portrait he has done of W. B. Y.[161] —

I had a bad moment when I first came over —

[pages missing]

his Irish blood — & such a poor little face, I didn't feel as if I was sitting next the Commander in Chief of the British Army[162] — Lecky, very encouraging about the "Letter Box" — says he knows nothing of that period — that all is known up to the Union & after the famine, but that is a blank — Dined also with the Frederic Harrisons — & twice with the Lyalls — & with Raffy — where I was much disgusted with the greediness of W. S. Lilly,[163] calling for more food, calling for champagne out of his turn, eating like a wild beast — M. Morris says he is the same everywhere — & Henry James says having met him once at dinner he refused to meet him again — Dined also Mrs. Kay — sat between 2 pleasant adventurers — Sir Leopold McClintock & Sir Alan Johnson[164] — I had some nice little dinners here too — Yeats always — partly for his sake & partly for my own, to make all go off well, for he is always brilliant & charming — First, Frederic Harrisons & Clodd[165] — Second Leckys — E. Martyn — Sharps — Miss Lyall[166] — Third, Reginald Smith, publisher, Mrs. Dugdale & Martin Morris — My little room held out nicely tho' on the Lecky

[160] WBY spoke at a dinner for Dairy Co-operators during the Annual Agricultural Organization Conference in Dublin on 3 November 1897. His speech was reported in *The Irish Homestead* 6 November, pp. 741–42.

[161] Plunkett's "one day" in London was 20 November, for which he recorded seeing Lecky, Lady Gregory and Gerald Balfour (Diary, Plunkett Institute). Balfour, then Chief Secretary of Ireland, was preparing to introduce the 1898 Local Government Bill, which authorized the granting of occasional licenses for theatrical performances. Plunkett had interviewed AE (who had in fact already resigned from Pim's on 3 November) for a job as agricultural organizer the previous day. AE's "cheery letter" of *c.* 27 November (Berg) expresses the "hope that I will be able do do one half of what my good friends who do not know my capacities prophesy" and promises by separate mail a chalk head of WBY, probably that reproduced in *The Irish Homestead* 13 November 1898, p. 765.

[162] Presumably Garnet Wolseley (see p. 113 n. 26).

[163] William Samuel Lilly (1840–1919), barrister, and Secretary of the Catholic Union of Great Britain from 1873.

[164] Allen Bayard Johnson (1829–1907), a general and then military secretary in the India Office 1877–89. Uncle to both Lionel Johnson and Olivia Shakespear.

[165] Clodd's diary records this dinner as taking place on 11 November. See Genevieve Brennan, "Yeats, Clodd, *Scatalogical Rites* and the Clonmel Witch Burnings" *Yeats Annual* 4 p. 214.

[166] Probably Sophie Lyall, Sir Alfred Lyall's daughter.

evening I sent my men to smoke in Mr. Monckton's room — I took Mrs. Hills[167] to the play "La Poupee"[168] to cure her of a "nerve strain" & I went with Nevill Geary to "The Little Minister"[169] & supper at the Savoy — He has gone to India, rather sorry, but brave —

Paul & Ethel well, don't see them often — so best — The baby a nice little thing[170] — Ethel carried off a picture by Jack B. Yeats for it in lieu of the promised silver mug[171] —

Dec[ember] 11 — Off to buy a curtain at Harvey & Nichols — & back for my Irish lesson with Miss Borthwick (an Irish teacher at last) & then to lunch with the Cunninghams — a large party — George [W. E.] Russell & Sir Alan Johnson & Sir Gerald Fitzgerald & Miss Trench[172] & a Mr. Riley — Dined Birches, they had asked me to bring Yeats to make his acquaintance & we found a pleasant little party there — the Comyns Carr[173] — & Lady Edmund Fitzmaurice — & Sir Bartle Frere[174] — visions & spiritualism after dinner & Yeats talked well & we didn't break up till near 12 —

12 — A wet Sunday — but not wasted — I wrote up this diary & corrected & indexed proofs — & wrote letters — & Martin Morris came to see me in the afternoon much pleased at some favourable notices of his "Transatlantic Traits" — Made some buttered eggs for dinner & escaped going upstairs — & peaceably read Tennyson's life[175] —

13 — Corrected proofs & wrote — & Hugh Lane dropped in to lunch wanting

[167] A fellow resident of Queen Anne's Mansions.

[168] *La Poupee*, a three act comic opera adapted by Arthur Sturgess from the work by Edmond Audran (music) and Maurice Ordonneau (libretto) which ran for nearly 600 performances at the Prince of Wales's Theatre between February 1897 and September 1898.

[169] *The Little Minister* by J. M. Barrie (1860–1937), playwright, novelist and author of *Peter Pan*, played for 330 performances at the Haymarket Theatre, November 1897–October 1898.

[170] Susan Harvey (1897–*fl.*1967). The only child born to the Harveys, she later became an accomplished photographer, publishing her work under the pseudonym Merlyn Severn.

[171] Jack Butler Yeats (1871–1957), WBY's younger brother, at this point just beginning to gain recognition as an artist. AG's gift was a watercolour titled "The Runaway", painted in 1897. The Harveys subsequently gave the picture away, as a wedding present to a Mr. and Mrs. Onions, in 1907. See Hilary Pyle, *Jack B. Yeats: His Watercolours, Drawings and Pastels*, Item 36.

[172] Probably either Charlotte (b.1871) or Sarah (b.1873), younger sisters of Willie Trench (see p. 16 n. 83).

[173] J. W. Comyns Carr (1849–1916), art critic and dramatist. Founder and Editor of *The English Illustrated Magazine*, Founder and Director of the New Gallery, and Managing Director of the Lyceum Theatre in the 1890s. His wife Alice Vansittart Strettel (b.1850), was a highly successful popular novelist.

[174] Sir Bartle Compton Frere (1854–1933), retired soldier, and son of Colonial Governor Sir Henry Bartle Frere.

[175] Hallam Tennyson's newly published biography, *Alfred, Lord Tennyson: A memoir by his son*.

me to try & arrange his return to the Carlton Gallery[176] — Mr. Popham having told him I was a "born diplomatist"! — A nice letter from poor E. Martyn who is low about the theatre — pouring rain, but got to Hampstead to call on Sharps — rather interested as Sharp showed me a portrait of Miss Gonne — a very lovely face — & a drawing by AE & some new poems of his — back & started to dine at Chelsea with Paul & Ethel who by some mistake didn't expect me — back & kept awake by mice or rats or both all night —

14 — Irish lesson & proofs — Afternoon to 18 Woburn Buildings to measure W. B. Y.'s window for a curtain[177] — Found his father there sketching him, & not very successfully — probably knows his face too well — He has been at him for 3 days — W. writes that "it was very difficult to make him begin & now it is still more difficult to make him leave off" — The sitting room is very nice — large & low — looking on a raised flagged pavement where no traffic can come — & the bedroom, very small & draughty looks out on St. Pancras church with its caryatides & trees — But I wish poor W. cd be a little better waited on — his room had not yet been done up — & remains of breakfast (cooked by himself) still there — He received me with the announcement he had "lost his coals" — & the fire was going out — & finally, when his father left a bucket of coal was sent in & stowed away — One cold night that he dined with me I asked him if he wd find his fire in when he went back & he said, no, he had carefully raked it out, so that the landlady when she came might make it up for lighting next morning, & otherwise he wd have to make it up himself, & the mornings are so cold for that — His father was to set out for Dublin in the evening, to paint Standish O'Grady's portrait — but I heard next day he had with W. started for the station, then found he had left his sketchbook & went back for that — & just as he had taken his ticket at Euston, the train steamed off — So then he decided to go by the next train & left his things at the cloak room & went back to Woburn Buildings — Then they set out the second time — & again he had left his sketch book — the other one, & had to return — but still they were in pretty good time at Euston, & they changed the ticket — but when he went to the cloak room, he had lost his luggage ticket & had to make a declaration — & while it was being made, the train went off! & then he was ashamed to go back to his family — & so went to the hotel for the night, & has been no more heard of —

14 — To Smith & Elder with photos of bust[178] — & then to Carlton Gallery

[176] AG gives no account of Hugh Lane working at the Carlton Gallery in her biography *Hugh Lane*. After his acrimonious break with Colnaghi, Lane had worked for a year at the Marlborough Gallery, leaving in a dispute which involved a court case. He opened his own premises as a dealer in Pall Mall Place in February 1898.

[177] WBY had moved from Fountain Court to rooms in 18 Woburn Buildings in February 1896, after resolving to become Olivia Shakespear's lover. This remained his London address until after his marriage in 1917.

[178] Of Under-Secretary Gregory, for the frontispiece to *Mr. Gregory's Letter-Box*.

to palaver Horsely[179] about H. Lane's return — which seemed possible — Lunched Birchs — called on Mrs. Halsey — who told me all the story of Francis Thompson having lived by selling matches, & sleeping under arches — & was rescued by the Meynells who had seen some of his poems — but he had got into opium taking — & is still sometimes found asleep in a stupor on the hearth rug[180] — W. B. Y. came to dine with me on the way to his '98 committee — he talked much of Miss Gonne — all the old story — poor boy, it interferes sadly with his work — as he says, his reveries go to her & not to it — I advised him not to press her while she is so taken up with '98 — He agrees but says "When one is a writer one gets into the belief that a phrase will do everything" —

15 — Irish lesson, the last — have got on pretty well, through the first book — <??> — H. Lane to lunch with some pictures — I bought a nice picture by <?Bristmore> of terriers & a weasel for Robert — £2-10/- & an entombing for the nuns' bazaar & a portrait of Buffon[181] for Frank — I wrote by Hugh's wish to Horsely — but have had an unsatisfactory answer — he has heard things of him since he left (probably his boasting that he made the gallery) & can't take him back "with any self respect" — Dinner at home, Flora Shaw (to interest her in the Celtic movement) Yeats — Willy Peel — Sir Alan Johnson (uncle to Lionel) — young Comyn Carr who has just left Oxford & is going in for literature[182] — very amusing — for W. B. Y. was excited by Miss Shaw's dogmatic commonplace ultra English mind — & let off fireworks all the evening — declaiming against men of science — they are poor & paltry on every other subject, they are but a <?man> in their own discoveries — A man of letters like Goethe, of all embracing wisdom so different — Yes Parnell was a representative Irishman he lived for an idea — Englishmen will only live for an institution — Sir Frederic Leighton[183] ought to have been King of England, & the Queen President of the Royal Academy — "Oh" says Miss Shaw seriously — "but do you not confess she is an excellent constitutional monarch?" Sir A. Johnson rather amusing, meant to crush him about Mme. Blavatsky who he had some stories about — & said "Do you confess Mme. Blavatsky was an imposter?" "Well, as to her being an imposter — it is like

[179] John Calcott Horsely R.A., (1817–1903), Treasurer to the Royal Academy (1882–97).

[180] Poet and critic Wilfrid Meynell (1852–1948) first met the visionary religious poet Francis Thompson (1859–1907) in 1888, after publishing one of his works in the journal *Merry England*, of which he was then editor. Meynell and his wife Viola (1886–1900) rescued Thompson from destitute condition, introduced him to a wide range of literary figures (including WBY) and encouraged him to resume writing. After Thompson's death from tuberculosis, hastened by his long opium addiction, the Meynells edited his collected works.

[181] George, Compte de Buffon (1707–88), French philosopher and naturalist.

[182] Philip Comyn Carr (1874–1957), who had just completed a B.A. at Brasenose College. He did not subsequently publish anything in book form, but became a prominent drama critic and producer, later founding the Mermaid Repertory Theatre.

[183] Sir Frederic Leighton (1830–96), painter and President of the Royal Academy 1878–96, created Baron Leighton the day before his death.

Newman being asked if he believed that the sun really stood still in the valley of Ajalon"[184] — & he said "There are so many ways of interpreting the words 'stood still' — that it must remain an uncertain question" —

Miss Shaw when leaving said pityingly "He's very young" — I asked Sir A. Johnson if his nephew Lionel talked like that & he says, not to me, but I daresay he does when they're together — which amuses W. B. Y. very much — Lionel being the most gloomy, serious & discreet of men — save & except when he is drunk — Then he draws on imaginary reminiscences — including a conversation of an hour with Gladstone at Oxford — which he never varies — his family who are Tory disapprove of, but are at the same time proud of this interview[185] —

17 — To see Sir F. Burton — He is amused at hearing Ingram's song is made so much of for the '98 centenary — as he says he never was a young Irelander or sympathized with the movement but that one evening he was roused by O'Connell in a speech throwing some disparagement on '98 — & he went home & wrote the verses[186] —

18 — Stores & letters — & called on Mrs. Kay & had Hugh Lane to tea — & W. B. Y. & Mrs. Emery to dinner —

[184] John Henry Newman (1801–90), ordained as an Anglican Minister in 1825, became a leading member of the Tractarian movement in the 1830s, urging the disestablishment of the Church of England. Converted to Catholicism in 1845, leading many others to follow his example. For the Biblical text Newman was asked to elucidate, see *Joshua* 10.12.

[185] For WBY's account of Johnson's imaginary conversations with Gladstone and Newman see *Au* pp. 305–6.

[186] John Kells Ingram (1823–1907), poet and economist, and Professor of Oratory and later of Greek at Trinity College, had written the popular Nationalist poem "Who fears to speak of Ninety-Eight?" in 1843.

1898

Jan[uary] 1 — 1898

Sunday 19th — Lunched with Lady Dorothy, bringing W. B. Y. there — Sir Francis Jeune, the Francis Hollands,[1] Sir Arthur Birch & Una — pleasant enough — Then W. B. Y. & I set out for Chiswick — where he had heard of "an old lady with folk lore & a weakness for bullseyes" — We found & interviewed her, & got some stories — a reward for what had seemed rather a wild goose chase[2] — Then tea with his sisters — one pretty & soft & delicate — the other "the dangerous one" I fancy keeps the house going[3] — Then back to Qmansions & dined there —

20th — A tiring, packing day — & heard of F. Lawley's dangerous illness, & went to offer to have the little grandson, Dick, with us for the holidays — Met Flora Shaw at Hatchard's, buying "Herodotus" as an Xmas box for her sister — She professed herself charmed with Yeats — on literary subjects — but is suspicious of him on others — had asked Traill to have "his book well reviewed" in "Literature" — but Traill said too much space had already been given to Celtic subjects — Wyndham Waithman[4] came to be taken charge of, & I took him to Euston & met Robert there, well & bright — We set out — & the boys had room to lie down & the fur rug — but I sat erect & shivering till we got to the boat — & was very tired when we got to Dublin — no time for

[1] Probably a slip for "Bernard" Holland following her entry "Francis" Jeune, but also possibly Bernard Holland's younger brother Francis.

[2] This visit followed a tip from Ford Madox Hueffer (later Ford), who had informed WBY of the old lady and her stories in November 1897.

[3] Susan Mary "Lily" Yeats (1866–1949) and Elizabeth Corbet "Lollie" Yeats (1868–1940), later the dominant partnership behind the Dun Emer Industries (1902–07) and the Cuala Press. Lily, a lifelong sufferer of respiratory problems, was in 1897 still recovering from the effects of typhoid fever contracted in 1895. Lollie, whose relationship with her family was frequently strained, was at this point the major breadwinner through her teaching of brushwork painting.

[4] Robert Waithman's grandson Henry Wyndham Waithman (b.1887), born to Waithman's only son William Waithman (d.1922).

breakfast — At Athenry bought "Internationalist" with a beautiful essay of AE's in it, on "the hero in man"[5] —

A very busy Xmas — Peyton [Persse] & Geraldine [Beauchamp] arrived next day — & the house had to be provisioned & the stores unpacked — & the Xmas tree for schoolchildren prepared — & Xmas boxes to so many — Robert gave me "Old Harrow Days"[6] Paul "Lavengro"[7] — the Sharps sent "Lyra Celtica" & "Vistas".[8]

28th & 29th the shooting, spoiled by bad weather — Arthur & Frank came for a night — Douglas Hyde for four[9] — & was very cheery & very interesting — so enthusiastic about his Gaelic League — He says of Yeats "his ideas come as fast as rabbits" — He seemed to enjoy the shoot very much — Robert shot so well that Arthur has asked him to the first shoot at Chevy [Chase] — quite an event!

Jan[uary] 1 — I do hope for a little peace now, for I have been overworked & headache & sickness have as usual followed — A peaceful day — sketched "Mr. Gregory's Letter Box" for the book cover — & helped Geraldine with a dress for the Gort fancy ball! & interviewed Noon about the Agricultural Organisation — our farmers are a little slow in joining — & saw Mrs. Mike John who told me she had got some new stories — but they are but varieties.

Jan[uary] 30 — The holidays have passed quickly & pleasantly, except that R. has not got over the eczema he came from school with — & it is unpleasant for him to go back with it — Peyton went as he came quietly, without demonstration, a curiously subdued lad — Our organisation has been started — a successful meeting, in the servants' hall — it is sure to do well as Frank has taken it up —

Yesterday I had the last proofs of the "Letter Box" — & did the Index — a great relief the heavy work being over — but now the time of publication comes near, I grow nervous, & think I ought not to have left in this or that — & that it will be very ignominious if it falls flat! — I have made designs for the Convent & started work, for the Lansdowne House Ex[hibition]. & the '98

---

[5] "The Hero in Man" *The Internationalist* 15 November 1897, pp. 35–38.

[6] *Old Harrow Days* (1898), by James George Minchin.

[7] The classic 1857 autobiographical novel of his life among the gypsies by George Borrow (1803–81).

[8] *Lyra Celtica*, an anthology of work by Irish women writers, edited by Sharp's wife Emilia (1856–1932), was published in 1896. *Vistas*, a collection of short dramatic pieces by Sharp, had just been published.

[9] Hyde arrived at Coole on 27 December, and left on 30th.

pilgrims[10] — & designed a bath rug which the nuns are going to give Horace Plunkett —

Mrs. Noon hopes her son will marry, but doesn't know how it will be managed "for he is so taken up with books, he'd die in a week if he married a dunce — & if he married a girl that was in any way cocked up in herself, it 'ud kill me!" — just as I may be thinking of R. — some day!

We went on our last Sunday to service at Killinane to see little "Kathleen Mary" christened[11] — but not to the afternoon party — I don't like the idea of Sunday parties being started unnecessarily in the neighbourhood —

Poor Fanny's troubles have culminated in the premature birth of twins, & I have promised to go to her for a bit, poor thing[12] —

Arranging tree planting — R. & I having marked 30 spruce for the people, & to leave gaps for the shooting, I am ordering 300 spruce, 300 larch, 100 silvers to take their place —

Standish O'Grady has taken over the "Kilkenny Moderator" — & asked me & his other friends to subscribe — I think he will ruin himself on it[13] — W. Yeats writes with a very downcast letter from AE who hates the organization work — & asks me to write & find out if he is permanently depressed or if it was only a passing mood[14] — Poor W. — he finds what a responsibility there is in trying to help others!

Feb[ruary] 10 — Clonodfoy[15] — got here 31st. — Fan[ny Trench]. very glad to have me as she has been shut up for so long — so I am glad to help her for

[10] A sale of Irish Industries goods at the Lansdowne House Exhibition took place in mid-March 1898 (see p. 180). "'98" pilgrims, Nationalists from Britain, Europe and the U.S.A., arrived in Ireland from July 1898 on, to visit key sites such as Wolfe Tone's grave. AG had no known subsequent connection with the '98 Centennial movement.

[11] Kathleen Mary Persse (22 December 1897–1979), first child of Major William Arthur Persse and Katy Gehle Persse. AG would eventually act as matchmaker for Kathleen Persse in her marriage to Edmund Maturin Persse in 1930 (see *Journals* vol. 2, pp. 412, 581).

[12] Fanny Trench's premature twins died in infancy, and their birth is not listed in *Burke's Peerage*.

[13] *The Kilkenny Moderator*, which ran from 1898–1900, indeed came close to ruining O'Grady. In 1900 he started the *All Ireland Review*, which he produced in Dublin from 1901 following a libel case, and edited until 1907.

[14] For WBY's letter encouraging AE to stay with the Agricultural Organization see *L* p. 294. AG herself received a downcast letter from AE the next day in which he wrote of his his new work as a "mistake. I was lured thereto by the poetical glamour thrown over it by my friend WBY and disregarded the still small voice" (Berg). AG in response sent AE a copy of Thoreau's *Walden*, which seems to have had the intended restorative effect on his morale.

[15] Home of the Trenches in Co. Limerick.

a bit, & now she is down & out in Bath chair, so over the worst — Tête à tête meals with Willie [Trench] — whose mind & soul are immersed in a Fish Oil Co. — in which he has made £2000 & is now speculating again — I began by a touch of regretful envy — for £2000 would make such a difference to me — but now I think I would, the mortgage once paid, throw my money out of the window rather than become so engrossed in the turning out of £. s. d. — It is like a man in the play, coming in always with the same sentence — at breakfast he has usually had a letter about it — at lunch a telegram — at dinner he wonders what news the morning will bring —

I am stronger in body from the rest, but growing dulled in mind so that it is an effort to write an Irish exercise or a letter — however I have finished & sent off a paper on "Tree Planting" to the Homestead[16] — & have done a Celtic design for blind in the hall, & for exhibition at the "Industries" — Smith & Elder send no word about the book & I feel rather stranded — but have two nice letters from AE — more cheerful in tone than W.'s —

Feb[ruary] 14 — Left Clonodfoy on Saturday — The nuns sent me the shamrock & fleur de lys cushion,[17] very successful, & a nice letter, saying they had been sent £10 from <??> by someone who had read my old Erin article ["Gort Industries"] — & the Homestead came with half my "charming article" on trees, the rest to follow in the next number — so I felt a revival of activity — A very unpleasant journey, rough crossing & crowded carriage, & my rooms not quite ready at Qmansions & the chimney smoking — & after unpacking I went to bed with a bad headache — still bad in the afternoon & after a lunch of tea & rusks went out & first met Dr. Maclagan in St. James's Park — who greeted me pleasantly & said they had wanted me to dine the day before — Walked to Savile Row & found Sir H. Thompson sitting with Enid — When he left she told me of all her servant worries (how happy am I to have so few!) & then walked back with me — & reappeared just as W. Yeats had arrived, to dine with us as her niece had not turned up — I was rather sorry, as W. B. Y. had so many things to tell me, however while she stayed he was charming & brilliant tho' rather above her head — & she went soon after 9 & he stayed till 12[18] — His time is terribly cut up with these '98 meetings & the fights & squabbles involved leading to nothing as far as he is concerned, except ill will — but he has the satisfaction of thinking himself useful to Miss

---

[16] "Tree Planting" *The Irish Homestead* 12 February, pp. 141–42 and 19 February, p. 164.

[17] Designed by AG, and illustrated in *The Daily Graphic* 18 March, p. 5.

[18] "[13 February] Lady Gregory came having this very morning returned from Ireland. . . . She asked me to go in & dine with her to meet Yates [*sic*] the Poet. . . . He is tall, refined & good looking & unaffected—but talked a good way over my head. . . . He had long thick black hair & allows a straight lock to fall over his forehead. This seems to me to be his only affectation. He was nicely and cleanly dressed in black—He seems full of enthusiasm & to have a great love of his Ireland" (Layard Diary, British Library).

Gonne, though by no means sure he is coming any nearer the fulfilment of his hopes — but "thinks perhaps she is keeping him to fall back on in old age" — which is quite likely — I was horrified when he told me that her new plan is to go to one of the "famine" districts — relieve the people, for which purpose she is selling her jewels — and then she is going to persuade them to rob — to kill the landlords' cattle for food — though she dislikes seeing pain inflicted on animals she will stand by & see it done — She expects the Govt. will interfere & perhaps fire on the people — & so draw attention to their case — W. had told her it was a political mistake, but that if she wished he would go with her, but she said she did not think it was in his line — I was aghast, & spoke very strongly, telling him first that the famine itself is problematic, that if it exists there are other ways of meeting it, that we who are above the people in means & education, ought, were it a real famine, to be ready to share all we have with them, but that even supposing starvation was before them it wd be for us to teach them to die with courage [rather] than to live by robbery — that the attempt would end in arrests — Miss Gonne would, if she suffered by imprisonment also gain by it the notoriety she wants — but the poor people sent to prison would have no such consolation — In all the crimes that have been condoned in Ireland, sheepstealing has been held in horror by the people, & it wd be a terrible responsibility to blunt their moral sensitiveness by leading them to it — He was very much struck & said he had only thought of the matter as it wd affect her — not as it would affect the people, (which I fancy is her point of view also) but that now he saw how wrong such a line would be & he would try to dissuade her from it[19] — He goes with her to Ireland today[20] — Poor boy, she is for the second time breaking up his life — And Knowles sent back his 2nd article very curtly, saying it was "too like the first" — however the Fortnightly has accepted it "If it is like the first"[21] — & his funds are evidently low — Some Hermetic seer has had a vision in which he has been given a message to "tell Maude Gonne to light the seven stars" — This will set her off on a new war path — He says all she does is

[19] Maud Gonne began touring distressed areas in the West of Ireland in March 1898. She had just co-authored a leaflet with James Connolly which advised those afflicted by hunger that Church doctrine held that "no human law can stand between starving people and their RIGHT TO FOOD including the right to take that food . . . with or without the owner's permission." WBY would recall that even at their first meeting in 1889 MG had vexed his father "by praise of war, war for its own sake . . . as if there were some virtue in excitment itself" (*Au* p. 123) and that "she thought almost any means justified in their success" (*Mem* p. 42). AG's warnings regarding sheepstealing proved astute, with Maud Gonne receiving a decidedly lukewarm response when proposing it in the West (see Samuel Levenson, *Maud Gonne* pp. 136–37). AG's caution as to whether there was indeed a "real famine" reflects contemporary press reports suggesting that allegations of distress in the Erris peninsula were unfounded, and a distaste for previous exaggerations of distress for political gain (see diary entry for 21 February 1898).

[20] This trip was in fact put off, and WBY went instead to Liverpool with Maud Gonne on 19 February, where they both addressed a '98 Centenary meeting.

[21] "The Broken Gates of Death", the third in a series of six folklore articles on which WBY and AG had collaborated, was published in *The Fortnightly Review* April 1898, pp. 524–36.

dictated by "voices" — & that if all this was known she might be locked up as mad — His account of the '98 squabbles is painful, even his own committee in London is fighting with the Dublin branch over Miss Gonne's £500[22] — I tell him they are like the S. London militia who had to be drilled back to back for fear they wd pick each other's pockets —

14 — Headache still, & a good deal of writing — & lunched with E. Layard — New Gallery to see the Rossettis[23] — Tea with Lady Lyall — home very tired — Paul came to dinner — a strange & troubled interview — Poor boy —

15 — Index proof to correct, at it till after 2 — Then to Harrow to see R. — found him well & cheery — He

[page missing]

18 — A telegram from Frank telling of Gerald's illness at Primrose Club[24] so went there & found him in bed with pneumonia — serious, 2 nurses — sat with him for a time & went for grapes for him — Dined Clays — Sir A. pleasant, but party dullish, Beadons & Dr. Farquharson M.P.[25] who asked me whether the '98 rebellion was before or after the Union — He is against a Catholic University but says he would have voted for it he thinks had the motion been put directly after Dillon's speech it was so powerful[26] —

19 — To St. Margaret's where Eyton preached, on the duty of giving — To the Primrose [Club] & found G[erald]. better — Barry O'Brien called — took my proofs to do some reviews — & took Finance Catechism to show to a Committee he is on[27] — He is all for keeping up the '98 spirit, as it is with

[22] Maud Gonne had decided to give part of the money she had collected during a recent fund-raising tour in U.S.A. to the '98 Centennial Committee. The Dublin and London branches of the Committee were divided principally by conflicting visions of the means necessary to gain Irish independence, with London, aligned with the Irish National Alliance, favouring constitutional methods, and Dublin, aligned with the Irish Republican Brotherhood, favouring direct action.

[23] This important exhibition, which considerably enhanced the stature of the pre-Raphaelites, ran from late December 1897 to March 1898. WBY, Maud Gonne and Synge all attended during its run.

[24] The Primrose Club, at 4, Park Place, was founded around 1890 by AG's brother Dudley. She reported that subsequent owner Jocelyn Persse (see p. 47 n. 142) received "about £120,000" when the Club was amalgamated with The Royal Overseas League in 1925 (Private MS).

[25] Dr. George Murray Farquharson (1835–99).

[26] Dillon had moved proposed legislation to establish a Catholic University in Dublin in a strong speech on 1 July 1897. His amendment was debated on 17 February 1898, but quickly foundered for lack of support.

[27] This was almost certainly the editorial committee for the Tower Pamphlets series. AG's *A Short Catechism on the Financial Claims of Ireland*, was accepted for the series, and set up in type (proofs with her corrections survive in the Berg Collection), but it is unclear whether it was published, as no copies appear to be extant.

that we will get concessions from England — Martin Morris afterwards, stayed to dinner — has spoken in favour of a Cat[holic] University but acknowledges that he is very glad to have been educated at Trinity instead — he wd have been "in a tight hole" had it existed when he was going to the University.[28]

21 — Miss Borthwick for an Irish lesson — stores & visits, only saw Lady Lovelace — Horace Plunkett & W. Yeats came and dined with me — The former anxious about the famine districts — says the distress tho' limited in area is very acute — He wants to get money just to keep the people from starving for the present, & he wants to make future famines impossible by teaching the people to help themselves — He is a good man, one feels the presence of goodness in the room — I think W. felt it also, & that his conscience begins to smite him — Miss Gonne had made a speech at Liverpool preaching pure insurrection[29] — whenever a chance may come — & he feels that there is a great responsibility involved in supporting & endorsing this — But "her wish is his law" — & also he feels he is of use to her & that she has many enemies & slanderers & that it would be a treachery to leave her — And there is always the hope, though I think it is a failing hope — of her accepting him at last — The Liverpool meeting had been most enthusiastic — tho' he still says she does not speak very well, it is her beauty that moves them —

I urged H. Plunkett to write a statement to the Times on the famine — his word will be accepted[30] — whereas the Nat[ionalist]. politicians have made so much capital out of possible famines for years past no one regards them now — He is enthusiastic about AE's work "the highest ideals & more practical than any of us" — & thinks if funds permit he may get him to train a pupil or two — & be free to come to his Dublin work when he likes —

W. B. Y. brilliant as ever — H. P. said Parnell was un-Irish — & he denies it — The Englishman he says, is reserved because of his want of sensibility — Parnell was reserved in spite of it — When he was taunted by Forster in the House he answered with no change from his usual cold manner — but afterwards it was seen blood was streaming from his hands, wounded by the

[28] The Morris family, though Unionist in their politics, were Catholic. Attending a Catholic University would have damaged Morris's standing with his core Unionist constituency, while failing to attend would have greatly limited his chances of winning swing votes from Catholic Nationalists.

[29] For a report on Maud Gonne's inflammatory speech at Liverpool on 20 February 1898, see *United Ireland* 26 February, p. 3.

[30] Though Plunkett had spoken forcibly about the famine in Preston on 18 February, he passed over this suggestion, but in his next letter to *The Times*, 31 March 1898 p. 10, a long critique of Government policy towards Ireland, he did briefly allude to the "chronic" situation.

clutch which had driven in the nails[31] — The Irish are a feminine nation with masculine ideals, the English are a masculine nation with feminine ideals — The English novel shows this — compare Balzac & Zola with Thackeray & Dickens — the English novelist knows nothing of the tenacity that makes a man write 40 novels in sequence, or that made Balzac keep himself awake with coffee for a week while he wrote — But England would never take a masculine ruler, Napoleon or Parnell as Ireland would do.

24 — Wrote to AE about W. & his difficulties — a delightful letter from him with verses enclosed — that is, delightful as showing his soul is awake again, but it gave a sad account of the poverty of the people — I sent it to Mr. Plunkett to use[32] — Kilkenny Moderator has my paper on Tree Planting & a paragraph on my intellectual sympathies![33] Went to see Gerald who is much better & sat with him — & was caught in the rain & so home — Dined Cheyne Row —

26 [i.e. 25] — Pains & langour, & shivering & when I went to see G. very knocked up & came home thinking I was in for influenza, but went to bed early after a cup of bovril & awoke all right —

26 — Irish lesson — called at Raffy's — Miss Gribbell says Mr. O'Brien can't get into Parliament for another 2 years & is getting restless — that is why he is attacking "gubbers" again[34] — He won't hear a good word of Horace Plunkett, says he is "not in earnest" — On to Lady Fingall, who promises to look after Gort work at the sale — On with her to Lady Arran[35] who says we must get round Miss Keatinge to get a good place so Lady F. is to interview her

[31] Probably the exchanges of 22–23 February 1883, when ex-Chief Secretary William Forster accused Parnell of being the inspiring force (though not organizer) of the Phoenix Park murders, and Parnell made a scornful response. See *Hansard Parliamentary Debates*, 3rd Series, CCLXXVI, pp. 607–33, 716–25.

[32] In his letter, sent from Crossmolina on 21 February 1898, enclosing the lyric "Carrowmore", one of his most distinctively Yeats-influenced poems, AE argued that the poor should be helped to help themselves, rather than just be given charity (Berg Collection). Instead of using the letter in a speech, Plunkett called on AE to give direct testimony to a House of Commons Committee reviewing development plans for the West of Ireland (see p. 184 n. 97).

[33] "Tree Planting" (reprinted from *The Irish Homestead*) was published in two parts, *Kilkenny Moderator* 23 February, p. 4 and 26 February, p. 5. The paragraph on AG, 23 February, p. 4, presumably by O'Grady, praises her "very beautiful, unaffected, and, so far as we can judge, wise and prudent paper . . . upon a theme in which poetry and financial enterprise seem to meet. Lady Gregory . . . takes a deep interest in everything relating to the welfare of her native land. . . . Irish writing men and women of the new school owe much to her sympathy, encouragement, personal friendship and good counsel."

[34] In a letter of 26 February 1898 (published widely in the Dublin press, and reprinted in *The Times* 1 March, p. 13) William O'Brien attacked Gerald Balfour for insinuating in Parliament that O'Brien was responsible for organizing recent agrarian violence, and for general incompetence in handling Irish affairs. Raffalovich's sister Sophie had married O'Brien in 1890, hence Miss Gribbell's prior knowledge of the letter.

[35] Winifrid, Lady Arran, née Reilly (d.1921), wife of the the 5th Earl.

— Hurried home to dress — W. Yeats to dinner & on to the Literary Society, Graves's lecture on Clarence Mangan — hopeless drivel, Graves looking like an owl trying to be sprightly & trying to make a "funny man" of poor stricken Mangan, quoting only his "funny" pieces — & a scrap or two of his translations[36] — very hard to listen to in patience — Yeats didn't, but read United Ireland[37] for a bit, & examined & admired his new blackthorn — Then Rolleston[38] made rather a prosy speech, claiming gr things for Mangan & reading a slightly better poem — Then J. F. Taylor, disappointing, as I had heard he was an orator, but the audience was too much for him — Then old McDermot, the last of the '48 men, prosed away interminably, reading, it was supposed an unpublished life of Mangan he has written, but so toothless it was difficult to hear him[39] —

Yeats had grown desperate, asked me for pencil & paper, I had only a blank cheque (the one to be filled up for Smith!) which I gave him & he dotted down some notes — Then when McDermot sat down he sprang up & said "I entirely disagree with Mr. Rolleston & I entirely disagree with Mr. Taylor — They claim too much for Mangan in claiming a mass of fine poetry for him — He did not do many fine things — he did 2 or 3 that were very fine — "Dark Rosaleen" & "O'Hussey's Ode to the Maguire" I do not look on as perfection but I look on them as as near perfection as anything that has ever been written — The poetry of Ireland is ballad poetry, & in the ballad poetry of all countries few men have written more than one or two of the best, & the rest has been rubble — It is absurd to claim for Mangan that he kept up to the high level of Shelley or Keats — In England there is a tradition of literature & of literary

[36] Graves's lecture was published as "James Clarence Mangan, Poet, Eccentric and Humorist" in *The Cornhill Magazine* March 1898, pp. 328–339. Mangan (1803–49), was for WBY the one Irish nineteenth-century poet "raised to the first rank by intensity" (*Au* p. 265). His lyric intensity, his disappointment in love, and the way in which his poetic genius set him apart socially made him a sympathetic figure for WBY in the 1880s and '90s, sparking an admiration that endured long after his enthusiasm for the work of Thomas Davis and Ferguson had waned.

[37] A radical Nationalist weekly paper.

[38] Thomas W. Rolleston (1857–1920), became a nationalist (and briefly a member of the IRB) under the influence of John O'Leary (see p. 173 n. 43), and edited *The Dublin University Review* 1885–87, which published WBY's earliest works. Co-member of The Rhymers' Club with WBY and helped found the Irish Literary Society, but his relationship with WBY was lastingly strained by his part in enabling Gavan Duffy (see p. 178 n. 71) to control the New Irish Library project in 1892 (*Mem* p. 81). A staunch supporter of Horace Plunkett, and worked from 1899 to 1905 for the Irish Department of Agriculture. Published an important anthology *A Treasury of Irish Poetry in the English Tongue* (1900), two volumes based on Gaelic mythology, and various poetical and philosophical writings, but increasingly subordinated his creative energies to his Civil Service work.

[39] Martin MacDermott (1823–1905), a Young Irelander, contributor to *The Nation*, and veteran of the abortive 1848 uprising. Served as architect to the Khedive of Egypt from 1866 and oversaw the rebuilding of Alexandria after the British bombardment of 1882. Founding member of the Irish Literary Society, author of a number of popular Irish ballads, and edited *The New Spirit of the Nation* (1884), a Young Ireland anthology (harshly reviewed by WBY, see *UP1* p. 333).

culture — In Ireland this has had to be created in later years — Mangan was one of the first creators — By these few fine ballads he inspired Poe, who inspired so much in modern French literature, & in England — He was the creator of a new style — And I disagree with Mr. Taylor in his ideas as to the end of art — Art should only be used for its own sake — In literature the art that aims at morals ends in the copybook & the head line — in Ireland many have an idea that literary art should be used for political ends, & this would lead us to Spirit of the Nation after Spirit of the Nation to the end of time — Art should be for its own sake only, that is the sake of the heavenly vision, & "its end should be for peace" — It is often my misfortune to have to combat with the enthusiasms of my elders!"[40]

He spoke with such life & vigour he put life into the assembly, but he says it was "lifting a dead weight" all the time — Strachey[41] was in the chair & had been listening with contemptuous tolerance, but his expression changed when this speech began, & he told him afterwards he was in full agreement with him — Stephen Gwynn, usually his enemy stood up & said Mr. Yeats had expressed his own ideas better than he could have done it himself[42] — & all ended well.

I had a little talk with Barry O'Brien, who is much excited over my book & the light it throws on [Dublin] Castle Government — He introduced me to Graves, who had been reading my Tree Planting articles with gr interest — & Yeats introduced me to Rolleston, & we had a little talk on industries & the A[gricultural]. O[rganization]. — Yeats came back with me, still excited with indignation at the poorness of the speaking — & read me "Dark Rosaleen" before he left.

Mar[ch] 1 — W. B. Y. dined with me — Gave an amusing account of Rolleston — who came from a German University, & fell under the influence of

---

[40] This assessment of Mangan broadly follows WBY's arguments in his 1887 article "Clarence Mangan" (*UP1* pp. 115–19) and his 1889 essay "Popular Ballad Poetry of Ireland" (*UP1* pp. 147–162), though WBY's experiences with "elders" (and Gavan Duffy in particular) who privileged patriotism over literary merit, had in the interim convinced him of Mangan's clear superiority to his contemporaries Davis and Ferguson. *The Spirit of the Nation*, edited by Duffy, a highly popular anthology of Young Ireland ballads and songs reprinted from the Nation magazine, was the embodiment of the kind of narrowly Nationalist literary aesthetic WBY was at this period trying to eclipse. WBY's comments about the ends of art rehearse arguments he would use in *Samhain* in 1905, in which he again cites Coventry Patmore's dictum "The end of art is peace".

[41] John St. Loe Strachey (1860–1927), Editor of *The Cornhill Magazine* 1896–97, and of *The Spectator* 1898–1925.

[42] Stephen Lucius Gwynn (1864–1950) journalist, critic, poet, Nationalist M.P. for Galway City 1906–18, and author of many Irish biographical and travel volumes. Grandson of 1848 Nationalist leader William Smith O'Brien.

O'Leary[43] — Then he came under the influence of old Gwynne[44] & became a Unionist — then a Parnellite — Has no instinct for forces, & so won't succeed — He had done well as editor of a University Review — "Oldham[45] was the prospective editor though he knew nothing of literature — but in Ireland every man who can do anything thinks he can do everything" — It was the great amusement among his mischief loving friends to propose something to him, & make him believe he had proposed it himself, when he was sure to carry it out — "So I went to him one day & suggested in this way that he should make Rolleston editor — So next time I went to see him he told me that he was not at all pleased with the present editor, Lough[46] — Oldham lived in a top room at Trinity, & he complained that when Lough came in to see him 'every man on the way up comes out & talks to him, & he arrives in my room holding the opinions of the man on the next floor — Then I talk sense to him for half an hour & he goes down again, & by the time he goes out into the street he holds the opinion of the man on the ground floor — Now there is a man called Rolleston who lives 25 miles out of Dublin, & I am going to make him editor, & I can go & talk to him when I have anything to say, & there will be no one to get at him & remove the impression' — so Rolleston was appointed & for once asserted himself & threw Oldham over & did the work very well" — "George Moore is a good natured fellow with an absorbing love of literature, who has reasoned himself out of all the moral codes as other people reason themselves into them — His tongue is terrific — He has quarrelled with Zola & with Mrs. Craigie & has only one word with which to describe both, that of pig! — He was never looked on by Mrs. Craigie as anything but a clever & agreeable man who it was rather a distraction to her to have following her, but he was never her lover — He was reading his new novel to Symons the other day & said 'Mrs. Craigie won't like that remark about her' — 'What remark' said Symons — 'Why that it is unpleasant to meet your mistress afterwards & find her both middle aged & middle class' — 'I did

---

43 John O'Leary (1830–1907), a key member of the Irish Republican Brotherhood in its early years, and editor of the IRB newspaper *Irish People* 1863–65. Arrested for conspiracy in 1865 and sentenced to twenty years imprisonment, but was released in 1871 on condition he not return to Ireland before 1885. Lived in exile mainly in Paris, but following his return to Ireland became a major influence on WBY's politics, conception of nationalism and knowledge of Irish literary history. In a hyperbolic act of homage, WBY would later write "From [Young Ireland Society] debates, from O'Leary's conversation, and from the Irish books he lent or gave me has come all I have set my hand to since" (*Au* p. 101).

44 Rev. John Gwynn (1827–1917), Stephen Gwynn's father. Regius Professor of Divinity at Dublin University 1888–1907.

45 Charles Hubert Oldham (1860–1926). Top scholar in his year at Trinity College, and founder in 1885 of The Contemporary Club, a key forum for discussion of literary and political questions, which itself led to the foundation of *The Dublin University Review*, for which he served as Managing Director. From 1909, Professor of Commerce at Trinity.

46 Possibly Thomas Lough (1850–1922), founder of the Home Rule Union in 1887. An M.P. for London 1892–1918, and a member of the London Irish Literary Society.

not know that applied to Mrs. Craigie' said Symons — 'Well, she will!' says G. M.[47] — Symons himself is so far reformed that he has become more fastidious, at the same time that he has lost the power of idealising — I told him the other day that he keeps the desire of sinfulness, without the inclination — Stead told someone the other day that there was no truth in the scandal about Lady Warwick & the Prince — 'How do you know?' — 'I asked her,' said Stead!!"[48]

4th — Dined Leckys — only a judge from the Transvaal (Morris) & his wife & a Dutch Baron — Lecky grieves over the exaggerated statements of the finance reformers. I pressed land purchase as the solution for our troubles — but he says, what is true, "it means changing every £100 into £70" — He thinks Parliament lessens one's interest in political questions — so much connected with them is of no value, & there is so much empty noise — Talking of Robert's future he said "It's a great thing after all to have a competence behind one" — He said he had been brought up for the Church — then found he could not enter it & went abroad & drifted, never thinking he wd marry & leading a solitary life — & so took to letters "& succeeded".

The old Dutchman talked to me after dinner, of religion — a Christian & an idealist — "We are on a journey home, & the ticket is taken the moment we are born" — "My mother would only when we were children read us the part

[47] Pearl Craigie (1867–1906), novelist and dramatist under the pseudonym "John Oliver Hobbes". Moore collaborated with Mrs. Craigie on several plays in the early 1890s, but as with most of Moore's collaborative ventures, quarrels ensued. His claim that she had been his mistress is characteristic; in Sarah Purser's celebrated quip, Moore invariably "didn't kiss, but told". An incident in Moore's *Memoirs of My Dead Life* in which he recounts kicking Craigie's bottom in public remains the most notorious event of their personal relationship, though likely also fictitious and a product of his resentment. They reunited for a final collaboration in 1904 which predictably ended in acrimony and failure. Craigie, who had joined the Catholic church after divorcing in 1895, has been suggested as an inspiration for Moore's novels *Evelyn Innes* (1898) — the "new novel" referred to above—and its sequel *Sister Teresa* (1901), both of which involve a sensual, gifted woman who becomes a nun. Moore modelled most of his early novels on the naturalistic style of French novelist Emile Zola, his friend in the 1880s, but broke with him both personally and stylistically from 1888 onwards. By the 1890s, partly no doubt in resentment at being tagged the "English Zola", Moore began to openly ridicule his former master.

[48] William Thomas Stead (1849–1912), Editor of *The Pall Mall Gazette* 1883–89, and founder and Editor of *The Review of Reviews*. Stead was the dominant crusading journalist of the late Victorian period. His exposés of the vice, squalor and hypocrisy rife in London challenged and often affronted the complacency of his many readers. In a sensational 1885 case he purchased a thirteen year old girl in order to dramatize the institutionalized state of child prostitution in the city, and was jailed for three months as a result. Met Lady Warwick in 1892, and immediately impressed her with his insistence that she should use her wealth in philanthropic causes, and through his tactful assertion that she could use her influence with the Prince of Wales (of whose decadence he was an outspoken critic) for social and moral good. Stead's comment on the relationship of Lady Brooke and the Prince is either apocryphal or an unrecognised irony, since the connection was his "favourite topic of conversation" with Lady Brooke (see Margaret Blunden, *The Countess of Warwick* pp. 85–86). One of the few leading journalists strongly opposed to the Boer War, Stead died in the sinking of the Titanic in 1912.

of the Bible that was about Paradise, for she said, children always walk in Paradise, they can wait till later to learn of the world & its wickedness".

6th — My book comes out tomorrow & I am getting anxious about it — Smith says it has been "very fairly well subscribed", about 150 copies taken, which is a good start — but much will depend on the reviews — Lunched Lyalls — Sir A. thanked me for book, & I said "I don't suppose Irish politics are much in your line" & he said "Oh yes, it sent me back to Lecky" — Later he said he thought I was wrong in saying Napoleon flourished his cane at Lord Whitworth[49] — I said my authority was Sir T. Moffett, Pres[ident] of Queen's College — Then he said it was badly bound, in which he is right — & that I ought to speak to Smith — & he had noticed the date on cover being different from title page — This not very encouraging! & I went home rather low — Lady Blake came in for a talk — & then Sir H. Cunningham — & then Mr. Lecky — who when the others had gone spoke quite with enthusiasm of the book — so full of interest — so brightly written — the narrative so skillfully interwoven with the letters — I was quite cheered, for I had been more anxious for his good opinion of it than anyone else's — He thinks I am a little hard on Plunket & that he was not a proselytiser — because he remembers a saying of his to his son the B[isho]p. of Tuam "leave the Catholics alone" — but I am sure I have authority[50] — He also thinks I am a little severe to George III — but Sir F. Burton who came afterwards said "I am glad you have come down on the real culprit, George III" — & quoted one or two people who had said his obstinacy was the cause of so many of Ireland's troubles[51] — He is much pleased with the book but says "I see a tendency to Home Rule in your own part" — I said "no, not to Home Rule, but I defy anyone to study Irish ~~politics~~ history without getting a dislike & distrust of England!" He was silent for a time & then said "That is my feeling" — & told me how patriotic he had been as a boy — though disliking O'Connell & his gang — W. Yeats to dinner — getting very tired of his committees & politics — & feeling the want of money, his work has been so much interrupted —

7th — Got up after rather a bad night — looked at Times — no notice at all in it! But a very good one in Chronicle written by Barry O'Brien[52] — & a

49 See *Mr. Gregory's Letter-Box* p. 34.

50 "Although [1st Baron] Plunket was sincerely in favour of religious freedom, he had . . . too much of a Moses-like sense of spiritual superiority. He wished to emancipate [the Catholics] first and to protestantize them afterwards" *Mr. Gregory's Letter-Box* pp. 122–23.

51 "Liberal measures were brought in again and again, and were dashed to pieces against the dead wall of [King George's] obstinacy. He had been brought up by his mother in a German cradle, and he could never stretch his limbs to the length of his English bedstead." *Mr. Gregory's Letter-Box* p. 27.

52 *The Daily Chronicle* 7 March, p. 3. O'Brien's lengthy review deftly outlines the historical contexts of AG's book and concludes that the work places "all students of Irish history under obligations . . . which should not be forgotten."

charming letter from Ld. Rosebery—who had been "absolutely unable to put the book down"—& must have read it carefully for he corrects a date—July 1 of Peel's letter on [the] C[atholic].Q[uestion] which ought to have been Feb 1 — & which, in consultation with Smith we found he had written Jany — & then put a scratch to make it Feby — which converts it to July[53] — Up to the reading room, & found a fairly good article in Daily News — a poor one in Standard, which wants to know who I am! An old gentleman had annexed the Daily Telegraph & I had to wait a long time before I cd get it, & see F. Lawley's gushing notice[54] — but the Chronicle much the most interesting — Went to Smith who thought I ought to be very well content with 4 reviews on first day — & Ld. R.'s letter — Lunched E. Layard & back to receive Mr. Barry O'Brien — Paul came in for a moment — & Sir A. Birch for some time — went to a little ev. party of Yeats[55] — Sharp & a Mr. Johnson[56] — & Nora Hopper[57] & Miss Giles[58] — W. read out some of Miss Hopper's poems & decided she had spoiled the last verse of King of Ireland's Son by an alteration[59] — but neither he or she cd remember how it had been until I repeated them — Then we left — & W. walked with me — & then came on by bus, & then we had some soup at Gatti's — for he wanted to talk over a letter just recd from Miss Gonne — a history of wretched intrigues at their committees which he is expected to go over & waste his time in trying to settle — She says she has begun her efforts (to teach the people to rob) under the auspices of the priests[60] — but this I

53 See above p. 155 n. 153.

54 *The Daily News* 7 March, p. 6; *The Standard* 7 March, p. 4—"It is greatly to be wished that [this] singularly interesting book . . . had been placed in the hands of some experienced editor before it was given to the public. Lady Gregory vouchsafes us no information about herself, her husband, or her husband's father. She relies, we presume, on the probability that enough will be remembered of Sir William Gregory's Autobiography, which appeared a few years ago, to make further annotations unnecessary. But in this she is very much mistaken"; *The Daily Telegraph* 7 March, p. 10—"delightful volume . . . one of the most instructive Irish books that have ever come into our hands."

55 This was apparently AG's first attendance at one of WBY's "Monday evenings".

56 Lionel Johnson, whom AG seems to have failed to connect at this point with WBY's stories of him (see p. 150 n. 129). She nonetheless subsequently asked Johnson to dinner, with WBY, via whom the invitation was issued, in the last week of March. WBY informed her in advance that Johnson did most of his drinking at home and would prove safe dinner company.

57 Nora Hopper (1871–1906), poet, novelist and free-lance journalist. Her early volumes of poetry, particularly *Under Quicken Boughs* (1895), earned WBY's praise, and he included her *Ballads in Prose* (1894) in a list of thirty "essential" Irish books in 1895 (*L* pp. 246–47), but she achieved little subsequent recognition either from him or the general reading public.

58 Althea Gyles (1867–1949), designer and symbolist painter. Studied at art school with WBY, was briefly a member of the Dublin Theosophists, and a co-member with WBY of the Golden Dawn. Designed covers for *The Secret Rose, Poems* (1899) and *The Wind Among the Reeds*. For WBY's relationship with her see Ian Fletcher "Poet and Designer: W. B. Yeats and Althea Gyles" *Yeats Studies 1* pp. 42–79. See also below p. 209 n. 46.

59 WBY singled out this poem, from the story "Daluan" in *Ballads in Prose*, for particular praise in his review "The Poems and Stories of Miss Nora Hopper" (*UP2* pp. 124–28), and in a letter of 1907 would call it the "one exception" of lasting value in her work (*L* p. 483).

60 See *Always Your Friend: The Gonne-Yeats Letters*, pp. 86–88.

doubt — I told him to go to Dublin if he thought it necessary but not to the West, lest he shd find himself endorsing doctrines that he cannot approve of — Poor boy — he is in a tangle —

8th — Nice letter from Lord Peel, & a cheery one from R. who says "I have begun to read your book & like it very much though I did not think it would suit me" — & is going in for scholarship exam — which may awaken his ambition — Dined Enid Layard — (after expedition for Fanny's curtains) — We went through Sir Henry's letters to Lord Lytton, from Madrid, & sitting with my back to a draught I got a stiff neck — Enid says Lady Lytton told her the Queen had been quite nervous when Lady Currie[61] came to Windsor & said to her "I hear she is a very vulgar woman & talks very loud — I hope she won't do that — you had better speak to her about it" — Lady Currie also arrived very nervous — & when Lady Lytton had said to her "You see we have all to speak very low here" she was terrified — & at dinner never spoke above a whisper.

9th — Getting into my Irish work again, the "Letter Box" excitement having subsided — Tea with Lady Morris, who said she cd not get Ld. M. to bed the night before, he was so taken up with it — Saw him also — he made one or two small corrections — W. B. Y. to dinner at 7 — & I saw him off at Euston, to Ireland — where I hope he won't get into mischief — We don't quarrel about '98, for as I told him the rebellion was two things — one in intention — the other in execution — In intention it was an attempt for national freedom, & if it had succeeded we should all now be celebrating it (he says he wd not, he wd be against the existing Govt. then!). In execution it was a massacre of Protestants, & I have no idea of celebrating that, but if he likes to celebrate the intention, well & good — Only, I beg him to keep out of the stirring up of troubles in the West —

10th — To Harrow to see R. — found him well & lively — doing work well, tho' the day he had done badly (through having mislaid his book the night before) Mr. Welldon had told him he was "on the brink of trouble" — Mr. Bowen caught him skirmishing about the House one day & told him he was "making more noise than he was worth" — but otherwise there are no complaints — Back at 7 & Willie Peel came in, I said I had been expecting a visit — having written so nicely of his grandfather — but he said he thought I had rather showed him up — however he had only read the reviews, & I lent him the book — He stayed till 8-30, then I poached some eggs & went to bed

[61] Mary Montgomerie Currie, née Lamb (1843–1905). Established herself as a fashionable hostess, and successful poet and novelist under the pseudonym "Violet Fane", during her first marriage, as Mrs Singleton. Married Philip Currie in 1894, a year after her first husband died, and continued to publish, including a volume of poetry *Under Cross and Crescent* (1896), written at Constantinople.

— Very good review in Scotsman.[62]

12 [i.e 11] — Times notice, short but good[63] — Irish lesson — then Irish Industries for the Gort things were arriving & I had slept with a pyramid of parcels in the middle of my room — wired for Miss Bentley & undid them all & found some of the things had no tickets — & none of the tickets had Gort name — so had a good deal of trouble — & finally took them off to Motcombe St. & deposited them there[64] — Then went to E. Layard for tea & stayed to dine & finish going through the letters from Constantinople — in 1879 — Sir H. beginning to see through his friend the Sultan — Pall Mall fairly good review[65] —

12 — Wrote & did Irish & called Tennants & Mrs. Dugdale & Blakes & dined with M[a]cBride & Major Thackwell — rather sad — recalling six years ago!

13 — Fog — Lunched Reays — not very interesting — Bernard Mallet & his mother,[66] & Mr. Henley[67] (honble, not poet!) but talked to Ld. R[eay]. about Westcote St. School & he has promised to go & see it[68] —

14 — Lunched Lady Dorothy — only Sir Hubert Stephens there[69] — Pottered about — met Miss Ida Taylor at the Lyalls — who is writing on "Pamela" & says she will demolish her character but prove her legitimacy[70] — Quiet evening, reading Gavan Duffy[71] —

[62] *The Scotsman* 7 March, p. 2: "Lady Gregory has the rare gift of being able to treat controversial politics with humour."

[63] *The Times* 11 March, p. 13.

[64] The headquarters of The Irish Industries Association were at 20 Motcomb Street.

[65] *Pall Mall Gazette* 11 March, p. 4: "really interesting" despite being "rather carelessly compiled."

[66] Bernard Mallet (1859–1932), Private Secretary to Arthur Balfour 1891–92, and Commissioner of Inland Revenue 1897–1909. Married Marie Adeane (b.1859) at this point Maid of Honour to Queen Victoria, in 1891. His mother was Lady Frances Mallet, née Pellew.

[67] Hon. Frederic Henley (1849–1923), who succeeded his father, as 4th Baron Henley, in November 1898.

[68] The London School Board school at Wescott and Tabard Streets, Southwark, for which AG raised funds.

[69] Sir Herbert Stephen (1857–1932), lawyer.

[70] Ida Ashworth Taylor (d.1929), daughter of dramatist and poet Sir Henry Taylor (1800–86). Her *Life of Lord Edward Fitzgerald* includes discussion of the ambiguous family origins of his wife, Pamela, (?1776-1831).

[71] Sir Charles Gavan Duffy (1816–1903), co-founder of the Nationalist newspaper *The Nation* with Thomas Davis and John Blake Dillon in 1842, and a leading member of the Young Ireland group. Though elected as a Nationalist M.P., Duffy gradually became pessimistic as to the prospects of reform in Ireland by constitutional means and emigrated to Australia, becoming Prime Minister there in 1871–72. Returned to Ireland in the late 1880s, and published a biography of Davis in 1890 and a two volume autobiography *My Life in Two Hemispheres*—most likely the work AG was reading—in 1898. For WBY's struggle with Gavan Duffy for control of the New Irish Library see p. 171 n. 38.

15 — A very saddening letter from Mr. Bowen — saying R. has been formally reported for idleness, & turned to the bottom of the class — no chance of course of his ever being head of the school[72] — & a shock to me as I thought he was doing well — It was only when I had read it that I remembered that it is my birthday! a painful celebration for it — I wrote to R. & to Mr. B[owen] — & had my Irish lesson — & went to lunch with E. Layard — Ly. Duncannon & "illconditioned" Mrs. Elliot there — & Mr. Alderson — On to Irish concert Miss Borthwick had asked me to go to — then tea at Murrays — John there — He spoke of [a] dinner he had presided at of correctors of the press & I asked what they sprang from, if they had failed in literature like critics — & he says — "Well I think, but I refrained from saying it at the dinner that they are old University men who have taken to drink"!

Ld. Salisbury worse from the Cabinet Council the other day — Nellie Alderson had called to see Lady S. — & she said "the Council is going on now in the house, & there are two men at the door to see that I don't listen."

A splendid review of *me* & my book in the World & I sent away some copies[73] — but my heart is heavy all the time, I wd rather my book had failed & my boy done well — It is nothing worse than carelessness — but it is hard that William's mother shd have been so proud of her boy at school — & that I should be kept unsure — However William also once went down & came up again[74] — & I pray that R. may take the disgrace to heart & begin to do his best.

16th — Dined Morris — to meet Alice Newton & her husband[75] — Sat between Lord Denbigh[76] & Sidney Colvin — not much interested — & would have liked to talk to Atkinson the Attorney Gen[era]l[77] — but he went off to the Speaker's Levée after dinner — Ld. Morris in gr humour, puffing my book (so it must be a success!) & is sending a copy to Lady Londonderry — Mr. Peel who came with me says Ld. Acton was very full of it at Trinity [College, Cambridge] — I say, the worst of the "World" review is, people will expect me when I dine out to be as amusing as Lord Morris — "So you are" says Lady M. — & I say in return it was necessary for me to have good reviews or Martin wd not acknowledge me, but his L[or]dship says "Ah sure Martin's is only a

72 RG's father and grandfather had both been Head Boy at Harrow.

73 *The World* 16 March, pp. 13–14.

74 After distinguishing himself at Harrow and making an impressive start at Oxford (twice placing second for the Craven Scholarship), WHG had failed to take a degree, and entered a ruinous gambling phase only belatedly atoned for by his political and diplomatic career.

75 Alice Newton, née Cochrane (d.1914), daughter of the 11th Earl of Dundonald, and her husband George Newton (d.1900).

76 Rudolph Fielding (1859–1939), 9th Earl Denbigh. Lord-in-waiting to Queen Victoria 1897–1901.

77 Rt Hon. John Atkinson, Q.C. (1845–1932), Attorney General for Ireland 1895–1905.

tuppeny halfpenny ephemeral sort of thing, but yours is a book of importance — As Lecky says, it deals with a time that has passed out of memory, but has not passed into history"

17th — Heavy hearted still — & a very tiring day — Irish lesson — & off to Lansdowne House to arrange stall — & then all the afternoon standing selling for Gort — Lady Fingall helping at intervals, & Lady Morris also — Better than last year when I & my blinds were alone! but I feel it ignominious, all this talk & professions about helping the poor Irish — & then fashionable people come, & buy from other fashionable people, getting as much as they can for their money, either in goods, or other commodities — & the extravagance of their dress makes one think of the poor workers at home! Back very tired — & dined Walpoles — late, from cabby losing his way — & found it dullish — I suppose I was so —

18 — A letter from R. written on Monday telling of his trouble — Poor child he seems to feel it very much — "it is so hopeless, now I can never get back to my old place in class" — & Mr. Moss seems to have treated him harshly, never having warned or prepared him for punishment — It may be all for the best, for he was careless — even in writing to me — but it is a hard lesson for him & for me — Lunched E. Layard — & the sale again — Alfred Graves there — says Lecky is reviewing my book for the Spectator — a gr compliment — & that his brother is going to ask me to write something for the Cornhill[78] — Sold most of the things, owing chiefly to Lady Fingall's help — cleared about £16 or £17 — very hard work for the money! — Home very tired — & Mr. MacBride called & took me to "The Liars"[79] — amusing after the first act which drags —

19 — Lecky's article in the Spectator takes the first place, very important & interesting — I wd have recognised it anyhow, as he is down on me for being down on Ld. Plunket — & also he speaks of the "excellent narrative" I have interspersed the letters with[80] — He is a very good & sincere friend — To "Industries" meeting at Londonderry House — all the smart ladies in smart clothes — & Horace Plunkett still bad from influenza speaking with gr difficulty, on co-operation — All this talking & fuss leads to a gain of £2000 per ann. — *most* of which goes to Ireland.

---

[78] Possibly a slip for *The Spectator*, of which Charles Larcom Graves (1856–1944) was subsequently assistant editor 1899–1917. *The Cornhill Magazine* had strongly promoted Irish material under Strachey's editorship 1896–97, but AG's only contribution to the magazine was to be "The Felons of Our Land" in 1900 (see p. 267 n. 192).

[79] *The Liars*, a four act comedy by Henry Arthur Jones, ran at the Criterion for 328 performances from early October 1897.

[80] *The Spectator* 19 March 1898, pp. 410–12.

On to buy a Spectator — & looking at the Athenaeum found it also has a first page review, very good — & I think more likely to attract readers than the others — tho' it criticizes the "brilliant unorthodoxy" of my editing — & is down on me for the wrong date on title page — tho' it is really the cover for which I am not responsible that has the wrong date — & the Athenaeum itself — while heading the article "Mr. G.'s letter box" has in the table of contents immediately above it "Mr. Gregory's Post Box" so needn't boast of accuracy![81]

Home & entertained Mrs. Aylmer Gowing at tea — Yeats & E. Martyn to dine & on to Literary Society "original evening" — Poor Yeats with a bad cold — caught in Ireland — where he spent his week trying to reconcile incompatible differences — & had to make a speech in the Phoenix Park[82] — The Celtic Theatre project looking up — as there is now an "amateurs protection society" formed in Dublin — proposing various schemes of circumventing the theatre managers — Lit. Society not very lively — so I soon took refuge in the other room, & sat with Graves & W. B. Y. — Graves says tho' his brother Charles gets credit for the Blarney Ballads it was he & his brother Arnold who wrote half of them — & his father one whole one[83] —

20 — Lunch Ricardos — Mr. R. enthusiastic about the "Letter Box" — begs for a repetition of the dose — "more of the same mixture" —

21 — Dined Lady Layard — Nellie Alderson came in from driving with Lady G[wendoline]. Cecil — says Lord Salisbury's one query is "Any letter from Beaulieu" where Lady S. has gone — & has only written once from — A nice article in "Echo"[84] — & the "Gort Convent Industries" have been illustrated in Daily Graphic[85] —

22 — Dined Sir A. Clay — met Richmond Ritchies — Mrs. R. unhappy about some sketch books of her father's that are being put up for sale[86] — They had been carried off at his death by the butler — she believes not as a theft but as

[81] *Athenaeum* 19 March 1898, pp. 365–66: "edited . . . in a brilliantly unorthodox style. She has paid little attention to dates, as her title-page shows, and she scorns footnotes."

[82] WBY's speech, at a meeting in Phoenix park on 13 March celebrating the '98 Centenary, urged the patriotic support of Nationalist demands. For a report see *The Irish Daily Independent* 14 March, p. 5.

[83] *Blarney Ballads* (1888), verses satirizing Gladstone and his Home Rule policy, had been published as authored by Charles Larcom Graves. Arnold Graves (1847–1930) was the third of the three Graves brothers. Their father, Charles Graves (1812–99), was Bishop of Limerick 1866–99.

[84] *The Echo*, March 19, p. 1: "a delightful and instructive book."

[85] *The Daily Graphic* 18 March, p. 5.

[86] Novelist William Makepeace Thackeray (1811–63) studied art as a young man, and continued to sketch and paint after achieving success as a writer.

a souvenir — & now his grandson is putting them up for sale — & they go at such high prices she can't redeem them — On to Blumenthals, music & diamonds — enjoyed it for once in a way —

23 — "Kilkenny Moderator" with a badly written review by Rolleston — using such a phrase as "conversation with well informed persons" — it sends one back to Sandford & Merton & the Fairchild family[87] — Tea with Lady Simeon — Pember Q.C. there —

25 — Snow all the morning — kept Miss Borthwick & went with her to I[rish]. L[iterary]. Society to hear a very poor lecture by Mr. Whyte on Irish actors of the century[88] — the society will become a scoffing & a derision if they have such wretched lecturers — Wyndham[89] in the chair, looking ill, but spoke amusingly — & the afternoon was redeemed by Bernard Shaw, who spoke very wittily — extinguished poor Whyte who he said, truly enough, had enumerated the best actors & actresses — & then said they were not Irish — but yet had proceeded to hold forth about them — As to what an Irishman is, he said, is a complex question — for wherever he may have been born, if he has been brought up in Ireland, that is quite sufficient to make him an Irishman — It is a mistake to think an Irishman has not common sense — it is the Englishman who is devoid of common sense — or at least has so small a portion of it that he can only apply it to the work immediately before him to do — that is why he is obliged to fill the rest of his horizon with the humbug & hypocrisy that fill so large a part of English life — The Irishman has a better grasp of facts & sees them more clearly — only, he fails in putting them into practise & has a great objection to doing anything that will lead to any practical result — It is also a mistake to think the Irishman has feeling he has not — but the Englishman is full of feeling — What the Irishman has is imagination, he can imagine himself in the situation of others — But the Irish language is an effete language — & the Irish nature is effete, & as to saying there are good Irish actors, there are not — & there won't be until the conditions in Ireland are favourable for the production of drama — "& when that day comes I hope I may be dead"[90] —

---

[87] Despite its laboured style, Rolleston's review, *The Kilkenny Moderator* 23 March, p. 3, is highly complimentary, defining AG's editorial work as "beyond all praise". *The History of Sandford and Merton*, by Thomas Day (1748–89), and *The History of the Fairchild Family* by Mary Sherwood (1775–1851), were celebrated children's books.

[88] Frederic Whyte (b.1867), who lectured on "Irish Actors and Actresses of the Century", subsequently published a volume *Actors of the Century* (1898) and a biography of William Stead.

[89] Charles Wyndham (1841–1919), actor, from 1876–99 Manager of the Criterion Theatre, and founder and proprietor of Wyndham's Theatre and The New Theatre.

[90] This was probably AG's first meeting with mercurial dramatist and critic George Bernard Shaw (1856–1950), who later embodied these revisionist theories of the differences between Irish and English character in his play *John Bull's Other Island* (1904). Despite the general antipathy between Shaw and WBY, AG and Shaw became firm friends.

Dined Lovelaces — sat between a Judge Lushington[91] I didn't care for, & Lord Morpeth[92] — Also there, Lord & Lady Tennyson[93] — She is a nice woman — told me that a lady had said to her husband at Oxford — "I hear young Tennyson is here — is he as great a fool as most great men's sons are?" — He said, quite — Mr. Wallop, Ld. Portsmouth's brother who I drove home — & Humphrey Wards — pleasant altogether —

26th — Lunched E. Layard, & rain came on & I came home & presently had a telegram "Gerald died in my arms this morning after a brief illness — Rose Persse"[94] —

Poor child — poor boy — he is gone — & what is saddest is, one cannot wish him back again — A life of great possibilities spoiled by some weakness of will or defects in bringing up —

27 — Very sad about poor G. — This last week was full of engagements, & I am putting all off of course — It is a dreary wind up to my visit & I shall be glad to get away — Sir H. Blake came in & I broke down — Sidney Colvin — & I sat up & said nothing — made no sign — The shock as usual fell inside & I have been retching all day — & lunched on bovril & biscuits[95] —

Ap[ril] 3 — Such a long week after those that had gone so quickly! & my physical strength has failed — I got through necessary shopping etc & dined usually with E. Layard — Wilfrid Blunt back from Egypt — but in poor health & low spirits — I think starved — suffers internal neuralgic pain, & says he wishes for death — but still hopes to live to see the break up of the British Empire. I brought W. Yeats to see him — but the visit did not go off very well though Yeats did a vision on him — & succeeded in making him see a flower in the "Golden Square"[96] —

[91] Vernon Lushington (1832–1912), Judge of the County Courts for Surrey and Berkshire 1877–1900. For the long friendship of the Tennyson and Lushington families see John Waller, *A Circle of Friends*.

[92] Charles Howard (1867–1912), Viscount Morpeth, who succeeded his father, as 10th Earl of Carlisle, in 1911.

[93] Hallam Tennyson (1852–1928) and his wife Audrey, née Boyle (d.1916). Hallam, 2nd Baron Tennyson, succeeded his father, the Poet Laureate, in 1892, and in a brief diplomatic career served as Governor–General of Australia 1902–04.

[94] Gerald Persse (1857–26 March 1898) was the fourth of AG's brothers to die, but the first of those near to her in age, and with whom she had grown up.

[95] "[28 March] Lady Gregory came & dined but was very miserable about her brother & cried bitterly" (Layard Diary, British Library).

[96] Blunt's diaries record a visit from AG on 29 March, of which he noted that she had become a "strong Nationalist", and a second in company with WBY on 1 April. Though in accord with WBY in hoping for "the coming doom of England", Blunt found his evocations of visions "imperfect, not to say null" (*My Diaries* [New York, 1921] vol.1, pp. 290–91). Blunt, whose health and morale recovered, lived for more than twenty more years.

I went one evening to dine with W. Yeats, not feeling up to the restaurant here — & after dinner AE appeared, his only day in London having come to give evidence on money lending before the H[ouse]. of Lords[97] — He looks much better & brighter than in the summer — & is full of life & energy — evidently doing his work well — & feeling that he is doing so — He makes me more hopeful about the state of the poor — for tho' the famine is bad now he does not think there will be actual death from starvation — & he thinks things may be remedied in the future — by co-operation — rural bonds — co-op stores & poultry farming — the people suffering so terribly now from the "gombeen men"[98] — & the shop keepers — W. tells him his literary style is improved — & I say his getting into the habit of speaking may have helped to do this — but he says — "Well I don't know that my style of speaking does — I have to straddle across a platform with a broad smile on my face & begin "Men of Killybegs" — However he says he doesn't care about his literary style — & W.B.Y. says "Ever since I have known you you have renounced literature every 6 months".

April 9 — Home again — very glad to leave London — my rooms seemed like a living tomb — & my strength seemed to have failed — W. R[obert]. G[regory]. came & dined with me, & we set off together & had a fairly good journey[99] — Geraldine [Beauchamp] met us here — Fine dry weather — I went round the first day with Mike to mark trees — dead & dying ash for the people — firing being very scarce — Their potatoes however seem to be holding out — & they are delighted with the new seed from the A[gricultural]. O[rganization]. & the manures — The Gort shopkeepers are "sitting idle" — though they have lowered manure prices £3 per ton —

7th — An unlucky day — for Prempeh, the black calf, got a fit & died — of "blackleg" Mike says — Then R. got his cricket ground arranged & started to play, & a rash & itching came on so that he had to stop — He says it has been coming on lately — Sent him in to the Dr. — who didn't throw much light on it — Then I got a violent headache & had a bad night —

Have done up my accounts & find myself very low in funds, only £150 left for five months! I can't afford London more than once a year — but don't see where else to economise — except in giving —

May 4 — The holidays passed peaceably — R. looked much better the last week — seemed very content all through — tho' not much going on — made

97 AE gave evidence to the Select Committee on Money Lending on 31 March 1898. See *Parliamentary Papers*, 1898 vol. 10, pp. 237–43.

98 Money-lenders who charged usurious interest rates. From the Gaelic "gaimbín".

99 AG and RG left London on 4 April (Layard Diary).

a kite — & played with the dogs & watched the lambs — & was wildly excited at the breaking out of war between America & Spain[100] —

He left 26th & as Geraldine was going to <?Clonmel> on May 2, I took advantage of freedom to come away for a little — for I have never been well since the shock of poor G[erald]'s death — appetite, strength & energy have failed & it seems such waste of time trying to live without energy — I thought of Aran, where I cd learn Irish for W. R. G. & pick up folk lore for W. B. Y. — & sketch to replace my lost book — but weather broke & steamers were too early — So set out for Cashla Connemara — using the half hour wait in Galway to drive to see G.'s grave with Rose, which upset me very much — Rain came on, & I had a dreary journey & drove on car in floods of rain from <?Recar> — & was not expected, my letter only arrived with me — Hotel very comfortable — & next day lovely — but no Irish teachers in school, tho' an Irish speaking district — & the people rather ungetatable, either at their own work, or in a gang under a Govt. inspector, making a wall along a short bit of the road — for no earthly reason — Miss O'L. says there are 9 men employed, & 4 paid to look after them — I talked to an old man who had been to Gort & asked "if Mr. Gregory was living yet" & tried for folk lore but in vain — Storm came on — & I didn't sleep — & am going back to Galway to try & make a rush for Aran by the morning boat —

5th — Off at 6-30 — A lovely morning & a breezy voyage — I was afraid of being disenchanted at Inishere — but when I had been dropped into the corragh & a rush of men had dragged us on the beach, I found it as fascinating [as] before — & spent all the morning there — The sand is silver — the colours extraordinarily delicate, the soft blues of the Connemara hills, the green sea water — the evening tints turning the sea to opal & the wet sands to amethyst — There was a sort of amphibious & familiar mingling of God's creatures on the beach — men & children un-concernedly wading in & out in soft cowskin slippers — children sitting at the edge of the water playing with shells, gulls stalking along like barn door fowl, but suddenly rising heavily when they had secured a morsel, & flying off pursued by quicker comrades — The men were pulling in a net they had carried a little way out in a corragh — They Three at each end, dragging at a rope, the wet its yellow coils growing into substantial heaps at their feet as the net grew heavier & came nearer — Then its wooden handles appear & a purple semi-circle looms below the green water — children in red flannel & a little exe barking fox terrier rush excitedly down — gleams of silver are seen thro' the meshes of the net — then

[100] Following the destruction of a U.S. ship at anchor in Havana on 15 February, allegedly by a Spanish submarine, war broke out between the two countries, long antagonistic due to U.S. claims to Cuba. Defeated by superior U.S. military strength, Spain ceded the Phillipines to the U.S., along with Puerto Rico, Cuba, and other Caribbean possessions, in a treaty signed in August.

with two or three great heaves it is pulled on shore & emptied of its contents
— chiefly alas heavy seaweed <?twists> & <?branches> — but about a dozen
red spotted plaice, & 3 or 4 gurnet & a black polack — These are thrown into
a square kish standing on the sand — the baby flat fish are thrown to the
children, & they in their turn pounce on little crabs & give them to the dog,
who snaps & dances round them, tearing off the claws with sudden dashes, &
<?losing> & <?worrying> them — Then the coracle is put out again, & the
process lasting altogether about an hour is repeated — Costello's[101] — very
comfortable — gurnet for breakfast — lobster for lunch — plaice for dinner
— the air delightful & exhilarating — (a little school of sea larks is playing with
the rippling waves — dashing out as they draw back — then at the turn
scuttling in out of reach — With little brown legs & tucked up grey & black
feathers — Then a sudden thought strikes them & they fly away) —

7th — An old woman says — It was St. Goban built that church — She was a
king's daughter, & could have married rich nobles, but she came here, to live
with the Saints — And her friends came to persuade her, but she wouldn't
go[102] —

When a sea fog comes & makes all landmarks invisible, you begin to feel that
you may have slipped anchor & have drifted in very truth into mid ocean —

"Why wouldn't we have courage to go to America — Sure we all have brothers
or sisters or children there — there's near as many of us there as here on the
island"

"My brother that died in Boston would have given thousands if he had them
to be buried in the clean churchyard here at home" —

In calm weather weed boats & hookers can anchor by the rocks — but when
there is a swell it is only the frail curragh that can ~~face the~~ make its way
through the thundering dashing surf —

~~It is a matter of pride~~ — Pride tempers the grief of father or mother if the lost
child has been summoned away by the touch of the Sidh ~~to live its life out in
that mystic region~~ — For it is known that it is the best that is always called, the
first in beauty or in dancing or in singing, to live his life out in that mystic
shadowy region — {A remote ethereal region} —

---

[101] The public house on Inishmaan, owned by Michael Costello.
[102] Teampall Ghobnait [St. Gobnet's Church] on the Northern end of Inishere. St. Gobnet
lived on Aran in the fifth century, allegedly to escape a family feud. In later life she established
a nunnery at Ballyvourney.

The dark sailed boats sweep out at night — the Enterprise, the Sailor Lad — the Morning Star — followed by the anxious eyes of women who have known the cruelty of the sea, & come back in the morning {at sunrise} piled with shining silver heaps that quickly turn into heaps of gold —

£5 per 1000 for mackerel after the middle of April —

"It was 15 year ago a French boat came into this harbour, with about £300 worth of fish on board — And we never knew anything about them till then — And from that day Father O'Donoghue never stopped writing & working, till he & Mr. Green[103] got the boats started at last" —

"The people of the South Island talk with a drawl like the Munsters — & the north island is too near Connemara & there they have too much English scattered through their talk" —

June 20 — Tête à tête with Geraldine — & at last after many delays W. B. Y. arrived[104] — He brings his father's sketches of Douglas Hyde & George Russell to begin my gallery of my best countrymen — both very good, especially AE's[105] —

26 — Began to teach Irish to W. B. Y. — & to read "War & Peace" to him —

27 — Mr. Synge came, from Aran[106] —

28 — Went again to see the poor Farrell girl, whose brother has died — it is very sad "Mike, Mike Machree! — my <?loughy> Mike! — I went out into the

[103] Rev. William Spotswood Green (1847–1919), Government Inspector of Fisheries 1889–1914 and Commissioner of the Congested Districts Board 1892–1909. For an account of his work initiating springtime deep sea mackerel fishing off the Aran islands see Stephen Gwynn *Experiences of a Literary Man* pp. 196–99.

[104] A romantic interest between WBY and Geraldine Beauchamp (1875–1975), who spent several summers at Coole, has been suggested. Asked about this by her son in 1969, when she was ninety-five, she dismissed the rumour roundly, recalling WBY as self-absorbed and "a very grubby man" (tape of interview, courtesy of E. C. Merriweather).

[105] AG had commissioned these and other sketches from John B. Yeats, both to keep him in funds and with a view to promoting his work. As WBY observed to Lily Yeats, AG intended to hang the sketches in her London flat "so somebody may see them there and want a portrait of themselves" (*L* p. 302). See also William M. Murphy, *Prodigal Father* p. 203.

[106] John Millington Synge (1871–1909), dramatist, and co-Director of the Abbey Theatre with WBY and AG until his early death from Hodgkin's Disease. This was Synge's first visit to Coole, where he stayed until 29 June, visiting Edward Martyn at Tillyra on 28th. AG had seen Synge on Aran during her own visit in May, but they had not met, and her invitation to him was relayed via WBY who had met Synge in Paris in 1896 and first encouraged him to visit the islands (see *Theatre Business* ed. Ann Saddlemyer, p. 27). Synge had been on Aranmore 10–24 May and 9–25 June, and on Inishmaan 24 May–9 June.

night to look for Mike, & when I came back there were two cateens[107] in the bed — We were like one when we were children, & we'd be telling one another stories when all the world was asleep — & when I'd laugh he'd laugh — This day fortnight he was annointed — & after when I went in to him his eyes were turned up like the dear Lord's — & except myself & the great God there was no living Christian with him when he went —

I hope your Ladyship will have a high place in heaven & that when you get to heaven the blessed Virgin will come to meet you — for she was the highest lady that ever lived in the world, & was always meek & mild — & you are the same yourself — for Mike would say "She's like a little beggarwoman & I can talk to her as if she was my mother" for he never liked proud people —

Bill Farrell, boxing with Mulkere was seized round the neck & called out "I couldn't box now if I was the Queen of England!"

I took Jack Ford & Daly to the wood for spruce trees they wanted for their haycocks — Daly found one he thought wd do, but when guiding me to see it, he could not come across it again — & J. F. called out "has it gone astray on you!" — The basket maker says: May the Lord Jesus be a travelling man at the end of the universe to lead you straight to heaven —

Aug[ust] 15 — Robert safe at home, well & grown — rather older, much excited about Navy matters & reads the papers with great interest — I am a little behindhand, having been taken up with Druids etc —

W. B. Y. — has left for '98 commemorations — Henry, Geraldine, Irene[108] here —

1st Sept[ember] — To Galway Feís[109] with W. B. Y. to support the Gaelic movement — very glad we went, for none of "the classes" were there to support it unless priests can so be called —

Greaney, the young Spiddal schoolmaster gave a recitation with gr vigour — & as Deeney the other master was giving the next, W. B. Y. asked Greaney what they were all about & he said "Both poems are called 'Thoughts on Ireland' — my one tells how the Sassenachs baffled us entirely, & the one he's giving tells how the Sassenach murdered us a while ago" — very characteristic "Thoughts on Ireland" —

---

[107] A Gaelic-English hybrid, meaning literally "little cats".
[108] Gwendoline Irene Persse, eldest daughter of AG's brother Arthur.
[109] Lit. "festival".

3rd — Cricket match — Ennis v Kiltartan — chiefly sappers — but a report went out that "the pick of Innis" had arrived — Our men were nervous and went down like ninepins, till Shaugnessy the giant & teetotal publican went in, & he looked on the visitors only as possible customers & strode about the field — didn't do very much but looked as if he did — R. redeemed the game — played with gr composure & style — made 22 in 2nd innings — & then only "last ball" — & we beat them to our gr satisfaction —

When the umpire made a mistake about "overs" Meade squatted in the gravel & scooped some up & cried "Can't you take five stones in your hand, & can't you put them one after another in to the other hand according as the balls go" —

The Ennis capt, very fat, said when going in "Don't expect me to run" — "Is it a caravan you want us to get for you" cries one of his side — When he was reproached for carelessness he cried "I tell you I had my eye on the flight of that ball all the time" —

Miss Green says to Miss Grubb "Are there XI on each side? Oh dear me, on each side — What a very strong team!" —

Miss E. Franks asks Robert "why were they beaten? Why did you beat them when they had come so far"!!

Mike John says the jennet walked by the pheasant coops & all the hens began to crow — "I'm sure they thought he was an elephant" says M. J.

20th Sept[ember] — holidays ended — happily on the whole — All left, Robert — Henry — Geraldine — Frances [Beauchamp] — Yeats stayed & G. Russell arrived, & I stayed till Saturday [24th], to let them have a pleasant time together — & they argued on all subjects — symbols & Judge[110] especially — G. R. certainly I think happier than last year when in Pims, but won't allow it — He had renounced life, & now he has come into it again — In Pims he says he found five mystics "five avenues into eternity" — They went into Lydicaun Castle & saw visions of a man in armour & a black pig & a tall woman & a black man — AE saw all these — Yeats some only — We drove to Chevy they liked the boat & roaming in the woods — Very sorry to leave them & Ireland on

---

[110] William Quan Judge (1851–96), co-founder of the Theosophical Society with Madame Blavatsky and Col. H. S. Olcott. After Blavatsky's death in 1891, Judge vied with Annie Besant for leadership of the organization, producing messages allegedly sent by Tibetan mahatmas in support of his plans. Charges of fraud followed but he refused to allow authentication of the messages and in 1895 formed a breakaway organization, the American Theosophists, which he headed. AE and the Dublin Lodge professed loyalty to Judge, in contrast to WBY, who suspected Judge of fraud.

Sep[tember] 24 — To London to 3 Savile Row —

26 — To Venice with Enid arrived 29th —

In London she told me Sir George Gray had married long ago, & soon afterwards, making a coastal voyage, he found his wife playing some pranks — So he made the Capt put back to the last port, & left his bride there — He never saw her till forty years later, when some friend persuaded him to receive her — & they were together again for a short time — & a year ago she died — & he has now "put back to the last port" & rejoined her[111] —

30th — Old Curtis[112] says Browning told him the reason he & Alfred Austin disliked one another — so that he makes "sauce tin" rhyme with Austin in some poem — is that long ago at a riding school they both attended there was a young lady who Austin was making up to — & when she snubbed him as she did, he got it in his head then quite erroneously that it was through Browning's interference & never forgave him[113] — Curtis once asked Browning what he did if an idea came to him at night, if he got up & wrote it down — But he said no, he wrote poetry for a couple of hours every morning & at no other time — He had written "Childe Roland" in one morning at a time when he had resolved to write a lyric every day — but this resolve he failed to keep.

3rd [October] — Strongs to lunch — He is librarian of H[ouse] of Lords[114] — says it was in gr disorder & the Lords don't read much but Ld. Acton comes sometimes to consult a cyclopedia which is not to be found at Cambridge — Thinks J. F. Taylor very brilliant & has recommended him to Lord A. to write on Philip IV[115] — A gr admirer also of John O'Leary — thinks it a privilege

[111] Sir George Gray (1812–20 September 1898), Governor of New Zealand 1846–54, 1861–67, of the Cape of Good Hope 1854–61, and Premier of New Zealand 1877–91. His wife Eliza, née Spencer, with whom he was reconciled for some eighteen months after an estrangement of more than thirty years, died within a fortnight of him.

[112] Daniel Curtis (1825–1908), a Bostonian who had settled in Venice with his wife Ariana, née Wormeley (1833–1922), in the early 1880s, and became close friends with Browning in his last years. The couple, who jointly authored a play The Spirit of Seventy-Six, published in 1864, were hosts to most of the visiting British and American literary and social figures of the period.

[113] Browning's antipathy towards Alfred Austin, fueled by Austin's repeated attacks on both his poetry and his supposed snobbery, simmered for many years before finding a crude outlet in his poem "Of Pacchiarotto and How He Worked in Distemper" published in 1876. Lines 533–34 of the poem read: "'Dwarfs are saucy,' says Dickens: so, sauced in / Your own sauce, . . . *." The asterisk is keyed to a footnote which reinforces the stress on Austin's diminutive stature: "Who would be satirical / On a thing so very small." In another poem of the period, Browning rather more elliptically compares Austin's poetry to flatulence.

[114] Sanford Arthur Strong (1863–1904), Professor of Arabic at University College London and Librarian to the House of Lords. Married Eugenie Sellers 1897.

[115] Neither Taylor nor Acton subsequently published in book form on Philip IV.

to know him, & says he lives for the ideal — Thinks the Trinity College body a very brilliant one — but that they live "on board ship & have no current of communication with the country" —

Oct[ober] 5 — Mr. Curtis says Mrs. Strong told him that once when she was receiving at Rome, a good many strangers, half known & unknown as usual "Mr. Alfred Austin" was announced — & she greeted him with "Very glad to see you — are you a son of Miss Jane Aus*tin*?"

Mr. Strong says Sir Frederic Leighton fulfilled the dream of a tobacconist's apprentice — velveteen — curls — & all the rest of it — And that like Royalty (as observed at Chatsworth) he regulated the number of fingers given in a handshake, sometimes bringing them down to one!

Strong says Ld. Bowen's definition of metaphysics was "a blind man in a dark room looking for a black hat that isn't there"[116] —

13th Oct[ober] — A gala day — All Venice decorated — King & Queen came to see Emperor & Empress of Germany off — The processions passed this house — The Queen looked handsome & dignified, tho' very stout & her hair new dyed bright gold — The Emperor fat too, but pleasant face — recognised Lady Layard in the balcony & waved his hand & touched his cap two or three times — The Empress plain & dowdy, a haus frau — with hideous black hat — All so amiable to each other, the Emperor carrying the Queen's parasol as they came down the side of the vessel, one wonders if they will ever be at each other's throats — The King they say still devoted to the lady he spent his wedding night with, & has never been able to bear the Queen, tho' he admires her & attributes all he has of popularity to her[117] —

Taxes very high — Mrs. Eden says it is a charity to take a little packet of salt to a poor person — it costs so much they don't eat enough of it, & madness is sometimes the result — Coffee also very dear, & sugar — & petroleum, a pint of which costs as much as a qt in England — And the conscription takes all young men away for at least a year — & sometimes when they come back there is no place for them in their old workshop — & they suffer distress for a time —

Mme. Canevaro, at the Monday ev reception gets up as if to go, but it is only to put one leg under her, & she sits down again —

[116] Charles Synge Bowen (1835–1894), eminent Mayo–born lawyer who spent almost all of his career in England. Created a life peer in 1893 as Baron Bowen of Colwood.

[117] The German Emperor and Empress arrived in Venice to embark for Constantinople on 13 October 1898. Hosted by King Umberto I (1844–1900) of Italy, and his wife Margherita (d.1926), they were rowed along the Grand Canal to a public farewell at St. Mark's.

Oct[ober] 28 — Cortelazzo[118] met us at the station with a hired carriage, not the brougham lined with blue satin he had once bought at Milan — He drove us about the town[119] to see the theatre built by Palladio after Greek models — The town itself is after the Venetian model, with a little Piazza & Piazetta of the same shape but not the same size — & with pillars with St. Theodore & St. ____ as at Venice — even an imitation bridge of sighs from the old heavily grated prison — Many of the house[s] are of the beautiful Renaissance work of Palladio — their beautiful <?porticoes> remain in the mind — Poultry is being sold in the streets, & wooden soled shoes for the winter, & pottery of bold designs & vivid colours, sold for centimes ~~at the~~ for they are made here — We went into a little old fashioned shop where one sees at first nothing but wooden cupboards & shelves, & a few ecclesiastical parasols — Beautiful silks are to be had here, made at Vicenza — The owner shows us one of splendid crimson & one crimson on a yellow ground & gold & yellow on a white ground, & then some black, covered with flowers — "I have made none of that for 60 years" he says "& it is so beautiful I would not like to part with it now, except to so conspicuous a person as the Signora — Eccelenza" — After lunch at the inn, excellent soup with pasta & chicken cutlets, & grapes & Val____ wine, we go to Cortelazzo's own house for coffee, his town house, a large red one, simply furnished, but in a glass case are the few pieces of his own workmanship he still keeps by him — very few, for his working days are over now, & the masterpieces of his youth have found a home in other countries — in Russia — in Germany — in England, where they are to be found in the possession {collections} of Lord Wimborne, of the Duke of Westminster, of Sir W. Drake. I myself have a bacillus & a vase —

Then we drive through lanes that would look English with thin hedges of hornbeam & hazel, garlanded with traveller's joy, but for the cypresses that stand here there in groups, & the vineyards that the hedges enclose. Cortelazzo takes us to his own villa, the joy of his heart — It is in a garden full of chrysanthemums coming into flower & sweet scented verbena, & behind it are vines & drying bundles of maize — It is covered with frescos, bold renaissance designs — His own portrait, life size, appears at one side, & in front portraits of Sir Henry & of Lady Layard — There is an inscription in the centre, "No prophet has honour in his own country" & under it "Se c'é un Dio, Layard é il mio"[120] — The sitting room has photographs round the walls of his works — & a table cloth formed of match box covers fitted together — In the kitchen, with its copper pots & wide raised hearth, is a tiny working bench where some of his later work has been done — ~~He tells me~~ I ask him which

---

[118] Antonio Cortelazzo (1820–1903), artist and designer. First met Sir Henry Layard around 1855, and rose to prominence with the help of his patronage.

[119] Vicenza.

[120] i.e. "If there is a God, Layard is mine".

of his pieces he considers the best, & he says "the first" & points to the pictures of the salver made for Sir H. Layard & tells me how he came to make it — "I was working for the antiquarians, making seals, & I got 15 c[entimes] a day, & my wife & I lived in a garret where the rain came through the roof, on to our bed at night — It was then that I came to know Layard — After he had talked with me, & I had told him I knew I could do good work if I had money to buy material to work on, I had a letter one day from Blumenthal, the banker in Venice, saying I was to come to see him for he had fifty lire lodged there for me — I thought 50 lire would not go very far, for I have to buy gold & silver to work with, and the work will take a long time, and I and my wife must eat while it is going on, & it would be better for me to keep to my work at 15 c a day — However I went to Venice & to Blumenthal's, & he came to the counter & said "Here is the money I have to pay you" — & he put down, instead of the 50 paper lire I expected, 50 gold pieces, one after another & pushed them over to me — I looked at them & he said "Why don't you take them up?" & I said "Am I mad or are you mad?" for I had never known that the 50 lire would be lire sterling — I took them at last & put them into my pocket & went to the station with my head going round & round — And when I got into the train the idea of the bacile came to me — divide it into 12, 12 signs of the Zodiac — then etc, etc — When I got I saw it all before me then — When I got home to our room my wife was there, & I put my hands in my pockets & pulled out the gold pieces & threw them down on the floor in handfuls, & then I lay down on them — My wife thought I had gone mad — and she thought so after that, for I could think of nothing but my work, the designs I had made at first did not satisfy me, & even at meals I had the plans beside me & worked at them between every mouthful — Then I set to work at the plate — Sir Hudson[121] came to see me one day, & he was astonished when he saw what I was doing & where I was doing it, for the plate I was working at was bigger than my work bench — He took a piece of charcoal then & wrote on the wall _ _ _ _

27th — Monday ev. — Hilda Montalba[122] says "I hope I do hope Dreyfus is innocent!" & I say, in hoping that, you hope that a great many are guilty[123] — & someone says to Admiral Hahn "Do you believe he is innocent" — & Hahn

[121] Sir James Hudson (1810–85), British Minister at Turin 1852–63, who had been Cortelazzo's patron, and assisted his defense in 1883 when Cortelazzo had been accused in a poisoning case.

[122] One of four artist sisters, near neighbours of Lady Layard at Palazzo Trevisan, Venice, two of whom had sculpted busts of Browning in the 1880s.

[123] Alfred Dreyfus (1859–1935), a French soldier courtmartialled and transported to Devil's Island for treason in 1894. In 1898 Emile Zola issued his famous appeal J'Accuse, which charged that Dreyfus was the victim of anti-Semitism and forgery, causing turmoil in France. Dreyfus's original conviction was overturned in June 1899, but in a retrial that September he was once again found guilty though extenuating circumstances were allowed. Finally, in 1906, the verdict was reversed. Clear documentary evidence of his innocence and a conspiracy to scapegoat him emerged in 1930. Dreyfus fought for France in WW1, winning the Legion of Honour.

shouts across his imaginary quarter deck "I believe de worst all round!" — re ghosts — Hilda Montalba says she was dining at Kensington Palace with Princess Louise[124] — & after dinner they were going up to the Princess' rooms, & she was left for a moment, & a deep voice said from below "Who is there" — She was surprised at anyone calling this out in that place, & the Princess came running out looking scared & said "Did you hear anything" — & when she told her, the Princess said "Yes others have heard it too, it is George IV".

Ach, says Hahn, "we hear sthories of ghosts, & they are got up by people that want to keep the place for shmuggling" — (Kensington Palace!)

13th [December] — Left Venice — I had grown fond of it in the end, the little bright streets & the feast of colours & sunshine — but one's mind goes asleep there —

A long tiring journey — got to London 6-00 14th[125] — Sent to War Office to ask Paul to dine & he came — He says war was very near for a time & the danger is not over yet — In the unsettled state of France some revolution will probably take place — Their secret information says the Bonapartists are very strong & they & the military party may succeed in a coup d'état, & then as their desire is to rehabilitate the army they will make a rush on London — But this they can't do before March — partly because they have just got in a lot of raw recruits & partly because of the fear of sea sickness![126] — There has been a gr row between the W[ar]. O[ffice]. & the Queen — She asked for some information which was sent — But not content with this, she got a Surgeon Genl. Taylor[127] who is in gr favour at Court, to get her the papers on the subject — He did so, & made extracts from them, giving his own side — H[er]. M[ajesty]. then wrote to Ld. Lansdowne saying the information she had recd did not agree with that recd elsewhere — upon which he went to Ld. Salisbury & declared he wd resign office if H. M. doubted his word — & the Queen had to climb down & make some sort of apology —

15 — To Harrow — found R. at his work — so didn't stay long — he is well & seems to have been doing well — thank God —

---

[124] Louise Caroline (1848–1939), Victoria's fourth daughter.

[125] Lady Layard's diary records AG's arrival in London as being on on 15 December.

[126] Suspicion of France was at its zenith amongst British officials during this period, reflecting both general Imperial anxiety over the increasing military and diplomatic power of U.S.A. and Germany, concern over relations with the Boers, and more specifically tensions provoked by French incursion into British territory in Sokoto, West Africa, in February 1898.

[127] Sir William Taylor (1843–1917), a career military surgeon who served as Principal Medical Officer of the Ashanti expedition (after which he was appointed Surgeon-General). Later served briefly as Honorary Physician to Edward VII.

16 — Lunched with Sir A. Birch, to ask if the boys wd come over which they are inclined to do — He says Sir W. Harcourt is resigning because he had no followers left but John Morley, & he is likely to drift out of politics with Gladstone's life[128] —

To see Sir F. Burton — who reproved me for having become a red hot Nationalist! & declared I had no Irish blood in my veins but I convinced him I have — both Irish & French[129] — To tea with Wilfrid Blunt — who looks very well again — hunts five days a week — but is put to bed afterwards & massaged — His secretary, Mr. Cockerell, was there part of the time — They are going to write a history of the Horse[130] — & he is writing an epic poem on the wickedness of society — & Herbert Spencer has written to beg him to write one against war & killing, an outline of which he sends him, Satan wandering about, & arguing with men — not much of an idea, but H. S's letter interesting — says that tho' an invalid since 1855 he had in (I think) '83 joined Frederic Harrison & John Morley in getting up a demonstration against bloodshed — & had permanently ruined his remaining health by the effort[131] — Mr. Blunt thinks Mr. Harcourt has resigned leadership because of the jingoism of the whole Liberal as well as Conservative party — the Liberals are worse if possible — & there is no one but Labby to say a word against it — He had written to Harcourt & had an answer "Dear Blunt, like yourself I am out of jail & rejoicing in my freedom" — He says W. H[arcourt]. is quite in earnest in his

[128] Harcourt had announced his intention to resign as Liberal leader in an open letter to John Morley on 8 December 1898. Morley followed suit, announcing his intention to resign his own seat soon after. He subsequently re-entered politics, returning to Cabinet office as Secretary of State for India 1905–10, and Lord President of the Council 1910–14. His monumental three volume biography of Gladstone was published in 1903.

[129] Though AG's Persse ancestors were overwhelmingly English Protestant settlers, she could claim some "Irish" blood via her mother's family. In *Seventy Years* and in her notes to *The Canavans*, she writes of a French great-grandmother (again on her mother's side), Frances Aigoin (given as Algoin in *Seventy Years*), whom she ascribes as the source of both her mother's stress on courtesy and her own "light-heartedness."

[130] Sydney Carlyle Cockerell (1867–1962), friend of Ruskin, and served as private secretary to William Morris and as Secretary of the Kelmscott Press in the early 1890s. Cockerell acted as Blunt's secretary for two years from November 1898, and remained his lifelong friend. Their history of the horse was not completed, though the central aim of the projected work was achieved by Blunt's daughter Judith in her book *The Authentic Arabian Horse and His Descendants* in 1945. Cockerell was subsequently Director of the Fitzwilliam Museum in Cambridge 1908–37, expanded and renovated the Museum with distinction, and was knighted in 1934.

[131] Blunt completed the poem inspired by Spencer's suggestion as *Satan Absolved* (1899), an impassioned attack on imperialism, which met with a predictably hostile reception on its publication during the Boer War. This seems to have also satisfied his plan for an epic on the wickedness of society. Herbert Spencer (1820–1903), the philosopher and social and economic theorist, had joined with Morley and Harrison in 1885 to protest British involvement in the Sudan. Spencer's disability, cardiac palpitations which afflicted him from 1853 onwards, has generally been seen as hysterical and related to his fear that his friendship with George Eliot might lead to marriage (see Gordon Haight, *George Eliot*).

Church letters[132] — He was much disgusted at the way bishops are appointed — He knew that the D[uke]. of Devonshire had recommended Page Roberts[133] for a bishopric — not that he knew him — but someone had asked him to — however, he was not appointed — When the Duke asked Ld. Salisbury why he had not done so he said "Why, that was the man who {stood against} denounced us at Walworth (?)" — he had mistaken him for Page Hopps![134] Wilfrid said "Well, that shows the Holy Spirit is looking after the Church, or it would have gone to wreck long ago with such Government".

18 — Dublin — W. Yeats to see me, he had been writing distracted letters about M[aud]. G[onne]. & something that had happened[135] — but it seems to be all for good — if marriage with her will be a good — He had begged me to come that he might talk to me — so I hurried from London[136] — We went to lunch with T. P. Gill[137] & Rolleston came later — Gill nice & quiet — but I couldn't help thinking a conversation between him & Horace Plunkett must take a long time! Yeats tried to urge Rolleston to work up the Literary Society — The "theatre" is to be joined with it to give it a lift — They are pleased with the paper I sent on "The Italian Literary Theatre"[138] & are going to have some more written — on the same movement in other countries to come out in the Express & prepare the way — I suggested to Rolleston adding Lord Bowen's "Shadow Land" to his anthology — he had not thought of it, or known Ld. B.

[132] Harcourt had begun a campaign in the Commons and in letters to *The Times* against the spread of ritualistic practices in the Church of England, and against the usurpation by the Church hierarchy of the authority residing in the Book of Common Prayer. His letters to *The Times* were reprinted in 1899 in *Lawlessness in the National Church*, and he continued to write on the subject into the new century.

[133] Rev. William Page-Roberts (1836–1928), Canon of Canterbury 1895–1907.

[134] John Page Hopps (1834–1911), Unitarian Minister and religious journalist.

[135] This was the double dream WBY describes in *Mem* pp. 131-34, which initiated his "spiritual marriage" with Maud Gonne, and after which she told him of her relationship with Millevoye. In a letter to AG on 8 December WBY had written: "Today & yesterday I have gone through a crisis that has left me worn out. MG is here & I understand everything now" (*CL1* p. 490). WBY evidently told AG about these events only in general terms, writing to her in February 1899, for instance: "of course I have not been able to tell you all, as you know" (*L* p. 312).

[136] In *Mem* p. 134, WBY would incorrectly recall AG as returning "at once" from Venice, rather than London, on receiving "an incoherent letter" from him.

[137] Thomas Patrick Gill (1858–1931). Nationalist M.P. 1885–92, but retired from politics after the fall of Parnell and the resulting split in the Irish party. Edited *The Dublin Daily Express* between July 1898 and December 1899, the period of Horace Plunkett's ownership of the paper. Was appointed Secretary of the Department of Agricultural and Technical Instruction by Plunkett after the sale of *The Express* to Lord Ardilaun in January 1900, a position he retained until her retired in 1923.

[138] An essay on D'Annunzio's play "Dream of a Spring Morning", published in *The Dublin Daily Express*, 8 April 1899, p. 3, under the title "An Italian Literary Drama".

was an Irishman[139] — Yeats gave an account of the meeting of the Pan Celtic committee — Lord Castletown in a <?ugly> lavender kid glove — suggestion made, that nothing shd be done without Ld. C.'s consent — that he shd co-opt the whole committee — etc — Hyde writes that he is not allowed to join it by his council! They are afraid of its taking money from the G[aelic]. L[eague] & the Feís people are afraid it will take money from the Feís — Gill calls the Gaelic people the Firbolgs![140] — W. dined with me — And in the evening Miss Gonne came to call! A shock to me — for instead of beauty I saw a death's head[141] — & what to say to him I knew not — She does not know I know anything so it was constrained — however we got on amicably —

[139] Rolleston's anthology *A Treasury of Irish Poetry in the English Tongue*, which he co-edited with Stopford Brooke (his father-in-law), was published in 1900, but included no poems by Bowen. AG subsequently wrote a letter published in the *All Ireland Review* 10 March 1900, p. 2, under the title "An Irish Poet", calling attention to Bowen's Irish roots.

[140] In Irish mythological accounts, the Firbolgs (lit. "Fir Bolg", either "people with big stomachs" or "bag people") were a race who gained control over Ireland in the period prior to the arrival of the Tuatha de Danann. As here, they were generally regarded as antediluvian.

[141] Maud Gonne had been "very ill" with bronchitis in Spring 1898, and as WBY reported to AG in June, a broken arm suffered in a fall from a carriage had compounded this condition, leaving her "looking pale and ill" (*L* p. 299). Her correspondence for late 1898, however, gives no indication of continued sickness. Significantly, AG was still unable to find any trace of Maud Gonne's celebrated beauty at their next meeting, though acknowledging she looked "less ill" (see diary entry for 6 March 1899).

1899

Jan[uary] 1 — 1899

No time to possess my soul since I last wrote — My Monday in Dublin busy —
Yeats took me to see Hughes the sculptor,[1] & the portrait of Parnell just given
to the N[ational]. Gallery — And then we went to the Gaelic League to see
Miss Borthwick, who has just resigned, worn out with work — And to Oldham
at the Contemporary Club — a waxwork manner, pulled by strings &
mechanical voice — but Y. says a good & disinterested man — And Gill came
to tea, very long winded — And at dinner I had Yeats & AE & "John Eglinton"[2]
a nice quiet young fellow, dragged away from his tea by the rushing Yeats —
Very tired & headache — & had to pack after they left — & leave at 6 next
morning — R. missed the train so got home alone, but he turned up later, well
& cheery — A busy time, Xmas — & the day after came Arthur & Katy [Persse]
& Col. Woods & Ione[3] & Frank to shoot — Dr. Moran & Mr. Bagot as day boys
— A frightful storm the first day & the birds would not rise, & 2 days total 42
pheasants, 47 cock — However party went off well, & it is my only chance of
showing a little civility to my relatives — The week wound up with a hockey
tea in Gort — troublesome, but successful — I looked in at the Workhouse
to see the infirmary old men who I had missed on Xmas day — & brought tea
& sugar to the infirmary old women — One said "Is is the truth you are telling,
for I would not like you to be making a jest" — & we had to give her the lb.

[1] John Hughes (1864–1941), a fellow student of AE and WBY in the early 1880s at the
Metropolitan School of Art in Dublin, where he later taught until 1902. He exhibited work at
the Royal Academy in the 1890s but left for Paris in 1902, where he eventually abandoned his
work in discouragement. AE had recently reviewed his work in *The New Ireland Review*, November
1898.

[2] John Eglinton, pseudonym of William Kirkpatrick Magee (1868–1961). A classmate of
WBY at school, and a co-member of the Dublin Theosophical Society with his close friend AE.
Active in literary circles as an essayist, and acted as reseacher for George Moore during the
novelist's Dublin years. Worked at the National Library of Ireland 1895–1921.

[3] Ione Woods, née Persse, Major William Norton Persse's youngest daughter, and her
husband Col. Adrien Woods.

tin, & she held & fondled it in her lap —

A paragraph has got into the papers that Lady Gregory is to be elected not only a guardian, but Chairman of the board![4] I laughed at the idea, but Frank says if offered election I should accept —

Ev[ening] before last at dinner R. asked me when the next gen[era]l elections wd be — I said one could not tell, but the Conservatives seem not to be losing ground & may last their full seven years — "& perhaps the election won't come until you are able to support, as I hope, the Liberal side?" — He grew a little red & said "I would not do that — They will never spend as much money on the navy as the Conservatives" — I said Ld. Rosebery was as Imperialist as anyone cd be & so was Chamberlain, & Frances[5] being there we let the matter drop — This is rather an epoch, for he has assented to my opinions until now — He must work out his own salvation & anyhow I think he will always be fond of Ireland & the people —

The year has brought no great sorrow for poor Gerald's death has long been discounted by our anxieties — Mr. Bowen has written me, voluntarily, a very nice letter about R. — speaking of the improvement he notices in him — We are still on good terms with our people — The "Letter Box" has been a quite sufficient success, it was an anxiety at the beginning of the year — & my XIXth Century "Ireland" has won me good words also[6] — & I have advanced in Irish, & I hope in power of thought — & I have been able to help some — chiefly W. Y. on their way — His friendship has been a great good to me — & that of AE also & has lead me to think less of the things that are seen & more of those that are unseen — My hopes for this year are chiefly connected with R.'s last terms at Harrow & first at Oxford — He received the Communion with me last Sunday —

Jan[uary] 9 — '99

Another busy week — Monday came Tony & Wyndham [Birch] — Keen as ever after sport & making the house very cheery for R. — Wed came Dr. Hyde & Miss Borthwick[7] — & I had a long visit from W. S[hawe].Taylor — Thursday, took lunch to the boys, shooting at Inchy — & in the afternoon had a meeting at Kiltartan school — Dr. Fahey in the chair — he made a speech in Irish, with

4 "We understand that the people of the electoral district of the Gort Union, where Lady Gregory resides, intend putting her name forward as a guardian for that division, and should she be elected it is not unlikely she will be chosen Chairman of the Union. Lady Gregory is an admirable woman of business" *Tuam Herald* 17 December 1898, p. 4.

5 Frances Morris (d.1952), Martin's sister, who became a Carmelite nun in 1900.

6 "Ireland Real and Ideal" *Nineteenth Century* November 1898, pp. 769–82.

7 Hyde and Norma Borthwick were at Coole 4–11 January 1899.

a very English accent & condescending manner — then one in English in
which he alluded to the example of "that young gentleman who though
acquainted with the languages of Athens & Rome as well as modern ones was
studying Irish, & who he hoped wd grow up 'more Irish than the Irish
themselves'" — Dr. Hyde made a very eloquent speech in Irish, not that I cd
understand it, but it roused the people — then he made one in English in
which he drew attention to the inferiority of the vocabulary of the English
peasant to that of the Irish — all very good except that he came a little too near
what may be taken for politics in saying "Let the English go their road & let
us go ours — & God forbid their road should ever be our road" — A branch
of the League was formed, & Miss B[orthwick]. is to start classes[8] —

Friday, Xmas tree — very hard work, a holy day — & the boys went off to Tillyra
& took the Mikes, so I cd get no helper but Marty — had to set up Punch &
Judy show — & when I proposed to decorate tree heard it was still in the
woods! However John Rourke appeared & dug up a small silver, to be planted
again — A lot of children, over 100, more than usual at Xmas — however
provisions & presents held out, the latter chiefly Italian pottery I had brought
home — Punch & Judy a gr success — first Wyn[dham] & Frances did it, &
then Dr. Hyde & Miss B. — in Irish, & this brought down the house — Dr. H.
chastising the baby much applauded, the children had probably themselves
been chastised in the same words! He made the "pilér" speak in English, &
then abused him in Irish, & said the paisdin had fallen out of the window by
himself! A success on the whole but very tiring[9] — 25 in the breakfast room
to tea! A[rch]. D[eacon]. Daly etc — Old Diveney says "that gentleman has
very good Irish, only his tongue is a little hard & sharp because he's Englified
— but I am but a common labourer, & so I speak flat".

Sat[urday] — the boys to the bogs, but didn't get much, but R. & Dr. H. got
a pheasant & 2 cock when they got back.

Sunday, to church, very stormy — After lunch I took Dr. H. across the lake to
Fahy's & left him there but he didn't get much except my story of Usheen &
says mine was just as good in English, & very accurate — Fahy says "Father
Fahey has good Irish but he's that talented the people can't well understand
it" — He also says they can't understand more than half what he says in
English — Miss Borthwick found about 60 at Mrs. Hanlon's — so couldn't
teach — but they had songs etc — (On Kilmacduagh bog Dr. Hyde went into
a house to change his boots & conversed with an old woman who hadn't much

[8] An anonymous report of this meeting, almost certainly written by AG, was published in
Fainne an Lae under the title "The West Awake", 21 January 1899, p. 19.

[9] In *Poets and Dreamers* (p. 136), AG would claim this Punch and Judy show as "the beginning
of modern Irish drama". The "pilér" is the policeman, the "paisdin [páistín]" the baby.

English, not having any "new learnments" — when she heard he was from Mayo she laughed very much & repeated a line of a song to the effect "There'll be boots on me yet says the man from the c[oun]ty Mayo!")

Sunday ev[ening] — Old Power the basket maker to be cross-examined, but without much result — An irrelevant story of a beggar who went to Castle Daly to ask for alms & Old James Daly[10] gave him a halfpenny & said "that's for my father & mother's soul" — & the beggar added another halfpenny to it & laid it down on the step & said "There's a halfpenny for my father's soul & a halfpenny for my mother's, & I wouldn't go to the meanness of putting them both in one" —

11th — Dr. Hyde just gone — Power came again, & gave him some information & a tolerably good song — has never written one himself because "the measuration of verses is a very ticklish thing" — I kept old "Cracked Mary" for him, but she wd only sing "Shule Agra"[11] over & over again, but with quite the sound of the spinning wheel — & some English ones such as
"I wish you were dead my dear old man
I wish you were dead & the sod on your head
And I'd marry poor Jack the journeyman —
There's broth in the pot for you old man
There's broth for me & cabbage for you
& beef for Jack the journeyman"[12] —

Tony Hynes came last night & Dr. H. got some songs from him — the best was by Raftery "Mary Hynes of Ballylee" — & there was "Mary Brown" — & "Raftery & Death" too long to be all taken down[13] — Miss Borthwick had 30 young men at her class — & they got thro' 50 pages! — Wyn[dham] left — the others shot the bogs & got a nice mixed bag —

[10] James Peter Daly (1808–81), AG's father's contemporary, whose parents had both died in the 1840s.

[11] "Siubhal aghradh" ("Walk beloved"), a Gaelic song probably dating from the Jacobite period.

[12] As WBY acknowledged in his notes to *The Pot of Broth*, Cracked Mary's song provided the "words and the air of 'There's Broth in the Pot'" in the play (*Variorum Plays* p. 254, and see Richard Finneran *Editing Yeats's Poems: A Reconsideration* p. 188, for a discussion of the source of the ballad). Cracked Mary also later served as an inspiration for WBY's "Crazy Jane".

[13] In his *Songs Ascribed to Raftery* (1903), the first published collection of work by the blind Gaelic poet Anthony Raftery (c.1784–1835), Hyde credits "Mr. Thomas Hynes, of Cilltartan" a relative of the Mary Hynes of Raftery's song, for giving him versions of "Mary Hynes" and "Raftery and the Death." The volume is dedicated to AG, with a verse praising her as a patron of poets and saviour of Raftery's fame, and credits her with locating an important manuscript volume from which he took versions of 17 Raftery songs. This was not the volume she traced in 1897 (see p. 154 n. 145), but one she obtained near Raftery's birthplace in December 1899 (see p. 223).

Jan[uary] 29 — The holidays over — all gone — "fada an lá gan Cloinne Uisnig"[14] — I went to Moyne for a couple of days — R. W[aithman]. much taken up with his incubator — chickens expected but not arriving — probably because the eggs were handled too much — but R. W. says because when he was ill he sent a maid down several times a day to report on the thermometer, & she always said it hadn't moved — When he got well, it was several degrees too low — He reproached her but she said "Sure the black figures never moved but stopped in the same place" — Back here alone — The workmen have made a bond only to speak Irish when together — & John Rourke knows the lst book by heart & has sent for the 2nd — & Mike says "there isn't a child you'll meet in the road now but will say 'God save you' in Irish".

30 — At the convent, Sister Frances tells me that last year £2 was sent for the poor, after the appeal, with a letter — written in a strange language — They puzzled over it & thought the signature was a Turkish one, so the Rev[erend] Mother thought it must be a gift from the Sultan, sent thro' the Turkish Ambassador in Paris, & wrote to thank the latter — His secretary wrote back to say H[is]. E[xcellency]. knew nothing of it — Then they took the letter to Dr. Fahey, who burst out laughing — for it was written in Irish![15] They have begun teaching the little boys their prayers in Irish —

Yesterday at Patsy Riley's I was trying for legends of Usheen & on mentioning Tir nan Og the old woman, sitting up straight & almost sightless by the fire said "Tir na-n-Og — that is not far from any of us" — And she told how a tall thin stranger had sat next her at Lebane chapel, & when she asked where he came from he said "From Tir na-n-Og — and that is near to where you live" — "And I think" she says "I had seen him before"[16] —

Feb[ruary] 12 — A few days at Clonodfoy — blank, except some increase of family kindliness for I think Fanny enjoyed my visit — Then to London — rough & tiring — The first week as always rather trying — getting into decent clothes — & leaving cards — & feeling one is not particularly wanted in the big city — however I keep my purpose in mind, Robert's good — & have been

---

[14] "Long is the day without the sons of Usnach." The quotation is from Deirdre's lament after the killing of Naoise, Ainnle and Ardan in the Tain bo Cuailgné (The Cattle Raid of Cooley), the central tale of the Cuchulain sagas, which AG would later translate and include in *Cuchulain of Muirthemne.* Her familiarity with the Gaelic text at this early point is indicative of her efforts with both the language and its literature, and lends considerable weight to her claim to have been considering translating the Tain for some time prior to broaching the subject to WBY in November 1900 (see p. 290).

[15] This anecdote is reported in *An Claidheamh Soluis* ["The Sword of Light"] 29 July 1899, p. 312, in an editorial column either written or inspired by AG.

[16] WBY included this anecdote in his 1899 article "The Literary Movement in Ireland" *UP*2 p. 191. Tir-na-n-Og—"The Country of the Young"—was the paradise of pre-Christian Irish mythology.

kept in mind of it by various things — E. Martyn said the other day "You are right to go to London — you have nice friends there — I never had any friends there" — & I don't want R. to have to say that — Then, the first ev I went to Lady Arthur Russell's, & Conrad was there, from Balliol, & said he wd look out for R. — and one evening I was at tea with Mrs. Dugdale & her boy came in, from <?school>, so different coming into *home* from the day's cramming from poor Paul as I remember him in his Manchester St. lodging — so I feel encouraged to keep a sort of *milieu* for R. —

Yeats in Paris "following after shadows" & depressed — G. Moore came yesterday — very much pleased with his own "Esther Waters" which he has been reading again & is much struck with —

12th — To Westminster Abbey — To lunch Haliburtons — Ev[ening] Ed. Martyn, J. B. Yeats & Jack B. Yeats to dinner —

13th — Dinner & play with E. Martyn — "The Ambassador"[17] —

14th — To Harrow — Had a talk with Mr. Bowen — He is quite enthusiastic about the improvement in R. — so strong & trustworthy, has "put away childish things" — He, with some awkwardness lest I should think him interested, suggested that he should stay another year at Harrow — The advantage wd be that he will be head of the house, & the authority & responsibility good for his character — The drawback wd be, that if he shd grow tired of the school, he wd lose interest in getting on —

19th — Pretty well got thro' clothes & card leaving — On Friday Willie Yeats came back from Paris & came to dine — poor boy with cough & remains of influenza — & depressed by his time in Paris — agrees altogether with my view that he was not on his own ground there, & she was on hers — & so he lost rather than gained ground — I am afraid she is playing with him, from selfishness — & vanity[18] —

Saturday, I went to Bedford Park to call on the Yeatses & found Edward

[17] *The Ambassador*, a four act comedy by "John Oliver Hobbes" (Mrs. Pearl Craigie), which ran for 160 performances at St. James's Theatre 1898–99.

[18] WBY had gone to Paris on 31 January specifically to propose to Maud Gonne, who refused him, as she had done once before in 1891. Despite her caustic focus on Maud Gonne, and her implication that she had advised WBY against leaving his "own ground", it was apparently AG who had urged him to try and bring matters to a head. WBY would recalls her telling him soon after the double dream "not to leave Maud Gonne till I had her promise of marriage" (*Mem* p. 134). In a letter to Lady Layard *c.* 17 February, AG had written that Yeats was "still, I am afraid in a state of uncertainty, & I begin to feel about the lady as a man at Coole did about his step mother 'I don't wish her any harm, but God is unjust if she dies a quiet death!'" (Berg).

Martyn sitting for his portrait, which he is giving me — Mr. Yeats insisted on Miss Mitchell[19] singing to him while the work went on, to steady his countenance — I think it turned out well — I dined at the Lovelaces — sat between Strachey editor of the Spectator & "Mr. Fortescue" — who I happily asked if he was related to the writer of "The History of a Red Deer" — & found it was he himself[20] — I had heard Mrs. Severn say Ruskin was delighted with it[21] — & this much pleased him, as he is a disciple of his — Strachey a little too much the superior person, condescending to men of low estate — Is always glad when the Irish upper classes join in a movement, for it shows it is over — Is of course against the Irish language & in favour of a tunnel — I talked to Lecky afterwards, very down on Yeats for removing the chairs set for the Viceregal party at Miss Stokes's lecture at the Lit. Society[22] — I made the best defence I could, that they only recognised intellect, not patronage etc — but he was unconvinced & murmured 'silly' at intervals — Lady Lyttelton & Lord Welby[23] also there — & I drove Wilfrid Blunt home — He is now enjoying society & giving a series of dinners —

In the morning I went to the War Office to see Paul about R. staying on at Harrow — I am a good deal perplexed — E. Martyn very decidedly against it — "If he is ready for Oxford let him go there, & begin his work early" —

19th — To Westminster Abbey — Fog — so no one came during the day — Ev dinner here, Ed. Martyn — W. B. Yeats — Horace Plunkett, Mrs. Emery, Mrs. Dugdale — Pleasant talk, & Mrs. Emery read E. Bronte's "Remembrance" & a poem of AE's — & Yeats read from the "Love Songs of Connaught"[24] — H. Plunkett quite for the language movement now — I think AE, of whom he speaks with gr enthusiasm, has inspired him with the idea of a spiritual

[19] Susan Langstaff Mitchell (1866–1926), poet and satirist. Assistant Editor to AE on *The Irish Homestead* and subsequently *The Irish Statesman*. She lived with the Yeats family at Bedford Park from late 1897 to late 1899 as a paying guest and companion to Lily Yeats. Her 1916 volume *George Moore* treated the novelist to a satirical blast widely enjoyed in the wake of *Hail and Farewell*.

[20] John William Fortescue (1859–1933), author of the children's book *The History of A Red Deer* (1897).

[21] Joan Severn, née Agnew (1846–1924), was a cousin of author and art critic John Ruskin (1819–1900), and served as his housekeeper and companion in his later years, assuming considerable censorial powers over his social life and correspondence in the process. She was the model for Joanna in *Praeterita*, and, along with her husband, was Ruskin's heir and literary executor.

[22] WBY reviewed Margaret Stokes's lecture to the National Literary Society on "High Crosses of Ireland" on 14 January 1899 in *The Dublin Daily Express* (*UP2* pp. 142–45). He had insisted just prior to the lecture that no special seating be provided for Lady Betty Balfour and her party.

[23] Reginald Earle Welby (1832–1915), 1st Baron Welby, Permanent Secretary to the Treasury 1885–94.

[24] Douglas Hyde's influential 1893 collection of traditional Gaelic poems with his accompanying idiomatic translations. For WBY's admiring review of the volume, for him Hyde's greatest achievement, see *UP1* pp. 292–95.

nationality — He says my article has been a immense help to him, especially in America, where it had been a good deal read[25] — I teased him about his bull, that the best organizer was "an ex-firebrand who has sown his wild oats" — he says AE promised to do a picture for the [Irish] Homestead of the firebrand sowing wild oats & the crop that resulted! He told a story of Mahaffy complaining that he had once been birched for speaking the truth, & another Professor of T[rinity]. C[ollege]. D[ublin]., I forget who, squashed him by saying "Well, you must confess it was very efficacious!" — Mrs. Dugdale mentioned Gladstone's beautiful oratory, that once when he spoke of finance he said "a loan" — with such a pathetic inflection that it sounded like solitude! Mrs. Dugdale said she had left her sons as long as possible at Eton because they were so happy there, but they are not allowed to stay after 19 —

20th — Lunched with Florence Burke,[26] re Irish Industries, but found her very vague, not knowing anything about Lady Fingall's stall — Looked at Kensington lithographs —

21 — Martin Morris in the morning, bringing back Lord Talbot's letters which Ld. M. had borrowed for Lady Londonderry — She was much interested in them, & wondered if I had read all the family secrets & scandals — I hope she gives me credit for discretion in not publishing them! Jack Yeats exhibition, sketches of West of Ireland — very good — I bought "The Returned American" — rather sorry to part with my £5-5/- but had St. James's advice in my ear[27] — Stayed in in the evening, expecting Willie Peel to talk about R. but he didn't turn up —

22 — Tired — but wrote an "appreciation" of Jack Yeats's sketches & sent it to the Express — hoping it may be an advt[28] — Lady Lyall called, & I proposed driving with her, & quite enjoyed being off my feet — we went finally to Lady Clay's — a stupid afternoon party — & Lady Simeon drove me part of the way home from there — so I had quite a time of luxury — Dined Horace Plunkett's — with Yeats, E. Martyn — G. Moore — Florence Burke — Bernard Holland, Lord Lytton & Lady Betty Balfour[29] — very pleasant — Lady Betty gushing "so pleased to meet me" etc — G. Moore on very good behaviour,

[25] "Ireland Real and Ideal" (see p. 199 n. 6).

[26] Lady Fingall's sister (see p. 139 n. 85). She married Nevill Geary in 1906.

[27] *James* 2.8: "Love thy neighbour as thyself." AG evidently stepped up her efforts to subsidize Jack Yeats's career considerably during this period, as in a letter of May 1899 John Butler Yeats acknowledges her purchasing a total of £60 of Jack's work (Berg). She also wrote to numerous connections, urging them to buy Jack Yeats's work and to visit his exhibition "Sketches of Life in the West of Ireland," at the Walker Art Gallery, London.

[28] "Ireland in Bond Street" (signed G) *Dublin Daily Express* 25 February, p. 5.

[29] Victor Bulwer-Lytton (1876–1947), 2nd Earl Lytton, Lady Balfour's younger brother. Plunkett was a close friend of the Balfours, and had recruited Lady Balfour as an activist for the co-operative movement.

making himself agreeable to H. Plunkett — Bernard Holland rather out of touch, pressing about a selection from Crabbe he thinks of doing[30] — Ld. Lytton charming & boyish — Yeats of course the centre of all — E. M. very chirpy in spite of his fasting dinner[31] — Yeats confesses he has *lost* my MS of "Italian Literary Drama" — really rather a trial — for I have no fair copy — & my interest in it having waned it will be hard work writing it again —

23 — Wrote about Gort work to Ly Fingall & about Oxford to R. — & then started my "Spring Morning Dream" again — & found I got on quicker than I expected, got thro' by 3 — (no time for lunch) took it to be typed — called for it at 5 & corrected & got it off to Gill in time — so can put it from my mind — Called on Lady Geary — poor thing, sitting in a scruffy lodging, with some dry books laid out beside her — Nevill is not well, suffers from ulcerated feet, & she hopes he will soon come home — I hope I shan't live to see Robert in exile for want of money, one wd be tempted to do away with oneself & leave the jointure free — Dined John Murrays, sat between Buckle, Editor of the Times & Ld. Eustace Cecil[32] — Buckle has been *materialised* by the Times — I remember his advent as editor, slight & eager & intellectual — Now he is, in appearance at least, heavy & vulgar — I, as usual thinking if there was any friend I cd give a lift to, cried up Horace Plunkett's work — & he seemed surprised & said he had been told it [is] "mostly talk" — He probably heard this from Ld. Morris — who can't forgive H. P. for some disparaging remarks on Martin when he stood for Galway[33] — Ld. Eustace Cecil was charming, knew Wm. so well when they were in Parliament together, & sometimes asked news of me from Sir A. Birch — Says, what I never knew, that Ld. Clanricarde was at Harrow & had to leave for an unmentionable offence — He thought Harrow bad in that way & in bullying when he was there, & sent his sons to Eton — but does not think it any better — "Anthony Hope" [Hawkins] & Ld. Balfour & the Hallam Murrays & Sir Bartle Frere & the George Goughs[34] also there — a very cheery evening, one does enjoy good society once in a way & I feel very hopeful now about giving R. a good start — & then I can retire in peace —

[30] Holland's selection of poems by George Crabbe (1754–1832) was published the following year.

[31] Lent had just begun.

[32] Eustace Brownlow Cecil (1834–1921), M.P. 1865–85, brother of the Prime Minister, Lord Salisbury, and father of Evelyn Cecil.

[33] Martin Morris had stood unsuccessfully for Galway City in 1895, but subsequently won the seat in 1900 (see p. 282 n. 240). Ironically, when Morris's succession to his father's peerage left the seat vacant, Plunkett himself was nominated as the Unionist candidate. With minimal support from Morris, and facing a reunited Nationalist constituency eager to elect a veteran of the Boer "Irish" brigades, Plunkett, who needed police protection during the campaign, polled less than 500 votes in what would prove his final effort to return to politics.

[34] George Gough and his wife Hilda, née Moffatt.

24 — Called on Lady Lindsay & met there Ly. Reay & Lady Shrewsbury, who asked me to let her have Ld. Talbot's letters to see, which Ly. Londonderry has returned — She told me some curious things about him — that when Lady Talbot died he did not like to tell the children it was in consequence of her confinement, so said "it was from eating too much peppermint" — & that not many years ago Gerald Talbot told her "his mother had died through eating too much peppermint" having believed this all through his long life! Also she says that Lord Ingestre's body was not recovered for a long time after his death — but this was not told to Lord Talbot — & he sent one of the other sons to bring the body home, & he had to bring an empty coffin, which was interred with gr solemnity at Ingestre — When the body was found afterwards it was buried at Vienna[35] — went on to Lady Haliburtons — Lady Dorothy came in, very smart — having entertained the Prince at lunch — He had proposed himself on short notice — wanted Mrs. Brown Potter[36] & others asked to meet him — She got her, but Lord Onslow[37] who he wanted could not be found — "And what did you give him to eat?" said Lady H. — "Oh, there was the difficulty — those wretched servants! — I ordered what he was sure to like, boiled beef, & chickens, & bacon & beans, & marrow bones — but I told them to bring up the beef & chickens together — & they thought they knew best & brought the beef first — & he said "No, I am going to have chicken" & he had to wait till it came — Then he always likes bacon & beans, that I always have for him, tho' of course there are only flageolets to be had now, but he likes them on separate dishes — & that wretched cook squashed them all on to the same dish" — However he had stayed from 10 to 2 [p.m.] to 1/4 past 4 [p.m.] — so must have enjoyed himself — Teck[38] is now quite out of his mind, & will only wear a blanket, which is awkward for visitors — as it hangs loose —

Dined Smith Elders — Canon Page-Roberts, a nice old man — Humphrey Wards — Madeline Shaw Lefevre — Miss Millais,[39] Ld. Robert Cecil[40] — Mr.

[35] Lady Talbot, née Frances Lambart (b.1782), wife of Charles Talbot (1777–1849), 2nd Earl Talbot, died in 1819 shortly after bearing their ninth son, Gerald (1819–85). Charles Thomas Talbot (1802–26), Viscount Ingestre, their oldest son, was killed in an accident in Vienna. AG had included a letter to Under-Secretary Gregory from Lord Talbot (who was Lord Lieutenant of Ireland 1817–21), giving an apparently spurious account of the death, in *Mr. Gregory's Letter-Box* p. 183.

[36] Cora Urquhart Potter (1858-1936), an actress.

[37] William Onslow (1853–1911), 4th Earl.

[38] Frances Paul Alexander (1837–1900), *cr.* Prince of Teck 1863, and married Mary (1833–97), daughter of the 1st Duke of Cambridge (Queen Victoria's uncle) in 1866. Their daughter (Victoria) Mary (Augusta Louisa) was later Queen as wife of George V.

[39] Probably Mary Millais (b.1860), daughter of Sir John Everett Millais, painter and President of the Royal Academy 1896. Millais's wife Euphemia was Albert Gray's sister.

[40] Edgar Robert Gascoyne Cecil (1864–1958), third son of Prime Minister Salisbury. M.P. 1906–23, Lord Privy Seal 1923–24, and created Lord Cecil of Chelwood 1923.

Scott Gatty was next me[41] — Smith took me in — Pleasant enough — but not a patch on Murrays dinners — & the house, one they have not long had, is furnished rather in modern art fashion — Smith says John Morley took up Parnell's life in Bain's shop & looked at a page or two & said "Three lies already" & put it down.[42]

25 — A telegram from Robert saying there was no football, & that he was expecting me — Paul came in, very strong against R. putting off his start in life — but I had already pretty well made up my mind on the subject — He is rather of opinion that a H. of Commons clerkship wd be good, if he thinks of politics afterwards — Then Willy Peel came in, stronger still — "such nonsense — I know the old game — don't hear of such a thing — I left Harrow at 17, & I had learned all then they were likely to teach me" — He is for Foreign Office, says a chap with brains can make his way there very well — & that he wd never stand the H. of C. clerks' life — however there is plenty of time to think of that — So went to Harrow, & told R. my decision, which, as ever, he took very well — Mr. Bowen not quite so gracious — much taken aback — & foolishly began arguing that there wd be plenty of time to cram for the H[ome]. O[ffice]. & that he cd never attempt the F. O. without living abroad for a couple of years — & we parted rather constrainedly — R. well & cheery — & likes Dr. Woods[43] so far — got books from Mudie's, among them Grant Duff's Indian Diaries, & find several extracts from my agreeable conversation! & some rather feeble jokes[44] — Yeats came to dine — His article again not in the Fortnightly! He has got a little loan from his uncle,[45] & says that last Wednesday he had only 2/6-. Then he was late dressing for dinner because his landlady's daughter was doing up his room — & to his grief had to take a hansom to H. Plunkett's — which left him with 6d — So he has not been going about lest he shd want a cup of tea — Poor boy, I wish all his troubles sat as lightly on him as this — My little puff of Jack Yeats's exhibition in the Express —

[41] Alfred Scott–Gatty (1847–1918), York Herald of the College of Arms.

[42] *The Life of Charles Stewart Parnell, 1846–1891* by Barry O'Brien, had just been published by Smith Elder.

[43] His House Master and classics teacher at Harrow.

[44] *Notes From a Diary 1881–1886* which had just been published (in two volumes) by John Murray. Vol.2 pp. 175–77 records Grant Duff's first meeting with AG, in India in 1886, and includes various of their conversational exchanges, including an Irish story she had told him.

[45] WBY had lived with his uncle George Pollexfen (1839–1910) in Sligo for several months over the winter of 1894–95, a period when he was unusually hard up. Pollexfen shared WBY's interest in occultism, giving "his nights to astrology and ceremonial magic" in later life (*Au* p. 70), and the men became lasting friends. According to one source, Pollexfen from this period on gave WBY "a pound a week, which was continued for some years until Willie's nationalist sympathies angered him and he stopped the grant" (William M. Murphy, *Prodigal Father* p. 176).

26 — Westminster Abbey — Afternoon Lord Lovelace came, sat from 4 to 5-30 luckily alone, for one gets better at his ideas — He was much interested in Miss Giles's pictures in "the Dome" — said he wd order it & the "Secret Rose"[46] — Alfred Cole afterwards — very quick with his ideas, or rather opinions — chiefly on America where he was at the breaking out of the war — Yeats came to dine —

27 — To Southwark, to see Mrs. Hills, with some money for the children's breakfasts[47] — Went into a china shop in Tabard St. to get a jubilee mug — & bought a figure of Moody, that had been on the shelf for 20 years, but all the Sankeys had been sold[48] — Lady Westmeath came in at tea time — so very retrograde Irish! — the badness of the people, & the hopelessness of the country, & is afraid the study of the language may create bad feeling [in] England — Dined Raffalovich — Mr. Harris,[49] & Miss Violet Hunt[50] — & <?Henry> Walsh who I sat next — a blatant creature, his mouth full of the names of great ladies — but perhaps useful in his sphere — He says he wrote an article on co-operation — but has been going round with it in vain — all editors say "Lady Gregory has exhausted the subject" — Such a comfort talking to good restful Ed. Martyn afterwards! & went on with him to a Celtic "evening" at Yeats's — Miss Purser[51] & Mrs. Emery, & G. Moore & Dr. Todhunter[52] —

[46] Three drawings by Althea Gyles accompanied WBY's article on her work, "A Symbolic Artist and the Coming of Symbolic Art" in *The Dome*, December 1898. She had designed the cover for *The Secret Rose*.

[47] Mrs. Mary Hills, schoolmistress at the Southwark School.

[48] Dwight Moody (1837–99) and Ira Sankey (1840–1908) were the most successful evangelical preachers of their era, touring U.S.A. and the British Isles extensively to hold open air missions.

[49] Frank Harris (1856–1931), author, Editor of the *Fortnightly Review* 1887–94, and friend of Oscar Wilde, whom he was at this point supporting financially. Now best remembered for his 1916 volume *Oscar Wilde: His Life and Confessions*, and his scandalous personal memoirs *My Life and Loves*, published posthumously.

[50] AG may have met the novelist Violet Hunt (1866–1942), whom Oscar Wilde had praised in uncharacteristically clichéd manner as the "sweetest violet in England", prior to this dinner, as Hunt had been mistress to Oswald Crawfurd, her neighbour at Queen Anne's Mansions, since 1892, an affair Hunt later fictionalized in her 1904 volume *Sooner or Later*. Hunt and Crawfurd parted acrimoniously during the course of 1898, Hunt later becoming Ford Madox Ford's mistress from 1908 to 1915.

[51] Sarah Purser (1848–1943), portrait painter and patroness of Irish arts. Founded the stained glass workshop An Tór Gloin with Edward Martyn in 1903.

[52] Dr. John Todhunter (1839–1916), close friend of John B. Yeats and a near neighbour of the Yeats family in Bedford Park. A sympathetic encourager of WBY in the 1890s and a co-member with him of the Rhymers' Club and other literary societies. Turned to Irish themes in *The Banshee and other Poems* (1888) under WBY's influence, and also contributed to *Poems and Ballads of Young Ireland*, though his principal career remained as a medic. His verse drama *A Sicilian Idyll*, first performed at Bedford Park in 1890, greatly impressed WBY, but was his sole success in the genre. He published little after 1896.

Someone said to Mrs. Emery — George Moore looks like a boiled ghost —

28 — To J. Yeats gallery, & found Horace Plunkett has bought one of his pictures, I gave him a card & asked him to go the night he dined here, so it is satisfying to find at least one of my efforts has been successful — To Chelsea, & had tea with Lady Lovelace, & Ld. L. came in — He is vexed with Murray for publishing too much in the Byron book — but that is the fashion of the day — & Lady L. had previously told me it was his own fault, as he had gone to the Alps instead of sticking to the editing of it — Dined Herbert Studds — dullish I confess — Ross Of Bladensburg pertinacious about the Catholic University — Herbert trying to take a polite interest in it — Denis Lawless[53] not very enlivening, & a Col. & Mrs. _____ that seemed to have no connection with anything — On to Lady Arthur [Russell]'s & talked to Bernard Holland, & Lady Sligo,[54] & Lecky — who I told to try & counteract Ld. Morris's influence on Buckle, & get Horace Plunkett given his due place — Found a rather disagreeable letter from Paul on my return — He attacked his mother-in-law for saying Walter did not suit Ethel, & Ethel for saying he goes to sleep in the evening — & both simply deny it! But in his heart he must know that my truth & memory are not likely to have failed.

March 1 — Lunched with Mrs. Marwood Tucker[55] — & talked over the Beauchamp girls — She had been staying with the Balfours for the Countess Kathleen tableau[x], says they were very good — She was surprised to find the Balfours & Lady de Vesci taking the Nationalistic spirit in Ireland so seriously, & so anxious about it[56] — Went on to see Grant Duff, he was pleased with the translation of the Moschus lines he gives in his diary — I had read it long ago — "Alas alas when mallows die!"[57] He is very anxious about Lord Halifax's statement at the meeting of the church delegates that they will not submit to

---

53 Denis Lawless (1854–1900), one of Emily Lawless's five brothers.

54 Isabelle Browne, née de Peyronnet (d.1927), widow of the 3rd Marquess of Sligo (d.1896). Lady Arthur Russell's sister.

55 Etheldreda Tucker, née Beresford-Hope (d.1928), second wife of Edmund Beauchamp's younger brother, Marwood Tucker. Beauchamp's patronymic was also Tucker, but he adopted Beauchamp, his mother's maiden name.

56 Nine tableaux vivants of key episodes from *The Countess Cathleen* were staged in January 1899 at the Chief Secretary's Lodge in Phoenix Park, Dublin, with Countess Fingall and Ruth Balfour (Lady Elizabeth Balfour's eldest daughter) being among the performers. WBY had been invited to rehearse the tableaux but had declined on the grounds that the venue was symbolic of Unionist Government in Ireland. Lady de Vesci, neé Lady Evelyn Charteris (d.1939), was wife of the 4th Viscount, and eldest daughter of Lord Wemyss (see p. 14 n. 63).

57 Grant Duff had included a poem by Moschus, Greek poet of the 2nd century B.C., in his *Notes From A Diary 1881–1886* vol. 2 p. 47, without a translation. He subsequently included an account of AG's visit, and the English translation she subsequently gave him (not her own), in his 1905 volume *Notes From A Diary 1896–1901*, vol.2 p. 92.

any authority but that of their own church[58] — he thinks there will be a large secession to Rome — & an intolerant High Church party as a result — He showed me some sapphires & moonstones just come from Ceylon, & told me to choose a sapphire from among them — on to see the Albert Grays — Dined Sir A. Clays — the electric light had just gone out when we came, so we groped, but I got Sir A. Lyall into the chimney corner & we sat there placidly — At dinner I was between Sir Arthur & Strachey — the latter delighted with the election ballad "What happened [to] all the rest" — I wrote it down for him.

2nd — Walked over to Christie's to see some pictures — a beautiful Hoppner[59] — a beautiful Sir Joshua,[60] with the sunlight on it — Telegram from Yeats, asking if I wd be at home at 4-30 — but with illegible address for reply — so I had to go to post office & wire to have it repeated & went into Westminster Abbey meanwhile — Then to the Pastel exhibition — very few that were good — Clausen, Rothenstein & some foreign ones[61] — Home, & Mrs. Emery came in, just from choosing costumes for the plays — I impressed on her that there ought to be music with them, & she says that is the opinion of every actor who has read the "Heather Field" but that it wd add to the expense[62] — but Mrs. Tucker told me Dr. Culwick had specially arranged music, old Celtic airs for the "Countess Cathleen" tableau[63] — & I think we might get the benefit of it — Telegram from Lady Fingall about the nuns' work, that it must be sent at once, so had to write & wire to them — Then Yeats came — with article he has written in reply to Dr. Atkinson's attack on the Irish language & folk lore[64] — very good but not legible enough to go without

[58] Charles Lindley Wood (1839–1934), 2nd Viscount Halifax, had been Ecclesiastical Commissioner for England since 1886, and was key figure in the English Church Union. A meeting of the Union on 31 January (reported in *The Times* 1 February, p. 7) sparked off an acrimonious debate over ritualism in the Established Church, with Lord Halifax, a supporter of confession and incense, pitted against Sir William Harcourt, whose distate for the "Romish" tendencies of supporters of ritual was well established (see p. 196 n. 132). For Halifax's positions see his letters to *The Times*, 11 February p. 14, 1 March p. 11, 2 March p. 10, and 21 March p. 14.

[59] John Hoppner (*c.*1758–1810), English portrait painter.

[60] Sir Joshua Reynolds (1723–92), portrait painter, first President of the Royal Academy (1768–90).

[61] Inveterate Academy exhibitor George Clausen, A.R.A. (1852–1944), and William Rothenstein (1872–1945), artist and art critic. WBY had sat to Rothenstein for a lithograph portrait for AG's collection in summer 1898.

[62] Edward Martyn's play *The Heather Field* was in rehearsal along with WBY's *The Countess Cathleen* for production by The Irish Literary Theatre in May (see p. 221 n. 101).

[63] James Cooksey Culwick (1845–1907), composer and music historian.

[64] WBY's article "The Academic Class and the Agrarian Revolution" (*UP*2 pp. 149–152, initially published as a letter in *The Dublin Daily Express* 11 March 1899) was a counterblast to the disparaging remarks on Gaelic expressed by Robert Atkinson (1839–1908), Professor of Romance Languages and Sanskrit at Trinity College, during hearings of the Intermediate Education Committee on the question of teaching Irish in schools. Countering testimony by Douglas Hyde in favour of Gaelic being taught, Atkinson asserted that "all folklore was at bottom

typing — & no time for that — so it must wait another week — He is in good spirits — is pulling himself together, & says he is determined to 'put a roof over his head' & work, by short articles, till he gets his affairs straight. He has written to Miss G[onne]. to say he hopes she will be in Dublin in May — for that after that he will be in the country until the autumn — All very well, but if she whistles him back again he will hardly have strength to resist — however it is a step in the right direction — He had been to dine with & speak to a Socialist Society, & had a very good discussion which he enjoyed[65] — & his poems are to be out in a week[66] — He went on to dine with George Moore — & I dined off my remaining sandwich! & some tea cake — & then by a gr effort of will, at bed time, dressed & went to Lady Trevelyan's — I get a sort of passion to keep going in society now Robert's appearance here is comparatively near — but I was tired & (as the ev before) sick while dressing — A dullish party after all, & only met Lady Clancarty[67] & Sir G. Fitzgerald — the latter very full of his brother in law's marriage to Lady Peggy — He was staying at Dalmeny last May — & was much taken with her then[68] — She is not pretty but very clever & amusing — Very full also of his own boy — who intends to be Lord Chief Justice —

3rd — Called, in an incautious moment, on Lady Cork — who expressed gr joy at seeing me — & attacked me to help her in her crusade for women's rights — I tried to escape after a time — but she held me with cold fingers & a glittering eye — a regular lunatic — On to Mary Studd, to see her return from the drawingroom — Lady Clancarty drove me for some calls after that — W. B. Y. dined — Althea Giles has been to attack him about letting the poster be dropped, & above all for having consented that his brother shd do one[69] — "just because Lady Gregory suggested it & because she is a person of title!" — She had done a back design for his poems, but now says he is not

abominable" and claimed that most Irish texts were "silly or indecent". Atkinson's comments reinforced WBY's longstanding hostility to Trinity as symbol of colonial rule, and spurred both Hyde and AG to a campaign of criticism. Atkinson himself was the main target, as "Dr. Mac Hatkin", in Hyde's satire "Pleusgadh na Bulgoide" ["The Bursting of the Bubble"], which AG translated and included in *Poets and Dreamers* in 1903.

[65] WBY spoke on the Celtic Renaissance to the City Socialist Circle, London, on 1 March 1899. No report of the speech appears to have survived.

[66] *The Wind Among the Reeds.*

[67] The widow of the 3rd Earl was still alive (aged in her late eighties), as was Lady Adeliza Trench, née Hervey (d.1911), wife of the 4th Earl, but this was probably the wife of the 5th Earl, William Le Poer Trench (1868–1929), Isabel, née Bilton (d.1906), whom AG had known before her marriage in 1889.

[68] Lady Margaret Primrose (d.1967), Lord Rosebery's youngest daughter, married Robert Milnes (d.1945), 1st Marquess of Crewe, in May 1899. Gerald Fitzgerald had married Milnes's sister Amicia (d.1902) in 1881. Dalmeny, West Lothian, was Lord Rosebery's principal country residence.

[69] The poster was presumably for the forthcoming production of *The Countess Cathleen*. No record of this quarrel appears to have survived.

worthy of it, & he shall not have it but must put up with an ordinary one —
J. B. Yeats says of Atkinson "he has the smallest & the quickest brain I ever
knew" — We went to see "The Fenian" at the Imperial theatre close by — very
funny — a Trinity lad the villain, in cap & gown, with a background of Ceylon
palm trees! Then a coast guard, an old woman from a cabin, a Fenian
midnight meeting in a cave (or forest) where, in spite of secrecy, the band was
playing Irish airs on brass instruments! Hubert O'Grady the writer of the
piece played the comic part very well, & it was very amusing on the whole[70] —

4 — Wilfrid Blunt came to lunch — rather drifting I think — & still hoping
for the break up of the British Empire — He says some of the reviews of Grant
Duff's book say my contributions are the best — I went to see G. D. afterwards
& take him the Moschus lines, & found him better, he had been at the
Breakfast Club — Tea at Raffy's — Ev at home — to bed early & a good sleep
— a good thing for I was tired out, & the last 3 evenings I had been sick &
retching before going out —

5th — To Westminster Abbey — Lunched Westmeaths, the Morrises there &
Sir Wm. & Lady Everett[71] — Ld. W. rather aggravating, with a sort of
assumption of Lecky's little superior manner, down on E. Martyn's plays —
down especially on the Irish language — "Ireland is a part of England & ought
to be *under* England" — He approves of H. Plunkett & has helped to establish
a branch "but if *I* gave it up it wd collapse — The people have no common
sense, no energy — no industry" — I hope Robert will never grow like that!
Martin Morris still in Galway trying for County Council — has secured the 5
priests "by telling lies" Frances says complacently — telling each priest the
others had promised to support him — If he gets in "Papa" says he will go over
& shake the priests by the hand & thank them — If he doesn't he will go over
& revenge himself as much as possible, by taking the land over the people's
heads etc — Altogether it was not an inspiriting atmosphere! Ed. Martyn
came in at 6 — rather depressed about his actors etc — Had asked G. Moore
to dine, & Yeats, who was to dine here, so I asked him to bring G. M. — & we
cd all dine here — & he did so —

After dinner he & Moore made an attack on Mrs. Emery, & deposed her as
stage manager — Yeats taking it well, but put out, & I seeing it must be done,
only said it must be done courteously — but it will be a little awkward — Yeats
full of Keats, he is reading Endymion for the first time with appreciation —
Also full of Shelley says they had a philosophy, which he is trying to get at, &

[70] *The Fenian* by Hubert O'Grady (1841–99) remained unpublished, though a text of the
play, registered with the Lord Chamberlain's Office, survives in the British Library.
[71] William St. George (1870–1933), 11th Earl of Westmeath, a diplomat, died unmarried.
For his mother, see p. 27 n. 14. Sir William Everett (1844–1908), retired Civil Servant and War
Office Intelligence Officer, and his wife Marie, née Calogeras.

will write on, something like Blake's philosophy[72] — I asked if Blake had influenced him & he says no, he knew nothing of him, but that minds act on each other — "If you shut yourself up in this room & think with sufficient vigour, you will impress your thought on others"[73] —

6th — This day seven years [ago] my husband died — The years have gone by more happily than I could have expected — No serious cause for anxiety about R. — tho' a little disappointment he has not left more mark at Harrow — Coole peaceful, & we are I think on closer & more sympathetic terms with the people — Here in London friends are still kind — & I feel that Robert will have good houses open to him, whether I am here or not — In Ireland I have found much happiness & given some help — new interests joining with old, the ag[ricultural] organisation, the folk lore — the idealising, or revealing the ideal side of our people's life, the language — I feel if there are still some years before me there is work to do in these — And I think Robert, in spite of his young enthusiasm for Imperialism, will always understand & care for his own people —

I went to Jack Yeats's exhibition — found my picture the "Returned American" had been sold — so chose another — & foolishly, but with good intent, took some trouble about the exchange of another — wrote to H. Plunkett & went to see E. Martyn — but it came to nothing — Afternoon, went to meet Lady Betty Balfour at Motcombe St. ab[ou]t the Gort convent work at the "Industries" — & then she asked me to go to her house in Addison Road & see the photos of the "Countess Kathleen" tableaux — not very good — Ly. Fingall pretty & graceful[74] — but Rolleston & Coffee[75] very prosperous & substantial & amiable demons — She is a nice simple girlish woman, opened the hall door herself, for she had bicycled home before me — I borrowed the photos to take to Yeats in the ev — Then back to entertain the Lanes at tea — had just lighted my spirit lamp when the Duchess of Bedford came in, very sweet & gracious — Ruth Lane[76] arrived, & was introduced to her first Duchess! H. Percy [Lane] not till past 6 — & after they left I went off to Argyll Road (getting into wrong trains & a long time on the journey) to get Yeats's poems from Sir F.

72 WBY subsequently published "The Philosophy of Shelley's Poetry" in *The Dome*, July 1900.

73 The idea that "minds can flow into one another" underlay many of WBY's mystical experiments around this time, and formed one of the central premises of his essay "Magic", published in *The Monthly Review* in September 1901.

74 Lady Fingall had taken the role of the Countess.

75 George Coffey (1857–1916), archeologist, and Keeper of Irish Antiquities at the National Museum of Science and Art 1897–1914. In *Mem* (pp. 117–18) WBY claimed that both Coffey and Rolleston received Government posts soon after their performances in the tableaux, and noting that Rolleston had compromised his Nationalist credentials quite openly by "urging Dublin to give an enthusiastic reception to Queen Victoria". Coffey, however, had in fact been appointed to the National Museum more than a year prior to the tableaux.

76 Hugh Lane's sister, later Ruth Shine.

Burton, as a copy can't be had, & one is wanted to show to possible actors[77]
— He I was grieved to find is in bed with pleurisy — & one dreads any illness
at his age — not up to seeing me but I got the book & carried it off — Eat my
sandwich at home, & then off to Woburn Buildings (had missed a visit from
Horace Plunkett while out) — Found E. Martyn — Mr. & Mrs. Ernest Rhys
(told her how I admired "Mary Dominic"),[78] Mr. Grene the actor[79] — Althea
Gyles — & then Miss Gonne & her sister came in[80] — She looked less ill than
in Dublin — but her beauty I look for in vain — we conversed amiably for a
time — & then I made off, being indeed tired out —

7th — Wrote letters all the morning — afterwards to see Sir F. Burton, & sat
with him for a while — he is still suffering pain from the pleurisy & coughed
a good deal but was cheery — We spoke of Mitchel's "Jail Journal" which he
had never read[81] — & he said "I did not like his appearance when I saw him,
Davis[82] took me to see him somewhere — His skin was blotched — & he had
ginger coloured hair — he was a regular Northener & he did not make a good
impression on me" — Took my Moody statuette to Lady Arthur Russell —
who was delighted with it — Then back, & Horace Plunkett came to talk about
the proposed banquet to be held in Dublin for the plays — a very good idea
if funds are forthcoming — I suggested the Lord Mayor to give it — but he
says the Ld. Mayor was so tipsy at the financial meeting he had to be held up

[77] While the 1895 edition of *Poems* appears to have been out of print at this time – it was
important that the first edition be sold out well before the appearance of the second – it is
probable that the last copies were bought by Elkin Mathews, for in 1904 he was including the title
in his catalogue as if it were his own publication, noting "A few copies only remain". Yeats wished
to use his revised text for the forthcoming production of *The Countess Cathleen* in Dublin in May,
and to provide texts for use in rehearsal, WBY's publisher T. Fisher Unwin had to print a short
run of copies of the play. See Colin Smythe "*The Countess Cathleen*: a note" *Yeats Annual 3* pp. 193–
97.

[78] Ernest Rhys (1859–1946), editor, critic and poet, founded the Rhymer's Club with WBY
in 1890, and under WBY's influence turned to the mythology of his Welsh background for
inspiration, publishing *Welsh Ballads* in 1898. Editor of the Camelot Series (for which WBY
compiled *Fairy and Folk Tales of the Irish Peasantry* and *Stories from Carleton*), and later of the
Everyman's Library. His wife Grace Rhys, née Little (d. 1929), was editor of *Banbury Cross* 1895–
96 and had published her first novel, *Mary Dominic*, a tale of Donegal life, in 1898.

[79] Probably J. T. Grein (1862–1935), who, though not an actor, was a key figure in founding
the Independent Theatre Company, and who shared WBY's enthusiasm for alternatives to
commercial theatre.

[80] Mrs. Thomas Pitcher, née Kathleen Gonne (1867–1919), Maud Gonne's younger sister,
the "beautiful mild woman" who inspired WBY's line "we must labour to be beautiful" in "Adam's
Curse".

[81] John Mitchel (1815–75), Young Irelander and Editor of *The United Irishman* 1847–48.
Urged agrarian uprising during the Famine and was convicted of sedition in 1848. His *Jail
Journal* recounts the events of his trial and transportation to Australia. Mitchel escaped to the
U.S.A. in 1853.

[82] Thomas Davis (1814–45), poet, patriot, journalist and leader of the Young Ireland
movement. Founded the influential Nationalist newspaper *The Nation* with Charles Gavan Duffy
and John Blake Dillon in 1842. Died of fever and exhaustion.

by the coat tails! Poor Ireland! — He is to try to get Ld. Russell to preside[83]
— & will come & lunch Friday to talk to Yeats about that, & about what he is
to say at the Lit. Society on Saturday —

8th — Got to Walton at last[84] — a long journey — first to Waterloo — then
back & forwards in the station — then nearly an hour to Walton — arrived
rather exhausted & cold — but the garden & the house had to be inspected
before food & fire were allowed — & then there were many draughts — & it
was depressing altogether — low rooms & too set out to be homelike — Susan
[Harvey] a nice little thing — I got back with cold & sore throat — longing
for bed — but Yeats turned up to dinner, a very good thing, as I eat something
& had quite a nice evening — Miss G[onne] playing with him, will not let him
go — he had made & told her his decision not to see her during the summer
— & she says "Oh but I will come to the West" — so the same work will begin
again —

9th — Suffering from yesterday's chill — sore throat & retching — so set to
work to make a new will, some little things wd have worried me if I had got
really ill — Struggled to Sir F. Burton & had a talk with him — left some cards,
& coming back I turned in at Mrs. Dugdale's & found a party going on —
wanted to make off but she wouldn't let me, & said how much she had enjoyed
her dinner with me — & how brilliant Yeats had been — I had a talk with Mr.
Albert Gray & with Mrs. Blumenthal — 2 new laid eggs in my muff all the time!
destined for my dinner — but luckily no mishap occurred —

10 — W. Peel came down to my room to sit for a sketch to Mr. [J.B.] Yeats[85]
— pleasant talk over Irish & English characteristics — Mr. Yeats says we are
too quick — the English too slow both in work & thought — He thinks English
children being set to work so young a gr drawback to them — He says Ireland
is what England was before Puritan influence came in — Then came W. B. Y.
— & Horace Plunkett for lunch & Ed. Martyn — We decided to try for Lord
Russell for a banquet chairman — & failing him, to think of the Ld. Mayor —
H. P. suggested getting the Ld. Lieutenant to give it! but W. B. Y. said he cd

---

[83] Daniel Tallon, Mayor of Dublin 1898–99, slid further into disrepute as the year progressed,
being "hissed & booed" for missing a pro-Boer meeting in October 1899 according to Maud
Gonne (*Always Your Friend: The Gonne-Yeats Letters*, p. 113). Sir Charles Russell (1832–1900),
eminent lawyer, was Attorney General 1886, 1892–94, and Lord Chief Justice of England from
1894. Raised to the peerage as Lord Russell of Killowen, 1894. Irish-born, Russell was one of
the most prominent Catholics in British public life, and a staunch promoter of Irish cultural
enterprisessuch as the Irish Literary Society, of which he was a founding member and Vice
President. The "banquet" for the Literary Theatre, a luncheon held on 22 February 1900 at the
Gresham Hotel, was eventually presided over by Dr. George Sigerson (see p. 243 n. 99).

[84] Where Paul and Ethel Harvey were then living.

[85] Peel had recently taken an apartment in Queen Anne's Mansions.

not go in that case — & of course none of the Nat[ionalist] guarantors wd —
it wd be like kneeling to the host in Prot[estant] eyes — H. P. says a rich
Englishman has half promised £5000 for the organization — but wants some
return — probably knighthood — & the Govt. won't promise this beforehand
— H. P. thinks if he can get him to give it, he can then by threatening to turn
Fenian squeeze the reward out of the Govt! I went to see Sir Frederic — he
was excited & incredulous over Atkinson's evidence against the Irish language in which he says all Irish books are filthy & all folk lore is at bottom
abominable — W. B. Y. is in gr triumph, having been to Nutt who is furious
& has written to the Express saying he has read every Irish book that has been
translated in the last 30 years & has not found the "filth" & if Atkinson cannot
prove his case, he will call him a liar![86] — Came home tired & aching, this cold
still on me — & Ed. Martyn came in, & said there was a report of Nevill Geary's
death — He went on to dine with George Moore, but I put on my things again
& went off to Lady Geary — found she had evidently heard nothing — poor
old thing she is very bothered — & so I trust the report is false — Called & sent
off a card to Ed. M. telling him this — & to bed very tired —

11 — From 11 to 5 assisting at W. Peel's portrait! — rather exhausted from
talking in the end — but he declared the time had gone by unnoticed! J. B.
Yeats is I confess rather an "enfant terrible". When I spoke of Welldon's
sermon on {the two ideals for a boy} "the British Empire & the Church of
Christ" he exclaimed "& both shams"! — We looked at each other — & he said
"I didn't know I was exploding a bomb shell" — Then he abused Ld. Morris
for his severity as a judge & at home — said he had dined in the house next
his one day, & there was a gr noise & scrambling going on next door — & his
host said "It's always like this when they get Morris out of the way" — I,
knowing this wd be repeated to Martin was on pins & needles — Then he wd
attack England on every point, & W. Peel who had been amused by this the
day before did not like its continuance so well — & when we went up to lunch,
very hungry, & at liberty to gesticulate, he let his tongue & temper loose &
spoke very violently & offensively of the Irish members, attacking & snarling
at the Empire, out of jealousy & without honest intention — I said their
manner & method was bad, but the underlying idea was that Ireland had
suffered thro' being under England, & that they wanted to give a word of
protest & sympathy when any other part of the world came under English rule
— but he wd [have] none of this — I felt he had been provoked to it so kept
my temper, & when we came down to coffee & cigarettes all went well again
& the portrait was finished by 5 — & we all parted friends — W. Peel says his
father wrote a very full diary while Speaker, & has been offered large sums for
it, but of course can't publish it at present, if ever — He himself is anxious to
write a life of Chatham, & when Morley took up Gladstone's life he went to

[86] Nutt's letter was published in *The Dublin Daily Express*, along with WBY's, on 11 March. See
UP2 p. 149.

MacMillan's to ask if there was an opening for it — but they said Morley still intends to write it when he has done with the G[rand]. O[ld]. M[an][87] —

Ed. Martyn came in, to say there has been a telegram from N. Geary who is all right — Off to see Sir F. Burton — & back to dress in a hurry for dinner at the Leckys — Old Leveson Gower — Mrs. H. Reeve — Ly. Sligo & Miss de Peyronnet[88] — Sir C. & Miss Dalrymple[89] — the Goldsteins — I sat between Evelyn Ashley, who I was very glad to meet again,[90] & Mr. Eyre Crowe of the Foreign Office, who says he has been in it for 15 years & had nothing to do but lick envelopes![91] Some pleasant talk with E. Ashley — it was rather a resurrected feeling meeting him & Mrs. Reeve & F. Leveson Gower again! Old Goldstein bored me afterwards — but E. Ashley brought his wife to introduce, & laughed & chatted a while — All the better for the outing —

Ap[ril] 4 — I write after a long time, influenza having stepped in & given me a "touch" — Sunday, March 5 I was suffering from a cold but went out & about — to lunch Studds, to see Sir Frederic, to tea with the Yeatses, & W. B. Y. came back to dinner with me — That night I tossed with fever, parched with thirst, sick at intervals, lay till the housemaid looked in after 10, & cried with joy when she brought me some tea — Then lay for hours, no one near, struggled up to call down the tube, when a boy appeared, sent off some necessary notes & a telegram for old Miss Bentley, who came for the next four days, & kept me supplied with bovril, eggs etc — for I was very unwell, weakness after the fever left — Heard of Horace Plunkett's accident — so sad that he of all people shd be laid aside for a time — The night before he had spoken at the I. Lit. Society on "The Irish Cabin" & won golden opinions by his gentleness & enthusiasm — It seemed such a martyrdom — the fall from the bicycle — the broken thigh, the move to St. George's Hospital for setting — the move from there to Harley St. — & then the pain & sleepless nights[92] —

[87] Neither Morley nor Peel subsequently wrote on William Pitt "the younger", the 2nd Earl of Chatham. For Morley's biography of Gladstone see p. 195 n. 128.

[88] Either a sister or niece of Lady Arthur Russell and Lady Sligo.

[89] Sir Charles Dalrymple (1839–1916), 1st Bart, and probably his eldest daughter Christian Elizabeth (b.1875).

[90] Rt. Hon Anthony Evelyn Ashley (1836–1907), 4th son of the 7th Earl of Shaftesbury. Private Secretary to Palmerstone 1858–65 and M.P. 1874–85. Ashley had known WHG during his early parliamentary career, and had been an occasional guest of the Gregorys in the 1880s.

[91] Eyre Crowe (1864–1925), Clerk in the Foreign Office 1885–1906, but thereafter graduated to Senior Clerk 1906, Assistant Under-Secretary of State 1912, Minister Plenipotentiary 1919, and Permanent Under-Secretary for Foreign Affairs 1920–25.

[92] Plunkett presided at The Irish Literary Society meeting on 11 March 1899. His remarks in response to Michael MacDonagh's paper "In an Irish Cabin" are reported in The Irish Literary Society Gazette June 1899, pp. 3–4. His cycling accident next day, in Kensington High St, was followed in June by a renewed breaking of his thigh bone when he fell from his crutches when returning to the House of Commons.

Above: pencil drawing by Robert Gregory of the Garden Quad at New College, Oxford, *c*.1899. Below: two sketches by John Butler Yeats of James Joyce in Lady Gregory's copy of *Samhain*, October 1902. This, and the cover of *Beltaine* on the next page are reproduced by courtesy of the Berg Collection, New York Public Library.

Above: cover of Lady Gregory's copy of the April 1900 issue of *Beltaine*, adorned by Jack B. Yeats, 'In the graceful year 1900 George Moore and Victoria returned to Ireland', 'Lady Fingall drops Edward Martyn' and (in Lady Gregory's hand 'W.B.Y. plays the organ'. Below: left, A John Butler Yeats sketch of Lady Gregory, dated June 8 1903; right, a studio photograph of Robert Gregory by Soames of Oxford, June 1902.

Above: A scene from the 14 January 1904 revival of Lady Gregory's play *Twenty Five*, with Maire ni Garbhaigh (Mary Garvey), Honor Lavelle (Helen S. Laird). P. J. Kelly and Seumas O'Sullivan (James Starkey). Below: a scene from the first production of *Cathleen ni Houlihan* by W. B. Yeats and Lady Gregory on 2 April 1902, with Maud Gonne in the title role.

Lady Gregory's fans: that shown above includes the signatures of John Bright, Sir Edward Malet, Sir Arthur Sullivan, Sir Auckland Colvin, Wilfrid Scawen Blunt, Ahmed Arabi, W. E. Gladstone, Lord Northbrook, Lord Rosebery, A. W. Kinglake, Sir George Trevelyan, W. E. Forster, and Sir Henry Layard. The other side of the fan (not illustrated includes signatures of James McNeill Whistler, Lord Tennyson, G. F. Watts, the Marquess of Dufferin and Ava, and Lord Randolph Churchill. That below (the more recent) includes, Viscount Goschen, Henry

James, W. E. H. Lecky, Lord Morley, Sir William Orpen, Bret Harte, Mark Twain, Theodore Roosevelt "alone in cabin", Antonio Mancini, Sir Horace Plunkett, Thomas Hardy, Ramsay MacDonald, Ellen Terry, Robin Flower, Finley Peter Dunne, Augustus John, Rudyard Kipling, H. H. Asquith, Fridtjof Nansen, G. Bernard Shaw, J. M. Synge, George Moore, John Eglinton (W. K. McGee), Sean O'Casey, An Craoibhín (Douglas Hyde), Jack B. Yeats, Edward Martyn, George Russell – "A.E.", James Stephens, and W. B. Yeats.

Above: pen and ink sketches by Robert Gregory of George Moore and Edward Martyn, possibly on the occasion of Martyn's visit to Coole when Moore was staying there, on 20 September 1900 (p.279). Below: George Moore leaving Coole, probably 5 October 1900, with W. B. Yeats, who stayed a few days longer (p.281).

Above: Coole Park in winter. Below: a pen and ink sketch by Jack B. Yeats of AE, Lady Gregory, the back of T. A. Harvey's head, and W. B. Yeats in the library at Coole, July 1900 (p.274).

Draw on him now

Jack B. Yeats
August 1902

And I'm
the man
That
drew
The Two
of ye

And I'm the man
that came from
America to hear
you say the same

I'm the man that buried Raftery
I'm the man That held The Candle

Above: Sketch by Jack B. Yeats of John Quinn and the "man that buried Raftery", August 1902. Below: a Jack B. Yeats ink and wash sketch of W. B. Yeats swimming in Coole Lake, entitled 'The Bather'. All illustrations by John Butler Yeats and Jack B. Yeats are reproduced by permission of Anne Yeats and Michael Yeats.

15th — Struggled to a dinner at Mrs. Kay's — It was dull or I was — The Lyalls next day seemed the same — indeed I was not fit to go out — I sat next Haldon Q.C.[93] who spoke sympathetically of Ireland —

17th — That dreadful sale of Irish Industries at Downshire House — I was only able to go in the afternoon & hold on to a chair & try to sell the poor Gort goods — Too many things sent & too various — & too dear — but the whole thing seems to me humiliating; more sellers than buyers, smart ladies in extravagant dresses, buying a little here & there from entertainers who will ask them in return to dinner — What I sold was almost exclusively to Irish people — & then one hears "What London has done for the Irish poor" — London being extremely anxious all the time to get full value for its money — Lady Betty Balfour pleasant, & bought a child's frock —

In the midst of my weakness & illness, I heard that Robert had to go to Oxford for some days for his Responsions, & cd not be given rooms in college, so must stay at a hotel — This seemed a poor beginning for his Oxford life, & I didn't like to think of him, lounging in the coffee rooms — didn't like to propose going myself lest I shd be in the way — asked various people, who didn't help me — but a note to Fischer Williams brought the result of rooms in New, all right — Then I wrote to Charlie Morris at Balliol & had a nice note from him, & all went off well — R. passed all right, & enjoyed himself also —

18th — Dined Grant Duffs — sat next Sir Wilfrid Lawson[94] — he was enthusiastic about the "Life of Parnell" so I asked him to meet Barry O'Brien & Yeats next day at dinner, & he came & we had very pleasant talk — B. O'B. told us that Lewis told him he had gone to Brighton to take Parnell's directions about the case, & Mrs. O'Shea came in & interrupted & gave her opinion — Lewis said "I am employed by Mr. Parnell" but she said "He will do as I wish", & Parnell sat there quite meek & mild.[95]

My last week was quiet, but somehow rather pleasant, Robert got on all right at Oxford — I went to see Sir Frederic every day & enjoyed my quiet little talks with him — Tuesday ev I dined with W. B. Yeats — When I was leaving there was a letter in the box, from E. Martyn — He opened it, & it was to say that he had conscientious scruples as to the "Countess Kathleen's" orthodoxy, &

93 Richard Burdon Haldane (1856–1928), Liberal M.P. 1885–1911, and Q.C. 1890. Raised to the peerage 1911. Later Lord High Chancellor 1912–15 and 1924.

94 Sir Wilfrid Lawson (1829–1906), 2nd Bart., M.P. 1859–65, 1868–1900, 1903–06. Lawson had been a close ally of AG in supporting Arabi in 1882–83.

95 Sir George Henry Lewis (1833–1911), Parnell's solicitor during the Pigott letters trial and, until his services were dispensed with by Mrs. O'Shea, during the early stages of the O'Shea divorce suit. Created a Baronet in 1902.

had consulted 'some one' who confirmed his opinion, & he must withdraw from the whole scheme, & not support it, financially or otherwise! A thunderbolt, for if he withdrew his guarantee why shd not the other guarantors do likewise — & what a scandal it wd make, poor Ireland quarrelling as usual, & about religion! We walked nearly home, Yeats much upset— Luckily he had to go & see his uncle, which gave me time for thought — Next day, as he was to come to lunch, I sent & asked George Moore & by gr luck T. P. Gill also came in, a good Catholic, making little of Ed.'s objections — & declaring the scheme must not be given up — G. Moore furious — declares Ed. keeps part of his conscience in his stomach, the rest round the corner — declares this decides him, "I shall never marry, my brother's son will inherit my property, now I have decided I will write & order him to be brought up a Protestant" — At last we get him to write, & then Yeats writes, & in the end, E. M. consents that the question shd be submitted to Father Barry at Oxford, or Father Finlay in Dublin — & both pass the play— so there is no excuse for not going on with it — but E. M. is rather restive wd still draw back if anyone 'in authority' pronounced against it[96] — Dined at George Moore's one evening — Lunched Haliburtons — Lady Betty Balfour sent an express asking me to bring Yeats to lunch "I know he won't go into an official residence but thank God we are not official here, & my husband wd like so much to meet him" — However I was engaged, & not sure if he cd go, & know he was busy so made an excuse of this[97] —

Wrote to ask Geraldine over, to make the holidays cheerful for Robert — Mrs. B[eauchamp] wrote refusing leave, as "the summer wd suit us better"[98] — so I pocketed my pride, & asked her to stay over the summer, & she was allowed to come — Took her to "The Musketeers"[99] & lodged her in Mr. Monckton's flat — & am rewarded for the holidays have been wet, & without her & chess R. wd have been dull —

The County Council elections have been taking place — not much excitement — R. went to Kiltartan schoolhouse — but voters were only dropping

96 Father William Barry (1849–1930), novelist, translator, and active member of the London Irish Literary Society, was Rector of a parish near Oxford. Rev. Thomas Finlay, S.J. (1848–1940), a Dublin economist at this point closely associated with Horace Plunkett in the co-operative movement, was also a literary activist and a founding member of the National Literary Society. AG included the text of Barry's letter to WBY, sanctioning the play, in *Our Irish Theatre* p. 26. For the lingering furore over the play's orthodoxy, see *Au* pp. 414–17.

97 Lady Balfour's invitation to her private residence followed WBY's refusal to enter the Chief Secretary's Lodge to see the *Countess Cathleen* tableaux. See p. 210 n. 56 and *Mem* pp. 117–18.

98 Louisa Beauchamp, née Jones (d.1934), Edmund Beauchamp's third wife.

99 *The Musketeers*, a series of tableaux adapted by Sydney Grundy from Dumas's novel, starring Beerbohm Tree in the role of D'Artagnan, performed 19 times at Her Majesty's Theatre in June and July 1899, following a run of 160 performances in 1898.

in one by one — Burke, a Gort publican, & W. S[hawe]. Taylor & Benny Murray the candidates — Mike & Marty express gr indignation at the expense the district is put to — £3 paid to John Gormally to go to Peterswell voting place, & £1 to his uncle as A. D. C. & car hire as well — And, old Diveney says, we don't like the Kilbecanty men to be coming down to bully our men voting for their own candidate — There's be curses enough after them for this day's work — And Marty says everyone in Gort was drunk in the evening, Mr. Burke having to treat his supporters, & Benny Murray having left money to treat his.

8th [April] — The Jack Yeatses arrived yesterday — He is too good an artist to leave to Devonshire, I want to keep him to Irish things[100] —

April 24 — Robert has gone — the holidays went off quietly & well — he played chess with G[eral]dine & fired at jackdaws & did his little Irish lessons — & he liked J. Yeats very much & they fraternized — The only gaiety was a clay pigeon match at Ashfield where he won 2 silver spoons — Mr. Aldridge came for a couple of days. The County Council elections have gone by, the people have kept the power in their own hands, & this is best, they will learn by responsibility, and — "le sang qui coulait, etait il donc si pur" — My cold still bad — Oh Paul! that visit to Walton has avenged you! A great exodus to America — Bridget Diveney has just been to say good bye —

July 12 — There was so much to say that I have never said it — The Literary theatre — well, it is in the newscutting books[101] —

August 28 —

My guests have been W. B. Yeats who came in May — Geraldine Beauchamp who came in April, they are still here —

---

[100] Jack Yeats had moved to Strete, near Dartmouth, Devon, in 1896, two years after marrying Mary Cottenham "Cottie" White (1868–1947), whose trust funds had given them a substantial assured income. Strete remained their residence until 1910, AG's hopes notwithstanding. Despite John B. Yeats's evident eagerness that AG's patronage be extended to his second son— he wrote to her flatteringly on 19 May 1899 "I expect to see them greatly improved & *expanded* by the liberating influence of your house and presence—I notice a subtle alteration in Jack's letters—as if his horizon had altered" (Berg)—the visit failed to reduce Jack Yeats's reserve with AG, largely in consequence of the "too obvious dislike" she showed towards Cottie. On this occasion, and again when visiting in 1900, Jack failed to send a thank-you letter following his stay at Coole (see William Murphy, *Prodigal Father* pp. 209, 585).

[101] The Irish Literary Theatre presented *The Countess Cathleen* (directed by Florence Farr) on 8 May 1899, with further productions on 10, 12 and 13 May; and Edward Martyn's *The Heather Field* on 9, 10 and 13 May. From 1899 onwards, AG collected reviews of Literary Theatre performances, and general press material concerning WBY, into newscutting books, now at NLI. She subsequently employed a cutting agency to gather such material for her. Her extensive cutting books on her own work are now at Emory.

Emily Lawless[102]
E. V. Longworth[103]
2 Gill boys
Douglas Hyde & wife[104]
John Eglinton
G. W. Russell [AE] (left today)

Robert has come back, having said good bye, regretfully to Harrow — Mr.
Bowen has written nicely of him — AE has done a picture of him in pastel —
Mr. Harvey, holiday tutor & cricketing companion is a great success[105] — nice
& boyish & musical —

W. B. Y. is writing "The Shadowy Waters" & has done an article on the Literary
Movement for the N[orth]. American Review, which has given him £40 — &
is doing a little article on Raftery[106] — I have been writing a little miracle play
for the school children, but haven't submitted it as yet to Dr. Fahey[107] — & I
did an account of our Irish meeting at Gort for the Speaker[108] — We spent
some days at Chevy where I got a good deal of folk lore, & I go on with Irish,
but proceed slowly —

We have beaten Ennis at cricket —

[102] This visit was apparently not a success as Lawless and WBY "did not get on very well"
(*Seventy Years* p. 386). In her Journal for 1924, AG recalled that Lawless had argued that "an artist
or poet should lay aside his gift if by working at an ordinary trade he could better help his family",
a position WBY would undoubtedly have resisted (*Journals* vol. 2, pp. 152, 424).

[103] Ernest Victor Longworth (1874–1935), barrister and Editor of *The Dublin Daily Express*
1901–04. AG's letter introducing Joyce to Longworth in 1902 resulted in Joyce briefly acting as
a reviewer for the paper.

[104] Lucy Hyde, née Kurtz (d.1937).

[105] Thomas Arnold Harvey (1878–1966), a scholar at Trinity College, Dublin, subsequently
entered the priesthood and was Bishop of Cashel and Waterford 1935–58. In his "Memories of
Coole" (*Irish Times* 23–4 November 1959) Harvey recalled that his common interest with Robert
"in classics and cricket laid the foundations of a friendship, and of the next ten years not one
passed without a visit." He remained a lifelong friend of Jack B. Yeats. In subsequent entries he
is invariably referred to as "Harvey" or "Mr. Harvey" while Paul Harvey is exclusively referred to
as "Paul".

[106] "The Literary Movement in Ireland", *North American Review* December 1899 (*UP2* pp.
184–96). WBY's "Raftery" article became "Dust Hath Closed Helen's Eye" published in *The Dome*
October 1899, and reprinted in revised form in *The Celtic Twilight* (1902).

[107] *Colman and Guaire*, a verse play based on the legend of St Colman and King Guaire of Gort.
When finally publishing the work in 1930 as *My First Play*, AG recalled that her original aim was
"a little play in rhyme [which] might perhaps be learned and acted by Kiltartan schoolchildren;
and it was on the railway journey home [from Venice] . . . that to the rythm of the engine I began.
. . . Monsignor Fahey, then our parish priest, was pleased with it and approved. But I was by that
time taken up with the practical work of the theatre in Dublin, and this was laid aside." As she
recognised when preparing it for the press in 1929, the play was no more than "gentle doggerel"
(*Journals* vol. 2, p. 495).

[108] "The Language Movement in Ireland" *The Speaker* 12 August, pp. 151–52.

R. has shot his first buck, at Kilcornan —

4th Sept[ember] — Mr. Ussher, Irish teacher has arrived, & I am taking lessons[109] —

Dec[ember] 31
All left in October — but after 2 or 3 weeks W. B. Y., Geraldine & Ruth [Lane] came back for a fortnight — then I was alone again — I spent my time alone chiefly in collecting materials re Raftery — I found his place of burial at Killeenan, & borrowed a MS book of his poems, & went to the lodge by moonlight each evening to translate them with Mulkair's[110] help — & then wrote my article[111] —

Some unpleasantness about E. Martyn's "Tale of a Town" — Moore & Yeats having pronounced against it in the state he left it, he gave it over to them to alter — They did this at Tillyra, & made too much mystery over it, & vexed him till he "hated the sight" of them both — & then Moore stayed in Dublin, still re-writing & showing it to Gill & Russell each day — This vexed him naturally, & he has lost interest in the play — But I believe it will be a success & that he will find himself all the higher for his sacrifice[112] —

To Roxboro' for the shooting — Pleasant & cheery — & I got some more Raftery lore by walking miles in the rain, to Illerton & beyond Kilchriest —

12th Dec[ember] — R. came back from his first term at Oxford — not much changed, a little more independent in doing for himself, but very gentle & good — He likes his tutor, Nowell Smith, & is reading for Honour Mods[113] — He has taken a great fancy for music, which unluckily we haven't much means of gratifying here — On the whole I am pleased, he is cheery & open & sensible — We had our shoot directly after he came, Arthur & Katy & the Wynnes[114] & Frank & the Doctor — The next week he did 3 days shoot at

[109] Mathew Usher [sic], Vice-President of the Galway Branch of the Gaelic League.

[110] Pat Mulkere, a neighbouring tenant farmer.

[111] AG's article "Raftery, Poet of the Poor" was published in An Claidheamh Soluis 14 October 1899, pp. 488-89. She announced her discovery of Raftery's burial place in a letter published in An Claidheamh Soluis 2 December 1899, p. 605, in which she appealed for funds for a memorial stone.

[112] Martyn's subsequent withdrawal of his play The Tale of a Town, and Moore's completion of a new play, The Bending of the Bough, loosely based on Martyn's, is documented in subsequent entries. Martyn eventually published his original version in 1901.

[113] RG had matriculated at New College, Oxford, in October to read Classics. Charles Nowell Smith (1871–1961), Fellow and Tutor in Classics at New College, 1897–1905, was subsequently Headmaster of Sherborne School 1909-27.

[114] Maud Wynne, née Morris (d.1957), third daughter of Lord Morris, and her husband Capt. Graham Wynne (d.1939), whom she had married in 1897.

L[ough]. Cutra, & Frank S[hawe]. Taylor & Miss Joyce came here for it —
then F. S. T. asked him over for a harrier hunt, gave him a mount, & he went
all right over his first stone walls — Xmas tree, Workhouse, presents as usual,
leaving me rather tired —

On the 12th Kate Wale died — Poor thing a death is sad that there is no one
to grieve for[115] — She left a will in our favour, & though she had lost a good
deal through dishonest attorneys, we shall get something, & whatever I get
will be a help in rolling my snow ball up hill —

On the whole the year has passed well — This was the only death in the family
— Robert has begun his Oxford time happily — No trouble with tenants —
Was able to help W .B. Y. by his long stay here, which was in itself a pleasure
— The Lit[erary]. theatre was successful — On good terms I think with
neighbours — I have been a little too long at home, however, & am tired of
housekeeping & entertaining, & welcome Robert's suggestion that we shd go
to Venice for Easter.

---

[115] Katherine Henrietta Wale, AG's half-sister and the oldest of her siblings, died on 11
December 1899. Her husband Commander George Wale, whom she had married in 1862, had
died in 1879.

1900

Jan[uary] 1 — 1900

Jan[uary] 24 — Q. A. Mansions — The holidays went off fairly well, a gr deal of rain, however R. had a good deal of shooting, at home & at Dunsandle, & Roxboro' & Lough Cutra, & 2 hunts, his first, one with harriers one with [the Galway] Blazers — a little shooting party of Gus Kelly & Mr. Richardson & the Miss Comyns came,[1] & Mr. R. stayed on till the end —

On the 18th we came over — Arrived 19th — R. went to the Birchs, I came here, very tired — R. came later full of war gossip, complaints of Ld. Methuen chiefly, the officers under him have been writing of the hopeless disorder & confusion of the attack[2] — R. off to see the London Volunteers drilled before their departure & then off to New [College] — Paul came in late, dreadfully busy at the W[ar]. O[ffice] — says Buller has written every week (there are reports that he had not) but his letters are so confused & contradictory they can't, even for his own sake publish them[3] — Methuen is not to be allowed to do any more — They are having a good deal of trouble in W. O. — about

---

[1] Gustavus Blake Kelly (1878–1951), from Co. Roscommon, was a friend and contemporary of RG at Oxford. Eily Comyn (b.1877), of Westwood, Co. Cork, subsequently married Gus Kelly in September 1900. She and her sister Geraldine (1875–1944), were great-grand-daughters of Daniel O'Connell.

[2] This was the severe defeat at Magersfontein on 11 December 1899 of British forces under the command of Paul Sanford Methuen (1845–1932), 3rd Baron Methuen, Lieut. General in S. Africa 1899–1902. After a chaotic night march, Methuen's troops frontally attacked a strong Boer position that had barely been reconnoitred, and more than 900 British troops were killed. Methuen continued as a senior General, and his troops suffered a succession of smaller defeats during the British advance towards the Tugela River in January 1900. He was eventually demoted in February 1900.

[3] Lord Roberts had arrived at Cape Town on 10 January to assume overall command of British forces, but though he advised Redvers Buller to remain in a defensive position until Roberts was familiarized with the situation, Buller managed to gain approval for an attack intended to relieve the British forces at Ladysmith. Buller's vagueness of command and the ponderous forward movement of the British forces brought a succession of severe defeats, culminating in Spion Kop.

the seizure of the German ships, & are much afraid of serious trouble with France[4] —

Yeats came to tea & stayed to dinner but had to go to some mystical meeting then[5] — Shadowy Waters on its way to America, for the N. A. Review[6] — He had received an [un]expected cheque, 25 guineas from the "Academy", a "prize" for the best book of poems in the year,[7] & is as pleased as a baby, especially as some mystic had foretold he was to come into some money he had not earned — He brought me the cheque to be changed, & is going to buy a new suit of clothes, & some books — He believes a new period of political activity is coming on in Ireland, but does not think it will be agrarian, because of the strength of the artisans in the towns — His occult ideas make him think there may be a revolution coming on, for Miss Gonne believes that she has been "sent" to stir up disloyalty, & though he thinks her hopes unreasonable, he thinks a prophet is "an unreasonable person sent by Providence when it is going to do an unreasonable thing".

20th — To see Sir F. Burton, found him much aged & shaken & weak, but able to talk & be interested in all that goes on — Yeats came to dine — He thinks, as I do, Phillips's "Paulo & Francesca" a poor thing, insincere — Accounts for its good reception by its being in the beaten track of ideas, that people are prepared for & need not exert their mind for — & partly because they have long been calling out for a poet playwriter who was also an actor & here they have one,[8] — but there are occasional felicities in it —

21 — Sunday — Went to see Lady Layard who is busy making "fisher caps" for sick soldiers, & sewing little Union Jacks on to various garments — Of course she is, like other British, in a frenzy of rage with the Boers — There is no use saying anything, people think it is because one is Irish & wishing for the downfall of England, & to state one's reasons is, as Bagehot wd say, like "giving

---

4 On 29 December 1899, British warships seized the German steamer Bundesrath, alleging that it was carrying German volunteers and munitions to aid the Boers, and in the following week several other German vessels were seized on the same pretext. The German Government portrayed the action as a petulant response to recent British defeats by the Boers, and the ships were soon released without incident. Establishment concern at rising strength of Nationalist parties in France is epitomised by the multi-column editorial in *The Times* 3 January 1900, p. 6 (and see also p. 194 n. 126).

5 Probably a meeting of The Golden Dawn.

6 *The North American Review*, May 1900.

7 See *The Academy*, 20 January 1900, p. 63.

8 With the publication of the verse drama *Paolo and Francesca*, Stephen Phillips (1868–1915), who had hitherto enjoyed scant success as an actor and poet, enjoyed a meteoric rise to critical acclaim, with many critics dubbing him Tennyson's successor. Two other verse dramas, *Herod* and *Ulysses*, were also well received, but thereafter critical enthusiasm for his simple neo-romanticism faded.

a tract to a Bull of Bashan"9 — On to lunch with the Morrises — who are by no means in that line — Wolseley, both Ld. M. & Lady L[ayard]. say, is going wrong in the head & forgets things — so no wonder the W[ar]. O[ffice]. is in confusion, especially as Paul says Knox is so cross at being forbidden by Lord L[ansdowne] to make any more cock-a-hoop speeches that they are hardly on speaking terms, which impedes work — I was telling Lord M. about Buller drinking "most of the champagne" at Lisdoonvarna — & he says he has taken quantities out with him, & that he was on a committee of Grillon's Club with him, & there was an accumulation of money to spend, & deliberations as to using it for portraits of members etc, but Buller insisted, in such a bullying way that they gave in, that it should be spent on champagne, at £1 a bottle! That is a general to put against praying Boers! — George Moore in the afternoon — has *signed* the re-written "Tale of a Town" & called it "the bending of a bough"10 —

22 — Dined Ly. Layard, & on to a party at Yeats to meet Miss Milligan — whose play, or a part of it is going to be performed11 — but there was nearly a row as George Moore, who is resolving himself into a syndicate for the re-writing of plays wanted to alter hers, & she refuses to let any hand touch it but her own — However that calmed down — then a row about Mrs. Emery, who W. B. Y. thought had been promised some parts, but G. M. has given them to someone else.

23 — Some shopping & cards — Dinner at home, the Barry O'Briens, G. Moore, E. Martyn, Yeats — & pleasant talk enough — G. M. has been writing an article on "the decadence of England"12 — a subject we all agree on — B. O'Brien had written to Gavan Duffy that my proposal that his Nationalist relics, or objects, shd be bought by subscription & given to the Nat[ional]. Lit[erary]. Society, was the only practical one, & he agrees it is the best13 —

9 See *Psalms* 22.12. AG is probably referring to Walter Bagehot (1826–77), the critic, constitutional scholar and Editor of *The Economist* 1860–77, known for his pithy sayings.

10 Moore had almost certainly privately intended to sign the play for some time, as he began negotiating with Fisher Unwin for its publication as early as November 1899.

11 Alice Milligan (1866–1953), poet and dramatist. An active nationalist despite her Ulster Presbyterian background, she lectured widely under the auspices of the Gaelic League in its early years. Co-founded and edited the Belfast-based radical political magazine *The Shan Van Vocht* 1896–99 with Ethna Carbery. Her play *The Last Feast of the Fianna* was staged by the Irish Literary Theatre in 1900 (see p. 242 n. 92), but met with minimal success and was her only involvement with the theatre movement.

12 This became his speech "The Irish Literary Renaissance and the Irish Language" delivered at the National Literary Society banquet in Dublin on 23 February 1900. AG gives some account of its evolution in succeeding entries (and see p. 240 n. 81).

13 Gavan Duffy's collection of Irish books, newspapers and manuscripts, which included letters by O'Connell, Thomas Davis, John Blake Dillon and John Mitchel, and literary manuscripts by Carleton, Davis, and Lady Wilde, was subsequently purchased as AG suggested. A summary catalogue of the collection is included in the *Irish Literary Society Gazette,* June 1899.

I offered £10 & Ed. will give £15 — B. O'B. says it is coming out more & more clearly that the P[rince]. of Wales was concerned in the [Jameson] Raid — Hawksley[14] as good as told him that Chamberlain was in it — And our B[isho]p of Armagh in his formal prayers returns thanks that we are not guilty of the 'crimson sin' of having begun the war! — They got on to Caesar & Bonaparte, B. O'B. says Pompey was a better general than Caesar, but he had more character — G. M. said it was striking to read Tolstoy's account of Bonaparte's efforts to get to Moscow, & the Russian efforts to keep him from reaching it,[15] & if he had not reached it he wd not have lost his army — I said it was like the anxiety the Boers had had for a seaport, & the determination of the English they shd not have one, & now the gr hope for the Boers was their having no place that the British Navy could reach — G. M. very low about an actor for his Jasper Dean,[16] the present one being hopelessly inert.

24 — Enid Layard after lunch, took her to call on Sir Frederic, who, braver than I, ventured a word in favour of the Boers — Then to Mrs. Green, much interested abt L. Theatre[17] — With Ed. Martyn to dine at Criterion & to "Midsummer Night's Dream" beautifully put on the stage, & Tree delightful as Bottom & music charming[18] — Ed. had been to see me in the morning also, & says the rehearsal of G. Moore's version is going very badly, Delange the manager says he can make nothing of it — this accounts for G. Moore's low spirits[19] — Edward of course pleased, as he had foretold its failure, Delange asked to see his version, but he won't show it without a written statement from "a majority of the Committee" that they wish for his play & withdraw theirs — I ask who "the Committee" are except Yeats, Moore & himself — He says I am one, which I deny, but they have evidently been using me in that capacity to bring pressure to bear on him — His temper is up & he says truly that he is being badly treated, never consulted, his opinion put aside, but he means to shake off "those chaps" — He says "the only one who was at all nice to me about my play was you" — I am troubled about the whole business —

---

[14] Bourchier Hawksley, the London solicitor for Cecil Rhodes's British South Africa Company. Hawksley's office had been the co-ordinating point for much of the telegram traffic prior to the Jameson Raid, material he concealed in the face of strong questioning when testifying at the Raid inquiry. He later helped Rhodes draft his Will, and assisted in designing the Rhodes scholarship programme.

[15] In *War and Peace*.

[16] The central character in Moore's *The Bending of the Bough*.

[17] Alice Stopford Green (1847–1929), niece of Stopford Brooke and widow of historian John Richard Green (d.1883).

[18] A production which ran for 153 performances at Her Majesty's Theatre between January and March 1900 starring actor and theatre manager Herbert Beerbohm Tree (1853–1917).

[19] The rehearsals prompted Moore to a flurry of revisions. As he wrote to Fisher Unwin on 21 January: "My second act is bad very bad. I wrote a new act yesterday" (Helmut Gerber, *George Moore in Transition* p. 189). Herman De Lange (1851–1929), enjoyed a long career as an actor, Stage Manager and Director in London.

25 — Lunched Haliburtons — Ld. H. says Wolseley is no good for office work, & Buller shines there, but in war Wolseley has imagination, which Buller is lacking in, & cd see "what was on the other side of the hill" — while Buller can only go at the hill doggedly & get to the top — Ly. Shrewsbury there, & Mr. F. Schuster,[20] & Mr. Howard Sturgis[21] — Ev[ening], Yeats dined, says he & Moore have re-written 3rd act & it is going better — won't even think of such an idea as withdrawing it — He read me "Shadowy Waters" in its final state — very beautiful, but it has lost more than it has gained by the alterations made at Moore's dictation, is simpler, more rounded, more equal, but much of the imaginative beauty gone — it seems to be as a planet now, but it was a star —

The taking of Spion Kop was announced[22] —

26 — At rehearsal of "Bending of a Bough" 12-00 to 3-30, & only 3 acts through then — very amusing, Delange the stage manager a splendid general, drilling & placing them all, letting nothing pass — Moore smartly got up, watching closely, & near his temper — Ed. Martyn who has been requested by Moore not to make any more comments, made them only in depreciating whispers to me — Yeats suggesting new alterations, & pining for lunch —

Posters announce "Spion Kop abandoned" after all the triumphs of yesterday.

To Sir F. Burton — who was not yet down at 4 — & decidedly weaker, I am afraid he will not last very long — He told me he had a portfolio of sketches made in Connemara in 1839 which he wishes to give me, if he can find it, but it is in his studio & he will look for it "if I get over this illness, for I would like the sketches of that happy time to be in your keeping" — Dined Lady Layard, only Lord Duncannon there — furious with the Salisbury-Balfour regime, both in Ireland & S. Africa — wishes for Chamberlain with a free hand, & Rosebery to help him — He says last May he dined at Ly. Selkirk's, & Montague White[23] was there, & had a long talk with him & told him of the Boer armaments, & that they wd take the field in October because they

[20] Possibly Francis Schuster (1823–1906), father of the 1st Bart.

[21] Howard Sturgis (1854–1920), author of the novel *Belchamber*. Friend of Henry James and Edith Wharton.

[22] The triumphant despatches announcing the occupation of Spion Kop were grossly premature, as British forces had in fact only occupied a secondary summit in the face of minor Boer resistance, and reflected British desperation to announce victorious news after a string of defeats. Next day, Boer troops overwhelmed the ill-positioned British troops, killing more than 400 and wounding over 1000.

[23] Montagu [*sic*] White (1857–1916), Consul-General in London for the S. African Republic 1892–1900.

believed the independence of their country was threatened — And if he knew & was ready to tell that, why did not the Govt. know it? And the same way with the [Jameson] Raid — Freddy Guest[24] on his way out to S. Africa wrote back from shipboard that the rising at Johannesburg was to take place at such a time — & why did not the Govt. know it? And who is responsible, the Govt. or their military advisers for the insufficient preparations & inadequate guns? — Evelyn Wood[25] is under petticoat influence, & the whole W[ar]. O[ffice]. more or less under it — He has seen a letter, ready for publication giving a list of officers sent out at the bidding of certain ladies — And he was told by the mother of a young officer that he was anxious to go but couldn't get leave, but a lady who had taken a fancy to him said she cd manage it, went down to the W. O. and at once he was attached to a reg[imen]t going out — Then she took a fancy to go out herself, took her ticket, asked him if he would like to come in the same ship — He said he was under orders to sail a week earlier — She said that didn't matter, went again to the W. O. & he got orders to go in her ship — It seems like the decadence of England! — In Ireland, the crowning sin of the Govt. is having thought of putting Gill into the B[oar]d of Agriculture, an ex-Parnellite, & it must be said a shady one[26] — Ld. D[uncannon]. wrote to the D[uke]. of Devonshire to ask if it was true, expecting an indignant denial, but he wrote back to say Ld. Cadogan was coming over soon & he wd talk to him about it[27] —

27 — Lunched Sir A. Lyall — B. Holland there & Sir Spencer Walpole — Talked of dreams — Sir A. wonders if Daniel really knew what Nebuchadnezzar's dream was, or whether he thought of one, & conveyed it hypnotically to him[28] — Of Kipling, Sir A. says he has gone down very low with "Pay, pay, pay" — & will lose his poetic reputation, tho' "Recessional" saves it still — S. Walpole says "Pay, pay" is all right, as it serves its purpose — I say a collecting box with a slit in it will do that, but it isn't poetry[29] — Sir A. wonders why a gr poetic voice has not come from Ireland, which has had miseries enough to inspire it — I tell him of the break in its literature caused by the change in the language —

[24] Frederick Guest (1875–1937), third son of Lady Layard's brother Lord Wimborne.

[25] General Sir Evelyn Wood (1838–1919), Adjutant-General to the Armed Forces 1897–1901.

[26] Plunkett's appointment of Gill, a Catholic and Parnellite activist during the Plan of Campaign, to the Department of Agriculture and Technical Instruction, was subsequently a key factor in Plunkett's loss of his Parliamentary seat. See p. 297 n. 7.

[27] George Cadogan (1840–1915), 5th Earl, was Lord Lieutenant of Ireland 1895–1902. Spencer Compton Cavendish, 8th Duke of Devonshire, had been Chief Secretary of Ireland 1870–74, and was now in the Cabinet as Lord President of the Council.

[28] See *Daniel* 1–2.

[29] "Pay—pay—pay" is the closing refrain in each stanza of "The Absent-Minded Beggar", a hugely popular poem by Rudyard Kipling (1865–1939) which appeals for money for the wives and children of British "Tommies" fighting in S. Africa.

Some visits, & Yeats to dine — very angry with Martyn, & with me for defending him — says Moore claims that no one can have more than one conscience, & his is an intellectual conscience — & no one with that can forgive Martyn's want of intelligence — I say if I have but one conscience it is a conscience of friendship — Our practical quarrel is about Beltaine, which I say he ought to be let see before it is printed, as a right act, & an act of courtesy — He is angry, says when an editor is trusted he shd be let alone, & that Martyn may object to some <??> sentence[30] — Then he declares that Moore wrote most of "The Heather Field" & a gr part of "Maeve" — (a new story) — says Moore told him so & he believes him — (all very well, but he doesn't believe him when he attacks Miss Gonne's morality) — We go to I. Literary Society — & he makes a very good little lecture on the Theatre & the idealising of Ireland[31] — Some vulgar recitations that made me cross — Home, & Y. went off to make more suggestions of corrections to G. Moore —

28 — Sunday, & fog & snow — & headache — so sat quiet & read "The Ancient Wisdom" Yeats had left me[32] — Ed. Martyn afternoon — delighted that his "Maeve" has gone so well, & very cheery — I begged him not to publish "Tale of a Town" as he intended, as it cd not hold its own with the others as literature whatever it may be as a play, & he assented — He brought news of Redvers Buller's telegram announcing the retreat across the Tugela![33] After all the triumph of Spion Kop — Dined Grant Duffs, but the news, which I brought, of the retreat depressed Sir M[ountstuart]. & the others were chiefly miscellaneous girls and young men — Sir M. agreeing that the Boers had been badly treated, but very bloodthirsty for all that, & in spite of his

[30] WBY's editorial comments for the February 1900 issue of *Beltaine* ranged over *The Bending of the Bough, The Heather Field* and *Maeve* (all of which were potentially touchy subjects for Martyn), and also the brief essay Martyn had contributed, "A Comparison between English and Irish Theatrical Audiences."

[31] No report of WBY's lecture on "The Irish Literary Theatre" to the ILS on 27 January 1900 appears to have survived.

[32] *The Ancient Wisdom* by Annie Besant. Mrs. Besant had been converted to theosophy by Madame Blavatsky's *The Secret Doctrine* in 1889, and worked briefly with WBY in the Esoteric Section of the Society. She was this point head of one of the factions into which the Theosophical Society had split after Blavatsky's death.

[33] After the defeat at Spion Kop, British troops withdrew across the Tugela river to be regrouped under Lord Roberts's command. The retreat earned Redvers Buller the nickname "Sir Reverse" and a subsequent withdrawal across the river prompted the nickname "the Ferryman of the Tugela". The whispering campaign against Buller reached its height following Spion Kop, and he became the scapegoat for British failures. Thomas Pakenham's comprehensive account, *The Boer War*, largely rehabilitates Buller for being the only British General to devise effective strategies to counter Boer guerilla tactics and to recognise the defensive advantages resulting from long-range, smoke-free repeating rifles and the use of trenches. Buller's later campaigns, from his relief of Ladysmith until he left for England in October 1900, were overwhelmingly successful, but he was nonetheless sacked in 1901.

depression repeating little jokes such as of the young fellow rejected for Yeomanry as having a bad tooth who said "Well, it is to kill Boers I want, not to eat them" — He is very down on Redvers Buller, says he can do two things well, embroidery & choosing wine, of which he takes too much, but nothing else — Mr. Thomas, an engineer next me, devoid of humour, but scientifically intelligent — Drove home with Rd. Ward[34] —

29 — To National Gallery — & to various horrors, trying on coat, trying on stays & dentist — who says a tooth must come out — Sat with Sir Frederic — Ev. quiet —

30 — G[eral]dine came up, & we set out together to Oxford to see Robert — a great delight seeing him there, well & happy in his own snug little rooms — I wd rather have had him to myself, but owed a treat to G. — Tea with [Gus] Kelly — Back & straight to theatre — "The Canary" & "The Sacrament of Judas"[35] — G. delighted — Worked in the morning at article for "Beltaine".[36]

31st — A tooth out! & spent the afternoon in seclusion at Savile Row, typing article for Beltaine — Ly. Layard excited about her scheme for villa hospitals at Madiera for officers — My belief is they would not stay there, within 4 days of friends & home — And then she went off excitedly to have safety pins made with little Union Jacks on, for Tommy to fasten his bandages with — Dined with Ly. Shrewsbury to meet Lady Londonderry, Ld. Morris, Edmund Gosse,[37] Mr. Cockerell & Bishop Rendall[38] — very pleasant, there is certainly an <??> in a perfectly ordered & arranged dinner & the refinement of a charming house — The talk too much of the war to be really good — all friends of Buller, but Lady L. wanting to know why he changed his plans when he went out, what pressure was brought to bear on him — Lord M. says a man

34 Richard Ward, son of "Ideal" Ward of the Oxford Movement, and brother of theologian and prominent Catholic Wilfrid Ward (see below p. 260 n. 159).

35 *The Canary*, a three act comedy by "George Fleming" (Constance Fletcher, 1858–1938) with Mrs. Patrick Campbell in the principal role, ran for 50 performances at the Prince of Wales's (November–December 1899) and Royalty Theatre (January–February 1900). *The Sacrament of Judas*, a one-act play by Louis Tiercelin (translated by Louis Parker) and also starring Mrs. Patrick Campbell, opened at the Prince of Wales Theatre in October 1899, and played as a double-bill with *The Canary* from November onwards.

36 "Last Year", a compendium of approving reviews of the performances by the Irish Literary Theatre in May 1899, published in *Beltaine* in February 1900.

37 Edmund Gosse (1849–1928), dismissed by WBY in 1886 as an "admirable but altogether trivial, English poet" (*UP1* p. 92), gradually rose to prominence as a critic and literary establishment figure and was knighted in 1925. WBY had by this point been friendly with Gosse for several years, and was his frequent dinner guest. For Gosse's part in assisting WBY gain a Civil List pension in 1910, and the tensions caused by an insulting letter he sent AG in the process, see *Mem* pp. 250–58.

38 Dr. James Leslie Randall [*sic*] (d.1922), Bishop of Reading 1889–1908.

in Galway said to him "We are for the Boers — but we are not for the Orange Free State!"[39] The Union of the Irish party has taken place on the basis that every man in it is to do as he likes![40] I had a talk with Gosse, a slightly condensed Sharp, abt Yeats, who he gushes over — The Bishop who had been with the Army in the Soudan, pining to be in fights again —

[February] 1st — Sat with Paul at his breakfast — he says the Govt. will throw the Generals over & they deserve it — To Irish Industries meeting — not much done, except sale settled for Patrick's Day in spite of the War — It was proposed it shd be put off till the summer — but who knows but England may be in a worse plight then! Lady Betty Balfour offered me the U[nder]. Sec[retary's]. Lodge to put up at in Dublin, she will be away but "her family" there — Horace Plunkett spoke, looking weak & shaky still — Lunched with the Morrises — Ld. M. very humorous & in good humour — To see Mrs. Frederic Harrison who says her husband's anti-war lecture the night before was very successful & well received[41] — She says it was dreadful before the war began how all women in Society were urging it on — but now there is a feeling springing up against it — To Sir F. Burton — & home where Yeats came to dine, & read me his own paper & Moore's for "Beltaine"[42] — I told him there *must* be a general for the 3 years of our theatre, & he assented, but Martyn & Moore have had another row & it may be difficult to help it — After he left at 11-30 Paul came in, had been from breakfast to 6 answering questions for Parliament, then had his own work to do, & had only just finished — He thinks the Govt. must go, the public are getting so vexed at the shilly shally debate going on, & cry for drastic measures — but there are none to take — Buller is going to make another attack but in a different way this time — one must hope very different!

2nd — To Baly[43] — & lunched with Sir A. Birch who rails chiefly against Rhodes — says it was he who clamoured for war, assuring the Govt. that the Boers would cave in as soon as attacked — I asked if Chamberlain had really known the Raid was coming up, & he said "They all knew it — I did for one" — Miss Keyser, the rich Jewess with whom the Prince constantly sups, has by

39 The speaker presumably suspected that the Orange Free State, which had formally allied with the Transvaal in the war, was related to the Protestant "Orange" Order.

40 The competing Nationalist factions had entered a period of rapprochement, mainly through their common opposition to British policy during the Boer War. The union was cemented by the anti-Parnellites' acceptance of Parnellite John Redmond as chairman of the United Irish League.

41 Harrison's speech, "The Two Republics", arguing the futility of British intervention in Cape Colony and Boer affairs, was delivered at the Queen's Hall on 31 January. For a report see *The Times* 1 February, p. 6. His wife Ethel, née Harrison, d.1916.

42 WBY contributed "Plans and Methods" and "'Maive' and Certain Irish Beliefs" to the February issue of *Beltaine*. Moore's contribution was "Is the Theatre a Place of Amusement?"

43 Charles Baly and son, AG's Harley Street dentists, who also treated WBY extensively.

his suggestion given up dinner parties, & offered the first floor of her house for wounded officers, to be kept free of charge[44] — It is she & Mrs. Rd. Chamberlain[45] who have Evelyn Wood in hand, chiefly — Looked in at Ly. Layard, found her preparing for a committee meeting re Madiera Hospital — Sleet came on & I had to come home for the rest of the day —

3 — Snow kept me in for the morning — Then went & sat with Annie Maxwell, recovering from influenza — She railed at the United Irish League[46] — & tried to make me say I was for the war, but I "kept silence for good & evil" — Then to Mrs. Dugdale — Mrs. Russell came in (Miss Bailey of long ago)[47] & they talked war — one young fellow lately killed had lunched with Mrs. D. before he left, looking so well & handsome — It seems rather cruel to his family that the report sent back to them says he was only found two days after the battle, dead (I think Magersfontein) & the wound was such a slight one he wd probably have been saved if it had been attended to in time — An officer's wife told Mrs. D. that her husband had written her a terrible acct of the flight of the Highlanders [at Magersfontein] — they ran over him & trampled him, they were howling with fright, some of them on hands & knees, quite demoralised & terror stricken — Dined Reginald Smith & sat next him — We spoke of the indignation expressed against the Dean of Durham for his sermon against sending soldiers out drunk, & showing that he disapproved of the war — The Ld. Chancellor as well as Judge Grantham have abused him for alluding to politics in the pulpit[48] — well & good if it were applied to all — but I have had to sit under A-D. Daly with his "Rebellion is as the sin of witchcraft"[49] & R. Smith had heard Canon Farrer preach at Canterbury this

44 Agnes Keyser (1852–1941), daughter of a wealthy stockbroker, devoted her career and income to nursing. Prince Edward, whom she first met in early 1898, appears to have been attracted to her as a mother-figure, and she was probably not his mistress. During the course of the Boer War, she converted her house in Grosvenor Crescent into a fully-equipped hospital, aided by funds from a trust set up by Prince Edward. After his accession to the throne, it became the King Edward's Hospital for Officers. She continued to enjoy the patronage of most of the Royal Family, including that of George V, after Edward's death.

45 Mrs. Richard Chamberlain, widow of Joseph Chamberlain's brother, who had died in 1899. An ardent Imperialist, she had spent part of the winter of 1899–1900 at the Cape during the build-up of British military strength prior to the first major advances against the Boers.

46 The United Irish League, founded in early 1898 by William O'Brien, sought to redistribute agricultural land to the benefit of smallholders by coercing large estates to sell. Though never as violent in its methods as the Land League, the UIL drew on massive and effective support, and helped usher in the Wyndham Act in 1903 which made Government funds available for land purchase and redistribution.

47 Philippa Russell (née Baillie), wife of Maj. General Frank Russell (1840–1912), career soldier, and M.P. for Cheltenham 1895–1900.

48 For a report quoting the sermon preached on 21 January 1900 by Dr. Kitchin (1827–1912), Dean of Durham 1894–1912, and Judge William Grantham's hostile response on 26 January, see The Times 29 January 1900, p. 11. Grantham (1835–1911) was Justice of the Queen's Bench Division of the High Court from 1886.

49 Samuel 15:23.

winter on the war which he declared to be an absolutely right one — & he said in his sermon "And what shall we say for the noble boy from this town who killed three Boers with his own hand?" — I told him of Sir Alfred Lyall saying the only thing that makes him believe in eternal punishment is the existence of Farrer — Sidney Lee,[50] & the Thackeray Ritchies, & Mary Hynes, I didn't know the others —

4 — Fog, but to Westminster Abbey — Lunched Ly. Layard — Horace Plunkett in the afternoon, full of cares of his new Board[51] — & I think far more Unionist than before his illness — seems to think the grant for the Board satisfies our financial claims, & that we ought to be grateful — I say no, if we are owed the money let us have it, there is no question of gratitude, and we ought not to have to sit up and beg for it every time — He says he sympathizes with the Boer farmers in the war — but if so, why did he go out of his way to make a speech in favour of it[52] —

5th — G[eral]dine & Hugh Lane to lunch — he is rather over<?bearing>, but tells of his successes, how he sold on Saturday for [£]40 a "Cuyp" he had bought in Dublin for 15/- etc[53] — With Geraldine to rehearsal of "Maeve", to take Peg Inerney's costume, & to show "Maeve" G.'s red petticoat, Edward Martyn wishing her to wear one[54] — She however rejects it, saying Maeve was supposed to have a sense of beauty! — The rehearsal went well, though the acting is not good — but the play is beautiful, and gives just the impression I had when I first read it in MS of taking one into a beautiful dream world — Tea with Yeats & G[eral]dine — Then to Sir Frederic — He says 2 of his

[50] Sidney Lee (1859–1926), Shakespeare scholar, and Editor of *The Dictionary of National Biography* 1891–1917.

[51] The Department of Agriculture and Technical Instruction, a State Ministry which addressed and funded a broad range of self-help and agricultural improvement programmes. Plunkett served as a Vice-President of DATI until forced to resign in 1907.

[52] In a speech to the Primrose League at Kingstown on 4 December 1899, Plunkett had moved a motion of "cordial support to Her Majesty's Government in the policy they have adopted in regard to the war in South Africa." Plunkett, who had in fact avoided taking a position on the war for as long as possible, argued that Boer treatment of Uitlanders had made British military intervention inevitable. His remarks were entirely free of jingoism, and urged a generous policy towards the Boers and the ensurance of religious and personal liberty regardless of national origin once the war ended. AG's distaste for the speech probably stemmed more from Plunkett's swingeing attacks on pro-Boer Irish Nationalists as "un-Christian and unintelligent" for harbouring hatred of England on account of the Famine, and earlier events such as the 1798 uprising, "which it was about time to forget." For a comprehensive report, see *The Irish Times* 5 February 1899, p.3.

[53] AG gives a different account of Lane's discovery of a painting by Dutch landscape artist Jacob Cuyp (*c.*1575–*c.*1650), father of the better-known artist Albert Cuyp, in *Hugh Lane* pp. 39–41.

[54] The role of Maeve in Martyn's play was taken by Dorothy Hammond, who also played in *The Bending of the Bough* and *The Last Feast of the Fianna*. She subsequently took no further part in the theatre movement.

pictures were burned in the Pantechnicon, put in by different possessors — "The Fisherman's Burial" & a portrait of 2 sisters — Promised me an engraving of the "Blind Girl" — his model for her was a younger daughter of Petrie[55] — It was bought by Genl. d'Aguilar,[56] & is now in the possession of his son's widow — Home eating some oysters on the way luckily, for G. Moore came in soon after 8, with his preface to "Bending of the Bough" & a wild scheme for having "The Shadowy Waters" translated into Irish for next year's theatre — that he may make the announcement in a speech he is going to make — He is now taking the Irish language under his patronage, & evidently thinks he is the only man to save it — I have no idea of consenting to let Shadowy Waters be translated, & will hold to its being acted next year in its own beautiful language — I believe what gives him his force is his power of only seeing one thing at a time, at the moment he only sees the language — whereas I see that the Theatre is the work in hand, & our immediate duty — Poor Shadowy Waters! it would appear to the audience as "Three men in a Boat"[57] talking gibberish!

Then when he had gone Paul came in, at 11 — very tired & depressed — will give no news, by which I suppose Buller is marching, but doesn't seem hopeful —

6 — To Mudies, for books for Sir Frederic, & for Mrs. Lecky (Celtic movement) & then bought sandwiches & took them to picnic lunch with Yeats, who looks ill still — Then to some calls, only Mrs. John Murray at home, & back very tired — Dined with Albert Ball at Albermarle Club — Mrs. Green & some young ladies — sat between Richard Ward & a Mr. Strett, author of "Diary of a Boy" which I haven't read,[58] but I didn't care for him — Mrs. G. told me of meeting the Bullers at the Lyalls, & Sir A. came & said "I can't stay talking to Lady L[yall].[59] any longer — she will call me Sir Audrey"! Paul came in when I got back, tired & depressed with the crossedness of things —

7 — Baly, for a long hour, nerve removed & tooth stopped — Lunched Ly. Layard, Lady Humphrey[60] there — To Sir F. Burton — & to see Clara Jackson[61] & Comyns Carrs & home very tired — Dinner Yeats, E. Martyn —

55 George Petrie (1798–1866), Irish painter and antiquary.

56 General George Charles d'Aguilar (1784–1855), Commander of British forces in China in the 1840s.

57 Jerome K. Jerome's classic 1889 comic novella, recounting the (mis)adventures of three young Londoners on a boat trip up the Thames.

58 George Slythe Street (1867–1936), author of *The Autobiography of a Boy* and numerous other works of fiction.

59 Cora, Lady Lyall, née Cloete.

60 Probably May Humphry, née McNab, widow of Sir George Humphry (d.1896), a distinguished surgeon.

61 Clara Huth-Jackson, formerly Grant Duff (see p. 70 n. 24).

Albert Ball & Philip Comyn Carr — pleasant enough, a good deal of theatre talk — C. Carr much inclined to come over for theatre —

8th — A dullish dinner at the Clays — had 3 other invitations but theirs came first — Herbert Marshalls[62] — Cockerell —

9th — Half expecting Robert, but a telegram to say he couldn't come — & expecting Yeats & another telegram that he had a cold & couldn't come — To lecture on Gaelic Literature — with Mrs. Green, at Grosvenor H[ou]se Club — Alfred Nutt lectured — read extracts from Bricriu's feast etc — Audience looking for jokes — When he spoke of Celtic chivalry & told how Cuchullin sent a part of the herbs brought to heal him across the ford to his wounded enemy, all burst out laughing[63] — such a joke! — certainly so unlike the conduct of the present war — Snow came on —

10 — To see Yeats, found him just up, coughing terribly — I made his breakfast & brought fruit etc — He says Barry O'Brien was at the war debate & said Tim Healy's speech was wonderful — He led the House on to a trap — telling how the Morning Post had published a letter from Winston Churchill giving an account of the splendid courage, coolness & gallantry of the Irish soldiers, & saying that they were the finest infantry in the world — (cheers) — This had been copied into 9 English papers (cheers, to emphasize English magnanimity) — Yes — into 9 English papers but in every one of them the word "Irish" had been left out! — Stony silence, & the House at the end of his speech sat cowering as if it had been whipped[64] — The Union of parties will rather spoil the effect of our play, that is the worst[65] — On to Sir F. Burton, so spent my day between two invalids —

11 — Sunday — Snow & slush, so went to see Yeats & tell him he must not venture out — Lit his fire & got his breakfast ready — He said Symons who dined with him the night before had discussed the question as to whether any man with self respect cd wear goloshes — as he, like Yeats, arrives at houses he dines at with muddy boots — I went on to lunch with Lady Layard — Lord Robert Cecil there so I consulted him & he said snow-shoes are the thing now

[62] Herbert Menzies Marshall (1841–1913), architect and artist. Arthur Clay's contemporary as a student at Cambridge.

[63] For AG's version of Bricriu's Feast see *Cuchulain of Muirthemne* pp. 53–62. For her account of Cuchulain's sharing of herbs during his fight with Ferdiad, see *Cuchulain of Muirthemne* pp. 180–81. Nutt's own volume *Cuchulainn, the Irish Achilles* appeared later in 1900.

[64] See *Hansard's Parliamentary Debates*, 4th Series, **VOL?**, pp. 865–66 (7 February 1900). Churchill's letter appeared in *The Morning Post* 26 January 1900, p. 5. Tim Healy (1855–1931), Nationalist M.P. 1880–1918, and Governor-General of the Irish Free State 1922–28, was an outspoken opponent of Parnell after the split.

[65] *The Bending of the Bough* is a satire on the long-running divisions in the Irish Parliamentary Party. One of the characters was based on Tim Healy.

— He is very sorry for himself, having joined the Volunteers in a moment of enthusiasm, & not liking the drill — Enid said she had joined a ladies' Volunteer reg[imen]t after the Crimean war, & practised shooting, she forgot what at — something white — I suggested "a flag of truce" which amused Ld. R. — Evening back to Yeats with some cold chicken & beef & bread & wine, & dined, or picnicked with him —

12 — Baly & dressmaker — Una Birch came to see rehearsal of "Bending of the Bough" — Ed. Martyn took us there & we wandered thro' passages of theatres — Rehearsal began in a little room at the Vaudeville & ended on the stage at Terry's — It went well, at least it will go well in Dublin from all the local allusions, but 3rd act is weak, & it isn't much of a play if the truth be told, tho' there are some good bits — Tea with Una, George Moore & Yeats — G. M. full of the speech he is going to make at the banquet about the Irish language — which as is his way, he seems to think he has discovered! Dined with Enid Layard — She had asked Soveral,[66] the Portuguese Minister, why we had all the nations against us in this war & he said "because they think, as many people in England do, that it is an unjust one!" — she gasped but made no answer —

13 — Lunched Morrises, to ask if they wd help about Jack's exhibition,[67] but they were cautious & not very responsive — & Mrs. Barton writes coldly that their own water colour ex comes off next day, so she can't help — & Lady Fingall hasn't answered — Dine Birchs, sat between Sidney Colvin & Sir Mansfield Clark[68] — the latter who was Commissioner in Basutoland says there is a good deal to be said for the Boers — He says the real bitter pill to them after annexation was sending Sir Owen Lanyon who had black blood (his grandmother was a negress) which they have a horror of, to swagger & lord it over them[69] — British stupidity! Sidney Colvin abusing G[eorge]. M[oore]. (for Stevenson's sake) & Symons (for Phillips's sake) & singing Phillips's praises[70] — he is so fine & athletic & *reads* poetry so beautifully.

14 — To see Sir Frederic — & dined Haliburtons, a banquet, the Ld.

---

[66] Luis de Soveral (1862–1922), Portuguese Foreign Minister 1895–97, Portuguese Minister in London 1897–1910, and an intimate friend of Prince Edward.

[67] Jack Yeats's exhibition, "Sketches of Life in the West of Ireland", opened at the Leinster Hall, Dublin, the following week.

[68] Sir Charles Mansfield Clark (1839–1932), Commissioner of Basutoland 1880–81, Quartermaster-General to the Armed Forces 1899–1903, and subsequently Governor of Malta 1903–07.

[69] Sir William Owen Lanyon (1842–87), administrator of the Transvaal 1879–81. Spurious rumours about his "black blood" started to circulate soon after his appointment to the Transvaal, as a result of his personal unpopularity, gaining credence from Lanyon's naturally dark complexion, and from his having commanded black troops throughout much of his career.

[70] See p. 226 n. 8.

Chancellor & Ly. Halsbury[71] — Ld. Wolseley, Sir Ed. Bradford, Ld. & Ly. Cork, Lady D. Nevill, Ld. & Ly. Duncannon, Sir Algernon West[72] — Mr. Watts Russell (Tony)[73] for the Halsbury girl[74] & another — I sat, well guarded, between the Chief Commissioner of Police & the Commander in Chief of the British Army! Sir Ed. charming, & pro-Boer in principle, but would like to kill them himself now we are at war — Ld. W. affable, but grew cross & excited talking of the Boers, so I left him to Lady Duncannon — "Dirty — ignorant — odious, uncivilised — never have a flower near their houses — not a flower" as if that was a reason for slaughtering them! — He doesn't think much of the Madiera hospital scheme — He looks much aged, his poor little mean face shrunken — Protests he has not a drop of Irish blood in his veins, & abuses Irish soldiers "hard to manage & drunken"[75] —

15 — Took Lady Morris, Una Birch, T. Watts Russell, Ethel, Mr. Cockerell & Capt. Ulick Brown,[76] to a rehearsal of "Maeve" at a tiny top room at the Vaudeville — First "[The Last Feast of] the Fianna" which I thought a poor & tawdry little piece — but "Maeve" went beautifully, a lovely thing, & all seemed to appreciate it — George Moore came to see me afterwards full of the speech on the language he is going to give at the Lit. lunch on Thursday — He is more gaedhilge[77] than Hyde or Concannon[78] now! wants me to write something to publish with it in a pamphlet — W. B. Y. to dine — we are both a little low about "Bending of the Bough" — it is not really a good play, & we feel that a play we produce ought not to depend on political allusions for its success — However we must make the best of it —

17 [i.e. 16] — A telegram from R. saying he cd come up, & I had to go to Baly & Durrant & so miss his arrival — He brought news of Kelly's engagement to Miss Comyn — She had written to say it was partly brought about by the visit to Coole — so my reputation as matchmaker will increase! We set out to rehearsal, with Ethel, Yeats & his sister — but they had promise of a stage at

[71] Harding Stanley Giffard (1823–1921), Lord Halsbury, Lord High Chancellor 1885–86, 1886–92, 1895–1905, and his wife Wilhelmina, née Woodfall (d.1927).

[72] Sir Algernon West (1832–1921), Gladstone's secretary when Prime Minister, and at this point Chairman of the Board of Inland Revenue.

[73] Formerly Tony Birch.

[74] Constance Mary Giffard (d.1962).

[75] Wolseley's family had been in Ireland for generations, and he was himself born and raised in Ireland. His protestations reflect a typical late-Victorian anxiety over cultural origins.

[76] George Ulick Brown (1856–1935), Captain in the Bengal Cavalry during the Afghan War, and succeeded his father as 6th Marquess of Sligo in 1913. Nephew of Lady Arthur Russell.

[77] Probably used here in the sense "cuír na gaedhilge" or "for the Irish language".

[78] Tomás Ua Concheanainn (1870–1960), also known as Thomas Concannon, born on the Aran islands, and served as a Gaelic League organiser and Irish language teacher 1898–1911. Wrote a number of Gaelic text books, plays and stories, often under the pseudonym Tomas Bhan. AG credited him with providing the inspiration for her play *The Rising of the Moon* during a visit to Coole (see *Journals* vol. 2, p. 428).

Terry's [Theatre], & it wasn't ready, & so we had to wait an hour outside the theatre door — & then all were cold & tired & a little cross, & the rehearsal seemed very forlorn — Edward rather pleased, abusing the play to me in whispers — & threatening to publish his own version — R. rather bored — It wasn't over till 7 — R. & I rushed to a restaurant, had some dinner, & went to "Florodora" which he wanted to see[79] — a dullish farce, but some pretty songs, <?? ?? ??> — Home tired — & said good night to my dear little man, very sorry to think of my early start, & that I should miss part of his visit, but I had promised Ed. Martyn to go, as the Nat. Lit. Society was to give a party in honour of the theatre, & he & the actors couldn't be in time — A letter from Lady Fingall saying she will bring Lady Cadogan[80] to the Private View, & will ask other <?fashionable> people (she is staying at the Castle) & H. Plunkett has forwarded some cards I sent him — & Lady Morris sends a few names — so my hopes rise —

17 — Up very early, & off to 8-30 train — Travelled with George Moore & Yeats — The former had brought his speech for us to read — very forcible in its paradoxical way — his point that the English language has been exhausted by all that has been written in it & especially by journalism, & that the literature of the future will be in the languages that are not used up, Irish, Welsh, Hungarian, perhaps Basque! — A very pleasant journey, a comfortable lunch in the train, the scenery lovely going thro' Wales — snow on the mountains & the sea blue as the Mediterranean — G. M. very amiable & really agreeable, & Yeats brilliant & fanciful[81] — A fine crossing — Y. came & dined at my lodgings, & we went, picking up G. M. on the way, to Lit. Soc. party — Douglas Hyde, between amusement & uneasiness at his new disciple, who is called by one of the papers "George the Baptist"[82] — Rolleston, delighted with "Bending of the Bough" which he has just read — & even his opinion is rather cheering — Yeats gave a beautiful little address on the plays — "Maeve, in which there is a wonderful literary invention, that of Peg Inerney — the old woman in rags in the day time, but living another, a second life, a Queen in the ideal world, a symbol of Ireland[83] — The financial question touched on

[79] *Florodora*, a highly successful musical farce, with libretto by Owen Hall (1854–1907), which ran for 455 performances at the Lyric Theatre 1899–1901.

[80] Beatrix, Lady Cadogan (d.1907), whose husband was then Lord Lieutenant of Ireland.

[81] For Moore's account of this trip and his delivery of the speech see *Ave* pp. 326–28. The speech was published in *Ideals in Ireland* as "Literature and the Irish Language".

[82] Nationalists were generally suspicious of Moore, as a result of his critical portraits of Irish life in *Parnell and his Island* and other early works, and his association with European "freethinkers" and Parisian life generally.

[83] In his article for the February 1900 issue of *Beltaine*, "'Maive' and Certain Irish Beliefs" (*UP*2 pp. 204–07) WBY enlarged on the folkloric basis of Peg Inerny [*sic*], the central character of *Maeve*, who is both peasant woman, incarnation of Queen Maeve, and symbol of Ireland. The theme provided a central inspiration for *Cathleen ni Houlihan*. For a report on WBY's speech, see *The Irish Times* 19 February 1900, p. 7.

in "Bending of the B." was chosen because in it all parties are united, but it means really the cause nearest to each of our hearts — The materialism of England & its vulgarity are surging up about us — it is not Shakespeare England sends us but musical farces, not Keats & Shelley but "Tit Bits" — A mystic friend of his had a dream in which he saw a candle, whose flame was in danger of being extinguished by a rolling sea — The waves sometimes seemed to go over it & quench it, & he knew it to be his own soul, & that if it was quenched, he wd have lost his soul — And now our ideal life is in danger from the sea of commonness about us"[84] —

18th — Wrote during the morning — Then went to Leinster Hall, & Willie[85] came then & we looked at Jack's pictures, a gr improvement in colour from last year, & as full of energy & imagination — but Miss <?Ling> ill still, & Miss <?Tennant> can't act as secretary — On to see Jack at Morehampton Road,[86] got there about 5 & he had just gone to see me — I waited till 8 there — he waited till 8 here so we missed, however I sent off more cards — & I went on to see Adelaide [Lane], & engaged Ruth as bookeeper for the week — Willie came in at 9-20 on his way to go round the papers — Has told Rolleston he must do something that will violently annoy the upper classes to redeem his character.[87]

19 — W. & Jack in, & we went to Leinster Hall, & were busy, arranging pictures, getting refreshments for reporters etc — I had put "At home 2-oo" — but at 2 no one appeared — at 3 a "gentleman" appeared, but it was to ask if we wd buy a Thom's Directory, or if we wanted any advertisements put in! However, about 4 [o'clock] people came quickly & thickly, Mahaffy, Lady Fingall, Lord Powerscourt,[88] Sir G[eorge] & Lady Morris,[89] Lady Arnott,[90] Martin & Richard Morris, Douglas Hyde, Lyster, Miss Stokes, Dr. Fitzgerald,[91] many I didn't know — The pictures much appreciated & admired, but alas, no sales — It was dark & the gas turned on, & some people said they wd come & see them by daylight — but anyhow buying wasn't in the air — Poor Jack ill after a working night — I went out for bovril & champagne for him & he

---

[84] This was presumably AE. WBY subsequently used the dream as the basis for a frontispiece illustration, designed by Thomas Sturge Moore (see p. 304 n. 32), which appeared in several Cuala Press editions of his work.

[85] AG addressed WBY as "Willie" from Autumn 1898 onwards in her letters, but this is her first use of the form in the diaries.

[86] Both Isaac Butt Yeats (1848–1930), Jack's uncle, and Jenny and Grace Yeats, his aunts, had homes on this street in Donnybrook.

[87] See p. 214 n. 75.

[88] Mervyn Wingfield, 7th Viscount Powerscourt (1836–1904).

[89] Elizabeth Morris, née Henchy (d.1912).

[90] Caroline, née Williams (d.1933), wife of Sir John Arnott (1853–1940), 2nd Bart.

[91] Probably George Fitzgerald (1851–1901), Professor of Philosophy at Trinity College 1881–1901.

cheered up — Ly. <?Cadogan> put off her visit —

Then the anxiety about the plays began[92] — W. Y. dined here & we set out together — found the Gaiety very well filled — A box was kept for the Committee, & we had it to ourselves. Douglas Hyde, who was in the stalls came now & again to talk to us, and Magragh[93] writing for the Freeman, came to consult about his report — Miss Milligan's tawdry little piece was well staged, but Finn & Usheen both very bad — & the language in the piece is to me intolerable — however it was very short & applauded — "Maeve" didn't begin very well, the long dialogue, & once the audience tittered, I think at old O'Heynes's fear that the rich son-in-law would not come back — but then things improved, & it went very well, the anti-English touches being much applauded & a little <?anti-hissing> cheered things. Ed called for at the end — appeared 3 times — & it may be called a success, & anyhow we are not discredited.

20 — W. & Jack, & to the Ex. , but a wet dark morning & hardly anyone came — Adelaide [Lane] to lunch, & back to the Ex. with me — poor thing, doing her best for the advancement of her children, but her ideas so far away from mine! Wants to put Eustace to the Bar — & to have Ruth presented at Court! either here or in London — this is Hugh's proposal![94]

Lady Cadogan & V[ice]. R[egal]. party came to Jack's Ex. from opening the Water Colour Ex. — & she bought "The Dance" so I feel my trouble rewarded, for it was my stirring up Lady Fingall that brought her — I bought the 2 horses, admiring it very much, & feeling that St. James had his eye on me to see if I carried my good wishes to "my brother" into practise! & Mr. Jackson, his uncle bought a picture[95] — so now his expenses are paid anyhow — People in to tea, & G. Moore very nice, walked round with Jack & gave practical criticisms of the pictures which will be of gt use to him, at the same time praising what was good, & I think looking at him with respect, when he found he works from sketches, & not models. This Moore says was the method of the old masters but it is a lost art — Whistler could do nothing at all without a model in his

92 The Irish Literary Theatre opened its second season on 19 February 1900 at the Gaiety Theatre, with a programme comprising Martyn's *Maeve*, Alice Milligan's *The Last Feast of the Fianna*, and the Martyn-Moore-Yeats *The Bending of the Bough*.

93 Probably John McGrath (1864–1956), Dublin literary journalist, who had assisted WBY in founding the National Literary Society in 1892. He was an inveterate reporter of Irish literary events, and crossed swords with WBY intermittently in the 1890s (see *CL1* p. 262).

94 Besides Hugh Lane, her eldest son, and her daughter Ruth, Adelaide had three other children: Harold, Ambrose Bassett and Eustace O'Grady Lane.

95 AG's purchase was a watercolour entitled "Playing Thimselves", which shows two horses racing on Sligo strand. See Hilary Pyle, *Jack B. Yeats: His Watercolours, Drawings and Pastels*, Item 257. Arthur Jackson, who had married Alice Pollexfen, younger sister of Jack's mother, Susan Yeats. Jackson had taken control of the Pollexfen shipping company in 1892.

studio[96] —

W. dined, & we went to the "Bending of the Bough" rather in trepidation, the last rehearsal had gone so badly — but we need not have been afraid, it went splendidly — acting splendid, meaning soon grasped, & applause tremendous — "Author" shouted for, but G. Moore had the grace not to appear — Poor Edward came round rather sadly, I had not seen him since the very qualified success of "Maeve" — but he spoke very nicely, said it was a gr piece of good luck this piece going so well it would save the venture — "Maeve" he says, truly, was very badly acted, & this very well — still he had been so confident that this wd fail as an acting piece that he has had two defeats as it were, & bears it very well — with no sign of irritation or bitterness — There his real goodness comes out —

21 — The gallery, & a rather poor matinée of "B. of B.", as far as audience was concerned, however a matinée is always flat — The papers are unanimous in praise of it, except Irish Times, which has a stupidly ferocious attack on it[97] — but unluckily its attacks keep away money tho' not intelligence — Martin & Richard Morris there, & I told Martin that it had suddenly struck me *he* was Jasper Dean, which was true enough to make him rather low[98] — They came to tea, & some of the actors & Hyde & Miss Milligan & others — Then Moore came here with me, & Yeats, till dinner time, & then we dined at the Shelbourne [Hotel] with Moore — talked of Byron & Shelley — off the theatre for a wonder! — I begged Moore to acknowledge Martyn's share in the work at his speech tomorrow & he promises to do so — "Maeve" went better, but a tiny audience, & it is lost in the big house, with such bad acting — Dalys there, very down on it — Jack had no sales, but the Dalys are nibbling.

22 — A rather dreary morning at the gallery, the Dalys who had promised to come, & all but promised to buy, not turning up — Russell came in then, but we had to hurry off to the lunch given by National Literary Society to Lit. Theatre — Dr. Sigerson[99] handed me down, but I told him he was to have an actress on each side of him, on which he exclaimed "God bless my soul!" —

[96] James McNeill Whistler (1834–1903), painter, society figure and wit.

[97] *Irish Times* 21 February 1900, p. 6. In dismissing the play bluntly—"Story none, dialogue dull, action weak"—the reviewer pointedly and repeatedly calls Moore's authorship of the work into doubt.

[98] Jasper Dean, the central figure in *The Bending of the Bough*, makes an initial stir as a public figure but then fades into political insignificance. Morris's robust campaign for political office in Galway (see p. 213) had by this point already sunk into mediocrity.

[99] Dr. George Sigerson (1836–1925), medic and writer, and long-time friend of the Yeats family. Sigerson edited a number of anthologies, most notably *Bards of the Gael and Gall* (1897), and published widely on Irish topics. A founding member with WBY of the National Literary Society, Dublin, in 1892, he served as a Free State Senator in his last years 1922–25. To WBY he was a "kind and even generous figure" but "exceedingly timid in action", and a man whose mind displayed "erudition without scholarship" (*Mem* p. 53).

I found myself next Oldham who was a nuisance, & opposite John O'Leary who was incoherent, & Richard Morris — G. Moore's great speech went off better than I expected, when it began the wretched waiters came clashing about with coffee cups, making a disturbance, & Moore's voice, with his mouth well in the MS didn't carry far — He paid a compliment to my industry in learning Irish, which was rec[eive]d with applause — Rolleston made a dull speech, & as usual left out his point, omitting "Maeve" (Miss Hammond) whose health he had particularly intended to propose — Yeats a fighting speech, calling on the M.P.['s] to use all their old methods of obstruction if necessary when the Amendment of Education Bill comes in, to insist on the teaching of Irish — He attacked Trinity College as provincial, which the Literary Society is not & the Gaelic League is not — We must fight against provincialism, & die fighting that, as Heine wished, a sword may be laid on our grave.[100]

Some of the people came on to tea with me, Magragh of the Freeman['s Journal] for one, who introduced a young man on the Irish Times — I remonstrated about the disparaging notices, & he said it was not the desire of the I. T. to show hostility, but that the writer of the notice was a "crank" & they were all vexed about it — I introduced him to Moore, so the poor young man had to run the gauntlet! He said they couldn't eat their own words, but wd put in a polite paragraph next day, which they did,[101] so my tea parties did so much good! I told him it was like the American paper which, when a gentleman remonstrated at having been put among the deaths said "We make a rule never to contradict anything that has appeared in our columns, but we will be happy, free of charge, to put you among the births tomorrow" — Then to "Bending of the Bough" a better house, & it went so well & was so much applauded it was decided to put it on again next day — Magragh is in gr enthusiasms over it, "there has never been anything like it, it will cause a revolution" — Hyde says "no young man can see that play and leave the house as he came into it" — O'Grady says it is "rather hard on Lord & Lady Castletown"[102] — I say there are so many Jasper Deans, they are like the chalk marks in Bagdad in Ali Baba's time, it is impossible to fix on the right door

[100] For reports on Moore's and WBY's speeches at the banquet, see *Dublin Daily Express* 23 February 1900, p. 6, and *Irish Times* 23 February 1900, p. 6. Heinrich Heine (1797–1856), the German poet who styled himself "the last romantic", concludes his *Autobiography* with the words "lay a sword upon my coffin, I pray you; for I have been a brave soldier in the wars of the liberty of mankind."

[101] *Irish Times* 23 February, p. 5.

[102] Castletown was a plausible model for Jasper Dean, having "made a famous speech declaring that Ireland must imitate the colonists, who flung the tea into Boston Harbour" when the Childers Commission reported on the over-taxation of Ireland (*Au* p. 418), but thereafter faded from prominence. In an insinuating editorial in *The Kilkenny Moderator* 24 February 1900, reviewing *The Bending of the Bough*, O'Grady made the connection clear without actually naming Lord Castletown. The editorial drew from AG a sharply critical demand for a rebuttal (see p. 249

— Gill, & Horace Plunkett & Rolleston may be fitted to it & when I said to Martin Morris "*you* are Jasper" I saw I had hit the mark, for he had made a great speech on financial reform, & had never been heard of since —

23 — Gallery, & was frightened at the sales, & ventured to buy a picture in Lord Gough's name, as he had told me to do so last year & I had not, as sales went so well then, & I wrote to Enid Layard, who had offered to buy one, to ask if she was still in the same mind — "Bending of the Bough" again, & the Lord Mayor there, but not such a good house as we expected, tho' the applause was rapturous — Hyde, & Russell in the box, besides Yeats — & Moore & Edward behind us, & Gill — The Gaelic League in gr force, sang "Fainne Geal" & "Shule Aroon" between the acts, & at the end "The Wearing of the Green" in Irish, & then when the "Author" wd not appear there were cries for "An Craoibhin" & Hyde was cheered—The actors delighted, say they never acted to so appreciative an audience but a little puzzled at the applause, not understanding the political allusions — Supper at Coffey's — very late.

24 — Our last day, & a tiring one — A wire from Enid, ordering a picture, which was a cheer up—I sat at the Gallery, too tired to stir, & Willie also. Then we lunched with the Gills — I took charge of the gallery for the afternoon as Jack & his wife & Ruth [Lane] wanted to go to the matinee — which was not very largely attended, but went off well — Gill came & bleated in his wise way about the necessity of Moore writing to say the play was partly Martyn's — I told him all his arguments were mine until yesterday, when Martyn, very cross, abused the play, said it was a poor & common thing, no better than "Frou-Frou"[103] — & not fit for a literary theatre — He also said that in future the only help he wd give wd be, if a play of his were produced, he would guarantee the theatre against loss on it — but that he wd not spend money on producing other people's plays — but he is out of sorts, & has a cold, & [I] feel sure his better nature will prevail in the end — His taking this attitude puts an end to the hope of Moore writing to the papers to acknowledge his share, which he had promised to do, as he can't father on Edward a play he thinks poor & common —

Russell sat almost all the afternoon with me, a gr pleasure, telling me of his new poems, & talking of Larminie's death, & his boy, & our friends & their

n. 115). WBY would later recall that Dean was intended for O'Grady himself (*Au* p. 427), though this was probably his confusion, long after the event, of the role of Dean with that of Kirwan, Dean's mentor in the play, who indeed seems to have been based on O'Grady.

[103] A popular comedy by Meilhac and Halévy, played numerous times on the London stage in the 1890s.

work[104] — Then Miss Borthwick and Miss O'Reilly came, & I had a Gaelic
League talk with them & found them amiable — Then the people from the
matinee began to arrive, but I was whirled off from them by E. Martyn, to the
library round the corner, re D[eputy]. L[ieutenant] business — The story is,
at that concert at Tillyra it was suggested "God save the Queen" shd be played,
& he said no, but without giving much thought to the matter — A-D. Daly
however & others chattered about it — When I met Fanny Trench in Dublin
she said "Is it true Mr. Martyn refused to have 'God save the Queen'?" I said
"Yes, & much worse than that, he wd not have [Kipling's] 'The Absent
Minded Beggar'!" which she took quite seriously — Lord Clonbrock came up
to E. M. in the smoking room at the Club the other day, & said he heard he
had refused to have "God Save the Queen" at his house — Ed. said yes, he did
not like songs that were party cries, & that someone else might have objected
to "The Wearing of the Green" — Clonbrock jabbered a lecture to him, & said
he shd remember his oath as D. L. & J. P. — Ed. said in that case he had better
resign — Clonbrock got frightened, begged him not to think of doing so, &
talked of other things — Next morning however Ed. sent in his resignation
to Lord Ashbourne — In the evening Clonbrock came to him, said he had
met Lord A. who was very much put out at his resignation (no doubt had given
Clonbrock a wigging) & wd write a letter to him (C) to show Edward & give
him a chance of withdrawing — This letter had now come, enclosed in one
from Clonbrock, begging Edward to reconsider his determination — He
came to consult me, but said he wished to resign, that he never wished for the
D.L. or J.P. & wd be freer without them — I was personally against his
resigning, as we are short of magistrates, that wretched Pery being our only
standby except Frank — Still, it is intolerable that in one's own house one shd
not be allowed to choose one's line of politics, & I begged him, if he did
resign, to put it on definite grounds & not leave his motives at the mercy of
every chatterer's invention — He made me write down what I proposed, &
said he wd bring draft of letter next day — Back to gallery — lots of people,
Walter Osborne,[105] Magee, who I am afraid is giving up writing, Richard
Morris, Longworth etc etc — My teas have certainly been a social success &
a help to theatre, & to Jack, in making the pictures known, & in Lady
Cadogan's purchase of one — "Bending of the Bough" in the evening — the
best house yet, & enthusiastic applause — Moore called for in vain — Then
calls for Yeats — & he said a few words from our box, thanking the audience
for the reception of the plays — claiming that they were at least patriotic in

[104] William Larminie (1849–1900), author of two volumes of poetry, *Glanlua* (1889) and
Fand (1892), and a folklore collection *West Irish Folktales* (1893), was an active member of the
National Literary Society in the 1890s. AE had married Violet North, a fellow theosophist who
had been a co-member of the "Household" in Ely Place, in June 1898. Their son Brian Russell
was born in early 1900. A first child, also called Brian, was born in March 1899, but had died
in infancy.

[105] Walter Frederick Osborne (1859–1903), at this point the most popular portrait artist in
Ireland.

intention, & promising that those for next year would be equally patriotic in intention — There will I am afraid be a disappointment, for we must try & keep politics out of plays in future — The "Bending" hits so impartially all round that no one is really offended, certainly not the Nationalists & we have not heard that Unionists are so — Curiously "Maeve" which we didn't think a Nationalist play at all, has turned out to be one, the audience reading & applauding the allegory, & there is such applause at "I am only an old woman, but I tell you that Erin will never be subdued" that Lady Mayo[106] who was at a performance reported to the Castle that they had better boycott it, which they have done — G. Moore has been received back as a prodigal with gr amiability & is delighted with his reception, tho' he grumbles at the houses not being better, & as Yeats says makes an Aunt Sally of "The Irish Times" , which at all events saves other heads from his missiles[107] — He is I think a little puzzled by his present political position, but I tell him & Edward "we are not working for Home Rule, we are preparing for it" — Supper at the Gills — I told the D.L. story, & the story of the police coming to Tillyra & calling E. M. to account for his United Irish League letter, & his taking it so meekly[108] — Gill begins his wise bleating about the necessity of Moore's acknowledging Ed's authorship of the "Bending" — Moore always shuts him up with — "I won't say anything — & I won't write anything" — Edward has again told him he will publish his version, which he feels will set him right — Yeats says "Edward Martyn has no sense" — & then Edward comes in — they attack him about Clonbrock & G. M. wants him to write a column & a half in "The Freeman['s Journal]" , showing up the landlords & officials & declaring his political convictions — Ed. says "My political convictions are those of the company I am in — I have no convictions but religious ones" — This settles that question!

25 — Sunday — The week over, & well over, for tho' there is financial loss we have gained rather than lost credit, have justified our existence & come into touch with national feeling on its best side, the side one wants to develop — News cuttings took a long time, & first Willie & then Jack came in — & Adelaide to lunch, & I had to go with her, & see her house, & how she has turned the coal hole into a larder etc, etc — Then back to Edward & his letter — He begins by stating his position something like this — "When you gave me the J. P. & D. L. — I was a Unionist, I had been brought up one, & in ignorance of the history of my country & of its language — Some years ago my eyes were

[106] Geraldine, née Ponsonby (d.1944), wife of the 7th Earl of Mayo.

[107] Moore evidently attributed the poor houses predominantly to the critical reception of *The Bending of the Bough* by the *Irish Times* (see p. 244 n. 101).

[108] *The Tuam Herald*, 31 March 1900, p. 2, reports that at a recent United Irish League meeting in Athenry "a letter was read by Canon Canton from the PP of Ardrahan stating that Mr. Martyn, of Tullyra, was perfectly willing to break up his lands and give it to his tenants (cheers)." Martyn's letter does not appear to have been published independently.

opened by reading Lecky's "History of Ireland in the 18th Century" — Since then I have gone on developing a dislike of England — I refused to have "God save the Queen" & "The Absent Minded Beggar" performed at a concert in my house because unfortunately in our country the Queen's name & Mr. Kipling's name have come to mean the same thing as the Union & the extinction of our distinctive nationality — If I am not free to act up to my convictions without being liable to be called to task in however a friendly manner by the Lieutenant of my county I have no alternative but to resign the J. P. & D. L. — I am however no politician & do not wish to take an active part in politics." — He had put that he had "half in jest" left out the Queen's name, but I struck that out — Clonbrock has succeeded in pushing him over the border — I am sorry, for I hoped we might all keep out of politics[109] — Yeats is sorry for he says he will compromise the party, that he will become a "leader of the Irish race, till Father Considine beckons to him, & then he will desert them"[110] — He was in a better mind about the plays — but he expects to have his done next year, & Moore expects to have his Grania,[111] & we have promised an Irish one, & Yeats has commissioned Bernard Shaw to write one, & my heart is set on "Shadowy Waters" — so how it will end I know not — Yeats came in to dine before I left, & then came to Westland Row,[112] & we found that he had wanted to come with me to London, & I had thought it was for politics & discouraged him — & so changed a pleasant journey for both into a dreary one — Crossed & slept at Holyhead —

26 — To London — a full carriage, but arrived much less tired than if I had gone straight through.

27 — Went to see Sir Frederic — "Cronje's surrender on the anniversary of Majuba" on the placards[113] — This will revive blatancy & renew the belief that God is on the side of big battalions — Sir Frederic in bed, & I fear — or indeed

[109] Martyn's correspondence with Clonbrock was not made public until 24 March 1900, at which point he published their exchanges to quell continuing speculation about his reasons for resigning (Dublin Daily Express p. 6).

[110] Father Thomas Considine, Parish Priest of Ardrahan, and President of the Galway branch of the Gaelic League.

[111] Moore and Yeats had begun collaborating on the play Diarmuid and Grania in October 1899. Due to their repeated quarrels over the project, the play was not produced until October 1901.

[112] The Pan-Celtic Association met in rented rooms at 3 Westland Row during this period.

[113] Pieter Cronje (1835–1911), rose to prominence as a Boer commander in the First Boer War, and became a national hero when he captured the Jameson raiders in 1896. Led the siege of Mafeking and commanded Boer forces on the southern front in the second Boer War, but surrendered with a force of 4000 to Lord Roberts on 22 February 1900, and was subsequently branded a traitor by many Boers. The defeat at Majuba Hill on 27 February 1881, at which 69 British soldiers were killed and 132 wounded to 1 Boer soldier killed and 6 wounded, had brought an ignominious end to the British offensive in the First Boer War, and spurred swift British agreement on peace terms.

must hope — the end is very near — Gangrene has attacked one of the legs, & he suffers a good deal — I went up to see him — he was clear but drowsy — at first a little inarticulate — but when I got up to go he held my hand a long time, speaking with great kindness, said I looked pale, asked for Robert, & how the plays had gone — I told him of them, & of the Times notice of "Maeve" with its idealism being so well recd by an Irish audience, & a notice on the same page that "Tess" in London had been jeered at by an audience who found it too serious[114] — he said "that is just what one would expect" — He asked if Robert has been abroad yet, & I said no, he was so fond of Ireland he had not cared to go until now, & that I myself found every year an increased delight & happiness in Ireland — He said "It is so with me, my best joys have been connected with Ireland" — Then he spoke of Celtic influence in English literature & said "there will be some day a great pan-Celtic empire" — I said "yes, & Ireland will be its soul" — & so we parted —

Some visits, & Yeats came to dinner, but we were both a little tired with our Irish week, & yet finding it hard to turn to other things — I wrote a short note to Standish O'Grady, asking him to contradict his statement in the Moderator that Jasper Dean was meant for Lord Castletown[115] —

28 — Wrote letters, & then to Sir Frederic — drowsy from morphia, & at first seemed wandering, but smiled while I sat by him & held his hand, & then said "What a dear good fellow Gregory was — so straight & kindhearted & a gentleman — If he was a little hot sometimes according to his nature, & I according to mine, we got over it afterwards because we were gentlemen" — After a time he brightened up — talked of George Eliot, how she told him she thought out characters, put them in certain circumstances & then they had to act according to their nature — Tho' a professed unbeliever he is sure she believed in a spiritual world, & she had said to him that the most stupendous conception she knew of was the Redemption — Some visits, & home, cold & tired & downhearted —

Mar[ch] 1 — Saw flags flying, & knew Ladysmith was relieved[116] — Began translating Douglas Hyde's poems — To see Sir Frederic, a little better, but Sir T. Martin came so I didn't stay[117] — Visits, & home to find a put off from dinner at E. Layard's, just as well, for G. Moore came in the evening, full of

[114] *The Times* 20 February 1900, p. 7 reported the enthusiastic reception of *Maeve* and *The Last Feast of the Fianna*, and on p. 9 deplored the crassness of the "suburban audience" that had hissed "Tess", a dramatization of Thomas Hardy's *Tess of the D'Urbervilles* by Hardy and H. A. Kennedy, which had opened at the Coronet Theatre the previous night.

[115] O'Grady published AG's letter, in which she noted having heard "at least six originals" suggested for Jasper Dean, *The Kilkenny Moderator* 3 March, p. 4.

[116] Ladysmith was relieved by forces under Redvers Buller on 1 March 1900, having been under seige by Boer forces since 2 November 1899.

[117] Sir Theodore Martin (1816–1909), lawyer and Parliamentary agent.

plans about next years' theatre, getting people to but seats instead of guaranteeing money, etc — He parted with Edward on good terms, so I hope all will go well —

2 — To see Yeats, took sandwiches & lunched there, & then he begged me to stay & hang his pictures, & went out for hammer & nails & wire, & we arranged & got them up — A pleasant little interlude, tho' destructive to my visits for the day — On to Sir Frederic, but for the first time I did not see him, he had had much pain, & morphia injections & was wandering — He had only made his will last week, leaving to his housekeeper £500 which is a relief to her mind — Dined with Enid, & had to listen to a great deal of war talk — Her enthusiasm about the Madiera hospital has rather faded, as only one officer has been got to accept a berth there! 7,000 beds have been offered in England for convalescent soldiers, but only 40 have been found to accept them! She said Venice wd be too cold to go to in March, & I was a little cast down, thinking perhaps she did not want us at her house —

3 — To Irish Industries, a scanty & feeble meeting — Then to Sir A. Birch, & found Una has not yet decided for Italy, so we may fit in with her, which would be splendid for R. — & we cd go to Florence or Rome — I wd like his first little trip to be a good one — Lunched with Mrs. Ricardo — Then to Mary Studd — but she is like gunpowder, all nerves & irritability, & indeed one is afraid not to agree with bloodthirstiness everywhere for fear of being hit with umbrellas like the people at last night's meeting — To Sir Frederic, too drowsy from morphia to see me — Dined Leckys — he rather X, took me down to dinner & said first thing "What silly speeches your Celtic people have been making!" "Moore?" I said, "Yes, & Yeats, oh, very silly" — He is in bad humour because Blackrock, which he has known & known to speak English all his life, has sent him copies of resolutions in favour of revival of Irish[118] — In revenge I told him how a D. L. was proclaiming himself a convert to nationalism on the ground of having been converted by his history — He shrugs his shoulders & says "People in Ireland are so one sided & only take up one part of one's argument" — I say I have a comfortable feeling I can be as one sided as I like, because the Irish average of impartiality will be kept balanced while he exists — I asked if he knew the new clerk of H. of Commons, as I want information about a clerkship, thinking of one for R. — & he was I think rather frightened lest I wanted him to ask for something, & shrunk up — Sir Charles Pontifex[119] on my other side, Anglo Indian, very

[118] Blackrock District Council had taken an active stance in promoting Irish products and the Gaelic language. See *An Claidheamh Soluis* 25 March 1899, p. 23, for their resolutions on Irish manufactures. In 1900, the Council resolved to change street signs to Gaelic, provoking considerable opposition.

[119] Sir Charles Pontifex (1831–1903), High Court Judge in Bengal 1872–82 and Legal Adviser to the Secretary of State for India 1882–92.

pleasant, Lord Welby opposite — Afterwards I talked with Mrs. Clemens, & then with "Mark Twain" himself, his picturesque grey hair the most striking thing abt him[120] — Then to Carson, Q.C., genial & shrewd[121] — He had congratulated Redmond on being chosen leader & he had replied gloomily — "I hope you may be able to congratulate me in 3 months time" — A talk with Mrs. Lecky about the war. She is a little bitter abt the papers & intolerance here — houses wrecked last night at Stratford because their owners were suspected of pro-Boer feelings.

4 — Sunday — To Sir F. & saw him for a moment but in great pain, the doctor says it is only a question of days now — To lunch with E. Layard — & afterwards to the New Gallery where Mr. Hallé had asked us to go in & see the pictures (Flemish & English) — He had been inspecting pictures for the Summer Ex. during the morning, & is to do so again next Sunday, so I was able to put in a word for Mr. Yeats's portrait of Willie, & he promised to look at it with attention[122] — Dinner, "Mark Twain" & Mrs. Clemens, & W. Yeats & Kathleen Morris[123] — I asked George Moore, but he refused on the ground of hating humourists, however he came in after dinner, and tho' I had been a little anxious, it was to me & I think to all a very pleasant evening — Yeats brilliant & bountiful — almost more than usual — Clemens rather slow in getting things out in his American drawl, but always got to the point at last — Talking of telepathy he said that dining at a hotel somewhere in America he tried to see some chromes on the wall, & thought one of them represented the Zulus killing "Lulu", Prince Napoleon — He said to his wife (who cd not see the pictures) "Do you remember that time we were in Paris" — & she went on "When we heard of Prince Lulu's death" — Afterwards he looked at the pictures & found they had nothing to do with Lulu at all![124] — Yeats read

[120] Samuel Langhorne Clemens (1835–1911), American novelist and author under the pseudonym "Mark Twain". His wife, Olivia, née Langdon, d.1904.

[121] Edward Henry Carson (1854–1935), lawyer and statesman. Rose to prominence representing the government in its prosecution of the Plan of Campaign, and was rewarded with election as Unionist M.P. for Dublin University 1892, a seat he held until 1918. Principal prosecutor in the trial of Oscar Wilde. Solicitor-General for Ireland 1900–06, Attorney-General 1915. As leader of the Irish Unionist party 1910–21, Carson was a champion of Ulster separatism, resisting the inclusion of Ulster in the 1913 Home Rule Bill, and promoting the organisation and arming of the Ulster Volunteers.

[122] Charles Hallé (1846–1919), was Director and Manager of the New Gallery. John B. Yeats had just completed a new oil painting of WBY, subsequently bought by John Quinn (see p. 312 n. 10), and later reproduced as the frontispiece of Essays and Introductions (1959).

[123] Mary Kathleen Morris (d.1954), fourth oldest of Lord Morris's daughters.

[124] Eugene Louis "Lou-lou" Napoleon (b.1856), the Prince Imperial, Napoleon III's only son, had been killed in May 1879 while serving unofficially in a British flying column in Zululand. The death caused a sensation both in France, where it ended any prospect of a restoration of the Bonapartes, and in Britain (where the Prince had lived since the fall of the Second Republic), where his determination to train in the British military school at Woolwich and desire to participate in the British Zulu war had made him highly popular.

translations from Irish after dinner, Hyde's and mine, which Clemens seemed delighted with — I asked him about his Joan of Arc,[125] for it always seems as if she had conquered him & his style in the writing, it is so unlike the other books — He said he had read a page from a French account of her trial as a boy, & had her in his mind all his life — G. Moore came in, enthusiastic about Benson's uncut Hamlet at the Lyceum,[126] & contrasts its length & exuberance with our fear of boring an audience for one single moment — He abuses the scenery of Mid[summer] Night's Dream, says people can't look at a Velasquez for half an hour without being tired, & why are they called on to look at a badly painted wood for 2 hours — Clemens however protests — "I like that wood, I like to see a wood on the stage that looks like a wood, & I like to see a <??> get up & act like a <??>!" — Moore & Yeats stayed on till after 12, — M. adding to his speech for New Ireland Review[127] — putting in the evil effects the S[outh]. A[frican]. war will have on England, how she will be smothered in S. Africa — Yeats says "She might have been Greece & she has chosen to be Persia" —

5 — MacBride, & walked over to Hugh Lane & to Christie's, as there were Simeon Solomons to be sold[128] — One a lovely little thing of a musician I set my heart on — within bounds of £2 or £3! However it went for £14 so I am trying to forget it, & Hugh sent me to make up, a present of an oil painting of a blind laurel-crowned poet-fiddler. Raftery of course! the eternal bard — Homer if you like, wandering thro' the ages[129] —

Lunched with the Birchs, & settled to join Una at Rome — which wd be delightful for R. — Saw Sir Frederic for a few moments, in gr pain, but forgot it for a little while he talked of his early life, his love of painting, & disappointment when he found the N[ational]. Gallery filled his time with routine work — His grandfather had been a very fair artist, which I had not known —

6th — A headache, & lay still & breakfastless till 12 — Then a note from Willy Peel asking me to lunch to meet his father, so I struggled up & went — &

---

[125] *Personal Recollections of Joan of Arc* (1896), a fictional memoir written as if by her page and secretary.

[126] Played in two parts over a matinee and then evening production, this "uncut" *Hamlet* ran for six performances in March 1900. Frank R. Benson (1858–1939), who played the title role, was the actor–manager of a Shakespearean company which played at Stratford and on tour 1886–1916. Mrs. Benson played Ophelia.

[127] "The Irish Literary Renaissance and the Irish Language" *New Ireland Review*, April 1900.

[128] Simeon Solomon (1840–1905), pre-Raphaelite painter. First exhibited at Royal Academy in 1858, but after a brilliant early career, lost favour due to his homosexuality and alcoholism. Died in poverty in a London workhouse.

[129] This oil was by Poussin (see *Hugh Lane* p. 33).

consulted Lord Peel about a H. of Commons clerkship for R. — He told me to write to Milman[130] direct — He is going to Oxford & promises to look in & see R. — Mrs. Peel[131] no beauty, & with a harsh voice, but devoted to Willy, & his luxurious home is certainly a contrast to his little flat here! Yet I would not like R. to do likewise — Then with W. Yeats to Benson's Hamlet, the unabridged text, lasting from 3-30 to 6-30 & then from 8-00 to 10-30 — A wonderful play, well as I knew it I had never known its extraordinary richness & variety before — & was never bored for one moment — And the acting did little for it, Benson jerky & laboured, & his soliloquies were those of a flea — hop — skip — wriggle — tho' in the quiet scenes & at the end, perhaps from being a little tired he grew better — Ophelia squeaky as to voice, jiggy as to action — Polonius about the best, reminded me of Gill, trying to settle everybody's business — W. delighted, except with the utterance, as he says, verse is considered of no account — they don't even try to give it, many lines were quite unintelligible — I am all the more anxious for Shadowy Waters to be properly done — A letter from Jack who has sold pictures to Lord Ashbourne, H. Plunkett & his uncle Isaac & seems content —

7 — Sir F. so low I did not go up to see him — Lunched with Mrs. Gowing, cracky & full of the war & a sonnet she had written on young Robert's death[132] — Called on the Strongs who were very glad to see me — he just going to give a Persian lesson to some lady — Dined with the Clemens, taking W. & Jack Yeats — Only themselves & 2 daughters — a quiet pleasant evening, all friendly — Mark Twain gives one the impression of genuine goodness & kindliness — Jack came out, & told anecdotes, & did a sketch of George Moore from memory which delighted them — & Willie read Mary Hynes, & some of the Rafterys — & they wanted to hear one of his own poems, & he couldn't remember one, & I wrote out "Angus" for him to read[133] —

8 — Translated some of Douglas Hyde's poems — Lunched with E. Layard — the streets crowded with people to see the Queen — The announcement

[130] Archibald John Scott Milman (1834–1902), Clerk assistant in the Commons 1886–1900, and Clerk of the House from 1900. Third son of Dean Milman (see p. 62 n. 201).

[131] Eleanor Peel, née Williamson (d.1949), eldest daughter of the 1st Baron Ashton, had married Willie Peel in April 1899.

[132] Lt. Frederick Roberts, Lord Roberts's only son, had been killed at Colenso on 15 December 1899, attempting under Buller's command to rescue British artillery subsequently abandoned to the Boers. Roberts learned about his son's death the same afternoon he received confirmation of his appointment to succeed Buller as head of the British forces.

[133] "Mary Hynes" was AG's translation of a Raftery poem collected by Hyde at Coole in January 1899 (see p. 201 n. 13), which WBY had included in his article "Dust hath closed Helen's Eye", published in The Dome, October 1899. Other translations from Raftery by AG he might have read include the lament he had quoted in his article "The Literary Movement in Ireland" in The North American Review, November 1899 (UP2 p. 189). "Angus" was WBY's lyric "The Song of Wandering Aengus", first published in 1897 and collected in The Wind Among the Reeds.

of her visit to Ireland was made today, & also that Irish soldiers were in future to wear the shamrock on St. Patrick's day — I met Miss Purser in Bond Street & she said "Well, what do you think of the shamrock? Rather hard isn't it, on the undivided Trinity in whose honour it has heretofore been worn!"

To Sir Frederic, very weak & low, but I stayed with him a long time as he would not let me go — I talked to his nephew & he joined in at intervals — He was not in pain — He told me again he wished me to have his Connemara sketches & mentioned particularly one of a girl, a singer near <?Maam>, & also of a piper, Paddy Connol[l]y, who was the best judge of sheep & cattle in the whole country — Home tired & did some more translating — A letter from Milman to whom I had written about nomination for Clerkship for H[ouse]. of C[ommons]. for R., refusing, though civilly, on the ground of his being too young at present.

9th — Strongs, who said they cd come any night to dinner can't come, when I have asked Hallé & Yeats to meet them — so after some fruitless wires, call at the Clays, & ask all them — Sir F. very weak — sat with him a little, but his eyes were closed & I would not let them rouse him — Visits, to Mrs. Courtenay among others, sad about the intolerance over the war[134] — someone said the other day there was a letter in the papers saying the Boers had treated English prisoners well, on which a lady got up & walked out of the room — Called on Albert Grays — Then back to dinner which went off fairly, Lady Clay rather heavy, & she & Yeats were in opposition & didn't get on well — & Sir A. is getting a little deaf & hidebound — Hallé charming, & Mrs. Emery read a little, & Yeats did, & he & Hallé took to each other, & stayed on, so I think his portrait shd be in the New [Gallery] —

10 — Translating poems — & Una Birch came to settle about Rome, & then the Waithmans, just arrived — & the Jack Yeatses to lunch — Saw Sir F. — but drowsy & weak — Called on E[mily]. Shaw Lefevre (pro-Boer) & dined with the Waithmans at the Grand Central Hotel — I came across the Queen on her way to Paddington — great crowds & great decorations & shouting — One cd just see a dab of pink, her face, & a dab of white, her hair, & white feathers — Dublin will look very small & dingy after this triumphal progress.

11th — To Westminster Abbey — met Hallam Murray outside the door, who said he had been hearing of Robert lately from the Dean of New, Spooner,[135]

---

[134] Catherine Courtney, née Potter, wife of Leonard Courtney M. P. (see p. 134 n. 67), one of the few strong critics of the Boer War.
[135] Rev. William Archibald Spooner (1844–1930), Tutor in Classics at New College and Warden 1903–24, for whom the misspeech "spoonerisms" are named.

& that he spoke well of him & seemed to have a great regard for him — this was a cheer up — To ask for Sir F. — too weak to see anyone, but I am distressed to find that he has proposed amputation of the leg — Says "it is hard to die" — One feels it wd be of no use, & trouble his end — The Comyn Carrs in the afternoon — & then Alfred Cole — who abused Yeats's prose "such intolerably bad style!" — I wonder what he has formed his judgement on — A quiet evening, translating — dined on hard boiled eggs & brown bread —

12 — Some translating — Lunch rather a terror, Mrs. Martin, very blind & tottering, with a sun hat & white veil, and Mrs. Aylmer Gowing in point lace & feathers, very deaf — And during lunch George Moore came in — However he knew Mrs. Gowing of old, & paid her compliments on her knowledge of Greek & French — Then I went down with him to look at a letter he has written on the Queen's visit to Ireland — not in the best taste, but moderate for him — only calling for "chill politeness"[136] — He wanted to know if I was shocked by anything in it — I said it did not shock me, but wd no doubt shock many people over here — but that he says he does not mind — If I were in politics, which I try to keep out of, I wd certainly show no welcome either to the head of the English state, or to a woman who has been callous to the failing & the famines in Ireland during a long reign — Then Arabella came — out with her, to trot abt shops — Home tired — Sir F. too weak for me to see —

13 — All the morning writing & paying bills & shopping — & to take tickets for Rome — & to Baly, & then took A[rabel]la out — Home at 5 — Lady Poynter came in — Also Yeats, with an article on Mohini for the "Speaker"[137] — delighted with my further translations from Hyde — O'Leary has written asking him to write on the Queen's visit & he thinks of doing so, suggesting that the M.P.s as natural leaders of the people should organise a meeting at the Rotunda expressing disapproval of public welcomes, as otherwise the demonstration against signs of rejoicing wd fall into "other" hands, & lead to riots[138] — Dined Lyalls — a family party, Sir James[139] & some cousins — Sir Alfred asked me about the Queen's visit, thinks it a mistake "such visits must be political" — & if he were a Nationalist he would object to expressions of welcome — Speaking of critics he quoted a sentence from Coleridge "Critics

[136] "The Queen of England's Visit" published in *The United Irishman*, 17 March 1900, p. 7.
[137] Mohini Chatterjee, a Brahmin Theosophist, had visited the Hermetic Society in Dublin in 1885 at the invitation of WBY and others, and helped established the Dublin Theosophical Lodge. WBY's article, "The Way of Wisdom" *The Speaker*, 14 April 1900 (reprinted in revised form in *Collected Works* 1908 as "The Pathway") recalls this visit. WBY subsequently commemorated Mohini's teaching again in his 1929 poem "Mohini Chatterjee".
[138] WBY followed this suggestion with "The Queen's Visit" *Dublin Daily Express*, 20 March 1900 (*L* pp. 335–37).
[139] Sir James Broadwood Lyall (1838–1916), younger brother of Alfred Lyall. Retired Indian Civil Servant, having been Lt Governor of the Punjab 1887–92.

are the eunuchs at the door of the temples of the Gods."[140]

14 — Translated a little — & lunched E. Layard — rather afraid to face her because of G. Moore's letter about the Queen's visit — reported in the Times[141] — but happily she had not read it! However we had a good deal of the war — She says of course Ld. Roberts must have a Dukedom — the D[uke] of Wellington got one[142] — & Ld. R. has done much more than he did! Very flattering to the Boers — To Motcombe St. to ask if the Gort nuns' work had arrived — & it has not — at least the best things have not come — what did come had no list, the linen had not the number of yards marked — the lace pieces did not agree with list — Very disheartening trying to help people who won't help themselves — I don't think I will go to the sale at all, as I shd be ashamed at a falling off instead of an improvement in our goods — Back to tea & W. Yeats came, & we went to call on the Clemens — not a very interesting visit, all tired — Then back to dress to dine at the Simeons — Sir Barrington & Sir Powlett Milbank[143] (who took me to dinner) in uniform for the Speaker's Levee — Mr. Bruce Lawson & Col. & Lady Emma Crichton[144] — & a Mr. <?Caton> — not very interesting, but all pleasant enough —

15 — My birthday — Letters, & clothes — & to see Waithmans — Then to W.B.Y. & he came on with me to Mudie's to have books bound — Then to Sir Frederic — very near his end — The housekeeper made me go up, as she thought he wd know I was there & it would please him — but I don't think he was conscious, tho' she thought so — Home, & read over "Raftery" with a view to shortening it[145] — Dined with Mrs. Green, a small party owing to 3 disappointments from illness — Harold & Ly. Victoria Russell — a Mr. & Mrs. Ilbert[146] — who had had to do with Venezuela arbitration — & Mr. Stopford, Mrs. Green's brother — Silence was threatened, but I roused myself up &

[140] Probably a corruption of Coleridge's dictum in *Lectures on Shakespeare and Milton*: "Reviewers are usually people who would have been poets, historians, biographers, etc., if they could: they have tried their talents at one or the other, and have failed; therefore they turn critics."

[141] *The Times* 14 March 1900, p. 6, notes Moore's "long and violent letter" and his central charge that Victoria's visit was a cynical effort to promote recruitment in Ireland.

[142] Roberts, whose appointment as Commander in Chief in S. Africa turned the course of the war, had led the forces which had captured Cronje and the Boer Western Army on 27 February 1900. He was elevated from Baron to Earl in 1901, and granted the sum of £100,000 by Parliament. Arthur Wellesley (1769–1852), had been created 1st Duke of Wellington in 1814, and capped his military career with the triumph over Napoleon at Waterloo the following year.

[143] Sir Powlett Charles Milbank (1852–1918), 2nd Bart., and M.P. 1895–1900.

[144] Col. Henry George Lewis Crichton (1844–1922) and his wife Jane Emma, née Baring (d. 1936), daughter of the 1st Earl of Northbrook. AG had attended their wedding in January 1890.

[145] Her article "The Poet Raftery", published in *The Argosy* January 1901, pp. 44–58, and reprinted in a revised form in *Poets and Dreamers* in 1903.

[146] Courtenay Ilbert (1841–1924), Assistant Parliamentary Council to the Treasury 1866–99, and his wife Jessie, née Bradley.

talked — & Mrs. G. produced rubbishy novels she is sent by MacMillan — & made me choose 2 for a birthday present!

16 — A telegram to tell of Sir Frederic's death — I wished for him to go & be at peace — & free from restlessness & suffering — but now he is gone I feel a strange blank — He had been my warm & constant friend for 20 years —

Writing, & A[rabel]la came in — To Argyll Road to take my last look at the cast off clothing of the spirit of my dear old friend — His nephew[147] told me he had twice impressed on him that he was to send me his sketches of Galway, Connemara & Aran — He is to be buried in Ireland, tho' he left no directions — I did not go to Mansion House sale, as the poor nuns had sent their work late & there was nothing new to show — George Moore, Philip Comyn Carr & Yeats dined — all abused Kipling's letter to the Times, calling for the hanging of Cape Colonists[148] — G. Moore said how much better a writer Bret Harte was, & I think it a just comparison as to prose, tho' Kipling's verse is better at its best — Talking of the Queen's visit & the impossibility of its being non-political, G. M. said it reminded him of Gladstone being asked to take part in some procession or meeting & saying "he would be happy to take a *small* part in it"! We went on to the New Gallery to see Miss Duncan's "Dance Idylls" — she is a pretty, graceful dancer[149] — & Miss Harrison recited the Idylls nicely tho' not very audibly — still it gave one an idea of Salomé & such old dancers — Then we went round the pictures with G. Moore — who was in one of his best moods, & listened to his criticisms — & he drove me home — Ly. Betty Balfour was there, says her husband is so much better they hope to get to Ireland next month, so I suppose he is going to hold on to the U. Secretaryship[150] —

17th — Walked across St. James's Park to lunch with Enid, the whole place like Burnam Wood marching, shamrocks as big as cabbage heads, tied with Union Jack ribbons on every ragamuffin — I wore an ivy leaf, feeling I must give up the poor shamrock till this calamity of vulgarising be overpast[151] — Enid very proud of wearing a shamrock "So *kind* of us" — I said I cd not wear one for fear of being mistaken for a Cockney — gr indignation on her part & Eda Alderson's, who like all the Aldersons connected with Ld. Salisbury

---

[147] Henry Bindon Burton, Sir Frederic's trustee and executor.

[148] "The Sin of Witchcraft" *The Times* 15 March 1900, p. 8. Kipling's letter urges that Cape Colonists active against British loyalists be tried for treason (for which the death penalty was in effect), but falls short of explicitly calling for hangings.

[149] Isadora Duncan (1877–1927), dancer. This was her first professional appearance in Britain, one of a series of three recitals at the New Gallery arranged by Charles Hallé.

[150] Gerald Balfour in fact ended his term as Under-Secretary later in 1900.

[151] Ivy was Parnell's symbol, and generally worn by Irish Nationalists on the anniversary of his death on 6 October 1891.

gives the impression "L'Empire, c'est moi" — Then they asked abt the
Queen's visit, & were annoyed when I said there would be rows — After lunch
I put my ivy leaf under my mantle, pinned with my diamond wheat ear,
thinking it really distressed Enid — We went off together to the Mansion
House sale, a crowd there, & bunches of shamrock — Whether the sales were
better than in less effusive years I know not — I had tea with Ly. Morris, talked
with Mrs. Lecky & slipped away, there being nothing to do there — Went later
to see the Haliburtons — Ld. H. decorated with shamrock — "Don't you think
this shamrock business will settle our difficulties in Ireland?" — I said "I doubt
that this sentimental affection will outlive the financial debate of next week"
— Then the Queen's visit — he like all intelligent men, reasonable, able to
separate the personal from the political aspect — She, like most women, got
cross — Home, & Mrs. Strong came in as I was lighting the fire & taking my
things off — When she went, I found my diamond wheat ear & the ivy leaf had
disappeared — & as I had been so much abt all the afternoon I felt low as to
prospect of ever seeing them again — Yeats called to walk on to George
Moore's with me, where we were dining, only Symons there — He brought
draft of letter to the papers on the Queen's visit — he had adopted my idea
of having a meeting on the ground of denouncing the Union, rather than the
visit, on this its Centenary, if dates wd fit in, & as luck wd have it, April 2, the
day the Queen leaves Windsor for Ireland, is the day the Union passed thro'
Parliament! — His letter, slightly modified is good — & if his advice is taken,
there will be a dignified protest instead of window breaking[152] — Moore still
enthusiastic on Irish things — I read my translations from Hyde, Symons as
well as the others, enthusiastic — I hope they are correctly translated! I asked
Symons why "Paolo & Francesca" is so much cried up — he says "because it
is the nearest approach to poetry people are able to understand" — Home,
& found my wheat ear awaiting me, sent on from Savile Row, so am comforted.

18 — Copying Yeats's letter on the Queen's visit for the papers, type offices
being shut — To Gr. Central Hotel, & lunched with A[rabel]la — Afternoon
Knowles came in — we talked of the Queen's visit — I said there wd be
disturbances, or at least some expressions of opinion against it — He was
indignant at the idea — I said I hoped it might be turned into an expression
of opinion against the Union, which wd be justifiable & dignified — but that
did not please him any better — there shd be nothing but a gushing reception
— or England would be in a state of fury — H. Plunkett & Lady Fingall then
came in — & Lady F. echoed Knowles, declared there wd be nothing but
loyalty "& at all events there are plenty of police" which gratified him — & he
was pleased at meeting a new Countess, & invited himself to Killeen, & asked

---

[152] WBY's letter urges Nationalists to protest the Queen's visit "with as much courtesy as is
compatible with vigour" and suggests prior organization of demonstrations so as to avoid the
"broken glass and rioting crowds" that had marred the Jubilee protests (see p. 148 n. 124).

H. Plunkett for an article, which pleased him, so all went off well[153] — H. P. pretty sure of losing his seat, because of the Gill appointment, & doesn't know what to do, he cd not get a Northern constituency as he is for a Catholic University — or a Home Rule one — I advised him to read Lecky's history & turn Nationalist like E. Martyn but Ly. Fingall who watched him all the time like cat & mouse, won't hear of that.[154]

My reflections![155]

It's a mistake to collect too many facts — more than you can consume in your own furnace —

The desire to possess the body is in reality the desire to discover the soul —

Money can't do everything, but it has long arms —

I dreamed that I had been writing some article & that W. B. Y. said "It's not your business to write — Your business is to make an atmosphere" —

The British public read the works of a laureate as they do the Authorized Version — other poets represent the Apocrypha —

Nov[ember] '99 — The people have grown to hate England through their love for Ireland — Our class is now through dislike of England growing to care for their own country —

Nov[ember] 99 — Very sorry for the fall of the trees at Trinity College[156] — about the only things there that were growing —

Feb[ruary] 1900 — We are not working for Home Rule, we are preparing for it —

---

[153] Plunkett completed Knowles's commission, contributing "Balfourian Amelioration in Ireland", an essay in favour of Balfour's Irish policies and analysing the part his support for them played in his electoral defeat, to *The Nineteenth Century* December 1900, pp. 891–904. Killeen Castle, Co. Meath was the seat of the Fingalls.

[154] Lady Fingall and Plunkett were almost certainly lovers, and he probably fathered one or more of her children. Plunkett's nephew Lord Dunsany gives a veiled account of the relationship in his roman à clef *The Story of Monah Sheehy* (1938). Trevor West acknowledges the close intimacy of the couple, but suggests that their relationship may have remained platonic (see *Horace Plunkett* p. 15).

[155] AG began a new exercise book with her entry for 19 March 1900. The series of aphorisms and observations included here are inscribed on the rear inside cover and last page of the volume she had just completed.

[156] The "great storm" which swept Dublin on 3 November 1899 damaged buildings and levelled many old trees at Trinity College. See *The Irish Times* 4 November 1899, p. 6.

To Argyll Rd — my last visit there — Mr. [Henry] Burton took me up to the studio & showed me 3 or 4 of the Irish sketches I am to have — He had left no other mementoes, except the Blake book to Fairfax Murray,[157] & 2 or 3 books to a niece & another relation — Yeats to dinner, & said good bye to him.

(of Kings)
To live in swaddling clothes until they become mummy clothes —

To learn to love your enemy, do him a kindness, & love will come of itself

Don't despise imagination, it is the corner stone of sympathy — (this was said to me in a dream) —

The weak point in marriage is that it legitimises selfishness —

Doing the hardest thing first instead of the easiest thing, becomes a habit —

To influence people, appeal to whatever is best in their nature —

Trying to write in Ireland where there is no reading public to respond is [like] trying to talk to sandbags[158] —

March 19 — Packing, & R. came from Oxford, & went shopping with him — Dined with Richard Ward, & sat next Wilfrid Ward, very popish[159] — His horror is great at Lecky having said to his wife at dinner one night, talking of Mrs. Craven's Life, that "to have religion as she had it was a disease"[160] — He asked me if Horace Plunkett was not "Secretary to Gerald Balfour" — poor Horace! — Home very tired, & then Paul came in, so I was late in bed —

20 — Off at 11 on our journey — A fine crossing — France monotonous, & didn't give R. a good impression of the Continent, but next morning 21st we had some lovely hours by Lucerne & across the Alps — Rain began on the

[157] Charles Fairfax Murray (1849–1919), prominent art collector and bibliophile. Murray's collection included a Blake MS he had loaned to WBY and Edwin Ellis in 1892 for their edition of *The Works of William Blake* (see *CLI* p. 281)

[158] This is the final entry of AG's "reflections", but a loose page inserted at this point bears in AG's hand "má's maith leat bheith buan, ól fuar agus tu" ("If you want to be long-lived, you must drink hot and cold") beneath the date 1900. AG frequently used this proverb to refer to the neccessity for political and ideological compromise.

[159] Wilfrid Ward (1856–1916), prominent Catholic and theologian, and sometime Editor of *The Dublin Review*. Son of "Ideal" Ward of the Oxford Movement. Subsequently biographer of Aubrey de Vere, Newman and others.

[160] Mrs. Augustus Craven, née Pauline de la Ferronays (1808–91), a best-selling author of biographies of Catholic figures and devotional novels. A biography of her by Maria Bishop had been published in 1895. Ward himself had also written an essay on her, subsequently collected in *Problems and Persons* (1903).

Italian side, & we got to Milan in rain, but went to the Hotel de la Ville, so got easily from there into the Cathedral & gallery — & then we saw an announcement of Lohengrin,[161] which R. had never seen, at La Scala, so got tickets & went there after dinner & saw a fairly good performance in the splendid opera house — So R. saw Lucerne, the Alps, Milan Cathedral & Lohengrin all in one day —

22 — To the Brera [Gallery], & then on to Rome, rain most of the time, but some fine hours in the Appenine gorges — Rome at midnight, Hotel de Rome —

23 — Looking at hotels, but could not get into any we wanted — Then Una Birch came, & we walked about with her, but there were many showers —

24 — To the Rospigliosi [Gallery] & saw the Aurora[162] — & in the afternoon de Basterot came, & gave us, in spite of showers, a delightful drive, showing S. Peter's to R. — & then out of the walls to S. Paolo, by gr good luck there were Croatian pilgrims there, in national costume, walking in processions & kneeling & praying at intervals & then bursting into hymns — Very pretty & R. did some sketches — Tea with Una —

25 — To the American Church, where the Burne Jones mosaics are finished[163] & after lunch de Basterot took us again about & outside, to S.___ in Monte, there we saw the graves of Tyrconnell & O'Neill[164] —

There has been a paragraph in the Times about Yeats's letter on the Queen's visit, & also about Edward Martyn resigning his D.L.[165] — This last put de B. very much out —

de B. says "the peasantry are the fountain of the world — the upper classes get worn out!"

26 — To the Capitol sculptures — Heavy showers —

27 — Baths of Diocletian with Una — R. drove with de B. — Dined de B. —

---

[161] Opera by German composer Richard Wagner (1813-83).

[162] "L'Aurore" by the Italian Baroque master Guido Reni (1575–1642).

[163] Burne-Jones had been commissioned to design mosaics for the apse and choir of the American Episcopal Church in Rome in 1880. He completed his designs in 1884, but the mosaics themselves were not finished until shortly after his death in 1898.

[164] Tyrconnel (d.1608) and Hugh O'Neill (c.1540–1606), the leaders who fled Ireland after the terminal defeat of the Gaelic forces at Kinsale in 1601, are both buried at the Church of San Pietro in Montorio, Rome.

[165] The Times 21 March, p. 16.

<?Brazzec> there, & some cousins of the Count — Pleasant enough, the cousins taken with R. — Countess de la Tour talks of Symons as "a vain boy".[166]

28 — S. Peter — & Vatican pictures —

29 — Barberini [Gallery] to see the Cenci[167] — & drove with de B. to the Hoffman villa & to Egeria's fountain — Evening we dressed for the Embassy party, & getting stuffy went first to the Beau Site to see Una & Mrs. Harris[168] — Then on to Embassy, Lady Currie very cordial, & a very pretty party — It is curious that my first great party & R.'s should be in the same Embassy[169] — The old Duke of Cambridge looking apoplectic but making himself agreeable to beautiful ladies — at least beautifully dressed ones — Mr. <?Bliss> there & Mrs. Lee & Kitty Hurlbert,[170] & Mme. <?Partiter> & Monsignor Stanley[171] & Hamilton Aide — I felt like a revenant, but very proud of my fair little sonnikin to show off, he did his mamma very nicely —

30 — Thunder & heavy rain, R. went out with Una & Mrs. Harris & after lunch with two Americans — Tea with Countess de la Tour — M[onsi]g[no]r Stanley there, very indignant about riots that have been going on in the Corso in front of our hotel — A popular preacher, Padre L____, has been preaching to gr crowds — who cheered him as we left — then other crowds gathered to cry "A basso i preti"[172] & gendarmes (carbinieri) had to come & disperse them — I was caught in the crowd yesterday, & clutched at by a frantic woman, & then saw the carbinieri charging at me, but got into the hotel at last — Stanley's indignation is against the students, who he says form the mob, & the statue of Giordano Bruno which he says excites them — & that G. Bruno was expelled from Oxford for unclean habits — & Mme. la Tour says it was for that

[166] Countess Victor Sallier de la Tour (1852–1912), a leading salon figure in Rome, and hostess to Symons (to whom de Basterot had introduced her) during Symon's stay in Rome in 1896. Symons stayed at her estate in southern France in 1898, and again in 1903, and dedicated his travel book *Cities* (1903) to her.

[167] A portrait of Beatrice Cenci, at this point attributed to Guido Reni (and now generally to Francesco Albani). Executed in 1599 for her part in the murder of her incestuous father, she is the central figure in Shelley's play *The Cenci*.

[168] Probably Edith Harris, née Remington (d.1926), previously Mrs. Clayton, wife of Frank Harris, from whom she was at this point estranged. She was a friend of Sir H. H. Johnston, Eliza Lynn Linton and others of AG's circle.

[169] AG's "first ball" had been at the British Embassy at Rome during her honeymoon in 1880 (*Seventy Years* p. 31)

[170] Widow of William Henry Hurlburt (1827–95), an American journalist who had been involved in a sensational breach of promise case in 1891.

[171] Monsignor Algernon Stanley (1843–1928), 4th son of the 2nd Baron Stanley. Canon of St. Peter's, Rome.

[172] i.e. "Down with the priests."

he was burned, & not for his beliefs[173] — Stanley is also indignant with the preacher, is jealous of him & says he has only a flow of words — Then I asked to see Symons's portrait, & Mme. de la Tour said "presently" & Stanley bolted — having it appears a gr horror of Symons — His portrait is too seraphic but the Countess says he is like that when he is "thinking of high things" i.e. the French Symbolists! — On to the Herrimans & looked at their pictures, Moreau's Edipus & the Sphinx — Millet's shepherd[174] —

31 — Vatican sculptures — Lunched with Mrs. Lee & tea with Ly. Louisa <???> — then went to say good bye to de Basterot — He was out & I waited & his servant lighted a lamp & brought me Cicero's Letters & 4 vols. Mahon's Hist[ory of] Eng[land] — to read from politeness I looked into the latter & found, what I had not known or had forgotten, an account of Dublin in I think 1753, when there was a rumour of a proposed Union, & the mob rose and seized Lords & M.P.s & made them swear in the streets they wd never agree to it[175] — Then de B. came in & announced that he was very cross with Yeats's letter which he had just been sent, but I think I made him understand it was written to keep the mob from violence, not to egg them on to it — Said good bye to him & rushed back to eat a bit & dress for the theatre, the Herrimans having given us their box for "Sappho"[176] — Una & Mrs. Mason joined us, & we had a very pleasant time, the music not much & the actors, except Sappho herself rather absurd — but the theatre (la Stanza) very handsome, & the dresses, more or less evening, with large hats to crown them, amusing — A downpour as we came out —

April 1 — Very heavy showers — to English church, & R. went to the

---

[173] Philosopher Giordano Bruno (1548–1600), born in Nola, Italy, and ordained 1572, fled from Italy after being accused of heresy in 1576. Lectured as a Professor at Toulouse, Paris and elsewhere, but caused contention wherever he lived, including at Oxford during a three-month stay in 1583. Denounced to the Inquisition soon after re-entering Italy, he was publicly burnt after refusing to recant his beliefs or to acknowledge the right of the Church to dictate in matters of philosophy. A statue of him was erected in the Piazza Campo de' Fiori in Rome in 1889.

[174] Brooklyn-born William J. Herriman (1828–1918), and his wife, who lived in Rome on account of her health. Herriman subsequently bequeathed "Oedipus and the Sphinx", by French painter Gustave Moreau (1826–98), to the Metropolitan Museum of Art, New York. French painter Jean-Francois Millet (1814–75), was renowned for rural scenes and studies of agricultural labourers.

[175] The relevant passage in the seven–volume *History of England* (1853) by Philip Stanhope (1805–75), 5th Earl Mahon, gives an account of Grattan's insistence on the dismantling of restrictive British tarrifs on Irish trade in 1779, not the question of Union itself. In response to Grattan's calls for greater economic and political autonomy "some four or five thousand of the Dublin populace rose in riot . . . calling out for a Free Trade and a Short Money Bill. They stopped the Speaker . . . in his coach, and endeavoured to administer an oath to him that he should vote as they desired. Several other Members were in like manner insulted and mal-treated" (vol. 7, p. 215).

[176] A five-act tragedy by Austrian poet and playwright Franz Grillparzer (1791–1872).

Haseltines — & then we had tea with Mrs. Abbott in the beautiful Aurora villa, painted by Guercino[177] — Walked in the Pincio —

2 — A lovely day, the first — so went by rail to Frascati — had a long walk thro' woods with carpet of anemones — view of Sabine hills — Home by 6 — but the day rather clouded by the loss of my ivory handled umbrella — given me so many years ago — & a headache —

3 — To Villa Borghese, the gallery shut, but the park lovely — Afternoon to the Forum — Walked about a little, & rain began & we took refuge in a temple turned into a carpenter's shop, & were followed by a flock of tourists, Cook's or Lunn's, listening to a lecture — & there we spent over an hour, then got out, & came in for another heavy shower — Tea with Mrs. Hurlbert at the Palazzo Sciarra —

4 — To look for Una at Beau Site — but she is knocked up & gone to Frascati — To Farnesina — & walked in the afternoon & took a wrong tram, & got to tea with Mrs. Abbott at 6 instead of 5 — Music in the evening, a papal singer "the Pope's angel" — for Lunn's tour, but we had the benefit — My umbrella was found in the morning, to my great joy —

4 — A fine day, so we drove to the Catacombs, & R. descended — After lunch I looked at the Times & saw that "Mr. Lecky has withdrawn his support from the Irish Literary Theatre in consequence of the discreditable utterances of Mr. W. B. Yeats, Mr. George Moore & other prominent supporters of the movement"[178] — It will do the theatre no harm, rather good I think, resting it again on a literary basis not helped by outsiders, but the little want of courtesy in his decision being sent to the papers with no private notice to me hurts me — On the other hand, I see that Parliamentarians & the Dublin Council (including the Lord Mayor!) have passed a resolution denouncing the Union, on the date of its introduction to the English H. of Lords — so my suggestion that this & not the Queen's visit should be the point of attack, has borne fruit.[179]

We drove to Borghese gallery, saw the statues & pictures — & then we went

---

[177] The Aurora fresco by Giovanni Francesco Guercino (1591–1666) at the Villa Ludovisi.

[178] *The Times* 3 April 1900, p. 6.

[179] "At a meeting of the Dublin Corporation yesterday afternoon . . . a resolution [was moved] declaring that as a section of the Unionist Press had misinterpreted the vote of the Council in favour of presenting an address to the Queen, the Council now assembled on the centenary of the passing of the Act of Union declared that that Act was obtained by fraud and shameful corruption, that the people could never give it loyal support, and that there would neither be contentment nor loyalty in Ireland until her National Parliament was restored" *Irish Times* 3 April 1900, p. 4.

to a horse jumping competition in the grounds at the back, which much amused R. — Then to tea at the Palazzo Mattei, (Mrs. <???>) a splendid set of splendidly done up rooms, but rather too much smelling of money — Then we dined at the Embassy — met Countess Passolini, & people I didn't know, & was taken in to dinner by Sir L. Alma Tadema[180] — & had a clever Italian who is over the excavations at the Forum on my other side — R. found that one of the attachés had been at New [College], had had his rooms, & his scout, a gr bond of union — Pleasant enough — & we drove Alma Tadema home, as cabs were scarce & rain had begun —

6 — Pouring rain — Drove to Vatican & saw the Sistine [Chapel] — Afternoon wet — got to tea at Herrimans — & chose photos at Almira's till dinner time —

7 — To the Colonna Gallery — & afternoon to Cappucini, & bought papal trays for schoolchildren — R. went to see Una in the ev —

8 — American church, & fine arts exhibition — & outside of S. Agatha, & after lunch garden of Knights of Malta — & tea at Mrs. Lee's — & very tired after all — And an offensive letter from Enid Layard about a new letter of Yeats's, calling to those who don't approve of the war to refrain from cheering as the Queen passes, & quoting Mirabeau's sentence "the silence of the people is the lesson of kings"[181] — For this Enid calls him "mad", no gentleman, without chivalry, ascribes a personal motive, & "deeply regret ever having shaken hands with such a creature" — I have answered, rather cruelly perhaps alluding to Sir Henry's letter about the Sultan & the Queen's resentment at it which cost him the peerage he wished for, but I must show her that duty to one's country comes before duty to a Queen[182] —

9 — To the Corsini [Gallery] to see Old Masters drawings — & walked & packed & dined at Beau Site with Una & the Harrises — dead tired —

10 — Off at 7-30 for Castellam[m]are — fairly good day — A lovely place —

[180] Sir Laurence Alma-Tadema (1836–1912), Dutch-born painter, knighted 1899.
[181] Yeats's letter had appeared in *The Dublin Daily Express* April 5 (*L* p. 338). Comte. Honoré Mirabeau (1749–91), revolutionary leader and orator, coined this maxim in a speech to the French Assembly in 1789.
[182] Layard's despatch of 27 April 1879, in which he freely acknowledged his lack of influence over the Sultan, effectively cost him his job as Ambassador to Constantinople as well as the peerage that would otherwise certainly have been his. The despatch compounded a grudge against Layard on the Queen's part begun by his outspoken criticism of the British military command during the Crimean War (for which she had blocked his appointment as Under-Secretary of War in 1855). WHG had lobbied energetically for Layard's elevation to the peerage in the 1880s.

11 — To Pompeii — a lovely day —

12–13–14 — Rode on donkeys up to Monte Capole[183] — And R. walked up
Vesuvius — good weather —

Paris — 10 Place de Laborde[184] — April 30 —
A pleasant day at Castellam[m]are — & then a driving tour for which Julia &
Frances Morris joined us, to Cava, Saleno, Paestum, Amalfi, Ravello —
Sorrento, Castellam[m]are, Naples — Lovely weather & all went well — 3
days at Naples — Then to Pisa, next day to Turin, a day there, & to Paris, where
R. & I parted, after a very happy 5 weeks together — Cost £115 — I came to
stay with de Basterot, who is kind & charming as possible, & it is a delightful
rest — He drove me to see Ex. buildings — which look like Arabian Nights
buildings, very pretty along the Seine — but most of them are but lath &
plaster & I grieve to hear of the trees cut down to make way for them —
Saturday Mrs. Lee Childe took me through some of the buildings, not many
of the exhibits open — I liked some Danish china best — Sunday we lunched
with Mrs. <?Cohen> — & drove [in] Bois de Boulogne — Saturday night I was
at the "Aiglon" — Sara Bernhardt's voice almost gone, hoarse when she raised
it, only good in the quiet parts[185] — I think it wd be a fine play if the last act
cd be cut off — It is the VIth! & interminable, Sara's death spun out, & the
gilt cradle brought in, & full of absurdities — But one is touched by the poor
young Duke making an effort to escape from his jail, & yet knowing he cannot
conquer his own weakness —

Ap[ril] 30 — Lee Childe called & took me to see Salomon Reinach & I had
a long Celtic talk with him[186] — He says what is most wanted just now is an
album of Irish antiquities, cheap — something like what Miss Stokes has done
for a series — but hers are all Christian[187] — Also there is a book of D'Arbois
he thinks shd be translated into English — with some of the chapters, now
obsolete, left out — "Mysteres de la religion Celtique" I think[188] — He was in

[183] Monte Coppola, rising some 1000 ft. directly outside Castellammare di Stabia, near
Sorrento, on the southern coast of the bay of Naples.

[184] De Basterot's Paris home.

[185] Sarah Bernhardt (1844–1923), the leading French actress of her time. This production
of *L'Aiglon*, by Edmond Rostand (1868–1918), had opened in Paris in March 1900, and
transferred to London for a short run at Her Majesty's Theatre in June 1901.

[186] Salomon Reinach (1858–1932), archeologist and historian. A long-standing friend of
WHG, and had reviewed his contribution to the National Gallery and British art in an 1895 article
"Sir W. Gregory et les collections Anglaises" in *Chronique des Arts*.

[187] Margaret Stokes had recently published a monograph, *The High Crosses of Castledermot and
Durrow* (1898), which Reinach had reviewed in *Revue Archeologique* in 1899. Her major work was
Early Christian Art in Ireland (1878).

[188] Henri d'Arbois de Jubainville (1827–1910), Celticist, historian and linguistic. His
seminal volume *Le Cycle Mythologique Irlandais et la Mythologie Celtique* (1884) was translated by
Richard Best in 1903.

Ireland last October, to see New Grange — He was struck with the ignorance of French in Ireland — astonished that neither Col. Plunkett[189] or Mr. Coffey cd speak Irish — & at the hostility of Trinity College to Irish things — "it is an English fort, nothing else, there is no chair of Irish literature or Irish archaeology, no lectures on them" — Its garrison, the students, had "gone out & broken the windows of a newspaper office" while he was there — He had spent an evening with Mahaffy who had been much astonished to find that he was no longer taken up with Greek things, finding Irish antiquities so much more interesting — He was delighted with the National Gallery, especially the Machiavelli picture, & gave me a pamphlet he has written on it[190] — Lunched with the Lee Childes — Then to the Ex. again to see the reproductions of Irish antiquities which Reinach had told me were ready — then to the Ceylon Court, & seeing Mr. Davidson's[191] name on a door I knocked & found him, & he was very glad to see me, said he had been thinking so much of us, knowing that of all people Sir William would have been the one most interested in the success of the Ex. — He showed me the exhibits & brought up the old goldsmith Mulalye & others to introduce to me, & I felt I had suddenly put on a crown!

My "Felons of our Land" had arrived, & de B. read it, & gave me a talking to in the evening — complimentary as to style, but thinks I am going too far away from the opinions of my husband & my son[192] — I told him I am convinced my husband would have been with me in all I have done so far — but that I had already determined not to go so far towards political nationalism in anything I write again as in the "Felons" partly because I wish to keep out of politics & work only for literature, & partly because if Robert is Imperialist I don't want to separate myself from him — so he preached to the converted — He winds up by saying in disgust that "that sort of patriotic doggerel makes him seasick" —

May 1 — To the Louvre — to look at the Salon Carré & the Venus of Milo —

[189] Presumably a slip for Count Plunkett. George Noble Plunkett (1851–1948), created a papal count, was a barrister with broad philological interests. He was at this point a Vice-President of the Society for the Preservation of the Irish Language. Father of Joseph Plunkett, leader in the 1916 Rising.

[190] "Un tableau de Machiavelli à Dublin" *Gazette des Beaux Arts*, 1 April 1900, pp. 278–82.

[191] Robert Davidson (1831–1913), Civil Servant who had been stationed at Madras 1852–84, and had met the Gregorys during their tour of India 1884–85.

[192] "The Felons of our Land" *Cornhill Magazine* May 1900, pp. 622–34. This article, one of the most overtly Nationalist of AG's writings, celebrates the heroes of Irish rebellions since 1798 in a discursive study of the ballads written about them. The Irish uprisings, she argues, were motivated by lofty idealism since those who fought did so in the expectation of death, and with no prospective personal gain. The essay explicitly aligns the executed rebels with Christ, himself "led to a felon's death", as uplifting examplars who provide a sharp contrast to the narrow-minded materialism and Jingoism of contemporary Britain.

After lunch to the Salon with Mrs. Lee Childe — miles of pictures, better painted I think than the London ones, but nothing very striking — But the little bronzes, medals, crescents etc — are charming & delicate & full of fancy — Took Mrs. Lee Childe to tea at Ceylon Court, & had asked Synge to come there — He is working at a book on Aran, & has sent an article to Harper's on it, which if taken he promises to get Jack Yeats to illustrate[193] — Dined with de B. — & then with him to the Cohens box at "Jean Bart" an absurd farce, but Coquelin[194] very funny — Home at midnight, very tired —

May 2 — The Luxembourg, & the Louvre again, & sketched de B.'s house from the "Place" — A nice quiet day —

3 — Off in the morning — A letter from "Cornhill" enclosing £13-13/-for my "Felons" so they shall build my chimney at Coole — A tiring journey — rough crossing, late arrival — A not very comfortable bedroom at Qmansions — & got off quickly to dine with Yeats — He has written nothing but his essay on "Symbolism" & a little article on Loyalty & Disloyalty in the United Irishman[195] — taking high ground — I wish that all who have read his letters on the Queen's visit could read this — but it would not make much difference — English people are in a fever & every attempt at reasoning acts as an irritant — He has been expelling MacGregor from the Kabbala[196] etc —

G. Moore had said sadly that he had thought his Queen letter splendid & powerful while he was writing it, but once written he thought it poor & flat — Yeats said "That is how Nature works — she holds out a lure before you, nothing would ever be done if that lure were not held before us — Then,

---

[193] Synge's article was not accepted by *Harper's*. He completed *The Aran Islands* in late 1901, but it was not published until 1907. Jack Yeats, who provided illustrations for the book, subsequently became one of Synge's closest friends.

[194] Either Constant-Benoit Coquelin (1841–1909), his brother Ernest-Alexandre (1848–1909), or his son Jean (1865–1944), who frequently performed together in London as well as Paris.

[195] "The Symbolism of Poetry" published in *The Dome* in April 1900 (and reprinted in *Ideas of Good and Evil*), and "Noble and Ignoble Loyalties" *United Irishman* 21 April (*UP2* pp. 211–13).

[196] Samuel Liddell Mathers (1854–1918), who later called himself MacGregor Mathers, was one of the founding Chiefs of the Order of the Golden Dawn in 1887 with William Wyn Westcott and W. R. Woodman. Mathers, who initiated WBY into the Order in 1890, and was the author of most of its rituals, lived in Paris from 1892 and continued to control the London temple of the Order through Florence Farr, but his dictatorial manner led to discontent among initiates. In February 1900, trying to consolidate his position, Mathers attempted to discredit Westcott by accusing him of forging the correspondence with the German adept Fraulein Sprengel on which the Order's charter had been based. The charge backfired, discrediting Mathers rather than Westcott, and after a dramatic seizure of the Order's archive by Mathers's agent, Aleister Crowley, was repulsed, Mathers was formally expelled from the London branch of the Order in April 1900. Mathers served as the basis for the figure "Maclagan" in WBY's unfinished novel *The Speckled Bird*.

when our work is done, it vanishes, is withdrawn" — That is true in many
things as well as writing, marriage among others —

He says there is a new recruit to the Celtic movement, a musician, O'Brien
Butler, who is writing an opera, & wants a libretto, & wants a cottage in Co.
Galway, where he can work — Moore had spent 2 hours listening to him &
said he is better than Stanford, & was delighted — Yeats had sent him to see
Nora Hopper, & to ask her to do a libretto — I thought he might be a useful
neighbour now R. is so fond of music, & said I wd come & see him[197] — Miss
Gonne taking an action against Irish Figaro for libel, she is accused of having
a Govt pension[198] — Macmillan in treaty with Yeats for his books — through
Stephen Gwynne — The latter says the Spectator didn't at all like putting in
his Queen article[199] — He says he was fighting his way into the Imperial hotel
through a crowd shouting for the Boers & being hustled by the police, & when
he got in he found the correspondent of the Chronicle writing an account of
the reception & saying how enthusiastic all the people were — He said "Had
you not better go out & see what is going on outside the hotel before you finish
that?" But he said "Thank you, I have quite enough material for my article".

3 [i.e. 4th] — A headache, but got out at 12 & went to see Horace Plunkett
about the Gort Convent, as the nuns want to turn it into a co-op & have me
on the Committee, & I waited to see him & know if it would be genuine — He
begged me to assent, as he says his department will have to fight with them,
& I will be someone reasonable to fight with! I don't like the idea of going on
to fight, but he suggested that I should stop in Dublin to see Father Finlay, &
talk to him, so wrote to him — He lamented the Queen letters "She was so
nice, & said the right things, & it is so sad the 'real and ideal' Ireland can't

[197] "T. O'Brien Butler" was the assumed name of Thomas Whitwell-Butler (1861–1915), a
composer who was a zealous convert to Irish cultural affairs. His collaboration with Nora Hopper
resulted in the opera *The Sea Swan*, later translated into Irish by Taidgh O'Donohue as *Muirgheis*.
Butler died in the sinking of the Lusitania. Charles Villiers Stanford (1852–1924), composer
and scholar of Irish music, was at this point best known for *Thirty Irish Songs* (1893) and his opera
"Shamus O'Brien" (see p. 140 n. 89).

[198] In the wake of "The Famine Queen", an inflammatory article by Maud Gonne in *The United
Irishman* (7 April 1900) denouncing Queen Victoria and her visit to Ireland, Ramsay Colles,
Editor of *The Irish Figaro* printed a defamatory attack which so incensed Arthur Griffith, Editor
of *The United Irishman*, that he and Colles came to blows. Colles printed a nominal retraction (21
April), which, however, asserted that Maud Gonne could not in good conscience attack Victoria
and her Government's military efforts against the Boers when she was in receipt of a British
pension as the daughter of a deceased British officer. Maud Gonne's libel action was completely
successful and forced *The Figaro* to publish a retraction admitting the charge was baseless (see
Samuel Levenson, *Maud Gonne* pp. 164–67).

[199] "The Queen in Dublin" *The Spectator* 7 April 1900, pp. 479–80. Gwynn's letter ostensibly
invokes high loyalty, alleging that all but extremist Nationalists want some form of dominion
status rather than separation, yet nonetheless hints at possible "disturbances" and alludes to the
rumour that Victoria's visit was principally intended as a recruiting measure for the Boer War.

work together" — Yeats had made such a beautiful speech that time they had a dinner, & he hoped we would work side by side — I defended Yeats, & on his persisting I said we cd still all work together "You made a speech on the war that made angels weep, but we have not given up the effort to help you because of that" — He said his speech on the war had offended some of his S. Dublin people by not being strong enough — & then he vexed me by saying "It is just as Balfour said in the H. of Commons, the Irish wd be against England in any war" — I said no, extremists wd be, & there wd be a bias against England, but I never remembered a war like this, in which each small farmer felt that the small farmers of another nation were being exterminated — It vexes me that he shd take his opinion of the opinions of Irish farmers from Balfour! However we parted friends — To see Sir A. Birch, & Enid Layard, people there, so we had no talk on the same subject, just as well — Private View at the Academy, got a card from Sir A. Birch, & had a run round — It looked vulgar after the Salon, but there were some good pictures, portraits by Sargent & boys by Clausen[200] — Then to tea with Yeats to meet O'Brien Butler — didn't think him very intelligent or attractive, but asked him for a few days when he comes over that he may look for a cottage — We discussed the folk lore of his opera — Yeats came back & dined, & we sat in Paul's sitting room till he came in, near 10, dead beat — He kept me till 12-30 talking — is depressed over the war, & his homeless life — as it is at present — He says Buller is a gr trial, cross grained & "cussed" & always throwing the blame on others — He wishes Ld. Lansdowne might resign that he cd have rest —

5 — Dressmaker, & house shopping — & afternoon to R[ichar]d III, Benson having given Yeats stalls in honour of Lit. Theatre — Too much of a spectacle, & all the acting overdone & jerky — Benson very painstaking, but restless, however he was fairly good in the great scenes of giving up the crown[201] — Dined at a restaurant & to bed very tired —

6 — Sunday — Went to Oxford to spend the afternoon with R. — His little room looked very nice — & we talked, & Gus Kelly came to tea, & we walked in the garden of S. John's [College] — & then ev. service, good singing & the beautiful chapel, a contrast to Gort! — got back about 11 — tired —

7 — Went in to tell the Morrises I could not dine with them, & Lord M. called me into his room & I sat talking with him a long while — He is down on Ed. Martyn for persisting in his resignation after Ld. Ashbourne's amiable letter — however he had shut up Clonbrock who had talked to him about it by

[200] The Royal Academy Exhibition included a number of portraits by American born painter John Singer Sargent (1856–1925), including two of Lord Russell of Killowen, and six works by George Clausen.

[201] In fact *Richard II*, played at the Lyceum Theatre between March and May 1900 in a series of Shakespeare plays performed by the F. R. Benson Company.

telling him that he had no more right to interfere with him as Lieut[enant] of the Co[unty] "than any crossing sweeper" — Much elated at an invitation to dine & sleep at Windsor, his invitation in Dublin having arrived too late — He says the Queen determined on going to Ireland quite by herself — Lord Salisbury told him that when he went to Windsor, Princess Henry[202] came in to the room & said "I am going to Ireland!" & that was the first he heard of it — Lord M. thinks it was the Irish massacres in the war that got on the Queen's mind — the In[n]iskillings going into action & coming out with 5 officers left out of 30 — 40 men out of 500[203] — "A member of the Royal Family" told Lord M. that it was John Brown[204] who kept the Queen from coming before — Whenever she spoke of it he wd say "Oh those Irish are good for nothing, come to Scotland, that's the place for you" —

Lunched Birchs — Sir A. says they are abusing Roberts now for having lost the waterworks & for other mistakes[205] — He saw a letter from an officer out there saying the cavalry were abusing the infantry & vice versa, & both the artillery — & meanwhile the terrific weekly expenses are mounting up — London decorated for the reception of the Naval Brigade — New Gallery with E. Layard — chiefly interested in Watts's portrait of W. Blunt[206] — Met Nora at Yapps — she says George's old wound came against him, & they knew by his letters of late his head was going — (He is said to have shot himself)[207] — Loaded my luggage at the Station & dined with Yeats & G. Moore — The latter says O'Brien Butler is very amateurish, & that it was only his general amiability since his conversion to Ireland that made him compliment him or sit two hours with him during which he was bored to death — However Miss Hopper arrived after dinner & they pounded out the libretto — & then W. B. Y. walked with me to the train — A good journey —

[202] Queen Victoria's daughter Beatrice (1857–1944), widow of Prince Henry of Battenburg (1858–96).

[203] At the battle of Colenso, 15 December 1899, Major-General Hart's Irish Brigade (2nd Royal Dublin Fusiliers, 1st Connaught Rangers, 1st Border Regiment and 1st Royal Inniskilling Fusiliers) were decimated in an attack conceived by Redvers Buller. Over 500 officers and men were killed or wounded, while the Boers suffered only a handful of casualties.

[204] John Brown (1826–83), Queen Victoria's loyal Highland servant, whose influence on and intimacy with the Queen had provoked widespread gossip in which she featured as "Mrs. Brown".

[205] After triumphantly relieving the beseiged garrison at Bloemfontein, Roberts neglected to post adequate defences at the town waterworks at Sannah's Post some 20 miles east, which were promptly captured by a Boer raiding party led by de Wet in late March.

[206] Painted in 1899 (and reproduced in Elizabeth Longford *A Pilgrimage of Passion* p. 340). Blunt had been proposed as Watts's pupil in 1854 when aged 13, but the idea had faded when the Blunts spent several months abroad shortly afterwards.

[207] Eleanor Persse's brother George Gough had shot himself in S. Africa on 29 March 1900. Gough was Wolseley's private secretary 1897–98, and served as Commanding Officer of the 9th Lancers in S. Africa, but had been sent back to the Cape in disgrace after incompetently leading a reconnaissance party to disaster on the Orange River front, the first C. O. so to be disgraced in the War. *The Tuam Herald* 14 April 1900, p. 2, reported that Gough had died from a "fever contracted in the discharge of his duty."

8 — Dublin, Gresham Hotel — Called on Mr. Burton about my pictures & he said he was to see them at Nat. Gallery where they are being sorted, at 3, & asked me to come — Lunched with Gills to meet Father Finlay & talked Gort Industries, & I decided not to join committee, unless a good business man is put on as well — Gill murmuring wisdom as usual — but not of a very convincing nature — Says, on Miss Stokes's authority, who was present, that Mahaffy when presented to the Queen said "Very happy to see yr Majesty — I met one of your nephews the other day" — The Queen glared at him & he withered by degrees — & now he says she is "a stupid old woman — doting — at least after dinner" — To Nat. Gallery — Miss Stokes there sorting the sketches — Mr. Burton had told me she was very jealous of mine, but she was very amiable — I think there are about a dozen for me — There is to be an exhibition of them, & Miss Stokes talks of writing a memoir — Then to see Russell & had a long talk with him, & he asked me to come in the evening & see his drawings — He has written a beautiful article on Imperialism in the All Ireland Review[208] — That, & Yeats's [letter] in the United Irishman put the question on a high level & one feels how futile ordinary newspapers or drawing room criticism is in dealing with it. Called on Ade[laide] but could not get in at her house — Ev. to Russells, saw Mrs. R. & the baby — & he read me part of his long poem, beautiful in single lines, but I did not hear enough of it to judge it as a whole[209] — He hopes Willie will soon be with me "& shut up in his room till you can hear him purr".

9 — Home — but missed train, & had a trying wait at Athenry, commercial travellers eating onions, & rain outside — & a very bad headache — however all was right when I got home — all green & clean & pleasant, tho' I missed old Ned Diveney's greeting —

10 — Getting things into their right places, & Ed. Martyn came over, in very good spirits, perhaps too much elated, at the reception his resignation has had — I told him I didn't like his letter to the Galway Union about landlords,[210] & that no one liked it, Gill amongst others & he was surprised & said Gill had said it was such a particularly good letter! He says I get the credit of his conversion! I don't know on what grounds — He has still some land troubles but is trying to settle them, & he is not at all reconciled to his own people, thinks them a horrid lot, & it makes him ill to see a countryman come into the yard to talk to him!

208 "Nationality and Imperialism" *All Ireland Review* 5 May 1900, p. 1.

209 "The Feast of Age", which AE never finished but later reworked as "The House of the Titans".

210 Probably Martyn's letter to the Galway Urban Coucil, published in *The Tuam Herald* 5 May 1900, p. 4, in which he suggested the formation of a National Landlord Party,

11 — Frank for rents — Says I am said to have influenced E. M. — I say I am flattered at being credited with so much influence —

12 — E. Martyn brought B[isho]p Healy[211] & Gill in the afternoon — A man had said to the Bp. "Mr. Martyn is a great man" — "What has he done?" — "He's after cutting the Government adrift!"

13 — To church — & then to the Convent to talk about the Industries — agreed to join their Committee if they can get a business man, Benny Murray or Huban in it —

18 — A quiet week — Have been translating Douglas Hyde's poems — got Mulkere to go through those I had done, & find them fairly correct — A good many of the people to see me, usually to ask for something!

Mulkere says "I think the Nationalists may take a back seat now" — I say "Oh yes, behind Mr. Martyn" & he says "Yes, & Lady Gregory" — And Cahel who I meet on the road says "You're the best lady in Ireland — sure we read it on the paper!"

Saturday 19th — I got a side of bacon for old Farrell, and Mrs. F. on being given it to take to him said "it would rise his heart after the bad news that was after coming" — "What bad news?" — "The Boers being bet!" (that is, the relief of Mafeking just known).[212] —

20th — Robert's birthday — Thank God we have got so far safely —

Lunched at Lough Cutra to see the new building — Hugh [Gough] anxious to know how we cd encourage enlisting! He thinks we might make the family at home more comfortable, & make a hero of the soldier — He is surprised that none of the tenants followed George to the war!

24th — Mr. Fahy from across the lake, hopes the English may win, because if not we'll have more taxes & they are heavy enough as it is — He understands that the Boers have been preparing for the last 15 years against the English, making portholes & setting traps.

27 — Too wet for church — A pleasant article in the "Pilot" by S. Gwynn partly

[211] Most Rev. John Healy (1841–1918), Archbishop of Tuam, a scholar of Irish Law, and active in promoting Irish agriculture.

[212] The British garrison at Mafeking, under seige by the Boers for 217 days, was relieved on 17 May 1900.

founded on my "Felons"[213]—At 5 I went to the gate to start my Irish class, only 3 little girls, F. Reilly, a Killeen & little Melville — but Mulkere came to help me & we got on nicely — 2 little Hanlons came in at the end — A beginning at all events —

June 10th — The next Sunday 6 little girls & Willie Moran — I sent my translations to D. Hyde to know if they were pretty correct & he seems delighted with them — didn't know how good they were! or how they would look in English[214] — Finished my article on them yesterday, but must keep it to show Yeats[215] — Went to a meeting at the Convent about Industries, but refused to go on c[ommit]t[ee], they have no notion of going straight poor things & I shd be alone to fight— Frank says when he made the plans for their new buildings, they wanted laundries built, but asked him to mark them "class rooms", thinking they wd get money more readily for these — Had the Workhouse children out for the day, & went to see the Ballylee people, which cost me boots for Brennan & a goat for Mrs. Quirk & a 1st communion dress for Fanny Reilly, & many extras — Rain came on, & it has been a quiet, wet week-end —

23 July— The Jack Yeats have come, & Mr. Harvey, & on the 17th the Russells — AE being only able to get his holiday now — The baby a dear little fellow, friendly & merry— Mrs. Russell very untidy & dirty in attire & hard in manner — slaps & shakes the child, says she hates it near her, & wd rather have a bundle of old manuscripts — but this must be partly put on, as she must be fond of such a dear little thing — The maids furious, as she sits reading a novel, or having her tea, while it is catching & eating flies at the window[216] — The end is, that I am chief nurse & am at this moment with it while asleep, Mr.

---

[213] "Irish Nationalist Poetry" *The Pilot* 19 May 1900, pp. 351–52. Gwynn's essay, a review of addresses by Rolleston and WBY to the Irish Literary Society that week, praises AG's "charmingly written [and] profoundly suggestive" article and notes that the poetry of rebellion will remain popular—notwithstanding the "serious literature" of the new school—until Ireland is no longer held "by coercion".

[214] "I was absolutely amazed at getting your translations of my Irish pieces, I had no idea you had translated anything like so many, or that you would have been able to translate them anything like so well. I had no idea that my things had any merit, but certainly your translations impressed me a little ! I have no idea how you did them so well" (Hyde to AG, 6 June 1900, Berg).

[215] "The Poet Raftery" *The Argosy*, January 1901, pp. 44–58.

[216] Along with the "too obvious dislike" she had shown for Cottie Yeats in 1899, AG's strong reaction to Violet Russell fitted a recurrent pattern of antipathy to women in general, and to the wives of men she admired in particular. Writing to John Quinn in 1906 she would complain at length of Lucy Hyde and her "sharp and even venomous tongue": "I should be content to have Jack Yeats and Douglas Hyde here for six months of the year, but a few weeks of their wives makes me hide in the woods! and I have felt the same with AE and his wife. It is not that they are particularly undesirable as guests, but one is not in sympathy with them or their attitude towards various things, and it makes a constant slight strain trying to find common grounds of sympathy" (Berg).

& Mrs. R[ussell]. being on the lake — R., the Jacks, Geraldine & Mr. Harvey at Athenry, where the County is playing Kiltartan — poor Kiltartan!

AE is doing wonderful pictures — he has begun oils, which have not the same charm as pastels, but are of course lasting — The deep pools delight him — He has painted 2 figures raising a cup, & seven figures holding a sword, & a Queen (at the deep hole) & some landscapes — I asked him what he thought these spirits are that he so constantly sees, & he says they are earth spirits that have not yet taken animal forms, but will probably when our race is extinct become a new race — He thinks them inferior to us, chiefly because, tho' more beautiful, they have not the look of being capable of complex emotions, or of understanding the nature of sacrifice — Anyone could see them, he says, who can detach their mind from the ordinary business of life, & wait for them — He is surprised I cannot see them by the shadowy pools, but I say I am like Martha, careful & cumbered with much serving[217] — His idea of our life is that we are making a daily sacrifice, consciously, but that the consciousness only comes in sleep, & can't be remembered afterwards — & that the verse "He giveth his beloved sleep" is really "He gives to his beloved in sleep"[218] — Even a drunkard is making a sacrifice in having consciously taken the nature of a drunkard, to work off the evil of the race (but this I don't follow quite clearly).

He doesn't like "Water of the Wondrous Isles" which W. Yeats is delighted with, he says "it is wall paper, mere decoration" — & that it is in imitation of Malory — Yeats says it is no more an imitation than Rossetti is imitation of early Italian pictures, the soul comes through, & that there cd be no art at all without tradition[219] —

23 — Kiltartan played the Co[unty]. at Athenry & beat it by 3 runs, a gr triumph — R. made top score, 27 —

R. dreamed that AE & Yeats wanted him to go with them & see visions, & that he was going, & then he thought "If I see visions it will spoil my eyesight & I won't be able to play cricket" — so he turned back —

AE doesn't like Swinburne, says there is nothing but words, nothing behind, while Wordsworth has faith behind him —

[217] See *Luke* 10.40.

[218] *Psalms* 127.2.

[219] *The Water of the Wondrous Isles* (1897) an Arthurian-style quest narrative by William Morris (1834–96). WBY, an habitué of Socialist League debates at Morris's Hammersmith home in the late 1880s, retained a lasting admiration both for Morris's prose romances, "the only books I was ever to read slowly that I might not come too quickly to the end" and for Morris himself, for his "spontaneity and joy" as "my chief of men" (*Au* p. 141).

24 — I left AE & Yeats at the big tree at Raheen, & they drew it, Yeats made a charming sketch — Russell a charming one also, but with a rather dreadful figure with long cloth ears under the tree — He says it was not very nice, but he wd like to pet it — When a man passed it shrank up, as if it wd climb the tree backwards — I showed it to <?Marty> who says his own brother-in-law had work to get his horse past that tree one night, but he is suprised that Mr. Russell can see these things in the daytime — Jack & R. sketching, & Mr. Russell has done some lovely figures & a Queen —

26 — All sketching — ev[ening] AE & Yeats tease each other — AE tells how Yeats found a "clairvoyant" in Miss Sigerson & put her to look in a crystal & invoked the Angel Gabriel — She looked & saw a golden palace — This was puzzling but she looked again & saw a white armed figure at the palace window — W. B. Y. was delighted, & prepared questions to put to the Archangel — but a rationalist who stood by, observed that the shop opposite had had a lot of gilding about it which was reflected in the crystal — & that there was a man in his shirt sleeves cleaning the window which was the Archangel![220] W. B. Y. says, when he once observed that one of AE's group dropped his h's — AE replied that "he functioned in a higher sphere"!

Aug[ust] 1 — AE & W. B. Y. had a fiery argument in the woods yesterday on the sword, whether it was the symbol of fire or air — & called each other "all the names" — but were good friends in the evening — W. has finished his lyric, on the withering of the boughs[221] — AE has done besides his spirit & landscape drawings, a charming little picture of baby for me — AE says, if he had money, he would go all over Ireland to look for the two men who are ruling its destinies at present — He has seen them & others have seen them in vision — One lives in a cottage beside a single-line railway, a log of wood in front — He is oldish, with a golden beard — The other, young & dark, lives in a park close by — There is a third, but he is vague, perhaps not in a physical body — The first time he saw them, he was filled with energy & life, so that he worked without effort & with joy for a long time after[222] — I suggest their being symbolic of the new spirit in people & landed gentry that will regenerate the country, but he declares they are real.

On Monday we went to Athenry for cricket match, & beat the County again

[220] Either Hester Sigerson (1870–1939), younger of George Sigerson's two daughters, who provided the "Uncle Remus" column in *The Weekly Freeman* in the 1890s, or more likely her elder sister Dora (1866–1918), who published a number of volumes of poetry and remained a lifelong friend of WBY. Dora Sigerson had married Clement Shorter, editor of *The Illustrated London News*, in 1896. The incident probably took place in 1891 (see *CL 1* p. 263).

[221] "The Withering of the Boughs", first published in *The Speaker* 25 August 1900.

[222] For AE's first visions of the avatars he believed had arrived in Ireland, see his letter to WBY in June 1896 (Alan Denson, *Letters From AE* pp. 17–18).

— Our men immensely proud.

Aug[ust] 27 — We went to Galway Feis on Thursday, more competitors & more people & more life than before — Robert came with me & Douglas Hyde & Yeats — Old men in white flannel jackets recited poems, some of Raftery's, one old man his own composition, a talk with death — He told how death swept away gr people, among others the Queen of England, & stopped to say "& that wouldn't be much loss" at which there was much applause among those who understood Irish — I found I understood a little more than last year, but still not much — A long wait on line, & late for Gort train at Athenry, & had to take a car home — late & tired —

24th — A cricket match here, Ennistymon came & played us, & was ignominiously beaten. They made 16 in their first innings — & Robert alone 19! A fine morning, but thunder & rain in afternoon — Many to provide for, fish lunch — & the "aristocracy" of the neighbourhood.

26 — After church we went off to Killeenan, to Raftery's grave, where the stone has been put up, to hold a meeting[223] — A long drive, seeming to lead to nowhere — & then we got to the village, found it decorated with evergreens, & Irish mottos — the band playing, a large crowd in best clothes, & Father McDonough who had been holding a religious service — There was a little platform, & we were led to it, & addresses of welcome presented to me, to Ed. Martyn, to Hyde, to Yeats — Then some speeches — Father McDonough, & the schoolmaster, & then Hyde, very eloquent, & reciting verses from Raftery, at which the people were delighted — They were pleased with the stone, only some objected to the word "Raftery" only, & I had to explain that Homer also had been known by one name only — "He is writing of this" one old man said "he was such a conversible man" — Tilly Redington then, had never heard of Raftery a month ago, & Father Considine had been for 2 years in the parish & had never heard of him —

Tea at Kilcornan[224] —

We had begun the day by church, where the Isle of Man preacher had said

[223] An account of this meeting in the *Tuam Herald*, 31 August 1900, which identifies participants and gives synopses of the speeches, is reprinted in *Poets and Dreamers* pp. 248–50, but the editorial note which accompanies the reprint, asserting that John Quinn and Jack B. Yeats were also present, is incorrect, and confuses this 1900 meeting with a similar event in 1902. As Hyde points out in *Songs Ascribed to Raftery* (p. 55): "Lady Gregory was the prime cause of the gathering. She raised a high and handsome stone above the grave . . . . It was she who thought of doing it, and it was upon her the cost, or the most of it, fell." Edward Martyn was the other principal contributor.

[224] Home of the Redington family.

how patriotic "we Britons" were — & no wonder with such a beautiful country!

27 — A cricket match with Ennis settled for Wednesday — Hyde said some one ought to write an account of yesterday's meeting to the Claidheam, & I did it to save him the trouble[225] — Took Mrs. Hyde in boat after — He began his "Twisting of the Rope" & got on splendidly[226] —

The cricket match a gr success — Ennis beaten all to nothing

"Twisting of the Rope" splendid —

The piper, Corly, came & Dr. Hyde interviewed him & took down some verses — He had spoken much of the change in Mr. Martyn, & what an ordeal it used to be going there in the old days, with fear in yr heart, & weakness in yr feet, & a sixpenny or maybe a threepenny thrust out at you then through the window — All the county talking of the change "& I have it in my heart & in my conscience, that it is the woman of this house that had been the cause of that change" —

Sunday 2nd Sept[ember] — Hyde at a meeting at Labane, & called in at my class on the way back, & we had asked a few men who were in earnest to come & meet him, & they came, Gillane & Jack Ford & Mulkere & Baldwin & J. Noone & W. Moran(!) Willie Hanlon, John Rourke, Michael Cahel (who I had met passing & sent in) — & Hyde proposed his "beal-direaca" League & they put themselves under gassa "not to speak any English amongst ourselves or with anybody else, except with stupid uneducated people who cannot understand the language of Ireland" — This is the first beginning of this league[227] —

3rd — Hydes left — He has begun a new play on matchmaking[228] — He had very good news from Father O'Hickey about the Archbishop & the language, but was not allowed to give us particulars[229] — Tired, & Yeats rowed me across the lake & we had tea at Inchy — He wandered, getting lines for his new lyric,

[225] "Raftery's Grave" *An Claidheamh Soluis* September 8 1900, p. 406.

[226] Hyde's diary records 28 August as the date of his start on the play (Dominic Daly, *The Young Douglas Hyde* p. 135).

[227] "Béal-díreach", literally "straight-mouth", is used here in the sense "right-talk". "Geasa" are "bonds" or "obligations".

[228] Hyde's play, *An Cleamhnas*, was subsequently published in Gaelic, and in an English version, *The Matchmaking*, translated by AG, in *Poets and Dreamers* pp. 205–14. See also p. 310, diary entry for 7 January 1902).

[229] Dr. Michael O'Hickey (1860–1916), Eugene O'Growney's successor as Chair of Irish at Maynooth 1896–1909, was a Vice President of the Gaelic League 1899–1903. A vigorous activist for the use of Gaelic, O'Hickey was dismissed from Maynooth in 1909 for his open criticisms of two bishops who opposed making Irish a compulsory subject at the National University.

of fair women, & was pleased, because, as a rhyme for dawn, I reminded him that Niam had appeared to Usheen as a fawn[230] —

4 — 2 Beauchamp girls arrived — & went up to Chevy — Another afternoon on the lake — very peaceful — but did not save me from exhausting sickness — R. away at Gus Kelly's wedding —

Sep[tember] 7 — To Duras to say good bye to de B[asterot]. — with Tim — & with Yeats, who all but got the last 4 lines of his new lyric —

8 — Lyric finished — begins "I have no happiness dreaming of Brycelinde"

11 — R. out shooting so went with Yeats to Chevy for the day — he taking "Shadowy Waters" which he is altering — A lovely day — I went to see old Mary Glynn who says "I hear the neighbours when they come in to light their pipes saying there's a power of the Queen's soldiers killed — And I have asked Pat Diveney to make me a little cabin in the wood, where I'll be near him when the war comes here — but he says the wood will be the first place they will try — They say it was the fault of the Queen beginning the war — well wasn't it foolish of her, & she so old, up to 80 years — But she knows that she herself is safe from slaughter, whatever may happen to anyone else" —

And Mrs. Hayes says — "There's no one from these parts gone to the war, but there's a gr many gone to America, and some of them boys that had business at home — but they were afraid of being brought off to the war by the Press" — I asked if they disliked all wars or this one in particular, & she said "Well, they don't like to be killed — Sure they're not brought up to it like the Captain!" —

Sept[ember] 21 — George Moore came a few days ago, to work at Grania with Yeats[231] — He likes "Twisting of the Rope" — & has made some small alterations in it — He will give £100 for the theatre, & I have renewed my £25 guarantee — He went over to Tillyra to see Edward who received him cordially, but refuses any guarantee, will pay for the production of his own play if it is accepted, but for nothing else — He came to dine yesterday ev., & I was alone with him before dinner, & begged him, for his own sake, to reconsider this — I told him it would be said that he had taken up the theatre only for the production of his own work, & not for the general good, & that he, who has written so strongly against music halls & low English plays, ought

[230] "Under the Moon", first published in *The Speaker*, 15 June 1901.
[231] Evidently tiring of collaboration by post, Moore had on 11 August invited Yeats to Moore Hall to finish the play (Berg). AG was almost certainly instrumental in quashing this plan, as her correspondence with AE in August and September signals their shared growing concern at the effect of the association on WBY. Moore's visit to Coole took place 15–17 September.

to help the Literary Theatre quite independently of his own work — But he is obstinate "will not pay a penny for the production of other people's work — Had his own play spoiled last year, & Maeve shelved, & will let these chaps find the money themselves now" — It is very sad & heartbreaking, it will do him so much harm —

Sep[tember] 29 — G. Moore been away in Dublin & just come back — He read his lst Act of "Grania" to Russell (rather spoiled by his altering the language) & Russell was indignant, thought the character of Diarmuid & of the Fianna was being taken away — So, he having written on Wednesday that the act was thin, & the Fianna were to be made more turbulent, he wrote on Thursday that they were to be endowed with all the virtues — so I telegraphed to him to come back, that they might arrive at some conclusion & write together[232] — I had a busy week, as Yeats was re-writing the 2nd Act, & I helped him with words as well as with typing —

Wrote to Gill to know if he would publish "Irish Ideals" at his own risk, but he refuses[233] —

30th — A letter from Seely Bryers,[234] refusing to publish at their own risk, but very civil, offering to do it as moderately as possible — G. Moore says he is going to take his new novel to a Dublin publisher — he thought Gill, but Yeats says Seely Bryers wd be better — & try to arrange publication, tho' it will probably mean loss of money to him, & he certainly won't get £500 in advance as he cd from a London publisher[235] — This is good of him, & if Seely takes

---

[232] Moore's account in *Ave* suggests that he made only one visit to Coole in summer 1900, which ended with his acquiescing to WBY's and AG's suggestion that he draft the play in French; this he claims to have begun in "a hotel sitting-room" in France (pp. 342–62). His double-visit was in fact punctuated by a stay at the Shelbourne Hotel, Dublin, from whence he telegraphed a message urging "turbulent fianne" on 22 September (Berg). After receiving sharp criticism from AE on 25th ("I broke Moore's heart over Grania last night. . . . I suggested that Diarmuid was supposed to be a man" AE to AG, Berg) Moore then wrote dismissing the draft of the first act as inadequate, and proposed to come back to Coole. Though he professed his inability to stay "for more than a couple of days" (Moore to AG, 26 September, Berg), he in fact stayed for two weeks.

[233] Henry Gill (1836–1903), a Dublin bookseller and occasional publisher who had issued *Poems and Ballads of Young Ireland* in 1888. "Irish Ideals" was AG's preliminary title for *Ideals in Ireland*. At this point the volume was still largely prospective, as only the contributions of AE and Moore were ready.

[234] Sealy Bryers and Walker, a Dublin publishing and printing firm (which had published WBY's *Mosada* in 1886).

[235] Moore's enthusiasm for Irish publication appears to have foundered on the rocks of practicality, and his "new novel" *Sister Teresa* was published by his long-suffering English publishers Fisher Unwin in 1901. He appears however to have arranged in 1901 for Fisher Unwin to act as distributors in England for copies of the first issue of *Samhain*, printed and published (in Ireland) by Sealy Bryers. Sealy Bryers also served as Fisher Unwin's printers for *The Untilled Field* in 1902, possibly at Moore's request.

it up, it may be a new epoch, having a genuine Irish publisher, so that we need not be dependent on English publishers who think only of what will suit the English market — "Grania" being altered a good deal —

Oct[ober] 1 — Irish class of 12 yesterday, 7 genuine pupils — G. Moore amused us at dinner with accounts of Dorothy Stanley's attempts to <?? ??> — This morning he has a letter from Ed. Martyn acknowledging his share in the "Heather Field", but hinting that he spoiled it! & also saying that he owed him no thanks as he had taken it up as a commercial transaction! He also says that he will not in future give any support to the I. Lit. Theatre, but if plays of his are accepted, he will have separate accounts kept, & will ensure the theatre being at no loss by them[236] — It is sad he shd cut himself away from what he had a share in starting, but for ourselves, it is better to have a definite statement —

1st Oct[ober] — Arabella came — Typing "Grania" —

2nd — Translating Douglas Hyde's little allegory about a field to read to the others — Pretty, but won't do for my book — We talked of words & their value in the ev. — teasing Moore a little for his "soldier" (Finn) & other words he used[237] — He got cross, lost his temper a bit —

3rd — Una Birch came — We read "Twisting of the Rope" in the ev. — R.'s last day — He went out shooting at [Lisheen] Cranagh in the morning, & took Moore & the girls out afternoon —

Oct[ober] 13 — London — R. left, & next day Una & G. Moore left — Wet weather — Very busy typing for Yeats, & making out an article of S. O'Grady's in "All Ireland Review"[238] — & sending off translation of "Lament for Ireland" to the "Leader"[239] — & going through "Grania" altering Moore's words —

---

[236] "As regards the help you gave me on the Heather Field, much of it was valuable & I am sure I always told you how much obliged I was for it. At the same time I accepted some things which I did not like . . . In all you did for [the play], you appear not to have been actuated solely with a wish to help me . . . You always stipulated you should get some of the receipts, if there were profits . . . Why make a great favour of what in reality was a matter of gain & business? . . . I feel I must adhere to my decision about not supporting any work in future except my own . . . If my play is accepted, separate accounts must be kept" (Martyn to Moore, 28 September 1900, Berg).

[237] For Moore's version of his disputes with WBY over the appropriate style of language for the play see *Ave* pp. 346–9.

[238] Probably the editorial column "The Great Enchantment" *All Ireland Review* 13 October, pp. 4–5, a disquisition on war and politics.

[239] "A Sorrowful Lament for Ireland", AG's translation of an undated Gaelic lament by an Irish priest, which she had first seen in *Revue Celtique* some years earlier. Published under the heading "An Irish Poem", *The Leader* 20 October 1900, pp. 123–24, and subsequently reprinted in *Poets and Dreamers*.

Very tired — On Monday Arabella & Geraldine left — & on Tuesday morning Yeats — & at midday I set out for Spiddal — At Galway the Leckys got out of the train, & Lord Morris was there with 'bus to meet us, but I drove with Martin in his little trap hearing all his election news — He had worked very well, & had very cleverly got small shopkeepers to canvass rural voters who knew nothing of the questions at issue & had made many promises, which I can't say he shows much intention of fulfilling — Redmond had trusted to the priests, & the priests had trusted to the power of their own wholesale orders, so they have lost Galway, & as Martin boasts "He is the first Unionist returned for 20 years in either Connaught or Munster — either Connaught or Munster"[240] — Arrived at Spiddal, tea was just being brought up, & I was given a telegram from R. saying he had been "sent down" till Nov[ember] 1 — & asking if he shd come back — A quite unexpected shock, for he was confident of passing his exam (divinity) — I was aghast — said nothing but slipped off to write & send a telegram — Could not have him back, for he would be idle, & there wd be so much talk, people wd think it was for bad conduct he had been sent back — So I wired that I wd come over — I had to tell Ly. Morris, & she was very sympathetic & thought me right to go — A beautiful sunset, & I kept up forced talk with Lecky about compulsory purchase which he thinks likely, tho' from his usual balancing mind, it is hard to say if he approves of it or not — At dinner forced myself into a fight for Irish — Ld. M. says he never spoke against it for he never heard a proposal at all made for it at the Board — if he had, he wd only have laughed at such an absurd craze — Lecky defending his Trinity Professors — & sneered at me for calling Irish a "modern language" — I said yes, in exactly the same sense as modern Greek — & Ly. Morris told him it was spoken all around there, & I told him that songs were still composed in it which astonished him — Lord M. asked me some Irish phrases which luckily I understood — so I came pretty well out of it — A bad night — & in the morning headache — Went to the school to ask Deaney & Greaney to collect some ballads for me[241] — then off in a car to Galway — dreading meeting anyone lest I shd be asked why I was going — A long journey, my head bad, & no rug or warm clothes for a cold night — Got to Qmansions Thursday morning — R. arrived evening, says out of 11 men who went up from New 6 were turned back — the Scripture questions seem unduly difficult & "catchy" — It seems foolish sending boys away because they

---

[240] Polling in the General Election for Galway City took place on 1 October 1900, with Martin Morris gaining victory over the Nationalist candidate by a modest margin. He was the first Unionist to hold the seat since the election of 1885. Morris had stood for the seat in 1895, coming a poor third despite a split in the Nationalist vote that year.

[241] AG's interest in ballads spurred a series of articles, which she revised and collected in *Poets and Dreamers*. Her "West Irish Folk Ballads" *The Monthly Review* October 1902, pp. 123–35 is the only one of these which suggests a specific debt to the Spiddal region: "It is chiefly in Aran, and on the opposite Connemara coast, that Irish ballads are still being made as well as sung" (*Poets and Dreamers* p. 254).

have been idle, instead of giving them extra work — & if other parents get no intimation from the dons, as I have got none, there may be young fellows amusing themselves & not telling their parents at all — Went to War Office to see Paul, who lent us rooms here for R. & talked the matter over — It didn't seem so bad when talked of, but I hope it won't be heard of in Galway — Head bad still & to bed early — Friday, R. went to Newman St. to start drawing, & we wrote & telegraphed about tutors — I went to see Birchs — but otherwise will stay away — Heard of Frances Beauchamp's engagement to Bobby Templar[242] —

13th — Letters, & to see Sir Frederic's old housekeeper, who has kept a plate for me, the one he used under his inkstand, & for R. the stick I had given Sir F. — from St. George's Place when I broke up — It is nice for R. to have it —

Oct[ober] 21 — We got thro' the week nicely, R. at his drawing lessons & at work, & copying the Longhi in my room — Nevill Geary in town, I helped him to furnish his rooms at the Temple — Jack Yeats turned up, & took R. to a boxing match — A week ago I wrote my preface for "Ideals in Ireland" — & the essays are nearly all ready, but Yeats is in Miss Gonne's clutches in Dublin & I am waiting for his — We dined at Birchs last night, & argued over Davitt's address to Kruger[243] — Sir A. thinking it scandalous — I thinking the style turgid & bad, but the sentiments only those of English radicals — R. appealed to, & tho' not agreeing with the views of the writer, thinks they are quite justified in expressing them —

28th — Got a bad cold on Sunday — & had a trying week — Struggled up on Thursday, for a small teaparty, a Miss Lockwood R. had asked, & Hugh Percy [Lane], & George Moore, & Yeats had come to lunch & stayed on — He read me 3rd Act of Grania, Moore's words very funny "the little mishaps of the birds" in allusion to 4 wild swans being blown into a tree — Rather disappointed, Diarmuid's death not made enough of — Yeats a little taken aback at finding all the papers had mentioned his being at the meeting of Transvaal Committee when vote of address of sympathy to Kruger was passed[244] —

[242] Frances, the eldest of AG's three Beauchamp nieces, married Robert Shawe Templar in January 1901.

[243] Kruger, who had fled the Transvaal, arrived in Belgium on 18 October 1900. In a letter to The Freeman's Journal 16 October, p. 4, Nationalist Michael Davitt (1846-1906), who founded The Land League in 1879, proposed to welcome him with an address from Irish opponents of the war. The text of the address was published in preliminary form in The Freeman's Journal on 18 October, p. 6, and in final form on 20 October, p. 5.

[244] WBY's attendance (along with Maud Gonne) at the Irish Transvaal Committee meeting of 10 October, at which a resolution was passed calling on Dublin Corporation to support a motion giving Kruger the Freedom of the City of Dublin, was reported widely in both the Irish and British press.

Paul came in, he had written that he wanted to talk to me about R. so we slipped off to Mr. Monckton's room — He had written to Nowell Smith about R. being sent down, & had an answer, which he did not show me, but told me contents of — N. Smith says R. is dreamy, does not do much work, & has no chance of taking a good place in schools — He has not a word to say against his character, says he is strong in expression & language — & has evidently a store of originality & power — but that it does not come into his work, & it is too late to make up for lost time, with a view to honours — Paul thinks I must reconsider his profession, & that a H. of Commons clerkship may be beyond him, as the exam is severe — However he agreed it was wise not to take him from Oxford for a crammer, but to wait, & watch his development —

I was tired, & my head aching, & it was rather an upset — but it is best to know — They were afraid my ambition was fixed on a 1st Class for him, but it is not, though I had thought he wd take a good place — It would have been worse if I had heard it alone, but R. is so good & gentle & affectionate, I feel that is better than having my pride satisfied by his success — But I must give my mind to what is best for his future — If his taste for pictures grows, he may join H. P. L[ane]. — A bad night, my poor head aching. On Saturday R. left for Oxford —

Nov[ember] 4 — Moorhurst Holmwood[245] — On Monday, after R. left, went to Oxford for the day, with W. Yeats, for Jack's exhibition, which looked a little forlorn, & he hadn't sold much — he ought to have waited till R. was back & could have introduced him to "men" — R. & I bought his "Harvestman"[246] between us — We escaped by being at Oxford the Saturnalia in London for the return of the C[ity]. I[mperial]. Volunteers — The police arrangements had broken down & there seem to have been disgraceful scenes[247] — Coming by Victoria, out of the beat, we got on all right, except that a young woman rushed at Yeats & tickled his face with a feather —

[245] Home of the Gibsons (see p. 286 n. 252).

[246] Jack Yeats's Exhibition, held at the Clarendon Gallery, Oxford, between 27–29 October 1900, appears to have received almost no advertisement. A brief notice in *The Oxford Review* 29 October p. 3 comments that the "sketches show considerable force and originality of treatment, but Mr. Yeats will do well to work steadily at the technique of his art", but the writer acknowledges only having entered the gallery in the first place in order to avoid a downpour. A rough sketch of "The Harvestman" had been published in *The Weekly Independent*, 3 March 1900, but the whereabouts of the original are currently unknown.

[247] The City Imperial Volunteers, a unit of more than 1000 professional and middle-class City men raised and paid for by the City of London in the wake of "Black Week" (the defeats at Colenso and Spion Kop) had fought impressively at the battle of Doornkop in May 1900, and returned from S. Africa in October 1900 when Lord Roberts judged (incorrectly) that the war was effectively over. Their march from London docks into the City on 22 October was treated like a victory parade (see *The Times*, 24 October).

I have not done very much this week — yet I don't know, it wasn't wasted — I had another talk with Paul — & he showed me Nowell Smith's letter — not very pleasant I must say, says R. is his most unsatisfactory pupil, unpunctual & brings very little work — has not a chance of doing well in schools — & is dreamy — On the other hand he has some original force, if it would wake up, & has taste in composition — I feel sure he will wake up some day, but I don't like the beginning of idle habits — though he is good as a boy can be —

Oldmeadow of the Dome accepted "Ideals in Ireland" & I went to see him[248] — he will take risk & give a royalty (if I get any money it will go to Gaelic League) — & will get up the book nicely — He proposed publishing Hyde's article (which had not yet arrived) in Irish as well as English if he can arrange with Claidheam about type — This will be a gr advertisement for the language — Thursday night Hyde's article came, in Irish, I was disappointed to find it was again a sort of allegory, about shooting a big crow, but next day read it and translated & altered it slightly, put a couple of his verses on the Fenians at the beginning & his poem "There's a change coming" at the end — Then took it to show to Yeats, who liked it in its altered form, it has a folk-fantastic touch about it[249] — Then to dictate it to a type writer — Then to Oldmeadow — Yeats walked back with me, & then I went with G. Moore to see "Mr. & Mrs. Daventry" — written by Frank Harris, & it is supposed Oscar Wilde[250] — A slight & skillfully constructed play, like a house of cards, & not of much interest — Moore introduced me to Bernard Shaw who was there — When we got back, at the door of Qmansions, the heel of my shoe caught in the cab, & I was flung to the ground, knee & shin much hurt, first turned deadly faint & then deadly sick — Moore very kind but vociferous, shouting for brandy & abusing them for not always keeping it in the hall for accidents! However I got to bed, tho' in too gr pain to sleep much —

Sat[urda]y — Better — Moore came to enquire, & also to try & persuade me that it would not matter if Grania was acted in London before it is acted in

---

[248] Ernest James Oldmeadow (1867–1949), novelist, music critic and editor. Managing Director of the Unicorn Press (which published *Ideals in Ireland* in 1901) and Editor of *The Dome* 1897–1900. In later life he converted to Catholicism and edited *The Tablet*.

[249] "The Return of the Fenians" *Ideals in Ireland*, pp. 65–73 (printed in both Gaelic and English). The crow in Hyde's allegory is the "English mind" blighting Ireland like a cloud. AG's additions of prefatory and closing poems frame the essay with a strong appeal to Fenian-style direct action which significantly inflects the otherwise benign metaphorical content of Hyde's text, in which the "arrow" that will slay the crow is the Gaelic League.

[250] "Mr. and Mrs. Daventry", a four act play, ran for 116 performances at the Royalty Theatre October 1900–February 1901, with Mrs. Patrick Campbell in the role of Mrs. Daventry. Harris wrote the play from a plot by Wilde, but Wilde himself was not involved in the writing. Moore had been to see the play already with WBY on 25 October; both were eager for Mrs. Campbell to play the role of Grania in the still incomplete *Diarmuid and Grania*.

Dublin — I think this wd be a gr downfall, & said so — He was vociferous, but if Alexander[251] takes it, he will say it must first be done in Ireland — He believes Alexander will take it, & that there is £5000 to £10,000 in it! I hope there may be! Afternoon, to Moorhurst (Mr. Gibson)[252] with Yeats & his sister — Found a Mr. Williams & a priest in a brown robe & cope, & Lord St. Cyres here[253] — Mr. Gibson in ancient Irish costume, kilt, shawl & bare legs — Mrs. Gibson pleasant, but not understanding English well enough to follow quick talk, things have to be repeated to her — A pretty old house — Talk in the ev. about original sin, & heredity — Mr. G. a very liberal Catholic — If a doctrine is proclaimed infallible by the Pope & he doesn't believe it, he simply says the Pope's infallibility failed — If a book is put on the Index that he wishes to read, & feels necessary for his intellectual development, he reads it, for it wd be a greater sin to starve his mind — I wonder how long this heterodoxy will be allowed! It is his liberalism that has made him take up Ireland — He finds the same spirit of Imperialism at Rome as there is in England, and wants to have more of independence & nationality in congregations — In England this is not possible, as Mivart's case shows,[254] so he has turned to Ireland — I have just been at ev service, where he & his gardener said the Rosary in Irish, & a set of little girls came in from a "home" they have established, & the Levite did a mass for the dead — Very pretty play acting, I wish they would settle in Ireland where the improvement of services would be a gr deed to do —

I forgot to put down that on the Saturday R. left I went to a meeting of Irish Lit. Society with Yeats — to hear Stephen Gwynn lecture on Irish Humour — The lecture began by 2 funeral orations by 2 judges on the late Ld. Russell of Killowen[255] — E. Gosse in the chair, introduced them in such a cheerful patronizing way, as if he was a grocer setting up 2 pots of jam — Gwynn's lecture, rather good, was chiefly to prove how little humour there is in Ireland — This annoyed the audience, & Graves made a long speech, quoting humourous anecdotes or what he considered as such — A Mr. Boyd asked if

[251] George Alexander (1858–1918), the influential and long-serving actor–manager at the St. James Theatre.

[252] William Gibson (1868–1942), also known as Ulliam Mac Giolla Bride, succeeded his father (see p. 31 n. 48) as Lord Ashbourne in 1913. Married Marianne de Montbrison (d.1953), a Frenchwoman, in 1896. Gibson had replaced A. P. Graves as Secretary of the Irish Literary Society in spring 1900.

[253] Stafford Harry Northcote (1869–1926), Viscount St. Cyres.

[254] St. George Jackson Mivart (1827–1900), converted to Catholicism in 1844, and as a distinguished Professor of Zoology became the most prominent Catholic scientist in England. Followed a broadly anti-Darwinian line in his early writings, but in later life began to criticize the conservatism of the Church's teachings. Excommunicated after a series of clashes with Catholic authorities, notably following his criticism of Pope Leo XIII's silence over the Dreyfus affair, and was buried in unhallowed ground.

[255] Lord Russell (see p. 216 n. 83) had died on 10 August 1900. The ILS meeting, at which Gwynn lectured on "Irish Humourists of the Nineteenth Century", took place on 27 October.

there was no such thing as "fun" in Ireland[256] — W. Yeats made a fighting speech, sat on Graves for telling as an Irish story one that had been current in India before Xtianity (3 monks speaking <?? ??> of <??> year) — & did not agree with Gwynn that Swift was un-Irish, as wherever he was born, his humour was the humour of insult, which is so much in the Irish nature — "The humour of insult has given us Swift, Mitchell, & Tim Healy, the humour of servility — this has given us Handy Andy" — "Tim Healy is only divided from Swift by an abyss of genius"[257] —

Oct [i.e. November] 18 — Got back from Gibsons, to find another article from Hyde "What Ireland is asking for" longer & more serious than the other — so set to work to translate it, & decided to publish both[258] — A good deal of trouble over essays, Moore's had to be patched — so had Moran's[259] — Yeats came back with a very bad cold, quite ill, I dined with him the Monday to entertain a new admirer who had sent him a book, a Mr. Masefield[260] — & the next few days I was very much with him, for he was far from well & had no one to look after him — One day I found him still foodless at 1-30 — he had not had energy to get anything ready — Towards end of week he roused up, & wrote a beautiful little "postscript" for the essays[261] —

I went to Oxford one day, to see Nowell Smith, but he was out — but had a pleasant afternoon with R. — I had finished the Longhi copy, & took it to show him, & he put in some touches — He had done a book plate for Una Birch, & a curious mystical drawing of a woman under a tree — & is certainly making strides in drawing, tho' I think it takes some of his mind from work

[256] Probably William Boyle (1853–1923), Irish born, but at this point resident in London working as a civil servant in the Inland Revenue. Published both poetry and short stories of peasant life, his best-known early volume being *A Kish of Brogues* (1899). Later emerged as a playwright, his works *The Eloquent Dempsey, The Building Fund* and *The Mineral Workers* being amongst the most successful early Abbey plays at the box-office, although disliked by both WBY and AG. *The Irish Literary Society Gazette* for December 1900 gives a synopsis of Gwynn's lecture and a list of attendees, which includes Boyle (who spoke at the meeting and was a regular participant at ILS meetings), but no Mr. Boyd.

[257] Satirist Jonathan Swift (1667–1745) was in fact Dublin born. John Mitchel's *Jail Journal* is far from humourous, but displays a disdain for his enemies that WBY evidently considered Swiftean. *Handy Andy*, a comic novel by Samuel Lover (1797–1868), epitomised for WBY the tradition of "stage-Irish" literature, with Irish characters represented as sentimental buffoons.

[258] "What Ireland is Asking For" *Ideals in Ireland* pp. 55–61 (given in AG's translation only), argues for the restoration of Gaelic in Irish schools.

[259] D. P. Moran (1871–1936), Editor of the Nationalist paper *The Leader*, which had begun publication in September 1900. Moran's essay "The Battle of Two Civilizations" urges the promotion of a new sense of Irish nationality, predicated on an independent notion of cultural values rather than hatred of England.

[260] John Masefield (1878–1967), poet, and Poet Laureate after the death of Robert Bridges in 1930. For AG's reminiscences of this first meeting and their subsequent friendship see *Seventy Years* pp. 386–88.

[261] "A Postscript" *Ideals in Ireland* pp. 105–07.

— However he says he is doing better, is pretty hopeful about Mods —

Lunch with Lyalls, a little hard to take up threads of conversation after so long — Dined Leckys — he kind but does seem to be going backwards — I think from want of faith — When talking of F[rances]. Morris's reception in the convent, & its being a life of prayer he said "And prayer is so useless!" — this from the representative of Trinity! He is sad at Ulster having taken up compulsory land purchase — thinks it will impoverish the country — sees no hope anyhow for congested districts — like that "incurable optimist" Horace Plunkett — When saying good bye I said "I will try to behave well in Ireland" & he said in his plaintive voice "please don't start anything incendiary!" — so I was afraid to mention my candlesticks![262] — Mrs. Green was there, just back from visiting the Boer prisoners at S. Helena — & gives a sad account of their down heartedness, hearing of defeat & the burning of their farms —

Poor Literary Theatre! An unhappy dispute now raging between the playwriters — Last Sunday Moore unhappily called on Yeats, found him altering the text, & got a little cross over it, attacked one passage, but by good luck a bit he thought was his own & held up to admiration, was really a bit by Yeats! One or two mistakes of this kind dumbfounded him, & they parted, slightly irritated — His type writer was to go & type an act for Yeats, but he determined afterwards he had better be free, & wrote to decline her services — On Thursday I met Moore in Victoria St.[263] — He turned to walk with me & burst out "I am afraid the play will break down — Yeats is so dictatorial I can't stand him" etc — I said we had better go to his rooms, which we did & he gave me tea & held forth — "Where there is collaboration, one must be master, and it is I who must be master — The conception of the characters is mine, & it is only I who can write the dialogue — God Almighty could not do it, it is only I, who have created them — Yeats claims to re-write the whole thing, flattens it out etc etc" Then he produced his absurd bit abt Grania in the woods "feeling a delicious singing in her breasts!" & said "I defy anyone to write it better than that" — I ventured to say I didn't think much of this passage! & told him also that Yeats is & will be immovable in matters of style — He says, concessions must be made on both sides, in collaboration, & that he will make nine if Yeats will make the tenth — I tell him, Yeats has already bowed to him in dramatic construction, & made many concessions, but words are his

[262] In her editorial introduction to *Ideals in Ireland*, AG holds up the candlestick maker as the type of the idealist. The cover of the volume has a candlestick design drawn by Jack Yeats, based on a rushlight holder made from a pike (to disguise it) at the time of the 1798 rebellion. The design signalled her aim that the book's call to idealism should be steeled by an underlying threat of direct action. WBY's "postscript" to the volume endorses this aim with its explicit acknowledgement that while a national rebirth must be largely intellectual and rely on "delicate talents", at times "the violence of the mob" is essential for change to occur.

[263] Moore was then living at 92 Victoria St.

religion, he will never let a sentence pass that he feels unable to sign — I told him also that he had better take care what sentences he chose to quarrel over, as if they are published, he may not be very proud of them in the end, and that from the very beginning the arrangement was that Yeats should set the language right at the end — We talked then of other things — the article Stead has published on the war, written by "a British Officer in the field" — (Maurice Moore) — M. had taken the article first to the "Contemporary" which refused it — then to Stead, who said, the worst was, it is so well written, no one will believe it is by an officer![264] — Also of Symons's engagement, to a ship broker's daughter[265] —

Yesterday Yeats came with two letters from Moore, less offensive than what he said to me, as there is nothing abt his being "Master" — Yeats has answered him, holding to the original agreement that he was to set the language right — Symons is to drop in on Moore this morning, & see what he can do[266] —

Have looked for a governess for Ashfield in vain, after much time spent on it — Hoped to get to Ireland last night, but Oldmeadow expecting proofs, & it will hurry matters if I stay & do them here —

I went to Northfleet & spent the afternoon with Elizabeth Persse, in her "cottage" — she seems content poor thing — W. Yeats to dinner — Has had a letter from Moore, mild in tone, but wants Yeats to write all Diarmuid says while he writes all Grania says! Absurd creature — He still wants Grania to have 'a singing in her breasts' — Yeats won't yield an inch, except that he will accept Symons as referee — & whether Moore will do this we know not — Says he lectured well on the Theatre last night, for the "Three Kings"[267] — Proofs of "Shadowy Waters" come but with absurd fancy type on title page, which

[264] While serving in S. Africa under Kitchener, George Moore's younger brother, Maurice, had sent him a letter detailing the cruelty of British forces, which Moore allowed W. T. Stead to publish over the signature "An Officer in Command" in a pamphlet entitled "The New War in South Africa and How It Is Being Carried On: Letter from an Officer in the Field" (London: November 1900). Further letters by Maurice Moore were published in November 1900 and January 1901, and provoked violent partisan debate about the British policy of burning Boer farms, and rumours that British troops were being told to take no prisoners. See Joseph Baylen, "George Moore, W. T. Stead, and the Boer War", *Studies in English* vol. 3 (1962), pp. 49–60.

[265] Symons married Rhoda Bowser (1874–1936), daughter of a wealthy shipbuilder, in January 1901.

[266] See *L* p. 347 (tentatively dated January 1901 by Wade), "our original compact was that the final words were to be mine". Moore's two letters are included in Robert Becker, *The Letters of George Moore 1863–1901* (Ph.D., University of Reading, 1980), where they are dated January 1901, following Wade. WBY had proposed Symons as a possible arbiter of the dispute in his letter to Moore, a role Symons did briefly assume.

[267] "The Fellowship of the Three Kings" was a society formed in January 1900 by WBY and others for the study of mystical and literary subjects. Yeats had previously lectured to the society on Shelley in February 1900.

must be altered²⁶⁸ —

19 — Nothing particular to do, waiting still for proofs — Yeats came to tea —
Moore has written to beg him to come for "ten minutes' talk" — but he wisely
won't, until things have been arranged in writing — Has broken his eyeglass,
& can't do anything without it — I read him proof of "Shadowy Waters" — &
wrote to Unwin & "Speaker" for him²⁶⁹ — Read a little Irish & "the Brass
Bottle"²⁷⁰ & so to bed —

20 — Waiting again — Irish, & to Mudie's — Yeats to dine, Symons had been
to see Moore & found him mild, & thinks Y. shd go & see him, so he will go
today — Shadowy Waters has a blank page, wants a dedication, so it is to be
dedicated to me after all —

I have had an idea floating in my mind for some time that I might put together
the Irish legends, into a sort of Morte d'Arthur, choosing only the most
beautiful or striking — but I was afraid about style, one cd not copy Morte
d'Arthur yet they shd be in something to answer to it — Now I think of ~~copying~~
{putting} each story into {the Irish idiom of} the original ~~& putting them into~~
— I consulted Yeats & after a short hesitation, he thinks the idea very good,
so I will try & carry it out, & am provided with work for the rest of my life".²⁷¹

Flowers from Wilfrid Blunt, in Egypt —

21 — Waiting! & a telegram from Oldmeadow saying "Proofs have been
posted by printers" — Bought some war handkerchiefs, & had tea with Mrs.
Dugdale — Then Yeats came, & we dined & went to Kensington to see Forbes
Robertson in Shaw's play "The Devil's Disciple" — a witty, pretty, romantic
play, I liked best of those I have seen²⁷² — Yeats had been with Moore & they

---

²⁶⁸ *The Shadowy Waters* had already appeared in *The North American Review* in May 1900. These
proofs were for the first book printing, issued in December 1900 by Hodder and Stoughton.

²⁶⁹ WBY's letter to Unwin probably related either to the forthcoming revised edition of *Poems*
(1895), issued in 1901, or to his efforts around this time to consolidate his work under one
publisher. WBY's letter to *The Speaker* presumably enclosed his introductory poem to *The
Shadowy Waters*, "I walked among the seven woods of Coole", which was published in *The Speaker*
on 1 December 1900 under the title "Introduction to a Dramatic Poem".

²⁷⁰ *The Brass Bottle* (1900), a novel by Anstey Guthrie.

²⁷¹ AG in fact completed the project by late 1901, *Cuchulain of Muirthemne* being published
by John Murray in spring 1902. WBY's recollection of her start on the work portrays her as
adopting a plan suggested to him by Alfred Nutt, to do for the Irish legends "what Malory had
done for the old French narratives", which he had been "too busy with my own work" to adopt
himself (*Au* p. 455–56).

²⁷² This production of *The Devil's Disciple*, featuring and produced by Johnston Forbes
Robertson (1853–1937), actor and theatre manager, was at the Coronet Theatre, Notting Hill
Gate.

got on amicably, re wrote the Grania passage, putting "laughter" in her breasts instead of "singing!" but I think they will get on all right now[273] —

22 — Waiting for proofs — & at 12-30 comes a letter from Oldmeadow saying they had been sent by the printers to Ireland! he knows not to what address — so if I had gone home I should have had them sooner — He says duplicates are being sent, & will arrive in the morning — I went to see him but he was out — I wished for George Moore's temper & power of expressing it for an hour! — A visit from Miss Hull, & picked up a little information about the Cuchullin stories[274] — Dined with Yeats — Home & in bed, after midnight, & Paul came & knocked me up — Has had offer of a Col[onial]. Sec[retar]y[ship]. in Bermuda but wd like something better[275] —

23 — Some proofs, at 1-00 — had already packed up — Corrected them, & went to see Yeats, meditating on a speech for a dinner of the Chaucer Society[276] — good bye to him, & then to Oldmeadow, who had the defaulting printer to meet me, & settled small matters — Off at night, very dark & cold.

24 — Arrived Dublin, Gresham Hotel — To see Mr. Burton, who says my pictures will be all right, are still at the N[ational]. Gallery, & date of exhibition not fixed, advised me to go to the Gallery which I did, & found Mr. Strickland[277] — He thinks Ex. will be opened next month & last a couple of months — Not all mine will be exhibited — but doesn't offer to give me over the others! Miss Stokes has left 2 beautiful pictures, the "Knight's Farewell", & portrait of Helen Faucit to the Gallery[278] — it will be nice to have them there — I think of writing something on Sir F.'s love of Ireland, as his long absence, & the Vice-regal opening may make people think he was a "West Briton"[279] — Then to see AE & had a long talk with him — He says Horace Plunkett believes

[273] The collaboration indeed went smoothly from this point on, and the play was finished in mid–December.

[274] Eleanor Hull (1860–1935), co-founder of the Irish Texts Society with F. York Powell, and sometime President of the Irish Literary Society of London. She had published *The Cuchullin Saga* in 1898, a version of the epic using translations by O'Curry, Whitley Stokes, Kuno Meyer, O'Grady and others—many of which AG was to use as the basis for *Cuchulain of Muirthemne*. Apparently undaunted by AG's success, Miss Hull subsequently published a further version, *Cuchulain, the Hound of Ulster*, in 1909.

[275] Harvey turned down the offer, and was appointed Commissioner on the International Financial Committee at Athens in 1903.

[276] No report of this speech appears to have survived.

[277] Walter G. Strickland (1850–1928), Director of the National Gallery of Ireland until 1916.

[278] In fact Margaret Stokes presented 11 works by Burton to the Gallery, including an 1849 sketch of Lady Helen Faucit (1817–98), later Lady Martin, as Antigone. "The Knight's Farewell" is probably the work now titled "Helellil and Hildebrand" (1864), which shows an armed Knight embracing a young woman.

[279] "Sir Frederic Burton", *The Leader* 8 December, pp. 231–32.

Ed. Martyn lost him his seat[280] — He was much amused by Moore's efforts to ascend the mountain of the Gods when with him, & his partial reformation so that he boasted "This is the first time in my life I have ever been able to lie for 2 hours on the grass, content with the sunshine, & without wanting a woman to amuse me!"[281]

25 — To AE, who read me the act he had written of his Deirdre, very poetic, & some beauty, especially her vision of the "three hunters from the heavenly fields" — It makes poor Grania seem very earthly! however it would never do for the stage, tho' AE has an idea which I encouraged, of having it acted by his own disciples, with scenery of his own painting[282] — Mrs. Russell has been ill, & baba farmed out, so I came back in the afternoon, & we went to his farmhouse, & found him fat & well, chasing chickens out of the house — He did not know me, but was friendly — Then to see the Lanes, & Adelaide came & dined with me — family gossip —

26 — Home — Rain, very heavy — It seems to have been raining most of the time I was away — The house cold, & small responsibilities begin, rats, & plumbing work wanted — & the paling at the monument taken for firewood — Mrs. Moran very ill, so went to see her, met Father Campbell there —

27 — Rain — Began typing bits from diary & letters, re Sir Frederic [Burton] — & out with Tim & Mike etc — Gillane says it is "heartbroken weather" —

28 — Some proofs (the old ones) from Oldmeadow & a rather cross letter to say Mr. Moore has called & wants proofs, & is afraid he may upset all the type — A telegram from Father Considine to say he will send Conolly, Irish teacher, tomorrow,[283] so sent for Treston — made store list — Treston came, & talked to him & wrote to Father Fahey about classes — Frank came, a little grumpy for him, & sneered at the Irish revival — repressing my enthusiasm! However we talked tenants, & how to settle Conyngham case without an eviction —

Dec[ember] 29 — A month since I last wrote — Had a quiet, wet, busy

---

[280] See p. 297 n. 7.

[281] For Moore's account of his travels with AE to Newgrange, the sacred mountain Slieve Gullion, and other "sacred places" see *Salve* pp. 38–79.

[282] AE finished *Deirdre* in January 1902, and the play was published serially in *All Ireland Review* July 1901–February 1902. The first two acts were first performed in the garden of George Coffey's Dublin house on 2 and 3 January 1902, with the parts played by AE and friends. The complete work was first staged in April 1902 by the Irish National Dramatic Company alongside the first production of *Cathleen ni Houlihan*.

[283] Sean Connolly, an Aran islander, stayed at Coole until early January 1901, giving AG Gaelic lessons, assisting her with translations, and also teaching Kiltartan Gaelic Leaguers.

fortnight, starting Conolly with classes, marking trees for tenants, who can't get turf from the wet bogs — Ceaseless rain — Had lessons from Conolly — rather disheartening, I understand so little by ear! Robert came, had passed his exam easily this time, & regrets having spent so much time preparing for it! Is working for Mods, at Greek sculpture & Greek plays — very intelligently if not very industriously — is really interested in his work — but shooting is a temptation — We had Frank, Dudley, <?Harvey>, Gus & Mrs. Kelly & Annie Redington for shoot — 40 woodcocks — 50 pheasants — All went off well — Douglas Hyde came on the Saturday — but Monday afternoon had a telegram saying his wife was very ill with quinsy so had to leave on Tuesday after an hour or so of shooting — a great pity — He came from Ballina where he had been entertained by 7 priests, given the best room in the hotel free, & a dinner beginning with champagne, ending with whisky punch, beginning at 4 ending at 7 — after which he held his meeting & made he says the best speech of his life, but I said, he has not seen it reported yet! One of the priests, a Father Smith, told him he has discovered an anagram, proving clearly that Bacon wrote Shakespear, & also enabling him to find out much of Shakespear's life — He finds for instance that Anne Hathaway was Ben Jonson's maid, & mistress, before Shakespear married her, & that Shakespear finding this out after they married, they blackmailed Ben Jonson for the rest of his life — The 2 grave diggers in Hamlet he says are Ben Jonson & Anne Hathaway — Horatio & Hamlet are falsehood & truth, for they go hand in hand to the end — He is anxious to publish, but afraid to leave his MS with a publisher lest his ideas should be stolen — Quite unexpected in a Ballina priest! — All the priests fiercely abused Mr. O'Brien, & declare that the farms left vacant in the neighbourhood are snapped up by local officials of the United Irish League.

Hyde rather snubs my idea of harmonising Cuchulain — I think his feeling is a scholar shd do it — & he is bewildered at my simple translations — I had got Conolly to put "Death of Cuchullin" into Irish, & had translated it back literally into English — "Of course an epic should not be translated in colloquial style" he says — which accounts for his translations of epic bits being heavy & formal, quite different from his folk tales & peasant poem translations — However he gave his consent, which is all I wanted — tho' I don't know yet if the task will be beyond my strength — & time.[284]

He had seen Moran, who told him he could not make head or tail of Yeats, or understand a word he said or wrote — however, he promised not to attack

[284] Hyde continued to view AG's plans as unrealistic during the early stages of her work—"I do think you are plucky to tackle the great cycle ... It is more difficult than it seems at first sight" (DH to AG, 13 March 1901, Berg)—and it was not until she made her determination clear in stream of letters asking for information that he began to demonstrate interest: "I am rejoiced to hear you have progressed so far with your Tain series. You are really wonderful. I shall be ever so curious to know and see what you have done" (DH to AG, 1 May 1901, Berg).

him (tho' he has not altogether kept that promise).[285] Hyde hinted that it was unwise to attack any but enemies, but Moran would by no means agree to this. "Your enemies don't mind what you say, but if you attack your friend, he is the boy that will feel it!" — He has already made a gr change in Ireland by the "Leader", & helps in the building up of the nation better than anyone else had done —

I wrote a little article on Sir F. Burton & his love for Ireland, & sent it to him [i.e. Moran], I had felt his exhibition was likely to be neglected — & it seems to have created interest. Sir F.'s nephew wrote to thank me, & Hyde says all the priests he met had read it & chaffed him about the reference to his age[286] — "Ideals" has never appeared yet — After my being rushed through the proofs, the binder failed, & it won't be out till the New Year — Just as well, for it wd be overbid by Xmas rubbish —

Xmas over! & has left me alive, tho' with an empty purse — A busy time, the poor at the door & my hand in my pocket — Then Workhouse, Xmas tree — presents to nephews & nieces, & letters — Yeats sent me "Shadowy Waters", which is dedicated to me — Good news of "Grania" — it is finished, & after a cold hearing from Forbes Robertson, Mrs. Pat Campbell has received it enthusiastically & will take it — some difficulty about Dublin, as she can't come over this spring — & we insist on having it in Dublin first — However she thinks she cd come in September, so I think we shall have its first performance then[287] —

Our first Xmas alone — but we are very good friends, & with work & shooting I don't think R. has been lonely — & it has been quite a treat to me — A letter from Edward [Persse] yesterday saying Aleck wd like to come to Galway[288] — & that Henry had been asked to C[astle]. Taylor for Xmas — but tho' he was ready to start, his invitation had not been renewed, so I have wired to ask both to come with Richard, on Thursday — He is just back from the Cape —

[285] WBY's contribution of a long letter "Irish Language and Irish Literature" to the first issue of *The Leader* (*UP*2 pp. 236–42) had provoked a somewhat acid response from D.P.Moran, who argued that only literature written in Gaelic could properly be called Irish literature. The debate in ensuing columns, featuring Moran, Moore, AE and Standish O'Grady, is reflected in *Ideals in Ireland* by AG's incorporation of the various writers' competing notions of Nationality. Moran remained a strong if occasional critic of Yeats.

[286] AG's article reports a conversation in which Burton asked her how old Douglas Hyde was: "My answer, or surmise, gratified him, and he said 'Then he will be able to work for a long time . . . I am so glad he is a young man.'"

[287] Mrs. Patrick Campbell (1865–1940), leading actress of the period. She proved unwilling to agree to a first performance of *Diarmuid and Grania* in Dublin, and the play eventually opened on 21 October 1901 in a production by F. R. Benson's company.

[288] Alexander Annesley Persse (1871–1941), Edward Persse's second son, had been serving as a Captain in the Boer War.

1901

Jan[uary] 1 — 1901 Beginning of the new Century — Alone, for Robert went to Dundemott yesterday for a couple of days[1] — but I was glad he shd have a cheery time, & was too busy to be lonely, began making notes for Cuchulain, & working at Raftery — and had still many letters to write, & went across to Lisheen [Crannagh] to see the herd & his wife — & mended R.'s stockings — und so weiter[2] — Sunday ev., Mulkere came down & we went through some of Raftery, & a little bit of the Cuchulain translation, but I must find a better translator than Conolly to put it into Irish, & Mulkere cd not read his flowing hand —

I am in pretty good heart at the opening of the new age, so many of my anxieties about R. over — he is safe through childhood & school — is now working for Mods — is as good & gentle & well behaved as a boy can be, & we are good friends — Whatever turn his ideas take, he will always I think be fond of home & of Ireland, & have a sense of duty to the people — & he has at all events heard both sides of all Irish questions — His choice of a profession is the chief anxiety, he has no decided bent, except for art, & it is hard to know if it is a real gift — The tenants are beginning to go into the Land Courts, which I hoped might be avoided, & compulsory purchase being agitated for, may stop free sale for a time, but I have had time to put by nearly enough to pay C. Gregory's mortgage, so I hope whatever happens we shall keep house & woods — I bought Lisheen Crannagh across the lake last year, which will save us some annoyance — Robert met Mr. Bagot, from his Land Commission a few days ago, & he said they had been raising a good many rents, that they find poor land is over rented, & good land under rented — He says compulsory purchase will be the beginning of a good time for landlords — I was glad R. should hear my own strong view thus supported —

The "Ideals" not out yet — I get a little nervous about them, but think I was

---

[1] Dundermot, Ballymoe, Co. Roscommon, home of RG's friend Gus Kelly.
[2] i.e. "and so on".

right in publishing, to show how strong the national spirit can be, without those who feel it being of necessity followers of William O'Brien or Tim Healy — The passionate love of Ireland in every Irish heart, that is the foundation to work on, & the first thing that has been done for some time is Moran's attempt in the Leader to turn the hatred of England into a hatred of the "works of the flesh" that come from England.

1st Jan[uary] — A peaceful day, like Sunday without church. Did notes for Cuchulain — Hyde sent me some more of his poems — Mike came from Gort market & says Ed. Martyn's tenants were attacking one another with sticks, so that all the people in Crow Lane had to keep their houses shut! He says in spite of E. M.'s sale of land, & nationalism he is not liked, neglects gracious things, for instance gives no firing to the people as we are doing, though his woods are full of decaying timber —

14th Jan[uary] — On the 3rd, R. & Harvey came, & the three Southampton boys, Alec, Richard, Henry, & we have had a busy pleasant time since then — Only one wet day — shooting constantly — at L. Cutra — Roxboro', here, all amicable — All nice & good & easily amused — the only drawback, that R. has given up his work — which he was doing well — However he is having a healthy time, for mind & body —

AE came for one day only,[3] full of life & fire — much more national than he used to be — Unluckily it was wet, so though I took him out in boat & woods he only got a couple of spotty sketches — He declares his psychical state has been injured for the present by all the A[gricultural]. O[rganization]. lectures he has had to give — He is so openly pro-Boer that I was a little afraid of a row with Alec, who is rather "permanent official" — but they got on fairly well & he was delighted with Richard, who has hedged by saying he tried to join the Boers first — & who said in his simple way "I don't see that the war was necessary — why couldn't Chamberlain have said 'We want the goldfields, what will you take for them?' It would have cost less than the war is costing" — Aubrey[4] was fired on in an ambulance waggon by the British, who mistook it for a Boer ambulance!!

"Grania" seems going well — tho' Mrs. Pat [Campbell] can't be got to give a definite promise about Dublin, so they showed it to Benson who is delighted with it, & would be in some respects better, for he is so very respectable, Merrion Sq. & Trinity College could hardly boycott him — And yesterday I had a letter from Ed. Martyn, approving of "Grania", & saying he & Moore were coming over together to Dublin, where Moore is taking a house, so that

3 11 January 1901.
4 Edward Aubrey Persse (1881–1918), another of Edward Persse's sons, who also served in the S. African War.

coolness is over, & all will I hope go well henceforth —

17th — R. left on Tuesday, for a day's shooting at Dunsandle & on to Oxford — I saw him off, & went to the convent about work, & the Dr. about patients, & came back to what has seemed a lonely house in spite of having the 3 Southampton boys — they leave today —

20th — Ed. Martyn came over, back from Rome, in exuberant spirits — Says George Moore apologised for the letters he had written him re theatre, & said he was very sorry to have got into the controversy but was "lead into it" — "They see now" says Ed. "that I can't be bullied or humbugged — they tried to knock money out of me after all I had spent, but I am a very firm chap, & very straight forward, & a bully is always a coward" etc etc etc — He says he believes Moore had never had any objection to his publishing "Tale of a Town" — I said neither had Yeats, that I had, because I did not think it so good as his other work — He says "it was Yeats that went about threatening things — he told Coffey all sorts of dreadful things wd be done if I published it" — What Yeats told Coffey was that he ought not to advise him to publish it without having read it, as it wd be laughed at by literary men — However Edward is triumphant — says the second act of "Grania" was read to him before he went abroad, was very poor & did not go — but he made suggestions as to its rewriting & Moore carried them out while he was away & now it is quite good! He & George came to Dublin together, & evidently Yeats was sacrificed on the altar of reconciliation — "he is growing barren because of thinking so much of words" — Moore says "Shadowy Waters" is the worst thing he has ever done, that he used to have a sort of inwardness, but that has left him & he thinks of nothing but pretty phrases![5] Such nonsense trying to have style in such a corrupt language as English, as if one word was not as good as another" — Poor Edward! He is also elated by having been asked to write for the Claidheamh!! I did not tell him I had been begged for also[6] — He declares Gill not only suggested his writing the Plunkett letter but pressed him to write it — & is now saying it caused H. Plunkett's defeat[7] —

[5] In *Hail and Farewell*, Moore would promote this theory of Yeats's "barrenness" at length, writing in *Ave* that "Yeats can no longer think with his body; it is only his mind that thinks. . . . The intellect outlives the heart, and the heart of Yeats seemed to me to have died ten years ago" (pp. 281–82), and in *Vale* that "his inspiration . . . did not seem to have survived his youth" (p. 168).

[6] AG published two articles in *An Claidheamh Soluis* in 1901; "A Nation's Words" 6 July, p. 262, and "The Last Class" (a translation from Daudet), 27 July, supplement, p. 1.

[7] As expected, Plunkett had lost his Dublin seat to a Nationalist candidate on 9 October, with the Unionist vote split between himself and an orthodox Unionist. Martyn's letter, published in *The Freeman's Journal* 2 October 1900, p. 7, had described Plunkett as "a gradual convert to Irish Nationality" and urged voters to be "generous to him as a convert on the way". For an assessment of Plunkett's difficult position in seeking re-election, and his courteous letter to Martyn after his defeat, acknowledging that the letter had done "some harm" see Denis Gwynn *Edward Martyn* pp. 288–89.

Jan[uary] 26 — A very quiet week, bad rough weather, but the trees came at last, & I was out a good deal with the men, planting <?plunk> in middle avenue — John Farrell says "Nursery men are more crafty than any other men within the four walls of the world" — Conolly went to Tillyra, I was rather glad to get rid of my Irish lessons, being at work on an article on Irish folk ballads,[8] & also translating Deirdre as an experiment towards my Cuchulain — & there are many minor matters to see to — The place so quiet that I felt as if sudden gaiety had begun one day, because the sheep had been put in the back lawn & I cd see them from the windows! the old black sheep, that always seems a friendly presence because William knew it, & the little cuckoo lamb, in an absurd lambswool <??> coat — Excitement enough outside, for the news of the Queen's illness was quickly followed by her death, on Tuesday[9] — Poor old Queen, good in England — very callous to Ireland — I won't go to London until the funeral festivities are over —

This, a very stormy day, has been a good one, for Yeats writes that "Ideals" is out, is good, & has been quite well taken by Dublin booksellers, Eason taking 100 — Frank writes that Kate's money will be paid directly & will be £1200[10] — I never dared hope for more than £1000 — And also that Conyngham has settled, will pay two years' rent, & accepts the valuation made — I am most thankful for this, for we seemed perilously near eviction — Mike says it is my help to his wife while sick that softened his heart — I don't know, I was afraid he wd look on it as yielding to him, but had to help the poor thing.

Worried by hearing from R. that though he got to Oxford all right, he lost his book box on the way — this will interrupt his work — & perhaps put him off it —

31st — Sunday was very stormy — no church, just as well, as I hear the A[rch]. D[eacon]. preached a funeral sermon in which he came down on those who did not sufficiently reverence the Queen — & said O'Connell had done so — but "O'Connell was a gentleman & came from Co. Kerry"! This of course aimed at Yeats, Moore & Martyn — Mr. Conolly walked over from Tillyra with a couple of ballads he has been sent from Aran — I went out in the storm to look at little trees, & when I came in E. Martyn was here — less excited & belligerent — but very funny — Says now that "Grania" is "fleshy" & hints that is why he refused to support it! he not having seen a line of "Grania" at the time — I said if the theatre went on it must be taken up on new lines by a larger committee, & he said "I won't have anything to do with a committee that picks & chooses plays — what I say is let every man back his own work"!!

[8] Probably "West Irish Folk Ballads", published in *The Monthly Review* October 1902 and reprinted in revised form in *Poets and Dreamers*.

[9] 22 January 1901.

[10] This was her half-sister Kate Wale's bequest.

Monday Frank came to lunch — & I was busy with "Children of Usnach" still, making a translation from the Irish[11] — & with my "Folk Ballads" — & out to see planting — Tuesday very busy — Tim's seed list took nearly 2 hours to go thro' & check — his usual absurd orders of the most expensive seeds, meant for experiments in high class gardens — Then letters & typing — then out at 2-00 to nut wood — found (snow having come on) the rabbits had been at last year's larch, & had killed some in the night — Cahel supposed to be tarring them, delicately with the point of a stick — Mike very boozy, either from a cold or what he has taken to cure it — holding silvers very sideways while <?Marty> planted them — I sent for more of the anti-rabbit mixture, & stayed there in the snow till 5-00, seeing Cahel & Jim put it on — Home soaking — Deirdre.

Wednesday awoke with bad headache & had a wretched morning, obliged to go thro' clothes preliminary to packing, & Olive Grubb came to lunch to measure chairs & sofa for covering — Got out for a bit, & was better, when Tim made a demand with some insolence, for a man "under his own command" in the garden — This I of course refused & said Mike wd send all the men in when required — He said that would not do — I said if he was not satisfied with the place he might leave — He said it would be as good for him — O! that he would, for his discontent & veiled insolence, his unfaithfulness & bad disposition have always made me suffer — & he is absolutely useless as a working gardener — A bad night in consequence of this — & R.'s book box has not yet got to him —

Feb[ruary] 7 — London — On Friday lst very busy & hardworked — & Tim sent for me — & again demanded a man "under his own command" & independent of Mike — I told him this was impossible — & he said he wd leave next day — I did not like to take advantage of his temper, & said he must give a week's notice & must write it to Mr. Frank — He followed me to the gate holding forth on his own merits, how he had "given us" grapes, melons, cucumbers, apples, etc etc etc — An upsetting interview, for though I know we should be better without him, I shall be abused for "turning away" an old servant — Indeed when I went in to write to Frank, the O'Haras called, & lamented his probable departure, tho' they cd say nothing in his favour but that he was good at vines — Dead tired —

8th — I packed in rather a scrimmage of last orders, & left for Galway, with Margery Glynn — Arrived at Waithmans 22 Dominick St. — a good house, & some nice furniture — all unsettled — A[rabe]ll[a] happier, brighter & more satisfied than I have ever seen her — But they are indignant at James's statement of accounts, re Wale will sent them, & are inclined to dispute it, R.

---

[11] "The Fate of the Sons of Usnach," the seventh chapter of *Cuchulain of Muirthemne*.

W[aithman] saying he will throw the whole thing into Chancery[12] — Certainly love of money is the least dignified of weaknesses — poor R. W. with his mind set on grasping & speculating is without any of the dignity or beauty of old age — a certain kindliness his only charm, & that very spasmodic — I spent Sunday in bed, with very bad headache, from over work & <??> — Rose brought the Templars to tea, Frances looks well in black — & seems happy —

9th — Monday — Left for London — still rather knocked up, & had the worst crossing I ever remember, storm all the way, & my sickness never ceased — however I had half a carriage to myself to London & was able to lie down — Found London under snow — Slept a while, & was unpacking when Yeats came in — Theatre a little unsettled as Benson has been nearly ruined by having to close his theatre for the Queen's death, & may break altogether, & Mrs. Pat is so cross having lost thousands from the same cause that she won't make a definite offer[13] — He came back & dined, & Moore came in after, delighted with "Ideals" which is out at last, I recd 2 copies on Saturday, but have lost interest in it by the long wait, & the cover is a disappointment, a very feeble candlestick in whitey yellow, instead of gold as was promised — I went yesterday to ask Oldmeadow if he had sent copies to my list, as I had recd no acknowledgements, but tho' I had written to make app[ointmen]t he was out & I had to leave after 1 1/2 hours wait — He publishes in a very sloppy slovenly way, & Yeats has not got his money out of him yet[14] — I went to see Lady Haliburton at tea time, she was cheery, says there has been gr squabbling already between the Earl Marshal & Ld. Chamberlain — the Windsor funeral muddled, poor Lecky was there & nearly died of cold & hunger, & said the seats at St. George's Chapel were not half filled — Now Queen Alex[andra] declares she won't live anywhere but where she has been used to live — so they can't go to Windsor or Buckingham Palace — I saw Mrs. Dugdale also, who said the Kaiser had won all their hearts, "so clean cut & rigid" & the King had "risen to the occasion & looked like Henry VIII!" Coming back from Lady H.'s I was knocked down by a carriage at the crossing at Wilton St., found myself struggling with the horses & then under their feet & thought "the wheel will come next" & tried to struggle away — Then I was picked up, & dragged to the pavement, & after a little got into a cab & home — covered with mud, my

[12] W. Charles James of Folkestone, Kent, Kate Wale's solicitor, had been a signatory to her Will, and was evidently suspected of being one of the "dishonest attorneys" who had reduced her estate (see p. 224 n. 115). The Will called for her assets to be split equally between her eight surviving half-brothers and sisters.

[13] Benson's company went into bankruptcy shortly after completing a run of *Coriolanus* at the Comedy Theatre 14–25 February as theatre audiences, already poor because of the Boer War, fell to disastrous levels following Queen Victoria's death. The company quickly reformed, however.

[14] AG had arranged a fee for WBY from Oldmeadow for his contributions to *Ideals in Ireland*, and for the royalties for the volume proper to go to the Gaelic League. Oldmeadow proved a slippery paymaster, and WBY eventually had to settle for half payment.

lip cut & cheek & one leg bruised, but a wonderful escape —

Sunday 11th — I read Yeats my translation of Sons of Usnach & of Cuchulain's death — & he was enthusiastic — says I must go on, & that it will be a great book — So I am encouraged[15] — & on Friday I went to the British Museum & asked for a reading ticket — The man asked what I was working at — I said "The Cuchulain Epic" & as that did not seem to convey much, I said "Ancient Irish History" — He asked how long I expected to be as it — I said I didn't know, perhaps 2 years — at which he jumped, having expected me I think to say two hours — Then he said I must make formal application & have a reference — I asked if Mr. Sidney Colvin wd do, & his respect increased & he said if I wd go to him, I cd get my order at once — So I found Sidney, looking rather long bearded, he was affable about ticket, but not very sympathetic about my scheme — says "the difficulty about harmonising is that there are so many different stories" — I say "yes, that is just why it is necessary" — Then he objects to the Sons of Ushnach having been overcome by enchantment — & he breaks off to say H. Trench has got more of the Celtic spirit into "Deirdre Wed" than any of our other poets, "though he is not in that set!"[16] Also he thinks Yeats has gone off (he writes next day attributing this to the influence of Arthur Symons!) — Then Sir Edward Thompson came in, said he knew me, anyhow gave me a reading order which made all the clerks bow before me like Joseph's sheaves[17] — & after a gr many intricacies, I got the books I wanted — never wd have got them but Yeats arrived — He is working there at his "Magic" essay[18] — all he is doing, for those wretched mystics are keeping him busy settling their small disputes — We lunched together — & I had tea with Una Birch, who is the first person I have met who has seen "Ideals" — She likes it, feels most stirred by Hyde's essay —

Worked again on Saturday at Museum getting on nicely, with Carmichael's "Deirdre"[19] which with a little alteration will fit on very well to the others — Went to see Morrises & met Miss Kinkead,[20] who is doing coloured woodcuts, so I have asked her to teach me that I may pass the knowledge on to R. — This

[15] As WBY would recall (*Au* p. 455) "now all in a moment, as it seemed, she became the founder of modern Irish dialect literature." AG recalled that "it was only when I had read him one day in London my chapter the 'Death of Cuchulain' that he came to look on me as a fellow writer" (*Seventy Years* p. 390).

[16] *Deirdre Wed and other Poems* (1901) by Frederic Herbert Trench (1865–1923).

[17] Sir Edward Thompson (1840–1929), Director and Principal Librarian at the British Museum 1888–1909. For Joseph's sheaves, see *Genesis* 37.7.

[18] "Magic" *The Monthly Review* September 1901.

[19] *Deirdire* [*sic*] *and The Lay of the Children of Uisne* a translation by folklorist and composer Alexander Carmichael (1832–1912), from a version he collected on the Island of Barra, Scotland.

[20] Alice S. Kinkead (1871–1926), a Tuam-born pastel and oil painter, who exhibited widely from 1897 on. She would paint an oil portrait of WBY in summer 1901.

seems to be a "working visit" to London! Went to Henry V — (Walkers) at Lyceum with Yeats[21] — A series of tableaus, fairly well spoken — but it is a "scattered" play for acting, & the constant change of scenery distracts the mind —

Going to Sussex Place, I found police & the street lined, rather thinly, with people — & came in for the King & Queen's public entry, their first[22] — He very fat & smiling, she bowing coldly but looking pretty under her veil — Read my folk ballad essay to Yeats who thinks it very good, but suggested a new bit at the end, leading up to the last fine ballad — I have done this today — & have been to church at S. Margaret's, & gone thro' Deirdre, & written heaps of letters for I was much behindhand —

I went yesterday to Jack's exhibition,[23] a little depressing — he has very few new pictures, & I don't see advance in them — And there is only one sold — Alec sent me a box of Cape peaches — beauties, I will send on to Robert —

16th — A busy week — Miss Kinkead came Monday & gave a lesson in woodcuts, which, like Irish, I am learning for R.'s sake — It seems difficult to cut the lines, wants practise & good sight — Una & Jack Yeats came also & had a lesson — All the other days I worked at B. Museum, at Cuchulain, find it very interesting & so far going easily — & Yeats is there & we lunch together — We went to "Coriolanus" one evening, & liked it very much as a play, tho' Benson is not very good in it, not proud enough & too romantic, but this will be all the better for Diarmuid[24] — Dined Lyalls — a "scattered" sort of a party — Mrs. Lyttelton speaking of the Queen's beauty said "it is all my loyalty has to hang on to now" — that is just why so much is made of it — Bernard Holland had been to Pretoria on Concessions Commission — says the war has been the triumph of the amateur, the Boers are amateurs — so are all the soldiers who did best — poor Tommy was nowhere, though he wd do a task set him well enough.

There was a very good review of "Ideals" in "Daily News" — & some rather silly ones elsewhere — None of the Irish papers except the "Leader" have yet noticed it[25] —

[21] This production, with Lewis Walker (1860–1915) in the principal role, and J. Comyns Carr as managing director, ran for 80 performances at the Lyceum Theatre between December 1900 and March 1901.

[22] King Edward VII (the former Prince of Wales) and his wife Alexandra.

[23] "Sketches of Life in the West of Ireland and Elsewhere" at the Walker Art Gallery, London.

[24] This production, with Benson in the role of Caius Marcus, ran for ten performances at the Comedy Theatre 13–25 February 1901.

[25] Daily News 11 February 1901, p. 6; The Leader 16 February, p. 403. AG had evidently not seen the favourable review in An Claidheamh Soluis 9 February, p. 761.

Saw various people — Ld. & Lady Lovelace — he has finally quarrelled with
Murray over the Byron book — He didn't want to publish scandal at all —
Murray thought the public wd be disappointed if there were none — "but
Murray himself only knows half the truth" & Lord L. doesn't want all to be
published, at least during his lifetime —

A lecture last night by Yeats, & chanting by Mrs. Emery & Miss Mather[26] —
amusing enough — but only a "fad" — Mrs. Emery's voice is better in ordinary
reciting, and Miss Mather hasn't much voice at all. Yeats didn't give a regular
lecture but warmed up after criticism by Todhunter & Herman Vezin,[27] &
said, in answer to one that all lyrics were sad, & that all the finest poetry was
the fruit of an austere sadness — He & Jack supped with me afterwards — C.
O'Hara wrote asking forgiveness for Tim, & I am negotiating it —

April 1 — Trieste! — A long time since I have written — I had a very busy time
in London — almost every day working at my "Cuchulain" at the British
Museum — very pleasant work, & then wd have lunch or tea with Yeats & talk
over what we were doing — then I would go to see people — & I had a good
many dinners to go to — people kind — Haliburtons, R[eginald]. Smiths,
Lady Lindsay, Alfred Cole, Lyalls, Leckys, Lovelaces, etc — but somehow I
have lost my interest in society for the present — All gatherings much the
same, a want of ideas — the war still spoiling any attempt at conversation, a
special correspondent at a dinner takes the place of the captured peer we
used to laugh at — The reaction beginning against the war shows itself in the
absurd excitement over "An Englishwoman's Love Letters" — This I heard
discussed at many houses, but did not trouble to read it till after I had left
London — Had I done so I could have settled the question as to their having
been written "many years ago" — for in one of the earliest is quoted a line "my
share of the world" from the Irish peasant poet who drops from absurd
exaggeration to this — This is taken from my translation of Mary Hynes,
published by Yeats in the "Dome" less than 2 years ago![28] — Also I learned
from Miss Kinkead to do woodcuts, Robert having wished to learn — this took
some days — & a week of feverish cold kept me in —

The last days very busy, giving up my rooms — Sent pictures home & stored

[26] WBY lectured on chanting to the Three Kings Society on 15 February 1901. Anna Mather
had played the role of Oona in the first production of *The Countess Cathleen*, and assisted Florence
Farr in demonstrating chanting sporadically until early 1909.

[27] Hermann Vezin (1829–1910), actor and dramatist.

[28] *An Englishwoman's Love Letters*, published anonymously by Laurence Housman (1865–
1959), brother of A. E. Housman, enjoyed immense popularity and was the focus of intense
speculation for several months in Spring 1901, with Edith Wharton, Oscar Wilde and others
being suggested as the author. Housman parodies "Irish" in various passages in the book. The
echo of AG's translation of Raftery from "Dust Hath Closed Helen's Eye" (see p. 253 n. 133)
features in letter 25.

furniture for Robert if he shd want it, for I don't think I shall set up in London again — tho' I will come for 2 years more, till R. is started[29] — He came on Mar[ch] 16 — & next day we set out for Venice —

Ten days there, rather bad weather, & R. who had been a little <?relaxed> at Oxford I think felt it — Lady L[ayard]. very kind, & every comfort — Lord & Lady Oranmore there on their wedding tour[30] — She is nice & cheery — he pleasant for a day or two — but too much cut up with small talk, his mind stored with small details as to hotels & railways — but ideas not to find — & in fact, I thought him a bore — Lady L. praised Robert very much, his nice manners & good looks, but thinks him shy, & says he ought to talk more — She also said "it must be an advantage to him having the opportunity of talking with a man like Lord Oranmore"!! — I said nothing — Poor Enid! — And as to talking, I myself have rarely felt it harder to get in a word, in so dead an atmosphere — The Duncannons expected, and we had settled to leave when they came, & thought of going to a hotel — but then thought of Trieste — then of exploring Istra — finally of Dalmatia, & at this moment of Montenegro! Anyhow here we are, delighted with Trieste, we came through snow on our way, then had a lovely view of the <?summery> sea — Sketched at cathedral — yesterday to church —

April 18 — 10 Place de Laborde, Paris — A tiring journey here, then comfort, a warm welcome, gr kindness — R. delighted with Louvre & Luxembourg [gardens] — weather not very good, so Paris doesn't look its best — De B[asterot]. suffering evidently from failure of limbs, but wonderfully brave & kindly —

May 12 — Coole — Safely back — Three days in London, at Savile Row — rather scrambly — Ran round private view New Gallery with Sir A. Birch — Went to "Coriolanus" with Yeats — but poor Irving's voice is quite gone, & sounds as if coming from a phonograph[31] — Yeats lingering on, but not doing much work — or any — Sturge Moore talks of getting up a performance of "Shadowy Waters"[32] — & he is going to the Stratford performances, by

[29] RG would graduate at Oxford in summer 1903. AG continued to use Queen Anne's Mansions as her London base after 1901, but as a short-term renter of the 'hotel' apartments in the building rather than taking out yearly leases on her own flat.

[30] Geoffrey Henry Browne (1861–1927), 3rd Baron Oranmore, and his wife Lady Olwen, née Ponsonby (d.1927), who had married on 2 January 1901.

[31] This production, with Henry Irving as Coriolanus and Ellen Terry as Volumnia, ran for 37 performances at the Lyceum in March–April.

[32] Thomas Sturge Moore (1870–1944), poet, playwright and designer, met WBY in 1898, became a lifelong friend, and subsequently designed the covers for *Responsibilities, The Tower* and other volumes by WBY. His plan to organize a performance of *The Shadowy Waters* came to nothing, but his discussions with WBY and others about forming a society to produce romantic drama did result in the foundation of the Literary Theatre Club, inaugurated later in 1901.

Benson, to report for the "Speaker"[33] — & he is still interested in his "chanting" & delighted with the one stringed lute from Montenegro[34] — Saw Wilfrid Blunt who is writing a history of the horse[35] — He says he has not heard anyone speak seriously of Edward VII — the ladies of his acquaintance call him "Edward the Caresser".

Came straight through home, as Punchestown [Race Meeting] was going on in Dublin, & have been alone ever since —

Mods list out, R. in the 3rd class — very little work wd have brought him into the 2nd, & it is certainly a little disappointment — & Frank seizes the opportunity of telling me that it is because he was "overworked at school" — & that boys to whom that happens are "never worth tuppence afterwards"! Poor Robert! —

Our land case, <?Healys>, has gone against us, he has £5 off his £30 rent — & others have given notice to go in — Frank is violently against selling, & talks of impeding their going to court by making them pay up the hanging gall if they do[36] — but I can't think this wd be right —

The little larch trees I last planted are doing well everywhere, but the silvers & spruce have withered up in cold winds —

I am working very hard at "Cuchulain", have done the fight with Ferdiad & Birth of Cuchulain, & am now at Bricriu's Feast.

May 18 — Another week gone by — I have done Bricriu & am still at the second part "the Championship of Ulster" — very fascinating work — Hyde has sent a bundle of "Irische Texte" & other books — & a MS that I'm afraid I can't read —

On Sunday there was a meeting at Kiltartan, to establish a branch of the United Irish League — Marian attended, says Mr. Duffy, M.P. from Loughrea,[37] & Mr. Lynam, evicted Portumna tenant, spoke well, but "the same old story

[33] WBY went to Stratford in April 1901 to see the Benson company perform a series of Shakespeare plays. His essay on the productions, "At Stratford-On-Avon" were published in *The Speaker* in May 1901.

[34] WBY refers to this gift from AG in his poem "Avalon".

[35] For Blunt's work with Arab horses see p. 29 n. 33. The projected book was eventually completed by his daughter Judith (see p. 195 n. 130).

[36] The "hanging gall" or "hanging gale" was arrears of rent, literally sums due on the previous 'gale' or rent-day.

[37] William John Duffy (b.1865), a Loughrea merchant who sat as Nationalist M.P. for S. Galway 1900–18.

ever since we were born, abuse of the landlords & Cromwell" — Some landlords were denounced, Dalys, Persses & others — however we were not mentioned — Mr. Macnamara the butcher, who has given offence by taking a Tillyra farm that was wanted by tenants, was alluded to as "Jack the Ripper" — Mr. Burke, publican & County Councillor spoke, Marian says "No better than baby Russell would — in a whisper as if he was selling a glass across the counter" — Father Campbell gave "a sort of a little sermon" — On Thursday, Ascension day, a branch was formed after mass, but a good deal of fighting, Quin of Corker objecting to Noon as secretary as he says he "did him out of £10" — & some attacked Patsy Regan, for holding too much land —

Monday, Frank collected rents — had a good collection, but some more said they were going into the Land Court — F. had said he would make those who go in pay up the hanging gall as a check — I objected to this, thinking it would not keep the bulk out if they wish to go in, but might fall heavily on poorer ones, who if they are over-rented, ought to have their chance — F. angry, says it is his business to get all he can out of the property — I say it is both our business to keep up its value, but at the same time to hand it over to Robert, in pleasant relations with the people, who have behaved very well, & the calling up the hanging gall might irritate them — He says however it has been done everywhere else, & they don't mind — so that closes for the present —

I have "done" the family this week, calling at Roxboro', & C[astle]. Taylor, & yesterday Katy [Persse] & little Kathleen came here — Walter [Shawe-Taylor] full of Frank's marriage & his own good behaviour over it[38] — Called on Blakeneys[39] also so feel very virtuous, & had the Workhouse children out for a day, the weather so fine —

20 — R.'s birthday, causing me to look before & after, with much thankfulness & much anxious thought —

A letter from Yeats, he has been to R[oyal]. I[rish]. Academy & seen the translation of Tain bo [Cuailgné], & thinks it will do for my purpose — a great relief, for I was beginning to feel the want of the great central tale to work at, & if I could not have got the Tain all my work would have had to lie by[40] — Rather a long day, walked to Kiltartan to see Treston about Irish teaching, &

38 Walter Shawe-Taylor's second son Francis (1869–1920) had married Agnes Ussher on 1 June 1901.

39 The Blakeneys, of Castle Blakeney, Co. Galway, had intermarried with Persses on various occasions dating back to 1671.

40 AG drew on two unpublished manuscript translations of the Tain Bo Cuailgné ["Cattle Raid of Cooley"], by O'Daly and O'Looney, held by the Royal Irish Academy, for *Cuchulain of Muirthemne*. Douglas Hyde had drawn her attention to these in a letter of 20 April 1901 (Berg).

he has done nothing, Father Fahey being away[41] — round to see elms planted in the winter, & a good many have failed — home to leave complaint of rats, which are eating the peas, red lead & all — A pleasant little talk with Mulkere who is <??> about an Irish singer he had heard in Gort, & about old manuscripts he has heard of, there is one with Raftery's poems he thinks can be still had — Then in, & found a letter from R., which Marian had left in the bag all day!

21 — Work as usual — a little tired of "the Championship of Ulster" — the first bit I have got tired of — A little depressed outside there are so many tumble down things, gates & walls, & cattle are breaking into the wood — & the rats have again eaten the peas!

29 — Had a nice Sunday at Killeaden — with Miss MacManus[42] — old men who remembered Raftery or were his cousins came, & young men from Kiltimagh chartered a car & came to greet me, they felt, I was told, that I had come from my own class to help theirs — A charming boggy country, bog cotton, & distant hills — & sunny fields about the house — On to Dublin Monday, a tiring journey — Tuesday, to R. I. Academy, & saw the MS of Tain bo — which I think will do quite nicely — I am to apply for leave to have it copied — Went to Spence about framing Sir F.'s pictures — then to AE, who came & spent the evening with me, read me some of his novel,[43] & told me his scheme of an Irish mythology — He had met Massingham who says he is convinced that the moral influence of England is injurious to the world.

G. Moore called in before dinner, happy in a fight with his landlord abt the painting of his door[44] —

---

[41] At Hyde's urging, AG had accepted election in May 1901 as delegate of the Kiltartan branch of the Gaelic League to the 1901 Oireachtas. As part of her efforts to promote Gaelic in the area, she was attempting "to get leave for Mulkere to teach in the school" (letter to Hyde 11 May, Berg). Later in 1901 she gained considerable notoriety by having the Coole carts marked in Irish as an expression of solidarity with a local farmer who had received a summons for doing likewise (see Maureen Murphy, "Lady Gregory and the Gaelic League" in *Lady Gregory: Fifty Years After* ed. Ann Saddlemyer and Colin Smythe).

[42] Charlotte Elisabeth MacManus (c.1850–1941), who achieved considerable popular success with serial and patriotic novels, and who was also active in the Gaelic League. Raftery had been born on her estate at Killeaden.

[43] This apparently remained unfinished, or may have been incorporated into one of the stories AE published during this period.

[44] "When [Moore] arrived in Dublin, all the doors in Ely Place had been painted white by an agreement between the landlords and the tenants. Moore had his door painted green ... insisted on his position as an art critic, that the whole decoration of the house required a green door— I imagine that he had but wrapped the green flag about him" (*Au* p. 444).

Jan[uary] 6 1902!

Eight months since I have written here, they have been very busy ones — Summer holidays passed pleasantly as usual — Yeats all through — Jack [Yeats] & Mrs. Jack the last month, Miss Kinkead the first month — Geraldine, (not improved), the W. Gibsons for some days — Violet Martin for a couple of nights[45] — Harvey about a month — R. & Jack wrote & acted a little play — "The Risin' Wind"[46] —

October, we broke up — R. went to lodgings this time, rather low, but found them comfortable in the end — I, & the Yeats[es] went to Dublin for the Lit. Theatre — (for which see cutting book in Yeats's keeping) — It was a success, quite respectable — even Times & Irish Times blessed us[47] — And Hyde's "Sugan" (I have carried off the real "Sugan" as a trophy) was a real & immense success[48] —

I stayed on for a while to read at R. I. Academy & Nat. Library —

I worked very hard through the summer at "Cuchulain", when not claimed by domestic duties, & finished it in the autumn — After an ineffectual attempt to deal with Bryers[49] (who has not yet sent me a definite answer!) I sent it to Murray who kept it a month — then sent it back with a rather disparaging & I must say silly letter from some wise man he had consulted — the point of which was, that I shd write it down to English comprehension, that is to the level of Jacob's fairy tales — & also prefix to it a history of Ireland & especially of Ulster at that time!! — I indignantly refused this suggestion & sent the MS to Yeats to dispose of — Then Murray wrote that he didn't mean to refuse the MS & was willing to publish at his own risk — So, Yeats having retrieved it from

---

45 Violet Martin visited Coole with her mother, staying 8–9 August 1901. For her interactions with WBY and AG during the visit see her letter to Edith Somerville in Maurice Collis, *Somerville and Ross* p. 129.

46 A typescript of this sketch survives, evidently preserved carefully by AG (doubtless in hopes that it presaged further creative work by RG), but it shows minimal dramatic merit.

47 *The Irish Times* 22 October, p. 4 reported that Yeats's "rare poetic gift and perfect mastery of his craft were never more finely demonstrated". *The Times* 22 October, p. 4 remarked circumspectly on the partisan political potential of the theatre movement, but applauded its "interesting" accomplishment to date.

48 Hyde's *Casadh an tSugáin*, with Hyde in the main role, was produced as the accompanying piece to *Diarmuid and Grania* by the Irish Literary Theatre in the third week of October 1901. AG's translation of the play, "The Twisting of the Rope" was published in *Samhain* at the time of the productions, and again in *Poets and Dreamers* (1903) pp. 200–15. The "tSugáin" was the rope of straw twisted by Hyde during the course of the play.

49 George Bryers (*c.*1849–1908), partner in the Dublin publishing firm Sealy, Bryers and Walker.

Fisher Unwin, it has so been arranged, & I am already revising proofs.[50]

I began in Dublin to read up the Gods — Then found the material too slight to make a whole vol., & turned to Finn — Found him hard to understand — why shd the sacred knowledge of the Hazel tree have been given to a mere militia captain? Then I reflected that he wasn't given the knowledge — he took it without leave, like Eve the apple, & as I think, the Gods had a grudge against him for it — I feel sure he was before Cuchulain's time, nearer to the spirit world — Anyhow I will do him from that point of view, in connection with the Gods.[51]

Xmas vac. began 12th & we have been busy — Shooting party, Ruttledge Fairs, Arthur, Frank, Gus Kelly, Hyde — Good shooting —

Then Xmas duties — 2 Xmas trees etc etc. Xmas in Galway, not a gr success — Trying to answer Xmas letters since then — & translating Hyde's matchmaking play — & reading mythologies — Mr. Rait here, Oxford don, examining papers at L. Cutra[52] — nice & cheery — Paul & Ethel for a couple of days — he is supposed to be cured, but I am afraid is not —

[50] In response to her initial enquiry on 31 October, Murray on 5 November sent a reader's report, which praised AG's translation and considered the book "might just pay its way" but argued in favour of a volume "which at once makes concessions to our ignorance" (Berg). AG interpreted this as a rejection, and sent the MS "straight off to W. B. Yeats telling him he must justify his belief in the book by finding me a publisher!" (AG to Murray, 10 December 1901, Murray). When Murray clarified the apparent rejection as in fact a cautious offer to publish, AG sent Yeats to discuss Murray's reservations: "though I did not want to send him, as it were, to press the book on you, I felt sure a talk with him would save you a good deal of trouble in writing to me" (AG to Murray, 16 December, Murray). At their meeting, as Murray informed her (14 December, Berg), Yeats "politely—but most uncompromisingly rejected every one of my critic's and my own suggestions, and I daresay he is quite right." AG agreed to modify certain colloquialisms in the volume, and to list her sources comprehensively, but to no other changes.

[51] This became *Gods and Fighting Men* (1903), to which AG refers below with the working titles "Gods and Champions" and "Finn".

[52] Robert Sangster Rait (1874–1936), Fellow in History at New College 1899–1913. His research at Lough Cutra was towards *The Life and Campaigns of Field Marshall Viscount Gough*, published in 1903.

1902

Jan[uary] 7 — Did a fine day's work yesterday — Wrote out notes from Cycle Mythologique & Voyage of Bran[1] — Finished translating Hyde's matchmaking play, not nearly so good as the sugan — walked to Raheen to condole with <?A.> O'Hara on the loss of the Mahony child — with May[2] — Read thro' & noted an Ossianic vol! & talked with Rait during the ev. — He says Robert bears a very high character at Oxford, is much "looked up to & respected" — Rashdall[3] likes his essays very much, when he gets them, but his work is spasmodic —

8 & 9 — Irene [Persse] came — 9th last ev. of Rait, read the fairy story I had got at Workhouse which seemed to give satisfaction — 8th, I went in with him to Gort & then went to Workhouse & got some bits of lore — Shooting at home — only the Ashfields & Mr. Kirkpatrick — not good — 7 couple woodcock <?barely> —

Left Coole on the 25th — I had ten days alone that ought to have been pleasant, for I was planting in the nut wood, but somehow were not, I was tired & sensitive to expectations & duties — And one day Frank came & after some of the slightly unpleasant words I still may say against, he brought out a letter from my husband promising him £100 if he wd act as executor, whereas he had only left him £50 (having afterwards put Algernon in with him & left each £50) — F. ought either to have spoken of this at once or not at all, for he has had a good deal of money from me since then & did not mention this till I had stopped my annual £25 for Geoffrey's schooling[4] — I sent him a cheque next day — but altered my will, so that Robert will be no poorer —

[1] AG used both de Jubainville's *Cycle Mythologique* (see p. 266 n. 188) and Alfred Nutt's *The Voyage of Bran* (1895) as sources for "The Birth of Cuchulain", the first chapter of *Cuchulain of Muirthmne*.

[2] May Persse (b.1882), eldest daughter of AG's brother Frank.

[3] Rev. Hastings Rashdall (1858–1924), Fellow of New College and Tutor in Classics 1895–1917.

[4] John Geoffrey Persse (1884–1915), Frank's eldest son, later killed in action at Gallipoli.

I got to Kilmacduagh one day & got a Fenian story — & on 25th I left by early train, stopped a few hours in Dublin to see Russell & get a system of Celtic mythology from him, & had a very helpful talk —

Then a terrible crossing, I fainted & found stewardess & steward bathing my face & giving smelling salts, they were very kind, & so was a young lady in the train —

26 — London, Qmansions, a new flat, same as the old, but 7th floor — Yeats to dine & I dined with him next day to hear Mrs. Emery chant on the new instrument, with moderate success[5] — I have had a very busy week — chiefly in Brit. Museum, reading up for next book — & proofs coming of the old one — & visits to pay — One big dinner at the Haliburtons where past years seemed to pass in procession — Sir Francis Jeune, Lady Reay, Lord Ashbourne, Lady Shrewsbury — Poynters, Walpoles, [Comyn] Carrs, Lady Dorothy [Stanley].

Jan[uary] 4 1903

I can only comfort myself for not having written here till now for a whole year, by thinking it is perhaps when one is doing least & so has least to tell, one has more time for writing it down — Anyhow this has been a busy year —

In London I worked very hard at Brit. Mus[eum] — beginning my "Gods & Champions" — And I had the proofs of "Cuchulain" to correct, sometimes finding them when I came in from dining out, & working at them till 2 am — A pleasant time enough — Yeats usually working at the Museum also —

In March Robert & I went to Florence for Easter — lovely weather, except for thunder storms, & Florence looking lovely — & he liked it — & people were kind — A few days in London then — I left for Coole about the very day "Cuchulain" was published[6] — How it did, let newscuttings speak —

A fortnight away at Hollybeach[7] & in Galway, looking for Finn stories, getting chiefly the folk stories I am putting in "Poets & Dreamers" —

Then Robert's coming of age home coming — bonfires — torches — dinner

[5] This performance by Florence Farr on the psaltery took place at WBY's rooms at Woburn Buildings on 27 January 1902. Farr's first public performace with the instrument, made by musician Arnold Dolmetsch (1858–1940), took place in June 1902. For WBY's account of the instrument, and his theory of chanting see his essay "Speaking to the Psaltery".

[6] AG left for Coole c. 28 April 1902.

[7] AG's letters from this period are addressed from Holly Park, Craughwell, Co. Galway, then the home of Helenus Peter Blake. Holly Park is a short distance from Moyode, then the seat of a branch of the Persse family, but AG's connection with Helenus Blake is not known.

& dance — presentations[8] — Thank God he is so well received & on such good terms with his people & has so good a name —

A long summer — many guests — Yeats, Hydes — Russell — Synge, Byrnes from America[9] — Jack Yeats — his friend Quinn for a night[10] — a great many of the family — Daphne, Irene, May, Richard, Peyton, Tom, Standish, Harold,[11] Rodolph[12] & Algernon — Very tired when all was over —

Worked a good bit at Finn, but Yeats's eyes were bad & I worked for him, from dictation, at "Hour Glass, "Pot of Broth" — & "Where There is Nothing" — And at his essay on Spencer[13] — And we made the scenarios of "Lost Saint" & "Nativity" & a "Fearful Dream" for Hyde[14] —

After the summer, at the end of October to Dublin for the plays "Kathleen ny Houlihan", "Pot of Broth" etc (see Samhain).[15] Then we worked over "Where

[8] Celebrations of RG's formal assumption of the Mastership of Coole took place on 28 June 1902. A draft of his response to a presentation by the tenants survives at Emory.

[9] James F. Byrne (1857–1942), a New York lawyer, and his wife Helen (1869–1945), a patroness of the arts. Byrne was a friend of John Quinn (see next note), and a leading activist in Irish-American circles.

[10] John Quinn (1870–1924), a New York lawyer of Irish extraction, visited Ireland for the first time in the week of 25–31 August 1902, after spending several days in London with Jack Yeats, with whom he had corresponded in 1901. Quinn, who bought numerous works by John and Jack Yeats both during and, by correspondence, prior to, his visit, was a well-read enthusiast of the Irish literary movement, and managed in his brief trip to meet and impress almost all the major creative figures of the Revival. For his mercurial subsequent career as patron and friend to Pound, Eliot, Joyce and others, and his long friendship with WBY and AG, see B. L. Reid, *The Man From New York*. Quinn stayed at Coole on the night of 31 August 1902 after attending a Feís in honour of Raftery at Killeenan. For his reminiscences of this and subsequent visits to Coole, see his essay "Lady Gregory and the Abbey Theater" in E. H. Mikhail, *Lady Gregory: Interviews and Recollections*.

[11] Probably Harold Lane, one of Hugh's younger brothers.

[12] Rodolph Algernon Persse (1892–1915), eldest son of AG's brother Algernon.

[13] WBY's first published version of *The Hour Glass* appeared in *The North American Review* September 1903. *The Pot of Broth*, first produced in October 1902, was first published in *The Gael* September 1903. *Where There is Nothing*, written with collaborative assistance from AG and Hyde in September 1902, was published as a supplement to *The United Irishman*, 30 October 1902 to coincide with the first production, was subsequently revised, and finally rewritten by WBY and AG in 1907–08 as *The Unicorn From the Stars*. WBY's essay "Edmund Spenser", finished in December 1902, formed the Introduction to his selected edition *The Poems of Spenser* (1906) and was reprinted in *Discoveries* (1908).

[14] AG subsequently translated Hyde's plays "The Lost Saint" and "The Nativity" and included them in *Poets and Dreamers*. The "Fearful Dream" was probably an early title for Hyde's play "Pleúsgadh Na Bulgóide", based on an idea by AG, which he completed at Coole in August 1902, and which she likewise translated (as "The Bursting of the Bubble") and published in *New Ireland Review* May 1903.

[15] *Cathleen ni Houlihan*, and *The Pot of Broth*, written jointly by AG and WBY in 1901–02, were produced by the Irish National Dramatic Company at the Antient Concert Rooms, Dublin, 27 October–1 November 1902.

There is Nothing" & did the little Christ play, the "Travelling Man"[16] —

Then home, alone, & worked very hard at Finn till vac[ation] began — Then shooting, Birchs & Gus Kellys — the former till after Xmas — the usual duties — very tired afterwards —

Now it is Jan[uary] 4 — And Robert & I are alone — & today Sunday he had a cold & we stayed at home & I have written letters & with sudden energy wrote this — The old year was a good one to me — R.'s age coming — "Cuchulain" finished — no griefs or land troubles — A good deal of happy friendship —

London Jan[uary] 25 — Marian writes — "Nora & myself went over to the school on Sunday & Monday to hear the lecture on fowl rearing, & indeed I think the women won't bother their heads about her talk, whitewash & ventilation and build a house 6 ft. wide & so on — they said it was an easy way for her to be earning money going about on cars, and anyone that wants the eggs they will have to go up to Kilbecanty for them, they will have to pay 1-a dozen — I don't think the Kiltartan women will sell their old hens at 1/3-each —

April 26 — London was hard work at Brit. Mus. — most of the time — & correcting proofs of "Poets & Dreamers", which only came out as I left —

Left Mar[ch] 13 for Dublin — Performance next day of the "Hour Glass" & "25"[17] — went well — a good audience — Gaelic League procession — Tea at Sir A. MacDonnells[18] —

Home 16th — The place sadly changed by storms of Feb[ruary] 26 — the accounts of which had disturbed me in London — 10 lime trees down between house & stables — & the big lime to the left (greatest loss of all) & the big evergreen oak in front lawn — & some parts of the woods laid flat —

A quiet Easter vac[ation] — R. busy reading for Greats — Yeats here, busy, &

---

[16] *The Travelling Man*, first published in *The Shanachie* in 1906, was not produced until 1910.

[17] *The Hour Glass* and AG's *Twenty-Five* were produced by The Irish National theatre Society at Molesworth Hall, Dublin, on 14 March 1903. *Twenty-Five* was subsequently renamed *A Losing Game* by the editorial staff of *The Gael* (New York), in which it was published in December 1902, as American readers were thought unlikely to know the card game referred to in the title. AG never reprinted the play, but in 1926 she rewrote it entirely as a new work, *On The Racecourse*.

[18] Sir Anthony MacDonnell (1844–1925), Civil Servant in India 1865–1901, and Under-Secretary of State for Ireland 1902–08. Raised to the peerage in 1908.

[19] This became *The King's Threshold*, first published in 1904.

I busy helping him, with scenario of "Senchan",[19] & re-doing "the Wild Horse"[20] — & arranging all the Folk Lore — I did a little "Finn" but hadn't time for much.

R. got some scratch hounds together from Gort, Ennis & Tubber & hunted hares at Ballylee & Lisheen & Lower Lavally — & a deer at Roxboro' — Olive & May & Harvey & Rodolph here at the end —

On Easter Sunday R. & I had a talk about his profession — He would have tried for H[ouse]. of C[ommons]. clerkship to please me, but his heart was on Art — I told him he shd choose as he liked — & he has chosen Art — I am glad he has so strong a bent towards anything & especially so high a profession — though the temptations to take work easily may beset him — But I believe he will succeed, he has imagination, & love of the country[21] — which has not yet found its expression —

Now all have gone & I am alone —

1903

[loose sheet begins here]

Coole Feb[ruary] 21, 1904 — Yes, I will begin to write this again — Now I have done with "Gods & Fighting Men" I have some hope never to be in a hurry again.

Today, alone, as I have been since Robert left early in Jan[uary]. — Yesterday it poured all day — Inside wainscot ripped up to try for leak in hot water pipes — I wrote my last letter to W. B. Y. in America[22] — put in his newscuttings — worked a little at "Saints".[23] Am trying to get everything in the house into order —

22 — Frank all day trying to get heating apparatus in order succeeded at last — [loose sheet ends]

[20] In early 1903, having failed to complete *The Travelling Man* with AG to their joint satisfaction, WBY attempted a 'pagan' version of the play, variously referred to as "The Wild Horse", "The Black Horse" and "The Country of the Young". For an account of this variant, which he left unpublished, see my "Recontextualizing the Lyric Moment: Yeats's "The Happy Townland" and the abandoned play 'The Country of the Young'" *Yeats Annual* 10, pp. 65–91.

[21] After leaving Oxford, RG studied at the Slade School of Art, and later in Paris under Jacques-Émile Blanche. He exhibited in London in 1912 and 1914, and painted many set designs for the Abbey Theatre. For reproductions of his work, see Colin Smythe, *Robert Gregory 1881–1918*.

[22] WBY spent the period November 1903–March 1904 lecturing in the U.S.A.

[23] *A Book of Saints and Wonders* (1906, rev. ed. 1907).

5 years interregnum in diary

Venice June 4 — 1909

What happened in these years? —

I wrote my plays — "7 Short Plays" — & "Kincora", "Dervorgilla", "Cockade", "Canavans" & in this last year "The Image"[24] —

I worked very very hard at the theatre — I spent a part of 2 summers working for & with Yeats on his "Deirdre"[25] — And then one on rewriting "The Unicorn [From the Stars]" — from "Where There is Nothing" — to please him but against my will[26] —

Robert's marriage.[27]

Before that, a beautiful month in Italy with him & W. B. Y.[28] —

Birth of Richard, (the darling) Jan[uary] 6 1909.[29] That is a great cheer up, & Margaret is charming & beautiful & I am quite satisfied with R.'s choice — But there have been troubles — Reduction of rents, still going on —

The "Playboy" row, leading to the Guardians' resolutions against letting the Workhouse children come to Coole — & to the threatening notice on the gate against our own schoolchildren if they accepted the tea & cake I had

[24] *Seven Short Plays*, comprising most of AG's one-act comedies, was published in 1909. Her plays *Kincora, Dervorgilla , The White Cockade* and *The Canavans* , were all published in book form in *Irish Folk-History Plays* (1912). *The Image*, first produced in 1909, was published in 1910.

[25] *Deirdre*, first published 1907 and later revised.

[26] "That I might free myself from what seemed a contamination [*Where there is Nothing*], I asked Lady Gregory to help me turn my old plot into *The Unicorn from the Stars*" (*Variorum Plays* p. 713). They completed this collaborative work in summer 1907.

[27] RG married Margaret Graham Parry, a fellow student whom he met at the Slade School of Art, in 1907.

[28] This was WBY's first visit to Italy. As AG recalled: "to please that student of Castiglione's *Courtier*... we drove over the Appenines to Urbino, & descended to Pisaro and Ravenna—Yeats had also set his mind on Ferrarra, on the way to Venice. . . . We came . . . not to the jangle and uproar of the railway station, but to the heart of the city's beauty, to [the] piazza of St. Mark— And as I left him there . . . he was as if entranced by the rich colouring, the strange beauty of the joyous Venetian night" (Holograph Memoirs, Berg).

[29] Richard Gregory (1909–81), the first of RG's and Margaret Gregory's three children.

promised[30] —

I have given up the school feast, it was another weapon to be used against me —

The disagreeable business about Hall the sawyer's marriage led to a slight coolness with Father Fahey — I blame the Archdeacon much more —

The splits & rows in the theatre very wearying & taking so much time — Poor Synge's death this spring a great sadness —

Yeats sometimes worried, restless, unwell, yet our friendship continues unbroken & I owe to him what I have done of late years — he gave me belief in myself —

Margaret's illness last year spoiled their Italy, & was a gr anxiety —

The tenants won't buy, & are getting reductions of about 25 p.c. in the Land Courts — Increased expenditure at this, we can't go on unless we earn —

---

[30] The furore over Synge's *The Playboy of the Western World* affected AG sharply. As she wrote to Wilfrid Blunt, she considered herself "the real sufferer" since "at the first attack Synge who is not fond of fighting his own battles kept in the background & Yeats was away—& I had to take responsibility—& the papers exaggerated this. I was at home for a few days & found a good deal of feeling had been stirred up . . ." (20 April 1907, Berg). Coolness towards her over the matter persisted from some quarters in Galway County for several years.

BIOGRAPHICAL APPENDIX

MAUD GONNE (1865–1953), the daughter of a British Army Captain, was brought up largely by governesses following the death of her mother in 1871. Her childhood was spent in Ireland from 1869–76, variously in England and France from 1876–81, and again in Ireland from 1882–86 as her father's military postings changed. The year after his death in late 1886 she came of age, inherited substantial independent means, and went to live in Paris. There, in 1888, she became the mistress of the Boulangist politician Lucien Millevoye. Under the influence of his strongly anti-British views, and as a result of having witnessed evictions in Ireland, she became a fervent convert to Irish Nationalism, and returned to Ireland in late 1888 determined to work for the cause of Irish independence. Through John O'Leary she met WBY for the first time in January 1889. WBY, who remained unaware of her relationship with Millevoye until 1898, sought to win her throughout the 1890s, writing *The Countess Cathleen* for her, collaborating with her in various Nationalist ventures, initiating her into the Golden Dawn in 1891, and writing many of the poems in which she features as his unnamed beloved. She bore two children by Millevoye—Georges (b.1890), who died aged one, and Iseult (1894–1954)—but their affair ended irrevocably in 1900. In 1903, to WBY's shock, she married Major John MacBride, leader of the pro-Boer Irish Brigade and later one of the sixteen leaders shot after the 1916 Rising, but their marriage was dissolved the following year in an acrimonious suit in which she charged him with physical abuse, drunkeness and a sexual assault on her half-sister. From 1905 to 1918 Maud Gonne was resident mainly in France, and during a visit in 1909 WBY appears to have briefly become her lover. She refused his final proposal in 1917. Following WBY's marriage shortly afterwards, their relationship cooled significantly save for a brief period of rapprochement in the 1930s, but she remained throughout an iconic figure in his poetry.

SIR WILLIAM HENRY GREGORY (1816–92), was the only son of Robert Gregory of Coole (1790–1847) and grandson of the Rt Hon. William Gregory (1762–1840), Under-Secretary for Ireland 1813–31. As heir presumptive to the Coole estates, totalling some 15,000 acres, he grew up indulged and well-connected, spending his formative childhood years in the Under-Secretary's Lodge in Phoenix Park, Dublin, during the period of his grandfather's greatest influence. After excelling academically at Harrow School, he matriculated in Classics at Christ Church, Oxford, in 1835, and seemed set for rapid advancement. His self-confidence and ambition were severely damaged, however, when he placed second in a series of University Prizes. He subsequently began to ignore his studies, developed a passion for gambling on the Turf, and eventually left Oxford in late 1839 without taking a degree. Supported by family money, and with extensive purchasing of votes, he was successfully elected as a Conservative member for Dublin in 1842. In Parliament he was in the unprecedented position of enjoying both the patronage of Robert Peel, the Prime Minister, in consequence of Peel's friendship with his late grandfather, and the personal regard of the Irish Nationalist leader, Daniel O'Connell. In 1846 Peel offered Gregory the Irish Lordship of the Treasury, which at the time would have given him a dominant position in Irish affairs, but he declined to accept. In 1847 he lost his seat by a substantial margin, largely as a result of his support for repeal of the Corn Laws, and for having forwarded an amendement to an Irish Poor Law Bill which prohibited Irish tenant farmers who held less than one-quarter of an acre from receiving relief—a measure which effectively sanctioned the clearance of smallholdings, given the straightened circumstances of tenants during the Famine. His defeat was narrowly preceded by the death of his father from typhus, contracted by ministering to Famine victims, and at age 31 Gregory thus became master of Coole. First-hand experience of his own tenants' privations quickly modified his views on the "Gregory clause" he had authored, and his generosity in famine relief and rent abatements likewise quickly transformed his reputation. His largesse, the reduced rents, a dishonest agent and his continued gambling expenditures, nonetheless all combined to drag the already encumbered estate into serious debt, and in 1857 he was forced to sell some 10,000 acres of his inheritance. Later in 1857, with his political prospects rehabilitated in the Galway area through his reputation as a model landlord and his promotion of local interests such as railway building, he was successfully returned as M.P. for Galway.

In the 1860s Gregory began to campaign actively for an appointment to redeem the wasted opportunities of his youth, and through the patronage of the influential Lady Waldegrave he was finally appointed Governor of Ceylon in 1871. The substantial salary the post entailed allowed him to marry Elizabeth Bowdoin, a recently widowed heiress, with whom he had been in love for many years. Her generous allocation of her private fortune in the marriage settlement substantially improved the financial position of the Coole estate. Gregory's liberal and energetic tenure in Ceylon, beginning in 1872, was marked by major public works, including the completion of a road network, irrigation improvements and the starting of a major harbour development at Colombo. He also initiated tea cultivation on the island in order to reduce over-reliance on the coffee crop. His wife's sudden death from fever in 1873, however, permanently sapped Gregory's enthusiasm for his position. Though he was knighted by the Prince of Wales, who spent a week in Ceylon in December 1875, he determined to resign, gave notice soon after his mother's death in 1876, and left in January 1877.

On his return from Ceylon, Gregory resumed a position as a popular figure in intellectual, political and artistic circles, spending much of the year in London. In January 1880 he proposed to Augusta Persse, the youngest daughter in a neighbouring landowning family, after an elliptical and cautious courtship clearly influenced by his sensitivity to the 35 year disparity in their ages. They were married in March 1880, and had one child, Robert, born in May 1881. The years of the marriage followed a fairly regular pattern consisting of winter travel in Europe, spring and autumn residence in London, and the summers spent at Coole. During the winter of 1881–82, while in Egypt, the Gregorys were drawn into the emerging political tensions between Arabi Bey, an Egyptian Colonel who had risen to prominence in pressing for Nationalist reforms, and the colonial bureaucracy then ruling the country. Allying with anti-Imperialist and poet Wilfrid Scawen Blunt, Gregory began a campaign of letter-writing to *The Times* in support of Arabi, suspending his efforts only when it became clear that Egypt would be annexed to satisfy Imperial interests. Along with Blunt, Lady Gregory continued a rearguard action in support of Arabi even after his capture by British forces in late 1882, and in 1883 she and Blunt began a brief and clandestine affair, ended that August by mutual agreement. In 1885–86 the Gregorys travelled widely in India and visited Ceylon, where Gregory was feted. His final return to the island in 1890 marked the beginning of a slow decline in energy, and increasing ill health. He died on 6 March 1892.

WILLIAM ROBERT GREGORY (1881–1918), Sir William and Lady Gregory's only child, was frequently separated from his parents as a child during their long trips in Egypt, India, Ceylon and Europe. He began boarding school at Park Hill School, Lyndhurst, in 1889, transferred to Elstree School in 1893 and then in 1895 began at Harrow School, where his father and grandfather had both been outstanding pupils. After matriculating as a scholar in Classics at New College, Oxford, in 1899, he enjoyed a chequered academic career, graduating with a third class degree in 1903. By the time he left college, Coole had become such a focal point for Lady Gregory's literary life that he was clearly reluctant to take over active ownership of the property, and instead spent most of his time in Paris and London. Embarking on a career as an artist, he studied at the Slade School, and then in Paris, and exhibited work in London in 1912 and 1914. In 1907 he married fellow art-student (Lily) Margaret Graham Parry, and they had three children, Richard (1909–81), Anne (b.1911) and Catherine (b.1913). He joined active duty with the Royal Flying Corps in 1916, and won the Military Cross and the Legion d'Honneur before being fatally shot down in 1918 on the Italian Front.

DOUGLAS HYDE (1860–1949), developed reasonable proficiency in the Irish language as a young man on his parents's estate in Roscommon. He took up residence at Trinity College, Dublin, in 1882, and quickly became known for his Irish poems written under the pseudonym "An Craoibhín Aoibhinn" ("The Pleasant Little Branch") and for his strong Nationalist views. His first book of folklore, *Leabhar Sgeulaigheachta*, published in 1889, was followed by *Beside the Fire*, which WBY praised as "incomparable" on its appearance in 1890. After a year in Canada teaching modern languages, Hyde returned to Ireland and founded the National Literary Society, to which he delivered his milestone address "The Necessity of De-Anglicising Ireland" in November 1892. The following year he helped establish The Gaelic League, which aimed to keep the use of the Irish langauge alive, and of which he was elected President, a position he retained until 1915 when he resigned in protest at the increasing politicization of the organisation. The idiomatic translations in his bilingual 1893 volume *The Love Songs of Connacht* represented for WBY the apogee of Hyde's poetic accomplishment, and paved the way for the poetic and idiomatic dialogue developed by Synge and Lady Gregory. Thereafter, WBY believed, Hyde's absorption in Gaelic League work beat "into prose / That noble blade the Muses buckled on". Hyde completed a monumental *Literary History of Ireland* in 1899, and several more volumes of Connacht *Songs*, but his energies were increasingly devoted to campaigning to establish Irish as a subject in school and University curricula, and to Gaelic League fundraising and organising. After his resignation from the League, he withdrew from public life save for an uneventful single term in the Free State Senate, and until 1932 held the post of Professor of Modern Irish at the National University to which he had been appointed in 1908. In 1938 he was drawn from retirement as de Valéra's choice to become first President of Ireland, in which capacity he served until 1944.

Hyde's period of closest alliance with AG was between 1897 and 1903, during which years he was a key encourager of her efforts to learn Irish and a scholarly advisor during her work on the Irish epics. Their joint interest in promoting Gaelic drama as part of the theatre movement also spurred their collaboration on a series of one-act plays during Hyde's numerous visits to Coole in these years, with AG and WBY providing him with scenarios and critical assistance. *Casadh an tSugáin*, written at Coole in 1900, was produced by the Irish Literary theatre in 1901 with Hyde in the central role. Hyde also assisted in the writing of *Where There is Nothing* in 1902, and offered AG substantial critical help in revising some of her first plays. By the time of the foundation of the Abbey Theatre in 1904, it was clear that Gaelic drama would have no significant part in its programme, and though AG herself remained an active and enthusiastic Gaelic Leaguer and a staunch ally of Hyde, their contact was thereafter only sporadic.

SIR AUSTEN HENRY LAYARD (1817–94), began work in a solicitor's office, but at age twenty-two determined to ride overland to Persia and then travel to Ceylon to start a new career. En route, he became fascinated with

Mesapotamian archeology, and organized a series of excavations of the mounds at Nineveh and Nimrud. Publication of his *Nineveh and Its Remains* in 1849 made him one of the most celebrated figures of his age. Lady Gregory would recall that in her childhood, a time when "Darwin was pulling nails out of Noah's Ark", he was heralded for his discoveries as "the man that made the Bible true" (*Seventy Years* p. 153). Layard subsequently turned his immense popularity to political advantage, and was elected to Parliament in 1852. With his outspokenness on British mismanagement during the Crimean War, however, he made many enemies, and lost his seat in 1857. In the early 1860s he was appointed Under-Secretary for Foreign Affairs by Palmerston, and thereafter embarked on a career as a diplomat, serving as British Minister at Madrid from 1869, and Ambassador at Constantinople from 1877. At Constantinople, Layard's pro-Turkish and anti-Russian views provoked repeated controversy, and in 1880 he was removed from office by Gladstone following the publication of a private letter in which he was critical of the Turkish Sultan, and candid about his own lack of influence. With his political career ended by this indiscretion, and denied a peerage, Layard divided his remaining years between Venice, at Ca' Capello, a palazzo on the Grand Canal he had bought in the 1870s, and London. His long friendship with Sir William Gregory was cemented by their shared artistic enthusiasms, and particularly in their work as Trustees of the National Gallery.

LADY LAYARD, née Enid Guest (1843–1913), eighth child of Lady Charlotte Guest (translator of *The Mabinogion*), married Layard in 1869, as his second wife, being aged 25 to his 52, a discrepancy of age which doubtless encouraged WHG, their best man, in making his own subsequent second marriage. The Layards hosted the Gregorys at Constantinople during their honeymoon tour, and quickly became protective and sympathetic friends to AG. AG's friendship with Lady Layard was at its closest in the period after both women were widowed in the early 1890s, as they offered one another mutual support in facing the difficulties of living alone. As AG's social and intellectual horizons broadened in the late 1890s, the friendship began to weaken, and though Lady Layard continued to host AG frequently both in London and occasionally in Venice, she was no longer a close confidante. As AG would recall: "Childless and with sufficient wealth, she had no anxieties such as mine, and her interests did not widen as mine did" (*Seventy Years* p. 285).

EDWARD MARTYN (1859–1923), AG's near neighbour at Tillyra Castle, Co. Galway, was prominent in the Irish revival as a playwright, patron, and founder of the Feís Ceoil. His important part in the foundation of the Irish theatre movement, and his eventual break from Yeats, AG and Moore, are broadly chronicled in the entries of this diary. Martyn continued to promote dramatic work after this break, most notably founding the Irish Theatre in 1914 to produce non-peasant Irish work and translations of foreign masterpieces, material he felt was excluded at the Abbey Theatre. As one of the few wealthy Catholic Nationalists in Ireland, he exerted considerable influence in both the Gaelic League, of which he served as an executive committee member, and as President of Sinn Fein from 1904–08. His generous patronage was influential in the European revival of Gregorian chant, and his endowments funded the Dublin Cathedral Palestrina Choir.

GEORGE MOORE (1852–1933), eldest son of a Mayo landlord, inherited substantial estates on his father's death in 1870. From 1869–75, he studied art in London and Paris, but then determined to become a writer. After publishing two meritless volumes of poetry, he became intent on commercial success, partly as a result of the fall in his rent income during the Land War in Ireland. He settled in London in 1881, and soon began to model his work after Zola, whom he met in 1882. His first novel *A Modern Lover* (1883) was banned by the circulating libraries for alleged immorality, earning Moore considerable notoriety and launching him on a career as a critic of censorship and provoker of controversy. *A Drama in Muslin* (1886) and *Parnell and his Island* (1887) likewise gave him a reputation as anti-Catholic, and provoked the lasting suspicion of Nationalists and landlords alike due to their critical portraits of Dublin social life. As a prolific reviewer and essayist, Moore gained a considerable reputation as an art critic in the late 1880s, consolidated in 1893 by his volume *Modern Painting*. His play *The Strike at Arlingford* (1893) enjoyed only modest success, but was followed by acclaim for his major novels *Esther Waters* (1894), later substantially revised, and *Evelyn Innes* (1898), in which the character Ulick Dean is modelled on Yeats. Increasingly attracted to the Irish literary movement through his friendships with Martyn and Yeats (with whom he collaborated on the play *Diarmuid and Grania* from 1899), Moore moved to Dublin in 1901, producing *The Untilled Field* (1903) a collection of mainly Irish-inspired short stories, and *The Lake*, which completed a hitherto gradual break from his earlier realism. He left Ireland in 1911 on the eve of publication of the first volume of his satirical autobiography *Hail and Farewell*. His final decades in London were marked by an increasingly lyrical style in works such as *The Brook Kerith* (1916), but declining critical and commercial success.

SIR HORACE CURZON PLUNKETT (1854–1932), third son of the 16th Baron Dunsany, spent his early years as a rancher in Wyoming before returning to Ireland to become the leading figure in Irish agricultural reform in his time, notably in promoting co-operation. He sat as a Unionist M.P. for South Dublin 1892–1900, but lost his seat due to friendships with prominent Nationalists and his employment of a former Parnellite M.P. to the Department of Agricultural and Technical Instruction for Ireland, of which he was Vice-President 1899–1907. Plunkett served as a Commissioner of the Congested District Board 1891–1918, and was President of the Irish Agricultural

Organization Society, which he founded, 1894–99. He was briefly proprietor of the Dublin *Daily Express* 1898–1900, during which time the paper was a strong supporter of the Irish literary movement.

GEORGE WILLIAM RUSSELL (1867–1935), was born in Co. Armagh, but moved to Dublin at the age of eleven. In the mid-1880s he studied at the Metropolitan School of Art, where he became a close friend of WBY. From 1890, he worked as a clerk in Pim's drapery store, devoting his free time to theosophy and poetry, until he was recruited to work for the Irish Agricultural Organisation Society by Horace Plunkett in 1897 as a promoter of rural banks. Russell was active in the Irish theatre movement in its early years, contributing a play, *Deirdre*, and serving as Vice-President of the Irish National Theatre Society until 1905, but he broke with the Abbey Theatre over its shift from democratic organisation to absolute directorial control by WBY, AG and Synge. Though they had been close friends and shared similar visionary, poetic and nationalist aims, WBY and AE became progressively estranged from this period on, as AE's tolerant, conciliating personal style became increasingly at odds with WBY's autocratic manner. Despite the success of his early volumes of poetry *Homeward: Songs by the Way* (1894) and *The Earth Breath* (1897), he turned increasingly to journalism in the new century, editing *The Irish Homestead*, and then *The Irish Statesman* (with which it merged in 1923) from 1905 until 1930.

INDEX